# BIOETHICS

## HEALTH CARE LAW AND ETHICS

### Eighth Edition

■ ■ ■

**Barry R. Furrow**

*Professor of Law and Director, Health Law Program*
*Kline School of Law, Drexel University*

**Thomas L. Greaney**

*Visiting Professor, UC Hastings College of Law*
*Distinguished Senior Fellow, UCSF/UC Hastings Consortium on Law, Science and Health Policy*
*Professor Emeritus, Saint Louis University School of Law*

**Sandra H. Johnson**

*Professor Emerita of Law and Health Care Ethics*
*Saint Louis University School of Law*

**Timothy Stoltzfus Jost**

*Robert L. Willett Family Professor of Law*
*Washington and Lee University*

**Robert L. Schwartz**

*Senior Visiting Professor*
*University of California Hastings College of the Law*
*Visiting Professor (Psychiatry), UCSF*
*Weihofen Professor of Law Emeritus, University of New Mexico*

**Brietta R. Clark**

*Associate Dean for Faculty*
*Professor of Law and J. Rex Dibble Fellow, Loyola Law School, Los Angeles*

**Erin C. Fuse Brown**

*Associate Professor of Law*
*Georgia State University College of Law*

**Robert Gatter**

*Professor of Law and Director, Center for Health Law Studies*
*Saint Louis University School of Law*

**Jaime S. King**

*Professor of Law, University of California Hastings College of the Law*
*Associate Dean and Co-Director, UCSF/UC Hastings Consortium on Law, Science and Health Policy*

**Elizabeth Pendo**

*Joseph J. Simeone Professor of Law*
*Saint Louis University School of Law*

**AMERICAN CASEBOOK SERIES®**

WEST
ACADEMIC
PUBLISHING

*American Casebook Series* is a trademark registered in the U.S. Patent and Trademark Office.

Printed in the United States of America

**ISBN:** 978-1-68328-841-1

To our wonderful colleagues—the health law students and teachers who have used this casebook over the last thirty years.

# PREFACE

This eighth edition of this casebook marks the thirty-first anniversary edition of our text, first published in 1987. Since that first edition, no part of the American landscape has changed more than the American health care system. The transformation in health care and in health law reaches deeply into issues that fall under the umbrella of bioethics. In 1987, the law relating to health care ethics issues was pretty lean, but in the years since, there has been a constant wave of state and federal legislation, judicial opinions, and administrative regulations addressing issues in bioethics.

While the perspective that we must bring to the legal analysis of issues relating to bioethics is necessarily more extensive now than it was thirty years ago, the fundamental concerns on which that analysis is brought to bear are surprisingly unchanged. As was the case in 1987, we want to know what role the law might play in promoting or mediating the values at issue in health care including individual rights in treatment decision making, access to necessary health care, competing interests and goals in medical research, and the balance of the individual and community in public health. We want to explore the nature of the relationship between law and health care ethics, both in areas where there are shared values and in areas where there are conflicts. We want to test basic legal and ethical principles in application to specific health care issues.

The eighth edition of this casebook continues to use the approach that teachers and students found so helpful in the prior editions. As was the case in previous editions, we employ materials from a variety of sources. This book continues to contain the most significant and useful judicial opinions, state and federal statutes, legislative history, administrative regulations, forms, and a host of other kinds of materials designed to bring the subject to life in the classroom. It also contains many classroom-tested problems that should be helpful in encouraging student engagement with these materials. While many of the problems and other materials have been brought forward from earlier editions of this book, every section of this casebook has been revised to reflect recent changes. Like other areas of health law, the law relating to bioethics is undergoing continuing and rapid change, especially in relation to federal administrative regulations. This book accounts for changes through early 2018, and teachers using this book can find updates and supplementary material in the Teacher's Manual and on the West website for the *Health Law* casebook. All cases, statutes, regulations, and other materials in the casebook have been edited to enhance their teaching value while assuring that they reflect problems faced by health care professionals, patients, policymakers, and lawyers coping with the health system in 2018 and beyond. The notes expose students to a range of the most subtle health law and bioethics inquiries under discussion at the time of publication.

Derived from the comprehensive material contained in our casebook, *Health Law: Cases, Materials, and Problems (West 8th ed.)*, this volume is custom made for courses focusing on issues in bioethics. *Bioethics: Health Care Law and Ethics* is one of three paperback volumes that collect chapters from our *Health Law: Cases, Materials, and Problems* casebook. The other volumes are *The Law of Health Care Organization and Finance* and *Law and Health Care Quality, Patient Safety, and Liability*. Each of these volumes is designed to present materials for courses with a more limited focus than what would be covered in a broader survey. Finally, there is also an abridged version of the comprehensive *Health Law* casebook which includes only limited coverage of bioethics.

Other than the first chapter, the chapters in this paperback volume are the same as they appear in the larger *Health Law* casebook. It is quite easy to teach the course with some students using the complete *Health Law* casebook and others using this volume. Students usually appreciate being able to have that choice.

The first chapter in *Bioethics: Health Care Law and Ethics* introduces students to fundamental theories of health care ethics, including codes of professional ethics, and to significant issues in the relationship between law and ethics. This chapter does not appear in the *Health Law* casebook, so teachers are welcome and have permission to distribute this first chapter to students in their class who may be using the larger casebook for the bioethics class.

This book addresses the current status of laws that regulate abortion, contraception, assisted conception, and human reproduction. It provides extensive discussions of the controversies over the definition of death, organ transplantation, the law of health care decision-making, and medically assisted dying. The casebook also includes a review of legal regulation of research involving human subjects, and it concludes with a chapter that addresses developments in public health. Throughout these chapters, we have included materials on genetics where appropriate and have expanded our treatment of disability. In addition, we have included a new chapter on issues of justice, equity, and discrimination across many dimensions. All of these materials have been reviewed to assure that a wide range of perspectives leaven the authors' analysis of health law. This casebook is designed to be a teachable book. We are grateful for the many comments and helpful suggestions that health law teachers across the United States (and from elsewhere, too) have made to help us improve this new edition. We attempt to present all sides of policy issues, not to evangelize for any political, economic or social agenda of our own. This task is made easier, undoubtedly, by the diverse views on virtually all policy issues that the several different authors of this casebook bring to this endeavor. A large number of very well respected health law teachers have contributed a great deal to this and previous editions by making suggestions, reviewing problems, or encouraging our more thorough investigation of a wide range of health law subjects. We are especially grateful to Charles Baron, Eugene Basanta, David Bennahum, Robert Berenson, Kathleen Boozang, Don Chalmers, Ellen Wright Clayton, Judith Daar, Dena Davis, Arthur Derse, Kelly Dineen, Ileana Dominguez-Urban, Stewart Duban, Barbara Evans, Margaret Farrell, Rob Field, David Frankford, Michael Gerhart, Joan McIver Gibson, Susan Goldberg, Jesse Goldner, Andrew Grubb, Sarah Hooper, Art LaFrance, Diane Hoffmann, Jill Horwitz, Amy Jaeger, Eleanor Kinney, Thomasine Kushner, Pam Lambert, Theodore LeBlang, Antoinette Sedillo Lopez, Mary Pareja, Lawrence Singer, Joan Krause, Leslie Mansfield, Thomas Mayo, Maxwell Mehlman, Alan Meisel, Vicki Michel, Frances Miller, John Munich, David Orentlicher, Vernellia Randall, Ben Rich, Arnold Rosoff, Karen Rothenberg, Mark Rothstein, Sallie Sanford, Giles Scofield, Jeff Sconyers, Charity Scott, Ross Silverman, Loane Skene, George Smith, Roy Spece, Jr., Carol Suzuki, Michael Vitiello, Sidney Watson, Lois Weithorn, Ellen Wertheimer, William Winslade and Susan M. Wolf for the benefit of their wisdom and experience.

We wish to thank those remarkable research assistants who provided support for our research and the preparation of the manuscript, Debra Au, Elizabeth Bertolino, Elysia Buckley, Erin O'Malley Gleim, Laura Hagen, Joshua Hasyniec, Delanie Inman, Min Ji Kim, Alexandra Montague, Kirstin E. Rodrigues and Anna Zaret. We are also very appreciative of the tremendous support and the publication assistance provided by Greg Olson, Jon Harkness and Cathy Lundeen of West Academic Publishing. We are also indebted to our casebook shepherds—Mary Ann Jauer for the first 25 years of the casebook, and now Cheryl Cooper. We appreciate those who were there for us during the nights and weekends we spent working on this project: Roger Fuse Brown, Maripat Loftus Gatter, Robert Johnson, Nancy Jones, James King, Donna Jo Napoli, Ruth Stoltzfus Jost, Ben Walker, Cary White and Jane Zwisohn. Finally, we wish to thank our deans, Roger Dennis, David Faigman, Dan Filler, Wendy Hensel, Steven J. Kaminshine, William Johnson, Sergio Pareja and Michael Waterstone.

It has been a splendid opportunity to work on this casebook. It has been a constant challenge to find a way to teach cutting edge issues influencing our health care system—at times before the courts or legislatures have given us much legal material for our casebook. Each time we have done a new edition, there have been developments that we find difficult to assess as to whether they will become more significant during the lifespan of the edition or are simply blips. It is always difficult to delete materials that required much labor and still remain quite relevant but that have been eclipsed in importance by others, and the length of each succeeding edition attests to our challenge. The good news is that this edition reverses one trend of the past thirty-plus years; it is actually shorter than its predecessor edition. We do not write this casebook for our classes alone, but for yours as well. We enjoy teaching, and we hope that comes through to the students and teachers who use this book.

Finally, this edition marks a substantial change in the authorship of the material. After thirty-one rewarding years writing and rewriting this casebook, the original authors are now passing off the torch (and the benefit that goes with it) to five thoughtful and inspired successors. This is not because the original five authors have grown tired of the endeavor—we all still love doing this quadrennial casebook labor. We have come to realize, though, that the casebook needs to be revisualized through the eyes of scholars and teachers who have come to this enterprise more recently and who have new and exciting approaches to teaching law more generally. We feel especially lucky to have found five brilliant health law scholars in complementing areas who are willing to take on this project and work collectively. In this edition, all ten authors worked to produce the final casebook. In the following editions, the new five authors will be responsible for all facets of the casebook. You will be able to find the original five authors in our respective pastures, blithely grazing (albeit still concerned about systemic health reform).

BARRY R. FURROW

THOMAS L. GREANEY

SANDRA H. JOHNSON

TIMOTHY S. JOST

ROBERT L. SCHWARTZ

BRIETTA CLARK

ERIN C. FUSE BROWN

ROBERT GATTER

JAIME KING

ELIZABETH PENDO

June 2018

# ACKNOWLEDGMENTS

American College of Obstetrics and Gynecology Committee on Ethics, The Limits of Conscientious Refusal in Reproductive Medicine, 110 Obstetrics Genecology 1203 (2007, reaffirmed 2016). Reprinted with permission.

American Medical Association, AMA Principles of Medical Ethics VI (adopted June 1957, revised June 1980, revised June 2001). Used with permission of the American Medical Association. All rights reserved.

American Medical Association, CEJA Medical Ethics Opinions 1.1.2, 1.1.7, 5.5, 5.6, 5.7, 5.8, 8.5, 11.1.4 (2016). Used with permission of the American Medical Association.

Austin, C.R., Human Embryos: Debate on Assisted Reproduction (1989). Copyright 1989, Oxford University Press. Reprinted by permission of Oxford University Press.

Battin, Margaret, The Least Worst Death, 13 Hastings Center Report (2) 13 (April 1983). Copyright 1983, The Hastings Center. Reprinted with permission of the Hastings Center. Reprinted with permission of the Hastings Center and the author.

Colorado Medical Orders for Scope of Treatment (2015 form). Reprinted with permission.

Crown copyright is produced with the permission of the Controller of Her Majesty's Stationery Office.

Devers, Kelly and Robert Berenson, Can Accountable Care Organizations Improve the Value of Health Care by Solving the Cost and Quality Quandries?, copyright 2009, The Urban Institute. Reprinted with permission.

Drescher, Jack et al., Minding the Body: Situating Gender Identity Diagnoses in the ICD-11, 24 International Review of Psychiatry 568 (2012). Copyright 2012, Institute of Psychiatry. Reprinted by permission of Taylor and Francis Ltd., http://www.tandfonline.com, on behalf of Institute of Psychiatry.

Enthoven, Alain, Health Plan: The Only Practical Solution to the Soaring Costs of Health Care 1–12 (1980). Copyright 1980 Alain Enthoven. Reprinted with permission.

Ethics Committee of the American Society for Reproductive Medicine, Informing Offspring of Their Conception by Gamete or Embryo Donation, 109 Fertilization and Sterilization 601 (2018). Reprinted with permission from Elsevier.

Fletcher, Joseph, Indicators of Humanhood, 2 Hastings Center Report (5) 1 (November 1972). Copyright 1972, the Hastings Center. Reprinted with permission of the Hastings Center.

Froedtert Hospital—Medical College of Wisconsin, Futility Policy. Reprinted with permission.

Gostin, Lawrence O., Public Health Law: Power, Duty, Restraint. Copyright 2000, University of California Press. Reprinted with permission of the University of California Press.

Hacker, Jacob S., and Theodore R. Marmor, How Not to Think About "Managed Care," 32 University of Michigan Journal of Law Reform 661 (1999). Copyright University of Michigan Journal of Law Reform. Used with permission.

Horney, James R. and Van de Water, Paul N., House-Passed And Senate Health Bills Reduce Deficit, Slow Health Care Costs, and Include Realistic Medicare Savings, Copyright, 2009, Center on Budget and Policy Priorities (used with permission).

Leape, Lucian L., Error in Medicine, 272 JAMA 1851 (1994). Copyright 1994, American Medical Association. Reprinted with permission of the American Medical Association.

National Conference of Commissioners on Uniform State Laws, Uniform Anatomical Gift Act. Copyright 2006, National Conference of Commissioners on Uniform State Laws. Reprinted with permission of National Conference of Commissioners on Uniform State Laws.

National Conference of Commissioners on Uniform State Laws, Uniform Determination Death Act. Copyright 1980, National Conference of Commissioners on Uniform State Laws. Reprinted with permission of National Conference of Commissioners on Uniform State Laws.

National Conference of Commissioners of Uniform State Laws, Uniform Health-Care Decisions Act. Copyright 1994, National Conference of Commissioners on Uniform State Laws. Reprinted with permission of National Conference of Commissioners on Uniform State Laws.

National Conference of Commissioners on Uniform State Laws, Uniform Parentage Act. Copyright 1973, 2000, 2002, and 2017, National Conference of Commissions on Uniform State Laws. Reprinted with permission of National Conference of Commissioners on Uniform State Laws.

National Conference of Commissioners on Uniform State Laws, Uniform Probate Code. Copyright, National Conference of Commissioners on Uniform State Laws. Reprinted with permission of National Conference of Commissioners on Uniform State Laws.

Randall, Vernelia, Trusting the Health Care System Ain't Always Easy! An African-American Perspective on Bioethics, 15 St. Louis U. Public L. Rev. 191 (1996). Reprinted with permission of the St. Louis U. Public Law Review.

Schneider, Eric C., et al., Mirror Mirror 2017: International Comparison Reflects Flaws and Opportunities for Better U.S. Health Care, Commonwealth Fund (2017).

Ulrich, Lawrence P., Reproductive Rights of Genetic Disease, in J. Humber and R. Almeder, eds., Biomedical Ethics and the law. Copyright 1986. Reprinted with permission.

# SUMMARY OF CONTENTS

# TABLE OF CONTENTS

# TABLE OF CASES

The principal cases are in bold type.

_____

# BIOETHICS

## HEALTH CARE LAW AND ETHICS

### Eighth Edition

# CHAPTER 1

## AN INTRODUCTION TO THE STUDY OF ETHICS AND ETHICAL THEORIES

### ■ ■ ■

### I.  THINKING ABOUT THE "ETHICS" IN BIOETHICS

At 4:30 on a Friday afternoon, you, as legal counsel for a 300-bed for-profit hospital, receive a telephone call from a physician, Dr. Rodriguez, asking your advice. For some time she has been caring for a 37-year-old man, Mr. Jones, who is in the late stages of lung cancer which has metastasized to his bones. Dr. Rodriguez predicts that Mr. Jones may live for another month or so if treatment is continued.

Treatment consists of chemotherapy (administration of drugs which slow the growth and spread of the cancer), and pain medication (injection of morphine which reduces, although does not eliminate, the pain Mr. Jones experiences). Mr. Jones also has a pacemaker to regulate his heart beat. Dr. Rodriguez has just admitted Mr. Jones to the hospital, and Mr. Jones makes a request that he has made repeatedly in the past. Specifically, Mr. Jones requests that all chemotherapy be stopped and that the pacemaker be deprogrammed immediately, so that his heart will malfunction and cause his death in a very short time. Dr. Rodriguez has talked at length with Mr. Jones about his request and she is convinced that the patient's thinking is clear, and that he is determined and consistent in his wishes. You mention to Dr. Rodriguez that a meeting with the hospital ethics committee or an ethics consultant at the hospital might be of help, and she asks, "How would that help me in this case? This is a legal issue, not an ethical one, right?"

Indeed, just what is meant by "ethics," especially as applied to health care decision making? There are a few inquiries required in approaching an answer to this question: first, we should define and distinguish certain terms that are used regularly in discussion; second, we should consider some of the processes used in applied ethics and health care decision making; third, we should recognize some strengths and limitations of this enterprise generally; and finally, we should attempt to figure out whether

1

this is an ethical question or a legal question and what difference that would make.[1]

### Definitions

While the terms "values," "morals," and "ethics" are sometimes used interchangeably, in this discussion they will be defined and used as follows. *Value* is, in the broad sense, the worth, goodness, or desirability attributed to something, whether moral or non-moral, such as tidiness, efficiency, honesty, and compassion. *Morals,* or morality, refer to those traditions of belief about what is right (or good) in human conduct that develop, are transmitted, and are learned, at least in part, independently of theoretical ethical analysis. Generally, morals are principles that are not amenable to logical proof. *Ethics* denotes that branch of philosophy or reasoned inquiry that studies both the nature of and the justification for general ethical principles governing right or good conduct.

Morality expresses society's basic instructions about what people may and may not do. Religious tenets can also be a source of moral judgments. Ethical theory, on the other hand, describes and justifies such traditions and is often divided into two quite separate areas: scientific and philosophical. The *scientific* branch of ethics gathers and reports accurate empirical information about existing moral beliefs, without evaluating the worth of moral judgments in any way. *Philosophical* ethics moves beyond description and either evaluates important moral concepts (for example, freedom, justice, the good) and moral reasoning from a logical, as opposed to a psychological, perspective, or establishes theoretical justifications for what is right and wrong (or good and bad) in human actions.

Special mention ought to be made of one component of formalized moral tradition that is not necessarily the product of formal ethical theory but which an important repository is, nevertheless, of and force for the moral beliefs of certain groups: codes of ethics. Sometimes they constitute a kind of oath that affirms the highest ideals and standards of the profession and that exhorts individuals always to strive for these standards. Sometimes they also provide rules for expected behavior and conduct, and they suggest, usually in general terms, certain ethical principles that professionals ought to consider when determining conduct. Professional codes are taken seriously and form an important expression of a profession's collective identity and mission at any given time. They are limited, however, in their effectiveness as rational tools for analyzing and resolving ethical issues and dilemmas; there is still a need for the more

---

[1]  This portion of the introduction was prepared in part by Dr. Joan Gibson. See Virginia Trotter Betts, Margie Nicks Gale and Joan McIver Gibson, Ethical and Legal Issues, in D. Critchley and J. Mavrin, eds., *The Clinical Specialist in Psychiatric Mental Health Nursing: Theory, Research, and Practice* 453, 454 (1985).

systematic, comprehensive, and internally consistent analysis of the issues they address.

### Ethics and Process

A somewhat different definition of ethics focuses on one aspect of philosophical ethics: establishing theoretical justifications for what is right and wrong in human actions. Why ought/ought not Dr. Rodriguez accede to Mr. Jones's wishes? Should deprogramming the pacemaker be evaluated in the same manner as stopping the chemotherapy? Indeed, it is asking "Why?" of specific moral value judgments, proffering good reasons in response to that question, and proceeding to ever more abstract reasons that characterize critical thinking generally.

For example, a comparison between the giving of good reasons in science, which is called "explanation," and the giving of good reasons in ethics, which is called "moral justification," reveals striking procedural similarities bordering on identity. Consider the following diagram:[2]

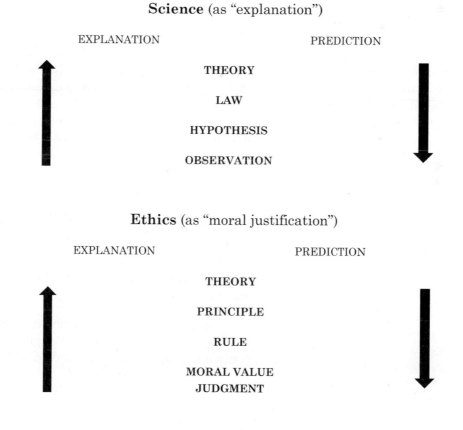

**Science** (as "explanation")

EXPLANATION                                        PREDICTION

THEORY

LAW

HYPOTHESIS

OBSERVATION

**Ethics** (as "moral justification")

EXPLANATION                                        PREDICTION

THEORY

PRINCIPLE

RULE

MORAL VALUE
JUDGMENT

---

[2] Adapted and expanded from T. Beauchamp and L. Walters, *Contemporary Issues in Bioethics* (8th ed. 2013).

## WHY?

. . . Did the pencil fall when dropped?

Because of the hypothesis that all objects fall when dropped.

. . . should Mr. Jones's pacemaker not be deprogrammed?

Because of the rule that you should never do an act that will kill another person.

Why?

Because of the law of gravity, i.e., because objects with mass attract each other.

Why?

Because of the principle of non-maleficence, i.e., you should never do something that will cause another harm.

Why?

Because of the theory of Newtonian Mechanics or General Relativity (which we will not try to describe here)

Why?

Because of the theory of (take your pick) Christianity, Judaism, Islam, Hinduism, Aristotelian virtue, Secular Humanism, Utilitarianism (and others which we will not try to describe here)

Of course, the right-hand column could have read:

. . . should Mr. Jones's pacemaker be deprogrammed?

Because of the rule that you should always do what a patient wishes. Why?

Because of the principle of autonomy, i.e., every person ought to control his own body and mind. Why?

Because of the theory of (take your pick) . . . .

Answering the question "Why?" moving up the column under "Science" is known as explanation: the accounting for observed phenomena at levels of increased abstraction, generalization, and simplification. Moving down the column, once the "Why?"s are answered, generates the power of prediction about future similar observations and phenomena.

And so it is with giving good reasons for individual moral value judgments, like whether Dr. Rodriguez ought to accede to Mr. Jones's wishes. Answering the question "Why?" moving up the column under "Ethics" is known as moral justification. Moving down the column, once the "Why?"s are answered, yields decisions about similar, future moral value judgments that must be made. Answering "Why?" (and thus moving up the column in either discipline) requires that reasons be elucidated and organized. Truth in science as well as in ethics derives not so much from discovering isolated, once-and-for-all answers, but rather from continually articulating, evaluating, and revising the reasons one gives for the continually modified propositions one asserts and the consistently reevaluated judgments one makes. Extrapolating into the future (predicting and making decisions) is only as sound as the integrity of prior explanations and moral justifications. Does this sound a great deal like the process of the development of the common law? Is it any surprise that the courts have been at the forefront of our society's debates on bioethics?

How does all of this apply to the case of Mr. Jones and Dr. Rodriguez? As we saw, Dr. Rodriguez, when considering whether to stop chemotherapy, might say, "As a rule I believe that patient wishes ought to prevail." The first level of abstraction above specific moral value judgments is the level of rule-making, a level of generalization with which most people who justify moral decisions are familiar. It is the "Why?" asked of rules themselves and the move up to principles, however, that has engaged the energies of bioethicists over the past several decades. Why should Dr. Rodriguez normally respect patients' wishes? Is there a harm that would arise if she were to deprogram Mr. Jones's pacemaker? Why should Dr. Rodriguez normally avoid harm? What is her professional responsibility as a physician?

# II. ETHICAL THEORIES

## A. CONSEQUENTIALIST AND DEONTOLOGICAL THEORIES

Most general ethical theories can be categorized as either consequentialist or deontological. Consequentialist theories (also known as teleological theories) judge the quality of an act by the end it achieves. If it maximizes the desired goal, it is the appropriate choice. Essentially, the end justifies the means. Deontological theories are those that justify the moral propriety of an act based solely on its compliance with chosen moral principles. A particular act that produces "good" results is still considered immoral in deontology if the act violates identified moral values.

Arguments centered on the consequences of a particular action or rule—e.g., what impact a particular rule may have on whether or not scientific research will flourish—often stand opposed to arguments that essential human characteristics demand certain restrictions on power—e.g., that human dignity requires that consent must precede the use of individuals as subjects in research. Although consequentialism and deontology are very different theories, they do not necessarily lead to different results in particular situations. So, for example, a consequentialist may argue that consent for participation in research should be required because it will produce scientific progress through better research design (to persuade subjects to participate) and more open sharing of results. In addition, as you will see in the sections that follow, neither approach is entirely absolutist in application. Consequentialist theories can make room for considerations beyond the result produced by the particular, discrete action at issue. Deontological theories likewise generally make room for shades of gray in the moral qualities of actions that might be considered inherently immoral, for example, by analyzing context and intent. Often, but not always, consequential analysis and deontological analysis arrive at the same place, although for different reasons.

Utilitarianism is the most familiar consequentialist theory; and Kantian ethics, the most prominent deontological theory. Both have had great influence in bioethics and in law. Most of us combine utilitarian and deontological reasoning when we confront ethical dilemmas. Courts and legislatures also tend to look at both the inherent moral qualities of acts and their consequences when they decide which actions should be mandated or prohibited by law.

The "trolley problem" is a classic illustration of an ethical dilemma that tests the boundaries and the opposition of consequentialist and deontological approaches.[3] Suppose you are standing at the switch on a series of train tracks when you see a runaway train about to run through the switch and into a group of people standing on the tracks beyond. If the current switch setting were maintained, the train would barrel through a group of five people gathered on one track, surely killing them all. If you were to pull the switch, though, the train would be sent off on a siding, where it would kill one person walking on that track. Should you pull the switch, thereby sacrificing one life to save five? Why? Why not? Before you make your final decision, consider the discussion in the following sections.

Now, suppose instead you were on a bridge overseeing this whole train wreck, and you knew that the lives of the five people on the train track could be saved if—and only if—you pushed the enormous man standing next to you off the bridge and onto the track below just as the train came by. Should you push your fellow train spotter onto the track, thereby

---

[3]    For a full discussion of the trolley problem, see J.J. Thomson, The Trolley Problem, 94 Yale L. J. 1395 (1985).

sacrificing his life to save five? Many of us feel comfortable pulling the switch and diverting the train, presumably because we serve the consequentialist end of saving five lives at the cost of one by doing so. We are far more reluctant to push our neighbor onto the track, sacrificing the life of a known innocent person to save others. It just doesn't seem right, even though the result is equally justifiable in terms of the consequences. It just doesn't seem consistent with the duty we owe another human being.

## B.  UTILITARIANISM

At its base, utilitarianism provides that the proper act is the one that maximizes the aggregate happiness, or "utility," of society as a whole. If an act tends to do so, it is the right act. If it does not, it is not. Two major branches of utilitarianism form the basis of modern consequentialist analysis. Act utilitarianism asks whether a particular, individual act serves to increase aggregate happiness or utility. Rule utilitarianism focuses on rules as a guide to correct conduct and judges whether a rule is correct by the consequences the rule produces. Rule utilitarianism asks what societal rules, rather than individual actions, are likely to maximize happiness in a society. Rule utilitarianism defines morally appropriate conduct as conduct that is consistent with those rules. Rule utilitarianism allows consequentialists to consider principles (perhaps you would call them moral principles) in judging whether a particular action that produces desirable outcomes in the individual instance is nevertheless unethical. As you can imagine, rule utilitarianism has been an especially powerful tool for legal agencies like courts and legislatures.

This simple description of utilitarianism leaves many questions unanswered, and philosophers have been debating the contours of utilitarianism over the past three centuries. First, it is hard to know just what counts as "happiness," and some utilitarian thinkers would prefer to use some other less hedonistic term to define the ultimate goal of all human conduct. Even if we knew what happiness were, though, we would have to figure out how to measure it (could there be a standard unit of happiness?). And, how demanding should we be in requiring that assumptions of what will happen, whether positive or negative, are grounded in empirical evidence? In addition, to judge whether aggregate utility is maximized, we would have to decide how to compare the happiness (or suffering) experienced by one person as a result of the action in question with that experienced by another. This challenge is magnified in the evaluation of the distribution of benefits and burdens (utility and disutility) across society. Most actions and rules produce uneven or unequal distributions of benefits and burdens even when the aggregate effect is to increase utility overall. Utilitarianism also has to confront the question of who counts when we do the math and add up all of the individual levels of happiness so that we can compare the results of different actions and decide which is morally superior. Are children to be treated the same way as adults? How about fetuses? How about unimplanted embryos? How about future generations, children not yet conceived? Those who lack consciousness? Are we to limit the calculus to increasing the utility levels of humankind, or should animals be included too? All animals, from insects to primates, or just some?

Consequentialism is most often criticized for leading to apparently immoral results. It is inconsistent with our notion of morality that an act that would result in the killing of an innocent person, for example, could be justified, even if it maximized happiness. Of course, some utilitarians argue that such results, while theoretically possible, would never govern a society that did the utilitarian calculus properly. Utilitarianism does not mark particular actions—such as murder, rape, lying, and fraud—as inherently unethical. Rather, the acts are to be measured by their aggregated consequences alone. Utilitarianism argues that a consequentialist analysis standing alone could itself reject such actions because of their negative consequences for society as a whole.

Return, then, to the problem at the beginning of these materials. Under utilitarian analysis, should Dr. Rodriguez discontinue the chemotherapy on Mr. Jones? Should she deprogram the pacemaker? Why? Are you applying act utilitarian analysis or rule utilitarian analysis? Are you satisfied with a utilitarian analysis of the potential actions in the trolley dilemma?

## C.  KANTIAN THEORIES

Immanuel Kant is the most influential deontological philosopher, and his work grounds much bioethics analysis. Kant's work is quite visible, for example, in the ethical framework for the regulation of research with human subjects and decision making at the end of life, among other areas in bioethics.

Kant, as a leading opponent of utilitarianism, argued that it is not the consequences that determine whether an action is right or wrong. Instead, Kantianism measures moral action primarily by whether it arises from a "good will." This sense of good will is not the equivalent of having a good heart or simply meaning to do well. Instead, good will for Kant refers to the individual's character or moral goodness. One who acts in a morally acceptable way merely because it produces benefits for himself rather than because he has a moral duty to do so is acting in a way that does not have intrinsic moral worth. True moral worth is evidenced by actions based on a sense of duty rather than personal inclination or the consequences of the act.

For Kant, moral principles (and the duties that proceed from them) are universal rather than subjective or relative. Kant's primary test for right action expresses the universalism of morality. His "Categorical Imperative" states: "I ought never to act except in such a way that I could also will that my maxim should become universal law."

This Categorical Imperative is the core Kantian command, and it is unconditional. While Kant is regarded as a deontologist, some argue that his Categorical Imperative is quite close to the assessment of consequences inherent in rule utilitarianism. There remains a significant distinction, however. Kant strongly asserted that it is not the consequences that determine the goodness or morality of an action but rather the moral principles that inhabit the action.

The Categorical Imperative relies on a critical, but only implied, notion in Kantianism; i.e., the moral equality of all persons. This relational aspect of Kantianism provides a core value in bioethics. It requires respect for all persons as moral beings and holds that persons may never be used merely as means to an end, even where the goal and likely outcome would be a great benefit to other persons. In Kantianism, persons are entirely distinguishable from things in that all persons have inherent worth and dignity that cannot be denied. The Kantian focus on respect for persons grounds the legal and ethical requirements of informed consent and protection of individuals participating as subjects in medical research.

The Categorical Imperative also appreciates individuals as autonomous beings with free will. Of course, Kant also argued that values are universal, and so the emphasis on will in the Categorical Imperative should not be taken to mean that values are subjective and dependent on an individual's personal analysis. Rather, one might expect that freely acting rational individuals will reason to and share universal moral values. The emphasis on individual free will associates Kant with a strong version of autonomy, although an autonomy that is morally bound by freely discerned and accepted principles.

Kant identifies two classes of duties: perfect duties and imperfect duties. Perfect duties are those which support a claim by others to our performance, i.e., rights. Imperfect duties do not support claims of right by others upon us. Examples of perfect duties may include the duty to refrain from unjustly harming another while the related imperfect duty may be the duty to contribute to the well-being of another. The first—the perfect duty to avoid harming another—carries a correlative right on the part of others to demand that this be done. The second—the imperfect duty to benefit others—carries no such rights and others cannot demand, as a matter of right, our efforts on their behalf. Kant argues that perfect duties cannot conflict, and that perfect duties, those that create rights in others, take priority over imperfect duties, which do not create those rights.

Kant's framework is apparent in bioethics in the United States, especially in its emphasis on the inherent worth, dignity, and autonomy of individuals. Although Kant's Categorical Imperative can be seen as being concerned about the well-being of the community, the framework, at least as adopted in bioethics, is criticized as emphasizing the individual to the detriment of the community or society as a whole. Also criticized is Kant's strong resistance to considering the consequences of actions in making moral judgments.

Under Kantian analysis, should Dr. Rodriguez discontinue the chemotherapy on Mr. Jones? Should she deprogram the pacemaker? Why? Are there perfect or imperfect duties that govern the relationship between Dr. Rodriguez and Mr. Jones? Does Kant's framework contribute to your solution of the trolley dilemma?

## D. RELIGIOUSLY-BASED ETHICS

Approaches to ethical reasoning in bioethics that are generally considered religious in nature are typically grounded in belief in the existence of a deity and rely on values that emerge from the guidance of a scripture, respected teachers and disciples, an authoritative central church authority, or highly personalized spiritual perceptions, insights and experiences or, often, a combination of all of these. Religious approaches to bioethics vary considerably, as would be expected with the diversity of religious viewpoints in the United States. Understanding the core principles—including those relating to the nature and purpose of personhood—and how those apply to particular medical treatment decisions often requires the investment of significant time and effort in study. Complicating that inquiry is that there is often significant diversity, and perhaps even conflict, within any particular religious tradition as to how a specific bioethics issue should be resolved.

The influence of religious belief and tradition upon medical treatment decision making by individual patients is well known even beyond the treatment decisions relating to Jehovah's Witnesses (regarding the refusal of blood transfusions) or Christian Scientists (regarding their practice of treatment for illness largely in contravention to customary medical standards). In practice, pastoral support is often engaged to help patients consider their treatment options. When an individual's religious perspective departs from customary or typical decisions, legal standards sometimes, although not always, accommodate that individual in making his or her own health care decisions. See, e.g., Chapters 4 and 5.

Scholarship from a religious perspective has contributed to the body of work in bioethics, and religious leaders certainly participate in public policy debates on science and medicine, some more vigorously than others. Some religious traditions or doctrines have had a significant influence on the legal framework for certain bioethics issues. In particular, Catholic tenets provided the framework used when the issue of decision making on withdrawal or withholding of treatment first reached the courts. Several early court decisions, such as In re Quinlan, 70 N.J. 10, 355 A.2d 647 (1976), which involved Catholic parents, relied on statements by Pope Pius XII supporting withdrawal of ventilator support and the primacy of the patient's choice. (See also Subsection E, below.) Similarly, the tenets of some forms of Judaism have influenced the adoption of choice options regarding neurological determination of death. See Chapter 4.

Applying religiously-based principles or doctrine to public policy in bioethics often engenders considerable conflict in our diverse society, especially when principles based on religious doctrines or perspectives depart from those held by most citizens. This is certainly the case with the use of contraception and access to abortion in many circumstances and appears to be the case with medical assistance in dying. On the public policy level, religious advocates argue that their perspective has a place in the public debate and that it offers principles that will preserve or create a better society. When religious perspectives are enforced at law, however, many argue that religious approaches to bioethics overstep appropriate boundaries and violate the tolerance that marks a civil, secular, and pluralistic society. These conflicts over religion and public policy intensified with the implementation of the Affordable Care Act (ACA) and the determination that contraceptive coverage is an "essential health benefit" within the basic package of benefits required to be offered. Ultimately churches were expressly exempted from this requirement. Other employers, including some that are formally religiously affiliated (such as non-profit religious hospitals and schools) as well as some that are organized as for-profit corporations, argued that offering any insurance that would cover contraception violates their religious liberty. Conversely, employees who do not hold the same religious views argued that denying them coverage violates their religious liberty as regards intimate decision making.

The Obama administration worked out a compromise through which religious non-profits could opt out of providing contraceptive benefits to their employees directly while allowing the companies that provide those non-profits with insurance coverage to provide the employees with the omitted coverage but outside the formal scope of the employees' employment. Ultimately, the Supreme Court decided, 5–4, that closely held family corporations whose owners' sincerely held religious views would be violated by the mandate to provide contraceptive coverage could be accommodated in exactly this same way, and that they must be under the Religious Freedom Restoration Act. Burwell v. Hobby Lobby, Inc., 134 S.Ct. 2751 (2014). For a more detailed discussion of this issue, see Chapter 3. As you can imagine, these battles over employers' obligations to provide contraceptive coverage to their employees reveal conflicts over not only the role of religion in society but other divisions within American society as well.

Finally, in medical treatment decision making, it is not always the patient who is asserting a right to make decisions consistent with their religious beliefs. Health care professionals and health care facilities also have asserted religious liberty rights to refuse to provide certain legally permitted medical interventions, even when their refusal conflicts with the autonomy, and perhaps the religious beliefs, of individual patients. See discussion in Section VI.A below.

## E.  NATURAL LAW

Traditional natural law theories of ethics rely both on the acceptance of a God who guides human beings through divine providence and on the inherent capacity of human beings to be rational actors who know and can choose to act in accord with the precepts of this divine guidance. Under natural law theory, the morally proper act is that to which human beings are naturally drawn by the perfection of human nature. St. Thomas Aquinas is widely viewed as the premier natural law theorist, grounding his theory in Catholic moral theology.

Many view the acceptance of a deity as essential to natural law theories, but some scholars more recently have argued that a secular natural law theory is possible, especially as a theory of law. These arguments proceed from a humanism that views human beings as transcendent, with an innate knowledge of right principles and values. Rather than draw the identification of the good from God, these theorists argue that the good can emerge from the nature of human beings. The foundational principle in our system of government that human beings are "endowed . . . with certain inalienable rights," for example, may evidence a natural law approach, but it is integrated within our legal system whether or not one believes that these rights come from "the Creator."

Natural law theory has had a persistent influence on legal norms. The continuing influence of natural law thinking, however, may be accounted for either as a remnant of the deity-based natural law approach that informed the early centuries of law in this country or as evidence of the continuing power of religious perspectives in our political system.

Like Kantian ethics, natural law is contrary to consequentialist theories of ethics in maintaining that the good holds inherent value, apart from any of its consequences or effects. Life, knowledge, procreation, friendship—all are aspects of the good under natural law theories without any calculation of benefits to individuals or the group. Also, like Kant, natural law theorists reject subjectivism and relativism that would argue that there are no shared concepts of the good.

Although natural law is criticized for its rigid adherence to a set of divine rules, it actually can accommodate a significant space for situational analysis and response. Natural law theory, as it conceives of humans as essential partners in the natural law as rational actors, accepts that the particulars of distinct situations require an individual to exercise her or his own rational capacity and virtue. Still, the theory steadfastly holds to the notion that some actions are intrinsically and absolutely evil. For example, the killing of an innocent is considered to be intrinsically evil in natural law. Yet, natural law theorists accept that some actions that one knows will result in the death of an innocent person are moral under certain circumstances.

### Natural Law and the Doctrine of Double Effect

One tool that the natural law theory uses to describe this paradox—that one can view killing as inherently evil but engage in actions that will surely result in death—is the principle of double effect. Double effect has been an influential principle in the development of health care ethics, with application to a range of health care decisions. The New Jersey Supreme Court in *Quinlan*, the first reported appellate case to allow a family to discontinue life-sustaining medical treatment, showcased a 1957 pronouncement by Pope Pius XII which relied on double effect to explain the moral permissibility of withdrawing life-sustaining respirator support from patients in particular circumstances. Its citation by that court gave prominence to the principle of double effect in subsequent cases.

Aquinas originally formulated the doctrine of double effect using the illustration of self-defense. Recognizing self-preservation as the good, and the killing of another as an evil, Aquinas argues that the value or duty of self-preservation is the objective and intent of self-defense and that the death of the other is the unintended consequence. The moral permissibility of killing in self-defense is entirely conditional and dependent on the proportionality and unavoidability of the response.

The dominant formulation of the doctrine of double effect requires the following four conditions:

1. the act itself must be morally good or at least indifferent;

2. the actor may not intend the bad effect and would avoid it if he could attain the good effect without the bad;

3. the good effect must be produced directly by the action and not by the bad effect itself; and

4. the good effect must outweigh the bad effect.

The principle of double effect is often credited as having improved care of the dying patient by encouraging the treatment of pain even if that treatment, as a byproduct, could also hasten the patient's death. The application of the doctrine of double effect to pain relief was explicitly recognized in Justice Rehnquist's opinion for the majority in Vacco v. Quill, 521 U.S. 793, 117 S.Ct. 2293, 138 L.Ed.2d 834 (1997), in which the Court rejected a claim of a Constitutional right to medically assisted dying. See Chapter 6.

In the context of pain relief, the principle of double effect holds that killing is intrinsically evil but that providing aggressive pain management, even if it may hasten the death of the patient, is morally acceptable, and some would say mandatory, if certain conditions are met. First, the intention of the caregiver must be to relieve the pain but not to directly kill the patient. In other words, the caregiver must intend to provide the good and avoid the evil, even when the particular action may have both effects— the double effect of good and evil. Second, the means chosen to relieve pain must be reasonably designed to do so; and, third, the pain relief must not be produced by the bad effect; i.e., the death of the patient. For example, using pain medication to relieve pain in the dying is acceptable, but using a drug such as potassium chloride that is designed to stop the heart is not even if it will relieve suffering. Finally, the fourth principle recognizes that the unintended bad effect—the death of the patient—is serious and undesirable and so requires that the good effect—the relief of pain— outweigh that effect. Thus, the doctrine of double effect as applied in such cases holds that relieving pain is a good and that good may be pursued, despite the foreseeable result of the patient's death, if the actor's intent is right and the actions themselves are reasonably designed to achieve the good and avoid, to the extent possible, the evil.

This application of the principle of double effect has been subject to serious criticism, however. The first criticism is a pragmatic concern. While the application of the principle to pain management at the end of life has had beneficial effects, it may have strengthened a largely mistaken perception that aggressive pain management actually hastens death. The repeated message to provide pain medication "even if it may hasten death" took on the character of a statement of fact (that pain medication does hasten death) rather than a statement of condition. Second, many reject the principle's premise that intentionally shortening the patient's life is an intrinsic evil rather than a legitimate aid in dying. Third, the intent requirement of the analysis is difficult to apply in practice, especially in a legal context. It is quite common that the family, patient, and professional caregivers near the end of a long dying will welcome death in some sense as a release from suffering. This does not mean that they intend to kill the patient, but testimony concerning conversations in which these parties agree that "it is time" or that "it would be better if he were to die" may be construed as evidence of an illegal killing rather than legitimate and necessary pain relief. The intent requirement is also sometimes viewed as a subterfuge in which health care professionals can use to disguise their true intentions. Natural law theory itself has been criticized by those who see the need for this elaborate double effect exception in order to allow for the humane treatment of some patients as a demonstration of its weakness.

Return one more time to the problem at the beginning of the chapter. Under a natural law analysis, should Dr. Rodriguez discontinue the chemotherapy on Mr. Jones? Should she deprogram the pacemaker? Why? What does natural law require in this case? Is the doctrine of double effect helpful? Does a natural law approach help at all in untying the knot of the dilemma in the trolley problem?

# III. PRINCIPLISM

Biomedical ethics has been dominated by a kind of "principlist" orientation over the past 35 years, and this approach is quite evident in judicial opinions addressing legal issues related to bioethics. The principles enunciated in this approach have been the hallmarks of bioethics debate ever since the National Commission for the Protection of Human Subjects of Biomedical and Behavioral Research issued its Belmont Report, the *Quinlan* case was decided, and Tom Beauchamp and James Childress published the first edition of their enormously influential *Principles of Biomedical Ethics*, all in the late 1970s.

The principlist approach does not necessarily bother itself with the underlying ethical theories that support the principles, and so it may be inappropriate to include it in a discussion of ethical "theories." Because the principles are untethered by specific theories, they are often referred to as "mid-level principles." Principlism can be criticized for operating without an agreed upon theoretical foundation, but it may be just that characteristic that has led to its great influence in law and public policy.

In principlism, ethical principles, "operate primarily as checklists naming issues worth remembering when considering a biomedical moral issue." K. Clouser and B. Gert, A Critique of Principlism, 15 J. Med. & Phil. 200 (1990). The most common checklist of principles includes at least the following:

1.   **Autonomy**. The principle that independent actions and choices of the individual should not be constrained by others.

2.   **Non-Maleficence (Do No Harm)**. The principle that one has a duty not to inflict evil, harm, or risk of harm on others.

3.   **Beneficence**. The principle that one has a duty to help others by doing what is best for them. Obviously, this principle is related to that of non-maleficence.

4.   **Confidentiality**. The principle that when information is divulged by one person to another with the promise, implicit or

explicit, that it will not be revealed to any other person that implicit promise should be respected.

5.  **Distributive Justice**. The principle that benefits and burdens ought to be distributed equitably, that resources (especially scarce resources) ought to be allocated fairly, and that one ought to act in such a manner that no one person or group holds a disproportionate share of benefits or burdens.

6.  **Truth Telling (Honesty, Integrity)**. The principle that one ought to accurately and fully disclose all pertinent information about a person to that person.

There is also one "meta-principle" which is often invoked by those engaged in bioethics discussion, the principle of Professional Responsibility. This principle provides that a professional has an obligation to observe the rules, principles, and moral precepts governing relations with patients, colleagues, the profession as a whole, and the community at large. Professional responsibility, as a normative principle, captures the fiduciary duty owed by health care professionals to their patients. It also can imply an obligation to abide by the virtues or codes adopted by the profession itself.

Some argue that principle-oriented bioethics needs major overhauling—an issue of special interest to those in the legal profession because the law still adheres to the principle-oriented approach with such tenacity. Principlism has provided clarity of thought, separation and identification of moral concepts and issues, and a common language of ethics applied to health care decision making. The approach has its limitations, and challenges to this now "traditional" method of analysis are increasingly frequent. See Section IV, below.

### The Principle of Distributive Justice

Although principlism includes distributive justice among the core principles for bioethics and health care decision making, that principle has largely remained on the sidelines in most of mainstream of bioethics. This marginalization of the principle of distributive justice is especially apparent in the use of principlism for analyzing medical treatment decision making "at the bedside," where autonomy and beneficence are elevated and distributive issues in health care have been minimized. The classic bioethics paradigm for the discussion of distributive justice in health care is not the social and financial constraints that impact decisions concerning end-of-life care but rather the selection of a recipient for transplantation of an available human organ where demand far outstrips supply. See Chapter 4. More recently, however, justice concerns arising in the context of health care disparities and barriers to medical care, especially for racial and ethnic minorities, persons residing in rural areas, LGBTQ persons, the poor, and disabled persons have attracted increased attention.

Application of general ethical theories to questions of distributive justice in health care typically begins with addressing one issue: whether health care is distinguishable from other goods and services that are generally governed by market transactions. Health care may be viewed as unique, or at least as special, because the social costs of disease and disability impair the functioning of society generally, or because health is required for human flourishing and identity, or because the relief of suffering is a special imperative, or because the unequal original distribution of health and illness among persons creates unfair competition among citizens for satisfaction of other needs. Others argue that health care is a consumer good like any other, and lack of health care is the result of personal choices and should remain so.

Any of the general theories of ethics discussed in this chapter may be employed in analyzing ethical issues in the distribution of or access to health care services. A utilitarian approach, for example, would assess the morality of a particular decision or system distributing health care resources by examining its consequences on society as a whole. A deontological approach may focus on analyzing the source of relevant moral duties and how respect for the moral equality of persons would be observed or violated in particular decisions or systems. Moreover, egalitarian and communitarian approaches argue that society has an obligation to its members to provide basic minimal care, however that may be defined, either because it is the only way to assure equal opportunity or because respect for persons requires it. Libertarians, for example, may support a market approach to access to health care because redistributing wealth by force of government power is unjust and that the government controls required to redistribute resources raises costs and limits personal autonomy. As with other ethical issues in bioethics, apparently conflicting theories may produce the same result in particular situations. So, for example, utilitarians may argue that providing health care as a matter of right creates disincentives for self-support, inefficiencies because of the added cost of the distribution system, and excessive utilization because of the separation of payment and consumption. On the other hand, a utilitarian approach may view the harmful societal consequences of denying health care to those unable to pay as outweighing the burdens of providing it.

Discrimination and unequal treatment in health care implicate norms of distributive justice, of course, but they also relate directly to other core principles in the principlist approach. Discriminatory exclusion from health care services, for example, impedes autonomy in health care decision making and can make that value illusory at best. In addition, discriminatory practices, whether intentional or not, can result in harming individuals by producing poor outcomes as compared to others with identical medical conditions. Systemic or structural barriers also can result in individual harms and unequal bearing of illness and disability among particular groups. For example, poorer, predominantly minority neighborhoods where there is a dearth of health care providers and facilities, are left without access to essential care. See Chapter 2.

# IV.  CONTEXTUAL THEORIES OF BIOETHICS

Critics of traditional theoretical ethics point out that not all theories can be neatly classified as utilitarian, Kantian, or natural law in origin. In addition, some bioethics scholars have questioned the application of the dominant principle-based ethical analysis as unnecessarily narrow. Not everything, they argue, can be parsed into manifestations of autonomy, beneficence, distributive justice, and the few other secondary principles (including non-maleficence, confidentiality, and truth telling).

There are a number of ethical approaches that offer an alternative to principlist methodology in bioethics. Some of these approaches represent a return to earlier ethical frameworks. For example, *virtue bioethics*, grounded in Aristotelian virtue ethics, argues that we can tell what ought to be done in particular circumstances by asking what a truly good or virtuous person would do. Personal virtues, including honesty and competency for example, lead to right action. Kant's approach, in fact, is closely associated with virtue ethics as it examines not only the moral principle underlying a decision but also its motivation, requiring that the actor be relying on values beyond his or her own self-interest. Virtue ethics dominated medical ethics for many decades and focused on the character of the good doctor as a source of guidance for decision making. Virtue ethics values the moral agency of health care professionals and argues that other approaches to bioethics mistakenly make professionals the instruments of the patients alone. In turn, critics argue that virtue ethics supports the hegemony of the medical profession.

*Casuistry* is also a centuries-old approach that derives principles from the analysis of individual cases. One example of casuistry, in fact, is the common law system; and not surprisingly, judges have been particularly comfortable with this form of practical, case-based reasoning. Casuistry focuses on the analysis and comparison of like cases. For example, this approach might ask whether it is ethical to deprogram a pacemaker by asking whether this action is more like the refusal of life-sustaining medical treatment by a competent adult (which is legally permitted as a general matter) or more like the purposeful commission of homicide (which is legally prohibited as a general matter). Casuistry seeks to discover the proper course of action through a close examination of the facts in each circumstance and asking whether the current case is more like or unlike other cases previously considered. Rather than deriving general principles from theory, casuistry develops principles from case analysis. Marshaling an accurate and adequately rich accounting of the facts to support a principled and generalizable resolution of a case is a challenge in casuistry just as it is in law. In a related approach, *narrative bioethics* suggests that we can learn a great deal from hearing the stories of those directly involved in episodes of challenging health care decisions. The argument is that hearing the narrative told by the participants produces a deeper understanding of how persons make decisions, how the context of care impacts these individuals and the caregivers, and the complexity of motivations and experiences in health care.

In another approach, a *new pragmatism*, which relies on several different strands of this Nineteenth Century American philosophy, has gained some influence. As applied to bioethics, pragmatism focuses on an empirical approach to problems that examines the context and the consequences of specific actions. This new pragmatism in bioethics is not entirely consequentialist, however, as many leading proponents of the approach argue that a vision of justice or sense of the good must animate judgments made in evaluating consequences. Pragmatism in bioethics often focuses on establishing process rather than specific rules to determine right outcomes, arguing that this method is consistent with the respect for democratic decision making and diversity in values in America. As you will see in many of the issues you study in this text, statutes and case law often resolve conflicts by prescribing procedures that should be followed in settling the dispute—including who should decide, what procedure should be followed, and what are the relevant considerations—rather than prescribing a particular outcome.

Several more recent and significant approaches to bioethics issues take a different approach by working from an in-depth analysis of the broader context in which health care is provided. These methods argue that this broader context—including discriminatory practices or effects, the shifting of hidden burdens to familial caregivers, disparities in access to care, and power disparities relating to gender, class, disability, and race, for example—are all relevant to ethical decision making in health care. This recognition of the impact of the social context of health care criticizes the facially neutral principlist approach as operating from privileged social and professional assumptions and culture. It also emphasizes that some morally significant choices for patients may be severely constrained by inadequate financial and social support, especially for minorities, the elderly, the disabled, and others who are marginalized in society.

Among the more influential of these contextual methodologies are Feminist Bioethics, Critical Race Theory, and Disability Theory. These three do not operate in separate spheres of issues and concerns. In fact, they share a central concern with context, particularly with the context encountered by marginalized persons, and often prioritize the same issues in health care. Furthermore, each of these critical theories explores the impact of intersectionality—the effects of intersecting systems of oppression faced by individuals by virtue of their membership in multiple marginalized categories, such as poor women of color or persons coping with disability and poverty.

## A. FEMINIST BIOETHICS

The feminist movement over the past five decades has focused on a good number of issues relating to health care, especially those affecting women, whether as patients or as the caregivers who most often will bear a direct burden in realizing the patient's choices. Originally focusing on women's health care issues relating to reproductive choice, including contraception, abortion, and choice in assistance in childbirth, the feminist movement reached into other areas of health care decision making. Feminist critiques of standard surgical interventions for breast and uterine cancer, the dearth of research on women's health issues, and the approval of new drugs on male-only research subjects have all had an impact. In addition, feminist analyses of the principlist approach to health care decisions, such as those at the end of life, emphasized that personal intimate relationships were neglected in the principlist focus on the physician-patient dyad and the autonomy of the patient. Feminist theorists also argued that embedded gender-biased power relationships can thwart theoretical autonomy in actual decision making.

There is a wide diversity of thought within feminist bioethics, however, and the various strands of feminist theory may conflict in the analysis of particular bioethics issues. Liberal feminism, for example, rests on a commitment to formal gender equality and argues that women are entitled to equal rights and equal opportunity. Liberal feminism distrusts the allocation of rights, responsibilities, and opportunities along gender lines, even when gender-specific rights would appear to work to the benefit of women, because female stereotypes have unjustly limited women under the guise of protection. Cultural feminism highlights gender differences and argues that apparently neutral rules that treat men and women the same can treat women unfairly. This form of feminist theory argues that male paradigms dominate apparently neutral value systems, including the principlist approach, and ignore an ethic of caring or a more relational approach to decision making that may be characterized as more female in nature. An ethics of caring fostered by this branch of feminist theory requires that we evaluate how the resolution of bioethical dilemmas will affect important human relationships. This approach stresses the caring, personal, and intimate nature of health care and distinguishes that from medicine's more purely scientific character. The emphasis on relationships also contrasts with the emphasis on bare rights that some argue has characterized legal resolution of conflicts over medical treatment decision making. Radical feminism also addresses gender differences, but argues that these are produced by the oppression of women, and that legal standards ought to protect women more actively from male oppression, especially in areas of sexual activity and male violence against women. See generally, Karen Rothenberg, New Perspectives for Teaching and Scholarship: The Role of Gender in Law and Health Care, 54 Md. L. Rev. 473 (1995). One way to understand the differences among these three is to use them to analyze an issue like medically assisted dying. See Chapter 6.

## B.  CRITICAL RACE THEORY

Critical race theory argues that legal and ethical decisions cannot be analyzed apart from the political, social, and economic systems within which they arise, and particularly as these relate to issues of race. Critical race theory argues, for example, that facially neutral principles reflect the dominant culture of white privilege and oppression of African Americans and other minorities. It argues that such principles obstruct the values that emerge from minority cultures within this country as well as values that would be developed in a more racially and cultural diverse society. Furthermore, the application of the professionally accepted principles in health care decision making works to the detriment of persons of color where social and economic systems, including health care, are inherently unjust. For example, this critical lens provides a powerful critique of forced medical intervention and confinement of pregnant women in the name of fetal well-being by exposing patterns that disproportionately harm racial minorities and the poor, illustrating intersectionality. See Chapter 3. Current debates over denial of health care to undocumented immigrants and their families touch upon many of these same issues.

At a minimum, critical race theory argues that the significant impact of race must be included in the development of principles and processes in bioethics to assure just outcomes. Study of the impact of racialized medicine in the United States reveals a pattern of race-based abuse and neglect. Race-based justifications, for example, undergird the forcible or deceptive use of African American individuals as subjects in unethical medical research; and racial discrimination and inequities in the health care system denied access to these important medical advances to the same racial minority. See Chapter 7. Health care disparities related to race persist in terms of access to care, treatment outcomes, and health status. See Chapter 2.

## C.  DISABILITY THEORY

Disability theory asserts that disability is a social, cultural, and political phenomenon, and not simply a medical one. It embraces a social model of disability rather than a medical model of disability, meaning that disability is a social construct rather than a biological fact and its disadvantages flow from societal attitudes and assumptions rather than physical or mental impairments. The classic example distinguishing the social model from the medical model is a person who uses a wheelchair who is unable to enter a building because the only means of entry is a staircase. The medical model suggests that the impairment and the use of the wheelchair are the problem. The social model suggests that the socially created barriers, such as a building design that involves the use of stairs and fails to include a ramp or lift, are the source of disablement.

Disability bioethics brings attention to the ways in which disability impacts health care decisions and experiences. It challenges the historical exclusion of disability perspectives in bioethics and argues that disability perspectives must be included in the analysis of bioethics issues. Those perspectives are informed by the cultural history of medicalized treatment of people with disabilities, including the denial of needed services; inadequate or inappropriate treatment; unnecessary institutionalization often under unacceptable conditions; involuntary sterilization; and other harms. Disability theory argues that disability is part of the diversity of human experience, and rejects the view that life with disability is pitiable or unworthy of living. For example, it calls for examination of assumptions and biases about quality of life that may impact decisions made by physicians on behalf of or when advising people with disabilities.

# V.  CODES OF ETHICS AND PROFESSIONAL OATHS

For the last few millennia, individuals and professional groups have attempted to distinguish themselves from others by adopting and applying principles which define ethically appropriate conduct in their professional roles. Sometimes these principles are accepted by individual professionals by the taking of an oath—a promise—to adhere to them, as in the case of the oath taken by followers of Hippocrates (and many doctors even today). Sometimes these oaths are expressed as contracts, promises, or even prayers, as in the case of the Prayer of Maimonides. Sometimes professional groups, such as the American Medical Association and the American Nurses Association, announce those principles that ought to apply to their membership, as they did in the Principles of Medical Ethics and the Code of Ethics for Nurses. As you read the oath, prayer, and sets of codes and principles which follow, ask yourself some questions about them. Are oaths, prayers, principles, pledges, and codes truly statements of ethics, or are they statements of professional convention and etiquette? Are they statements of fundamental principles, or parts of a contract among health care providers and between health care providers and their patients? Do they give rise to reasonable expectations among providers? Among patients? For the whole society? Which ethical theories are reflected in each of these documents? Does any one of them have any utilitarian element? Why is the utilitarian theory—so popular among philosophers and American courts—so little represented in these statements? Are they consistent with the principles identified in the principlist approach? Do you see imprints of Kantianism or virtue ethics?

Should any of these statements be enforceable in law? Should they be enforceable in some other way? Does it make sense to approve and accept these statements but maintain them as unenforceable exhortations? As you read the material in the rest of this casebook, ask yourself whether the expectations of these oaths and codes have been accepted by the courts, formally or informally, whether they have been rejected by the courts, or whether they have been ignored.

## OATH OF HIPPOCRATES

I swear by Apollo the Healer, by Asclepius, by Hygieia, by Panacea all the gods and goddesses, that, according to my ability and judgment, I will keep this Oath and this stipulation—to reckon him who taught me this Art equally dear to me as my parents, to share my substance with him, and relieve his necessities if required; to look upon his offspring in the same footing as my own brothers, and to teach them this Art, if they shall wish to learn it, without fee or stipulation; and that by precept, lecture and every other mode of instruction, I will impart a knowledge of the Art to my own sons, and those of my teachers, and to disciples bound by a stipulation and oath according to the law of medicine, but to none other. I will follow that system of regimen which, according to my ability and judgment, I consider for the benefit of my patients, and abstain from whatever is deleterious and mischievous. I will give no deadly medicine to anyone if asked, nor suggest any such counsel; and in like manner I will not give to a woman a pessary to produce abortion. With purity and with holiness I will pass my life and practice my Art. I will not cut persons laboring under the stone, but will leave this to be done by men who are practitioners of this work. Into whatever houses I enter, I will go into them for the benefit of the sick, and will abstain from every voluntary act of mischief and corruption; and, further, from the seduction of females, or males, of freemen or slaves. Whatever, in connection with my professional practice, or not in connection with it, I see or hear, in the life of men, which ought not to be spoken of abroad, I will not divulge, as reckoning that all such should be kept secret. While I continue to keep this Oath un-violated, may it be granted to me to enjoy life and the practice of the Art, respected by all men, in all times. But should I trespass and violate this Oath, may the reverse be my lot.

## PRAYER OF MAIMONIDES

Almighty God, Thou has created the human body with infinite wisdom. Ten thousand times ten thousand organs hast Thou combined in it that act unceasingly and harmoniously to preserve the whole in all its beauty—the body which is the envelope of the immortal soul. They are ever acting in perfect order, agreement and accord. Yet, when the frailty of matter or the unbridling of passions deranges this order or interrupts this accord, then forces clash and the body crumbles into the primal dust from which it came. Thou sendest to man diseases as beneficent messengers to foretell approaching danger and to urge him to avert it.

Thou has blest Thine earth, Thy rivers and Thy mountains with healing substances; they enable Thy creatures to alleviate their sufferings and to heal their illnesses. Thou hast endowed man with the wisdom to relieve the suffering of his brother, to recognize his disorders, to extract the healing substances, to discover their powers and to prepare and to apply them to suit every ill. In Thine Eternal Providence Thou hast chosen me to watch over the life and health of Thy creatures. I am now about to apply myself to the duties of my profession. Support me, Almighty God, in these great labors that they may benefit mankind, for without Thy help not even the least thing will succeed.

Inspire me with love for my art and for Thy creatures. Do not allow thirst for profit, ambition for renown and admiration, to interfere with my profession, for these are the enemies of truth and of love for mankind and they can lead astray in the great task of attending to the welfare of Thy creatures. Preserve the strength of my body and of my soul that they ever be ready to cheerfully help and support rich and poor, good and bad, enemy as well as friend. In the sufferer let me see only the human being. Illumine my mind that it recognize what presents itself and that it may comprehend what is absent or hidden. Let it not fail to see what is visible, but do not permit it to arrogate to itself the power to see what cannot be seen, for delicate and indefinite are the bounds of the great art of caring for the lives and health of Thy creatures. Let me never be absent-minded. May no strange thoughts divert my attention at the bedside of the sick, or disturb my mind in its silent labors, for great and sacred are the thoughtful deliberations required to preserve the lives and health of Thy creatures.

Grant that my patients have confidence in me and my art and follow my directions and my counsel. Remove from their midst all charlatans and the whole host of officious relatives and know-all nurses, cruel people who arrogantly frustrate the wisest purposes of our art and often lead Thy creatures to their death.

Should those who are wiser than I wish to improve and instruct me, let my soul gratefully follow their guidance; for vast is the extent of our art. Should conceited fools, however, censure me, then let love for my profession steel me against them, so that I remain steadfast without regard for age, for reputation, or for honor, because surrender would bring to Thy creatures sickness and death.

Imbue my soul with gentleness and calmness when older colleagues, proud of their age, wish to displace me or to scorn me or disdainfully to teach me. May even this be of advantage to me, for they know many things of which I am ignorant, but let not their arrogance give me pain. For they are old and old age is not master of the passions. I also hope to attain old age upon this earth, before Thee, Almighty God!

Let me be contented in everything except in the great science of my profession. Never allow the thought to arise in me that I have attained to sufficient knowledge, but vouchsafe to me the strength, the leisure and the ambition ever to extend my knowledge. For art is great, but the mind of man is ever expanding.

Almighty God! Thou hast chosen me in Thy mercy to watch over the life and death of Thy creatures. I now apply myself to my profession. Support me in this great task so that it may benefit mankind, for without Thy help not even the least thing will succeed.

## AMERICAN MEDICAL ASSOCIATION, PRINCIPLES OF MEDICAL ETHICS
(2001).

### PREAMBLE

The medical profession has long subscribed to a body of ethical statements developed primarily for the benefit of the patient. As a member of this profession, a physician must recognize responsibility to patients first and foremost, as well as to society, to other health professionals, and to self. The following Principles adopted by the American Medical Association are not laws, but standards of conduct which define the essentials of honorable behavior for the physician.

### PRINCIPLES OF MEDICAL ETHICS

I.   A physician shall be dedicated to providing competent medical care, with compassion and respect for human dignity and rights.

II.  A physician shall uphold the standards of professionalism, be honest in all professional interactions, and strive to report physicians deficient in character or competence, or engaging in fraud or deception, to appropriate entities.

III. A physician shall respect the law and also recognize a responsibility to seek changes in those requirements which are contrary to the best interests of the patient.

IV.  A physician shall respect the rights of patients, colleagues, and other health professionals, and shall safeguard patient confidences and privacy within the constraints of the law.

V.   A physician shall continue to study, apply, and advance scientific knowledge, maintain a commitment to medical education, make relevant information available to patients, colleagues, and the public, obtain consultation, and use the talents of other health professionals when indicated.

VI. A physician shall, in the provision of appropriate patient care, except in emergencies, be free to choose whom to serve, with whom to associate, and the environment in which to provide medical care.

VII. A physician shall recognize a responsibility to participate in activities contributing to the improvement of the community and the betterment of public health.

VIII. A physician shall, while caring for a patient, regard responsibility to the patient as paramount.

IX. A physician shall support access to medical care for all people.

## AMERICAN NURSES ASSOCIATION, PROVISIONS OF THE CODE OF ETHICS FOR NURSES
### (2014).

1. The nurse, practices with compassion and respect for the inherent dignity, worth, and uniqueness of every person.

2. The nurse's primary commitment is to the patient, whether an individual, family, group, or community.

3. The nurse promotes, advocates for, and protects the rights, health, and safety of the patient.

4. The nurse has authority, accountability and responsibility for nursing practice; makes decisions; and takes action consistent with the obligation to promote health and to provide optimal care.

5. The nurse owes the same duties to self as to others, including the responsibility to promote health and safety, preserve wholeness of character and integrity, maintain competence, and continue personal and professional growth.

6. The nurse, through individual and collective effort, establishes, maintains, and improves the ethical environment of the work setting and conditions of employment that are conducive to safe, quality health care.

7. The nurse, in all roles and settings, advances the profession through research and scholarly inquiry, professional standards development, and the generation of both nursing and health policy.

8. The nurse collaborates with other health professionals and the public to protect human rights, promote health diplomacy, and reduce health disparities.

9. The profession of nursing, collectively through its professional organizations, must articulate nursing values, maintain the

integrity of the profession, and integrate principles of social justice into nursing and health policy.

## Public Health Leadership Society, Principles of The Ethical Practice of Public Health
### (2002).

1.   Public health should address principally the fundamental causes of disease and requirements for health, aiming to prevent adverse health outcomes.

2.   Public health should achieve community health in a way that respects the rights of individuals in the community.

3.   Public health policies, programs, and priorities should be developed and evaluated through processes that ensure an opportunity for input from community members.

4.   Public health should advocate and work for the empowerment of disenfranchised community members, aiming to ensure that the basic resources and conditions necessary for health are accessible to all.

5.   Public health should seek the information needed to implement effective policies and programs that protect and promote health.

6.   Public health institutions should provide communities with the information they have that is needed for decisions on policies or programs and should obtain the community's consent for their implementation.

7.   Public health institutions should act in a timely manner on the information they have within the resources and the mandate given to them by the public.

8.   Public health programs and policies should incorporate a variety of approaches that anticipate and respect diverse values, beliefs, and cultures in the community.

9.   Public health programs and policies should be implemented in a manner that most enhances the physical and social environment.

10. Public health institutions should protect the confidentiality of information that can bring harm to an individual or community if made public. Exceptions must be justified on the basis of the high likelihood of significant harm to the individual or others.

11. Public health institutions should ensure the professional competence of their employees.

12. Public health institutions and their employees should engage in collaborations and affiliations in ways that build the public's trust and the institution's effectiveness.

### PROBLEM: DRAFTING A PROFESSIONAL CODE OF ETHICS

You are legal counsel to several medical professional organizations, including organizations of physicians, nurses, physical therapists, cafeteria workers, and health care administrators. You have been asked to draft codes of ethics for these organizations. Does this seem like an appropriate endeavor with respect to each of these groups? From whom would you seek advice as you began such a drafting process? What information would you need? Draft an appropriate code of ethics for any one of these professions, and also draft an oath (or affirmation) the professionals should take upon becoming a member of the organization.

## VI.  THE RELATIONSHIP BETWEEN ETHICS AND LAW

Law and ethics are not identical. In fact, some have viewed the participation of lawyers in the debate over ethical issues in health care as an intrusion into the physician-patient relationship; and some believe that the law is too blunt an instrument to deal with the delicate, intimate, and highly variable situations in which ethical concerns arise. Others argue that the law is essential to the protection of patients from medical dominance and overreaching and contributes important values to health care decision making.

It is tempting to assume that all substantial ethical obligations should be supported by the force of law. Paradoxically, however, the "legalization" of a moral obligation, like the "medicalization" of a personal or social problem, can have undesired consequences. While a specific law may be established to deter bad behavior, encourage desired behavior, protect those too vulnerable to protect themselves, or offer an effective nonviolent recourse for disputants, it may also encourage gaming, avoidance, and defensive action to the detriment of patients. Legal standards, usually oriented around ethical minimums, have been attacked as stimulating a drive to the bottom rather than to the optimal and a diminution of commitment to ethical behavior that, in turn, requires more enforcement for less compliance. Law is limited as an enforcer of ethics by the cost or intrusiveness of enforcement, the variability of context, and even by the lack of consensus on ethical norms. It is usually understood, then, that obligations defined by law do not encompass the complete moral obligations of the health care professional, the family, or the patient.

Law and ethics often converge, however, and the two disciplines influence one another. One point of convergence arises in some shared methodology. For example, the common law system in the United States develops principles on a case-by-case basis, with the courts looking for commonalities and distinctions in diverse fact situations. Casuistry, the development of principles from specific situations or cases as described in

Section IV, above, has been a key methodology in bioethics scholarship and education as well. The case method, as you will see in these materials, is a significant teaching and analytical tool in bioethics as well as law. Another point of convergence between law and ethics is evident in the explicit adoption of ethical norms and ethical modes of reasoning in regulation or case law. For example, the regulation of research with human subjects incorporated the ethical framework established in the Belmont Report, which rested on an early version of principlism, and is imbued with a Kantian approach to ethical reasoning. In contrast, the debate over stem cell research has implicated primarily natural law and utilitarian theories. Most case law on end-of-life decision making has explicitly adopted the principlist approach, depending especially upon the principles of autonomy and beneficence. Newer cases on the regulation of assisted reproduction tend to employ utilitarian analysis, while a great deal of the legal regulation of genetic information is explicitly based on Kantian principles.

As you read the legal material in the following chapters, ask yourself which theories are consistent with the judicial opinions in cases concerning bioethics. Consider the *Cruzan* case in Chapter 5, for example. What was the ethical basis of the decision of the Cruzan family to seek authority to terminate Nancy Cruzan's treatment? What was the ethical basis of the Missouri Supreme Court's majority opinion? How is it different from those ethical frameworks that appear to support the majority and the dissenting opinions in the United States Supreme Court? Do any of the United States Supreme Court opinions you will study appear to be based in utilitarianism? In Kantian analysis? In natural law? How do the very different ethical theories applied by different parties and judges in *Cruzan* play out in the context of physician assisted death?

Our law has a number of mechanisms that assure that the law does not directly contradict the demands of ethical behavior, especially on the part of health care professionals. It is common, for example, for courts and legislatures to defer to "professional custom" and "standards of the profession" for the content of legal obligations. Further, various decision making or consultative functions in health care—including institutional review boards that apply ethical and legal norms to medical research and hospital ethics committees that consider situations of individual patients, offer consultation on difficult cases, and establish policies for the hospital— are dominated by members of the health professions and have acquired official legal status. See Chapters 5 and 7. Accommodating or protecting the ethical norms of individual health care professionals, however, can further professional domination and conflict directly with the ethical norms and moral decisions of individual patients. In addition, legislative or institutional policies that allow an individual professional to refuse a patient's choice of treatment on grounds that providing it, although legal, would be inconsistent with the conscience of the provider raise significant concerns.

Despite instances of shared methodologies and the adoption of specific ethical norms, the culture of law emphasizes particular values itself. Law focuses on consistency or fairness, for example, as a primary principle. In addition, law expresses a very strong respect for process over specific outcome as legal institutions have resolved some thorny ethical issues in bioethics by specifying a procedure by which the conflict should be resolved rather than by deciding the substantive outcome. Finally, law generally champions individual rights and personal autonomy over social relationships; and this bias, too, appears within the dominant approaches to American bioethics. The values in law may cause friction with established ethical norms and the culture of the health care professions. In such cases, deference to professional standards and custom is not complete, and legal norms may have overtaken ethical norms in some circumstances. *Quinlan*, for example, intentionally reached beyond the medical custom and ethics of the time to shift authority, at least partially, from the doctors to the patient and family. In fact, the legal requirement of informed consent was established in contravention of established medical custom, although some argue that medicine was moving in that direction anyway. See Subsection B, below. Finally, the greatest culture clash arises with the law's confidence in the adversarial method of advocacy and decision making.

## PROBLEM: ETHICS AND LAW—NEVER THE TWAIN SHALL MEET?

The American Medical Association "Code of Medical Ethics," consists of the Principles of Medical Ethics," most recently revised in 2001, and the Opinions of the AMA Council on Ethical and Judicial Affairs (CEJA). The preamble to the Principles of Medical Ethics states:

> The following Principles adopted by the [AMA] are not laws, but standards of conduct which define the essentials of honorable behavior for the physician.

The AMA Code of Medical Ethics contains several provisions relating to access to care. These include the following:

> A physician shall, in the provision of appropriate patient care, except in emergencies, be free to choose whom to serve, with whom to associate, and the environment in which to provide medical care. (AMA Principles of Medical Ethics)

> . . . Physicians must also uphold ethical responsibilities not to discriminate against a prospective patient on the basis of race, gender, sexual orientation or gender identity, or other personal or social characteristics that are not clinically relevant to the individual's care. Nor

may a physician decline a patient based solely on the individual's infectious disease status. . . . (Code of Medical Ethics Opinion 1.1.2)

Individual physicians should: Take steps to promote access to care for individual patients, such as providing pro bono care in their office or through freestanding facilities or government programs that provide health care for the poor, or, when permissible, waiving insurance copayments in individual cases of hardship. . . . (Code of Medical Ethics Opinion 11.1.4)

Assume that you are a member of the state's medical licensure board: Would you recommend that the state adopt these standards, or perhaps some of them, as legal grounds for disciplinary action or conditions for license renewal? Should plaintiffs in private litigation be permitted to submit these ethical principles into evidence to prove the scope of legal obligations or the standard of medical care? Why or why not? See related discussion in Chapter 2.

[Physicians] should have considerable latitude to practice in accord with well-considered, deeply held beliefs that are central to their self-identities. . . . Physicians have stronger obligations to patients with whom they have a physician-patient relationship, especially one of long standing; when there is imminent risk of foreseeable harm to the patient or delay in access to treatment would significantly adversely affect the patient's physical or emotional well-being; and when the patient is not reasonably able to access needed treatment from another qualified physician. In following conscience, physicians should . . . inform the patient about all relevant options for treatment, including options to which the physician morally objects; . . . refer a patient to another physician or institution to provide treatment the physician declines to offer [and when conscience leads a physician to decline to refer], the physician should offer impartial guidance to patients about how to inform themselves regarding access to desired services. (Code of Medical Ethics Opinion 1.1.7)

Should this provision be enforceable in litigation by a patient concerning a physician's refusal to treat a particular patient or to provide a particular medical intervention which the physician is capable of providing? Should a physician be able to rely on this provision to defend against a hospital's requirement that all physicians holding staff privileges must provide legally mandated emergency care when the physician has a moral objection to providing certain interventions? Before you answer these questions, consider the following section.

## A.  CONFLICTS OF CONSCIENCE AND LAW

The law of bioethics in large part addresses the scope of individual liberties in regard to health care decision making. For example, case law and statutes set limits on abortion; prohibit or permit medical aid in dying;

and regulate the activities of researchers and the participation of individuals as research subjects. See Chapters 3, 6, and 7.

Debates over legal boundaries on individual choice typically contest the appropriate relationship of law and morality. Some argue that the use of the law's power to restrict care (such as abortions or medically assisted dying) believed necessary or desirable by an individual patient enforces a moral, ethical, or religious perspective illegitimately. Others argue that the law must restrict individual choices that they consider immoral because they damage the social fabric, violate foundational civic norms, or injure vulnerable persons. See Section II.D above.

Even where a particular medical intervention is permitted by law, patients and health care providers may disagree as to the morality of that intervention. In this context, both parties assert claims to moral agency, personal liberty, and, perhaps religious freedom. Individual patients claim a right to make their own moral judgment as to whether to receive treatment or not, and individual professionals and health care facilities claim a right to refrain from participating in actions they view as immoral even though permitted by law. These conflicts arise in any number of health care treatment decisions, but have most prominently concerned abortion, contraception, medical assistance in dying, and euthanasia. Beyond these categories, however, these conflicts can arise in medical treatment decision making in particular situations, for example, where health care providers claim that it is unethical to continue treatment that is futile. See Chapter 5.

Some argue that health care professionals and health care organizations surrender some personal liberty when they choose to enter the health care field and should be bound to provide all care allowed by law and chosen by patients as needed. If they are not willing to provide treatment that has been permitted through the democratic and social processes that produce legal rules, they should leave the practice or at least confine their field of work. Others argue that health care professionals are themselves moral beings who should never be forced by law to engage in activities that violate their moral principles or subject their own moral agency to the will of another. If the ethics and character of the health professions are compromised, they argue, the moral character of medicine itself is compromised. Most public policy responses to these claims of conscience seek to balance the claims of patients and health care professionals.

Legislative responses to conscience claims over the past four decades have carved out specific areas in which health care professionals can claim a legal right to refuse particular services as a matter of conscience despite the health burdens that may impose on the patient seeking care. Many of these statutes also try to accommodate the interests of health care facilities where particular interventions violate the religious mission of the facility. Some state statutes address how services are to be provided when individual employees or medical staff refuse to participate on moral or religious grounds. All of these efforts attempt to balance the moral agency of the patient and the moral agency of the health care professional within the context of the need for timely medical care. In some situations, these interests are amenable to compromise because the care is quite easily available elsewhere, although some advocates find any compromise unacceptable. In other circumstances, care will be delayed or denied, and no true compromise is available.

Typically, legislation and regulation extending legal protection (from liability, denial of government funding, or adverse employment actions) to health care providers refusing to provide legal health care services set boundaries on that right of refusal. These boundaries can include identification of the specific interventions (e.g., abortion) that may be refused; limitations on the categories of professionals who fall within the scope of protection; specification of the bases of objection (e.g., religious but not always moral or psychological) that trigger protection; conditional as compared to unconditional protection of refusals depending, for example, on the availability of alternative providers or particular preconditions such as specific notice to prospective patients, required referral systems for services, or timely notice to employers by objecting employee caregivers, and so on. Some legislative "conscience clauses" appear as a provision, or clause, within broader legislation. For example, it is quite common for state statutes on advance directives to include a provision recognizing a right of health care professionals to refuse to comply with specific directives under certain circumstances. See Chapter 5.

The most substantial limitations in these conscience clauses concern the scope of services and the character of the objections they address. Early legislative efforts on both the federal and state levels addressed particular identified services only, focusing primarily on abortion and certain forms of end of life care (often stated in terms of "euthanasia" or "mercy killing"). Some legislation extends a right of refusal to religious and to moral, non-religiously-based objections alike. These broad terms—"religious" and "moral"—can be difficult to define and to apply. Protecting religious objections may require deciding what counts as a religion or a religious objection. Similarly, expanding the scope of protection to non-religious moral perspectives raises questions as to what counts as a moral objection as opposed to objections made on other grounds. Those statutes extending protection to religious objections only favor religion over secular moral perspectives, raising the question of whether that is appropriate in the context of our pluralistic society.

Health care organizations experience the conscientious objection issue in two forms. First, as employers, these organizations are concerned about the effect of protection of individual refusals on their ability to deliver care to patients. Although most facilities provide some room for individual conscientious objections, the broader that is, the more challenging it is for the facility to provide care that is legally permitted or legally demanded as a matter of patient choice or legally enforced as customary medical standards of care. Second, religiously affiliated health care facilities themselves claim protection for their refusal to provide certain forms of treatment when to do so would violate their religious mission and obligations.

Extending conscience protections to health care organizations confronts a number of conflicts. Legally protecting health care organizations in claiming conscience objections, especially if those protections are accorded to religiously-based or faith-based facilities that actively and consistently implement their mission, recognizes that the organization carries the religious values of the individuals that created and lead it. It also recognizes the significant contribution that religious health care organizations have contributed and continue to contribute to serving health care needs. Religious health care organizations are critical to providing adequate health care services to many underserved areas, and they are willing to serve populations that for-profit providers would be happy to avoid.

On the other hand, religiously-based health care organizations accept very substantial support from public funds provided by all citizens, including Medicare and Medicaid payments, publicly funded research, support for residency training, and exemption from income and property taxes. In addition, in many circumstances, allowing a health care organization to deny treatment to patients if there are no other facilities that can provide timely access to care causes significant harm to those patients. Protection for a health care facility's choice to refuse certain services may compromise the moral agency of health care professionals working within that facility. A physician may agree with a patient's choice that a particular treatment is medically necessary and ethically appropriate, but be forbidden by the hospital from providing that treatment within the hospital because it violates the religious principles claimed by the institution. A hospital, for example, may refuse to allow tubal ligations following the delivery of a child to be performed in the hospital even if the patient explicitly requests it and the physician believes that another pregnancy might be dangerous for the mother. The patient can choose to have the tubal ligation sometime later at another hospital, if one is available, but she will have to risk a second surgery. Most conscience legislation, therefore, has permitted facilities to refuse to provide particular services only under certain limiting circumstances.

This remains a very contentious issue. In fact, conflicts over claims of religious liberty relating to the provision of health care have broadened and intensified. In 2018, the Office of Civil Rights (OCR) of HHS established a new Conscience and Religious Freedom Division that will focus on heightening enforcement of current federal statutes that allow health care professionals and organizations under certain circumstances to refuse to provide (or provide training in) abortions, sterilizations, medical aid in dying and other services. The Division is encouraging health care professionals claiming a conscientious objection to file complaints if those objections are not honored and characterizes the matter of conscience conflicts as raising issues of discrimination against religious health care providers. HHS also issued a proposed regulation that adopts a much broader interpretation of the scope of those statutes (by expanding the services, including referrals, that individuals may refuse to provide; the categories of individuals who may claim protection; and what counts as discrimination against an individual refusing to engage in certain health care services) than had been in place under prior regulations. The proposed regulation also provides OCR with strong enforcement remedies. 83 Fed. Reg. 3880 (Jan. 26, 2018).

## B.  INFORMED CONSENT: LAW'S IMPERFECT INTERSECTION WITH BIOETHICS

Informed consent exemplifies how the law pursues but often cannot achieve a bioethical ideal. The doctrine imposes two separate duties on physicians: a duty to obtain a patient's consent to treatment, and a duty to disclose material treatment information. Each is enforced through its own cause of action.

First, a physician must obtain a patient's consent prior to treatment except in emergencies, and this duty is enforced through the intentional tort of battery. Under the battery claim, treatment, in the absence of consent, constitutes "intentional" and "harmful or offensive touching," and even a successful treatment gives rise to damages.

Second, a physician, prior to seeking consent, must also disclose to a patient all information material to the patient's treatment decision. Breach of this duty is treated as professional negligence. States are divided evenly over the standard for materiality. In some, information is "material" if a reasonable person, in what the physician knows or should know to be the patient's position, would consider it significant to the treatment decision at issue. In the others, information is "material" if a reasonably prudent physician would disclose it to a patient in clinical circumstances similar to those of the patient. The two standards overlap significantly, requiring physicians to disclose a patient's diagnosis and prognosis, viable treatment options, and the risks and benefits of those options. To prevail, a plaintiff must also establish that a breach of the duty to disclose caused the patient to consent to treatment ("decision-causation") and that the breach also caused injury ("injury-causation"). Decision-causation exists when a reasonable person, in what the physician knows or should know to be the patient's position, would have refused treatment if that reasonable person knew about the undisclosed information. Meanwhile, injury-causation requires a plaintiff to show that the undisclosed risk actually materialized in the plaintiff's case and caused harm.

The failure-to-disclose claim in combination with the medical battery claim aligns the common-law informed consent with the bioethical principles of truth-telling and respect for individual autonomy. By requiring physicians to disclose to patients information that is objectively relevant to their treatment decisions, the doctrine encourages doctors to be honest with patients about their conditions and treatment options. Additionally, the doctrine forces the communication of information, which improves patients' understanding of their treatment choices and their ability to act autonomously.

As much as the informed consent doctrine exemplifies the convergence of law and ethics, it also demonstrates their incongruity. For example, under the bioethical ideal, a physician would provide all information necessary to enable a patient to make a treatment choice that reflects the patient's unique values. Yet, the law relies on objective disclosure standards and, thus, does not require physicians to serve the idiosyncratic informational needs of each patient. Consequently, the law cannot assure fully autonomous treatment decisions.

Additionally, the informed consent doctrine exemplifies how the law can undermine ethics by "legalizing" a moral obligation. Anxious to avoid liability, a physician may satisfy her common-law duty to disclose material treatment information by delivering a set of rote warnings like a police officer "mirandizes" a criminal suspect. This falls well short of the ethical ideal for a physician to help her patient make autonomous treatment decisions, and it may even erode cooperative decision making by introducing a bureaucratic or adversarial element to the doctor-patient interaction.

There is no question that patients are informed of much more today than they were before informed consent actions became an accepted part of malpractice law in the 1970s. How has that improved the ethical quality of the practice of medicine and the doctor-patient relationship, and how has it undermined it? On balance, were we better off leaving this issue to the discretion of legally unregulated providers, or are we better off subjecting it to the rather blunt instrument of the common law?

## *BIBLIOGRAPHICAL NOTE*

There is a great deal of literature on the principles underlying bioethics and the ethical theories that give rise to those principles. The foundational text in this area is Tom Beauchamp and James Childress, Principles of Medical

Ethics (7th ed. 2013). See also Albert Jonsen, Mark Siegler and William Winslade, Clinical Ethics: A Practical Approach to Ethical Decisions in Clinical Medicine (8th ed. 2015), Bonnie Steinbock, Alex John London, and John D. Arras, Ethical Issues in Modern Medicine (8th ed. 2012). Particularly useful readings can be found in Marsha Garrison and Carl Schneider, The Law of Bioethics: Individual Autonomy and Social Regulation (3rd ed. 2015). The most helpful online reference for those seeking an introduction to philosophy is the Stanford Encyclopedia of Philosophy, available at http://plato.stanford.edu/.

# CHAPTER 2

## DISCRIMINATION AND UNEQUAL TREATMENT IN HEALTH CARE

■ ■ ■

### I. INTRODUCTION

Access to health care depends on finding providers who are willing and able to treat you. But some people are refused medical care or given inadequate treatment for economic and social reasons unrelated to medical need. Among the cases you will read in this chapter are cases in which patients were denied care because they couldn't pay or they had a disfavored form of insurance; because of their race, ethnicity, or national origin; because they had a particular type of disability; or because of their gender.

In addition to individual refusals of care, patients may also experience systemic or structural barriers, indirectly or directly related to the same characteristics that motivate refusals. People with a lower socioeconomic status, and racial and ethnic minorities, are more likely to live in communities with an inadequate supply of providers. The combination of public hospital closures and provider "flight"—physicians and private hospitals leaving poorer, predominantly minority neighborhoods in favor of more affluent, predominantly white ones—has deprived entire communities of essential health resources. People with disabilities and transgender individuals are also at higher risk for not being able to find health professionals or facilities willing to provide the specific care they need. Imagine not being able to get a common diagnostic test, like an X-ray or MRI, at a hospital—this is the situation faced by many individuals with mobility impairments. Disparities in health care access and outcomes across race, gender, and disability persist, even after controlling for factors such as ability to pay and medical need.

Although a number of factors can impact health access and outcomes, this chapter focuses on the role of providers in shaping patients' access to care. Provider decisions about whether to treat patients, and the limits they place on their own capacity or willingness to treat certain groups, are important factors in determining health care access, raising ethical and legal questions about whether and how such decisions should be regulated. This chapter examines the extent to which doctors, hospitals and other types of providers may be legally obligated to treat patients needing medical care, and how effectively these legal obligations address the barriers described above.

This chapter begins with a consideration of the common law. We revisit the traditional legal principle of freedom of contract that governs the physician-patient relationship, which the physician may choose to enter or not. The main cases in this section reveal that the common law privileges the freedom to contract, typically finding no duty to treat regardless of motive for the refusal or seriousness of medical need.

This focus on providers' freedom to contract is consistent with a view of health care as an ordinary consumer good whose supply and demand should be subject to free market principles—a view that has dominated the United States approach to health care for much of its history. But a countervailing view—one that views health care as an essential public good to which everyone should have access—has gained increasing support in recent years and was a dominant theme in the push for the Affordable Care Act. See Chapter 1.

But one cannot talk about a "right" to health care without confronting the fact that this depends on creating a legal obligation to provide care or to ensure access to an adequate supply of providers. This, in turn, implicates questions about how resources should be allocated and who should bear the cost of care. In many of the cases you will read, access barriers are linked to cost concerns—the risk of being unable to collect payment or being undercompensated for service, as well as concerns about how to distribute limited health care resources, such as hospital services, across different communities. The Affordable Care Act has somewhat ameliorated, but has not eliminated, these concerns.

Although there is no universal right to health care in the U.S., there is a patchwork of federal statutes limiting providers' freedom to deny care under certain circumstances or for specific reasons. The remaining parts of the chapter examine this legal patchwork. Section III focuses on the Emergency Medical Treatment and Labor Act (EMTALA). Enacted to respond to the specific problem of "patient dumping" in hospital emergency departments, EMTALA creates a limited duty to treat and only under specific circumstances. Section IV reviews a set of statutes that apply nondiscrimination principles to the provision of health care in the following areas: race, color or national origin; disability; and sex discrimination. These antidiscrimination principles limit providers' right to refuse to treat patients based on particular characteristics and, at times, have been used to limit institutional policies or practices that result in unequal treatment or health care inequity based on protected characteristics.

# II.  COMMON LAW APPROACHES

## RICKS V. BUDGE
Supreme Court of Utah, 1937.
91 Utah 307, 64 P.2d 208.

EPHRAIM HANSON, JUSTICE.

This is an action for malpractice against the defendants who are physicians and surgeons at Logan, Utah, and are copartners doing business under the name and style of the "Budge Clinic." . . . [P]laintiff alleges that he was suffering from an infected right hand and was in immediate need of medical and surgical care and treatment, and there was danger of his dying unless he received such treatment; that defendants for the purpose of treating plaintiff sent him to the Budge Memorial Hospital [BMH] at Logan, Utah; that while at the hospital and while he was in need of medical and surgical treatment, defendants refused to treat or care for plaintiff and abandoned his case. . . .

\* \* \*

[T]he evidence shows that when plaintiff left the hospital on March 15th, Dr. [S.M.] Budge advised him to continue the same treatment that had been given him at the hospital, and that if the finger showed any signs of getting worse at any time, plaintiff was to return at once to Dr. Budge for further treatment; that on the morning of March 17th, plaintiff telephoned Dr. Budge, and explained the condition of his hand; that he was told by the doctor to come to his office, and in pursuance of the doctor's request, plaintiff reported to the doctor's office at 2 p.m. of that day. Dr. Budge again examined the hand, and told plaintiff the hand was worse; he called in Dr. D.C. Budge, another of the defendants, who examined the hand, scraped it some, and indicated thereon where the hand should be opened. Dr. S.M. Budge said to plaintiff: "You have got to go back to the hospital." . . . Within a short time after the arrival of plaintiff, Dr. S.M. Budge arrived at the hospital. Plaintiff testified: "He [meaning Dr. S.M. Budge] came into my room and said, 'You are owing us. I am not going to touch you until that account is taken care of.'" (The account referred to was, according to plaintiff, of some years' standing and did not relate to any charge for services being then rendered.) Plaintiff testified that he did not know what to say to the doctor, but that he finally asked the doctor if he was going to take care of him, and the doctor replied: "No, I am not going to take care of you. I would not take you to the operating table and operate on you and keep you here thirty days, and then there is another $30.00 at the office, until your account is taken care of." Plaintiff replied: "If that is the idea, if you will furnish me a little help, I will try to move."

[A]fter being dressed, he left [BMH] to seek other treatment. At that time it was raining. He walked to the Cache Valley Hospital [CVH], a few blocks away, and there met Dr. Randall, who examined the hand. Dr. Randall testified that when the plaintiff arrived at [CVH], the hand was swollen with considerable fluid oozing from it; that the lower two-thirds of the forearm was red and swollen from the infection which extended up in the arm, and that there was some fluid also oozing from the back of the hand, and that plaintiff required immediate surgical attention; that immediately after the arrival of plaintiff at the hospital he made an incision through the fingers and through the palm of the hand along the tendons that led from the palm, followed those tendons as far as there was any bulging, opened it up thoroughly all the way to the base of the hand, and put drain tubes in. . . . About two weeks after the plaintiff entered [CVH], it became necessary to amputate the middle finger and remove about an inch of the metacarpal bone.

\* \* \*

Defendants contend: (1) That there was no contract of employment between plaintiff and defendants and that defendants in the absence of a valid contract were not obligated to proceed with any treatment; and (2) that if there was such a contract, there was no evidence that the refusal of Dr. S.M. Budge to operate or take care of plaintiff resulted in any damage to plaintiff.

\* \* \*

Under this evidence, it cannot be said that the relation of physician and patient did not exist on March 17th. It had not been terminated after its commencement on March 11th. When the plaintiff left the hospital on March 15th, he understood that he was to report to Dr. S.M. Budge if the occasion required and was so requested by the doctor. Plaintiff's return to the doctor's office was on the advice of the doctor. While at the doctor's office, both Dr. S.M. Budge and Dr. D.C. Budge examined plaintiff's hand and they ordered that he go at once to the hospital for further medical attention. That plaintiff was told by the doctor to come to the doctor's office and was there examined by him and directed to go to the hospital for further treatment would create the relationship of physician and patient. That the relationship existed at the time the plaintiff was sent to the hospital on March 17th cannot be seriously questioned.

We believe the law is well settled that a physician or surgeon, upon undertaking an operation or other case, is under the duty, in the absence of an agreement limiting the service, of continuing his attention, after the first operation or first treatment, so long as the case requires attention. The obligation of continuing attention can be terminated only by the cessation of the necessity which gave rise to the relationship, or by the discharge of the physician by the patient, or by the withdrawal from the case by the physician after giving the patient reasonable notice so as to enable the patient to secure other medical attention. A physician has the right to withdraw from a case, but if the case is such as to still require further medical or surgical attention, he must, before withdrawing from the case, give the patient sufficient notice so the patient can procure other medical attention if he desires.[ ]

\* \* \*

We cannot say as a matter of law that plaintiff suffered no damages by reason of the refusal of Dr. S.M. Budge to further treat him. The evidence shows that from the time plaintiff left the office of the defendants up until the time that he arrived at [CVH] his hand continued to swell; that it was very painful; that when he left [BMH] he was in such condition that he did not know whether he was going to live or die. That both his mental and physical suffering must have been most acute cannot be questioned. While the law cannot measure with exactness such suffering and cannot determine with absolute certainty what damages, if any, plaintiff may be entitled to, still those are questions which a jury under proper instructions from the court must determine.

\* \* \*

FOLLAND, JUSTICE (concurring in part, dissenting in part).

\* \* \*

. . . The theory of plaintiff as evidenced in his complaint is that there was no continued relationship from the first employment but that a new relationship was entered into. He visited the clinic on March 17th; the Doctors Budge examined his hand and told him an immediate operation was necessary and for him to go to the hospital. I do not think a new contract was entered into at that time. There was no consideration for any implied promise that Dr. Budge or the Budge Clinic would assume the responsibility of another operation and the costs and expenses incident thereto. As soon as Dr. Budge reached the hospital he opened negotiations with the plaintiff which might have resulted in a contract, but before any contract arrangement was made the plaintiff decided to leave the hospital and seek attention elsewhere. As soon as he could dress himself he walked away. There is conflict in the evidence as to the conversation. Plaintiff testified in effect that Dr. Budge asked for something to be done about an old account. The doctor's testimony in effect was that he asked that some arrangement be made to take care of the doctor's bill and expenses for the ensuing operation and treatment at the hospital. The result, however, was negative. No arrangement was made. The plaintiff made no attempt whatsoever to suggest to the doctor any way by which either the old account might be taken care of or the expenses of the ensuing operation provided for. . . . Dr. Budge had a right to refuse to incur the obligation and responsibility incident to one or more operations and the treatment and attention which would be necessary. If it be assumed that the contract relationship of physician and patient existed prior to this conversation, either as resulting from the first employment or that there was an implied contract entered into at the clinic, yet Dr. Budge had the right with proper notice to discontinue the relationship. While plaintiff's condition was acute and needed immediate attention, he received such immediate attention at [CVH]. There was only a delay of an hour or two, and part of that delay is accounted for by reason of the fact that the doctor at [CVH] would not operate until some paper, which plaintiff says he did not read, was signed. Plaintiff said he could not sign it but that it was signed by his brother before the operation was performed. We are justified in believing that by means of this written obligation, provision was made for the expenses and fees about to be incurred. I am satisfied from my reading of the record that no injury or damage resulted from the delay occasioned by plaintiff leaving the Budge Hospital and going to [CVH]. He was not in such desperate condition but that he was able to walk the three or four blocks between the two hospitals. . . .

## CHILDS V. WEIS

Court of Civil Appeals of Texas, 1969.
440 S.W.2d 104.

WILLIAMS, J.

On or about November 27, 1966 Daisy Childs, wife of J.C. Childs, a resident of Dallas County, was approximately seven months pregnant. On that date she was visiting in Lone Oak, Texas, and about two o'clock A.M. she presented herself to the Greenville Hospital emergency room. At that time she stated she was bleeding and had labor pains. She was examined by a nurse who identified herself as H. Beckham. According to Mrs. Childs, Nurse Beckham stated that she would call the doctor. She said the nurse returned and stated "that the Dr. said that I would have to go to my doctor in Dallas. I stated to Beckham that I'm not going to make it to Dallas. Beckham replied that yes, I would make it. She stated that I was just starting into labor and that I would make it. The weather was cold that night. About an hour after leaving the Greenville Hospital Authority I had the baby while in a car on the way to medical facilities in Sulphur Springs. The baby lived about 12 hours."

[Dr. Weis] said that he had never examined or treated Daisy Childs and in fact had never seen or spoken to either Daisy Childs or her husband, J.C. Childs, at any time in his life. He further stated that he had never at any time agreed or consented to the examination or treatment of either Daisy Childs or her husband. He said that on a day in November 1966 he recalled a telephone call received by him from a nurse in the emergency room at the Greenville Surgical Hospital; that the nurse told him that there was a negro girl in the emergency room having a "bloody show" and some "labor pains." He said the nurse advised him that this woman had been visiting in Lone Oak, and that her OB doctor lived in Garland, Texas, and that she also resided in Garland. The doctor said, "I told the nurse over the telephone to have the girl call her doctor in Garland and see what he wanted her to do. I knew nothing more about this incident until I was served with the citation and a copy of the petition in this lawsuit."

\* \* \*

Since it is unquestionably the law that the relationship of physician and patient is dependent upon contract, either express or implied, a physician is not to be held liable for arbitrarily refusing to respond to a call of a person even urgently in need of medical or surgical assistance provided that the relation of physician and patient does not exist at the time the call is made or at the time the person presents himself for treatment.

\* \* \*

Applying these principles of law to the factual situation here presented we find an entire absence of evidence of a contract, either express or implied, which would create the relationship of patient and physician as between Dr. Weis and Mrs. Childs. Dr. Weis, under these circumstances, was under no duty whatsoever to examine or treat Mrs. Childs. When advised by telephone that the lady was in the emergency room he did what seems to be a reasonable thing and inquired as to the identity of her doctor who had been treating her. Upon being told that the doctor was in Garland he stated that the patient should call the doctor and find out what should be done. This action on the part of Dr. Weis seems to be not only reasonable but within the bounds of professional ethics.

We cannot agree with appellant that Dr. Weis' statement to the nurse over the telephone amounted to an acceptance of the case and affirmative instructions which she was bound to follow. Rather than give instructions which could be construed to be in the nature of treatment, Dr. Weis told the nurse to have the woman call her physician in Garland and secure instructions from him.

The affidavit of Mrs. Childs would indicate that Nurse Beckham may not have relayed the exact words of Dr. Weis to Mrs. Childs. Instead, it would seem that Nurse Beckham told Mrs. Childs that the doctor said that she would "have to go" to her doctor in Dallas. Assuming this statement was made by Nurse Beckham, and further assuming that it contained the meaning as placed upon it by appellant, yet it is undisputed that such words were uttered by Nurse Beckham, and not by Dr. Weis. . . .

[The court affirmed summary judgment in favor of the defendant.]

## WILLIAMS V. U.S.

United States Court of Appeals, Fourth Circuit, 2001.
242 F.3d 169.

NIEMEYER, CIRCUIT JUDGE:

* * *

The revised amended complaint in this case alleges that in October 1997, Berlie White, while at a restaurant in Cherokee, North Carolina, became short of breath, developing "various signs of respiratory distress." Asserting that he was suffering from a medical emergency, White presented himself at about 7:00 p.m. to the emergency room of the nearby Cherokee Indian Hospital [CIH], an Indian hospital operated on the Cherokee Reservation by the United States Public Health Service. Federal employees operating the hospital refused to treat White or to refill his oxygen tank because he was not Indian. [The hospital was funded under the federal Indian Health Care Improvement Act which prohibits the hospital from treating non-Indians, with the exception of emergency medical treatment which the hospital is permitted but not required to provide to non-Indians.] They referred him to the Swain County Hospital [SCH] . . ., approximately 10 miles away. When White arrived at [SCH], he was in extreme respiratory distress, and he died the next day. The complaint alleges that White's death was caused by CIH's "refusal to provide any treatment or assistance" and "the delay of his access to medical care."

The United States filed a motion to dismiss. . . . The district court agreed, dismissing the action. In doing so, it held that . . . North Carolina has no law creating a duty in favor of a private person to provide medical treatment or to recover for a discriminatory refusal to provide medical treatment. [The plaintiff, representing White's estate, brought several claims under federal law, all of which also were dismissed.]

* * *

The North Carolina Supreme Court has held that a physician has no duty to render services to every person seeking them. See Childers v. Frye, 201 N.C. 42, 158 S.E. 744 (1931). The *Childers* court based its decision on a contract theory, concluding that a physician's decision of whether to treat a person amounts to a decision of whether to enter into a contractual relationship. In the case of an unconscious patient, where a traditional contract relationship could not be formed, the court explained that liability would then be established only if "the physician actually accepted an injured person as a patient and undertook to treat him." Holding that the common law does not limit a medical provider's discretion to turn away potential patients, the court found it unobjectionable that the doctor had refused to treat the patient because he mistakenly believed the patient was drunk.

Despite the holding in *Childers,* Williams advances four theories as to why a healthcare provider in North Carolina has a duty not to discriminate in the provision of emergency medical care. First, [plaintiff] argues that N.C.G.S. § 58–65–85, which prohibits nonprofit hospitals from discriminating on the basis of race, color, and national origin, would provide her with a cause of action against a private hospital. This provision, however, is part of North Carolina's Insurance Code and applies only to nonprofit hospitals seeking reimbursement from the North Carolina Department of Insurance. Moreover, the statute does not apply to every private hospital. Most importantly, we have been unable to find any North Carolina case that interprets this statute to give rise to a private cause of action.

Second, [plaintiff] directs us to N.C.G.S. § 131A–8, a statute pertaining to hospitals receiving state financing, which states, "All health care facilities shall be operated to serve and benefit the public and there shall be no discrimination against any person based on race, creed, color or national origin." Again, this statute does not provide a private enforcement mechanism. Arguably, the North Carolina Medical Care Commission is authorized to enforce this nondiscrimination rule [ ] . . . . While § 131A–15 permits "[a]ny holder of bonds or notes issued under the provisions of this Chapter" to bring suit to enforce his contractual rights under the bond, this provision does not authorize a private enforcement action against a hospital that has discriminated in violation of § 131A–8.

Third, [plaintiff] relies on the Patients' Bill of Rights, § 3C.4103, a state agency rule promulgated pursuant to the Hospital Licensure Act, N.C.G.S. § 131E 75. Again, however, the legislature provided for enforcement of this Act only by the North Carolina Department of Health and Human Services.

Finally, [plaintiff], relying on a Georgia case, asserts a common law duty based on her theory that a hospital emergency room is a "public utility." See Williams v. Hosp. Auth., 119 Ga.App. 626, 168 S.E.2d 336, 337 (1969) ("To say that a public institution which has assumed this duty and held itself out as giving such aid can arbitrarily refuse to give emergency treatment to a member of the public who presents himself with 'a broken arm and in a state of traumatic injury, suffering mental and physical pain visible and obvious to the hospital employees' is repugnant to our entire system of government"). In *Williams,* however, the court "express[ed] no opinion on the [existence of a] duty of a *private* hospital in Georgia." (emphasis added). . . .

The scope of duties imposed by positive law is necessarily narrower than the reach of moral command, and this case presents a tragic circumstance, if the allegations of the complaint are true, that could have been avoided by simple obedience to a moral command. That individuals at [CIH] would deny Berlie White the most meager of medical assistance— that of refilling his oxygen tank when it had run out—at a time of extreme need is incomprehensible, particularly when these individuals were not prohibited by law from providing White with this assistance. If they did deny White this minimal care, the burden of their moral failure will surely remain with them.

AFFIRMED.

## NOTES AND QUESTIONS

1.     Why did the doctor refuse to treat Mr. Ricks? Ms. Childs? Mr. White? In determining whether a physician has a legal duty to provide care, should courts distinguish among such cases on the basis of the reason for the refusal, the circumstances of the refusal, or both? Consider the following ethical prescriptions adopted by the American Medical Association (AMA):

A physician shall, in the provision of appropriate patient care, except in emergencies, be free to choose whom to serve, with whom to associate, and the environment in which to provide medical care. AMA Principles of Medical Ethics VI (Adopted June 1957; revised June 1980; revised June 2001).

. . . Differences in treatment that are not directly related to differences in individual patients' clinical needs or preferences constitute inappropriate variations in health care. . . . [P]hysicians . . . ethically are called on to provide the same quality of care to all patients without regard to medically irrelevant personal characteristics. . . . [P]hysicians should [p]rovide care that meets patient needs and respects patient preferences[;] [a]void stereotyping patients[;] [e]xamine their own practices to ensure that inappropriate considerations about race, gender identity, sexual orientation, sociodemographic factors, or other nonclinical factors, do not affect clinical judgment. . . . AMA, Opinion 8.5 Disparities in Health Care, Code of Medical Ethics (2016).

. . . Individual physicians should . . . promote access to care for individual patients, such as providing pro bono care in their office or through freestanding facilities or government programs that provide health care for the poor, or when permissible, waiving insurance copayments in individual cases of hardship. . . . AMA, Opinion 11.1.4 Financial Barriers to Health Care Access, Code of Medical Ethics (2009).

The AMA considers these to be ethical principles, not legal ones. Creating an ethical principle that encourages caring for the poor is very different from creating a legal duty to treat that requires physicians to care for patients even if they cannot pay. Should we go this far? Or should the law merely narrow limits on when a provider can refuse treatment? If so, where would you draw the line? Even the AMA seems to draw certain lines in its ethical prescriptions. What factors seem most salient to the AMA's conceptions of physicians' ethical duty of care? What provider interests are implicated by creating a duty to treat?

2.     Although *Ricks* seemed to embrace the common law rule allowing physicians to refuse to establish a treatment relationship with a patient, the decision refers to "well-settled limits" on the physician's ability to terminate that relationship. One limit is that a physician must give the patient "reasonable notice so as to enable the patient to secure other medical attention." Does this mean that the physician must continue to treat the patient until the patient finds someone else to treat her? What if she can't find someone else to treat her? This is not merely a theoretical question; questions about the content of this duty are at the heart of challenges to hospital discharge practices of homeless patients. See e.g., Joseph Serna, Hospital Agrees to Pay $450,000 to L.A. to Settle Homeless Patient Dumping Lawsuit, L.A. Times (Oct. 25, 2016).

3.     In *Childs*, the court says that "it is unquestionably the law that the relationship of physician and patient is dependent upon contract, either express or implied," but this raises the question about what facts would support a finding of "implied" contract, especially in the context of an emergency. Presumably, a medical provider undertaking to care for a patient in an emergency evidences the willingness to enter into a physician-patient relationship; but what qualifies as such an "undertaking"? Does a medical professional have to begin administering treatment or is action that creates a reasonable expectation of treatment enough? See, for example, New Biloxi Hospital, Inc. v. Frazier, 245 Miss. 185, 146 So.2d 882 (Miss. 1962), in which the court held a hospital liable for the death of a patient who remained untreated in the emergency room for over two hours and died twenty-five minutes after transfer to a Veterans Administration hospital. The court based its holding on the hospital's breach of the duty to exercise reasonable care once treatment had been undertaken and it noted the special role of emergency professionals: "A hospital rendering emergency treatment is obligated to do that which is immediately and reasonably necessary for the preservation of the life, limb or health of the patient. It should not discharge a patient in a critical condition without furnishing or procuring suitable medical attention." The court described the scene in detail:

> . . . Sam Frazier was a 42 year old Negro man, who had lost his left eye and his left arm, just below the elbow, during World War II. He and his wife had two young children.

> . . . [Mr. Frazier was brought to the emergency department after being shot.] The blast made two large holes in the upper arm and tore away the brachial artery. . . . Ambulance attendants carried him into the emergency room, where one of the Hospital's nurses just looked at him and walked away. He was bleeding profusely at that time. There was blood all over the ambulance cot, and while waiting in the hospital, blood was

streaming from his arm to the floor, forming a puddle with a diameter of 24–30 inches. After about twenty minutes, another Hospital nurse came, looked at Frazier and walked away.

. . . Neither [the nurse] nor the doctor made any effort to stop the bleeding in any way. [The nurse] continued to come in and out of the emergency room on occasion, but simply looked at Frazier. He asked to see his little boy, and for water. His bleeding continued. * * *

This summary of the evidence reflects that Frazier was permitted to bleed to death. . . .

Tort principles have also been used by courts to find an implied duty to treat in emergency settings. See Wilmington Gen. Hospital v. Manlove, 174 A.2d 135 (Del. 1961), holding that a hospital must provide emergency care to a person who relies on the presence of an emergency department in coming to the hospital. The court analogized this to the negligent termination of gratuitous services because "such a refusal might well result in worsening the condition of the injured person, because of the time lost in a useless attempt to obtain medical aid." Given the unpredictable and inconsistent application of different states' common law principles to the denial of care in emergency settings, and the often devastating effects of such denials, the federal government eventually addressed the problem through federal statute. See Section III below.

4.    Physicians often commit by contract to treat a certain group of patients, for example in contracts with health plans or in employment contracts with health care facilities or employers. Physician specialists often have a contractual relationship with the hospital to be on-call for essential services, either for compensation or as required in the medical staff by-laws as a condition of staff privileges. These commitments to an organization may be sufficient to create a physician-patient relationship and trigger a duty to provide treatment. See e.g., Hiser v. Randolph, 126 Ariz. 608, 617 P.2d 774 (Ariz. 1980); Millard v. Corrado, 14 S.W.3d 42 (Mo. Ct. App. 1999). But see, Seeber v. Ebeling, 36 Kan.App.2d 501, 141 P.3d 1180 (2006), holding that no claim was available against an on-call specialist who refused to come to the hospital due to fatigue. See also, discussion of on-call physicians under EMTALA in Section III, below.

5.    Some states have statutes or regulations limiting hospitals' ability to refuse care in some circumstances, but this does not necessarily guarantee an enforceable right to treatment. For example, the most recent version of the regulations promulgated under the hospital licensure statute of North Carolina at issue in *Williams* provide that:

[a] patient has the right to expect emergency procedures to be implemented without unnecessary delay [and] the right to medical and nursing services without discrimination based upon race, color, religion, sex, sexual orientation, gender identity, national origin, or source of payment. 10A N.C. Admin. Code tit. 13B.3302(6) & (13).

The state licensing agency had authority to investigate violations of this provision, but *Williams* held that there was no private right of enforcement. In contrast, see Thompson v. Sun City Community Hospital, Inc., 141 Ariz. 597, 688 P.2d 605 (1984), where the court relied on state hospital regulations and private accreditation standards to find a duty to provide emergency care enforceable through private litigation.

6.    *Williams* considers state law governing not-for-profit organizations, but federal law also regulates tax-exempt hospitals, which have "charitable" obligations. To satisfy these charitable obligations, non-profit hospitals must provide some level of community benefit and they must meet certain standards relating to emergency care and financial assistance plans.

### PROBLEM: CHERYL HANACHEK

Cheryl Hanachek, a law student residing in Boston, discovered she was pregnant during an "action" called by the city's obstetricians in protest against Medicaid and discounted private insurance payment rates. Ms. Hanachek first called Dr. Cunetto, who had been her obstetrician for the birth of her first child two years earlier. Dr. Cunetto's receptionist informed Ms. Hanachek that Dr. Cunetto wasn't taking any patients covered by Ms. Hanachek's health plan.

About two weeks later, Ms. Hanachek called Dr. Simms, who had been recommended by her sister. Dr. Simms' receptionist told Ms. Hanachek that Dr. Simms was not taking any new patients as his malpractice premiums were so high that he was even considering discontinuing his obstetrical practice. In fact, however, Dr. Simms actually did not accept lawyers as patients. Ms. Hanachek reported to the receptionist that she was having infrequent minor cramping, and the receptionist told her that this was "nothing to worry about at this stage." Later that night Ms. Hanachek was admitted to the hospital on an emergency basis. Ms. Hanachek was in shock from blood loss due to a ruptured ectopic pregnancy. As a result of the rupture and other complications, Ms. Hanachek underwent a hysterectomy.

Ms. Hanachek has brought suit against Dr. Cunetto and Dr. Simms. If you were representing Ms. Hanachek, how would you proceed in arguing and proving your case?

## III.  EMTALA: THE EXCEPTION FOR EMERGENCY CARE

This Section and Section IV survey the statutory tools used to address certain barriers to health care. For each statutory tool, consider what particular barrier(s) the law is attempting to address, the scope of protection the law provides, and the limits of the statute. How effective is each statute at addressing the problem it was enacted to solve? What about as a tool for protecting health care access generally?

In 1986, the federal Emergency Medical Treatment and Labor Act (EMTALA), 42 U.S.C.A. § 1395dd, was enacted in response to "patient dumping," a practice in which patients are transferred from one hospital's emergency department to another's—typically from a private hospital to a public hospital—for other than therapeutic reasons.

Several empirical studies documented patient dumping as a widespread practice. See e.g., Robert L. Schiff et al., Transfers to a Public Hospital, 314 NEJM 552 (1986). Researchers determined that transferred patients tended to be uninsured or government-insured patients, with one study revealing that lack of insurance was the reason given for transfer in 87% of the cases. The findings also suggested a dramatic increase in transfers during the 1980s—coinciding with large cuts in government funding for health care and a growth in uninsured Americans from 25 million in 1977 to 35 million in 1987. Researchers also found that significant percentages of patients transferred were medically unstable at the time transfer and experienced an average delay of over five hours before receiving treatment. Finally, such transfers were found to disproportionately impact racial minorities. See also Robert L. Schiff & David Ansell, Federal Anti-Patient-Dumping Provisions: The First Decade, 28 Annals Emergency Med. 77 (1996).

EMTALA's focus is narrow: it creates limited duties to treat in the emergency setting. In other ways, however, EMTALA's reach is broad. Although EMTALA applies *only* to hospitals that accept payment from Medicare *and* operate an emergency department, almost all hospitals participate in the Medicare program. And while EMTALA does not require a hospital to offer emergency department services, some state hospital licensure statutes do. In addition, federal tax law encourages tax-exempt hospitals to offer emergency services, and Medicare Conditions of Participation require that all hospitals receiving Medicare payments be capable of providing initial treatment in emergency situations and have an effective procedure for referral or transfer to more comprehensive facilities. Perhaps most importantly, EMTALA applies to *all* patients of such hospitals and not just to Medicare beneficiaries. This means that its protections apply to the uninsured or those with disfavored forms of insurance.

EMTALA specifically empowers patients to bring civil suits for damages against participating hospitals, but does not provide a private right of action against a treating physician. The Office of the Inspector General (OIG) of HHS enforces EMTALA against both hospitals and physicians. Private EMTALA litigation has burgeoned, while government enforcement has been much less active. Administrative enforcement actions under EMTALA are few; monetary penalties are quite small; and exclusion from Medicare is almost unheard of. Despite the passage of EMTALA, and perhaps because of its lax enforcement by the agency, patient dumping continues. See Sara Rosenbaum et al., Case Studies at Denver Health: "Patient Dumping" in the Emergency Department Despite EMTALA, the Law that Banned It, 31 Health Affairs 1749 (2012).

## EMERGENCY MEDICAL TREATMENT AND LABOR ACT
### 42 U.S.C. § 1395dd.

**(a)  Medical screening requirement.** In the case of a hospital that has a hospital emergency department, if any individual . . . comes to the emergency department and a request is made on the individual's behalf for examination or treatment for a medical condition, the hospital must provide for an appropriate medical screening examination within the capability of the hospital's emergency department, including ancillary services routinely available to the emergency department, to determine whether or not an emergency medical condition . . . exists.

**(b) Necessary stabilizing treatment for emergency medical conditions and labor.**

(1)  In general. If any individual . . . comes to a hospital and the hospital determines that the individual has an emergency medical condition, the hospital must provide either—

(A)  within the staff and facilities available at the hospital, for such further medical examination and such treatment as may be required to stabilize the medical condition, or

(B)  for transfer of the individual to another medical facility in accordance with subsection (c).

\* \* \*

**(c)  Restricting transfers until individual stabilized.**

(1)  Rule. If an individual at a hospital has an emergency medical condition which has not been stabilized . . ., the hospital may not transfer the individual unless—

(A)(i)  the individual (or a legally responsible person acting on the individual's behalf) after being informed of the hospital's obligations under this section and of the risk of transfer, in writing requests transfer to another medical facility, [or]

(ii)  a physician . . . has signed a certification that[,] based upon the information available at the time of transfer, the medical benefits reasonably expected from the provision of appropriate medical treatment at another medical facility outweigh the increased risks to the individual and, in the case of labor, to the unborn child from effecting the transfer.

\* \* \*

(B) [and] the transfer is an appropriate transfer ... to that facility ....

\* \* \*

(2) Appropriate transfer. An appropriate transfer to a medical facility is a transfer—

(A) in which the transferring hospital provides the medical treatment within its capacity which minimizes the risks to the individual's health and, in the case of a woman in labor, the health of the unborn child;

(B) in which the receiving facility—

(i) has available space and qualified personnel for the treatment of the individual, and

(ii) has agreed to accept transfer of the individual and to provide appropriate medical treatment;

(C) in which the transferring hospital sends to the receiving facility all medical records ... related to the emergency condition for which the individual has presented, available at the time of the transfer ...; [and]

(D) in which the transfer is effected through qualified personnel and transportation equipment. ...

**(d) Enforcement.**

(1) Civil monetary penalties. [Fines for negligent violations of the statute by hospitals of up to $50,000 for each violation; and for physicians of up to $50,000 for negligent violation and exclusion from Medicare and Medicaid for gross and flagrant violations.]

(2) Civil enforcement.

(A) Personal harm. Any individual who suffers personal harm as a direct result of a participating hospital's violation of a requirement of this section may, in a civil action against the participating hospital, obtain those damages available for personal injury under the law of the State in which the hospital is located, and such equitable relief as is appropriate.

(B) Financial loss to other medical facility. Any medical facility that suffers a financial loss as a direct result of a participating hospital's violation of a requirement of this section may, in a civil action against the participating hospital, obtain those damages available for financial loss, under the law of the State in which the hospital is located, and such equitable relief as is appropriate. ...

\* \* \*

**(e) Definitions.** In this section:

(1)    The term "emergency medical condition" means—

(A)  a medical condition manifesting itself by acute symptoms of sufficient severity (including severe pain) such that the absence of immediate medical attention could reasonably be expected to result in—

(i)    placing the health of the individual (or, with respect to a pregnant woman, the health of the woman or her unborn child) in serious jeopardy,

(ii)   serious impairment to bodily functions, or

(iii) serious dysfunction of any bodily organ or part; or

(B)  with respect to a pregnant woman who is having contractions—

(i)    that there is inadequate time to effect a safe transfer to another hospital before delivery, or

(ii)   that transfer may pose a threat to the health or safety of the woman or the unborn child . . . .

\* \* \*

(3)(A) The term "to stabilize" means . . . to provide such medical treatment of the condition as may be necessary to assure, within reasonable medical probability, that no material deterioration of the condition is likely to result from or occur during the transfer of the individual from a facility. . . .

(B)  The term "stabilized" means . . . that no material deterioration of the condition is likely, within reasonable medical probability, to result from or occur during the transfer of the individual from a facility, or, with respect to an emergency medical condition described in paragraph (1)(B), that the woman has delivered (including the placenta) . . . .

\* \* \*

**(h) No delay in examination or treatment.** A participating hospital may not delay provision of an appropriate medical screening examination required under subsection (a) . . . or further medical examination and treatment required under subsection (b) . . . in order to inquire about the individual's method of payment or insurance status.

## BABER V. HOSPITAL CORPORATION OF AMERICA

United States Court of Appeals, Fourth Circuit, 1992.
977 F.2d 872.

WILLIAMS, CIRCUIT JUDGE:

Barry Baber, Administrator of the Estate of Brenda Baber, instituted this suit against . . . Raleigh General Hospital (RGH), Beckley Appalachian Regional Hospital (BARH), and the parent corporations of both hospitals. Mr. Baber alleged that the Defendants violated the Emergency Medical Treatment and Active Labor Act (EMTALA)[ ]. The Defendants moved to dismiss the EMTALA claim under Rule 12(b)(6) of the Federal Rules of Civil Procedure. Because the parties submitted affidavits and depositions, the district court treated the motion as one for summary judgment. See Fed.R.Civ.P. 12(b).

\* \* \*

Mr. Baber's complaint charged the various defendants with violating EMTALA in several ways. Specifically, Mr. Baber contends that Dr. Kline, RGH, and its parent corporation violated EMTALA by:

(a) failing to provide his sister with an "appropriate medical screening examination;"

(b) failing to stabilize his sister's "emergency medical condition;" and

(c) transferring his sister to BARH without first providing stabilizing treatment.

\* \* \*

After reviewing the parties' submissions, the district court granted summary judgment for the Defendants. . . . Finding no error, we affirm.

\* \* \*

. . . Brenda Baber, accompanied by her brother, Barry, sought treatment at RGH's emergency department at 10:40 p.m. on August 5, 1987. When she entered the hospital, Ms. Baber was nauseated, agitated, and thought she might be pregnant. She was also tremulous and did not appear to have orderly thought patterns. She had stopped taking her antipsychosis medications, . . . and had been drinking heavily. Dr. Kline, the attending physician, described her behavior and condition in the RGH Encounter Record as follows: Patient refuses to remain on stretcher and cannot be restrained verbally despite repeated requests by staff and by me. Brother has not assisted either verbally or physically in keeping patient from pacing throughout the Emergency Room. Restraints would place patient and staff at risk by increasing her agitation.

In response to Ms. Baber's initial complaints, Dr. Kline examined her central nervous system, lungs, cardiovascular system, and abdomen. He also ordered several laboratory tests, including a pregnancy test.

While awaiting the results of her laboratory tests, Ms. Baber began pacing about the emergency department. In an effort to calm Ms. Baber, Dr. Kline gave her [several medications]. The medication did not immediately control her agitation. Mr. Baber described his sister as becoming restless, "worse and more disoriented after she was given the medication," and wandering around the emergency department.

While roaming in the emergency department around midnight, Ms. Baber . . . convulsed and fell, striking her head upon a table and lacerating her scalp. [S]he quickly regained consciousness and emergency department personnel carried her by stretcher to the suturing room, [where] Dr. Kline examined her again. He obtained a blood gas study, which did not reveal any oxygen deprivation or acidosis. Ms. Baber was verbal and could move her head, eyes, and limbs without discomfort. . . . Dr. Kline closed the one-inch laceration with a couple of sutures. Although she became calmer and drowsy after the wound was sutured, Ms. Baber was easily arousable and easily disturbed. Ms. Baber experienced some anxiety, disorientation, restlessness, and some speech problems, which Dr. Kline concluded were caused by her pre-existing psychiatric problems of psychosis with paranoia and alcohol withdrawal.

Dr. Kline discussed Ms. Baber's condition with Dr. Whelan, the psychiatrist who had treated Ms. Baber for two years. . . . Dr. Whelan concluded that Ms. Baber's hyperactive and uncontrollable behavior during her evening at RGH was compatible with her behavior during a relapse of her serious psychotic and chronic mental illness. Both Dr. Whelan and Dr. Kline were concerned about the seizure she had while at RGH's emergency department because it was the first one she had experienced. . . . They also agreed Ms. Baber needed further treatment . . . and decided to transfer her to the psychiatric unit at BARH because RGH did not have a psychiatric ward, and both doctors believed it would be beneficial for her to be treated in a familiar setting. The decision to transfer Ms. Baber was further supported by the doctors' belief that any tests to diagnose the cause of her initial seizure, such as a computerized tomography scan (CT scan), could be performed at BARH once her psychiatric condition was under control. The transfer to BARH was discussed with Mr. Baber who neither expressly consented nor objected. His only request was that his sister be x-rayed because of the blow to her head when she fell.

* * *

Because Dr. Kline did not conclude Ms. Baber had a serious head injury, he believed that she could be transferred safely to BARH where she would be under the observation of the BARH psychiatric staff personnel.

At 1:35 a.m. on August 6, Ms. Baber was admitted directly to the psychiatric department of BARH upon Dr. Whelan's orders. She was not processed through BARH's emergency department. Although Ms. Baber was restrained and regularly checked every fifteen minutes by the nursing staff while at BARH, no physician gave her an extensive neurological examination upon her arrival. Mr. Baber unsuccessfully repeated his request for an x-ray.

At the 3:45 a.m. check, the nurse found Ms. Baber having a grand mal seizure. At Dr. Whelan's direction, the psychiatric unit staff transported her to BARH's emergency department. Upon arrival in the emergency department, her pupils were unresponsive, and hospital personnel began CPR. The emergency department physician ordered a CT scan, which was performed around 6:30 a.m. The CT report revealed a fractured skull and a right subdural hematoma. BARH personnel immediately transferred Ms. Baber back to RGH because that hospital had a neurosurgeon on staff, and BARH did not have the facility or staff to treat serious neurological problems. When RGH received Ms. Baber for treatment around 7 a.m., she was comatose. She died later that day, apparently as a result of an intracerebrovascular rupture.

* * *

Mr. Baber . . . alleges that RGH, acting through its agent, Dr. Kline, violated several provisions of EMTALA. These allegations can be summarized into two general complaints: (1) RGH failed to provide an appropriate medical screening to discover that Ms. Baber had an emergency medical condition as required by 42 U.S.C.A. § 1395dd(a); and (2) RGH transferred Ms. Baber before her emergency medical condition had been stabilized, and the appropriate paperwork was not completed to transfer a non-stable patient as required by 42 U.S.C.A. § 1395dd(b) & (c). Because we find that RGH did not violate any of these EMTALA provisions, we affirm the district court's grant of summary judgment to RGH.

Mr. Baber first claims that RGH failed to provide his sister with an "appropriate medical screening". He makes two arguments. First, he contends that a medical screening is only "appropriate" if it satisfies a national standard of care. In other words, Mr. Baber urges that we construe EMTALA as a national medical malpractice statute, albeit limited to whether the medical screening was appropriate to identify an emergency medical condition. We conclude instead that EMTALA only requires hospitals to apply their standard screening procedure for identification of an emergency medical condition uniformly to all patients and that Mr. Baber has failed to proffer sufficient evidence showing that RGH did not do so. Second, Mr. Baber contends that EMTALA requires hospitals to provide some medical screening. We agree, but conclude that he has failed to show no screening was provided to his sister.

\* \* \*

While [the Act] requires a hospital's emergency department to provide an "appropriate medical screening examination," it does not define that term other than to state its purpose is to identify an "emergency medical condition."

\* \* \*

[T]he goal of "an appropriate medical screening examination" is to determine whether a patient with acute or severe symptoms has a life threatening or serious medical condition. The plain language of the statute requires a hospital to develop a screening procedure[6] designed to identify such critical conditions that exist in symptomatic patients and to apply that screening procedure uniformly to all patients with similar complaints.

[W]hile EMTALA requires a hospital emergency department to apply its standard screening examination uniformly, it does not guarantee that the emergency personnel will correctly diagnose a patient's condition as a result of this screening.[7] The statutory language clearly indicates that EMTALA does not impose on hospitals a national standard of care in screening patients. The screening requirement only requires a hospital to provide a screening examination that is "appropriate" and "within the capability of the hospital's emergency department," including "routinely available" ancillary services. 42 U.S.C.A. § 1395dd(a). This section establishes a standard, which will of necessity be individualized for each hospital, since hospital emergency departments have varying capabilities. Had Congress intended to require hospitals to provide a screening examination which comported with generally-accepted medical standards, it could have clearly specified a national standard. Nor do we believe Congress intended to create a negligence standard based on each hospital's capability. . . . EMTALA is no substitute for state law medical malpractice actions.

---

[6] While a hospital emergency room may develop one general procedure for screening all patients, it may also tailor its screening procedure to the patient's complaints or exhibited symptoms. For example, it may have one screening procedure for a patient with a heart attack and another for women in labor. Under our interpretation of EMTALA, such varying screening procedures would not pose liability under EMTALA as long as all patients complaining of the same problem or exhibiting the same symptoms receive identical screening procedures. We also recognize that the hospital's screening procedure is not limited to personal observation and assessment but may include available ancillary services through departments such as radiology and laboratory.

[7] Some commentators have criticized defining "appropriate" in terms of the hospital's medical screening standard because hospitals could theoretically avoid liability by providing very cursory and substandard screenings to all patients, which might enable the doctor to ignore a medical condition. [ ] Even though we do not believe it is likely that a hospital would endanger all of its patients by establishing such a cursory standard, theoretically it is possible. Our holding, however, does not foreclose the possibility that a future court faced with such a situation may decide that the hospital's standard was so low that it amounted to no "appropriate medical screening." We do not decide that question in this case because Ms. Baber's screening was not so substandard as to amount to no screening at all.

* * *

The Sixth Circuit has also held that an appropriate medical screening means "a screening that the hospital would have offered to any paying patient" or at least "not known by the provider to be insufficient or below their own standards."

* * *

Applying our interpretation of section (a) of EMTALA, we must next determine whether there is any genuine issue of material fact regarding whether RGH gave Ms. Baber a medical screening examination that differed from its standard screening procedure. Because Mr. Baber has offered no evidence of disparate treatment, we find that the district court did not err in granting summary judgment.

* * *

Mr. Baber does not allege that RGH's emergency department personnel treated Ms. Baber differently from its other patients. Instead, he merely claims Dr. Kline did not do enough accurately to diagnose her condition or treat her injury.[ ] The critical element of an EMTALA cause of action is not the adequacy of the screening examination but whether the screening examination that was performed deviated from the hospital's evaluation procedures that would have been performed on any patient in a similar condition.

* * *

Dr. Kline testified that he performed a medical screening on Ms. Baber in accordance with standard procedures for examining patients with head injuries. He explained that generally, a patient is not scheduled for advanced tests such as a CT scan or x-rays unless the patient's signs and symptoms so warrant. While Ms. Baber did exhibit some of the signs and symptoms of patients who have severe head injuries, in Dr. Kline's medical judgment these signs were the result of her pre-existing psychiatric condition, not the result of her fall. He, therefore, determined that Ms. Baber's head injury was not serious and did not indicate the need at that time for a CT scan or x-rays. In his medical judgment, Ms. Baber's condition would be monitored adequately by the usual nursing checks performed every fifteen minutes by the psychiatric unit staff at BARH. Although Dr. Kline's assessment and judgment may have been erroneous and not within acceptable standards of medical care in West Virginia, he did perform a screening examination that was not so substandard as to amount to no examination. No testimony indicated that his procedure deviated from that which RGH would have provided to any other patient in Ms. Baber's condition.

* * *

The essence of Mr. Baber's argument is that the extent of the examination and treatment his sister received while at RGH was deficient. While Mr. Baber's testimony might be sufficient to survive a summary judgment motion in a medical malpractice case, it is clearly insufficient to survive a motion for summary judgment in an EMTALA case because at no point does Mr. Baber present any evidence that RGH deviated from its standard screening procedure in evaluating Ms. Baber's head injury. Therefore, the district court properly granted RGH summary judgment on the medical screening issue.

Mr. Baber also asserts that RGH inappropriately transferred his sister to BARH. EMTALA's transfer requirements do not apply unless the hospital actually determines that the patient suffers from an emergency medical condition. Accordingly, to recover for violations of EMTALA's transfer provisions, the plaintiff must present evidence that (1) the patient had an emergency medical condition; (2) the hospital actually knew of that condition; (3) the patient was not stabilized before being transferred; and (4) prior to transfer of an unstable patient, the transferring hospital did not obtain the proper consent or follow the appropriate certification and transfer procedures.

* * *

Mr. Baber argues that requiring a plaintiff to prove the hospital had actual knowledge of the patient's emergency medical condition would allow hospitals to circumvent the purpose of EMTALA by simply requiring their personnel to state in all hospital records that the patient did not suffer from an emergency medical condition. Because of this concern, Mr. Baber urges us to adopt a standard that would impose liability upon a hospital if it failed to provide stabilizing treatment prior to a transfer when the hospital knew or should have known that the patient suffered from an emergency medical condition.

The statute itself implicitly rejects this proposed standard. Section 1395dd(b)(1) states the stabilization requirement exists if "any individual . . . comes to a hospital and the hospital determines that the individual has an emergency medical condition." Thus, the plain language of the statute dictates a standard requiring actual knowledge of the emergency medical condition by the hospital staff.

Mr. Baber failed to present any evidence that RGH had actual knowledge that Ms. Baber suffered from an emergency medical condition. Dr. Kline stated in his affidavit that Ms. Baber's condition was stable prior to transfer and that he did not believe she was suffering from an emergency medical condition. While Mr. Baber testified that he believed his sister suffered from an emergency medical condition at transfer, he did not present any evidence beyond his own belief that she actually had an emergency medical condition or that anyone at RGH knew that she suffered from an emergency medical condition. In addition, we note that Mr. Baber's testimony is not competent to prove his sister actually had an emergency medical condition since he is not qualified to diagnose a serious internal brain injury.

. . . [W]e hold that the district court correctly granted RGH summary judgment on Mr. Baber's claim that it transferred Ms. Baber in violation of EMTALA.

\* \* \*

Therefore, the district court's judgment is affirmed.

### NOTES AND QUESTIONS

1. The Affordable Care Act (ACA) leaves EMTALA intact, although it adopted other measures favorable to the provision of emergency care. Most notably, it incentivized states to expand Medicaid coverage, mandated that individuals have minimal health coverage, and subsidized the cost of private coverage for those who cannot afford it. Significantly, the ACA also authorizes states to allow hospitals to make presumptive Medicaid eligibility determinations for individuals, which should reduce the volume of uncompensated care that is provided to individuals eligible for but not enrolled in Medicaid. The ACA also requires insurers to pay for emergency care under a prudent layperson standard, a provision welcomed by hospitals concerned about insurers refusing to pay for emergency services that they deem unnecessary but that hospitals were obligated to provide under EMTALA. 42 U.S.C. § 300gg–19a. The more significant anticipated impact of the ACA, of course, was that it would decrease patients' reliance on emergency department care as a safety net and decrease preventable emergency conditions by providing greater access to primary care. Early evidence suggests, however, that insurance may not significantly reduce emergency department visits in the short term and that other factors, such as primary care wait times, also influence emergency department use. See Scott M. Dresden et al., Increased Emergency Department Use in Illinois After Implementation of the Patient Protection and Affordable Care Act, 69 Ann. Emerg. Med. 172 (2017).

2. In contrast to the standard for medical screening, the standard applied to the question of whether the patient was unstable when discharged or transferred is an objective professional standard and not defined by the specific hospital's policy. How should plaintiffs structure discovery to meet each of these two standards? What is the role for expert testimony, if any, in an "unstable transfer or discharge" claim? In an "inappropriate screening" claim?

3. Improper motive is not required for a violation of the EMTALA requirement that the patient be *stabilized*. Roberts v. Galen of Va., Inc., 525 U.S. 249, 119 S.Ct. 685, 142 L.Ed.2d 648 (1999). The Court expressed no opinion as to whether proof of improper motive is essential for a claim of failure to provide an appropriate screening. The Circuits, except for the Sixth Circuit

in Cleland v. Bronson Health Care Group, 917 F.2d 266 (6th Cir. 1990), uniformly have held that EMTALA reaches beyond economically motivated decisions and that proof of motive is not required for either a screening or a stabilization claim. Could proof of improper motive be useful to the plaintiff in distinguishing negligent misdiagnosis from an EMTALA claim? How might such proof assist the plaintiff in making his or her case? How would you go about proving motive once the physician and hospital claim medical judgment as the basis for discharge or transfer?

4.    One of the sticky issues in EMTALA is whether a patient has "come to" the hospital's emergency department. In a rather notorious case, a hospital emergency department refused to aid a teenager who had been shot and lay dying 35 feet from the ER doors. Kristine Marie Meece, The Future of Emergency Department Liability after the Ravenswood Hospital Incident: Redefining the Duty to Treat?, 3 DePaul J. Health Care L. 101 (1999). After years of court opinions with conflicting results, HHS promulgated regulations in 2003 (42 C.F.R. § 489.24(b)) under which a patient is determined to have "come to" an emergency department when the patient:

- "present[s] on hospital property";

- "is in a ground or air ambulance owned and operated by the hospital . . . even if the ambulance is not on hospital grounds [unless the ambulance is directed to another hospital by a communitywide emergency medical service or is operated at the direction of a physician unaffiliated with the hospital]"; or

- "is in a ground or air nonhospital-owned ambulance on hospital property [unless the hospital directs the ambulance elsewhere because the hospital is on 'diversionary status' and the ambulance abides the hospital's direction]."

5.    For many years, courts reached conflicting results as well on the issue of whether a patient who had been admitted to the hospital would be covered by EMTALA or whether the EMTALA obligations of the hospital ceased upon admission. Finally, in 2003, HHS promulgated regulations providing that EMTALA's obligations end when an emergency department patient is admitted in good faith to the hospital as an inpatient. See 42 C.F.R. 489.24(d)(2). Most courts have deferred to this interpretation of the statute. See e.g., Thornhill v. Jackson Parish Hospital, 184 F.Supp.3d 392 (W.D. La. 2016). A lone circuit held, in dicta, that the regulations are contrary to the plain language of the statute, Moses v. Providence Hosp. & Med. Ctrs., 561 F.3d 573 (6th Cir. 2009). Several federal district courts, including the Court in *Thornhill*, have disagreed with that holding. In 2010, CMS asked for comments on its 2003 regulations and ultimately decided not to change them. 77 Fed. Reg. 5213 (Feb. 2, 2012). See the Problem, below.

6.    Treatment in the emergency department often will require the services of an on-call specialist. The hospital generally doesn't employ on-call specialists, but may contract with individual physicians to provide on-call

services or may require on-call coverage by physicians as a condition of receiving admitting privileges. The division of labor inherent in the ED/on-call relationship can be contentious and raise EMTALA risks. Consequently, the management of on-call services remains an intractable problem for hospitals. See Sarah Coyne et al., Using Deferred Compensation to Incent On-Call Coverage, 23 Health Law. 28/No4 (2011) and the Problem below.

7.    EMTALA, while helpful, has not ended the problem of "patient dumping" particularly among our most vulnerable sub-populations. Several hospitals in Los Angeles, for example, have settled claims that they improperly discharged homeless patients from their emergency departments back on to the streets. See Maria Castellucci, "Calf. Hospital Pays $1 Million to Settle Patient-Dumping Case," Modern Healthcare (June 24, 2016). At least some of these "skid row dumping" cases involved allegations that patients were discharged while in unstable conditions. See Editorial Board, "No Excuse for 'Patient-Dumping' in L.A.'s Skid Row," L.A. Times (Jan. 20, 2014). EMTALA does not prohibit a hospital from discharging a person who does not have an emergency medical condition or whose emergency condition the hospital has stabilized.

### PROBLEMS: EMTALA

Ms. Miller

On May 21, Ms. Nancy Miller, who was eight months pregnant, called her obstetrician, Dr. Jennifer Gibson, at 2:00 a.m. because she was experiencing severe pain which appeared to her to be labor contractions. Dr. Gibson advised Ms. Miller to go to the emergency department of the local hospital and promised to meet her there shortly. Ms. Miller was admitted to the emergency department of General Hospital at 2:30 a.m., and Dr. Gibson joined her there at 3:14 a.m. After examining Ms. Miller, Dr. Gibson concluded that Ms. Miller had begun labor and that, despite the fact that the pregnancy had not reached full-term, the labor should be continued to delivery. At that time, Dr. Gibson asked that the on-call anesthesiologist, Dr. Martig, see Ms. Miller to discuss anesthesia during the delivery. At the same time, the procedure to admit Ms. Miller to the hospital's maternity floor was begun. The nurse informed Ms. Miller that there would be a short wait because there was no space available at that point.

Dr. Martig saw Ms. Miller at 4:00 a.m. When asked, Dr. Martig informed Ms. Miller that he was not qualified to and would not be able to perform an epidural (a spinal nerve-block anesthesia, often used in childbirth). Instead, he gave her Demerol and left the emergency department.

At 4:30 a.m., Ms. Miller was admitted to the labor and delivery floor. At 4:45 a.m., the obstetrical nurse observed fetal distress and called Dr. Gibson. At 4:50 a.m., Dr. Gibson concluded that Ms. Miller had a prolapsed umbilical cord and ordered an emergency caesarean section. The OB nurse paged Dr. Martig, but he could not be located. (Dr. Martig later stated that his pager had malfunctioned.) Because Dr. Martig could not be located, Dr. Gibson and a resident performed the C-section without an anesthetic and delivered the child healthy and alive. (These facts are based on Miller v. Martig, 754 N.E.2d 41 (Ind. Ct. App. 2001).)

Assume that Ms. Miller has brought suit against the hospital and Dr. Martig. What federal and state claims might Ms. Miller make? Assume that Dr. Martig and the hospital have filed a motion for summary judgment on all claims. What result?

Mr. Liles

Jesse Liles has no health insurance but went to a local hospital (NMC) complaining of fever and shortness of breath. He was admitted to the hospital with a diagnosis of severe dehydration, bilateral pneumonia, and adult respiratory distress syndrome. According to Mr. Liles, the hospital attempted to transfer him on eighteen separate occasions during the course of his stay between December 28, 2009, and January 24, 2010. Mr. Liles charges that two physicians at NMC falsely certified that he was stable for transfer from the hospital. At 3:35 a.m., on January 1, 2010, EMS from the local privately owned ambulance service came at the hospital's request to transfer Mr. Liles to another hospital. Liles went into cardiac arrest in the ambulance where he was resuscitated by EMS personnel and brought back inside NMC. He was placed on a ventilator in the ICU and stayed at the hospital until he was discharged to home on January 24.

On January 26, 2010, Liles called the same ambulance company because of his acute respiratory distress. The EMS personnel called NMC en route, but NMC told them to take Mr. Liles to some other hospital because there was no pulmonologist available at NMC. The ambulance was already at the entry to the hospital grounds, and continued to be in contact with NMC to get further instructions. Staff at NMC made a number of calls to potential "receiving hospitals" to identify a facility willing to accept Mr. Liles. Ultimately, he was taken to another hospital where he was admitted to the ICU and underwent surgery for a collapsed lung. (These facts are based on Liles v. TH Healthcare, Ltd., 2012 WL 3930616 (E.D.Tex.).)

Assume that Mr. Liles has sued the hospital for EMTALA violations. You are the hospital's attorney. What arguments do you expect Mr. Liles to make? What are your best defenses to Liles' claims?

# IV. FEDERAL ANTIDISCRIMINATION STATUTES

This Section examines the federal statutes enacted to address problems of discrimination in health care based on certain protected characteristics. These characteristics define the groups that have historically been subjected to some kind of discrimination—whether through outright denial of care, unequal treatment in how care is delivered, or inequity in the distribution of health care resources. These laws have been used to challenge operations at the health system level as well as decisionmaking at the individual, patient-provider level.

## A. TITLE VI OF THE CIVIL RIGHTS ACT

U.S. hospitals and other health care facilities were segregated by law well into the late 1960s and by custom for some time thereafter. White-only hospitals refused admission to African American citizens, and those white-dominated hospitals that did admit African Americans segregated them into separate units. Even publicly owned hospitals and hospitals funded by the federal government were segregated by race. A post-World War II federal health care funding program, known as Hill-Burton, invested millions of federal tax dollars in the construction of hospitals across the country. Yet the legislation specifically institutionalized race discrimination by allowing federally funded hospitals to exclude African Americans if other facilities were available. The segregated facilities available were hardly equal. For example, the ward for African Americans in the community hospital in Wilmington, North Carolina, held only 25 beds and two toilets in a building separated from the main building so that surgery patients had to be transported across an open yard. And neither of the two hospitals (one public and one private) in Broward County, Florida, admitted patients from the more than 30,000 African Americans residing in the county. Segregation even trumped ability to pay. For example, in 1950s Chicago, African American union members with generous health insurance plans were steered almost entirely to Cook County Hospital despite closer facilities. See David Barton Smith, Health Care Divided: Race and Healing a Nation (1999). Not until 1962, did a federal Court of Appeals declare the "separate but equal" provision of the Hill-Burton Act unconstitutional. Simkins v. Moses H. Cone Mem'l Hosp., 323 F.2d 959 (4th Cir. 1963), cert. denied, 376 U.S. 938 (1964).

Despite the eradication of legal barriers to care, racial disparities in health care access and quality persist. Such disparities are not captured entirely in the story of geographic segregation or socioeconomic status. For example, disparities in treatment decisions appear in a great variety of medical conditions. See Rene Bowser, The Affordable Care Act and Beyond: Opportunities for Advancing Health Equity and Social Justice, 10 Hastings Race & Poverty L. J. 69 (2013), citing studies documenting that African-American and Latino patients are categorized as needing less urgent care by emergency department personnel than whites with the same cardiac symptoms; are less likely to receive aspirin upon discharge after heart attack; and are less likely to receive appropriate pain medication in the emergency department for problems like bone fractures. In 2002, an Institute of Medicine report found serious racial and ethnic disparities, defined as "racial or ethnic differences in the quality of healthcare that are not due to access-related factors or clinical needs, preferences and appropriateness of intervention." Institute of Medicine, Unequal Treatment: Confronting Racial and Ethnic Disparities in Health Care (2002). See also, National Health Care Quality and Disparities Reports (2011), by the federal Agency on Healthcare Research and Quality, reporting that African Americans and Latinos receive lower quality care than do non-Hispanic whites on approximately 40% of quality measures.

Title VI of the Civil Rights Act of 1964, 42 U.S.C.A. § 2000d, prohibits discrimination on the basis of race, color, or national origin by any program receiving federal financial assistance. Title VI regulations go even further to prohibit the use of criteria or methods of administration that have the effect of subjecting individuals to discrimination on the basis of race, color, or national origin. 45 C.F.R. 80.3(b)(2). Thus, Title VI has been used to combat both intentional discrimination in health care and health care polices or practices that have discriminatory effects.

Beginning in 1965, Medicare and Medicaid provided federal payments to physicians, hospitals, nursing homes, and other health care organizations, creating significant leverage for enforcement of Title VI. Despite this leverage, regulators initially decided to limit Title VI's reach. Hospitals were considered compliant even if they extended admitting privileges to physicians who refused to admit African Americans and even if doctors who would admit more broadly were excluded from privileges. Originally, the federal government threatened enforcement against such hospitals, but then retreated. See David Barton Smith, Healthcare's Hidden Civil Rights Legacy, 48 St. Louis U. L.J. 37 (2003). In addition, the regulatory agency charged with overseeing Medicare declared that Title VI did not apply to physicians who received payment under Part B of Medicare, interpreting that program as a "contract of insurance" rather than payment of public funds. This narrow interpretation has recently been displaced by Section 1557 of the Affordable Care Act, discussed in Section C of this chapter.

The Office of Civil Rights (OCR) within HHS is charged with Title VI enforcement, although it has long been criticized for not being proactive in monitoring hospitals' compliance and for responding too slowly and ineffectively to patients' complaints. OCR's enforcement priorities depend on its leadership, and persistent resource, organizational, and political challenges have made administrative enforcement of Title VI uneven. See Sara Rosenbaum & Joel Teitelbaum, Civil Rights Enforcement in the Modern Healthcare System: Reinvigorating the Role of the Federal Government in the Aftermath of Alexander v. Sandoval, 3 Yale J. Health Pol'y, L. & Ethics 215 (2003).

Title VI is also enforceable through private litigation. Private litigation has been seen as an important tool to fight policies or practices that result in discrimination, especially during periods of inactivity by regulators. Yet, this tool has been a limited one for a couple of reasons. First, proving discrimination can be difficult, even under the more generous "effects" test allowed under Title VI regulations. Second, the Supreme Court has severely limited the types of claims that private plaintiffs can bring under Title VI. See Rosenbaum & Teitelbaum, supra.

## LINTON V. COMMISSIONER OF HEALTH AND ENVIRONMENT

United States District Court, Middle District, Tennessee, 1990.
779 F.Supp. 925.

JOHN T. NIXON, DISTRICT JUDGE.

Plaintiffs are before the Court seeking to enjoin a Tennessee policy through which only a portion of the beds in Medicaid participating nursing homes are certified to be available for Medicaid patients. Plaintiffs allege that this policy artificially limits the accessibility of nursing home care to indigent Medicaid patients and fosters discrimination against indigent patients by nursing homes. Plaintiffs claim that, as a result of the challenged policy, they and other individuals similarly situated face delay or outright denial of needed nursing home care, as well as displacement from current residency in nursing home facilities. Plaintiffs bring this action under [ ] Title VI of the Civil Rights Act of 1964.

\* \* \*

## FINDINGS OF FACT

The present case was initiated on December 1, 1987 on behalf of Mildred Lea Linton. Ms. Linton suffers from rheumatoid arthritis and has been a patient for four years at Green Valley Health Care Center in Dickson, Tennessee [hereinafter "Green Valley"]. A Medicaid patient who had been receiving skilled nursing facility (SNF) level care throughout her stay, the plaintiff received notice from State Medicaid officials that she no longer qualified for such care. The same notice advised her that she would have to move to another nursing home, an intermediate care facility (ICF), to receive the level of care to which the State believed she should be downgraded. Green Valley provides ICF care, and in fact the bed occupied by Ms. Linton was dually certified for Medicaid purposes for provision of both SNF and ICF levels of care. However, Green Valley was unwilling to care for Ms. Linton at an ICF level of reimbursement. The nursing home, which had directed the State to certify only part of its ICF beds as available to Medicaid patients, reserved the right to decertify the plaintiff's bed for Medicaid ICF participation. This decertification would have compelled the plaintiff's involuntary transfer to another facility.

On December 11, 1989, plaintiff Belle Carney, an 89 year old black woman, requested intervention. She had been diagnosed in July 1987 as requiring nursing home treatment due to Alzheimer's disease, however, no nursing home placement was found for her. Plaintiff Carney asserts that the State's limited bed certification policy, which the State refers to as distinct part certification, creates an artificial restriction on the number of available Medicaid beds and that it fosters discrimination against Medicaid patients by nursing homes. Plaintiff Carney's health deteriorated over a period of several months as she was moved from one inadequate placement to another. Finally, Carney's condition declined to the point that she required emergency hospitalization. . . .

\* \* \*

A.   *The Tennessee Medicaid Program*

Tennessee participates in the federal Medicaid program to provide medical assistance to those recipients who are eligible to receive such assistance in accordance with the requirements of Title XIX of the Social Security Act. [ ] . . . The types of medical assistance that are provided under the Tennessee Medicaid program include, among others, services by skilled nursing home facilities [(SNFs)] and intermediate care facilities [(ICFs)]. [ ] [ICF services include institutional, health-related services above the level of room and board, but at a level of care below that of hospital or SNF care. SNF care consists of institutional care above the level of ICF services but below the level of a hospital. The Tennessee Department of Health and Environment (TDHE) is the single state agency responsible for administration of the Medicaid program. The Department is administered under the direction of the defendant Commissioner.] TDHE also acts as the State licensing agency for nursing homes or long term care facilities and certifies such facilities for Medicaid. . . .

\* \* \*

Tennessee has previously had a "Medicaid Bed Management program" which represents an attempt to place a percentage limitation on the number of available Medicaid beds in nursing homes. Federal auditors recommended that this policy be discontinued, and Tennessee abolished this program on October 1, 1985.

Plaintiffs challenge what they refer to as an unwritten limited bed certification policy. Defendants assert that this policy is instead simply Tennessee's version of distinct part certification. [Federal law authorizes State agencies to certify facilities for either SNF or ICF reimbursement. Such certification may be of a "distinct part of an institution." According to federal policy, the term "distinct part" denotes that the unit is organized and operated to give *a distinct type of care within a larger organization which otherwise renders other types or levels of care.* "Distinct" denotes both organizational and physical distinctness. A distinct part SNF must be physically identifiable and be operated distinguishably from the rest of the institution. *It must consist of all the beds within that unit such as a separate building, floor, wing or ward.*] The Court finds, however, that the Tennessee policy varies markedly from federal "distinct part" certification.

Perhaps the most fundamental difference between Tennessee's limited bed certification policy and federal "distinct part" certification is to be found in the different purposes served by the respective policies. Federal distinct part certification is intended to accommodate the delivery of qualitatively different types of health care within the same facility. Tennessee's policy, however, appears to serve the interests of nursing homes who wish to participate in the Medicaid program while also maintaining a separate private pay facility offering the same type of care.

\* \* \*

Federal Medicaid law mandates that states set their Medicaid payments to nursing homes at levels which are "reasonable and adequate to meet the costs which must be incurred by efficiently and economically operated facilities in order to provide care and services in conformity with applicable State and Federal laws, regulations and quality and safety standards . . ." [ ]

By contrast, private pay rates are set by the market, a market in which there are more patients seeking care than there are beds to accommodate them. There are waiting lists to gain admission to nursing homes throughout Tennessee. As a result of this situation, unregulated private pay rates are substantially higher than Medicaid payments, and nursing home operators prefer private pay patients. Tennessee's present certification program allows nursing home operators to give preference to private pay patients by reserving for their exclusive use beds which are, due to lack of certification, unavailable to Medicaid patients.

. . . The [limited bed certification] policy leads to disruption of care and displacement of Medicaid patients after they have been admitted to a nursing home. Such displacement often occurs when a patient exhausts his or her financial resources and attempts transition from private pay to Medicaid. In this situation, a patient who already occupies a bed in a nursing home is told that his or her bed is no longer available to the patient because he or she is dependent upon Medicaid. . . . Involuntary transfers are triggered on other occasions when a patient already on Medicaid at SNF level of reimbursement is reclassified to an ICF level of care [with lower reimbursement].

. . . [T]he Court finds that the limited bed certification policy has caused widespread displacement. . . . The Court is persuaded by the depositions, affidavits and exhibits concerning the severe impact of the limited bed certification policy. Finally, the Court is mindful of the Medicaid eligibility rules which allow eligibility for relatively more affluent patients already residing in nursing homes than those seeking initial admission. This phenomenon combined with the limited bed certification policy often renders the poorest and most medically needy Medicaid applicants unable to obtain the proper nursing home care.

### B.  *Disparate Impact on Minorities*

The Court finds that the plaintiff has established by a preponderance of the evidence that the Tennessee Medicaid program does have a disparate and adverse impact on minorities. Because of the higher incidence of poverty in the black population, and the concomitant increased dependence on Medicaid, a policy limiting the amount of nursing home beds available to Medicaid patients will disproportionately affect blacks.

Indeed, while blacks comprise 39.4 percent of the Medicaid population, they account for only 15.4 percent of those Medicaid patients who have been able to gain access to Medicaid-covered nursing home services. In addition, testimony indicates that the health status of blacks is generally poorer than that of whites, and their need for nursing home services is correspondingly greater. Finally, such discrimination has caused a "dual system" of long term care for the frail elderly: a statewide system of licensed nursing homes, 70 percent funded by the Medicaid program, serves whites; while blacks are relegated to substandard boarding homes which receive no Medicaid subsidies.

### CONCLUSIONS OF LAW

* * *

### B.  *Plaintiffs' Claims Under Title VI of the Civil Rights Act of 1964*

Title VI of the Civil Rights Act of 1964 provides, in relevant part:

> No person in the United States shall on the ground of race, color or national origin . . . be subjected to discrimination under any program or activity receiving Federal financial assistance.

[ ] Regulations under Title VI provide that a state in its administration of the federally funded program can not:

> . . . directly or through contractual or other arrangements, utilize criteria or methods of administration which have the effect of subjecting individuals to discrimination because of their race, color, or national origin, or have the effect of defeating or substantially impairing accomplishment of the objectives of the program as respect individuals of a particular race, color or national origin.

45 C.F.R. § 80.3(b)(2).

* * *

The plaintiffs have shown that the defendants' limited bed certification policy has a disparate impact on racial minorities in Tennessee. The burden of proof next falls upon the defendants to show that the disparate impact is not unjustifiable. The defendants state that the "self-selection preferences" of the minorities, based upon the minorities' reliance upon the extended family, lack of transportation, and fear of institutional care, adequately explain the disparate impact. [ ] This explanation, however, is not sufficient justification for minority underrepresentation in nursing homes. Therefore, the defendants have failed to meet their burden of proof . . . .

\* \* \*

The Court recognizes that under Title VI, deference is accorded to the Title VI administrative agency to cure the discriminatory effects of the particular program. To be sure, THDE employs Ms. Beverly Bass as a director to monitor Title VI compliance. However, even Bass concedes that under the TDHE certification policy black Medicaid recipients are displaced or denied admission to nursing homes. Further, it is noteworthy that the Bed Management Program that was instituted in 1981, was not repealed as TDHE policy until October 13, 1987. Prior TDHE studies identified the status of minority citizen in Tennessee's Medicaid Program and the reasons for lack of minority participation. Yet, despite these studies, the Commissioner implemented a policy that fosters and continues the egregious status of minority Medicaid patients within the program. In these circumstances, continued deference to the administrative agencies is inappropriate. To cure the effects of this policy, judicial intervention is necessary. To accomplish this, the Court ORDERS the Commissioner, in consultation with [the federal agency overseeing Medicaid], to submit a plan for court approval that will redress the disparate impact upon eligible minority Medicaid patients' access to qualified nursing home care due to the THDE certification policy and the State's past noncompliance with Title VI.

\* \* \*

## BRYAN V. KOCH

United States Court of Appeals, Second Circuit, 1980.
627 F.2d 612.

NEWMAN, CIRCUIT JUDGE:

This litigation challenges New York City's decision to close Sydenham Hospital, one of its 17 municipal hospitals, on the ground that the City's proposed action would constitute racial discrimination in the use of federal funds in violation of Title VI of the Civil Rights Act of 1964, *42 U.S.C. § 2000d* et seq. Like most American cities, New York has struggled mightily to provide adequate municipal services with limited financial resources; its difficulties have become particularly severe since its budget crisis that began in the mid-1970's. Closing Sydenham is one of the many painful steps that the City has undertaken or proposed in an effort to maintain financial stability. The discrimination claim in this case arises from the fact that Sydenham, located in central Harlem, serves a population that is 98% minority (Black and Hispanic). Three related cases have been brought to prevent the closing of the Hospital, or at least to ameliorate the effects that the closing would have on the minority population it serves. This consolidated appeal is from the denial of a preliminary injunction. . . .

\* \* \*

In April, 1979, Mayor Koch appointed a Health Policy Task Force to examine ways of reducing costly excess hospital capacity while maintaining access to high quality health services. The Task Force report, issued June 20, 1979, recommended a series of steps that the City's Health and Hospital Corporation (HHC) estimated would save $ 30 million in fiscal year 1981. With respect to the 17 hospitals of the municipal hospital system, the report proposed that some hospitals be replaced, that some hospitals reduce the number of beds, and that two hospitals, Sydenham and Metropolitan, both located in Harlem, be closed. The HHC approved the report on June 28, 1979. On August 12, 1979, the first of the three cases in this litigation, Bryan v. Koch, was filed on behalf of a class of low income Black and Hispanic residents of New York City who use the municipal hospital system. Defendants are the City and State of New York, the HHC, the State Health Department, and various city and state officials, including Mayor Koch. The U. S. Department of Health and Human Services (HHS) (formerly Department of Health, Education and Welfare) was joined as a defendant, though not charged with any violation of law. . . . [The] suits, which have been consolidated, allege that the City's proposed plan for the municipal hospital system violates various federal civil rights statutes, primarily Title VI. . . .

\* \* \*

. . . [T]he findings that the City acted without discriminatory intent are fully supported by the evidence.

\* \* \*

. . . Even under the effects standard, we conclude that the judgment of the District Court should be affirmed. Applying that standard, we agree with the plaintiffs that they have sufficiently shown a disproportionate racial impact to require justification by the defendants. Disparity appears from comparing the 98% minority proportion of the Sydenham patients with the 66% minority proportion of the patients served by the City's municipal hospital system. Whether the impact of this disparity is sufficiently adverse to create a prima facie Title VI violation is a closer question. The District Court was satisfied with the City's estimates for the care of Sydenham patients in nearby municipal and voluntary hospitals. Nevertheless, the District Court acknowledged that at least a small number of patients, those admitted to the emergency room because of gunshot or knife wounds or drug overdoses, would suffer adverse consequences if the nearest emergency room treatment available were at even slightly more distant locations. Moreover, we share the plaintiffs' concern that the City's estimates for alternative care of Sydenham's patients rests on projections about the availability of bed space without sufficient assurance that the voluntary hospitals on which the City relies will admit all of Sydenham's patients in financial need. Whether these hospitals will admit Sydenham's Medicaid patients remains an issue in some dispute, and even if Medicaid patients will be admitted, it is also unclear what will happen with those eligible for Medicaid who are unable to establish their eligibility at the time hospital admission is needed.

* * *

We therefore consider it appropriate to complete an assessment of plaintiffs' Title VI claim by examining the justification advanced by the City for closing Sydenham. As the District Court found, that justification is both the reduction of expenditures and the increase in efficiency within the municipal hospital system. Though the plaintiffs dispute the amount of savings the City claims will be achieved, they acknowledge that there is sufficient evidence to support the District Court's finding that closing Sydenham will reduce expenditures to some extent. However, saving money, while obviously a legitimate objective of any governmental plan to close a public facility, cannot be a sufficient justification in a case like this where public officials have made a choice to close one of 17 municipal hospitals. In such circumstances it is the choice of this particular hospital that must be justified.

To provide a basis for making this choice the Task Force report initially assessed each of the municipal hospitals against four sets of criteria: (a) hospital size, scope of patient services, and extent of usage; (b) patient access to comparable alternative facilities; (c) quality of plant and operations; and (d) present and predicted fiscal performance. Among the several hospitals considered deficient in this assessment, recommendations for closure were made for those hospitals with disproportionately high operating deficits and obsolete plants, located within 30 minutes of other municipal hospitals with comparable or broader services. These criteria are reasonably related to the efficient operation of the City's municipal hospital system, and the evidence abundantly justifies the selection of Sydenham based on these criteria. . . .

If any of the municipal hospitals are to be closed, plaintiffs do not dispute that Sydenham is an appropriate choice for closing. Their claim is that the closing of a federally funded facility resulting in a disproportionate racial impact violates Title VI unless the defendants establish the unavailability of alternative measures that would save equivalent money with less disproportionate impact. Proceeding from this premise, plaintiffs further contend that instead of closing any municipal hospitals, the City could save as much money or more and avoid a disparate racial impact by such alternatives as hospital mergers, regionalization of services, increasing Sydenham's services to reduce its deficit, or increasing Medicaid reimbursement.

Neither Title VI nor the HHS regulations explicitly require a federal fund recipient to consider alternatives to a proposed placement or closing of a public facility. It is unlikely that challenges to such governmental actions were even contemplated when Title VI was enacted in 1964. The focus at that time was on federally aided facilities that denied access to minorities or admitted them only to segregated portions of a facility. [ ] The argument for consideration of alternatives in placing or closing facilities stems from two sources. HHS has expressed its view as the administrator of federal medical care funds that its regulations should be interpreted to require consideration of alternatives. On March 5, 1980, the Undersecretary of what was then HEW wrote to Mayor Koch, in connection with the proposed closing of municipal hospitals, that if closings were to create a disparate racial impact, the City would have an opportunity to establish that they are "necessary to achieve legitimate objectives unrelated to race or national origin and that these objectives cannot be achieved by other measures having a less disproportionate adverse effect." . . .

. . . [H]owever, the inquiry could frequently become too open-ended. If, for example, a court were to assess alternative ways of saving funds throughout the administration of a city or even throughout the administration of the health care function, it would seriously risk substituting its own judgment for that of the city's elected officials and appointed specialists. We are skeptical of the capacity and appropriateness of courts to conduct such broad inquiries concerning alternative ways to carry out municipal functions. Once a court is drawn into such a complex inquiry, it will inevitably be assessing the wisdom of competing political and economic alternatives. Moreover, such policy choices would be made without broad public participation and without sufficient assurance that the alternative selected will ultimately provide more of a benefit to the minority population.

. . . [W]e do not believe Title VI requires consideration of alternatives beyond an assessment of all the municipal hospitals in order to select one or more for closing. . . . The alternatives plaintiffs wish to have considered are more appropriate for examination by administrative, legislative, and other political processes than by the courts.

Without expressing any views as to the wisdom of closing Sydenham Hospital, we conclude that the plaintiffs have shown no likelihood of success in establishing that its closing would violate Title VI, and the District Court therefore did not err in denying a preliminary injunction.

\* \* \*

## NOTES AND QUESTIONS

1.    In 2001, in Alexander v. Sandoval, 532 U.S. 275, 121 S.Ct. 1511, 149 L.Ed.2d 517 (2001), the Supreme Court dealt a significant blow to private Title VI litigation. The Court held that only intentional discrimination is actionable through private suit under Title VI. The five-to-four majority strictly construed the text of Title VI, and held there was no private cause of action to enforce regulations that went beyond the scope of the statutory prohibition. The Court held that enforcement of regulations prohibiting policies or criteria with racially disparate effects was exclusively in the purview of OCR. *Sandoval* proved to be the death knell for private disparate impact litigation like that in *Linton and Bryan*—that is, until the ACA. There is an open question as to whether the ACA's antidiscrimination provision will breathe new life into private disparate impact litigation. See Section C below.

2.    As noted in the cases above, Title VI regulations prohibit policies that have a discriminatory effect. Is an "effects" test designed merely to help root out pretext for intentional discrimination? Is the goal to eliminate health inequity more broadly? Or does the goal lie somewhere in-between: is Title VI a vehicle for distinguishing unjustifiable policies that have discriminatory effects from justifiable policies that may have the unfortunate, but not illegal, effect of exacerbating health disparities?

3.    In *Bryan* and *Linton*, there was no evidence of discriminatory intent, but plaintiffs were able to establish a prima facie case based on disparate racial impact. What evidence did plaintiffs offer to prove disparate impact? Consider that race-based residential patterns originally established as a matter of *de jure* segregation in housing have produced a legacy of *de facto* racial segregation still engraved on the U.S. health care system today: Hospitals and nursing homes continue to avoid predominantly African-American neighborhoods; only one-quarter of pharmacies in these neighborhoods carry necessary prescription medications; and health insurers market different and more limited health plans, if they market at all, than they do in predominantly Caucasian neighborhoods. See Sidney Watson, Section 1557 of the Affordable Care Act: Civil Rights, Health Reform, Race, and Equity, 55 How. L. J. 855 (2012); David Barton Smith, Healthcare's Hidden Civil Rights Legacy, supra; Ruqaiijah Yearby, African Americans Can't Win, Break Even, or Get Out of the System: The Persistence of "Unequal Treatment" in Nursing Home Care, 82 Temple L. Rev. 1177 (2010).

4.    In *Bryan*, the court found that plaintiffs showed a disproportionate *racial* impact, but noted that "[w]hether the impact of this disparity is

*sufficiently adverse* to create a prima facie Title VI violation is a closer question." Sydenham was a public hospital, owned and operated by the municipal hospital system. Public hospitals are an important part of the health care safety net because they are required by state or local law to treat indigent patients. As a result, they have been the primary source of treatment for patients who otherwise could not afford care or find providers willing to treat them. The City claimed that, after the closure, Sydenham's patients would still be able to get the care they needed from private hospitals in neighboring areas; plaintiffs' questioned this claim and the court shared plaintiffs' concern. Was this concern well-founded?

5.     These cases introduce you to two essential parts of the U.S. health care safety net. In *Linton*, the plaintiffs depended on Medicaid, known primarily as the public insurance program for the poor. Medicaid, which is jointly funded by federal and state government, is the primary source of payment for institutional and long term care. In *Bryan*, the plaintiffs depended on a local public hospital system, which could not refuse to treat anyone based on ability to pay. Although there is no universal right to health care in the U.S., states may require local governments to ensure a minimal level of service to indigent residents. See e.g., Cal. Welf. & Inst. Code § 17000 ("[E]very city and county shall relieve and support all incompetent, poor, indigent persons, and those incapacitated by age, disease, or accident, lawfully resident therein, when such persons are not supported and relieved by their relatives or friends, by their own means, or by state hospitals or other state or private institutions.") Nonetheless, local governments may have great discretion in how they satisfy this duty.

6.     *Alexander v. Sandoval*, described in Note 1 above, does not preclude administrative actions on disparate impact grounds. OCR can pursue cases under both intentional discrimination and disparate effects theories, including, for example, intervening in hospital closures or relocations that could have a discriminatory impact. For example, in 2010 the OCR responded to complaints about a decision by the University of Pittsburgh Medical Center (UPMC) to close its hospital in Braddock, Pennsylvania, which was in a predominantly African American community, and to relocate services to a new facility in a predominantly white area that was a great distance away. Although HHS did not stop the closure, it did reach an agreement with UPMC to ameliorate the effects on access by providing door-to-door transportation services from Braddock to its new outpatient facilities and expanding support for primary and urgent care services locally. See U.S. Department of Health and Human Services, Press Release, UPMC Agrees to Expand Access to Care After Closure of UPMC Braddock (Sep. 2, 2010). The OCR has used its power to challenge a broad range of discriminatory actions. See Speech by Thomas Perez, Director, Office for Civil Rights, Discrimination and Health Disparities (Apr. 13, 1999) (describing actions targeting home health care chains engaging in medical redlining—a policy of refusing to serve people in predominantly minority neighborhoods; a hospital's policy of not giving epidurals to women who did not speak English; hospital segregated maternity wards; and a pharmacy's

repeated failure to fill the prescription of an African-American Medicaid recipient).

7.    Discussions of race discrimination tend to treat race and ethnicity as interchangeable concepts because of the commonality in forms of discrimination and disparities experienced by groups identifying as racial and/or ethnic minorities. Nonetheless, discrimination based on national origin presents distinct legal issues, such as language barriers to access. According to the 2015 American Community Survey from the U.S. Census Bureau, a record 64.7 million people spoke a language other than English at home, and more than 25.9 million people were "limited English proficient" (LEP). Data from this annual survey is available at the U.S. Census Bureau's official website. LEP individuals experience linguistic barriers to care that impact both the ability to access care and the quality of care received. In 1974, the Supreme Court in Lau v. Nichols, 414 U.S. 563, interpreted Title VI regulations as prohibiting conduct that has a disproportionate effect on individuals with limited English proficiency as a form of national origin discrimination. (As noted above, however, *Sandoval* subsequently limited enforcement of such violations to agencies). In 2000, Executive Order 13166, titled "Improving Access to Services for Persons with Limited English Proficiency," was issued, explaining that federal funding recipients were "required to take reasonable steps to ensure meaningful access" for LEP persons. 65 Fed. Reg. 50121 (Aug. 11, 2000). This requirement was reaffirmed most recently through the final rule implementing the ACA's nondiscrimination requirement. See Nondiscrimination in Health Programs and Activities, 81 Fed. Reg. 31375 (May 18, 2016) (codified at 45 C.F.R. Part 92).

8.    Perhaps the most challenging aspect of national origin discrimination is conduct motivated by or linked with immigration status. Since enactment of the Personal Responsibility and Work Opportunity Reconciliation Act of 1996 (PRWORA), Pub. L. No. 104–193, 110 Stat. 2105, federal law has severely curtailed public healthcare benefits for immigrants who are here legally, illegally, and whose legal status is uncertain. The ACA excludes all U.S. residents not "lawfully present" in the U.S. from access to the health insurance exchanges and subsidies for insurance. The ACA also continues the five-year waiting period for Medicaid applied to lawfully present immigrants, as well as the exclusion of undocumented immigrants. See Health Coverage for Immigrants, The Henry J. Kaiser Family Foundation (Dec. 2017). Funding restrictions on immigrants' access to health care are often part of a broader package of immigration-related initiatives limiting immigrants' access to public services as a means of discouraging illegal immigration. Despite evidence to the contrary, this perceived link between benefits and illegal immigration persists in popular culture, negatively impacting the willingness of some providers to treat immigrants. See Brietta R. Clark, The Immigrant Health Care Narrative and What It Tells Us About the U.S. Health Care System, 17 Annals of Health Law 229 (2008). There are also reports that such restrictions have contributed to a climate of fear that makes some immigrants

less willing to seek care, regardless of their status. See Wendy E. Parmet & Elisabeth Ryan, New Dangers for Immigrants and the Health Care System, Health Affairs Blog (Apr. 20, 2018). Lack of health insurance has also been linked to the practice of medical repatriation, which occurs when a hospital sends critically injured or ill immigrant patients back to their native country without their consent. In these cases, hospitals sometimes also fail to ensure that the patient is being properly discharged to a facility that can appropriately meet the patient's post-discharge medical needs. See Center for Social Justice at Seton Hall Law School and the Health Justice Program at New York Lawyers for the Public Interest Joint Project Report, Discharge, Deportation, and Dangerous Journeys: A Study on the Practice of Medical Repatriation (2012).

## B.  ADA AND SECTION 504 OF THE REHABILITATION ACT

Individuals with disabilities have experienced a history of unequal treatment in medicine and health care, including denial of needed services; inadequate or inappropriate treatment; unnecessary institutionalization often under unacceptable conditions; involuntary sterilization; and other harms. The legislative history of the Americans with Disabilities Act (ADA) documents significant and persistent discrimination against individuals with disabilities across society, including in medicine and health care. The treatment of individuals with disabilities also is discussed in later chapters addressing sterilization (Chapter 3), life and death decisions (Chapter 5), medically assisted death (Chapter 6), and research with individuals with mental disabilities (Chapter 7).

Despite passage of the ADA in 1990, inequities and barriers to care for individuals with disabilities persist. In 2005, 15 years after the passage of the ADA, the Surgeon General's *Call to Action to Improve the Health and Wellness of Persons with Disabilities* highlighted inequities such as poorer reported health status and specific risk of secondary conditions, as well as barriers to health and health care including lack of transportation, provider attitudes and misconceptions, and inaccessible facilities and services. A few years later, the National Council on Disability published its evaluation of decades of research on health inequities and barriers experienced by people with disabilities. Its 2009 report, *The Current State of Health Care for People with Disabilities,* found that people with disabilities report poorer health status than people without disabilities, use fewer preventative services despite using health care services at a significantly higher rate overall, and face more problems accessing health care than other groups. The report identified lack of training on disability competence issues and on legal requirements for health care practitioners among the most significant barriers.

Reports from governmental agencies, advocacy organizations, academic researchers, and others continue to document inequities in health and health care. See e.g., Gloria Krahn, Persons with Disabilities as an Unrecognized Health Disparity Population, 105 Am. J. Pub. Health S198 (2015); Jana J. Peterson-Besse et al., Clinical Preventative Service Use Disparities Among Subgroups of People with Disabilities: A Scoping Review, 7 Disability & Health J. 373 (2014).

The Americans with Disabilities Act (ADA) was enacted to end a history of discrimination based on disability to ensure integration in the community and full participation in society. Title I of the ADA (42 U.S.C. § 12111) applies to employment; Title II (42 U.S.C. § 12131) applies to state and local government services, including state and local public hospitals and health programs such as Medicaid; Title III (42 U.S.C. § 12181) applies to public accommodations, including private health care facilities and offices open to the public; Title IV (42 U.S.C. § 12201) includes miscellaneous provisions, including important provisions regarding insurance.

Section 504 of the Rehabilitation Act of 1973 (29 U.S.C. 749) also prohibits discrimination on the basis of disability in federal employment and in programs and activities that are funded by federal agencies. The ADA and Section 504 are quite similar in most respects, and courts have used cases under the Rehabilitation Act to assist in interpreting the later ADA. There are some significant differences, however. See *Howe*, below. In addition, Section 504, in contrast to the ADA, applies only to programs and services receiving federal funding. As discussed below, the Affordable Care Act broadens the reach of Section 504 significantly.

The U.S. Department of Justice is charged with enforcement of Titles II and III of the ADA and Section 504 and has broad authority to investigate, mediate, litigate, and settle individual and class-based claims. Private individuals and groups can also enforce the ADA and Section 504 through litigation raising disparate treatment and disparate impact claims. Public and private ADA enforcement actions and settlement agreements have addressed a wide range of barriers to health care services for individuals with disabilities. However, many experts claim that the ADA and Section 504 are underenforced.

The following materials explore the impact of the ADA and Section 504 on health care for individuals with disabilities and the promise and challenge of using these laws to address different forms of discrimination based on disability in health care.

## BRAGDON V. ABBOTT
Supreme Court of the United States, 1998.
524 U.S. 624, 118 S.Ct. 2196, 141 L.Ed.2d 540.

KENNEDY, J., delivered the opinion of the Court, in which STEVENS, SOUTER, GINSBERG, and BREYER, JJ., joined. STEVENS, J., filed a concurring opinion. REHNQUIST, C.J., filed an opinion concurring in the judgment in part and dissenting in part, in which SCALIA and THOMAS, JJ., joined, and in Part II of which O'CONNOR, J., joined. O'CONNOR, J., filed an opinion concurring in the judgment in part and dissenting in part.

. . . We granted certiorari to review . . . whether the Court of Appeals, in affirming a grant of summary judgment, cited sufficient material in the record to determine, as a matter of law, that respondent's infection with HIV posed no direct threat to the health and safety of her treating dentist.

I

Respondent Sidney Abbott has been infected with HIV since 1986. When the incidents we recite occurred, her infection had not manifested its most serious symptoms. On September 16, 1994, she went to the office of petitioner Randon Bragdon in Bangor, Maine, for a dental appointment. She disclosed her HIV infection on the patient registration form. Petitioner completed a dental examination, discovered a cavity, and informed respondent of his policy against filling cavities of HIV-infected patients. He offered to perform the work at a hospital with no added fee for his services, though respondent would be responsible for the cost of using the hospital's facilities. Respondent declined.

\* \* \*

. . . Notwithstanding the protection given respondent by the ADA's definition of disability, petitioner could have refused to treat her if her infectious condition "posed a direct threat to the health or safety of others."[ ] The ADA defines a direct threat to be "a significant risk to the health or safety of others that cannot be eliminated by a modification of policies, practices, procedures, or by the provision of auxiliary aids or services."[ ] . . .

The ADA's direct threat provision stems from the recognition in School Bd. of Nassau Cty. v. Arline[ ] of the importance of prohibiting discrimination against individuals with disabilities while protecting others from significant health and safety risks, resulting, for instance, from a contagious disease. In *Arline,* the Court reconciled these objectives by construing the Rehabilitation Act not to require the hiring of a person who posed "a significant risk of communicating an infectious disease to others."[ ] . . . [The ADA's] direct threat provision codifies *Arline.* Because few, if any, activities in life are risk free, *Arline* and the ADA do not ask whether a risk exists, but whether it is significant.[ ]

The existence, or nonexistence, of a significant risk must be determined from the standpoint of the person who refuses the treatment or accommodation, and the risk assessment must be based on medical or other objective evidence.[ ] As a health care professional, petitioner had the duty to assess the risk of infection based on the objective, scientific information available to him and others in his profession. His belief that a significant risk existed, even if maintained in good faith, would not relieve him from liability. To use the words of the question presented, petitioner receives no special deference simply because he is a health care professional. It is true that *Arline* reserved "the question whether courts should also defer to the reasonable medical judgments of private physicians on which an employer has relied."[ ] At most, this statement reserved the possibility that employers could consult with individual physicians as objective third-party experts. It did not suggest that an individual physician's state of mind could excuse discrimination without regard to the objective reasonableness of his actions.

. . . In assessing the reasonableness of petitioner's actions, the views of public health authorities, such as the U.S. Public Health Service, CDC, and the National Institutes of Health, are of special weight and authority.[ ] The views of these organizations are not conclusive, however. A health care professional who disagrees with the prevailing medical consensus may refute it by citing a credible scientific basis for deviating from the accepted norm.[ ]

[An] illustration of a correct application of the objective standard is the Court of Appeals' refusal to give weight to the petitioner's offer to treat respondent in a hospital.[ ] Petitioner testified that he believed hospitals had safety measures, such as air filtration, ultraviolet lights, and respirators, which would reduce the risk of HIV transmission.[ ] Petitioner made no showing, however, that any area hospital had these safeguards or even that he had hospital privileges.[ ] His expert also admitted the lack of any scientific basis for the conclusion that these measures would lower the risk of transmission.[ ] Petitioner failed to present any objective, medical evidence showing that treating respondent in a hospital would be safer or more efficient in preventing HIV transmission than treatment in a well-equipped dental office.

We are concerned, however, that the Court of Appeals might have placed mistaken reliance upon two other sources. In ruling no triable issue of fact existed on this point, the Court of Appeals relied on the CDC Dentistry Guidelines and the 1991 American Dental Association Policy on HIV.[ ] This evidence is not definitive. . . . [T]he CDC Guidelines recommended certain universal precautions which, in CDC's view, "should reduce the risk of disease transmission in the dental environment."[ ] The Court of Appeals determined that, "[w]hile the guidelines do not state explicitly that no further risk-reduction measures are desirable or that routine dental care for HIV-positive individuals is safe, those two conclusions seem to be implicit in the guidelines' detailed delineation of procedures for office treatment of HIV-positive patients."[ ] In our view, the Guidelines do not necessarily contain implicit assumptions conclusive of the point to be decided. The Guidelines set out CDC's recommendation that the universal precautions are the best way to combat the risk of HIV transmission. They do not assess the level of risk.

Nor can we be certain, on this record, whether the 1991 American Dental Association Policy on HIV carries the weight the Court of Appeals attributed to it. The Policy does provide some evidence of the medical community's objective assessment of the risks posed by treating people infected with HIV in dental offices. It indicates:

> "Current scientific and epidemiologic evidence indicates that there is little risk of transmission of infectious diseases through dental treatment if recommended infection control procedures are routinely followed. Patients with HIV infection may be safely treated in private dental offices when appropriate infection control procedures are employed. Such infection control procedures provide protection both for patients and dental personnel."[ ]

We note, however, that the Association is a professional organization, which, although a respected source of information on the dental profession, is not a public health authority. It is not clear the extent to which the Policy was based on the Association's assessment of dentists' ethical and professional duties in addition to its scientific assessment of the risk to which the ADA refers. Efforts to clarify dentists' ethical obligations and to encourage dentists to treat patients with HIV infection with compassion may be commendable, but the question under the statute is one of statistical likelihood, not professional responsibility. Without more information on the manner in which the American Dental Association formulated this Policy, we are unable to determine the Policy's value in evaluating whether petitioner's assessment of the risks was reasonable as a matter of law.

\* \* \*

We acknowledge the presence of other evidence in the record before the Court of Appeals which, subject to further arguments and examination, might support affirmance of the trial court's ruling. For instance, the record contains substantial testimony from numerous health experts indicating that it is safe to treat patients infected with HIV in dental offices.[ ] We are unable to determine the import of this evidence, however. The record does not disclose whether the expert testimony submitted by respondent turned on evidence available in September 1994.[ ]

There are reasons to doubt whether petitioner advanced evidence sufficient to raise a triable issue of fact on the significance of the risk. Petitioner relied on two principal points: First, he asserted that the use of high-speed drills and surface cooling with water created a risk of airborne HIV transmission. The study on which petitioner relied was inconclusive, however, determining only that "further work is required to determine whether such a risk exists."[ ] Petitioner's expert witness conceded, moreover, that no evidence suggested the spray could transmit HIV. His opinion on airborne risk was based on the absence of contrary evidence, not on positive data. Scientific evidence and expert testimony must have a traceable, analytical basis in objective fact before it may be considered on summary judgment.[ ]

[P]etitioner argues that, as of September 1994, CDC had identified seven dental workers with possible occupational transmission of HIV.[ ] These dental workers were exposed to HIV in the course of their employment, but CDC could not determine whether HIV infection had resulted.[ ] It is now known that CDC could not ascertain whether the seven dental workers contracted the disease because they did not present themselves for HIV testing at an appropriate time after their initial exposure.[ ] It is not clear on this record, however, whether this information was available to petitioner in September 1994. If not, the seven cases might have provided some, albeit not necessarily sufficient, support for petitioner's position. Standing alone, we doubt it would meet the objective, scientific basis for finding a significant risk to the petitioner.

\* \* \*

We conclude the proper course is to give the Court of Appeals the opportunity to determine whether our analysis of some of the studies cited by the parties would change its conclusion that petitioner presented neither objective evidence nor a triable issue of fact on the question of risk.

JUSTICE STEVENS, with whom JUSTICE BREYER joins, concurring.

. . . I do not believe petitioner has sustained his burden of adducing evidence sufficient to raise a triable issue of fact on the significance of the risk posed by treating respondent in his office. . . . I join the opinion even though I would prefer an outright affirmance.[ ]

CHIEF JUSTICE REHNQUIST, with whom JUSTICE SCALIA and JUSTICE THOMAS join, and with whom JUSTICE O'CONNOR joins as to Part II, concurring in the judgment in part and dissenting in part.

\* \* \*

II

I agree with the Court that "the existence, or nonexistence, of a significant risk must be determined from the standpoint of the person who refuses the treatment or accommodation," as of the time that the decision refusing treatment is made.[ ] I disagree with the Court, however, that "in assessing the reasonableness of petitioner's actions, the views of public health authorities . . . are of special weight and authority."[ ] Those views are, of course, entitled to a presumption of validity when the actions of those authorities themselves are challenged in court, and even in disputes between private parties where Congress has committed that dispute to adjudication by a public health authority. But in litigation between private parties originating in the federal courts, I am aware of no provision of law or judicial practice that would require or permit courts to give some scientific views more credence than others simply because they have been endorsed by a politically appointed public health authority (such as the Surgeon General). In litigation of this latter sort, which is what we face here, the credentials of the scientists employed by the public health authority, and the soundness of their studies, must stand on their own. The Court cites no authority for its limitation upon the courts' truth-finding function, except the statement in School Bd. of Nassau Cty. v. Arline,[ ] that in making findings regarding the risk of contagion under the Rehabilitation Act, "courts normally should defer to the reasonable medical judgments of public health officials." But there is appended to that dictum the following footnote, which makes it very clear that the Court was urging respect for *medical* judgment, and not necessarily respect for "official" medical judgment over "private" medical judgment: "This case does not present, and we do not address, the question whether courts should also defer to the reasonable medical judgments of private physicians on which an employer has relied."[ ]

Applying these principles here, it is clear to me that petitioner has presented more than enough evidence to avoid summary judgment on the "direct threat" question . . . . Given the "severity of the risk" involved here, i.e., near certain death, and the fact that no public health authority had outlined a protocol for *eliminating* this risk in the context of routine dental treatment, it seems likely that petitioner can establish that it was objectively reasonable for him to conclude that treating respondent in his office posed a "direct threat" to his safety.

* * *

## NOTES AND QUESTIONS

1.   *Bragdon* established that the analysis of "direct threat" as a defense to a claim under the ADA must rely on scientific evidence rather than stereotyping or misconceptions. On remand, the First Circuit upheld the District Court's grant of summary judgment in favor of the plaintiff:

The [American Dental] Association formulates scientific and ethical policies by separate procedures, drawing on different member groups and different staff complements. The Association's Council on Scientific Affairs, comprised of 17 dentists (most of whom hold advanced dentistry degrees), together with a staff of over 20 professional experts and consultants, drafted the Policy at issue here. By contrast, ethical policies are drafted by the Council on Ethics, a wholly separate body. Although the Association's House of Delegates must approve policies drafted by either council, we think that the origins of the Policy satisfy any doubts regarding its scientific foundation.

For these reasons, we are confident that we appropriately relied on the Guidelines and the Policy. . . . Thus, we again conclude, after due reevaluation, that Ms. Abbott served a properly documented motion for summary judgment.

We next reconsider whether Dr. Bragdon offered sufficient proof of direct threat to create a genuine issue of material fact and thus avoid the entry of summary judgment . . . . The Supreme Court suggested that one such piece of evidence—the seven cases that the CDC considered "possible" HIV patient-to-dental worker transmissions—should be reexamined. Since an objective standard pertains here, the existence of the list of seven "possible" cases does not create a genuine issue of material fact as to direct threat. . . . Each piece of evidence to which [defendant directs] us is still "too speculative or too tangential (or, in some instances, both) to create a genuine issue of material fact."

Abbott v. Bragdon, 163 F.3d 87 (1st Cir. 1998), cert. denied, 526 U.S. 1131, 119 S.Ct. 1805, 143 L.Ed.2d 1009 (1999).

2.    The CDC reports only one confirmed case of occupational transmission of HIV to a health care worker since 1999. CDC, Occupational HIV Transmission and Prevention Among Health Care Workers (2015). The CDC recommends "universal precautions" (using barriers such as gloves; handwashing; and design and use of sharps to reduce accidental needle sticks) against transmission of infectious diseases (including hepatitis, which is much more prevalent than HIV) be taken. For HIV in particular, the CDC recommends a specific protocol of post-exposure treatment following any exposure to prevent seroconversion in the exposed health care worker. The risk of transmission of disease from needle stick is 0.23% for needles contaminated with HIV.

3.    Empirical studies demonstrate that a significant number of health care professionals refuse to provide care for persons with HIV/AIDS. See Brad Sears et al., HIV Discrimination in Dental Care: Results of a Testing Study in Los Angeles County, 45 Loy. L.A. L. Rev. 909 (2012), including results of studies from 2003–2008 demonstrating that 46% of skilled nursing facilities, 55% of OB/GYNs, and 26% of plastic surgeons in Los Angeles County refused to treat persons with HIV. See also, Ronda Goldfein, From the Streets of Philadelphia: The AIDS Law Project of Pennsylvania's How-To Primer on Mitigating Health Disparities, 82 Temp. L. Rev. 1205 (2010). The Department of Justice has brought actions against several providers for explicit refusal to

treat patients with HIV. Settlement agreements are available on the DOJ website.

4.     In 2006, the CDC significantly altered its policy on routine screening for HIV. Under the new policy, routine HIV screening is to be "a normal part of medical practice" for all adults unless the prevalence of HIV infection is documented to be less than 0.1% in a particular provider's patient population. In addition, informed consent, beyond a general consent to medical treatment, is not required. Instead, the health care professional need only notify the patient that an HIV test will be performed unless the patient declines. Finally, the CDC asserts that counseling need not be provided for HIV testing. CDC, Revised Recommendations for HIV Testing of Adults, Adolescents, and Pregnant Women in Health-Care Settings, Sept. 22, 2006. The aim of the CDC policy is to prevent AIDS transmission among the general public and to lead persons with HIV to get treatment by addressing the fact that 20–25% of persons with HIV don't know they have the virus. The new policy raises issues concerning access to treatment for those testing positive; confidentiality of results; and whether routinization of testing will lead to a practice of testing without notice. Studies documenting continuing discrimination against persons with HIV raise substantial concern over routine testing. The new screening recommendations may be barred by state law, but the CDC encourages states to revise their statutes. See generally Sarah Schalman-Bergen, CDC's Call for Routine HIV Testing Raises Implementation Concerns, 35 J. L. Med. & Ethics 223 (2007). The U.S. Preventive Services Task Force issued proposed guidelines that mirror the CDC guidelines making it likely that HIV testing will become part of the preventive care package that must be offered by insurers under the ACA at no cost to patients.

5.     Only persons with disabilities are covered by the ADA and Section 504. In *Bragdon*, a deeply divided Court concluded that asymptomatic HIV could be considered a disability under narrow circumstances. In a series of cases after *Bragdon*, however, the Court established a very narrow interpretation of the ADA statutory definition of disability. Congress enacted the Americans with Disabilities Act Amendment Act of 2008 (ADAAA) specifically to reject the Supreme Court's narrow interpretation of the ADA, stating that Congress expected the courts would interpret the term as they had for Section 504. The ADAAA directs that regulations adopt a more expansive interpretation of the ADA definition of disability. A person is disabled if he or she has "a physical or mental impairment that substantially limits one or more major life activities of such individual; a record of such impairment; or [is] regarded as having such an impairment." 42 U.S.C. §§ 12101–12213.

## HOWE V. HULL

U.S. District Court, Northern District, Ohio, 1994.
874 F.Supp.779.

JOHN W. POTTER, SENIOR DISTRICT JUDGE.

\* \* \*

Plaintiff brought suit in the current action alleging that on April 17, 1992, defendants refused to provide Charon medical treatment because he was infected with HIV. Plaintiff claims that defendants' actions violate the Americans with Disabilities Act (ADA) [and] the Federal Rehabilitation Act of 1973 (FRA). . . . The defendants vehemently dispute these claims and allegations and have moved for summary judgment on all of plaintiff's claims.

\* \* \*

On April 17, 1992, Charon and plaintiff Howe were travelling through Ohio, on their way to vacation in Wisconsin. Charon was HIV positive. That morning Charon took a floxin tablet for the first time. Floxin is a prescription antibiotic drug. Within two hours of taking the drug, Charon began experiencing fever, headache, nausea, joint pain, and redness of the skin.

Due to Charon's condition, Charon and plaintiff checked into a motel and, after consulting with Charon's treating physician in Maine, sought medical care at the emergency room of Fremont Memorial Hospital. Charon was examined by the emergency room physician on duty, Dr. Mark Reardon. There is some dispute over what Dr. Reardon's initial diagnosis of Charon's condition was.

Dr. Reardon testified that Charon suffered from a severe drug reaction, and that it was his diagnosis that this reaction was probably Toxic Epidermal Necrolysis (TEN).[2] This diagnosis was also recorded in Charon's medical records. Dr. Reardon also testified regarding Charon's condition that "possibly it was an early stage of toxic epidermal necrolysis, although I had never seen one." Dr. Reardon had no prior experience with TEN, other than what he had read in medical school.

Plaintiff's medical expert Calabrese, however, testified that, after reviewing the medical records and Reardon's deposition, while Charon did appear to be suffering from a severe allergic drug reaction, Calabrese "did not believe that [TEN] was the likely or even probable diagnosis. . . . "

Prior to Charon's eventual transfer to the Medical College of Ohio, Dr. Reardon called Dr. Lynn at MCO and asked Lynn if he would accept the transfer of Charon. Dr. Lynn testified that at no time did Dr. Reardon

---

[2]   TEN is a very serious, very rare, and often lethal skin condition that causes an individual's skin to slough off the body.

mention that plaintiff had been diagnosed with the extremely rare and deadly TEN. Dr. Reardon also did not inform the ambulance emergency medical technicians that plaintiff was suffering from TEN.

Dr. Reardon determined that Charon "definitely needed to be admitted" to Memorial Hospital. Since Charon was from out of town, procedure required that Charon be admitted to the on-call physician, Dr. Hull. Dr. Reardon spoke with Dr. Hull on the telephone and informed Dr. Hull that he wanted to admit Charon, who was HIV-positive and suffering from a non-AIDS related severe drug reaction.

While Dr. Reardon and Dr. Hull discussed Charon's situation, the primary area of their discussion appears to have been whether Charon's condition had advanced from HIV to full-blown AIDS. Dr. Hull inquired neither into Charon's physical condition nor vital signs, nor did he ask Dr. Reardon about the possibility of TEN. During this conversation, it is undisputed that Dr. Hull told Dr. Reardon that "if you get an AIDS patient in the hospital, you will never get him out," and directed that plaintiff be sent to the "AIDS program" at MCO. When Dr. Hull arrived at the hospital after Dr. Reardon's shift but prior to Charon's transfer, he did not attempt to examine or meet with Charon.

\* \* \*

Charon was transferred to the Medical College of Ohio some time after 8:45 P.M. on April 17. After his conversation with Dr. Hull and prior to the transfer, Dr. Reardon told Charon and plaintiff that "I'm sure you've dealt with this before. . . . " Howe asked, "What's that, discrimination?" Dr. Reardon replied, "You have to understand, this is a small community, and the admitting doctor does not feel comfortable admitting [Charon]."

\* \* \*

Charon was admitted and treated at the Medical College of Ohio (MCO). Despite the TEN diagnosis, Charon was not diagnosed by MCO personnel as having TEN and, in fact, was never examined by a dermatologist. After several days, Charon recovered from the allergic drug reaction and was released from MCO.

\* \* \*

Before examining the merits of defendants' contentions, the Court must look at and compare the applicable parameters of the ADA and FRA. There are three basic criteria plaintiff must meet in order to establish a prima facie case of discrimination under the ADA:

a)   the plaintiff has a disability;

b)   the defendants discriminated against the plaintiff; and

c)   the discrimination was based on the disability.

42 U.S.C. § 12182(a); 42 U.S.C. § 12182(b). The discrimination can take the form of the denial of the opportunity to receive medical treatment, segregation unnecessary for the provision of effective medical treatment, unnecessary screening or eligibility requirements for treatment, or provision of unequal medical benefits based upon the disability. [ ] A defendant can avoid liability by establishing that it was unable to provide the medical care that a patient required. [ ]

Similarly, to establish a prima facie case under the FRA the plaintiff must show

a)    the plaintiff has a disability;

b)    plaintiff was otherwise qualified to participate in the program;

c)    defendants discriminated against plaintiff solely on the basis of the disability; and

d)    the program received federal funding.

29 U.S.C. § 794(a).

[A] reasonable jury could conclude that the TEN diagnosis was a pretext and that Charon was denied treatment solely because of his disability. Further, there is no evidence to support the conclusion that Memorial Hospital was unable to treat a severe allergic drug reaction. In fact, the evidence indicates that Dr. Reardon initially planned to admit Charon for treatment. Therefore, Charon was "otherwise qualified" for treatment within the meaning of the FRA. . . .

The FRA states that "no otherwise qualified individual with a disability . . . shall, solely by reason of his or her disability . . . be subjected to discrimination. . . .". 29 U.S.C. § 794(a). The equivalent portion of the ADA reads "No individual shall be discriminated against on the basis of disability. . . ." 42 U.S.C. § 12182(a). It is abundantly clear that the exclusion of the "solely by reason of . . . disability" language was a purposeful act by Congress and not a drafting error or oversight * * *.

The inquiry under the ADA, then, is whether the defendant, despite the articulated reasons for the transfer, improperly considered Charon's HIV status. More explicitly, was Charon transferred for the treatment of a non-AIDS related drug reaction because defendant unjustifiably did not wish to care for an HIV-positive patient? Viewing the evidence in the light most favorable to the plaintiff, the Court finds plaintiff has presented sufficient evidence to preclude a grant of summary judgment on these claims. Defendant Memorial Hospital's motion for summary judgment on the plaintiff's ADA and FRA claims will be denied.

## NOTES AND QUESTIONS

1.    Although persons with HIV/AIDS require very specialized treatment, most also need the same medical services as other generally healthy individuals and as other chronically or intermittently disabled persons. The AMA Medical Code of Ethics provides that "physicians [may not] decline a patient based solely on the individual's infectious disease status." AMA, Opinion 1.1.2 Prospective Patients, Medical Code of Ethics (2016). What is the significance of the AMA's use of the word "solely"? Many state legislatures have amended their medical practice acts to provide that discrimination against persons with HIV is grounds for disciplinary action. See e.g., Wis. Stat. § 252.14.

2.    The ADA and Section 504 address a range of barriers in health care settings. These laws require: physical access to services and facilities, including accessible spaces and the removal of barriers; effective communication, including auxiliary aids and services such as the provision of sign language interpreters or materials in alternative formats; and reasonable modification of policies, practices, and procedures when necessary to accommodate individual needs. 28 C.F.R. 35.130(b)(7); 42 U.S.C. 12182(b)(2)(A), 12183(a). The Affordable Care Act (ACA) also prohibits discrimination on the basis of disability, and the final rule incorporates many of the ADA's regulatory requirements, including those for effective communication. See Section C below. Provision of sign language interpreters for deaf patients has been an active issue in ADA and Section 504 litigation. See e.g., Loeffler v. Staten Island University Hospital, 582 F.3d 268 (2d Cir. 2009), holding that an action for damages under Section 504 could proceed where facts alleged by plaintiff husband (the patient) and wife, both deaf, could support a conclusion that the hospital acted with deliberate indifference in refusing repeated requests for a sign language interpreter for the patient, forcing his minor children to interpret for him. The Department of Justice has brought a number of suits against providers for failing to provide sign language interpreters, and settlement agreements are available on the DOJ website.

3.    Access to medical care for persons with disabilities has been greatly compromised by providers' failure to choose medical diagnostic equipment such as examination tables, dental and eye examination chairs, weight scales, and mammography equipment, that is accessible for persons with mobility limitations. For a thorough discussion, see Elizabeth Pendo, Reducing Disparities Through Health Reform: Disability and Accessible Medical Equipment, 2010 Utah L. Rev. 1057 (2010), including a review of litigation approaches and provisions of the Affordable Care Act requiring promulgation of standards for accessible medical equipment. Class action litigation has targeted health care facilities for violation of the ADA regarding physical access. See e.g., Settlement Agreement in United Spinal Association et al. v. Beth Israel Medical Center et al., No. 13-cv-5131 (S.D.N.Y., filed Nov. 17, 2017). In accordance with the ACA, the U.S. Access Board issued a final rule that delineates minimum technical criteria for the accessibility of examination tables, examination chairs, weight scales, mammography equipment, and

other diagnostic imaging equipment. Architectural and Transportation Barriers Compliance Board, Standards for Accessible Medical Diagnostic Equipment. 82 Fed. Reg. 2810 (Jan. 9, 2017) (codified at 36 CFR Part 1195). The standards become mandatory when adopted by a federal agency.

4.    *Howe* correctly notes that the ADA and Section 504 differ significantly on what the plaintiff must prove as the reason for the defendant's action. For seventeen years, the Sixth Circuit applied the "solely" standard from Section 504 to ADA cases. Finally, it held: "Our interpretation of the ADA not only is out of sync with the other circuits, but it also is wrong." Lewis v. Humboldt Acquisition Corp., 681 F.3d 312 (6th Cir. 2012). In the course of correcting itself, the court provides a very good analysis of the difference in standards.

It may be difficult in a particular case to prove the reason for the refusal of treatment much less meet the requirement that the disability be the "sole" reason for denial of adequate treatment. In Lesley v. Hee Man Chie, 250 F.3d 47 (1st Cir. 2001), the District Court adopted the following standard:

> The case requires us to determine how far courts should defer to a doctor's judgment as to the best course of treatment for a disabled patient in the context of discriminatory denial of treatment claims. We hold that the doctor's judgment is to be given deference absent a showing by the plaintiff that the judgment lacked any reasonable medical basis.

Is the court's deference appropriate? Consistent with the statute? How would you go about proving or defending against a claim that the medical judgment defense is a subterfuge? Haavi Morreim offers the following as indicators of discriminatory decisions to withhold treatment: where the medical judgment is based on "inaccurate facts" resulting from presumptions or prejudices against persons with the patient's medical condition; where the reasoning underlying the treatment decision is "irrational" as, for example, where a surgeon would decide not to perform surgery only because of the high risk of mortality even though the surgery would provide the patient's only hope of survival; or where the decision is based on "inappropriate values" such as a conclusion that certain persons are by race or gender inherently inferior. E. Haavi Morreim, Futilitarianism, Exoticare, and Coerced Altruism: The ADA Meets Its Limits, 25 Seton Hall L. Rev. 883 (1995). See also Mary A. Crossley, Of Diagnoses and Discrimination: Discriminatory Nontreatment of Infants with HIV Infection, 93 Colum. L. Rev. 1581 (1993).

5.    During the 1980s, the case of Baby Doe focused attention on denial of care to seriously ill newborns based on disability. In 1983, Baby Doe was born with Down syndrome and a tracheoesophageal fistula which would require repair to allow him to consume nutrition orally. The parents decided not to authorize the necessary surgery because of the Down syndrome, and the baby was given phenobarbital and morphine until he died, six days after birth. A lawsuit by the hospital in the local children's court was rendered moot by Baby Doe's death.

Several political groups, including right-to-life groups and advocacy groups for the developmentally disabled, were outraged by the circumstances of Baby Doe's death. The Secretary of HHS issued emergency regulations pursuant to Section 504 to assure that no hospital would deny treatment to seriously ill newborns based on disability. After a furious political battle, a compromise was reached in the form of the Child Abuse Amendments of 1984, 42 U.S.C.A. § 5102, that conditions each state's receipt of some federal funding on the maintenance of procedures for dealing with reports of the medical neglect of newborns. Regulations issued under the Child Abuse Amendments interpret "medical neglect" to include "the withholding of medically indicated treatment from a disabled infant with a life threatening condition." 45 C.F.R. § 1340.15(b)(1). Further, the regulations provide that the "'withholding of medically indicated treatment' means the failure to respond to the infant's life threatening conditions by providing treatment (including appropriate nutrition, hydration, and medication) which in the treating physicians' . . . reasonable medical judgment will be most likely to be effective in ameliorating or correcting all such conditions." 45 C.F.R. § 1340.15(b)(2). There is no obligation to provide care to an infant who is "chronically and irreversibly comatose," when the treatment would "merely prolong the dying process" of the infant and not ameliorate or correct the underlying medical problem (and thus be futile), or when the treatment would be "virtually futile" and "inhumane." *Id.*

6.     In the landmark 1999 case *Olmstead v. L.C*, the SCOTUS held that unnecessary segregation of persons with disability constitutes discrimination in violation of Title II of the ADA. Olmstead v. L.C. ex rel. Zimring, 527 U.S. 581, 592 (1992). The Court held that public entities, including state Medicaid programs, must provide community-based services to persons with disabilities when such services are appropriate, desired by the recipient, and can be reasonably accommodated by the public entity. The Court relied on the "integration mandate" in the Title II regulations that requires public entities to "administer services, programs, and activities in the most integrated setting appropriate to the needs of qualified individuals with disabilities." The regulations define the "most integrated setting" as one that "enables individuals with disabilities to interact with nondisabled persons to the fullest extent possible. . . ." This means individuals with disability, including persons with cognitive and intellectual disabilities and persons with mental illness, cannot be required to live in institutions or group settings to obtain the health care and other services they need. Some states are expanding their Medicaid programs to expand coverage for home and community-based care.

## NOTE: DISCRIMINATION BASED ON GENETIC INFORMATION

The ability to read (and, perhaps, change) a person's genetic characteristics has created tremendous hopes and terrible fears. There is a fear that the terrifying history of eugenics will repeat itself. In Buck v. Bell, 274 U.S. 200 (1927), for example, the Supreme Court tragically misunderstood and misused genetics and decided that the forced sterilization of a woman perceived to be intellectually disabled, whose mother and grandmother were also believed to be so, was not a violation of her Constitutional rights. Justice Holmes, in a now infamous declaration, stated that it is desirable "to prevent those who are manifestly unfit from continuing their kind . . . . Three generations of imbeciles are enough." For a full history of that case and the family, see Paul Lombardo, Three Generations, No Imbeciles: New Light on Buck v. Bell, 60 N.Y.U.L.Rev. 30 (1985). About 8,000 Virginians who were low-income, uneducated and believed to have intellectual disabilities were sterilized as part of a eugenics program in that state between 1924 and 1979. Thirty states engaged in such programs, and 65,000 individuals nationwide were involuntarily sterilized. Similarly, government efforts targeted people with sickle cell based on mistaken genetic assumptions:

> In the 1970s, large scale screening [for sickle cell] was undertaken with the goal of changing African American mating behavior. Unfortunately, the initiative promoted confusion regarding the difference between carriers and those with the disease. This confusion resulted in widespread discrimination against African Americans. Some states passed legislation requiring all African American children entering school to be screened for the sickle-cell trait, even though there was no treatment or cure for the sickle-cell disease. Some states required prisoners to be tested, even though there would be no opportunity for them to pass on the trait. Job and insurance discrimination were both real and attempted. The military considered banning all African Americans from the armed services. African American airline stewardesses were fired. Insurance rates went up for carriers. Some companies refused to insure carriers. During that period, many African Americans came to believe that the sickle-cell screening initiative was merely a disguised genocide attempt, since often the only advice given to African Americans with the trait was, "Don't have kids."

Vernellia R. Randall, Trusting the Health Care System Ain't Always Easy! An African American Perspective on Bioethics, 15 St. Louis U. Public L. Rev. 191 (1996). See also, Norman-Bloodsaw v. Lawrence Berkeley Laboratory, 135 F.3d 1260 (9th Cir. 1998), involving employment-based testing for sickle cell.

Fear of discrimination based on genetic traits is not just a matter of history. In 2008 Congress passed and the President signed the Genetic Information Nondiscrimination Act of 2008 (GINA), P.L. 110–233, which regulates the collection and use of genetic information by group health plans, by those marketing individual policies for health insurance, and by employers. GINA amends ERISA, HIPAA, and the Internal Revenue Code, and adds a provision to the federal employment discrimination statutes. The EEOC has promulgated regulations to enforce the statute in the employment context, while the Office of Civil Rights of the Department of Health and Human Services and other agencies have issued regulations to enforce the statute in other contexts.

Unlike the other federal anti-discrimination laws discussed in this section, GINA does not regulate the delivery of health care services. However, it addresses related concerns. The Preamble of the Act describes the rationale for its enactment:

> Deciphering the sequence of the human genome and other advances in genetics open major new opportunities for medical progress. New knowledge about the genetic basis of illness will allow for earlier detection of illnesses, often before symptoms have begun. Genetic testing can allow individuals to take steps to reduce the likelihood that they will contract a particular disorder. New knowledge about genetics may allow for the development of better therapies that are more effective against disease or have fewer side effects than current treatments. These advances give rise to the potential misuse of genetic information to discriminate in health insurance and employment. The early science of genetics became the basis of State laws that provided for the sterilization of persons having presumed genetic "defects" such as mental retardation, mental disease, epilepsy, blindness, and hearing loss, among other conditions. . . . [T]he current explosion in the science of genetics, and the history of sterilization laws by the States based on early genetic science, compels Congressional action in this area.

> Although genes are facially neutral markers, many genetic conditions and disorders are associated with particular racial and ethnic groups and gender. Because some genetic traits are most prevalent in particular groups, members of a particular group may be stigmatized or discriminated against as a result of that genetic information. . . . To alleviate some of this stigma, Congress in 1972 passed the National Sickle Cell Anemia Control Act, which withholds Federal funding from States unless sickle cell testing is voluntary.

GINA prohibits health insurers, in both group health plans and in the individual market, from making insurance decisions based on "genetic information." Genetic information is defined broadly as genetic tests, the genetic tests of family members, and the manifestation of a disease or disorder in family members, with exceptions. See 42 U.S.C. § 2000ff. Insurers may consider genetic diseases that have manifested themselves in ways other than genetic tests. However, the ADA may apply for manifested diseases that meet the definition of "disability." While some of the insurance protections mandated under GINA will become unnecessary as the ACA becomes effective, it will continue to be an additional source of support for those who face discrimination in health insurance eligibility, price, or conditions because of their genetic status. Note that GINA does not reach discrimination issues other than genetic discrimination in employment and health insurance. It generally provides no protection against discrimination in the disability and long-term care insurance markets, for example. GINA also applies to workplace wellness plans.

## NOTES AND QUESTIONS

1.    Concerns over discrimination related to genetic characteristics relate both to the predictive reliability of the information and to the legitimacy of the interests served by the practice in question. While we may have broad agreement that a decision based on information that is inaccurate or misunderstood is a "bad" decision, is it also discriminatory? Categorizing a decision as discriminatory generally requires that one identify a group against which this individual is treated differently; e.g., women, differently from men; older, differently from younger; or one race differently from another. What is the relevant comparable group for genetic discrimination; i.e., are groups to be identified by specific genetic characteristic? Is the decision discriminatory only if it relates to characteristics that are beyond the individual's control? Are there any legitimate reasons to use genetic traits in decision making, for example, in making decisions about medical treatment? See generally, Radhika Rao, A Veil of Genetic Ignorance? Protecting Genetic Privacy to Ensure Equality, 51 Vill. L. Rev. 827 (2006).

2.    Given our often moralistic attitudes toward sickness and the continuing human history of exclusion and discrimination against minorities and the disabled, will "imperfect humans" be devalued and penalized? This is a familiar dynamic in history, but the new power of genetics may widen the net for imperfection. Increased opportunities for control of genetic traits in reproductive decision making, for example, raise questions of choice and consequences. See Eric Rakowski, Who Should Pay for Bad Genes, 90 Cal. L. Rev. 1345 (2002), arguing that parents who choose to bear such a "genetically disadvantaged" child should incur a greater liability for the costs of the child's care. On the other hand, others are concerned about the drive toward "genetic enhancement" and the creation of a genetically perfect person (or society). See Maxwell Mehlman, Law of Above Averages: Leveling the New Genetic Enhancement Playing Field, 85 Iowa L. Rev. 517 (2000); Michael Malinowski, Choosing the Genetic Makeup of Our Children: Our Eugenics Past—Present, and Future, 36 Conn. L. Rev. 125 (2003). Reproductive decision making is discussed in detail in Chapter 3.

3.    Genetic information is likely to have implications for groups. The idea that groups may have concerns, interests, and perhaps rights is one that is hotly debated in genetic research. See e.g., Joan L. McGregor, Population Genomics and Research Ethics, 35 J.L. Med. & Ethics 356 (2007); Laura Underkuffler, Human Genetics Studies: The Case for Group Rights, 35 J.L. Med. & Ethics 383 (2007). See also the discussion of research with the Havasupai tribe in Chapter 7.

Sometimes the distribution of genetic traits may appear to parallel what have been called "folk notions" of race or ethnicity. Pilar Ossorio, Race, Genetic Variation, and the Haplotype Mapping Project, 66 La. L. Rev. 131 (2005). For example, the sickle cell trait is more common in persons with ancestors from sub-Saharan Africa, Latin America, Saudi Arabia, India, and Mediterranean countries; and Tay-Sachs is more common in Jews of Eastern European extraction (although 1 in 250 persons in the general population also carries the gene for the disease and it is found in higher than general rates in French Canadians and Cajuns). Each of these common claims of association of genetic traits with particular geographically based populations is extraordinarily imprecise and overgeneralized, however. Keith Wailoo & Stephen Pemberton, The Troubled Dream of Genetic Medicine: Ethnicity and Innovation in Tay-Sachs, Cystic Fibrosis, and Sickle Cell Disease (2006). See also, Mark Rothstein, Legal Conceptions of Equality in a Genomic Age, 25 Law & Ineq. 429 (2007).

4.    Genetic discrimination is of substantial concern beyond the United States, and international human rights law has taken notice of the possibility of inappropriate genetic discrimination. In 1997 UNESCO issued a Universal Declaration on the Human Genome and Human Rights that requires that "no-one shall be subjected to discrimination based on genetic characteristics that is intended to infringe or has the effect of infringing human rights, fundamental freedoms and human dignity." United Nations Educational, Scientific, and Cultural Organization, Universal Declaration on the Human Genome and Human Rights art. 6 (Nov. 11, 1997). UNESCO's International Declaration on Human Data notes that "every effort should be made to ensure that human genetic data are not used for purposes that are discriminatory or in any way that would lead to the stigmatization of an individual, a family or a group." United Nations Educational, Scientific, and Cultural Organization, International Declaration on Human Data art. 7 (Oct. 16, 2003). Many other countries have laws regulating such discrimination, as do international regional organizations. For an interesting account of Australian practices with regard to employment, see M. Otlowski, et al., Practices and Attitudes of Australian Employers With Regard to the Use of Genetic Information, 31 Comp. Lab. L. & Pol'y J. 637 (2010).

## C.  SECTION 1557 OF THE ACA

Section 1557 of the ACA, 42 U.S.C. § 18116, builds upon and expands the reach of existing antidiscrimination protections. It provides:

(a)  . . . [A]n individual shall not, on the ground prohibited under title VI of the Civil Rights Act of 1964 (42 U.S.C. 2000d et seq.), title IX of the Education Amendments of 1972 (20 U.S.C. 1681 et seq.), the Age Discrimination Act of 1975 (42 U.S.C. 6101 et seq.), or section 504 of the Rehabilitation Act of 1973 (29 U.S.C. 794) . . . be excluded from participation in, be denied the benefits of, or be subjected to discrimination under, any health program or activity, any part of which is receiving Federal financial assistance, including credits, subsidies, or contracts of insurance, or under any program or activity that is administered by an Executive Agency or any entity established under this title (or amendments). The enforcement mechanisms provided for and available under title VI  shall apply for purposes of violations of this subsection.

(b) . . . Nothing in this title . . . shall be construed to invalidate or limit the rights, remedies, procedures, or legal standards available to individuals aggrieved under title VI of the Civil Rights Act of 1964 [ ], title IX of the Education Amendments [ ], section 504 of the Rehabilitation Act [ ] or to supersede State laws that provide additional protections against discrimination on any basis described in subsection (a).

Under the Obama administration, the HHS Office of Civil Rights issued a lengthy and comprehensive Final Rule for the implementation of Section 1557 in May of 2016. See Nondiscrimination in Health Programs and Activities, 81 Fed. Reg. 31375 (May 18, 2016) (codified at 45 C.F.R. Part 92). The final rule clarified and codified existing nondiscrimination requirements and set forth new standards to implement Section 1557, particularly with respect to the prohibition of sex discrimination in health programs. The fate of Obama-era regulations and interpretations of Section 1557 have been called into question with the election of President Trump. The Trump administration has already signaled its disagreement with various parts of the May 2016 Final Rule and its intent to propose new rules that would narrow antidiscrimination protections under Section 1557 regulations. This section describes the state of the law as it exists at the beginning of 2018, highlighting aspects of Section 1557 enforcement already in contention and starting to wend their way through the courts. This is an area that should be watched closely.

## 1. Expanding the Reach of Existing Antidiscrimination Protections

Section 1557 incorporates the rights and remedies under Title VI and Section 504 (discussed above) among other statutes, and it expands the reach of these protections in important ways. First, it broadens the application of the prohibitions. HHS regulations define federal financial assistance to include grants, loans, credits, subsidies, and insurance contracts. 42 C.F.R. § 92.4. Under this definition, Section 1557 antidiscrimination prohibitions apply to health insurers that receive premium tax credits or cost-sharing reduction payments for enrollees. Section 1557 also applies to most providers, though there are some limits. For example, HHS maintains that payments for patient care under Medicare Part B (the program that pays for physician services for Medicare beneficiaries) do not count as "Federal financial assistance," and providers paid directly by covered health insurers are not deemed to have received "assistance" for purposes of Section 1557. Nonetheless, most of these physicians probably receive federal assistance in other forms, and the statute does apply to all physicians who receive Medicaid or meaningful use information technology (IT) funding (which ends in 2018).

Second, Section 1557 seems to strengthen private enforcement of antidiscrimination law. Individuals may sue directly under section 1557 in federal court. Also, HHS has interpreted Section 1557 as providing a new, health-specific, anti-discrimination cause of action subject to a single standard, regardless of the plaintiff's protected class status. This is significant because this could mean that an individual would be able to bring a private disparate impact claim, even though a private disparate impact claim may not otherwise be available based on the underlying statutory prohibition (as in the case of Title VI, discussed at Section A). There is already litigation over this question, with courts coming to different conclusions.

In Rumble v. Fairview Health Services, No. 14-CV-2037 SRN/FLN, 2015 WL 1197415 (D. Minn. Mar. 16, 2015), the court held that Congress intended to create a new, health-specific, anti-discrimination cause of action that is subject to a singular standard, regardless of a plaintiff's protected class status, because holding otherwise "would lead to an illogical result." The court explained that applying different standards would mean a plaintiff bringing a race discrimination claim under Section 1557 could allege only disparate treatment, but plaintiffs bringing a disability or sex discrimination claim under the same statute could allege disparate treatment or disparate impact. This argument was rejected by a different court, however. In Southeastern Penn. Transp. Auth. v. Gilead Sciences, 102 F. Supp. 3d 688 (E.D. Pa. 2015), the court found that Congress created a private right of action for Section 1557 violations, but that "Congress's express incorporation of the enforcement mechanisms from . . . four federal civil rights statutes . . . manifests an intent to import the various different standards and burdens of proof into a Section 1557 claim." The court then applied Title VI standards to require plaintiffs to raise an inference of intentional race discrimination in pleadings for a Section 1557 violation.

Finally, HHS has clarified that compensatory damages are available in 1557 actions and that attorneys' fees and class action rules that apply under the underlying statutes also apply to 1557 claims.

## 2.   A New Prohibition on Sex Discrimination

The last decade has seen an increase in attention to gender-based disparities in health care, with a particular focus on the health care barriers and poorer health outcomes experienced by women and transgender individuals. For example, studies in the U.S. have demonstrated that women tend to receive less intensive treatment for acute myocardial infarction, have an increased chance of misdiagnosis of stroke, and suffer higher rates of mortality from sepsis than men. See Viola Vaccarino et al., Sex and Racial Differences in the Management of Acute Myocardial Infarction, 1994–2002, 353 NEJM 671 (2005); David E. Newman-Toker et al., Missed Diagnosis of Stroke in the Emergency

Department: A Cross-Sectional Analysis of a Large Population-Based Sample, 1 Diagnosis 155 (2014); Anthony P. Pietropaoli et al., Gender Differences in Mortality in Patients with Severe Sepsis and Septic Shock, 7 Gender Med. 422 (2010). There is also evidence that women are more likely to be undertreated for or inappropriately diagnosed and treated for pain, as compared to men. See Diane E. Hoffman and Anita J. Tarzian, The Girl Who Cried Pain: A Bias Against Women in the Treatment of Pain, 29 J. L. Med. & Ethics 13 (2001). In some cases, women have been refused treatment because of pregnancy, such as where pregnant women seek drug treatment services.

Transgender individuals also experience health care barriers and unequal treatment. Barriers include lack of access to transition-related care, such as hormone therapy and sex reassignment surgery, due to a lack of qualified providers and inadequate training of medical professionals generally with respect to the medical needs of transgender patients. Such barriers can have serious health consequences, including an increased chance of depression and suicide, and physical and mental health risks for those who attempt to self-medicate. See National Center for Transgender Equality and National Gay and Lesbian Task Force, Injustice at Every Turn: A Report of the National Transgender Discrimination Survey, 5–6 (2011). Transgender individuals also have the same health care needs as other patients, but they may be denied care or receive worse treatment because of their transgender status. In a 2010 survey on discrimination against LGBT people, nearly 27% of transgender respondents reported being denied medically necessary care outright because of their transgender status. See Lamba Legal, When Health Care Isn't Caring: Survey on Discrimination Against LGBT People and People Living with HIV (2010). In the same survey, 70% reported being treated poorly by health care providers, in ways that create serious dignitary harms and potentially jeopardize health. Survey participants described a broad range of such treatment by physicians: refusing to touch them or using excessive precautions; using harsh or abusive language; being physically rough or abusive; or blaming the patients for their health status. Examples of poor treatment by hospital staff were also reported, including: laughter, pointing, taunting, use of slurs, and other negative comments; violations of confidentiality; use of improper name and/or pronoun for patient; exceptionally long waits for care; inappropriate questions or exams, including needless viewing of genitals; and failure to follow standards of care. See Lamba Legal, supra.

Section 1557 creates a new prohibition on sex discrimination in health care (incorporating by reference Title IX, which prohibits discrimination on the basis of sex in educational programs and activities that receive federal financial assistance, 20 U.S.C. § 1681). Implementing regulations finalized during the Obama administration define sex discrimination broadly to include discrimination "on the basis of pregnancy, false pregnancy, termination of pregnancy or recovery therefrom, childbirth, or related medical conditions, sex stereotyping and gender identity." 45 C.F.R. § 92.4. Gender identity is defined in the regulation as "an individual's internal sense of gender, which may be male, female, neither, or a combination of male and female, and which may be different from an individual's sex assigned at birth." Id. The definition further notes that the way one expresses gender identity is often called "gender expression" and this may or may not conform to social stereotypes associated with that particular gender. The regulations also require that covered entities treat individuals in accordance with their gender identity or expression, with one important clarification: this requirement cannot be used to deny medically necessary care. 45 C.F.R. § 92.206. For example, the final rule explains that a covered entity could not deny treatment for ovarian cancer based on an individual's identification as a transgender male, where that treatment is medically indicated.

One of the earliest cases to interpret Section 1557 involved a claim of discrimination on the basis of transgender status. See Rumble v. Fairview Health Services, supra. In *Rumble*, the plaintiff, who self-identified as a "female-to-male transgender man," alleged treatment by health care providers that mirrored many of the examples of discrimination described in the Lambda survey above: hostile and abusive touching by a physician, misclassification of the plaintiff's gender, unnecessary disclosures revealing his status, and subjection to unnecessary and improper exams. There was also evidence the plaintiff did not receive adequate pain treatment or a timely diagnosis, and that the delay could have been life-threatening. Based on this evidence, the court refused to grant defendants' motion to dismiss and found that the nature and degree of defendants' "unprofessional" and "assaultive" actions were sufficient to raise an inference of discriminatory intent under Section 1557.

This interpretation of sex discrimination—as including discrimination on the basis of gender identity—is currently being challenged. Although the final rule explained its inclusion of gender identity discrimination within the definition of sex discrimination as "well-grounded" in law, the Trump administration has signaled its disagreement with this interpretation, and courts confronting the question have come to different conclusions. Compare Franciscan Alliance v. Burwell, 227 F. Supp. 3d 660 (N.D. Texas 2016) (holding that "HHS's expanded definition of sex discrimination [to include gender identity] exceeds the grounds incorporated by Section 1557" and issuing a nationwide preliminary injunction blocking application of the prohibition of gender identity discrimination) with Prescott v. Rady Children's Hospital-San Diego, 265 F. Supp. 3d 1090 (S.D. Cal. 2017) (reviewing cases interpreting Title IX and a federal law prohibiting sex discrimination in employment, and holding that "because [those statutes] recognize that discrimination on the basis of transgender identity is discrimination on the basis of sex, the Court interprets the ACA to afford the same protections). Litigation on this question is certain to continue, as it presents an issue of statutory interpretation that may or may not depend on HHS's interpretation of sex discrimination. See e.g., id. (noting that "the Court does not rely on the HHS's regulation in concluding that the claim survives").

## NOTES AND QUESTIONS

1.    Does discrimination "on the basis of sex" include discrimination on the basis of sexual orientation? The final rule does not list sexual orientation among the categories of sex discrimination that are prohibited, and the OCR expressly refused to resolve the issue as part of the final rule. It left the question open, noting that it would continue to monitor the evolving law in this area. But in doing so, it highlighted cases and federal agency decisions that have found discrimination on the basis of sexual orientation to constitute unlawful sex discrimination under other statutes. See e.g., Videckis and White v. Pepperdine Univ., No. 15-00298, 2015 WL 8916764 (C.D. Cal. Dec. 15, 2015) (concluding that the distinction between gender stereotyping and sexual orientation discrimination is illusory and artificial, and that sexual orientation discrimination is not a category distinct from sex or gender discrimination under Title IX); U.S. Equal Employment Opportunity Comm'n Appeal No. 0120133080, Agency No. 2012-24738-FAA-03 (July 15, 2015) (finding that sexual orientation is inseparable from and inescapably linked to sex and an allegation of discrimination based on sexual orientation is necessarily an allegation of sex discrimination under Title VII). Other courts have disagreed, however. See e.g., Hinton v. Virginia, 185 F. Supp. 3d 807 (E.D. Va. 2016) (rejecting the Equal Employment Opportunity Commission's 2015 interpretation of Title VII as encompassing sexual orientation discrimination claims). Under the Obama Administration, OCR and HHS expressed support for a prohibition on sexual orientation discrimination "as a matter of policy" and pointed to existing CMS regulations that expressly prohibit sexual orientation discrimination by most health insurance issuers.

2.    Does discrimination "on the basis of sex" protect individuals born with atypical sex characteristics or traits? On this question, the final rule was clear that sex discrimination includes discrimination on the basis of "the presence of atypical sex characteristics and intersex traits (i.e., people born with variations in sex characteristics, including in chromosomal, reproductive, or anatomical sex characteristics that do not fit the typical characteristics of binary females or males)." Nondiscrimination in Health Programs and Activities, supra. Such individuals, who may identify as "intersex" individuals or as individuals with "disorders of sex development," can experience discrimination similar to the kind of discrimination that transgender people face. For example, the rule noted that such individuals have been denied care or coverage for medical care that is classified as "sex-specific," where the treatment classification did not match the person's registered sex; but this

denial would be prohibited under Section 1557. The rule fails to explicitly address, however, concerns that have been raised about medical interventions performed on intersex infants and children to conform their sexual or reproductive anatomy to a binary sex norm. Although the most extreme examples of these interventions have been rejected by the mainstream medical community and have largely disappeared, medically unnecessary surgical alteration of infants still occurs. See Julie A. Greenberg, Intersexuality and the Law: Why Sex Matters (N.Y.U. Press 2012), arguing that this practice should be considered a form of sex discrimination, and providing a thorough exploration of the medical, ethical, and legal issues arising out of this practice.

3.    The focus of this chapter has been on discriminatory refusals and unequal treatment by different types of health care providers, but antidiscrimination law also applies to public and private insurance. As discussed elsewhere in this book, the laws studied in this chapter have been used to challenge insurance benefit exclusions or denials. Consider, for example, whether the categorical exclusion of sex reassignment surgery or other transition-related care would constitute discrimination on the basis of gender identity under Section 1557? What about the exclusion of reproductive health care that is woman-specific—would this be sex discrimination under Section 1557? Would the exclusion of certain kinds of mental health coverage or prosthetic devices violate the ADA or Section 1557? For more information on woman-specific reproductive health exclusions, see Chapter 3, Sections III & IV (Abortion and Contraception).

# CHAPTER 3

## REPRODUCTION AND BIRTH

■ ■ ■

## I.  INTRODUCTION

As the other chapters in this book have demonstrated, health policy can be motivated by diverse economic, political, cultural, and social justice goals. These goals, in turn, are often shaped by deeply held beliefs about the ethical principles and moral values that should inform government's role in society. Perhaps no area of health law stimulates as much passionate debate and reveals as sharply diverging views on the appropriate role of government, as the regulation of reproduction and birth.

One reason for this is that regulation of reproduction implicates questions of personhood. The rights, obligations, privileges, and relationships previously described in this book are generally rights, obligations, privileges, and relationships of people. But who ought to be recognized as a person, subject to the legal principles that regulate our rights and obligations? When does a person, entitled to formal legal respect as such, come into existence? Can such answers be resolved through an analysis of medicine, philosophy, law, social history, anthropology, theology and other disciplines which seek to answer the basic questions of human existence?

Physicians and lawyers have necessarily been involved in these questions, as demonstrated by conflicts over government regulation of abortion and contraception, compelled medical intervention of pregnant women, and legal questions about the treatment of embryos arising out of the growing use of assisted reproductive technology. It is therefore appropriate to consider these issues in this text. The deeply contested and complex legal and philosophical questions around personhood are surveyed in the first portion of this chapter, and this issue is an important theme in the legal and ethical questions considered throughout the rest of the chapter.

The issues surveyed in this chapter also raise important gender, racial, disability, and socioeconomic justice concerns, which have motivated complaints of both too much and too little government regulation in the area of reproduction. Gender concerns are most obviously implicated, because although both men and women have reproductive health care needs, women's ability to get pregnant means they bear unique health and social consequences of being denied care that enables, prevents, or terminates pregnancy. Socioeconomic concerns are implicated because the ability to control the timing and manner of pregnancy impacts women's and families' well-being and socioeconomic opportunities.

While reproductive *rights* advocates have traditionally focused on women's ability to prevent pregnancy, a more recent movement around reproductive *justice* has shone a light on government actions that create barriers to procreation. For example, assumptions about who *ought* to be a parent, or who can be trusted to parent effectively, have motivated government sterilization programs targeting people with developmental disabilities, the poor, racial and ethnic minorities, and women in prison. In addition, state and federal laws have traditionally made it more difficult for some groups to realize their procreative dreams through assisted reproductive technology, though this is changing.

The remaining parts of this chapter are not intended to be a comprehensive analysis of all of the legal and ethical questions raised by reproduction. The goal of this chapter is to provide structure for an analysis of issues surrounding procreation and reproduction that are likely to be of special concern to attorneys representing health care professionals, institutions, and their patients.

## II. WHEN DOES HUMAN LIFE BECOME A "PERSON"?

This society has had difficulty defining who is a "person." In part, this arises out of the different and inconsistent purposes for which we seek a definition. The "person" from whom we wish to harvest a kidney for transplantation may be defined differently from the "person" who is protected by the Fourteenth Amendment, federal civil rights laws, and various other federal and state laws. Even when the purpose of the definition is settled—such as who is a person able to bring an action under state tort law—there is no consensus on when the status of "personhood" first attaches. The most obvious definition of personhood is a recursive one: a human being (and, thus, a "person") is the reproductive product of other human beings. Even if we accept this "human stock" definition of person, however, the inquiry remains open. Does that human stock become a person, for tort law or other purposes, upon conception? Upon quickening? Upon viability? Upon birth? A year after birth? Upon physical maturity?

The definition of "person" is not limited to various stages in the development of human stock. "Personhood" could commence upon ensoulment, upon the development of self concept, upon the development of a sense of personal history, or upon the ability to communicate through language although none of these points is easy to identify in individual cases. The resolution of the question appears to require a resort to first principles.

In the vast majority of cases, it is not difficult to distinguish a person from something else. You are easily distinguishable from your arms, your dog, your insurance company and your gold bust of Elvis, as close as you may feel to each of them. The most difficult questions tend to arise at the very beginning and at the very end of human life. Just as you may be able to identify the fact that you were in love, but not be able to identify exactly when it began, or the moment when it ended, the beginnings and the endings of "personhood" are the fuzzy portions.

There are limits to what may reasonably be considered a "person," even when we limit our consideration to human stock. Few suggest that anything independent of the unified sperm and ovum, or its consequences, ought to be considered a person, although advances in cloning and cellular manipulation may challenge this assumption. A great many religious groups consider "personhood" to attach at conception. Aristotle viewed the development of the person as a three stage process, going from vegetable (at conception), to animal (in utero), to rational (sometime after birth). For many centuries, Christian theology fixed the point of "immediate animation" when the fetus was "ensouled" as forty days after conception for males and eighty days after conception for females. St. Thomas Aquinas determined that the ensoulment took place at the time of quickening, usually fourteen to eighteen weeks after conception, and his determination had a very substantial effect on the development of the common law in England and in this country. Recently some philosophers have suggested that "personhood," at least to the extent that it includes a right to life, depends on attributes that are not likely to be developed until sometime after birth.

One thoughtful and oft-cited set of attributes of personhood has been developed by Joseph Fletcher, a bioethicist. Consider his fifteen criteria, described below, and determine whether some or all of them can be used to properly define who is your colleague in personhood and who is not. Consider whether the fact that many of these criteria disqualify fetuses, newborns, and the seriously developmentally disabled affects their acceptability as standards. Further, does the fact that some animal or machine might eventually fulfill all of these criteria cause you to doubt their validity? What are the consequences of our failure to define as a person a clone, a highly intelligent and communicative ape, a robot, or a manufactured cell that can be brought to term in an artificial womb, with regard to our conceptions of "democracy" and "slavery," for example?

### JOSEPH FLETCHER, "HUMANNESS," IN HUMANHOOD: ESSAYS IN BIOMEDICAL ETHICS
12–16 (1979).

Synthetic concepts such as human and man and person require operational terms, spelling out the which and what and when. Only in that way can we get down to cases—to normative decisions. There are always some people who prefer to be visceral and affective in their moral choices, with no desire to have any rationale for what they do. But ethics is precisely the business of rational, critical reflection (encephalic and not merely visceral) about the problems of the moral agent—in biology and medicine as much as in law, government, education, or anything else.

To that end, then, for the purposes of biomedical ethics, I now turn to a *profile of man* in concrete and discrete terms. * * * There is time only to itemize the inventory, not to enlarge upon it, but I have fifteen positive propositions. Let me set them out, in no rank order at all, and as hardly more than a list of criteria or indicators, by simple title.

#### 1.   Minimum Intelligence

Mere biological life, before minimal intelligence is achieved or after it is lost irretrievably, is without personal status.

#### 2.   Self-awareness

* * *

#### 3.   Self-control

If an individual is not only not controllable by others (unless by force) but not controllable by the individual himself or herself, a low level of life is reached about on a par with that of a paramecium. * * *

#### 4.   A Sense of Time

* * *

#### 5.   A Sense of Futurity

How "truly human" is any man who cannot realize there is a time yet to come as well as the present? Subhuman animals do not look forward in time; they live only on what we might call visceral strivings, appetites. Philosophical anthropologies (one recalls that of William Temple, the Archbishop of Canterbury, for instance) commonly emphasize purposiveness as a key to humanness. Chesterton once remarked that we would never ask a puppy what manner of dog it wanted to be when it grows up. * * *

#### 6.   A Sense of the Past

* * *

### 7.   The Capability to Relate to Others

Interpersonal relationships, of the sexual-romantic and friendship kind, are of the greatest importance for the fullness of what we idealize as being truly personal. * * *

### 8.   Concern for Others

Some people may be skeptical about our capacity to care about others (what in Christian ethics is often distinguished from romance and friendship as "neighbor love" or "neighbor concern"). * * * But whether concern for others is disinterested or inspired by enlightened self-interest, it seems plain that a conscious extra-ego orientation is a trait of the species. * * *

### 9.   Communication

Utter alienation or disconnection from others, if it is irreparable, is dehumanization. * * *

### 10.   Control of Existence

It is of the nature of man that he is not helplessly subject to the blind workings of physical or physiological nature. He has only finite knowledge, freedom, and initiative, but what he has of it is real and effective. * * *

### 11.   Curiosity

To be without affect, sunk in *anomie,* is to be not a person. Indifference is inhuman. Man is a learner and a knower as well as a tool maker and user. * * *

### 12.   Change and Changeability

To the extent that an individual is unchangeable or opposed to change, he denies the creativity of personal beings. It means not only the fact of biological and physiological change, which goes on as a condition of life, but the capacity and disposition for changing one's mind and conduct as well. Biologically, human beings are developmental: birth, life, health, and death are processes, not events, and are to be understood progressively, not episodically. All human existence is on a continuum, a matter of becoming. * * *

### 13.   Balance of Rationality and Feeling

* * * As human beings we are not coldly rational or cerebral, nor are we merely creatures of feeling and intuition. It is a matter of being both, in different combinations from one individual to another. * * *

### 14.   Idiosyncrasy

The human being is idiomorphous, a distinctive individual. * * * To be a person is to have an identity, to be recognizable and callable by name.

### 15. Neocortical Function

In a way, this is the cardinal indicator, the one all the others are hinged upon. Before cerebration is in play, or with its end, in the absence of the synthesizing function of the cerebral cortex, the person is nonexistent. Such individuals are objects but not subjects. This is so no matter how many other spontaneous or artificially supported functions persist in the heart, lungs, neurologic and vascular systems. Such noncerebral processes are not personal. * * *

## NOTES AND QUESTIONS

1.    Some commentators have concluded that the real consensus requirement of personhood is the capacity for conscious experience. Do you think that it is a necessary attribute? A sufficient attribute? Does it encompass many—or all—of the attributes described by Fletcher? Capacity for conscious experience is also relevant to questions about the determination of death. See Chapter 4.

2.    Fletcher commenced a serious debate over whether the persons protected by law ought to be defined in terms of attributes we wish to protect or in terms of the human stock from which the person is created. Both forms of definition may be valuable for different purposes. We provide some rights to people because they possess many or all of the attributes that distinguish human beings. The right to make medical decisions, based on the autonomy of individuals, is not accorded to those without some "minimum intelligence." On the other hand, we provide minimally adequate housing, food, medical care, and other necessities for those of human stock, even when they do not meet some of Fletcher's criteria, and even when we do not provide those same benefits to others, (e.g., animals) who fail the same criteria. In the end, the Fletcher propositions may be useful in determining some of the rights of persons and the "human stock" definition may be helpful in determining others. Just as property is often described as a bundle of rights, it may turn out that "personhood" is a bundle of attributes that need to be separated out and individually analyzed.

## PROBLEM: DOES THINKING MAKE IT HUMAN?

Assume that a laboratory has learned enough about neuroscience and the operation of the brain, artificial intelligence, robotics and psychology to create a machine that acts in a way that is indistinguishable from a human being. Assume that without actually seeing the mechanical interior of this machine it would be effectively impossible for a person to distinguish the machine from any another human being. It speaks well, it "sees" accurately, and it has reactions that we would expect from one with all of the attributes, including the emotional attributes, of a human being. Further, it looks like any other human being—at least from the outside—and it has an ability to learn and change the way human beings do. It does not have the ability to reproduce the way other human beings do, but it does have the ability to reconstruct itself in the workshop, and thus can continue its line. Those of you with a background in philosophy or artificial intelligence will recognize this as a slightly updated version of the renowned "Turing test" first proposed by the brilliant computer scientist Alan Turing in one of the most influential philosophical works of the last century. A. Turing, Computing Machinery and Intelligence, 49 Mind 433 (1950). See also Stuart Russell and Peter Norving, Artificial Intelligence: A Modern Approach (2d ed. 2003).

For legal and other purposes, should this machine be treated as a human being? Should it be able to vote or otherwise be protected by the Fourteenth Amendment? If you don't think it should be treated like a human being, why is that? What attribute is it missing? What if it had that attribute, too? Is there some attribute of the human mind (or the human being more generally) that is not a part of the physical human brain? What are the consequences of treating this machine as a person? What are the consequences of failing to do so? Should "natural" persons be able to enslave our robotic brothers and sisters?

What if a natural human being whose brain had failed as a result of an utterly disastrous stroke had her brain replaced by an electronic version. Would that still be a person? Would it be the same person? What is the relationship between the mind, the brain, our individual histories and values, and our personhood? Is there a place for the consideration of the "soul" in this discussion? Are the questions raised here the same as the basic questions raised by the "mind vs. brain" debate over the past millennia?

There has been a great deal of discussion of the issue of machine-as-human recently. Several provocative books and articles have been written by Ray Kurzweil, an entrepreneur, scientist and futurist whose most recent book is the controversial *How to Create a Mind: The Secret of Thought Revealed (2012)*. There has also been discussion of intellectual property issues that may grow out of nontraditional human beings. See, e.g., Eric Zylstra, Presumed Sapient: A Proposed Test for the Constitutional Personhood and Patentability of Human-Animal Chimeras and Hybrids, 46 U.S.F.L.Rev. 1075 (2012).

Is the only way out of this dilemma to define a human being as one created through human stock—that is, one who is born (in more or less the traditional way) of other human beings? Of course, as we saw earlier, even the adoption of a "human stock" definition does not answer the question of when that human stock becomes a person. What is the attribute of the human stock that makes it a person—genetic uniqueness? Responsiveness? The potential to be born? The appearance of a human being? Consider the following list of the alternative medical points of personhood.

### C.R. AUSTIN, "WHEN DOES A PERSON'S LIFE REALLY BEGIN?" IN HUMAN EMBRYOS: THE DEBATE ON ASSISTED REPRODUCTION

22–31 (1989).

* * * Probably most people who were asked this question would answer "at fertilization" (or "conception"). Certainly, several interesting and unusual things happen then—it is really the most *obvious* event to pick— but for biologists the preceding and succeeding cellular processes are *equally* important. Nevertheless, "fertilization" continues to be the cry of many religious bodies and indeed also of the august World Medical Association, who, in 1949, adopted the Geneva Convention Code of Medical Ethics, which contains the clause: "I will maintain the utmost respect for human life from the time of conception." So we do need to look more closely at this choice, for a generally acceptable "beginning" for human life would be a great help in reaching ethical and legal consensus.

In the first place human *life,* as such, obviously begins before fertilization, since the egg or oocyte is alive before sperm entry, as were innumerable antecedent cells, back through the origin of species into the mists of time. A more practical starting point would be that of the life of the human *individual,* so it is individuality that we should be looking for, at least as one of the essential criteria. Now the earliest antecedents of the eggs, as of sperm, are the primordial germ cells, which can be seen as a group of distinctive little entities migrating through the tissues of the early embryo. When they first become recognizable, they number only about a dozen or two, but they multiply fast and soon achieve large numbers, reaching a peak of 7–10 million about 6 months after conception. Then, despite continued active cell division, there is a dramatic decline in the cell population, which has tempted people to suggest that some sort of "selection of the fittest" occurs, but there is no good evidence in support of this idea; nor is there any good reason to look for individuality in that mercurial population. In due course, the primordial germ cells, while still undergoing cell divisions, settle down in the tissues of the future ovary, change subtly in their characteristics, and thus become oogonia; and then, soon after birth, *cell division ceases,* the cells develop large nuclei and are now recognizable as primary oocytes. From now on, there are steady cell losses but no further cell divisions * * *; it is the same entity that was a primary oocyte, becomes a fertilized egg, and then develops as an embryo. The primary oocytes are very unusual cells, for they have the capacity to live for much longer than most other body cells; the *same* oocytes can be seen in the ovaries of women approaching the menopause—cells that have lived for about 40 years or longer. And it is with the emergence of the primary oocytes that we can hail the start of *individuality*. Then, in those oocytes that are about to be ovulated, the first meiotic division takes place—another important step, for the "shuffling" of genes that occurs at that point bestows *genetic uniqueness* on the oocyte. So both individuality and genetic uniqueness are established before sperm penetration and fertilization; these processes have distinctly different actions—providing the stimulus that initiates cleavage and contributing to biparental inheritance. Thus, the preferred choice for the start of the human individual should surely be the formation of the primary oocyte, but there is certainly no unanimity on this score.

Passing over now the popularity of fertilization, for many people it is instead the emergence of the embryonic disc and primitive streak that most appeals as the stage in which to identify the start of "personhood" (one or more persons, in view of the imminent possibility of twinning), and there is much to support this opinion. Here, for the first time, are structures that are designed to have a different destiny than *all the rest of the embryo*— they represent the primordium of the fetus, and the developmental patterns of embryo and fetus progressively diverge from this stage onwards. An additional point is that this new emergence is not inevitable, for in around one in two-thousand pregnancies the embryo grows, often to quite a large size, but there is no fetus * * *.

At the time of appearance of the embryonic disc, and shortly beforehand, the process of implantation is occurring, and this is considered by many to have special significance in relation to embryonic potential—so far as we know, implantation cannot occur once the development of the embryo has passed the stage when interaction with * * * the uterus normally takes place.

But despite all that has been said, there are still many folk who remain unconvinced—is the being at this stage sufficiently "human" to qualify as the start of a person? After all, the disc is just a collection of similar cells, virtually undifferentiated, poorly delineated from its surroundings, about a fifth of a millimetre long, non-sentient, and without the power of movement. It is in no way a "body" and it does not bear the faintest resemblance to a human being—*and* the soul cannot enter yet, for the disc may yet divide in the process of twinning, and the soul being unique is indivisible. Also, it is argued that we should be looking for some spark of personality, and a moral philosopher has proposed that some sort of responsiveness is an essential feature.

One of the earliest succeeding changes in the direction of humanness could be the development of the heart primordium, and soon after that the beginnings of a circulatory system; the first contractions of the heart muscle occur possibly as early as day 21, with a simple tubular heart at that stage, and in the fourth week a functional circulation begins. With the heart beats we have the first movements initiated within the embryo (?fetus) and thus in a way the first real "sign of life." The conceptus is now about 6 mm long. During the fifth and sixth weeks, nerve fibres grow out from the spinal cord and make contact with muscles, so that at this time or soon afterwards, a mechanical or electrical stimulus might elicit a muscle twitch; this is important for it would be the first indication of sentient existence—of "responsiveness." At this stage, too, the embryo could possibly feel pain. But, still, some would find cause to demur: only an expert could tell that this embryo/fetus, now 12–13 mm in length, with branchial arches (corresponding to the "gill-slits" in non-mammalian embryos), stubby limbs, and a prominent tail, is human. A marginally more acceptable applicant is the fetus at 7½ weeks, when the hands and feet can be seen to have fingers and toes, and thereafter physical resemblance steadily improves; also at this time, a special gene on the Y-chromosome (the "testis-determining factor" or TDF) is switched on, and the fetuses that have this chromosome, the males, proceed thenceforward to develop *as* males, distinguishable from females.

At about 12 weeks, electrical activity can be detected in the brain of the fetus, which could signal the dawn of consciousness. Here, we would seem to have a very logical stage marking the *start* of a person, for the cessation of electrical activity in the brain ("brain death") is accepted in both medical and legal circles as marking the *termination* of a person—as an indication that life no longer exists in victims of accidents or in patients with terminal illnesses. Around the fourth or fifth month of pregnancy, the mother first experiences movements of the fetus ("quickening"), which were regarded by St. Thomas Aquinas as the first indication of life, for he believed that life was distinguished by two features, knowledge and movement; moreover, it would seem logical that the fetus would move when the *animus* (life or soul) took up residence. * * *

At about 24 weeks, the fetus reaches a state in which it can commonly survive outside the maternal body, with assistance. * * * Just which stage marks the start of a person's life is a matter of personal opinion. Much of the foregoing argumentation may seem to some people difficult to comprehend, especially if they have not had formal training in biology, and to others may even seem irrelevant, in view of the firm line taken by many church authorities. But it really is important that we should try to reach a consensus on just when a person's life should be held to begin, for the decision does have important practical consequences—it directly affects the rights of other embryos, of fetuses, and of people.

# III. ABORTION

Abortion is the area where the most high profile and controversial debates have occurred over questions about when life begins, as well as how the answer to this question should inform government regulation of reproduction. We begin this section with the seminal case, *Roe v. Wade*, defining abortion as a privacy right. This right has been subject to several decades of legal contests. In most of these, a state has enacted legislation that regulates or restricts access to abortions, and patients or providers challenge the laws on constitutional grounds. Abortion restrictions or regulations have tested, and often narrowed the boundaries of the constitutional right to abortion established in *Roe*. At this point, *Roe* still stands, but in what could be viewed as an altered form.

## A. ABORTION AS A PRIVACY RIGHT

### ROE V. WADE
Supreme Court of the United States, 1973.
410 U.S. 113, 93 S.Ct. 705, 35 L.Ed.2d 147.

MR. JUSTICE BLACKMUN delivered the opinion of the Court.

\* \* \*

We forthwith acknowledge our awareness of the sensitive and emotional nature of the abortion controversy, of the vigorous opposing views, even among physicians, and of the deep and seemingly absolute convictions that the subject inspires. One's philosophy, one's experiences, one's exposure to the raw edges of human existence, one's religious training, one's attitudes toward life and family and their values, and the moral standards one establishes and seeks to observe, are all likely to influence and to color one's thinking and conclusions about abortion.

In addition, population growth, pollution, poverty, and racial overtones tend to complicate and not to simplify the problem.

Our task, of course, is to resolve the issue by constitutional measurement, free of emotion and of predilection. We seek earnestly to do this, and, because we do, we have inquired into, and in this opinion place some emphasis upon, medical and medical-legal history and what that history reveals about man's attitudes toward the abortion procedure over the centuries. We bear in mind, too, Mr. Justice Holmes' admonition in his now-vindicated dissent in Lochner v. New York[ ]:

> [The Constitution] is made for people of fundamentally differing views, and the accident of our finding certain opinions natural and familiar or novel and even shocking ought not to conclude our judgment upon the question whether statutes embodying them conflict with the Constitution of the United States.

\* \* \*

The principal thrust of appellant's attack on the Texas statutes is that they improperly invade a right, said to be possessed by the pregnant woman, to choose to terminate her pregnancy. Appellant would discover this right in the concept of personal "liberty" embodied in the Fourteenth Amendment's Due Process Clause; or in personal, marital, familial, and sexual privacy said to be protected by the Bill of Rights or its penumbras,[ ]; or among those rights reserved to the people by the Ninth Amendment[ ]. Before addressing this claim, we feel it desirable briefly to survey, in several aspects, the history of abortion, for such insight as that history may afford us, and then to examine the state purposes and interests behind the criminal abortion laws.

## VI

It perhaps is not generally appreciated that the restrictive criminal abortion laws in effect in a majority of States today are of relatively recent vintage. Those laws, generally proscribing abortion or its attempt at any time during pregnancy except when necessary to preserve the pregnant woman's life, are not of ancient or even of common-law origin. Instead, they derive from statutory changes effected, for the most part, in the latter half of the 19th century.

[The Court then reviewed, in great detail, ancient attitudes, the Hippocratic Oath, the common law, English statutory law, American Law, the position of the American Medical Association, the position of the American Public Health Association, and the position of the American Bar Association.]

## VII

Three reasons have been advanced to explain historically the enactment of criminal abortion laws in the 19th century and to justify their continued existence.

It has been argued occasionally that these laws were the product of a Victorian social concern to discourage illicit sexual conduct. Texas, however, does not advance this justification in the present case, and it appears that no court or commentator has taken the argument seriously. * * *

A second reason is concerned with abortion as a medical procedure. When most criminal abortion laws were first enacted, the procedure was a hazardous one for the woman. * * * Thus, it has been argued that a State's real concern in enacting a criminal abortion law was to protect the pregnant woman, that is, to restrain her from submitting to a procedure that placed her life in serious jeopardy.

Modern medical techniques have altered this situation. Appellants and various amici refer to medical data indicating that abortion in early pregnancy, this is, prior to the end of the first trimester, although not without its risk, is now relatively safe. Mortality rates for women undergoing early abortions, where the procedure is legal, appear to be as low as or lower than the rates for normal childbirth. Consequently, any interest of the State in protecting the woman from an inherently hazardous procedure, except when it would be equally dangerous for her to forgo it, has largely disappeared. Of course, important state interests in the area of health and medical standards do remain. The State has a legitimate interest in seeing to it that abortion, like any other medical procedure, is performed under circumstances that assure maximum safety for the patient. * * *

The third reason is the State's interest—some phrase it in terms of duty—in protecting prenatal life. Some of the argument for this justification rests on the theory that a new human life is present from the moment of conception. * * * Logically, of course, a legitimate state interest in this area need not stand or fall on acceptance of the belief that life begins at conception or at some other point prior to live birth. [R]ecognition may be given to the less rigid claim that as long as at least potential life is involved, the State may assert interests beyond the protection of the pregnant woman alone.

* * *

It is with these interests, and the weight to be attached to them, that this case is concerned.

## VIII

The Constitution does not explicitly mention any right of privacy. In a line of decisions, however, going back perhaps as far as[ ] 1891 the Court has recognized that a right of personal privacy, or a guarantee of certain areas or zones of privacy, does exist under the Constitution. In varying contexts, the Court or individual Justices have, indeed, found at least the roots of that right in the First Amendment,[ ] in the Fourth and Fifth Amendments,[ ] in the penumbras of the Bill of Rights, Griswold v. Connecticut,[ ] the Ninth Amendment,[ ] or in the concept of liberty guaranteed by the first section of the Fourteenth Amendment.[ ] These decisions make it clear that only personal rights that can be deemed "fundamental" or "implicit in the concept of ordered liberty,"[ ] are included in this guarantee of personal privacy. They also make it clear that the right has some extension to activities relating to marriage,[ ] family relationships,[ ] and child rearing and education[ ].

This right of privacy, whether it be founded in the Fourteenth Amendment's concept of personal liberty and restrictions upon state action, as we feel it is, or, as the District Court determined, in the Ninth Amendment's reservation of rights to the people, is broad enough to encompass a woman's decision whether or not to terminate her pregnancy. The detriment that the State would impose upon the pregnant woman by denying this choice altogether is apparent. Specific and direct harm medically diagnosable even in early pregnancy may be involved. Maternity, or additional offspring, may force upon the woman a distressful life and future. Psychological harm may be imminent. Mental and physical health may be taxed by child care. There is also the distress, for all concerned, associated with the unwanted child, and there is the problem of bringing a child into a family already unable, psychologically and otherwise, to care for it. In other cases, as in this one, the additional difficulties and continuing stigma of unwed motherhood may be involved. All these are factors the woman and her responsible physician necessarily will consider in consultation.

On the basis of elements such as these, appellant and some amici argue that the woman's right is absolute and that she is entitled to terminate her pregnancy at whatever time, in whatever way, and for whatever reason she alone chooses. With this we do not agree. * * * [A] State may properly assert important interests in safeguarding health, in maintaining medical standards, and in protecting potential life. At some point in pregnancy, these respective interests become sufficiently compelling to sustain regulation of the factors that govern the abortion decision.

\* \* \*

## IX

\* \* \*

Appellee argues that the State's determination to recognize and protect prenatal life from and after conception constitutes a compelling state interest. [W]e do not agree fully with [this] formulation.

[ ] The appellee and certain amici argue that the fetus is a "person" within the language and meaning of the Fourteenth Amendment. In support of this, they outline at length and in detail the well-known facts of fetal development. If this suggestion of personhood is established, the appellant's case, of course, collapses, for the fetus' right to life is then guaranteed specifically by the Amendment. The appellant conceded as much on reargument. On the other hand, the appellee conceded on reargument that no case could be cited that holds that a fetus is a person within the meaning of the Fourteenth Amendment.

The Constitution does not define "person" in so many words. Section 1 of the Fourteenth Amendment contains three references to "person." The first, in defining "citizens," speaks of "persons born or naturalized in the United States." The word also appears both in the Due Process Clause and in the Equal Protection Clause. "Person" is used in other places in the Constitution: in the listing of qualifications for Representatives and Senators [ ]; in the Apportionment Clause [ ][53] in the Migration and Importation provision [ ]; in the Emolument Clause [ ]; in the Electors provisions [ ]; in the provision outlining qualifications for the office of

---

[53] We are not aware that in the taking of any census under this clause, a fetus has ever been counted.

President [ ]; in the Extradition provisions, [ ], and the superseded Fugitive Slave Clause; and in the Fifth, Twelfth, and Twenty-second Amendments, as well as in §§ 2 and 3 of the Fourteenth Amendment. But in nearly all these instances, the use of the word is such that it has application only postnatally. None indicates, with any assurance, that it has any possible prenatal application.[54]

\* \* \*

All this, together with our observation \* \* \* that throughout the major portion of the 19th century prevailing legal abortion practices were far freer than they are today, persuades us that the word "person," as used in the Fourteenth Amendment, does not include the unborn. \* \* \*

\* \* \*

Texas urges that, apart from the Fourteenth Amendment, life begins at conception and is present throughout pregnancy, and that, therefore, the State has a compelling interest in protecting that life from and after conception. We need not resolve the difficult question of when life begins. When those trained in the respective disciplines of medicine, philosophy, and theology are unable to arrive at any consensus, the judiciary, at this point in the development of man's knowledge, is not in a position to speculate as to the answer.

It should be sufficient to note briefly the wide divergence of thinking on this most sensitive and difficult question.

\* \* \*

## X

In view of all this, we do not agree that, by adopting one theory of life, Texas may override the rights of the pregnant woman that are at stake.

\* \* \*

With respect to the State's important and legitimate interest in the health of the mother, the "compelling" point, in the light of present medical knowledge, is at approximately the end of the first trimester. This is so

---

[54] When Texas urges that a fetus is entitled to Fourteenth Amendment protection as a person, it faces a dilemma. Neither in Texas nor in any other State are all abortions prohibited. Despite broad proscription, an exception always exists. The exception contained in Art. 1196, for an abortion procured or attempted by medical advice for the purpose of saving the life of the mother, is typical. But if the fetus is a person who is not to be deprived of life without due process of law, and if the mother's condition is the sole determinant, does not the Texas exception appear to be out of line with the Amendment's command?

There are other inconsistencies between Fourteenth Amendment status and the typical abortion statute. It has already been pointed out [ ] that in Texas the woman is not a principal or an accomplice with respect to an abortion upon her. If the fetus is a person, why is the woman not a principal or an accomplice? Further, the penalty for criminal abortion specified by Art. 1195 is significantly less than the maximum penalty for murder prescribed by Art. 1257 of the Texas Penal Code. If the fetus is a person, may the penalties be different?

because of the now-established medical fact * * * that until the end of the first trimester mortality in abortion may be less than mortality in normal childbirth. It follows that, from and after this point, a State may regulate the abortion procedure to the extent that the regulation reasonably relates to the preservation and protection of maternal health. * * *

This means, on the other hand, that, for the period of pregnancy prior to this "compelling" point, the attending physician, in consultation with his patient, is free to determine, without regulation by the State, that, in his medical judgment, the patient's pregnancy should be terminated. If that decision is reached, the judgment may be effectuated by an abortion free of interference by the State.

With respect to the State's important and legitimate interest in potential life, the "compelling" point is at viability. This is so because the fetus then presumably has the capability of meaningful life outside the mother's womb. State regulation protective of fetal life after viability thus has both logical and biological justifications. If the State is interested in protecting fetal life after viability, it may go so far as to proscribe abortion during that period, except when it is necessary to preserve the life or health of the mother.

* * *

## XI

To summarize and to repeat:

1.   A state criminal abortion statute of the current Texas type, that excepts from criminality only a *lifesaving* procedure on behalf of the mother, without regard to pregnancy stage and without recognition of the other interests involved, is violative of the Due Process Clause of the Fourteenth Amendment.

(a)   For the stage prior to approximately the end of the first trimester, the abortion decision and its effectuation must be left to the medical judgment of the pregnant woman's attending physician.

(b)   For the stage subsequent to approximately the end of the first trimester, the State, in promoting its interest in the health of the mother, may, if it chooses, regulate the abortion procedure in ways that are reasonably related to maternal health.

(c)   For the stage subsequent to viability, the State in promoting its interest in the potentiality of human life may, if it chooses, regulate, and even proscribe, abortion except where it is necessary, in appropriate medical judgment, for the preservation of the life or health of the mother.

* * *

## NOTES AND QUESTIONS

1. *State Regulation of Abortion.* The Court rejected Texas' ability to apply its "theory of life" to "override the rights of the pregnant woman at stake," but the Court also acknowledged the state's interest in protecting prenatal life. How did the Court understand the various interests at stake and what balance did it strike?

2. *The State's "Theory of Life."* In *Roe*, the Court was confronted with the question of when personhood begins for purposes of determining rights under the Fourteenth Amendment of the Constitution, but Justice Blackmun refused to answer "the difficult question of when life begins." Indeed, the Supreme Court has never formally determined when a fetus becomes a "person" for Constitutional purposes. This has left an open question about whether the substantive provisions of the Constitution (as interpreted by the Court) put any limit on the way that states may define "person" for *other* purposes? In 1989, the Supreme Court faced this question in Webster v. Reproductive Health Services, 492 U.S. 490, 109 S.Ct. 3040, 106 L.Ed.2d 410 (1989). The Supreme Court reviewed a Missouri statute that restricted the availability of abortions in several ways. The statute also included a preamble that defined personhood:

1. The general assembly of this state finds that:

    (1) The life of each human being begins at conception;

    (2) Unborn children have protectable interests in life, health, and well-being;

    * * *

2. [T]he laws of this state shall be interpreted and construed to acknowledge on behalf of the unborn child at every stage of development, all the rights, privileges, and immunities available to other persons, citizens, and residents of this state, subject only to the Constitution of the United States, and decisional interpretations thereof * * *.

3. As used in this section, the term "unborn children" or "unborn child" shall include all unborn child or children or the offspring of human beings from the moment of conception until birth at every stage of biological development.

    * * *

Vernon's Ann.Mo.Stat. § 1.205. This preamble was attacked on the grounds that it was beyond the constitutional authority of the state legislature to define personhood, at least to the extent that the definition extended personhood to pre-viable fetuses. The Supreme Court sidestepped that question by concluding that the preamble was nothing more than a state value judgment favoring childbirth over abortion, and that such a value judgment was clearly within the authority of the legislature. It noted that the preamble itself did not regulate abortions and could be interpreted to do no more than offer protections to unborn children in tort and probate law.

Questions about personhood have influenced states' decisions to expand statutory and common law rights for fetuses outside the abortion context. The debate over the common law recognition of the personhood of the fetus has been waged primarily over whether a fetus may recover under state wrongful death and survival statutes. Today, many states allow such claims as a matter of common law or through statute. See Ex Parte Ankrom, 152 So.3d 397, 425–428 (Ala. 2013) (Parker, J. concurring) (noting that forty states and D.C. allow recovery for the wrongful death of an unborn child when post-viability injuries to that child cause its death before birth, and eleven of these states allow recovery regardless of stage of pregnancy). One reason given is the perception that a live birth requirement is an arbitrary line that serves no purpose of the wrongful death and survival statutes. Others, more influenced by the arguments over abortion, have urged that such actions should be recognized because the fetus is a full human being entitled to all protections accorded to all other human beings. Indeed, debates about extending protections to fetuses in these contexts are often shaped by the fear or hope that doing so will influence abortion jurisprudence, allowing for greater restrictions on a woman's right to have an abortion.

Consider that over the past several years, some states have made the penalties for feticide commensurate with the penalties for homicide. Typically such statutes were used to allow recovery or impose punishment on third parties who harmed a fetus. Id. at 423–424 (noting that a majority of states treat killing an unborn child as criminal homicide unless it occurs as the result of a medical abortion). Increasingly, however feticide laws are being used to punish pregnant women who want to carry a pregnancy term, but who suffer a miscarriage or still birth believed to be the result of harmful or risky behavior by the woman. For a discussion of how feticide and other "fetal protection" laws are used to regulate women's behavior during pregnancy, see Section VI of this chapter.

3.    *The Role of Sexual Morality in Reproductive Regulation.* In exploring the reasons for the emergence of abortion bans, the Court mentions, but quickly dismisses, the argument that such laws were the product of a "Victorian social concern to discourage illicit sexual conduct." But does the Court give this short shrift? When it says no court or commentator has taken the argument seriously, is it that the Court does not believe that this is an underlying motivation of such laws? Or is it dismissing its legitimacy as a state interest for purposes of this analysis? If there is evidence that a state's desire to regulate sexual morality motivated abortion regulation, what impact, if any, should that have on a court's constitutional analysis? For a history of the relationship between sex, religion, and reproductive regulation, see Geoffrey R. Stone, Sex and the Constitution (2017).

4.    *Bans on Use of Government Resources for Abortion. Roe* invalidated a criminal ban on abortion, but access to health care also depends on having the resources to access a particular service. A 2014 survey found that three-fourths of abortion patients were low income—49% living at less than the federal poverty level, and 26% living at 100–199% of the poverty level. See Jenna

Jerman et al., Characteristics of U.S. Abortion Patients in 2014 and Changes Since 2008, Guttmacher Institute (May 2016). Traditionally, the poor have been less likely to be employed in jobs that offered health insurance, and have been more likely to depend on public resources, such as public hospitals or public insurance. Pregnant women are eligible for Medicaid coverage only if their income is low enough to qualify. Immediately after *Roe*, the battle over abortion quickly moved into the realm of funding. To the extent that federal and state governments were funding or providing health care services, did the privacy right in *Roe* have anything to say about government's ability to exclude abortion from these programs?

In a series of cases, the Supreme Court has made clear that the constitution does not prevent the government from excluding abortion from public insurance coverage or from banning abortions in government run facilities. Beal v. Doe, 432 U.S. 438, 97 S.Ct. 2366, 53 L.Ed.2d 464 (1977); Maher v. Roe, 432 U.S. 464, 97 S.Ct. 2376, 53 L.Ed.2d 484 (1977); Poelker v. Doe, 432 U.S. 519, 97 S.Ct. 2391, 53 L.Ed.2d 528 (1977). In 1980, in Harris v. McRae, 448 U.S. 297, 100 S.Ct. 2671, 65 L.Ed.2d 784 (1980), the Court addressed the constitutionality of the Hyde Amendment, which limits federal Medicaid funding for abortions. The Hyde Amendment only funds abortions in cases of life endangerment, rape or incest. It excludes funding for abortions that may not be viewed as life threatening but are otherwise medically necessary because carrying a pregnancy to term would pose a serious danger to a woman's health or may even shorten her life. Examples of cases where abortions may be deemed medically necessary, though not immediately life threatening, are where pregnancy would exacerbate medical risky conditions, such as heart conditions, diabetes, or cancer, and could lead to permanent damage to the woman's health. The Supreme Court upheld the Hyde amendment against due process and equal protection challenges, with Justice Stewart writing for the court:

> * * * [R]egardless of whether the freedom of a woman to choose to terminate her pregnancy for health reasons lies at the core or the periphery of the due process liberty recognized in Roe v. Wade, 410 U.S. 113, 93 S.Ct. 705, 35 L.Ed.2d 147 (1973), it simply does not follow that a woman's freedom of choice carries with it a constitutional entitlement to the financial resources to avail herself of the full range of protected choices. [A]lthough government may not place obstacles in the path of a woman's exercise of her freedom of choice, it need not remove those not of its own creation. Indigency falls in the latter category. The financial constraints that restrict an indigent woman's ability to enjoy the full range of constitutionally protected freedom of choice are the product not of governmental restrictions on access to abortions, but rather of her indigency. Although Congress has opted to subsidize medically necessary services generally, but not certain medically necessary abortions, the fact remains that the Hyde Amendment leaves an indigent woman with at least the same range of choice [ ]as she would have had if Congress had chosen to subsidize no health care costs at all. * * * Although the liberty

protected by the Due Process Clause affords protection against unwarranted government interference with freedom of choice in the context of certain personal decisions, it does not confer an entitlement to such funds as may be necessary to realize all the advantages of that freedom. * * *

Quoting another case that upheld a similar abortion restriction by a state, the Court made clear that " 'the constitutional freedom recognized in Roe v. Wade and its progeny, did not prevent [government] from making a value judgment favoring childbirth over abortion, and . . . implement[ing] that judgment by the allocation of public funds.' " Id. (quoting Maher v. Roe, 432 U.S. 464 (1977).

5. *Impact of the ACA.* The ACA reinforced Hyde Amendment restrictions, which have been attached to Medicaid and other relevant appropriations by the U.S. Department of Health and Human Services (HHS) since the 1970s. The ACA extended federal funding limits on abortion in significant ways. It excludes abortion from the required essential health benefits, requires each health insurance exchange to offer at least one multi-state plan that does not include abortion coverage, and allows states to forbid exchange plans from covering abortion. Most state laws banning abortion coverage provide narrow exceptions for life endangerment, rape, or incest, but Louisiana and Tennessee do not provide any exceptions.

The ACA permits plans to cover abortion, but establishes strict rules for how this can be done. 42 U.S.C.A. § 18023. Plans that offer abortion coverage must essentially do so by selling a separate abortion rider; that is, they must charge a separate, actuarially segregated premium for that service, which is paid separately by each insured who desires that coverage (and each insured's employer, if the employer contributes to the employee's health coverage). The actuarial value of this coverage may not count savings arising from the performance of an abortion (such as prenatal care or delivery). These restrictions have created administrative barriers to abortion coverage, as well as confusion among enrollees as to whether certain plans even cover abortion. For example, a 2016 review of marketplace plans found that six states that did not have laws restricting abortion coverage (and thus allowed plans to cover it) still had no marketplace plans that included coverage. See Alina Salganicoff et al., Coverage for Abortion Services in Medicaid, Marketplace Plans and Private Plans, The Henry J. Kaiser Family Foundation (Jan. 2016). Before the ACA, most private health insurance plans covered abortion. Now, federal restrictions shape insurance company choices in ways that limit abortion access beyond what is actually required by law.

Finally, the ACA contains a provision providing that nothing in the ACA shall be construed as preempting state law regarding the prohibition of or requirement of coverage, funding, or procedural requirements on abortion. 42 U.S.C.A. § 18023(c)(1). This has been understood to preserve state power to regulate abortion coverage, outside of the specific limits mentioned above. But see the Note on Federal Conscience Protections at the end of Section III of this chapter.

6.   *State Approaches to Funding Abortion.* In the face of federal funding restrictions on abortion (pre and post-ACA), states have responded very differently. See Salganicoff, supra. Most states have followed the federal government's lead in restricting abortion coverage. In Medicaid, thirty-three states prohibit coverage of abortions excluded by the Hyde Amendment, and one state is even more restrictive, only covering abortion in cases of life-endangerment. Congress has also prohibited the District of Columbia from using local funds to cover medically necessary abortions. For private insurance, twenty-six states prohibit marketplace plans from offering abortion coverage, and eleven of those prohibit all insurers from providing abortion coverage. Again, most laws allow narrow exceptions similar to those in the Hyde Amendment.

On the other hand, some states have responded by filling in the gaps. Seventeen states provide entirely state-funded Medicaid abortions. Some state legislatures have done this voluntarily, while others have been required to do so by the courts. See, e.g., Right to Choose v. Byrne, 91 N.J. 287, 450 A.2d 925 (1982); Moe v. Secretary of Administration and Finance, 382 Mass. 629, 417 N.E.2d 387 (1981); Committee to Defend Reproductive Rights v. Myers, 29 Cal.3d 252, 172 Cal.Rptr. 866, 625 P.2d 779 (1981). Since *Harris v. McRae*, thirteen state supreme courts have recognized a state constitutional right to have state Medicaid programs pay for abortions as it does other medical procedures. In the case of private insurance, however, only three states require nearly all insurance plans to provide abortion coverage, including marketplace plans.

7.   *Beyond Abortion Funding: Attempts to Defund Planned Parenthood & the Fungibility Theory.* For decades, anti-abortion advocates have gone further than simply seeking bans on funding for abortion; they have proposed absolute bans on clinics that perform abortions or have an affiliation with abortion advocacy from receiving any government funding. Planned Parenthood, widely recognized as a provider of abortion and advocate for access to legal abortion services, has been the primary target of such defunding attempts. It is important to distinguish this from bans on funding used for abortion: as noted above, there have long been prohibitions on the use of federal funding for abortion except in extreme cases, and many states have taken this approach with state funding as well. Funding bans targeting clinics, like Planned Parenthood, would deprive such clinics of government funding for *any* service—they would not be able to receive funding to provide the non-abortion services they typically provide, such as health checkups, cancer screenings, disease prevention, and contraception. In addition, some of the bans proposed to date would apply to Planned Parenthood clinics that do not even perform abortions. The theory behind this more sweeping funding ban is the "fungibility" of money—the presumed interchangeability of government and private funds. The argument is that any amount of government money that funds such clinics frees up money to be used to provide abortion, thus funding it indirectly.

These bans have been challenged on a number of grounds. The most successful challenges have come in the context of exclusions from the Medicaid program. Almost every circuit to hear such a challenge has struck down the state's attempt to exclude Planned Parenthood and similar clinics from receiving Medicaid payments, as violating a provision in the Medicaid Act that guarantees patients the freedom to choose their provider. Challenges to state exclusions from other federally funded programs have yielded mixed results. See, e.g., Planned Parenthood Ass'n of Utah (PPAU) v. Herbert, 828 F.3d 1245 (10th Cir. 2016) (finding PPAU established a likelihood of success on its claim that the Governor's directive to a state health department official to stop distributing federal grant funds to PPAU violated the First and Fourteenth Amendments under the unconstitutional conditions doctrine, where the denial of funding was likely retaliation for PPAU's role in providing abortions, advocacy for abortion rights, and its affiliation with Planned Parenthood Federation of America, Inc.). See also Planned Parenthood of Greater Ohio v. Hodges, 201 F.Supp.3d 898 (S.D. Ohio 2016), aff'd, 888 F.3d 224 (6th. Cir. 2018) (invalidating a state law prohibiting the distribution of federal funds to entities that perform or promote nontherapeutic abortions, or contract with or become an affiliate of any entity that performs or promotes nontherapeutic abortions, on similar grounds). But see Planned Parenthood Ass'n of Hidalgo County Texas, Inc. v. Suehs, 692 F.3d 343 (5th Cir. 2012) (upholding a narrower state ban on Women's Health Program (WHP) funds to entities that perform or promote elective abortions, in light of WHP's stated goal of subsidizing non-abortion family planning).

Attempts to defund Planned Parenthood at the federal level have been unsuccessful so far, but Republican legislators are hoping to revive such proposals. Bans targeting Planned Parenthood by name have been introduced, but have not passed both houses of Congress. See, e.g., Defund Planned Parenthood Act of 2017, H.R. 354, 115th Cong. (2017) (providing that for one-year, no federal funding "may be made available for *any purpose* to Planned Parenthood Federation of America, Inc. [(PPFA)] or *any affiliate* or *clinic* of [PPFA], unless such entities certify that [PPFA and its] affiliates and clinics will not perform, and will not provide any funds to any other entity that performs, an abortion during such period.") (emphasis added). A similar provision was part of the ACA repeal and replace bill approved by the House in May 2017. See American Health Care Act, H.R. 1628, 115th Cong. (2017).

8.   *After Roe v. Wade.* The Court's decision invigorated political forces opposed to abortion, encouraging state legislatures to seek creative ways to discourage abortions without directly running afoul of the right articulated in *Roe.* Outside of the funding context, *Roe* was proving to be a formidable check on state abortion restrictions. The "compelling interest" standard was used to strike down a number of state regulations of abortion. For example, a requirement that all second-trimester abortions be performed in a hospital was struck down as an unreasonable health regulation in light of evidence that such abortions could be safely performed in an outpatient clinic. City of Akron v. Akron Center for Reproductive Health, Inc., 103 S. Ct. 2481 (1983), *overruled*

*by* Planned Parenthood v. Casey, 505 U.S. 833, 112 S.Ct. 2791 (1992). In another case, the Court invalidated a state's requirement that physicians must provide certain information to women before an abortion, such as descriptions of fetal characteristics or locations of agencies providing alternatives to abortion. The Court viewed the information as medically irrelevant, emphasizing that "[s]tates are not free, under the guise of protecting maternal health or potential life, to intimidate women into continuing pregnancies." Thornburgh v. American College of Obstetricians and Gynecologists, 476 U.S. 747, 106 S.Ct. 2169, 90 L.Ed.2d 779 (1986), *overruled by* Planned Parenthood v. Casey, 505 U.S. 833, 112 S.Ct. 2791 (1992). Other state abortion restrictions repeatedly landed in court and were used to test the boundaries of this privacy right.

At first the Supreme Court resisted attempts to limit the underlying rights recognized in 1973, but the number of justices supporting that decision declined over time. *Roe* was reaffirmed more than a dozen times in its first decade, but by 1986 the 7–2 majority was down to 5–4, Thornburgh v. American College of Obstetricians and Gynecologists, 476 U.S. 747, 106 S.Ct. 2169, 90 L.Ed.2d 779 (1986), and by 1989 the Court appeared to be evenly divided, with Justice O'Connor unwilling to confront the issue. Webster v. Reproductive Health Services, 492 U.S. 490, 109 S.Ct. 3040, 106 L.Ed.2d 410 (1989). Some of the same types of laws that had been invalidated by the Court under the reasoning of *Roe v. Wade*, made it back to the Supreme Court in 1992, in *Planned Parenthood v. Casey* (below). Although the Court explicitly affirmed *Roe's* "essential holding," *Casey's* reasoning and outcome signaled a significant re-shaping of abortion jurisprudence that would open the door to increased state regulation.

## B. *ROE* REVISITED: THE "UNDUE BURDEN" TEST

### PLANNED PARENTHOOD OF SOUTHEASTERN PENNSYLVANIA V. CASEY

Supreme Court of the United States, 1992.
505 U.S. 833, 112 S.Ct. 2791, 120 L.Ed.2d 674.

JUSTICE O'CONNOR, JUSTICE KENNEDY, and JUSTICE SOUTER announced the judgment of the Court and delivered the opinion of the Court with respect to Parts I, II, III, V-A, V-C, and VI, an opinion with respect to Part V-E, in which JUSTICE STEVENS joins, and an opinion with respect to Parts IV, V-B, and V-D.

I.

Liberty finds no refuge in a jurisprudence of doubt. Yet 19 years after our holding that the Constitution protects a woman's right to terminate her pregnancy in its early stages,[ ] that definition of liberty is still questioned.
* * *

At issue in these cases are five provisions of the Pennsylvania Abortion Control Act of 1982. * * * The Act requires that a woman seeking an abortion give her informed consent prior to the abortion procedure, and specifies that she be provided with certain information at least 24 hours before the abortion is performed.[ ] For a minor to obtain an abortion, the Act requires the informed consent of one of her parents, but provides for a judicial bypass option if the minor does not wish to or cannot obtain a parent's consent.[ ] Another provision of the Act requires that, unless certain exceptions apply, a married woman seeking an abortion must sign a statement indicating that she has notified her husband of her intended abortion.[ ] The Act exempts compliance with these three requirements in the event of a "medical emergency," which is defined in the Act.[ ] In addition to the above provisions regulating the performance of abortions, the Act imposes certain reporting requirements on facilities that provide abortion services.[ ]

* * *

After considering the fundamental constitutional questions resolved by *Roe*, principles of institutional integrity, and the rule of stare decisis, we are led to conclude this: the essential holding of Roe v. Wade should be retained and once again reaffirmed.

It must be stated at the outset and with clarity that *Roe's* essential holding, the holding we reaffirm, has three parts. First is a recognition of the right of the woman to choose to have an abortion before viability and to obtain it without undue interference from the State. Before viability, the State's interests are not strong enough to support a prohibition of abortion or the imposition of a substantial obstacle to the woman's effective right to elect the procedure. Second is a confirmation of the State's power to restrict abortions after fetal viability, if the law contains exceptions for pregnancies which endanger a woman's life or health. And third is the principle that the State has legitimate interests from the outset of the pregnancy in protecting the health of the woman and the life of the fetus that may become a child. These principles do not contradict one another; and we adhere to each.

II.

* * *

Men and women of good conscience can disagree, and we suppose some always shall disagree, about the profound moral and spiritual implications of terminating a pregnancy, even in its earliest stage. Some of us as individuals find abortion offensive to our most basic principles of morality, but that cannot control our decision. Our obligation is to define the liberty of all, not to mandate our own moral code. The underlying constitutional issue is whether the State can resolve these philosophic questions in such a definitive way that a woman lacks all choice in the matter, except perhaps in those rare circumstances in which the pregnancy is itself a danger to her own life or health, or is the result of rape or incest. * * * Abortion is a unique act. It is an act fraught with consequences for others: for the woman who must live with the implications of her decision; for the persons who perform and assist in the procedure; for the spouse, family, and society which must confront the knowledge that these procedures exist, procedures some deem nothing short of an act of violence against innocent human life; and, depending on one's beliefs, for the life or potential life that is aborted. Though abortion is conduct, it does not follow that the State is entitled to proscribe it in all instances. That is because the liberty of the woman is at stake in a sense unique to the human condition and so unique to the law. The mother who carries a child to full term is subject to anxieties, to physical constraints, to pain that only she must bear. That these sacrifices have from the beginning of the human race been endured by woman with a pride that ennobles her in the eyes of others and gives to the infant a bond of love cannot alone be grounds for the State to insist she make the sacrifice. Her suffering is too intimate and personal for the State to insist, without more, upon its own vision of the woman's role, however dominant that vision has been in the course of our history and our culture. The destiny of the woman must be shaped to a large extent on her own conception of her spiritual imperatives and her place in society.

* * *

While we appreciate the weight of the arguments made on behalf of the State in the case before us, arguments which in their ultimate formulation conclude that *Roe* should be overruled, the reservations any of us may have in reaffirming the central holding of *Roe* are outweighed by the explication of individual liberty we have given combined with the force of stare decisis. We turn now to that doctrine.

III.

A.

[In this section, the court discussed the conditions under which it is appropriate for the Court to reverse its own precedent.]

So in this case we may inquire whether *Roe's* central rule has been found unworkable; whether the rule's limitation on state power could be removed without serious inequity to those who have relied upon it or significant damage to the stability of the society governed by the rule in question; whether the law's growth in the intervening years has left *Roe's* central rule a doctrinal anachronism discounted by society; and whether *Roe's* premises of fact have so far changed in the ensuing two decades as to render its central holding somehow irrelevant or unjustifiable in dealing with the issue it addressed.

* * *

The sum of the precedential inquiry to this point shows *Roe's* underpinnings unweakened in any way affecting its central holding. While it has engendered disapproval, it has not been unworkable. An entire generation has come of age free to assume *Roe's* concept of liberty in defining the capacity of women to act in society, and to make reproductive decisions; no erosion of principle going to liberty or personal autonomy has left *Roe's* central holding a doctrinal remnant; *Roe* portends no developments at odds with other precedent for the analysis of personal liberty; and no changes of fact have rendered viability more or less appropriate as the point at which the balance of interests tips. Within the bounds of normal stare decisis analysis, then, and subject to the considerations on which it customarily turns, the stronger argument is for affirming *Roe's* central holding, with whatever degree of personal reluctance any of us may have, not for overruling it.

### B.

[The Court next distinguished the rule in the abortion cases from the rules in *Lochner* and the "separate but equal" cases, two areas in which the Supreme Court did reverse its well settled precedents this century. The Court also explained that it should not expend its political capital and put the public respect for the Court and its processes at risk by reversing *Roe*.]

### IV.

From what we have said so far it follows that it is a constitutional liberty of the woman to have some freedom to terminate her pregnancy. We conclude that the basic decision in *Roe* was based on a constitutional analysis which we cannot now repudiate. The woman's liberty is not so unlimited, however, that from the outset the State cannot show its concern for the life of the unborn, and at a later point in fetal development the State's interest in life has sufficient force so that the right of the woman to terminate the pregnancy can be restricted.

* * *

We conclude the line should be drawn at viability, so that before that time the woman has a right to choose to terminate her pregnancy. We adhere to this principle for two reasons. First, as we have said, is the doctrine of stare decisis. * * *

The second reason is that the concept of viability, as we noted in *Roe,* is the time at which there is a realistic possibility of maintaining and nourishing a life outside the womb, so that the independent existence of the second life can in reason and all fairness be the object of state protection that now overrides the rights of the woman. * * *

The woman's right to terminate her pregnancy before viability is the most central principle of Roe v. Wade. It is a rule of law and a component of liberty we cannot renounce.

\* \* \*

Yet it must be remembered that Roe v. Wade speaks with clarity in establishing not only the woman's liberty but also the State's "important and legitimate interest in potential life."[ ] That portion of the decision in *Roe* has been given too little acknowledgment and implementation by the Court in its subsequent cases. Those cases decided that any regulation touching upon the abortion decision must survive strict scrutiny, to be sustained only if drawn in narrow terms to further a compelling state interest.[ ] Not all of the cases decided under that formulation can be reconciled with the holding in *Roe* itself that the State has legitimate interests in the health of the woman and in protecting the potential life within her. In resolving this tension, we choose to rely upon *Roe,* as against the later cases.

\* \* \*

We reject the trimester framework, which we do not consider to be part of the essential holding of *Roe.*[ ] Measures aimed at ensuring that a woman's choice contemplates the consequences for the fetus do not necessarily interfere with the right recognized in *Roe*, although those measures have been found to be inconsistent with the rigid trimester framework announced in that case. A logical reading of the central holding in *Roe* itself, and a necessary reconciliation of the liberty of the woman and the interest of the State in promoting prenatal life, require, in our view, that we abandon the trimester framework as a rigid prohibition on all previability regulation aimed at the protection of fetal life.

\* \* \*

The fact that a law which serves a valid purpose, one not designed to strike at the right itself, has the incidental effect of making it more difficult or more expensive to procure an abortion cannot be enough to invalidate it. Only where state regulation imposes an undue burden on a woman's ability to make this decision does the power of the State reach into the heart of the liberty protected by the Due Process Clause.

\* \* \*

Not all burdens on the right to decide whether to terminate a pregnancy will be undue. In our view, the undue burden standard is the appropriate means of reconciling the State's interest with the woman's constitutionally protected liberty.

\* \* \*

A finding of an undue burden is a shorthand for the conclusion that a state regulation has the purpose or effect of placing a substantial obstacle in the path of a woman seeking an abortion of a nonviable fetus. A statute with this purpose is invalid because the means chosen by the State to further the interest in potential life must be calculated to inform the woman's free choice, not hinder it. And a statute which, while furthering the interest in potential life or some other valid state interest, has the effect of placing a substantial obstacle in the path of a woman's choice cannot be considered a permissible means of serving its legitimate ends. * * *

Some guiding principles should emerge. What is at stake is the woman's right to make the ultimate decision, not a right to be insulated from all others in doing so. Regulations which do no more than create a structural mechanism by which the State, or the parent or guardian of a minor, may express profound respect for the life of the unborn are permitted, if they are not a substantial obstacle to the woman's exercise of the right to choose.[ ]

[The Justices then summarized their new undue burden test:]

(a)  To protect the central right recognized by Roe v. Wade while at the same time accommodating the State's profound interest in potential life, we will employ the undue burden analysis as explained in this opinion. An undue burden exists, and therefore a provision of law is invalid, if its purpose or effect is to place a substantial obstacle in the path of a woman seeking an abortion before the fetus attains viability.

(b)  We reject the rigid trimester framework of Roe v. Wade. To promote the State's profound interest in potential life, throughout pregnancy the State may take measures to ensure that the woman's choice is informed, and measures designed to advance this interest will not be invalidated as long as their purpose is to persuade the woman to choose childbirth over abortion. These measures must not be an undue burden on the right.

(c)  As with any medical procedure, the State may enact regulations to further the health or safety of a woman seeking an abortion. Unnecessary health regulations that have the purpose or effect of presenting a substantial obstacle to a woman seeking an abortion impose an undue burden on the right.

(d)  Our adoption of the undue burden analysis does not disturb the central holding of Roe v. Wade, and we reaffirm that holding. Regardless of whether exceptions are made for particular circumstances, a State may not prohibit any woman from making the ultimate decision to terminate her pregnancy before viability.

(e)  We also reaffirm Roe's holding that "subsequent to viability, the State in promoting its interest in the potentiality of human life may, if it chooses, regulate, and even proscribe, abortion except where it is necessary, in appropriate medical judgment, for the preservation of the life or health of the mother."[ ]

\* \* \*

## V.

\* \* \*

## A.

Because it is central to the operation of various other requirements, we begin with the statute's definition of medical emergency. Under the statute, a medical emergency is "that condition which, on the basis of the physician's good faith clinical judgment, so complicates the medical condition of a pregnant woman as to necessitate the immediate abortion of her pregnancy to avert her death or for which a delay will create serious risk of substantial and irreversible impairment of a major bodily function."[ ]

Petitioners argue that the definition is too narrow, contending that it forecloses the possibility of an immediate abortion despite some significant health risks.

[The Justices accepted the Court of Appeals interpretation of the statute, which assured that the "abortion regulation would not in any way pose a significant threat to the life or health of a woman," and determined that the definition imposed no undue burden on a woman's right to an abortion.]

## B.

We next consider the informed consent requirement.[ ] Except in a medical emergency, the statute requires that at least 24 hours before performing an abortion a physician inform the woman of the nature of the procedure, the health risks of the abortion and of childbirth, and the "probable gestational age of the unborn child." The physician or a qualified nonphysician must inform the woman of the availability of printed materials published by the State describing the fetus and providing information about medical assistance for childbirth, information about child support from the father, and a list of agencies which provide adoption and other services as alternatives to abortion. An abortion may not be performed unless the woman certifies in writing that she has been informed of the availability of these printed materials and has been provided them if she chooses to view them.

\* \* \*

\* \* \* If the information the State requires to be made available to the woman is truthful and not misleading, the requirement may be permissible. [The Court then rejects the argument that the physician's first amendment speech rights trump the state-mandated obligation to provide patients with identified truthful information.]

* * *

The Pennsylvania statute also requires us to reconsider the holding[ ] that the State may not require that a physician, as opposed to a qualified assistant, provide information relevant to a woman's informed consent.[ ] * * * Our cases reflect the fact that the Constitution gives the States broad latitude to decide that particular functions may be performed only by licensed professionals, even if an objective assessment might suggest that those same tasks could be performed by others.[ ] Thus, we uphold the provision as a reasonable means to insure that the woman's consent is informed.

Our analysis of Pennsylvania's 24-hour waiting period between the provision of the information deemed necessary to informed consent and the performance of an abortion under the undue burden standard requires us to reconsider the premise behind the decision in *Akron I* invalidating a parallel requirement. In *Akron I* we said: "Nor are we convinced that the State's legitimate concern that the woman's decision be informed is reasonably served by requiring a 24-hour delay as a matter of course."[ ] We consider that conclusion to be wrong. The idea that important decisions will be more informed and deliberate if they follow some period of reflection does not strike us as unreasonable, particularly where the statute directs that important information become part of the background of the decision.

* * *

C.

* * * Pennsylvania's abortion law provides, except in cases of medical emergency, that no physician shall perform an abortion on a married woman without receiving a signed statement from the woman that she has notified her spouse that she is about to undergo an abortion.

* * *

This information and the District Court's findings reinforce what common sense would suggest. In well-functioning marriages, spouses discuss important intimate decisions such as whether to bear a child. But there are millions of women in this country who are the victims of regular physical and psychological abuse at the hands of their husbands. Should these women become pregnant, they may have very good reasons for not wishing to inform their husbands of their decision to obtain an abortion. Many may have justifiable fears of physical abuse, but may be no less fearful of the consequences of reporting prior abuse to the Commonwealth of Pennsylvania. Many may have a reasonable fear that notifying their husbands will provoke further instances of child abuse; these women are not exempt from [the] notification requirement. Many may fear devastating forms of psychological abuse from their husbands, including verbal harassment, threats of future violence, the destruction of possessions, physical confinement to the home, the withdrawal of financial support, or the disclosure of the abortion to family and friends. * * *

The spousal notification requirement is thus likely to prevent a significant number of women from obtaining an abortion. It does not merely make abortions a little more difficult or expensive to obtain; for many women, it will impose a substantial obstacle. We must not blind ourselves to the fact that the significant number of women who fear for their safety and the safety of their children are likely to be deterred from procuring an abortion as surely as if the Commonwealth had outlawed abortion in all cases.

Respondents attempt to avoid the conclusion that [the spousal notification provision] is invalid by pointing out that it imposes almost no burden at all for the vast majority of women seeking abortions. * * * Respondents argue that since some of [the 20% of women who seek abortions who are married] will be able to notify their husbands without adverse consequences or will qualify for one of the exceptions, the statute affects fewer than one percent of women seeking abortions. For this reason, it is asserted, the statute cannot be invalid on its face.[ ] We disagree with respondents' basic method of analysis.

The analysis does not end with the one percent of women upon whom the statute operates; it begins there. Legislation is measured for consistency with the Constitution by its impact on those whose conduct it affects. * * * [A]s we have said, [the Act's] real target is narrower even than the class of women seeking abortions * * *: it is married women seeking abortions who do not wish to notify their husbands of their intentions and who do not qualify for one of the statutory exceptions to the notice requirement. The unfortunate yet persisting conditions * * * will mean that in a large fraction of the cases * * *, [the statute] will operate as a substantial obstacle to a woman's choice to undergo an abortion. It is an undue burden, and therefore invalid.

* * *

[The spousal notification provision] embodies a view of marriage consonant with the common-law status of married women but repugnant to our present understanding of marriage and of the nature of the rights secured by the Constitution. Women do not lose their constitutionally protected liberty when they marry. * * *

### D.

\* \* \*

Our cases establish, and we reaffirm today, that a State may require a minor seeking an abortion to obtain the consent of a parent or guardian, provided that there is an adequate judicial bypass procedure.[ ] Under these precedents, in our view, the [Pennsylvania] one-parent consent requirement and judicial bypass procedure are constitutional.

\* \* \*

### E.

[The Justices upheld all of the record keeping and reporting requirements of the statute, except for that provision requiring the reporting of a married woman's reason for failure to give notice to her husband.]

### VI.

Our Constitution is a covenant running from the first generation of Americans to us and then to future generations. It is a coherent succession. Each generation must learn anew that the Constitution's written terms embody ideas and aspirations that must survive more ages than one. We accept our responsibility not to retreat from interpreting the full meaning of the covenant in light of all of our precedents. We invoke it once again to define the freedom guaranteed by the Constitution's own promise, the promise of liberty.

\* \* \*

[In addition to those parts of the statute found unconstitutional in the three-justice opinion, Justice Stevens would find unconstitutional the requirement that the doctor deliver state-produced materials to a woman seeking an abortion, the counseling requirements, and the 24-hour-waiting requirement. His concurring and dissenting opinion is omitted. Justice Blackman's opinion, concurring in the judgment in part and dissenting in part, is also omitted.]

CHIEF JUSTICE REHNQUIST, with whom JUSTICE WHITE, JUSTICE SCALIA, and JUSTICE THOMAS join, concurring in the judgment in part and dissenting in part.

The joint opinion, following its newly-minted variation on stare decisis, retains the outer shell of Roe v. Wade,[ ] but beats a wholesale retreat from the substance of that case. We believe that *Roe* was wrongly decided, and that it can and should be overruled consistently with our traditional approach to stare decisis in constitutional cases.

\* \* \*

The end result of the joint opinion's paeans of praise for legitimacy is the enunciation of a brand new standard for evaluating state regulation of a woman's right to abortion—the "undue burden" standard. As indicated above, Roe v. Wade adopted a "fundamental right" standard under which state regulations could survive only if they met the requirement of "strict scrutiny." While we disagree with that standard, it at least had a recognized basis in constitutional law at the time *Roe* was decided. The same cannot be said for the "undue burden" standard, which is created largely out of whole cloth by the authors of the joint opinion. It is a standard which even today does not command the support of a majority of this Court. And it will not, we believe, result in the sort of "simple limitation," easily applied, which the joint opinion anticipates.[ ] In sum, it is a standard which is not built to last.

In evaluating abortion regulations under that standard, judges will have to decide whether they place a "substantial obstacle" in the path of a woman seeking an abortion.[ ] In that this standard is based even more on a judge's subjective determinations than was the trimester framework, the standard will do nothing to prevent "judges from roaming at large in the constitutional field" guided only by their personal views.[ ]

* * *

The sum of the joint opinion's labors in the name of stare decisis and "legitimacy" is this: Roe v. Wade stands as a sort of judicial Potemkin Village, which may be pointed out to passers by as a monument to the importance of adhering to precedent. But behind the facade, an entirely new method of analysis, without any roots in constitutional law, is imported to decide the constitutionality of state laws regulating abortion. Neither stare decisis nor "legitimacy" are truly served by such an effort.

* * *

JUSTICE SCALIA, with whom the CHIEF JUSTICE, JUSTICE WHITE, and JUSTICE THOMAS join, concurring in the judgment in part and dissenting in part.

* * *

The States may, if they wish, permit abortion-on-demand, but the Constitution does not require them to do so. The permissibility of abortion, and the limitations upon it, are to be resolved like most important questions in our democracy: by citizens trying to persuade one another and then voting. As the Court acknowledges, "where reasonable people disagree the government can adopt one position or the other." [ ] The Court is correct in adding the qualification that this "assumes a state of affairs in which the choice does not intrude upon a protected liberty,"[ ]—but the crucial part of that qualification is the penultimate word. A State's choice between two positions on which reasonable people can disagree is constitutional even when (as is often the case) it intrudes upon a "liberty" in the absolute sense. Laws against bigamy, for example—which entire societies of reasonable people disagree with—intrude upon men and women's liberty to marry and live with one another. But bigamy happens not to be a liberty specially "protected" by the Constitution.

That is, quite simply, the issue in this case: not whether the power of a woman to abort her unborn child is a "liberty" in the absolute sense; or even whether it is a liberty of great importance to many women. Of course it is both. The issue is whether it is a liberty protected by the Constitution of the United States. I am sure it is not. I reach that conclusion not because of anything so exalted as my views concerning the "concept of existence, of meaning, of the universe, and of the mystery of human life." [ ] I reach it for the same reason I reach the conclusion that bigamy is not constitutionally protected—because of two simple facts: (1) the Constitution says absolutely nothing about it, and (2) the longstanding traditions of American society have permitted it to be legally proscribed.

\* \* \*

I am certainly not in a good position to dispute that the Court has saved the "central holding" of *Roe*, since to do that effectively I would have to know what the Court has saved, which in turn would require me to understand (as I do not) what the "undue burden" test means. \* \* \* I thought I might note, however, that the following portions of *Roe* have not been saved:

• Under *Roe*, requiring that a woman seeking an abortion be provided truthful information about abortion before giving informed written consent is unconstitutional, if the information is designed to influence her choice[ ]. Under the joint opinion's "undue burden" regime (as applied today, at least) such a requirement is constitutional[ ].

• Under *Roe*, requiring that information be provided by a doctor, rather than by nonphysician counselors, is unconstitutional[ ]. Under the "undue burden" regime (as applied today, at least) it is not[ ].

• Under *Roe*, requiring a 24-hour waiting period between the time the woman gives her informed consent and the time of the abortion is unconstitutional. Under the "undue burden" regime (as applied today, at least) it is not[ ].

• Under *Roe*, requiring detailed reports that include demographic data about each woman who seeks an abortion and various information about each abortion is unconstitutional[ ]. Under the "undue burden" regime (as applied today, at least) it generally is not[ ].

\* \* \*

## NOTES AND QUESTIONS

1.    *Casey vs. Roe.* At the beginning of 2018, *Casey's* holding remains the governing law with regard to abortion. Does *Casey* really affirm *Roe*? As Scalia points out, several laws that had been struck down under *Roe* are being upheld under *Casey*. Which aspects of *Roe's* reasoning survived and which did not?

2.    *Parental Consent and Notification Requirements.* After *Casey*, states may require minors to obtain the consent of a parent to an abortion, as long as the state permits a court to dispense with that requirement under some circumstances. As of early 2013, thirty-seven states required some kind of parental involvement (either consent or notification, or, in four states, both). The Supreme Court has never determined if a two-parent consent requirement (with a proper judicial bypass provision) would pass Constitutional muster, and courts have reached different conclusions. Compare Barnes v. Mississippi, 992 F.2d 1335 (5th Cir.1993), cert. denied, 510 U.S. 976, 114 S.Ct. 468, 126 L.Ed.2d 419 (1993) (upholding two-parent consent requirement because involvement of both parents will increase "reflection and deliberation" on the process, and if one parent denies consent the other will be able to go to court in support of the child) and S.H. v. D.H., 796 N.E.2d 1243 (Ind.App.2003) (family court judge cannot require consent of both parents before an abortion is performed, even if the divorced parents have joint custody). The Supreme Court has suggested that a state requirement of mere parental notification (rather than consent) also requires a judicial bypass, and lower courts have generally assumed that it does. Ohio v. Akron Ctr. for Reproductive Health, 497 U.S. 502, 110 S.Ct. 2972, 111 L.Ed.2d 405 (1990). But states may have more robust state constitutional protections that limit their ability to require parental notification or consent. For example, one state supreme court has found that a parental notification requirement violates the state constitution's equal protection clause when it is imposed only on those who seek abortions, not on pregnant children making other, equally medically risky, reproductive decisions. Planned Parenthood of Central New Jersey v. Farmer, 165 N.J. 609, 762 A.2d 620 (2000).

3.    *Judicial Bypass.* It is not clear what Constitutional standard a court must apply in a "bypass" case. Under what circumstance is the court required to waive consent or notification: if it finds that the minor is sufficiently mature that she should be able to make the decision herself; if it finds that if she seeks consent from (or notifies) her parents she will be subject to abuse; if it finds that it is in her best interest to have the abortion; if it finds that it is in her best interest not to be required to notify, or get consent from, her parent; or some combination of these? See Lambert v. Wicklund, 520 U.S. 292, 297, 117 S.Ct. 1169, 137 L.Ed.2d 464 (1997) (per curiam).

4.    *Two-Trip Requirement and Waiting Period.* When a state imposes a waiting period between the time a pregnant woman is provided information under state informed consent requirements and the time of the medical procedure, this typically requires the pregnant woman make two trips to the medical facility. In *Casey* the Court announced that a 24-hour waiting period

did not constitute an unconstitutional undue burden, because it considered "[t]he idea that important decisions will be more informed and deliberate if they follow some period of reflection" to be reasonable, the statute was understood as not requiring the waiting period in a medical emergency, and "the record evidence show[ed] that in the vast majority of cases, a 24-hour delay does not create any appreciable health risk." A Tennessee Supreme Court, however, has determined that imposing what amounts to a three-day waiting period violated the *state* constitution's protected right of privacy. See Planned Parenthood of Middle Tennessee v. Sundquist, 38 S.W.3d 1 (Tenn.2000). The court cited evidence of the burdens such a requirement could impose:

> [P]atient mortality rates for abortions increase as the length of pregnancy increases. Studies also suggest that a large majority of women who have endured waiting periods prior to obtaining an abortion have suffered increased stress, nausea and physical discomfort, but very few have reported any benefit from having to wait. [Evidence also] indicates that the waiting period increases a woman's financial and psychological burdens, since many women must travel long distances and be absent from work to obtain an abortion . . . . [which] is especially problematic for women who suffer from poverty or abusive relationships.

As of early 2013, about half of the states imposed waiting periods of some sort. What if the woman must travel a very far distance to the facility and has difficulty accessing transportation? Should this impact an undue burden analysis of a waiting period requirement? A 2014 study of the distance that women would have to travel for an abortion revealed spacial disparities in abortion access. The median distance to the nearest clinic providing abortion services was less than 15 miles in 23 states, 15–29 miles in 16 states, 30–89 miles in eight states. In three states, at least half of all women had to travel more than 90 miles (168.49 miles in Wyoming; 151.58 in North Dakota; and 92.06 miles in South Dakota). The study also found that in states with a relatively low median travel distance (like Alaska), a sizeable percentage of women still had to travel over 150 miles to reach the nearest abortion clinic. See Jonathan M. Bearak et al., Disparities and Change Over Time in Distance Women Would Need to Travel to Have an Abortion in the USA: A Spatial Analysis, 2 Lancet Public Health 493–500 (Nov. 2017).

5. *State "Informed Consent" Requirements for Abortion.* In *Casey* the Court upheld a statute requiring that a state-approved packet of material be given to the pregnant woman as a part of the informed consent process, and that the consent process be obtained by the physician, not by anyone else. The only requirement the majority in *Casey* appears to put on the distributed material is that it is "truthful and not misleading." How should this be understood in the context of the summary of the "undue burden" test (offered in Part IV of the opinion by Justices O'Connor, Justice Kennedy, and Justice Souter), which allows the State to enact regulations that "further the health or safety of a woman seeking an abortion" but prohibits "[u]necessary health regulations that have the purpose or effect of presenting a substantial obstacle

to a woman seeking an abortion." This has led to a number of conflicts as state legislatures have enacted more expansive information requirements at the behest of groups that want to discourage women from having an abortion. Consider the following examples:

- *Information about Medical Risk.* In early 1996 a couple of epidemiological studies arguably suggested a very weak relationship between having an abortion and the subsequent risk of developing breast cancer and the severity of that cancer. Subsequent reports cast doubt on this relationship. See P.A. Newcomb, et al., Pregnancy Termination in Relation to Risk of Breast Cancer, 275 JAMA 283 (1996). A handful of states do require by statute that a woman seeking an abortion be told of the purported breast cancer risk. A handful of states also require that women be told that an abortion can jeopardize a woman's future fertility and can have serious mental health consequences, despite weak or contrary scientific support.

- *Information about Fetal Pain.* Nearly a dozen states require that a woman seeking an abortion be told of the possibility that the fetus can feel pain. Should courts scrutinize the scientific basis of this assertion? (See the Note on Fetal Pain Bans after *Gonzales v. Carhart* below).

- *Moral Information Laws.* How far can states go in promoting their preference for pregnancy over abortion? Should a state be able to require physicians to provide materials highlighting moral objections to abortion? Six states require that a woman be told that personhood begins at conception.

- *Mandatory Ultrasound & Viewing Laws.* Over the last few years, several states have added requirements that before a woman can have an abortion, she must be required or allowed to see an ultrasound of the fetus, to hear the fetal heartbeat, and to hear a description of the fetus (such as dimensions of the embryo or fetus, presence of cardiac activity, and the presence of external members and internal organs). Abortion is the only medical procedure in which the state requires a patient to undergo a particular diagnostic test even if the patient does not wish to do so and her doctor believes the tests will not have any diagnostic or therapeutic value. Some of these laws have been enjoined by court order. See, e.g., EMW Women's Surgical Center v. Behear, 283 F. Supp. 3d 629, 2017 WL 4288906, *appeal docketed*, No. 17–6183 (6th Cir. Oct. 12, 2017) (holding that Kentucky's mandatory "speech-and-display" ultrasound law violated physicians' First Amendment rights because it compelled ideological speech, it did not serve a substantial government interest, and it actually undermined the government's stated interest by inflicting psychological harm on the women instead of promoting psychological health). See also Stuart v. Camnitz, 774 F.3d 238 (4th Cir. 2014), *cert. denied* 135 S.Ct. 2838 (U.S. Jun. 15, 2015) (affirming the lower court's invalidation of North Carolina's mandatory ultrasound law based on similar reasoning). But see Texas Medical Providers Performing Abortion Services v. Lakey, 667 F.3d 570 (5th Cir. 2012) (finding Texas's law to be a constitutionally permissible regulation of the practice of medicine and consistent with *Casey*'s holding allowing required disclosure of "truthful, non-misleading information.")

6.    *State Disclosure Requirements on Pregnancy Centers.* The battle over what information should be provided to women seeking abortions has taken a different turn recently. There is growing attention to entities often referred to as "Pregnancy Centers," "Crisis Pregnancy Centers," or "Limited-Service Pregnancy Centers." These entities only provide support and assistance for those who want to carry a pregnancy to term. Some of these centers help women who want to keep their children but feel like they cannot afford to do so by connecting the women with resources and support, such as counseling, drug abuse treatment, and vocational training. See Michelle Oberman, The Women the Abortion War Leaves Out, N.Y. Times (Jan. 11, 2018). There is evidence, however, that some centers do not provide this kind of support and instead are focused on persuading women not to have abortions through false and misleading information about the health risks of abortion. See U.S. House of Representatives, Committee on Government Reform—Minority Staff, False and Misleading Information Provided by Federally Funded Pregnancy Resource Centers (July 2006). Findings from this report and some state investigations assert that some of these Centers intentionally "pose as full-service women's health clinics" despite their aim to discourage women from having an abortion, and then use "counseling practices that often confuse, misinform, and even intimidate women from making fully-informed, time-sensitive decisions about critical health care." See National Institute of Family & Life Advocates (NIFLA) v. Harris, 839 F.3d 823 (9th Cir. 2016).

Some states have responded to these concerns by requiring such Centers to make disclosures about the limits of the services they provide as well as information about where more comprehensive family planning, including abortion, can be accessed. Such disclosures have been challenged on First Amendment grounds, and courts confronting the question have reached different conclusions. See, e.g., Greater Baltimore Center for Pregnancy Concerns, Inc. v. Mayor and City Council of Baltimore, 879 F.3d 101 (4th Cir. 2018), *petition for cert. filed*, No. 17–1369 (U.S. Mar. 29, 2018) (invalidating the regulation on free speech grounds for failing to satisfy strict scrutiny; finding no compelling interest to justify the intrusion because the city failed to demonstrate that deception was taking place and that harm was caused by any deception; also noting that the regulation was overinclusive). But see NIFLA v. Harris, 839 F.3d 823 (9th Cir. 2016), *cert. granted*, 86 U.S.L.W. 3238 (U.S. Nov. 13, 2017) (No. 16–1140) (upholding the state law as a constitutional regulation of professional speech, satisfying intermediate scrutiny; finding that the law was narrowly drawn to achieve the state's substantial interest in ensuring its citizens have access to and adequate information about constitutionally-protected medical services like abortion). Soon, the Supreme Court will weigh in on the question of what kind of disclosures, if any, a state can require in these situations.

## GONZALES V. CARHART
Supreme Court of the United States, 2007.
550 U.S. 124, 127 S.Ct. 1610, 167 L.Ed.2d 480.

JUSTICE KENNEDY delivered the opinion of the Court.

These cases require us to consider the validity of the Partial-Birth Abortion Ban Act of 2003 (Act),[ ] a federal statute regulating abortion procedures. * * * We conclude the Act should be sustained against the objections lodged by the broad, facial attack brought against it.

* * *

I

A

[The Medical Procedure]

The Act proscribes a particular manner of ending fetal life, so it is necessary here[ ] to discuss abortion procedures in some detail. * * *

Abortion methods vary depending to some extent on the preferences of the physician and, of course, on the term of the pregnancy and the resulting stage of the unborn child's development. Between 85 and 90 percent of the approximately 1.3 million abortions performed each year in the United States take place in the first three months of pregnancy, which is to say in the first trimester.[ ] The most common first-trimester abortion method is vacuum aspiration (otherwise known as suction curettage) in which the physician vacuums out the embryonic tissue. Early in this trimester an alternative is to use medication, such as mifepristone (commonly known as RU-486), to terminate the pregnancy.[ ] The Act does not regulate these procedures.

Of the remaining abortions that take place each year, most occur in the second trimester. The surgical procedure referred to as "dilation and evacuation" or "D & E" is the usual abortion method in this trimester.[ ] Although individual techniques for performing D & E differ, the general steps are the same.

A doctor must first dilate the cervix at least to the extent needed to insert surgical instruments into the uterus and to maneuver them to evacuate the fetus.[ ] The steps taken to cause dilation differ by physician and gestational age of the fetus. * * *

After sufficient dilation the surgical operation can commence. The woman is placed under general anesthesia or conscious sedation. The doctor, often guided by ultrasound, inserts grasping forceps through the woman's cervix and into the uterus to grab the fetus. The doctor grips a fetal part with the forceps and pulls it back through the cervix and vagina, continuing to pull even after meeting resistance from the cervix. The friction causes the fetus to tear apart. For example, a leg might be ripped off the fetus as it is pulled through the cervix and out of the woman. The process of evacuating the fetus piece by piece continues until it has been completely removed. A doctor may make 10 to 15 passes with the forceps to evacuate the fetus in its entirety, though sometimes removal is completed with fewer passes. Once the fetus has been evacuated, the placenta and any remaining fetal material are suctioned or scraped out of the uterus. The doctor examines the different parts to ensure the entire fetal body has been removed.[ ]

Some doctors, especially later in the second trimester, may kill the fetus a day or two before performing the surgical evacuation. They inject digoxin or potassium chloride into the fetus, the umbilical cord, or the amniotic fluid. Fetal demise may cause contractions and make greater dilation possible. Once dead, moreover, the fetus' body will soften, and its removal will be easier. * * *

The abortion procedure that was the impetus for the numerous bans on "partial-birth abortion," including the Act, is a variation of this standard D & E.[ ] The medical community has not reached unanimity on the appropriate name for this D & E variation. It has been referred to as "intact D & E," "dilation and extraction" (D & X), and "intact D & X."[ ] For discussion purposes this D & E variation will be referred to as intact D & E. The main difference between the two procedures is that in intact D & E a doctor extracts the fetus intact or largely intact with only a few passes. There are no comprehensive statistics indicating what percentage of all D & Es are performed in this manner.

Intact D & E, like regular D & E, begins with dilation of the cervix. Sufficient dilation is essential for the procedure. * * * In an intact D & E procedure the doctor extracts the fetus in a way conducive to pulling out its entire body, instead of ripping it apart. * * *

Intact D & E gained public notoriety when, in 1992, Dr. Martin Haskell gave a presentation describing his method of performing the operation.[ ] In the usual intact D & E the fetus' head lodges in the cervix, and dilation is insufficient to allow it to pass.[ ] Haskell explained the next step as follows:

> " 'At this point, the right-handed surgeon slides the fingers of the left [hand] along the back of the fetus and "hooks" the shoulders of the fetus with the index and ring fingers (palm down).

> " 'While maintaining this tension, lifting the cervix and applying traction to the shoulders with the fingers of the left hand, the surgeon takes a pair of blunt curved Metzenbaum scissors in the right hand. He carefully advances the tip, curved down, along the spine and under his middle finger until he feels it contact the base of the skull under the tip of his middle finger.

" 'The surgeon then forces the scissors into the base of the skull or into the foramen magnum. Having safely entered the skull, he spreads the scissors to enlarge the opening.

" 'The surgeon removes the scissors and introduces a suction catheter into this hole and evacuates the skull contents. With the catheter still in place, he applies traction to the fetus, removing it completely from the patient.' " [ ]

This is an abortion doctor's clinical description. Here is another description from a nurse who witnessed the same method performed on a 26-week fetus and who testified before the Senate Judiciary Committee:

" 'Dr. Haskell went in with forceps and grabbed the baby's legs and pulled them down into the birth canal. Then he delivered the baby's body and the arms—everything but the head. The doctor kept the head right inside the uterus. . . .

" 'The baby's little fingers were clasping and unclasping, and his little feet were kicking. Then the doctor stuck the scissors in the back of his head, and the baby's arms jerked out, like a startle reaction, like a flinch, like a baby does when he thinks he is going to fall.

" 'The doctor opened up the scissors, stuck a high-powered suction tube into the opening, and sucked the baby's brains out. Now the baby went completely limp. . . .

" 'He cut the umbilical cord and delivered the placenta. He threw the baby in a pan, along with the placenta and the instruments he had just used.' " [ ]

[JUSTICE KENNEDY next describes other varieties of this procedure in equally vivid terms.]

* * *

D & E and intact D & E are not the only second-trimester abortion methods. * * *

B

[The Statute]

After Dr. Haskell's procedure received public attention, with ensuing and increasing public concern, bans on " 'partial birth abortion' " proliferated. By the time of the *Stenberg* decision [finding Nebraska's statutory partial birth abortion ban to be unconstitutional in 2003], about 30 States had enacted bans designed to prohibit the procedure.[ ] In 1996, Congress also acted to ban partial-birth abortion. President Clinton vetoed the congressional legislation, and the Senate failed to override the veto. Congress approved another bill banning the procedure in 1997, but President Clinton again vetoed it. In 2003, after this Court's decision in

*Stenberg*, Congress passed the Act at issue here.[ ] President Bush signed the Act into law. It was to take effect the following day.[ ]

The Act responded to *Stenberg* in two ways. First, Congress made factual findings. Congress determined that this Court in *Stenberg* "was required to accept the very questionable findings issued by the district court judge,"[ ], but that Congress was "not bound to accept the same factual findings,"[ ]. Congress found, among other things, that "[a] moral, medical, and ethical consensus exists that the practice of performing a partial-birth abortion . . . is a gruesome and inhumane procedure that is never medically necessary and should be prohibited."[ ]

Second, and more relevant here, the Act's language differs from that of the Nebraska statute struck down in *Stenberg*.[ ] The operative provisions of the Act provide in relevant part:

"(a) Any physician who, in or affecting interstate or foreign commerce, knowingly performs a partial-birth abortion and thereby kills a human fetus shall be fined under this title or imprisoned not more than 2 years, or both. This subsection does not apply to a partial-birth abortion that is necessary to save the life of a mother whose life is endangered by a physical disorder, physical illness, or physical injury, including a life-endangering physical condition caused by or arising from the pregnancy itself. * * *

"(b) As used in this section—

"(1) the term 'partial-birth abortion' means an abortion in which the person performing the abortion—

"(A) deliberately and intentionally vaginally delivers a living fetus until, in the case of a head-first presentation, the entire fetal head is outside the body of the mother, or, in the case of breech presentation, any part of the fetal trunk past the navel is outside the body of the mother, for the purpose of performing an overt act that the person knows will kill the partially delivered living fetus; and

"(B) performs the overt act, other than completion of delivery, that kills the partially delivered living fetus;

* * *

"(e) A woman upon whom a partial-birth abortion is performed may not be prosecuted under this section, for a conspiracy to violate this section * * *.

The Act also includes a provision authorizing civil actions [for damages following a "Partial Birth Abortion"] that is not of relevance here.[ ]

* * *

## II

### [The Holding in *Casey*]

The principles set forth in the joint opinion in *Casey* [ ] did not find support from all those who join the instant opinion.[ ] Whatever one's views concerning the *Casey* joint opinion, it is evident a premise central to its conclusion—that the government has a legitimate and substantial interest in preserving and promoting fetal life—would be repudiated were the Court now to affirm the judgments of the Courts of Appeals. *Casey* involved a challenge to Roe v. Wade[ ]. [One of the three essential principles of *Roe* that was upheld in Casey was] the principle that the State has legitimate interests from the outset of the pregnancy in protecting the health of the woman and the life of the fetus that may become a child. * * * [W]e must determine whether the Act furthers the legitimate interest of the Government in protecting the life of the fetus that may become a child.

To implement its holding, *Casey* rejected both *Roe*'s rigid trimester framework and the interpretation of *Roe* that considered all previability regulations of abortion unwarranted. * * *

We assume the following principles for the purposes of this opinion. Before viability, a State "may not prohibit any woman from making the ultimate decision to terminate her pregnancy."[ ] It also may not impose upon this right an undue burden, which exists if a regulation's "purpose or effect is to place a substantial obstacle in the path of a woman seeking an abortion before the fetus attains viability."[ ] On the other hand, "regulations which do no more than create a structural mechanism by which the State, or the parent or guardian of a minor, may express profound respect for the life of the unborn are permitted, if they are not a substantial obstacle to the woman's exercise of the right to choose."[ ] *Casey*, in short, struck a balance. The balance was central to its holding. We now apply its standard to the cases at bar.

## III

We begin with a determination of the Act's operation and effect. A straightforward reading of the Act's text demonstrates its purpose and the scope of its provisions: It regulates and proscribes, with exceptions or qualifications to be discussed, performing the intact D & E procedure.

Respondents agree the Act encompasses intact D & E, but they contend its additional reach is both unclear and excessive. Respondents assert that, at the least, the Act is void for vagueness because its scope is indefinite. In the alternative, respondents argue the Act's text proscribes all D & Es. Because D & E is the most common second-trimester abortion method, respondents suggest the Act imposes an undue burden. In this litigation the Attorney General does not dispute that the Act would impose an undue burden if it covered standard D & E.

We conclude that the Act is not void for vagueness, does not impose an undue burden from any overbreadth, and is not invalid on its face.

## A

### [Interpreting the Statute]

The Act punishes "knowingly performing" a "partial-birth abortion."[ ] It defines the unlawful abortion in explicit terms.[ ]

First, the person performing the abortion must "vaginally deliver a living fetus."[ ] The Act does not restrict an abortion procedure involving the delivery of an expired fetus. The Act, furthermore, is inapplicable to abortions that do not involve vaginal delivery (for instance, hysterotomy or hysterectomy). The Act does apply both previability and postviability because, by common understanding and scientific terminology, a fetus is a living organism while within the womb, whether or not it is viable outside the womb. * * *

Second, the Act's definition of partial-birth abortion requires the fetus to be delivered "until, in the case of a head-first presentation, the entire fetal head is outside the body of the mother, or, in the case of breech presentation, any part of the fetal trunk past the navel is outside the body of the mother." * * *

Third, to fall within the Act, a doctor must perform an "overt act, other than completion of delivery, that kills the partially delivered living fetus."[ ] For purposes of criminal liability, the overt act causing the fetus' death must be separate from delivery. And the overt act must occur after the delivery to an anatomical landmark. This is because the Act proscribes killing "the partially delivered" fetus, which, when read in context, refers to a fetus that has been delivered to an anatomical landmark.[ ]

Fourth, the Act contains scienter requirements concerning all the actions involved in the prohibited abortion. To begin with, the physician must have "deliberately and intentionally" delivered the fetus to one of the Act's anatomical landmarks. * * * In addition, the fetus must have been delivered "for the purpose of performing an overt act that the [doctor] knows will kill [it]." * * *

## B

### [Vagueness]

Respondents contend the language described above is indeterminate, and they thus argue the Act is unconstitutionally vague on its face. "As generally stated, the void-for-vagueness doctrine requires that a penal statute define the criminal offense with sufficient definiteness that ordinary people can understand what conduct is prohibited and in a manner that does not encourage arbitrary and discriminatory enforcement."[ ] The Act satisfies both requirements.

* * * Unlike the statutory language in *Stenberg* that prohibited the delivery of a " 'substantial portion' " of the fetus—where a doctor might question how much of the fetus is a substantial portion—the Act defines the line between potentially criminal conduct on the one hand and lawful abortion on the other.[ ]

* * *

## C

### [Undue Burden]

We next determine whether the Act imposes an undue burden, as a facial matter, because its restrictions on second-trimester abortions are too broad. A review of the statutory text discloses the limits of its reach. The Act prohibits intact D & E; and, notwithstanding respondents' arguments, it does not prohibit the D & E procedure in which the fetus is removed in parts.

* * *

A comparison of the Act with the Nebraska statute struck down in *Stenberg* confirms this point. The statute in *Stenberg* prohibited " 'deliberately and intentionally delivering into the vagina a living unborn child, or a substantial portion thereof, for the purpose of performing a procedure that the person performing such procedure knows will kill the unborn child and does kill the unborn child.' "[ ]. The Court concluded that this statute encompassed D & E because "D & E will often involve a physician pulling a 'substantial portion' of a still living fetus, say, an arm or leg, into the vagina prior to the death of the fetus." * * *

Congress, it is apparent, responded to these concerns because the Act departs in material ways from the statute in *Stenberg*. It adopts the phrase "delivers a living fetus,"[ ] instead of " 'delivering . . . a living unborn child, or a substantial portion thereof,' "[ ]. The Act's language, unlike the statute in *Stenberg*, expresses the usual meaning of "deliver" when used in connection with "fetus," namely, extraction of an entire fetus rather than removal of fetal pieces. * * *

The identification of specific anatomical landmarks to which the fetus must be partially delivered also differentiates the Act from the statute at issue in *Stenberg*. * * *

By adding an overt-act requirement Congress sought further to meet the Court's objections to the state statute considered in *Stenberg*. * * * The fatal overt act must occur after delivery to an anatomical landmark, and it must be something "other than [the] completion of delivery."[ ] This distinction matters because, unlike intact D & E, standard D & E does not involve a delivery followed by a fatal act.

The canon of constitutional avoidance, finally, extinguishes any lingering doubt as to whether the Act covers the prototypical D & E procedure. " 'The elementary rule is that every reasonable construction must be resorted to, in order to save a statute from unconstitutionality.' "[ ] It is true this longstanding maxim of statutory interpretation has, in the past, fallen by the wayside when the Court confronted a statute regulating abortion. * * * *Casey* put this novel statutory approach to rest. * * *

* * *

## IV

### [Substantial Obstacle]

Under the principles accepted as controlling here, the Act, as we have interpreted it, would be unconstitutional "if its purpose or effect is to place a substantial obstacle in the path of a woman seeking an abortion before the fetus attains viability." *Casey* [ ] The abortions affected by the Act's regulations take place both previability and postviability; so the quoted language and the undue burden analysis it relies upon are applicable. The question is whether the Act, measured by its text in this facial attack, imposes a substantial obstacle to late-term, but previability, abortions. The Act does not on its face impose a substantial obstacle, and we reject this further facial challenge to its validity.

### A

### [Congressional Purpose]

The Act's purposes are set forth in recitals preceding its operative provisions. A description of the prohibited abortion procedure demonstrates the rationale for the congressional enactment. The Act proscribes a method of abortion in which a fetus is killed just inches before completion of the birth process. Congress stated as follows: "Implicitly approving such a brutal and inhumane procedure by choosing not to prohibit it will further coarsen society to the humanity of not only newborns, but all vulnerable and innocent human life, making it increasingly difficult to protect such life."[ ] The Act expresses respect for the dignity of human life. Congress was concerned, furthermore, with the effects on the medical community and on its reputation caused by the practice of partial-birth abortion. * * *

There can be no doubt the government "has an interest in protecting the integrity and ethics of the medical profession." Washington v. Glucksberg,[ ] [reprinted in Chapter 6, below]. Under our precedents, it is clear the State has a significant role to play in regulating the medical profession.

*Casey* reaffirmed these governmental objectives. The government may use its voice and its regulatory authority to show its profound respect for the life within the woman. * * * The three premises of *Casey* must coexist.[ ] The third premise, that the State, from the inception of the pregnancy, maintains its own regulatory interest in protecting the life of the fetus that may become a child, cannot be set at naught by interpreting *Casey's* requirement of a health exception so it becomes tantamount to allowing a doctor to choose the abortion method he or she might prefer. Where it has a rational basis to act, and it does not impose an undue burden, the State may use its regulatory power to bar certain procedures and substitute others, all in furtherance of its legitimate interests in regulating the medical profession in order to promote respect for life, including life of the unborn.

* * * The Court has in the past confirmed the validity of drawing boundaries to prevent certain practices that extinguish life and are close to actions that are condemned. *Glucksberg* found reasonable the State's "fear that permitting assisted suicide will start it down the path to voluntary and perhaps even involuntary euthanasia."[ ]

Respect for human life finds an ultimate expression in the bond of love the mother has for her child. The Act recognizes this reality as well. Whether to have an abortion requires a difficult and painful moral decision.[ ] While we find no reliable data to measure the phenomenon, it seems unexceptionable to conclude some women come to regret their choice to abort the infant life they once created and sustained.[ ] Severe depression and loss of esteem can follow.[ ]

In a decision so fraught with emotional consequence some doctors may prefer not to disclose precise details of the means that will be used, confining themselves to the required statement of risks the procedure entails. From one standpoint this ought not to be surprising. Any number of patients facing imminent surgical procedures would prefer not to hear all details, lest the usual anxiety preceding invasive medical procedures become the more intense. This is likely the case with the abortion procedures here in issue.[ ]

It is, however, precisely this lack of information concerning the way in which the fetus will be killed that is of legitimate concern to the State.[ ] The State has an interest in ensuring so grave a choice is well informed. It is self-evident that a mother who comes to regret her choice to abort must struggle with grief more anguished and sorrow more profound when she learns, only after the event, what she once did not know: that she allowed a doctor to pierce the skull and vacuum the fast-developing brain of her unborn child, a child assuming the human form.

* * *

It is objected that the standard D & E is in some respects as brutal, if not more, than the intact D & E, so that the legislation accomplishes little.

* * * It was reasonable for Congress to think that partial-birth abortion, more than standard D & E, "undermines the public's perception of the appropriate role of a physician during the delivery process, and perverts a process during which life is brought into the world." * * * In sum, we reject the contention that the congressional purpose of the Act was "to place a substantial obstacle in the path of a woman seeking an abortion."[ ]

## B

### [Protecting the Health of the Mother]

The Act's furtherance of legitimate government interests bears upon, but does not resolve, the next question: whether the Act has the effect of imposing an unconstitutional burden on the abortion right because it does not allow use of the barred procedure where " 'necessary, in appropriate medical judgment, for [the] preservation of the . . . health of the mother.' "[ ] The prohibition in the Act would be unconstitutional, under precedents we here assume to be controlling, if it "subjected [women] to significant health risks." * * * Here, by contrast, whether the Act creates significant health risks for women has been a contested factual question. The evidence presented in the trial courts and before Congress demonstrates both sides have medical support for their position.

* * *

The question becomes whether the Act can stand when this medical uncertainty persists. The Court's precedents instruct that the Act can survive this facial attack. The Court has given state and federal legislatures wide discretion to pass legislation in areas where there is medical and scientific uncertainty.

* * *

In reaching the conclusion the Act does not require a health exception we reject certain arguments made by the parties on both sides of these cases. On the one hand, the Attorney General urges us to uphold the Act on the basis of the congressional findings alone.[ ] Although we review congressional factfinding under a deferential standard, we do not in the circumstances here place dispositive weight on Congress' findings. The Court retains an independent constitutional duty to review factual findings where constitutional rights are at stake.[ ]

As respondents have noted, and the District Courts recognized, some recitations in the Act are factually incorrect. * * * Uncritical deference to Congress' factual findings in these cases is inappropriate.

On the other hand, relying on the Court's opinion in *Stenberg*, respondents contend that an abortion regulation must contain a health exception "if 'substantial medical authority supports the proposition that banning a particular procedure could endanger women's health.' " * * *

*Stenberg* has been interpreted to leave no margin of error for legislatures to act in the face of medical uncertainty.[ ]

A zero tolerance policy would strike down legitimate abortion regulations, like the present one, if some part of the medical community were disinclined to follow the proscription. This is too exacting a standard to impose on the legislative power, exercised in this instance under the Commerce Clause, to regulate the medical profession. Considerations of marginal safety, including the balance of risks, are within the legislative competence when the regulation is rational and in pursuit of legitimate ends. * * * The Act is not invalid on its face where there is uncertainty over whether the barred procedure is ever necessary to preserve a woman's health, given the availability of other abortion procedures that are considered to be safe alternatives.

V

[Propriety of a Facial Attack on the Statute]

The considerations we have discussed support our further determination that these facial attacks should not have been entertained in the first instance. In these circumstances the proper means to consider exceptions is by as-applied challenge. * * * This is the proper manner to protect the health of the woman if it can be shown that in discrete and well-defined instances a particular condition has or is likely to occur in which the procedure prohibited by the Act must be used. In an as-applied challenge the nature of the medical risk can be better quantified and balanced than in a facial attack.

* * *

As the previous sections of this opinion explain, respondents have not demonstrated that the Act would be unconstitutional in a large fraction of relevant cases. * * *

The Act is open to a proper as-applied challenge in a discrete case. * * * No as-applied challenge need be brought if the prohibition in the Act threatens a woman's life because the Act already contains a life exception.[ ]

* * *

JUSTICE THOMAS, with whom JUSTICE SCALIA joins, concurring.

I join the Court's opinion because it accurately applies current jurisprudence, including *Casey* [ ]. I write separately to reiterate my view that the Court's abortion jurisprudence, including *Casey* and *Roe*[ ] has no basis in the Constitution.[ ] I also note that whether the Act constitutes a permissible exercise of Congress' power under the Commerce Clause is not before the Court. The parties did not raise or brief that issue; it is outside the question presented; and the lower courts did not address it.[ ]

JUSTICE GINSBURG, with whom JUSTICE STEVENS, JUSTICE SOUTER, and JUSTICE BREYER join, dissenting.

* * *

In reaffirming *Roe*, the *Casey* Court described the centrality of "the decision whether to bear . . . a child,"[ ] to a woman's "dignity and autonomy," her "personhood" and "destiny," her "conception of . . . her place in society."[ ] Of signal importance here, the *Casey* Court stated with unmistakable clarity that state regulation of access to abortion procedures, even after viability, must protect "the health of the woman."[ ]

Seven years ago, in *Stenberg*,[ ] the Court invalidated a Nebraska statute criminalizing the performance of a medical procedure that, in the political arena, has been dubbed "partial-birth abortion." With fidelity to the *Roe-Casey* line of precedent, the Court held the Nebraska statute unconstitutional in part because it lacked the requisite protection for the preservation of a woman's health.[ ]

Today's decision is alarming. It refuses to take *Casey* and *Stenberg* seriously. It tolerates, indeed applauds, federal intervention to ban nationwide a procedure found necessary and proper in certain cases by the American College of Obstetricians and Gynecologists (ACOG). It blurs the line, firmly drawn in *Casey*, between previability and postviability abortions. And, for the first time since *Roe*, the Court blesses a prohibition with no exception safeguarding a woman's health.

I dissent from the Court's disposition. Retreating from prior rulings that abortion restrictions cannot be imposed absent an exception safeguarding a woman's health, the Court upholds an Act that surely would not survive under the close scrutiny that previously attended state-decreed limitations on a woman's reproductive choices.

## I

### A

As *Casey* comprehended, at stake in cases challenging abortion restrictions is a woman's "control over her [own] destiny." * * * Women, it is now acknowledged, have the talent, capacity, and right "to participate equally in the economic and social life of the Nation."[ ] Their ability to realize their full potential, the Court recognized, is intimately connected to "their ability to control their reproductive lives."[ ] Thus, legal challenges to undue restrictions on abortion procedures do not seek to vindicate some generalized notion of privacy; rather, they center on a woman's autonomy to determine her life's course, and thus to enjoy equal citizenship stature.[ ]

In keeping with this comprehension of the right to reproductive choice, the Court has consistently required that laws regulating abortion, at any stage of pregnancy and in all cases, safeguard a woman's health.[ ]

We have thus ruled that a State must avoid subjecting women to health risks not only where the pregnancy itself creates danger, but also where state regulation forces women to resort to less safe methods of abortion. * * *

In *Stenberg*, we expressly held that a statute banning intact D & E was unconstitutional in part because it lacked a health exception.[ ] We noted that there existed a "division of medical opinion" about the relative safety of intact D & E,[ ], but we made clear that as long as "substantial medical authority supports the proposition that banning a particular abortion procedure could endanger women's health," a health exception is required.[ ] We explained:

> "The word 'necessary' in *Casey*'s phrase 'necessary, in appropriate medical judgment, for the preservation of the life or health of the [pregnant woman],' cannot refer to an absolute necessity or to absolute proof. Medical treatments and procedures are often considered appropriate (or inappropriate) in light of estimated comparative health risks (and health benefits) in particular cases. Neither can that phrase require unanimity of medical opinion. Doctors often differ in their estimation of comparative health risks and appropriate treatment. And *Casey*'s words 'appropriate medical judgment' must embody the judicial need to tolerate responsible differences of medical opinion. . . . "[ ]

Thus, we reasoned, division in medical opinion "at most means uncertainty, a factor that signals the presence of risk, not its absence."[ ] "[A] statute that altogether forbids [intact D & E] . . . consequently must contain a health exception."[ ]

### B

In 2003, a few years after our ruling in *Stenberg*, Congress passed the Partial-Birth Abortion Ban Act—without an exception for women's health.[ ] The congressional findings on which the Partial-Birth Abortion Ban Act rests do not withstand inspection, as the lower courts have determined and this Court is obliged to concede.

* * *

### C

* * *

During the District Court trials, "numerous" "extraordinarily accomplished" and "very experienced" medical experts explained that, in certain circumstances and for certain women, intact D & E is safer than alternative procedures and necessary to protect women's health.[ ]

According to the expert testimony plaintiffs introduced, the safety advantages of intact D & E are marked for women with certain medical conditions * * *. Further, plaintiffs' experts testified that intact D & E is significantly safer for women with certain pregnancy-related conditions, such as placenta previa and accreta, and for women carrying fetuses with certain abnormalities, such as severe hydrocephalus.[ ]

Intact D & E, plaintiffs' experts explained, provides safety benefits over D & E by dismemberment for several reasons [which Justice Ginsburg lists and describes]. * * *

* * *

Nevertheless, despite the District Courts' appraisal of the weight of the evidence, and in undisguised conflict with *Stenberg*, the Court asserts that the Partial-Birth Abortion Ban Act can survive "when . . . medical uncertainty persists."[ ] This assertion is bewildering.

* * *

II

A

The Court offers flimsy and transparent justifications for upholding a nationwide ban on intact D & E *sans* any exception to safeguard a women's health. Today's ruling, the Court declares, advances "a premise central to [*Casey*'s] conclusion"—i.e., the Government's "legitimate and substantial interest in preserving and promoting fetal life."[ ] But the Act scarcely furthers that interest: The law saves not a single fetus from destruction, for it targets only a *method* of performing abortion.[ ] And surely the statute was not designed to protect the lives or health of pregnant women.[ ]

* * *

Ultimately, the Court admits that "moral concerns" are at work, concerns that could yield prohibitions on any abortion.[ ] Notably, the concerns expressed are untethered to any ground genuinely serving the Government's interest in preserving life. By allowing such concerns to carry the day and case, overriding fundamental rights, the Court dishonors our precedent.[ ]

Revealing in this regard, the Court invokes an antiabortion shibboleth for which it concededly has no reliable evidence: Women who have abortions come to regret their choices, and consequently suffer from "severe depression and loss of esteem."[ ] Because of women's fragile emotional state and because of the "bond of love the mother has for her child," the Court worries, doctors may withhold information about the nature of the intact D & E procedure.[ ] The solution the Court approves, then, is *not* to require doctors to inform women, accurately and adequately, of the different procedures and their attendant risks.[ ] Instead, the Court deprives women of the right to make an autonomous choice, even at the expense of their safety.

This way of thinking reflects ancient notions about women's place in the family and under the Constitution—ideas that have long since been discredited. * * *

Though today's majority may regard women's feelings on the matter as "self-evident,"[ ] this Court has repeatedly confirmed that "the destiny of the woman must be shaped . . . on her own conception of her spiritual imperatives and her place in society." *Casey*[ ].

## B

* * *

The Court's hostility to the right *Roe* and *Casey* secured is not concealed. Throughout, the opinion refers to obstetrician-gynecologists and surgeons who perform abortions not by the titles of their medical specialties, but by the pejorative label "abortion doctor."[ ] A fetus is described as an "unborn child," and as a "baby,"[ ]; second-trimester, previability abortions are referred to as "late-term,"[ ]; and the reasoned medical judgments of highly trained doctors are dismissed as "preferences" motivated by "mere convenience,"[ ]. Instead of the heightened scrutiny we have previously applied, the Court determines that a "rational" ground is enough to uphold the Act [ ]. And, most troubling, *Casey*'s principles, confirming the continuing vitality of "the essential holding of *Roe*," are merely "assumed" for the moment [ ], rather than "retained" or "reaffirmed," *Casey*[ ].

## III

### A

The Court further confuses our jurisprudence when it declares that "facial attacks" are not permissible in "these circumstances," i.e., where medical uncertainty exists. * * *

Without attempting to distinguish *Stenberg* and earlier decisions, the majority asserts that the Act survives review because respondents have not shown that the ban on intact D & E would be unconstitutional "in a large fraction of relevant cases."[ ] But *Casey* makes clear that, in determining whether any restriction poses an undue burden on a "large fraction" of women, the relevant class is *not* "all women," nor "all pregnant women," nor even all women "seeking abortions."[ ] Rather, a provision restricting access to abortion, "must be judged by reference to those [women] for whom it is an actual rather than an irrelevant restriction."[ ] Thus the absence of a health exception burdens *all* women for whom it is relevant—women who, in the judgment of their doctors, require an intact D & E because other procedures would place their health at risk.[ ] It makes no sense to conclude that this facial challenge fails because respondents have not shown that a health exception is necessary for a large fraction of second-trimester abortions, including those for which a health exception is unnecessary: The very purpose of a health *exception* is to protect women in *exceptional* cases.

### B

If there is anything at all redemptive to be said of today's opinion, it is that the Court is not willing to foreclose entirely a constitutional challenge to the Act. "The Act is open," the Court states, "to a proper as-applied challenge in a discrete case."[ ] But the Court offers no clue on what a "proper" lawsuit might look like.[ ] Nor does the Court explain why the injunctions ordered by the District Courts should not remain in place, trimmed only to exclude instances in which another procedure would safeguard a woman's health at least equally well. Surely the Court cannot mean that no suit may be brought until a woman's health is immediately jeopardized by the ban on intact D & E. A woman "suffering from medical complications"[ ] needs access to the medical procedure at once and cannot wait for the judicial process to unfold.[ ]

\* \* \*

### IV

As the Court wrote in *Casey*, "overruling *Roe*'s central holding would not only reach an unjustifiable result under principles of *stare decisis*, but would seriously weaken the Court's capacity to exercise the judicial power and to function as the Supreme Court of a Nation dedicated to the rule of law." \* \* \*

Though today's opinion does not go so far as to discard *Roe* or *Casey*, the Court, differently composed than it was when we last considered a restrictive abortion regulation, is hardly faithful to our earlier invocations of "the rule of law" and the "principles of *stare decisis*." Congress imposed a ban despite our clear prior holdings that the State cannot proscribe an abortion procedure when its use is necessary to protect a woman's health.[ ] Although Congress' findings could not withstand the crucible of trial, the Court defers to the legislative override of our Constitution-based rulings.[ ] A decision so at odds with our jurisprudence should not have staying power.

In sum, the notion that the Partial-Birth Abortion Ban Act furthers any legitimate governmental interest is, quite simply, irrational. The Court's defense of the statute provides no saving explanation. In candor, the Act, and the Court's defense of it, cannot be understood as anything other than an effort to chip away at a right declared again and again by this Court—and with increasing comprehension of its centrality to women's lives.[ ] When "a statute burdens constitutional rights and all that can be said on its behalf is that it is the vehicle that legislators have chosen for expressing their hostility to those rights, the burden is undue."[ ]

For the reasons stated, I dissent from the Court's disposition and would affirm the judgments before us for review.

## NOTES AND QUESTIONS

1. *The Undue Burden Test.* The Court "assume[s]" for purposes of the opinion that a regulation would constitute an "undue burden" if the regulation's purpose or effect is to place a substantial obstacle in the path of a woman seeking an abortion of a nonviable fetus. How is a court expected to divine the purpose of challenged legislation? How does a court determine whether a challenged statute in "effect" creates a substantial obstacle? Is an obstacle substantial because it imposes a serious limitation on any identifiable woman, because it affects a large number of women, or because it affects a large percentage of the cases in which women would seek abortions?

2. *Health Justifications.* One justification offered by Justice Kennedy was based on the government's interest in protecting women from a lack of information about the specific nature of the abortion procedure because of the emotional harm that could result from finding out the details after the fact. Yet, Justice Kennedy admits "there is no reliable data to measure this phenomenon." If claims about potential health risks of a procedure are being asserted to ban that procedure, should those risks have to be substantiated with scientific or medical evidence in court? Or should it be enough that such harm is "self-evident" to the Court?

3. *The Health Exception.* Consider that, unlike the abortion regulations challenged in *Casey*, the Partial Birth Abortion Ban Act did not contain an exception for the preservation of the mother's health. (It only provided an exception for life-threatening emergencies). *Casey's* decision depended, in part, on its finding that "the abortion regulation would not in any way pose a significant threat to the life *or health* of a woman," and this was part of the reason why the partial-birth abortion ban in *Stenberg* had been struck down. Why was the absence of a "health" exception not fatal in *Carhart*? The Court notes that "there is uncertainty over whether the barred procedure is ever necessary to preserve a woman's health." Does this "medical uncertainty" weigh in favor of upholding the ban or striking it down?

4. *Stenberg vs. Carhart.* The Court distinguished its earlier decision striking down Nebraska's partial birth abortion ban in *Stenberg*. What were the relevant differences between the partial birth abortion ban that was rejected in *Stenberg* and the one accepted in *Carhart*? Was it the legislative findings that saved the federal statute? The more precise definition of the banned procedure? The scienter requirement? The fact that D & E abortions are still permitted? Some combination of these? Or was the change in the Court's approach due perhaps to the replacement of Justice O'Connor by Justice Alito?

5. *Other Criminal Bans on Abortion.* Consider the ethical and legal questions raised by other state abortion bans based on *type of procedure*, *timing of procedure*, or *reason for the procedure*—laws which are currently being or

have been challenged in court. For example, some states some have gone further than the federal partial birth abortion ban, by not allowing an exception for life endangerment, and some have banned D & E (the most commonly used form of abortion) in the second trimester, with limited exceptions. Seventeen states have enacted pre-viability bans on abortions at 20 weeks (with limited exceptions, such as life endangerment). This is often justified on the grounds the fetus may be able to feel pain at this point, despite contrary scientific evidence that the neural anatomy of a fetus is not sufficiently developed to be able to perceive pain until at least after 24 weeks of gestation. See I. Glenn Cohen & Sadath Sayeed, Fetal Pain, Abortion, Viability, and the Constitution, 39 J.L. Med. & Ethics 235 (2011). Eight states have enacted abortion pre-viability bans for reasons of sex selection, and a few states have outlawed abortion where the fetus may have a genetic anomaly, including a recently enacted Ohio law banning abortion after prenatal tests reveal Down syndrome in a fetus. Such laws have been challenged in court. See, e.g., Cleveland v. Himes, 2018 WL 1315019, ___ F.Supp.3d ___ (S.D. Ohio Mar. 14, 2018), appeal docketed, No. 18–3329 (6th Cir. Apr. 12, 2018) (issuing a preliminary injunction against the Ohio law on due process grounds); Planned Parenthood of Ind. & Ky., Inc. v. Comm'r Ind. State Dep't of Health, 265 F.Supp.3d 859 (S.D. Ind. 2017), appeal docketed, No. 17–3163 (7th Cir. Oct. 19, 2017) (finding unconstitutional a law that banned pre-viability abortions where the reason for the abortion was based on some characteristic of the fetus, such as sex, race, or Down syndrome diagnosis).

6.    *Regulating the Abortion Procedure. Carhart* invigorated attempts to target abortion providers for stricter regulations, effectively making access more difficult. Yet, important questions remained about exactly what kind of regulation or degree of impact would constitute an undue burden under *Casey*. After *Carhart*, restrictions targeting abortion providers were easily upheld in the lower courts; but when two such restrictions reached the Supreme Court in *Whole Woman's Health* (below), it seemed that, once again, the trajectory of abortion jurisprudence may have shifted.

## C.  AN UNDUE BURDEN TEST WITH TEETH?

### WHOLE WOMAN'S HEALTH V. HELLERSTEDT
Supreme Court of the United States, 2016.
136 S.Ct. 2292, 195 L.Ed.2d 665.

JUSTICE BREYER delivered the opinion of the Court.

In *Planned Parenthood of Southeastern Pa. v. Casey* [ ] a plurality of the Court concluded that there "exists" an "undue burden" on a woman's right to decide to have an abortion, and consequently a provision of law is constitutionally invalid, if the *"purpose or effect"* of the provision *"is to place a substantial obstacle* in the path of a woman seeking an abortion before the fetus attains viability." [ ] The plurality added that "[u]nnecessary health regulations that have the purpose or effect of presenting a substantial obstacle to a woman seeking an abortion impose an undue burden on the right." [ ]

We must here decide whether two provisions of Texas' House Bill 2 violate the Federal Constitution as interpreted in *Casey*. The first provision, which we shall call the *"admitting-privileges requirement,"* says that

"[a] physician performing or inducing an abortion . . . must, on the date the abortion is performed or induced, have active admitting privileges at a hospital that . . . is located not further than 30 miles from the location at which the abortion is performed or induced." [ ]

This provision amended Texas law that had previously required an abortion facility to maintain a written protocol "for managing medical emergencies and the transfer of patients requiring further emergency care to a hospital." [ ]

The second provision, which we shall call the *"surgical-center requirement,"* says that

"the minimum standards for an abortion facility must be equivalent to the minimum standards adopted under [the Texas Health and Safety Code section] for ambulatory surgical centers." [ ]

We conclude that neither of these provisions confers medical benefits sufficient to justify the burdens upon access that each imposes. Each places a substantial obstacle in the path of women seeking a previability abortion, each constitutes an undue burden on abortion access, [ ], and each violates the Federal Constitution. [ ]

I

A

In July 2013, the Texas Legislature enacted House Bill 2 [which is the subject of this litigation. A part of the Act, the admitting-privileges provision, was challenged on its face in *Planned Parenthood of Greater Tex. Surgical Health Servs. v. Abbott*. Ultimately, the Fifth Circuit upheld that provision, and no review was sought in the Supreme Court.]

* * *

B

[One] week after the Fifth Circuit's decision, petitioners, a group of abortion providers (many of whom were plaintiffs in the previous lawsuit), filed the present lawsuit in Federal District Court. They sought an injunction preventing enforcement of the admitting-privileges provision as applied to physicians at two abortion facilities * * * . They also sought an injunction prohibiting enforcement of the surgical-center provision anywhere in Texas. They claimed that the admitting-privileges provision and the surgical-center provision violated the Constitution's Fourteenth Amendment, as interpreted in *Casey*.

The District Court subsequently received stipulations from the parties and depositions from the parties' experts. The court conducted a 4-day bench trial. It heard, among other testimony, the opinions from expert witnesses for both sides. On the basis of the stipulations, depositions, and testimony, that court reached the following conclusions:

1.   Of Texas' population of more than 25 million people, "approximately 5.4 million" are "women" of "reproductive age," living within a geographical area of "nearly 280,000 square miles." [ ]

2.   "In recent years, the number of abortions reported in Texas has stayed fairly consistent at approximately 15–16% of the reported pregnancy rate, for a total number of approximately 60,000–72,000 legal abortions performed annually." [ ]

3.   Prior to the enactment of H.B. 2, there were more than 40 licensed abortion facilities in Texas, which "number dropped by almost half leading up to and in the wake of enforcement of the admitting-privileges requirement that went into effect in late-October 2013." [ ]

4.   If the surgical-center provision were allowed to take effect, the number of abortion facilities, after September 1, 2014, would be reduced further, so that "only seven facilities and a potential eighth will exist in Texas." [ ]

\* \* \*

7.   The suggestion "that these seven or eight providers could meet the demand of the entire state stretches credulity." [ ]

8.   \* \* \* After September 2014, should the surgical-center requirement go into effect, the number of women of reproductive age living significant distances from an abortion provider will increase [substantially]. [ ]

9.   The "two requirements erect a particularly high barrier for poor, rural, or disadvantaged women." [ ]

10. "The great weight of evidence demonstrates that, before the act's passage, abortion in Texas was extremely safe with particularly low rates of serious complications and virtually no deaths occurring on account of the procedure." [ ]

11. "Abortion, as regulated by the State before the enactment of House Bill 2, has been shown to be much safer, in terms of minor and serious complications, than many common medical procedures not subject to such intense regulation and scrutiny." [ ].

12. "Additionally, risks are not appreciably lowered for patients who undergo abortions at ambulatory surgical centers as compared to nonsurgical-center facilities." [ ].

13. "[W]omen will not obtain better care or experience more frequent positive outcomes at an ambulatory surgical center as compared to a previously licensed facility." [ ]

\* \* \*

On the basis of these and other related findings, the District Court determined that the surgical-center requirement "imposes an undue burden on the right of women throughout Texas to seek a previability abortion," and that the "admitting-privileges requirement . . . in conjunction with the ambulatory-surgical-center requirement, imposes an undue burden on the right of women \* \* \* to seek a previability abortion." [ ] The District Court concluded that the "two provisions" would cause "the closing of almost all abortion clinics in Texas that were operating legally in the fall of 2013," and thereby create a constitutionally "impermissible obstacle as applied to all women seeking a previability abortion" by "restricting access to previously available legal facilities." [ ] [T]he court enjoined the enforcement of the two provisions.

C

\* \* \*

[T]he Court of Appeals reversed the District Court on the merits. With minor exceptions, it found both provisions constitutional and allowed them to take effect. [ ]

\* \* \*

II

[In this part of the Opinion, the Court explains why the plaintiffs' claims are not barred by the doctrine of *res judicata*, also known as claims preclusion.]

\* \* \*

III

*Undue Burden—Legal Standard*

We begin with the standard, as described in *Casey*. We recognize that the "State has a legitimate interest in seeing to it that abortion, like any other medical procedure, is performed under circumstances that insure maximum safety for the patient." *Roe v. Wade* [ ]. But, we added, "a statute which, while furthering [a] valid state interest, has the effect of placing a substantial obstacle in the path of a woman's choice cannot be considered a permissible means of serving its legitimate ends." *Casey* [ ]. Moreover, "[u]nnecessary health regulations that have the purpose or effect of presenting a substantial obstacle to a woman seeking an abortion impose an undue burden on the right." [ ]

The Court of Appeals wrote that a state law is "constitutional if: (1) it does not have the purpose or effect of placing a substantial obstacle in the path of a woman seeking an abortion of a nonviable fetus; and (2) it is reasonably related to (or designed to further) a legitimate state interest." [ ] The Court of Appeals went on to hold that "the district court erred by substituting its own judgment for that of the legislature" when it conducted its "undue burden inquiry," in part because "medical uncertainty underlying a statute is for resolution by legislatures, not the courts." [ ]

The Court of Appeals' articulation of the relevant standard is incorrect. The first part of the Court of Appeals' test may be read to imply that a district court should not consider the existence or nonexistence of medical benefits when considering whether a regulation of abortion constitutes an undue burden. The rule announced in *Casey,* however, requires that courts consider the burdens a law imposes on abortion access together with the benefits those laws confer. [ ] And the second part of the test is wrong to equate the judicial review applicable to the regulation of a constitutionally protected personal liberty with the less strict review applicable where, for example, economic legislation is at issue. [ ] The Court of Appeals' approach simply does not match the standard that this Court laid out in *Casey,* which asks courts to consider whether any burden imposed on abortion access is "undue."

The statement that legislatures, and not courts, must resolve questions of medical uncertainty is also inconsistent with this Court's case law. Instead, the Court, when determining the constitutionality of laws regulating abortion procedures, has placed considerable weight upon evidence and argument presented in judicial proceedings. In *Casey,* for example, we relied heavily on the District Court's factual findings and the research-based submissions of *amici* in declaring a portion of the law at issue unconstitutional. [ ] (discussing evidence related to the prevalence of spousal abuse in determining that a spousal notification provision erected an undue burden to abortion access). And, in *Gonzales* the Court, while pointing out that we must review legislative "factfinding under a deferential standard," added that we must not "place dispositive weight" on those "findings." [ ] *Gonzales* went on to point out that the "*Court retains an independent constitutional duty to review factual findings where constitutional rights are at stake.*" [ ] (emphasis added). Although there we upheld a statute regulating abortion, we did not do so solely on the basis of legislative findings explicitly set forth in the statute, noting that "evidence presented in the District Courts contradicts" some of the legislative findings. [ ] In these circumstances, we said, "[u]ncritical deference to Congress' factual findings . . . is inappropriate." [ ]

Unlike in *Gonzales,* the relevant statute here does not set forth any legislative findings. Rather, one is left to infer that the legislature sought to further a constitutionally acceptable objective (namely, protecting women's health). [ ] For a district court to give significant weight to evidence in the judicial record in these circumstances is consistent with this Court's case law. As we shall describe, the District Court did so here. It did not simply substitute its own judgment for that of the legislature. It considered the evidence in the record—including expert evidence, presented in stipulations, depositions, and testimony. It then weighed the asserted benefits against the burdens. We hold that, in so doing, the District Court applied the correct legal standard.

IV

## *Undue Burden—Admitting-Privileges Requirement*

Turning to the lower courts' evaluation of the evidence, we first consider the admitting-privileges requirement. Before the enactment of H.B. 2, doctors who provided abortions were required to "have admitting privileges *or* have a working arrangement with a physician(s) who has admitting privileges at a local hospital in order to ensure the necessary back up for medical complications." [ ] The new law changed this requirement by requiring that a "physician performing or inducing an abortion . . . must, on the date the abortion is performed or induced, have active admitting privileges at a hospital that . . . is located not further than 30 miles from the location at which the abortion is performed or induced." [ ] The District Court held that the legislative change imposed an "undue burden" on a woman's right to have an abortion. We conclude that there is adequate legal and factual support for the District Court's conclusion.

The purpose of the admitting-privileges requirement is to help ensure that women have easy access to a hospital should complications arise during an abortion procedure. [ ] But the District Court found that it brought about no such health-related benefit. The court found that "[t]he great weight of evidence demonstrates that, before the act's passage, abortion in Texas was extremely safe with particularly low rates of serious complications and virtually no deaths occurring on account of the procedure." [ ]. Thus, there was no significant health-related problem that the new law helped to cure.

[The Court then summarized the evidence that drew the trial court to that conclusion.]

* * *

At the same time, the record evidence indicates that the admitting-privileges requirement places a "substantial obstacle in the path of a woman's choice." [ ] [The Court pointed out that the evidence showed that many clinics closed when the admitting-privileges requirement went into effect.]

* * *

[There are many] common prerequisites to obtaining admitting privileges that have nothing to do with ability to perform medical procedures. See Brief for Medical Staff Professionals as *Amici Curiae* [ ] (listing, for example, requirements that an applicant has treated a high number of patients in the hospital setting in the past year, clinical data requirements, residency requirements, and other discretionary factors); see also Brief for American College of Obstetricians and Gynecologists [ ] ("[S]ome academic hospitals will only allow medical staff membership for clinicians who also . . . accept faculty appointments"). Again, returning to the District Court record, we note that Dr. Lynn of the McAllen clinic, a veteran obstetrics and gynecology doctor who estimates that he has delivered over 15,000 babies in his 38 years in practice was unable to get admitting privileges at any of the seven hospitals within 30 miles of his clinic. [ ] He was refused admitting privileges at a nearby hospital for reasons, as the hospital wrote, "not based on clinical competence considerations." [ ] The admitting-privileges requirement does not serve any relevant credentialing function.

In our view, the record contains sufficient evidence that the admitting-privileges requirement led to the closure of half of Texas' clinics, or thereabouts. Those closures meant fewer doctors, longer waiting times, and increased crowding. Record evidence also supports the finding that after the admitting-privileges provision went into effect, the "number of women of reproductive age living in a county . . . more than 150 miles from a provider increased from approximately 86,000 to 400,000 . . . and the number of women living in a county more than 200 miles from a provider from approximately 10,000 to 290,000." [ ]. We recognize that increased driving distances do not always constitute an "undue burden." [ ] But here, those increases are but one additional burden, which, when taken together with others that the closings brought about, and when viewed in light of the virtual absence of any health benefit, lead us to conclude that the record adequately supports the District Court's "undue burden" conclusion. [ ]

\* \* \*

[T]he dissent suggests that one benefit of H.B. 2's requirements would be that they might "force unsafe facilities to shut down." [ ] To support that assertion, the dissent points to the Kermit Gosnell scandal. Gosnell, a physician in Pennsylvania, was convicted of first-degree murder and manslaughter [as a result of the operation of an abortion clinic]. \* \* \* Gosnell's behavior was terribly wrong. But there is no reason to believe that an extra layer of regulation would have affected that behavior. Determined wrongdoers, already ignoring existing statutes and safety measures, are unlikely to be convinced to adopt safe practices by a new overlay of regulations. \* \* \* The record contains nothing to suggest that H.B. 2 would be more effective than pre-existing Texas law at deterring wrongdoers like Gosnell from criminal behavior.

V

*Undue Burden—Surgical-Center Requirement*

The second challenged provision of Texas' new law sets forth the surgical-center requirement. Prior to enactment of the new requirement, Texas law required abortion facilities to meet a host of health and safety requirements [which are listed in the opinion by the court]. * * *

H.B. 2 added the requirement that an "abortion facility" meet the "minimum standards . . . for ambulatory surgical centers" under Texas law. [ ] The surgical-center regulations include, among other things, detailed specifications relating to the size of the nursing staff, building dimensions, and other building requirements. [The Court went on to list the many requirements imposed on surgical-centers.]

There is considerable evidence in the record supporting the District Court's findings indicating that the statutory provision requiring all abortion facilities to meet all surgical-center standards does not benefit patients and is not necessary. The District Court found that "risks are not appreciably lowered for patients who undergo abortions at ambulatory surgical centers as compared to nonsurgical-center facilities." [ ] The court added that women "will not obtain better care or experience more frequent positive outcomes at an ambulatory surgical center as compared to a previously licensed facility." [ ] And these findings are well supported.

The record makes clear that the surgical-center requirement provides no benefit when complications arise in the context of an abortion produced through medication. That is because, in such a case, complications would almost always arise only after the patient has left the facility. [ ] The record also contains evidence indicating that abortions taking place in an abortion facility are safe—indeed, safer than numerous procedures that take place outside hospitals and to which Texas does not apply its surgical-center requirements. * * * Nationwide, childbirth is 14 times more likely than abortion to result in death, [ ] but Texas law allows a midwife to oversee childbirth in the patient's own home. Colonoscopy, a procedure that typically takes place outside a hospital (or surgical center) setting, has a mortality rate 10 times higher than an abortion. [T]he mortality rate for liposuction, another outpatient procedure, is 28 times higher than the mortality rate for abortion. Medical treatment after an incomplete miscarriage often involves a procedure identical to that involved in a nonmedical abortion, but it often takes place outside a hospital or surgical center. And Texas partly or wholly grandfathers (or waives in whole or in part the surgical-center requirement for) about two-thirds of the facilities to which the surgical-center standards apply. But it neither grandfathers nor provides waivers for any of the facilities that perform abortions. [ ] These facts indicate that the surgical-center provision imposes "a requirement that simply is not based on differences" between abortion and other surgical procedures "that are reasonably related to" preserving women's health, the asserted "purpos[e] of the Act in which it is found." [ ]

* * *

At the same time, the record provides adequate evidentiary support for the District Court's conclusion that the surgical-center requirement places a substantial obstacle in the path of women seeking an abortion. The parties stipulated that the requirement would further reduce the number of abortion facilities available to seven or eight facilities * * * . In the District Court's view, the proposition that these "seven or eight providers could meet the demand of the entire State stretches credulity." [ ] We take this statement as a finding that these few facilities could not "meet" that "demand."

The Court of Appeals held that this finding was "clearly erroneous." * * * [W]e hold that the record provides adequate support for the District Court's finding.

* * *

More fundamentally, in the face of no threat to women's health, Texas seeks to force women to travel long distances to get abortions in crammed-to-capacity superfacilities. Patients seeking these services are less likely to get the kind of individualized attention, serious conversation, and emotional support that doctors at less taxed facilities may have offered. Healthcare facilities and medical professionals are not fungible commodities. Surgical centers attempting to accommodate sudden, vastly increased demand, [ ] may find that quality of care declines. Another commonsense inference that the District Court made is that these effects would be harmful to, not supportive of, women's health. [ ].

* * *

We agree with the District Court that the surgical-center requirement, like the admitting-privileges requirement, provides few, if any, health benefits for women, poses a substantial obstacle to women seeking abortions, and constitutes an "undue burden" on their constitutional right to do so.

VI

[In this section the Court explains why the severability clause is of no assistance to Texas in this case.]

JUSTICE GINSBURG, concurring.

The Texas law called H.B. 2 inevitably will reduce the number of clinics and doctors allowed to provide abortion services. Texas argues that H.B. 2's restrictions are constitutional because they protect the health of women who experience complications from abortions. In truth, "complications from an abortion are both rare and rarely dangerous." [ ] Many medical procedures, including childbirth, are far more dangerous to patients, yet are not subject to ambulatory-surgical-center or hospital admitting-privileges requirements. [ ] Given those realities, it is beyond rational belief that H.B. 2 could genuinely protect the health of women, and certain that the law "would simply make it more difficult for them to obtain abortions." [ ] When a State severely limits access to safe and legal procedures, women in desperate circumstances may resort to unlicensed rogue practitioners, *faute de mieux,* at great risk to their health and safety. [ ] So long as this Court adheres to *Roe v. Wade* [ ], and *Planned Parenthood of Southeastern Pa. v. Casey,* [ ] Targeted Regulation of Abortion Providers laws like H.B. 2 that "do little or nothing for health, but rather strew impediments to abortion," [ ] cannot survive judicial inspection.

JUSTICE THOMAS, dissenting.

Today the Court strikes down two state statutory provisions in all of their applications, at the behest of abortion clinics and doctors. That decision exemplifies the Court's troubling tendency "to bend the rules when any effort to limit abortion, or even to speak in opposition to abortion, is at issue." [ ] As JUSTICE ALITO observes, [ ] today's decision creates an abortion exception to ordinary rules of *res judicata*, ignores compelling evidence that Texas' law imposes no unconstitutional burden, and disregards basic principles of the severability doctrine. I write separately to emphasize how today's decision perpetuates the Court's habit of applying different rules to different constitutional rights—especially the putative right to abortion.

To begin, the very existence of this suit is a jurisprudential oddity. Ordinarily, plaintiffs cannot file suits to vindicate the constitutional rights of others. But the Court employs a different approach to rights that it favors. So in this case and many others, the Court has erroneously allowed doctors and clinics to vicariously vindicate the putative constitutional right of women seeking abortions.

This case also underscores the Court's increasingly common practice of invoking a given level of scrutiny—here, the abortion-specific undue burden standard—while applying a different standard of review entirely. Whatever scrutiny the majority applies to Texas' law, it bears little resemblance to the undue-burden test the Court articulated in *Planned Parenthood of Southeastern Pa. v. Casey,* [ ] and its successors. Instead, the majority eviscerates important features of that test to return to a regime like the one that *Casey* repudiated.

Ultimately, this case shows why the Court never should have bent the rules for favored rights in the first place. Our law is now so riddled with special exceptions for special rights that our decisions deliver neither predictability nor the promise of a judiciary bound by the rule of law.

## I

This suit is possible only because the Court has allowed abortion clinics and physicians to invoke a putative constitutional right that does not belong to them—a woman's right to abortion. [Justice Thomas then explains why the medical plaintiffs in this case should not have standing to raise these claims, which really belong to women who seek abortions].

\* \* \*

There should be no surer sign that our jurisprudence has gone off the rails than this: After creating a constitutional right to abortion because it "involve[s] the most intimate and personal choices a person may make in a lifetime, choices central to personal dignity and autonomy," [ ] the Court has created special rules that cede its enforcement to others.

## II

Today's opinion also reimagines the undue-burden standard used to assess the constitutionality of abortion restrictions. Nearly 25 years ago, in *Planned Parenthood of Southeastern Pa. v. Casey* [ ] a plurality of this Court invented the "undue burden" standard as a special test for gauging the permissibility of abortion restrictions. *Casey* held that a law is unconstitutional if it imposes an "undue burden" on a woman's ability to choose to have an abortion, meaning that it "has the purpose or effect of placing a substantial obstacle in the path of a woman seeking an abortion of a nonviable fetus." [ ] *Casey* thus instructed courts to look to whether a law substantially impedes women's access to abortion, and whether it is reasonably related to legitimate state interests. As the Court explained, "[w]here it has a rational basis to act, and it does not impose an undue burden, the State may use its regulatory power" to regulate aspects of abortion procedures, "all in furtherance of its legitimate interests in regulating the medical profession in order to promote respect for life, including life of the unborn." [ ]

I remain fundamentally opposed to the Court's abortion jurisprudence. [ ] Even taking *Casey* as the baseline, however, the majority radically rewrites the undue-burden test in three ways. First, today's decision requires courts to "consider the burdens a law imposes on abortion access together with the benefits those laws confer." [ ] Second, today's opinion tells the courts that, when the law's justifications are medically uncertain, they need not defer to the legislature, and must instead assess medical justifications for abortion restrictions by scrutinizing the record themselves. [ ] Finally, even if a law imposes no "substantial obstacle" to women's access to abortions, the law now must have more than a "reasonabl[e] relat[ion] to . . . a legitimate state interest." [ ] (internal quotation marks omitted). These precepts are nowhere to be found in *Casey* or its successors, and transform the undue-burden test to something much more akin to strict scrutiny.

First, the majority's free-form balancing test is contrary to *Casey*. * * * Contrary to the majority's statements [ ] *Casey* did not balance the benefits and burdens of Pennsylvania's spousal and parental notification provisions, either. Pennsylvania's spousal notification requirement, the plurality said, imposed an undue burden because findings established that the requirement would "likely . . . prevent a significant number of women from obtaining an abortion"—not because these burdens outweighed its benefits. [ ]. And *Casey* summarily upheld parental notification provisions because even pre-*Casey* decisions had done so. [ ]

* * *

Second, by rejecting the notion that "legislatures, and not courts, must resolve questions of medical uncertainty," [ ] the majority discards another core element of the *Casey* framework. Before today, this Court had "given state and federal legislatures wide discretion to pass legislation in areas where there is medical and scientific uncertainty." * * *

Today, however, the majority refuses to leave disputed medical science to the legislature because past cases "placed considerable weight upon the evidence and argument presented in judicial proceedings." * * *

Finally, the majority overrules another central aspect of *Casey* by requiring laws to have more than a rational basis even if they do not substantially impede access to abortion. [ ] "Where [the State] *has a rational basis to act* and it does not impose an undue burden," this Court previously held, "the State may use its regulatory power" to impose regulations "in furtherance of its legitimate interests in regulating the medical profession in order to promote respect for life, including life of the unborn." [ ] No longer. Though the majority declines to say how substantial a State's interest must be, [ ] one thing is clear: The State's burden has been ratcheted to a level that has not applied for a quarter century.

Today's opinion does resemble *Casey* in one respect: After disregarding significant aspects of the Court's prior jurisprudence, the majority applies the undue-burden standard in a way that will surely mystify lower courts for years to come. As in *Casey,* today's opinion "simply . . . highlight[s] certain facts in the record that apparently strike the . . . Justices as particularly significant in establishing (or refuting) the existence of an undue burden." [ ] As in *Casey,* "the opinion then simply announces that the provision either does or does not impose a 'substantial obstacle' or an 'undue burden.'" [ ] And still "[w]e do not know whether the same conclusions could have been reached on a different record, or in what respects the record would have had to differ before an opposite conclusion would have been appropriate. [ ] All we know is that an undue burden now has little to do with whether the law, in a "real sense, deprive[s] women of the ultimate decision," [ ] and more to do with the loss of "individualized attention, serious conversation, and emotional support," [ ].

The majority's undue-burden test looks far less like our post-*Casey* precedents and far more like the strict-scrutiny standard that *Casey* rejected, under which only the most compelling rationales justified restrictions on abortion. [ ] One searches the majority opinion in vain for any acknowledgment of the "premise central" to *Casey's* rejection of strict scrutiny: "that the government has a legitimate and substantial interest in preserving and promoting fetal life" from conception, not just in regulating medical procedures. * * * Moreover, by second-guessing medical evidence and making its own assessments of "quality of care" issues, [ ] the majority reappoints this Court as "the country's *ex officio* medical board with powers to disapprove medical and operative practices and standards throughout the United States." [ ] And the majority seriously burdens States, which must guess at how much more compelling their interests must be to pass muster and what "commonsense inferences" of an undue burden this Court will identify next.

### III

The majority's furtive reconfiguration of the standard of scrutiny applicable to abortion restrictions also points to a deeper problem. The undue-burden standard is just one variant of the Court's tiers-of-scrutiny approach to constitutional adjudication. And the label the Court affixes to its level of scrutiny in assessing whether the government can restrict a given right—be it "rational basis," intermediate, strict, or something else— is increasingly a meaningless formalism. As the Court applies whatever standard it likes to any given case, nothing but empty words separates our constitutional decisions from judicial fiat.

* * *

The Court should abandon the pretense that anything other than policy preferences underlies its balancing of constitutional rights and interests in any given case.

### IV

It is tempting to identify the Court's invention of a constitutional right to abortion in *Roe v. Wade* [ ] as the tipping point that transformed third-party standing doctrine and the tiers of scrutiny into an unworkable morass of special exceptions and arbitrary applications. But those roots run deeper, to the very notion that some constitutional rights demand preferential treatment.

* * *

[Over the past 80 years, the] Court has simultaneously transformed judicially created rights like the right to abortion into preferred constitutional rights, while disfavoring many of the rights actually enumerated in the Constitution. But our Constitution renounces the notion that some constitutional rights are more equal than others. A plaintiff either possesses the constitutional right he is asserting, or not—and if not, the judiciary has no business creating ad hoc exceptions so that others can assert rights that seem especially important to vindicate. A law either infringes a constitutional right, or not; there is no room for the judiciary to invent tolerable degrees of encroachment. Unless the Court abides by one set of rules to adjudicate constitutional rights, it will continue reducing constitutional law to policy-driven value judgments until the last shreds of its legitimacy disappear.

\* \* \*

I respectfully dissent.

JUSTICE ALITO, with whom THE CHIEF JUSTICE and JUSTICE THOMAS join, dissenting.

The constitutionality of laws regulating abortion is one of the most controversial issues in American law, but this case does not require us to delve into that contentious dispute. Instead, the dispositive issue here concerns a workaday question that can arise in any case no matter the subject, namely, whether the present case is barred by res judicata. As a court of law, we have an obligation to apply such rules in a neutral fashion in all cases, regardless of the subject of the suit. If anything, when a case involves a controversial issue, we should be especially careful to be scrupulously neutral in applying such rules.

The Court has not done so here. On the contrary, determined to strike down two provisions of a new Texas abortion statute in all of their applications, the Court simply disregards basic rules that apply in all other cases.

[In Parts I and II of his opinion, Justice Alito explains why the plaintiffs' challenges to the admitting-privileges requirements (Part I) and the surgical-center requirements (Part II) are barred by the doctrine of claim preclusion.]

### III

Even if res judicata did not bar either facial claim, a sweeping, statewide injunction against the enforcement of the admitting privileges and ASC [i.e., surgical-center] requirements would still be unjustified. Petitioners in this case are abortion clinics and physicians who perform abortions. If they were simply asserting a constitutional right to conduct a business or to practice a profession without unnecessary state regulation, they would have little chance of success. [ ] Under our abortion cases, however, they are permitted to rely on the right of the abortion patients they serve. [ ]

Thus, what matters for present purposes is not the effect of the H.B. 2 provisions on petitioners but the effect on their patients. Under our cases, petitioners must show that the admitting privileges and ASC requirements impose an "undue burden" on women seeking abortions. *Gonzales v. Carhart* [ ]. And in order to obtain the sweeping relief they seek—facial invalidation of those provisions—they must show, at a minimum, that these provisions have an unconstitutional impact on at least a "large fraction" of Texas women of reproductive age. [ ] Such a situation could result if the clinics able to comply with the new requirements either lacked the requisite overall capacity or were located too far away to serve a "large fraction" of the women in question.

Petitioners did not make that showing. Instead of offering direct evidence, they relied on two crude inferences. First, they pointed to the number of abortion clinics that closed after the enactment of H.B. 2, and asked that it be inferred that all these closures resulted from the two challenged provisions. [ ] They made little effort to show why particular clinics closed. Second, they pointed to the number of abortions performed annually at ASCs before H.B. 2 took effect and, because this figure is well below the total number of abortions performed each year in the State, they asked that it be inferred that ASC-compliant clinics could not meet the demands of women in the State. [ ] Petitioners failed to provide any evidence of the actual capacity of the facilities that would be available to perform abortions in compliance with the new law—even though they provided this type of evidence in their first case to the District Court at trial * * * .

IV

[In Part IV of his opinion, Justice Alito explains why even if the Court were right to hold that res judicata does not bar this suit and that H.B. 2 imposes an undue burden on abortion access, it is still wrong to conclude that the admitting privileges and surgical center provisions must be enjoined in their entirety. He finds that H.B. 2 has an extraordinarily broad severability clause that must be considered before enjoining any portion or application of the law.]

* * *

## NOTES AND QUESTIONS

1. *Balancing the Benefit and Burden.* Justice Breyer says the undue burden test requires a balancing of the burdens imposed on the woman seeking the abortion against the asserted benefits of the law (in this case, women's health). The Court found that the law yielded few, if any, health benefits, but did pose a substantial obstacle to women seeking abortions, so the balancing

was easy. What if there were credible evidence that a law provides a small, but demonstrable health benefit? The dissents argue that there is no real standard for balancing, and that such balancing merely opens the door for the injection each Justice's personal views on abortion rights. What standards, if any, does the Court offer to guide such balancing?

2. *The Role of Science.* Was the Texas legislature's fatal flaw its failure to make formal findings regarding the health benefits of H.B. 2 and include them in the text of the statute? If the legislature had done so, would the result have been different? Should it be? Recall the question after *Carhart*: How closely should courts analyze the medical or scientific basis for state assertions that a regulation is justified by maternal or fetal health? Does *Whole Women's Health* reflect the Court's willingness to scrutinize such justifications more closely than in *Carhart*?

3. *Licensing Requirements & Scope of Practice.* Courts have had little trouble with the requirement (now in almost 40 states) that only licensed physicians, not physicians' assistants or others, perform abortions, because the authority granted with professional licenses is a matter of state law. Such licensing requirements are seen as an uncontroversial way of protecting the pregnant woman, not imposing a burden on her decision to have an abortion. More recently, some states have expanded their scope of practice laws to allow non-physician certified or licensed health care professionals with the relevant specialized training to perform abortions in limited circumstances, and a growing number of professional organizations are calling for an expansion of the pool of clinicians able to perform abortions. Yet, significant regulatory and political barriers to doing this remain. See American Public Health Association, Policy Statement, Provision of Abortion Care by Advanced Practice Nurses and Physician Assistants (Nov. 1, 2011) (noting that physician-only laws do not acknowledge the roles and experience of NPs, CNMs, and PAs, whose scope of primary and specialty practice includes management of conditions and procedures significantly more complex than medication or aspiration abortion; also noting evidence that with appropriate education and training, NPs, CNMs, and PAs can competently provide all components of medication abortion care). See also Chapter 2.

4. *The Future of Abortion Jurisprudence.* The cases in this section have revealed the more significant twists and turns that abortion jurisprudence has taken since abortion was established as a privacy right in *Roe v. Wade*. Despite the qualifications and limits that have been fleshed out since then, the Court has repeatedly affirmed the "essential" holding that anchors judicial scrutiny of abortion laws to a fundamental right of procreation. But how secure is this right? *Whole Women's Health* was a 5–3 decision, with Justices Ginsburg, Sotomayor, Kagan, and Kennedy joining Justice Breyer's majority opinion. Chief Justice Roberts and Justices Thomas and Alito dissented. Justice Scalia passed away before the case was argued. His vacancy has since been filled by Justice Gorsuch, nominated by President Trump who promised as a candidate to nominate Supreme Court justices who would overturn *Roe v. Wade*. People on both sides of the abortion debate believe that one new vacancy on the Court

under the Trump administration could result in yet another, and even more dramatic, shift in abortion jurisprudence.

## NOTE: FEDERAL CONSCIENCE PROTECTIONS

Soon after *Roe v. Wade* the federal government enacted legislation known as the "Church Amendments" creating conscience protections for those objecting to providing abortion or sterilization. 42 U.S.C. § 300a–7. These Amendments apply to federal funds and grants provided pursuant to Population Research and Voluntary Family Planning Programs, and they make clear that such funds cannot be used to require individuals to perform or assist in abortions (or sterilizations), if contrary to the individual's religious or moral beliefs. Such funds also cannot be used to require entities to make their facilities available for the performance of abortions (or sterilizations), or to make personnel available for such procedures, if contrary to the moral or religious beliefs of the entity or personnel, respectively.

In 2004, Congress passed the Weldon Amendment, originally adopted as section 508(d) of the Labor-HHS Division of the 2005 Consolidated Appropriations Act, Public Law 108–447, 118 Stat. 2809, 3163 (Dec. 8, 2004), and readopted in each subsequent HHS appropriations act. The Weldon Amendment provides that "[n]one of the funds made available in this Act may be made available to a Federal agency or program, or to a state or local government, *if such agency, program, or government subjects any institutional or individual health care entity to discrimination on the basis that the health care entity does not provide, pay for, provide coverage of, or refer for abortions.*" The term "health care entity" is defined broadly to include health care professionals, hospitals and other health facilities, and health care organizations, such as health insurance plans. These statutory conscience protections remain in effect after the ACA, and the ACA extended conscience protection to providers participating in health plans offered through the exchange. The ACA language largely tracks the Weldon Amendment, prohibiting exchange plans from *discriminating against any individual health care provider or facility because of its unwillingness to provide, pay for, provide coverage of, or refer for abortions.*

When the Weldon Amendment was passed, legal challenges were brought based on concerns that it would conflict with other federal or state obligations to patients, putting funding recipients in a Catch 22: they feared that by obeying one law, they risked violating the other, and either way they risked losing funding. For example, in National Family Planning and Reproductive Health Assn. v. Gonzales, 468 F.3d 826 (D.C. Cir. 2006), the plaintiffs alleged a potential conflict between the Weldon Amendment, on the one hand, and plaintiffs' ethical and legal duties as family planning grant recipients under HHS regulations, on the other. HHS regulations required recipients to offer pregnant women the opportunity to be provided information and counseling regarding pregnancy termination. If a caregiver objected to providing this information, one way the plaintiff might respond would be to reassign that caregiver to another job; this would accommodate the worker's religious objections while ensuring patients get information that is legally and ethically required. In the lawsuit, the plaintiff expressed the concern that if the caregiver wanted to retain a pregnancy counseling job, such a reassignment may be viewed as "discrimination" under the Weldon Amendment. Without ruling on the merits, the court noted the absence of any indication that the federal government would view a reassignment or other attempts to navigate such a conflict as discrimination.

A California district court came to a similar conclusion in California v. U.S., 2008 WL 744840 (N.D. Cal. 2008). California officials claimed that the Weldon Amendment appeared to be in conflict with EMTALA, the federal law that obligates hospitals with emergency rooms to provide emergency care, as well as a state law that tried to balance provider conscience protections against duties to patients in emergency cases. California's state conscience law exempted medical personnel and facilities from participating in abortions if they objected on moral, ethical, or religious grounds, but it contained an exception for medical emergency situations and spontaneous abortions. In an unreported opinion, the court did not resolve the potential conflict. Rather, it held that California could not show an injury in fact (and thus did not have standing), because there was no clear indication from either the text of the Amendment or the federal regulator that California's emergency exception would be viewed as "discrimination" under the Weldon Amendment.

Although actual conflicts did not materialize in the above cases, HHS has proposed a rule that is renewing concerns about how federal regulators will interpret the Weldon Amendment and other statutory conscience protections going forward. See Protecting Statutory Conscience Rights in Health Care; Delegations of Authority, 83 Fed. Reg. 3880 (Jan. 26, 2018). The proposed rule expresses concern about prior underenforcement of conscience protections, notes that HHS is delegating authority to OCR to enforce these protections, and describes the tools that OCR will use to both educate the public about their rights and more actively monitor and enforce compliance among recipients. Id. See also, HHS Announces New Conscience and Religious Freedom Division, U.S. Dep't of Health & Human Svc's News Release (Jan. 18, 2018) (announcing the formation of this new division in the HHS Office for Civil Rights).

The rule also proposes definitions of terms not defined in the statute. One new definition in the proposed rule is for the term "discrimination." HHS defines discrimination broadly as including "to withhold, reduce, exclude, terminate, restrict, or otherwise make unavailable or deny any grant, contract, subcontract, . . . license, employment, title, or other similar instrument, position, or status." Id. Unfortunately, the proposed rule does not discuss the potential impact on patients when medical professionals refuse to perform certain procedures and refuse to refer patients to someone who can help them in emergency situations. This creates the same kind of uncertainty about how the federal government will view providers' attempts to balance these competing interests that led to earlier challenges to the Weldon Amendment.

The proposed rule also identifies certain state laws as possible violations of the Weldon Amendment, suggesting those states may be targets for potential enforcement. Most states already have laws allowing health care providers to refuse to provide abortions, and some are broader to include other services. But, as the cases above demonstrate, there is concern that limits on state conscience protections that attempt to balance refusal rights against patient needs may be vulnerable to legal challenge. The rule also suggests that longstanding state laws requiring insurers to cover abortion services might violate conscience provisions where the employers that ultimately purchase the insurance object to abortion coverage, even if the insurers themselves have not raised any objection to providing such coverage. Because this is a proposed rule, these definitions and interpretations may be refined before final regulations are promulgated. But this rule clearly signals the Trump administration's intention to interpret conscience statutes more broadly than in the past and to use its enforcement power against state laws intended to protect abortion access. If OCR enforcement actions are viewed as jeopardizing providers' ability to accommodate conscience objections while ensuring patient access, or as targeting the kind of regulation that has long been understood as within the legitimate scope of state power, litigation will certainly result. For a discussion of the ethical considerations that inform conscience protections generally, see Section IV.C. below.

# IV.   CONTRACEPTION

Contraception, generally, has not been as controversial as abortion, and as we will in this section, the jurisprudence developed in response to contraceptive access questions has taken a somewhat different journey. This section begins with the constitutional origins of the right to procreative choice. Next, it explores how, over time, access to contraception has tended to receive broader public and private support, and even legal protection, based on health, economic, and gender equity concerns. Conflicts do arise, however, typically based on objections to certain forms of contraception as interfering with the reproductive process after "life" has begun, and often linked to religious freedom claims. The final part of this section reviews this conflict.

## A.   CONTRACEPTIVE USE AS A PRIVACY RIGHT

Government regulation of reproduction, in particular abortion and contraception, has ebbed and flowed throughout history. In Geoffrey Stone's book, Sex and the Constitution, he explains that during the 18th and early 19th centuries, there were no laws prohibiting either contraception or abortion before quickening. Indeed, during this time, he found that contraception and abortion were increasingly recognized as legitimate and morally acceptable practices to maintain and improve a family's economic welfare, and that advertisements for birth control products were commonplace. Social leaders concerned about overpopulation leading to poverty and social decline viewed birth control as a tool for promoting individual and societal well-being.

The increasing medicalization of the reproductive process, and a growing focus on the link between illicit sexual activity and reproductive control within powerful religious movements, brought greater public attention to reproduction, and this eventually led to greater regulation. In 1873, Congress enacted the Comstock Act, which prohibited anyone from mailing "any drug or medicine, or any article whatever, for the prevention of conception" or from mailing any information about how to obtain these articles. Anthony Comstock, the author of this act, considered contraceptive material "obscene" because it was believed to encourage immoral thoughts and behavior. According to Stone, Comstock wanted to outlaw birth control "because the availability of contraceptives reduces the risk that individuals who engage in premarital sex, extramarital sex, or prostitution will suffer the consequences of venereal disease or unwanted pregnancy."

In the next couple of decades, most states enacted similar criminal bans and some, like Connecticut went even further, criminalizing the *use* of contraception, as well as the act of helping someone to violate the law. This ban was ultimately invalidated by the Supreme Court in the seminal case Griswold v. Connecticut, 381 U.S. 479, 85 S.Ct. 1678, 14 L.Ed.2d 510 (1965). In *Griswold,* an official of the Planned Parenthood League of Connecticut and a Yale physician were charged with aiding and abetting "the use of a drug, medicinal article, or instrument for the purpose of preventing conception," a crime under Connecticut law, by providing contraceptives to a married couple. The Supreme Court reversed their conviction. Justice Douglas, writing for the Court, concluded:

> The present case * * * concerns a relationship lying within the zone of privacy created by several fundamental constitutional guarantees. And it concerns a law which, in forbidding the *use* of contraceptives rather than regulating their manufacture or sale, seeks to achieve its goals by means having a maximum destructive impact upon that relationship. Such a law cannot stand in light of the familiar principle so often applied by this Court, that a "governmental purpose to control or prevent activities constitutionally subject to state regulation may not be achieved by means which sweep unnecessarily broadly and thereby invade the area of protected freedoms." Would we allow the police to search the sacred precincts of marital bedrooms for telltale signs of the use of contraceptives? The very idea is repulsive to the notions of privacy surrounding the marriage relationship.

> We deal with a right of privacy older than the Bill of Rights—older than our political parties, older than our school system. Marriage is a coming together for better or worse, hopefully enduring, and intimate

to the degree of being sacred. It is an association that promotes a way of life, not causes; a harmony in living, not political faith; a bilateral loyalty, not commercial or social projects. Yet it is an association for as noble a purpose as any involved in our prior decisions.

381 U.S. at 484, 85 S.Ct. at 1681.

*Griswold's* articulation of the privacy right focused so heavily on preventing intrusions into the marital relationship that questions remained about the application of this right to non-married people. This was understandable in light of the moral aims of such laws to prevent premarital or extramarital sex. For example, three justices who concurred in *Griswold*, explained that they found the law invalid because they rejected the state's assertion of a rational relationship between the ban and the state's interest in discouraging extra-marital relations. But the justices went on to note that the Court's holding "in no way interferes with a State's proper regulation of sexual promiscuity or misconduct."

The Court was confronted with this question in 1972, in Eisenstadt v. Baird, 405 U.S. 438, 453, 92 S.Ct. 1029, 1038, 31 L.Ed.2d 349 (1972). The Court determined that a law that allowed married people, but not unmarried people, to have access to contraceptives violated the equal protection clause of the Fourteenth Amendment because there could be no rational basis for distinguishing between married and unmarried people in permitting access to contraceptives. The Court suggested that "if the right of privacy means anything, it is the right of the individual, married or single, to be free from unwarranted government intrusion into matters so fundamentally affecting a person as a decision whether to bear a child." In Carey v. Population Services International, 431 U.S. 678, 97 S.Ct. 2010, 52 L.Ed.2d 675 (1977), the Court confirmed this right not only prohibits bans on the *use* of contraception, it prevents *any unjustified intrusion* by the State, such as a ban on the *distribution* or *sale* of contraceptives.

But what constitutes an unjustified intrusion? Relying on *Roe v. Wade*, the Court in *Carey v. Population Services International* made clear that recognizing a privacy right for procreative choice does not "automatically invalidate every state regulation in this area." It noted that some regulations may not infringe on individual choice at all, and "even a burdensome regulation may be validated by a sufficiently compelling state interest." The FDA has authority to approve and monitor the safety of drugs and devices, including prescription contraception. States also have broad power to regulate health and safety. But in *Carey*, the Court struck down a state law limiting the distribution of *nonprescription* contraceptives to licensed pharmacists, noting that the limit on these "nonhazardous" forms of contraception bore no relation to the State's interest in protecting health. A plurality opinion also invalidated a provision banning distribution of nonprescription contraceptives to those under 16.

## NOTE: THE DISTINCTION BETWEEN CONTRACEPTION AND ABORTION

Early objections to the use and distribution of contraceptives tended to focus on their use for pregnancy prevention and they often applied to any type of birth control. More recently, however, objections or restrictions tend to target certain forms of contraceptives because of how and when they work.

Contraception is designed to work by preventing fertilization. Some forms are taken or used prior to intercourse, while others may be taken after intercourse. Two examples of medication that work after intercourse but prior to fertilization are Plan B (levonorgestrel) and ella (ulipristal acetate), also commonly referred to as "morning after pills." They are designed to avoid the development of pregnancy by inhibiting ovulation or follicle rupture. Questions have been raised, however, about whether such pills may alter the uterine lining and, possibly, make it less likely that a fertilized ovum will enter the uterus or implant in the uterine wall, though recent studies do not seem to support this theory. For those who believe that life begins at fertilization, concern that morning after pills may prevent implantation of a fertilized ovum has fueled opposition to the pills.

Plan B became available in 2006 after a long and highly political history. In 1999 an FDA advisory panel had recommended that the drug be made available over the counter for all purchasers, but objections (arguably political and arguably medical) caused the FDA to delay approval until 2003 and then require a prescription for this medication. After a threat by some members of the Senate to withhold confirmation of a newly appointed FDA Commissioner in 2006, Plan B was finally made available over the counter for persons over 18, and that age was subsequently lowered to 17. See Gardiner Harris, Morning-After Pill: Politics and the F.D.A., N.Y. Times (Aug. 28, 2015). Plan B, a two-dose regimen, was eventually replaced by Plan B One Step, which as the name suggests, is a one-dose regimen. Plan B One Step is effective at reducing the risk of pregnancy if taken within 72 hours of intercourse, and its efficacy increases if taken within 24 hours. Approved in 2010 after its own long medical and political battle, ella works in largely the same way, but can be effective within five days of having sex.

Devices and medication that prevent fertilization or implantation are considered *contraceptives*, that is a form of pregnancy prevention, by the medical community. Mifepristone (RU-486), on the other hand, is classified as an *abortifacient* because it works after pregnancy. It is designed to disrupt implantation of the fertilized embryo and to change the uterus to become less hospitable to the fertilized ovum, eventually expelling it. Mifepristone is available only through prescription and dispensed only by specially licensed physicians authorized to administer it. For a general account of the pharmacology and medical use of these medications, see Robert Hatcher et al., Contraceptive Technology (20th rev. ed. 2011).

The generally accepted medical definitions used to distinguish contraceptives from abortifacients may not be accepted by those who believe that life begins at fertilization. People who hold this belief may have no objections to contraception that prevents fertilization; but they view medications or devices that work after fertilization as terminating life and thus would characterize them as abortifacients. This definitional disagreement can be significant in a number of contexts. As described in this Note, it can fuel political opposition to government action that would facilitate access to certain drugs. But it may also be relevant to the question of how far government can go in requiring individuals or entities to provide contraception as part of health care, a question we revisit in Section C below.

## B.  ACCESS TO FUNDING FOR CONTRACEPTION

As noted in Section III, the Supreme Court has made clear that a constitutional right to have one's procreative choices protected from unwarranted government intrusion does not create an entitlement to government funding or subsidization of those services. Nonetheless, other legal and policy avenues have facilitated access to funding for contraception.

### ERICKSON V. THE BARTELL DRUG COMPANY
United States District Court, Washington, 2001.
141 F.Supp.2d 1266.

The parties' cross-motions for summary judgment in this case raise an issue of first impression in the federal courts whether the selective exclusion of prescription contraceptives from defendant's generally comprehensive prescription plan constitutes discrimination on the basis of sex. In particular, plaintiffs assert that Bartell's decision not to cover prescription contraceptives such as birth control pills, Norplant, Depo-Provera, intra-uterine devices, and diaphragms under its Prescription Benefit Plan for non-union employees violates Title VII, 42 U.S.C. § 2000e *et seq.,* as amended by the Pregnancy Discrimination Act, 42 U.S.C. § 2000e(k).

### A.  APPLICATION OF TITLE VII

Title VII makes it unlawful for an employer "to fail or refuse to hire or to discharge any individual, or otherwise to discriminate against any individual with respect to his compensation, terms, conditions, or privileges of employment, because of such individual's race, color, religion, sex, or national origin." 42 U.S.C. § 2000e–2(a)(1). Unfortunately, the legislative history of the Civil Rights Act of 1964, of which Title VII is a part, is not particularly helpful in determining what Congress had in mind when it added protection from discrimination based on sex. * * *

* * * What is clear from the law itself, its legislative history, and Congress' subsequent actions, is that the goal of Title VII was to end years of discrimination in employment and to place all men and women,

regardless of race, color, religion, or national origin, on equal footing in how they were treated in the workforce.

In 1978, Congress had the opportunity to expound on its view of sex discrimination by amending Title VII to make clear that discrimination because of "pregnancy, childbirth, or related medical conditions" is discrimination on the basis of sex. 42 U.S.C. § 2000e(k). The amendment, known as the Pregnancy Discrimination Act ("PDA"), was not meant to alter the contours of Title VII: rather, Congress intended to correct what it felt was an erroneous interpretation of Title VII by the United States Supreme Court in *General Elec Co. v. Gilbert,* 429 U.S. 125, 50 L. Ed. 2d 343, 97 S. Ct. 401 (1976). In Gilbert, the Supreme Court held that an otherwise comprehensive short-term disability policy that excluded pregnancy-related disabilities from coverage did not discriminate on the basis of sex. The Gilbert majority based its decision on two findings: (a) pregnancy discrimination does not adversely impact all women and therefore is not the same thing as gender discrimination; and (b) disability insurance which covers the same illnesses and conditions for both men and women is equal coverage. To the Gilbert majority, the fact that pregnancy-related disabilities were an uncovered risk unique to women did not destroy the facial parity of the coverage. The dissenting justices, Justice Brennan, Justice Marshall, and Justice Stevens, took issue with these findings, arguing that: (a) women, as the only sex at risk for pregnancy, were being subjected to unlawful discrimination; and (b) in determining whether an employment policy treats the sexes equally, the court must look at the comprehensiveness of the coverage provided to each sex. * * *

The language of the PDA was chosen in response to the factual situation presented in Gilbert, namely a case of overt discrimination toward pregnant employees. Not surprisingly, the amendment makes no reference whatsoever to prescription contraceptives. Of critical importance to this case, however, is the fact that, in enacting the PDA, Congress embraced the dissent's broader interpretation of Title VII which not only recognized that there are sex-based differences between men and women employees, but also required employers to provide women-only benefits or otherwise incur additional expenses on behalf of women in order to treat the sexes the same. * * *

Although this litigation involves an exclusion for prescription contraceptives rather than an exclusion for pregnancy-related disability costs, the legal principles established by Gilbert and its legislative reversal govern the outcome of this case. An employer has chosen to offer an employment benefit which excludes from its scope of coverage services which are available only to women. [T]he intent of Congress in enacting the PDA, even if not the exact language used in the amendment, shows that mere facial parity of coverage does not excuse or justify an exclusion which carves out benefits that are uniquely designed for women.

The fact that equality under Title VII is measured by evaluating the relative comprehensiveness of coverage offered to the sexes has been accepted and amplified by the Supreme Court. * * *

The other tenet reaffirmed by the PDA (*i.e.,* that discrimination based on any sex-based characteristic is sex discrimination) has also been considered by the courts. The Supreme Court has found that classifying employees on the basis of their childbearing capacity, regardless of whether they are, in fact, pregnant, is sex-based discrimination. *International Union v. Johnson Controls, Inc.,* 499 U.S. 187 (1991). The court's analysis turned primarily on Title VII's prohibition on sex-based classifications, using the PDA merely to bolster a conclusion that had already been reached. To the extent that a woman's ability to get pregnant may not fall within the literal language of the PDA, the court was not overly concerned. Rather, the court focused on the fact that disparate treatment based on unique, sex-based characteristics, such as the capacity to bear children, is sex discrimination prohibited by Title VII.

[T]he Court finds that Bartell's exclusion of prescription contraception from its prescription plan is inconsistent with the requirements of federal law. The PDA is not a begrudging recognition of a limited grant of rights to a strictly defined group of women who happen to be pregnant. Read in the context of Title VII as a whole, it is a broad acknowledgment of the intent of Congress to outlaw any and all discrimination against any and all women in the terms and conditions of their employment, including the benefits an employer provides to its employees. Male and female employees have different, sex-based disability and healthcare needs, and the law is no longer blind to the fact that only women can get pregnant, bear children, or use prescription contraception. The special or increased healthcare needs associated with a woman's unique sex-based characteristics must be met to the same extent, and on the same terms, as other healthcare needs. Even if one were to assume that Bartell's prescription plan was not the result of intentional discrimination,[7] the exclusion of women-only benefits from a generally comprehensive prescription plan is sex discrimination under Title VII.

Title VII does not require employers to offer any particular type or category of benefit. However, when an employer decides to offer a prescription plan covering everything except a few specifically excluded drugs and devices, it has a legal obligation to make sure that the resulting

---

[7] There is no evidence or indication that Bartell's coverage decisions were intended to hinder women in their ability to participate in the workforce or to deprive them of equal treatment in employment or benefits. The most reasonable explanation for the current state of affairs is that the exclusion of women-only benefits is merely an unquestioned holdover from a time when employment-related benefits were doled out less equitably than they are today. The lack of evidence of bad faith or malice toward women does not affect the validity of plaintiffs' Title VII claim. Where a benefit plan is discriminatory on its face, no inquiry into subjective intent is necessary.

plan does not discriminate based on sex-based characteristics and that it provides equally comprehensive coverage for both sexes. * * *

## B. SPECIFIC ARGUMENTS RAISED BY DEFENDANT-EMPLOYER

Bartell argues that opting not to provide coverage for prescription contraceptive devices is not a violation of Title VII because: (1) treating contraceptives differently from other prescription drugs is reasonable in that contraceptives are voluntary, preventative, do not treat or prevent an illness or disease, and are not truly a "healthcare" issue; (2) control of one's fertility is not "pregnancy, childbirth, or related medical conditions" as those terms are used in the PDA; (3) employers must be permitted to control the costs of employment benefits by limiting the scope of coverage; (4) the exclusion of all "family planning" drugs and devices is facially neutral; (5) in the thirty-seven years Title VII has been on the books, no court has found that excluding contraceptives constitutes sex discrimination; and (6) this issue should be determined by the legislature, rather than the courts. Each of these arguments is considered in turn.

### (1) Contraceptives as a health care need

An underlying theme in Bartell's argument is that a woman's ability to control her fertility differs from the type of illness and disease normally treated with prescription drugs in such significant respects that it is permissible to treat prescription contraceptives differently than all other prescription medicines. The evidence submitted by plaintiffs shows, however, that the availability of affordable and effective contraceptives is of great importance to the health of women and children because it can help to prevent a litany of physical, emotional, economic, and social consequences. * * *

Unintended pregnancies, the condition which prescription contraceptives are designed to prevent, are shockingly common in the United States and carry enormous costs and health consequences for the mother, the child, and society as a whole. Over half of all pregnancies in this country are unintended. A woman with an unintended pregnancy is less likely to seek prenatal care, more likely to engage in unhealthy activities, more likely to have an abortion, and more likely to deliver a low birthweight, ill, or unwanted baby. Unintended pregnancies impose significant financial burdens on the parents in the best of circumstances. If the pregnancy results in a distressed newborn, the costs increase by tens of thousands of dollars. In addition, the adverse economic and social consequences of unintended pregnancies fall most harshly on women and interfere with their choice to participate fully and equally in the "marketplace and the world of ideas." *Stanton v. Stanton,* 421 U.S. 7 (1975). See also *Planned Parenthood v. Casey,* 505 U.S. 833, 856 (1992) ("The ability of women to participate equally in the economic and social life of the nation has been facilitated by their ability to control their reproductive lives.").

* * * Although there are many factors which help explain the unusually high rate of unintended pregnancies in the United States, an important cause is the failure to use effective forms of birth control. [ ] Insurance policies and employee benefit plans which exclude coverage for effective forms of contraception contribute to the failure of at-risk women to seek a physician's assistance in avoiding unwanted pregnancies. [ ]

The fact that prescription contraceptives are preventative appears to be an irrelevant distinction in this case: Bartell covers a number of preventative drugs under its plan. The fact that pregnancy is a "natural" state and is not considered a disease or illness is also a distinction without a difference. Being pregnant, though natural, is not a state that is desired by all women or at all points in a woman's life. Prescription contraceptives, like all other preventative drugs, help the recipient avoid unwanted physical changes. * * *

(2) Pregnancy Discrimination Act

[I]t is clear that in 1978 Congress had no specific intent regarding coverage for prescription contraceptives. The relevant issue, however, is whether the decision to exclude drugs made for women from a generally comprehensive prescription plan is sex discrimination under Title VII, with or without the clarification provided by the PDA. The Court finds that, regardless of whether the prevention of pregnancy falls within the phrase "pregnancy, childbirth, or related medical conditions," Congress' decisive overruling of [*Gilbert*] evidences an interpretation of Title VII which necessarily precludes the choices Bartell has made in this case.

(3) Business Decision to Control Costs

Bartell also suggests that it should be permitted to limit the scope of its employee benefit programs in order to control costs. Cost is not, however, a defense to allegations of discrimination under Title VII. [ ]While it is undoubtedly true that employers may cut benefits, raise deductibles, or otherwise alter coverage options to comply with budgetary constraints, the method by which the employer seeks to curb costs must not be discriminatory. Bartell offers its employees an admittedly generous package of healthcare benefits [ ]. It cannot, however, penalize female employees in an effort to keep its benefit costs low. The cost savings Bartell realizes by excluding prescription contraceptives from its healthcare plans are being directly borne by only one sex in violation of Title VII. Although Bartell is permitted, under the law, to use non-discriminatory cuts in benefits to control costs, it cannot balance its benefit books at the expense of its female employees.

(4) Neutrality of Exclusions

Prescription contraceptives are not the only drugs or devices excluded from coverage under Bartell's benefit plan. Bartell argues that it has chosen to exclude from coverage all drugs for "family planning," and that this exclusion is neutral and non-discriminatory. There is no "family planning" exclusion in the benefit plan, however, and the contours of such a theoretical exclusion are not clear. On the list of excluded drugs and devices, contraceptive devices and infertility drugs are the two categories which might be considered "family planning" measures. Contrary to defendant's explanation, there appear to be some drugs which fall under the "family planning" rubric which are covered by the plan. Prenatal vitamins, for example, are frequently prescribed in anticipation of a woman becoming pregnant and are expressly covered under the plan.

\* \* \*

Although the Court's decision is a matter of first impression for the judiciary, it is not the first tribunal to consider the lawfulness of a contraception exclusion. On December 14, 2000, the EEOC made a finding of reasonable cause on the same issue which is entitled to some deference. Although the Commission's analysis focused primarily on the PDA, it [came] to the same conclusion reached by this Court.

(6) Legislative Issue

Although this litigation involves politically charged issues with far-reaching social consequences, the parties' dispute turns on the interpretation of an existing federal statute. \* \* \* The normal rules of statutory construction, not the give and take of a legislative body, will guide this determination. Contrary to defendant's suggestion, it is the role of the judiciary, not the legislature, to interpret existing laws and determine whether they apply to a particular set of facts. While it is interesting to note that Congress and some state legislatures are considering proposals to require insurance plans to cover prescription contraceptives, that fact does not alter this Court's constitutional role in interpreting Congress' legislative enactments in order to resolve private disputes.

## C. CONCLUSION

\* \* \* For all of the foregoing reasons, the Court finds that Bartell's prescription drug plan discriminates against Bartell's female employees by providing less complete coverage than that offered to male employees.

### NOTES AND QUESTIONS

1. *The Limits of Erickson.* As noted in *Erickson*, the court's decision was consistent with an EEOC decision finding that the exclusion of prescription contraception from a plan that provides comparable drugs and devices violated Title VII as amended by the Pregnancy Discrimination Act. EEOC Commission

Decision on Coverage of Contraception (Dec. 14, 2000), *available at* http://www. eeoc.gov/policy/docs/decision-contraception.html. But one circuit seemed to reject the approach taken by *Erickson* and the EEOC. See, e.g., In re Union Pacific Railroad Employment Practices Litigation, 479 F.3d 936 (8th Cir. 2007) (holding that an employer health plan, which excluded contraception when used for purposes of contraception, but not for non-contraceptive medically necessary purposes, did not violate Title VII, because it excluded coverage of all contraception for men and women, both surgical and prescription). There are not many cases addressing the issue of whether prescription contraception exclusions violate Title VII. This is likely due, in part, to the number of states that began requiring contraceptive coverage as part of state insurance mandates around the mid-1990s. See Note 2 below. It is also important to remember that Title VII only applies to employment-based policies; prior to the Affordable Care Act, there was no federal statute prohibiting sex discrimination in health care generally.

2. *Private Insurance Mandates.* Many states have enacted laws requiring insurers to cover prescription contraception as part of comprehensive prescription benefit plans. By the time of the ACA, 28 states already required some form of contraceptive coverage in at least some health insurance plans sold in their states. The ACA still brought about a significant change, though, because it required most group health plans and health insurance issuers to provide preventive services without cost-sharing. In defining the scope of services to be included, the relevant regulatory agencies adopted guidelines from the Health Resources Services Administration, based on recommendations by the independent Institute of Medicine (IOM). The IOM recommended that preventive services include all forms of contraception approved by the FDA, which meant that most health insurance policies would cover hormonal methods of contraception (i.e., birth control pills and post-intercourse emergency contraception like Plan B and ella), as well as intrauterine devices (IUDs), sterilization, and patient education and counseling. See, IOM, Clinical Preventive Services for Women: Closing the Gaps (National Academies Press, 2011). In adopting these recommendations, federal regulators acknowledged the gender disparities that existed in the insurance market prior to the ACA and noted that "[t]he contraceptive coverage requirement is . . . designed to serve . . . compelling public health and gender equity goals. . . ." Group Health Plans and Health Insurance Issuers Relating to Coverage of Preventive Services Under the Patient Protection and Affordable Care Act, 77 Fed. Reg. 8725, 8727–8729 (Feb. 15, 2012).

3. *Federal & State Family Planning Programs.* Various government health programs also provide coverage for prescription contraception for low income individuals. For example, Medicaid plays a critical role in providing family planning services, a federally mandated benefit, to low-income populations. Although states have discretion to determine the specific services they will cover through Medicaid, contraception is one of the primary services covered and most states offer broad coverage. Contraception is also an

important service in other federally funded family planning and disease prevention programs, such as the Title X Family Planning Program.

4. *Other State Actions to Facilitate Access.* Some states have enacted provider mandates to ensure access to certain kinds of contraceptive care. Seventeen states and the District of Columbia require emergency rooms to provide information about emergency contraception to sexual assault victims, and thirteen states and DC require emergency rooms to dispense the drug to sexual assault victims on request. Four states require either pharmacies or pharmacists to fill all valid prescriptions, and eight states allow pharmacists to dispense emergency contraception without a physician's prescription under certain conditions. States have also expanded minors' authority to consent to health care generally, but in particular relating to sexual and reproductive health care. See Guttmacher Institute, Fact Sheets on Emergency Contraception and Minors' Access to Contraceptive Services (Jan. 1, 2018).

## C. THE CLASH BETWEEN GOVERNMENT MANDATES AND RELIGIOUS OR MORAL BELIEFS

In response to government action to expand contraceptive access, political and legal challenges have emerged. In particular, those who object to certain medication or devices on religious or moral grounds have sought exemptions from government mandates to provide or pay for contraception. The most recent and well-known example of this is the controversy surrounding religious objections to the ACA's prescription contraceptive mandate.

### 1. Religious Objections to the ACA Contraceptive Mandate

Early in the process of issuing regulatory rules for coverage of preventive services, including the prescription contraception mandate, the Obama administration included a very narrow exemption for *religious employers* that (1) have the purpose of religious inculcation of religious values, (2) employ primarily people who share its religious values, (3) primarily serve people who share its religious tenets, and (4) are non-profit organizations established to be a church, association of churches or a religious order. See Coverage of Certain Preventive Services Under the Affordable Care Act, 78 Fed. Reg. 39870 (Jul. 2, 2013). Essentially, this exemption meant *churches* and other *houses of worship* did not have to provide contraception coverage, and it applied to some religious primary and secondary schools organized to inculcate religious views and designed for attendance by coreligionists only.

The exemption did not extend to most religious colleges and universities that had students of all faiths, nor to social service organizations that provided service to people of all faiths. These religious organizations would have to provide insurance that included contraception. Because the rule was later extended to cover student health plans, the fact that religious colleges (and, in particular, Catholic universities open to students of all faiths) were not exempt proved to be very significant. Although the scope of this exemption was consistent with the kinds of religious exemptions provided in state mandates at the time, it met with strong objections from religiously affiliated organizations that the exemption was too narrow. Opposition, led by the U.S. Conference of Catholic Bishops, evangelical Christians, and conservative politicians, believed the rule to be an unconscionable intrusion on religious liberty.

*Obama's Compromise: Accommodation for Religious Nonprofits*

In the face of deeply held and conflicting views on the issue, the Obama administration tried to fashion a compromise that would ensure women received coverage for contraception while allowing religious employers and universities to opt out of participation in the provision of any services they found to be morally objectionable. New regulations were issued, extending protection to the *religious nonprofits* (schools and social service organizations) previously left out, if they had religious objections to providing coverage for contraceptive services required by law. See Coverage of Certain Preventive Services Under the Affordable Care Act, supra. See also Robert Pear, Birth Control Rule Altered to Allay Religious Objections, N.Y. Times (Feb. 2, 2013).

Importantly, the regulations did not *exempt* these religious nonprofits from the mandate; instead they established an *accommodation* that would allow these religious nonprofits (classified as "*eligible organizations*" in the regulation) to "opt-out" of providing contraceptive coverage for their employees by formally announcing that they had religious objections to offering this coverage. This would not impede access, though, because it would trigger a process by which the health insurer or other third party would be required to provide the contraceptive coverage, with no cost sharing by the employee and without the employer having to pay for it or help arrange for its provision.

*Legal Challenges to the Obama Era Compromise*

There were two types of challenges to the Obama era rules worthy of note. The first was by for-profit companies, whose owners operated their companies in accord with religious principles, but who were not entitled to an accommodation under the Obama compromise. Numerous companies filed legal challenges to the contraceptive mandate on religious freedom grounds, and the first suit to reach the Supreme Court was Burwell v. Hobby Lobby, Inc., 134 S.Ct. 2751 (2014). In *Hobby Lobby*, the Supreme Court determined that closely held private corporations could assert the religious liberty interests of their owners, and that the ACA's mandate to provide contraception was a violation of the federal Religious Freedom Restoration Act (RFRA), 42 U.S.C.A. § 2000bb–1(a), (b).

Justice Alito, who wrote for the 5–4 majority finding that the contraceptive mandate violated RFRA, summarized his opinion this way:

We must decide in these cases whether the Religious Freedom Restoration Act . . . (RFRA) [ ] permits the United States Department of Health and Human Services (HHS) to demand that three closely held corporations provide health-insurance coverage for methods of contraception that violate the sincerely held religious beliefs of the companies' owners. We hold that the regulations that impose this obligation violate RFRA, which prohibits the Federal Government from taking any action that substantially burdens the exercise of religion unless that action constitutes the least restrictive means of serving a compelling government interest.

In holding that the HHS mandate is unlawful, we reject HHS's argument that the owners of the companies forfeited all RFRA protection when they decided to organize their businesses as corporations rather than sole proprietorships or general partnerships. The plain terms of RFRA make it perfectly clear that Congress did not discriminate in this way against men and women who wish to run their businesses as for-profit corporations in the manner required by their religious beliefs.

Since RFRA applies in these cases, we must decide whether the challenged HHS regulations substantially burden the exercise of religion, and we hold that they do. The owners of the businesses have religious objections to abortion, and according to their religious beliefs the four contraceptive methods at issue are abortifacients. If the owners comply with the HHS mandate, they believe they will be facilitating abortions, and if they do not comply, they will pay a very heavy price—as much as $1.3 million per day, or about $475 million per year, in the case of one of the companies. If these consequences do not amount to a substantial burden, it is hard to see what would.

Under RFRA, a Government action that imposes a substantial burden on religious exercise must serve a compelling government interest, and we assume that the HHS regulations satisfy this requirement. But in order for the HHS mandate to be sustained, it must also constitute the least restrictive means of serving that interest, and the mandate plainly fails that test. There are other ways in which Congress or HHS could equally ensure that every woman has cost-free access to the particular contraceptives at issue here and, indeed, to all FDA-approved contraceptives.

In fact, HHS has already devised and implemented a system that seeks to respect the religious liberty of religious nonprofit corporations while ensuring that the employees of these entities have precisely the same access to all FDA-approved contraceptives as employees of companies whose owners have no religious objections to providing such coverage. [Ed. Note: This refers to the opt-out scheme, described above.] The employees of these religious nonprofit corporations still have access to insurance coverage without cost sharing for all FDA-approved contraceptives; and according to HHS, this system imposes no net economic burden on the insurance companies that are required to provide or secure the coverage.

Although HHS has made this system available to religious nonprofits that have religious objections to the contraceptive mandate, HHS has provided no reason why the same system cannot be made available when the owners of for-profit corporations have similar religious objections. We therefore conclude that this system constitutes an alternative that achieves all of the Government's aims while providing greater respect for religious liberty. And under RFRA, that conclusion means that enforcement of the HHS contraceptive mandate against the objecting parties in these cases is unlawful.

As this description of our reasoning shows, our holding is very specific. We do not hold, as the principal dissent alleges, that for-profit corporations and other commercial enterprises can "opt out of any law (saving only tax laws) they judge incompatible with their sincerely held religious beliefs." [ ] (opinion of Ginsburg, J.). Nor do we hold, as the dissent implies, that such corporations have free rein to take steps that impose "disadvantages . . . on others" or that require "the general public [to] pick up the tab." [ ] And we certainly do not hold or suggest that "RFRA demands accommodation of a for-profit corporation's religious beliefs no matter the impact that accommodation may have on . . . thousands of women employed by Hobby Lobby." [ ] The effect of the HHS-created accommodation on the women employed by Hobby Lobby and the other companies involved in these cases would be precisely zero. Under that accommodation, these women would still be entitled to all FDA-approved contraceptives without cost sharing.

Burwell v. Hobby Lobby, Inc., 134 S.Ct. 2751, 2759–60 (2014).

The second type of challenge brought against the Obama era rule was based on objections to the opt-out process itself. Numerous religious organizations and employers filed suit alleging that the requirement they submit a formal written document asking to be relieved of the mandate violated RFRA, because it constituted facilitation of a sin. The legal issues at play in the courts were whether the opt-out process itself was a substantial burden, whether the governmental interest was compelling, and whether there was a less restrictive way of serving the same interest. All but one courts of appeals hearing these challenges held that the accommodation adequately protected plaintiffs' religious freedom. See, e.g., Little Sisters of the Poor v. Burwell, 794 F.3d 1151 (10th Cir 2016) (holding that the accommodation scheme does not substantially burden their religious exercise under RFRA or infringe upon their First Amendment rights). In October 2017, however, the Trump administration issued expansive new rules (described below) which appeared to relieve these entities of the procedural obligations to which they objected. The plaintiffs entered into agreements with the government to dismiss their cases because it looked like the new rules had settled the issue in their favor.

### Trump Era Rules: Expanding Exemptions & Reducing Access

On October 13, 2017, two interim final rules were issued by the regulatory agencies charged with implementation of the ACA. Religious Exemptions and Accommodations for Coverage of Certain Preventive Services Under the Affordable Care Act, 82 Fed. Reg. 47792 (Oct. 13, 2017), and Moral Exemptions and Accommodations for Coverage of Certain Preventive Services Under the Affordable Care Act, 82 Fed. Reg. 47838 (Oct. 13, 2017). These rules expand the scope of exemptions allowed in two important ways. First, the new rules allow any objecting religious employers or universities, even those who expressly hire and recruit people from diverse religious and ideological backgrounds, to get an exemption from the law, as opposed to requiring them to follow an opt-out process provided as an accommodation. The difference between accommodation and exemption means the difference between an employee or student getting contraceptive coverage or not. The opt-out process was created precisely to accommodate religious objections while protecting access to coverage. Granting these entities exemptions means that covered individuals will not be offered the objected to contraception by any means.

Second, the new rules allow those who were not previously eligible for either an exemption or accommodation to now claim an exemption, as long as they have *moral* objections to the rule. This means the exemption is no longer specifically linked to religious exercise, which is the basis of the protections in RFRA. It also increases the number of entities that can deny contraceptive coverage for employees or students. The rules did preserve the opt-out process as an option, but it would not be required.

### Legal Challenges to the Trump Administration Rules

Lawsuits challenging the new rules have already been filed by several states and public interest organizations. There are three common themes among the suits filed to date. First, challengers allege that the rules have the effect of advancing and endorsing a particular set of religious beliefs in violation of the Establishment Clause of the First Amendment. Second, they allege that targeting woman-specific benefits for an expansive exemption that denies women access to contraceptive coverage constitutes gender discrimination in violation of the Equal Protection Clause of the Fifth Amendment and the ACA's antidiscrimination provision (Section 1557). Finally, challengers allege procedural and substantive violations of the Administrative Procedure Act (APA), such as failing to follow proper notice and comment procedure, and failing to provide an evidence-based reason for the change in policy. As of December 2017, two courts granted preliminary injunctions against the rules. See Pennsylvania v. Trump, No. 17-4540, 281 F.Supp.3d 553 (E.D. Penn. 2017); California v. HHS, No. 17-cv-05783-HSG, 281 F.Supp.3d 806 (N.D. Cal. 2017).

### NOTES AND QUESTIONS

1. *RFRA Challenge: Substantial Burden on Free Exercise of Religion*. In *Hobby Lobby*, the plaintiffs objected to two forms of intrauterine devices and two forms of emergency contraception forms on religious grounds. They believed that these medications and devices worked after fertilization and thus were abortifacients. They claimed that requiring them to include these forms of contraception in their health plans substantially burdened their free exercise of religion. The Court did not engage in the debate over where the line should be drawn between abortion and contraception, for purposes of evaluating plaintiffs' claim of a substantial burden. In religious freedom cases, courts have been careful not to weigh or evaluate the relevant doctrines of faith. As long as a belief is sincere, the Court will not second-guess the underlying basis for claims that a particular action violates one's religious beliefs.

2. *RFRA Challenge: Does the Contraceptive Mandate Serve a Compelling Interest?* RFRA provides that government action imposing a substantial burden on religious exercise must serve a "compelling government interest." The majority did not, however, discuss whether it viewed the government's interest as compelling. It merely assumed such an interest was met for purposes of its analysis and found the mandate unconstitutional on a different basis.

Addressing potential unintended pregnancies is widely recognized as an important issue, but would a majority of the Court consider it compelling? Consider that around the time of this case, statistics showed that half of all pregnancies were unintended, a million women who do not want to become pregnant have unprotected sex each day, and 25,000 women become pregnant through sexual assault each year. See Gardiner Harris, F.D.A. Approves 5-Day Emergency Contraception, N.Y. Times (Aug. 13, 2010). Studies have also shown that cost-sharing can act as a barrier to women getting birth control, or the most effective form of birth control.

What about the recommendations of the IOM report? How much weight should these be given in assessing the strength of the interest? Should current federal regulators be bound by a prior administration's conclusions that the contraceptive mandate serves compelling public health and gender equity goals? What about claims that prescription contraception exclusions constitute sex discrimination—would this establish a compelling interest?

3.  *Challenge to Trump Rules Expanding the Exemption.* If a court were to find that the expanded exemption has a discriminatory effect on women, how should this be balanced against claims that the exemption is designed to protect religious and moral beliefs? Does the *Hobby Lobby* decision make this a more difficult claim to win or does it strengthen the case for why the exemption goes too far? Consider that in *Hobby Lobby* the Court's holding turned on the fact that the government had already created an opt-out program that could accommodate religious objections without impeding access to contraception. The opt-out accommodation was key to the Court's finding that the government had a less restrictive alternative for achieving its goal of ensuring access to prescription contraception. Should government have to require objecting entities to follow the opt-out process to preserve access, instead of simply giving them an exemption?

## 2.  Provider Conscientious Refusals

Just as some employers and schools object to funding certain forms of contraception, some health care professionals and entities, including hospitals and pharmacies, may also object to dispensing or even giving information about certain forms contraception. Twelve states have statutory conscience protections that allow health care providers to refuse to provide contraception-related services. As we saw above, however, some states require certain providers, such as hospitals or pharmacists, to dispense and/or provide information about contraception; sometimes these mandates target particular circumstances, such as emergency contraception for sexual assault victims; in other cases, the mandates may be broader.

Providers have raised religious objections to these mandates, but such challenges tend not to be successful. RFRA only applies to federal law. State law challenges are subject to the Free Exercise Clause of the federal constitution; unlike RFRA, the federal Free Exercise Clause does not require exemptions from neutral laws of general applicability. See, e.g., Storman's, Inc. v. Selecky, 794 F.3d 1064 (9th Cir. 2015), cert. denied 136 S.Ct. 2433 (2016) (holding that the Free Exercise Clause provided for only rational basis review of a state's requirement that a pharmacist dispense emergency contraception). Although state mandates have also been challenged under state constitutional free exercise protections, the results tend to be the same. See, e.g., Catholic Charities v. Superior Court, 85 P.3d 67 (Cal. 2004) (rejecting a state free exercise challenge to the state's Women's Contraceptive Equity Act).

### *NOTE: THE ETHICS OF CONSCIENTIOUS REFUSALS*

The materials in the first four sections of this chapter demonstrate that questions about the regulation of access to abortion and contraception can trigger sharply divided views shaped by deeply held beliefs. Such disputes implicate difficult ethical questions about how to balance protections for religious and moral objections to certain procedures with patients' health care needs and gender equity concerns. Claims for legal protections of providers and other entities that refuse to provide or pay for certain care on religious or moral grounds are grounded in claims about the importance of conscience. Consider how one bioethicist and physician has explained the role of conscience in such conflicts:

> Conscientious persons strive to preserve moral integrity. This requires that their external behavior be congruent with their conscience's internal dictates about what they take to be morally right and feel compelled to do. In our morally diverse world, conscientious persons may come into conflict with each other and with society's moral values. * * *

> Any society purporting to serve the good of its members is therefore obliged to protect the exercise of conscience and conscientious objection. However, this involves a serious dilemma for any pluralist, democratic, liberal, or constitutional state. On the one hand, such a society is committed to tolerance to religious diversity, freedom of individual choice, and "neutrality" with respect to religious belief. On the other hand, optimizing freedom of conscience for some individuals may often limit the legal rights, social entitlements, and moral beliefs of others.

Edmund D. Pellegrino, The Physician's Conscience, Conscience Clauses, and Religious Belief: A Catholic Perspective, 30 Fordham Urban L.J. 221, 221 (2002). In this essay, Dr. Pellegrino explored the ethical implications of religious health care professionals and institutions objecting to procedures considered standard in the medical community. He questioned whether conscience clauses can provide adequate protection for religious and moral beliefs, such as where they are written narrowly to only apply to certain kinds of providers. In addressing the conflict between patients' needs and physicians' conscience, he stated that physicians should make their positions publicly known so that patients know in advance of a crisis that what they want may not be care the physician is willing to provide. At the same time, he concluded that "[t]he only viable course for the religious physician is to maintain fidelity to moral integrity and dictates of conscience" by refusing to perform a morally objectionable procedure or treatment, even in emergencies or remote areas where the choice of physicians is limited. For some religious professionals, this would include refusing to refer a patient to another practitioner willing to perform the disputed treatment, because to do so would be cooperation in an illicit act, making the person a moral accomplice.

Compare this approach to the ethics opinion on conscientious refusals in reproductive health published by the American College of Obstetrics and Gynecology (ACOG). ACOG offered several recommendations, which it believes "maximize respect for health care professionals' consciences without compromising the health and well-being of the women they serve":

1. In the provision of reproductive services, the patient's well-being must be paramount. Any conscientious refusal that conflicts with a

patient's well-being should be accommodated only if the primary duty to the patient can be fulfilled.

2.  Health care providers must impart accurate and unbiased information so that patients can make informed decisions about their health care. * * *

3.  Where conscience implores physicians to deviate from standard practices, including abortion, sterilization and provision of contraceptives, they must provide potential patients with accurate and prior notice of their personal moral commitments. * * *

4.  Physicians and other health care professionals have the duty to refer patients in a timely manner to other providers if they do not feel that they can in conscience provide the standard reproductive services that their patients request.

5.  In an emergency in which referral is not possible or might negatively affect a patient's physical or mental health, providers have an obligation to provide medically indicated and requested care regardless of the provider's personal moral objections.

6.  In resource poor areas, access to safe and legal reproductive services should be maintained. * * *

7.  Lawmakers should advance policies that balance protection of providers' consciences with the critical goal of ensuring timely, effective, evidence-based, and safe access to all women seeking reproductive services.

The Limits of Conscientious Refusal in Reproductive Medicine. ACOG Committee Opinion No. 385. American College of Obstetricians and Gynecologists. Obstet Gynecol 2007; 110:1203–8 (reaffirmed 2016).

# V. STERILIZATION

Sterilization, like most forms of contraception, is generally considered less controversial than abortion. Nonetheless, as with abortion and contraception, some patients have had difficulty accessing sterilization procedures because of insurance exclusions and provider refusals to treat. Recall that the Church Amendments (discussed in the Note on Federal Conscience Protections at the end of the Section III of this chapter) provided that receipt of federal funding could not be used to require recipients to provide abortions or *sterilizations*. Sterilization is considered by some religious persons to be a sin, because it separates sexual activity from a procreative purpose. In fact, the Church Amendments were a response to an injunction initially issued by a Montana district court requiring a religiously-affiliated hospital to perform a tubal ligation despite religious objections, based in part on the fact it received federal funding. The injunction was eventually dissolved, however, based on the Church Amendments. See Taylor v. St. Vincent Hospital, 369 F. Supp. 948 (D.

Mont. 1973), aff'd, 523 F. 2d 75 (9th Cir. 1975). Today, eighteen states allow health care providers to refuse to provide sterilization services. Many of the issues discussed under the sections on abortion and contraception are thus relevant to sterilization as well.

Sterilization practices also highlight reproductive justice concerns often neglected in debates over access to contraception and abortion. While much of the "reproductive rights" movement has focused on barriers to preventing or terminating pregnancy, some individuals experience *barriers to choosing procreation*. There is a long and troubling history of forced and coerced sterilization of certain groups, which complicates discussions about sterilization as a reproductive health issue.

### *Forced and Coerced Sterilization*

Discussions about sterilization often begin with the development of the eugenics movement in the late 19th century. Among the groups targeted for sterilization were people believed to have intellectual disabilities, as well as those engaging in criminal behavior or behavior viewed as immoral, reflecting low intelligence, and/or reflecting poor character. Despite lack of evidence of a link between such characteristics and heritability, some believed society could "purify" its gene pool by sterilizing those who would "pollute" it. The aim of the eugenics movement was articulated in a now infamous decision by Justice Holmes in Buck v. Bell, 274 U.S. 200, 47 S.Ct. 584, 71 L.Ed. 1000 (1927). That case dealt with an attempt by the State of Virginia to sterilize Carrie Buck, who had been committed to the State Colony for Epileptics and the Feeble Minded. This action was opposed on the grounds that the statute authorizing sterilization violated the Fourteenth Amendment by denying Ms. Buck due process of law and the equal protection of the law. Justice Holmes responded:

> Carrie Buck is a feeble minded white woman who was committed to the State Colony above mentioned in due form. She is the daughter of a feeble minded mother in the same institution and the mother of an illegitimate feeble minded child * * *.

> [The lower court found] "that Carrie Buck is the probable potential parent of socially inadequate offspring, likewise afflicted, that she may be sterilized without detriment to her general health and that her welfare and that of society will be promoted by her sterilization." * * * We have seen more than once that the public welfare may call upon the best citizens for their lives. It would be strange if it could not call upon those who already sapped the strength of the state for these lesser sacrifices, often not felt to be such by those concerned, in order to prevent our being swamped with incompetence. It is better for all the world if instead of waiting to execute degenerate offspring for crime, or to let them starve for their imbecility, society can prevent those who are manifestly unfit from continuing their kind. The

principle that sustains compulsory vaccination is broad enough to cover cutting the fallopian tubes.[ ] Three generations of imbeciles are enough.

\* \* \*

The Supreme Court has never overturned the decision in *Buck v. Bell*, although it is of questionable precedential value today. Society's perception of people with disabilities has undergone significant change and, especially after the Nazi experience, for which *Buck v. Bell* was cited as precedent, arguments based upon eugenics are now held in low regard. In fact, when Carrie Buck was discovered in the Appalachian hills in 1980, she was found to be mentally competent and extremely disappointed that throughout her life she was unable to bear another child. Subsequent research determined that Carrie Buck's illegitimate daughter Vivian, who was conceived as the result of a rape by a relative of Carrie Buck's foster parents, was an honor roll student. At the trial that, on appeal, gave rise to Justice Holmes' regrettable opinion, Carrie Buck was poorly represented by a lawyer who did not develop the evidence or the legal arguments necessary to overcome the statute or its application to his client. For an engaging account of this case by a scholar who met Ms. Buck in the 1980s, and for pictures of Ms. Buck and her daughter, see Paul Lombardo, Facing Carrie Buck, 33 Hastings Ctr. Rep. (March–April) 14 (2003).

The Supreme Court addressed eugenic sterilizations once more, in Skinner v. Oklahoma, 316 U.S. 535, 62 S.Ct. 1110, 86 L.Ed. 1655 (1942). The Court determined that the equal protection clause prohibited Oklahoma from enforcing a statute requiring sterilization of persons convicted of repeated criminal acts, but only if the crimes were within special categories. White collar crimes were exempted from these categories, and the Supreme Court's holding was based on the state's irrational distinction between blue collar (sterilizable) and white collar (unsterilizable) crimes. The Court was asked to, but did not, overrule *Buck v. Bell*. The Governor of Virginia apologized for the sterilization of Carrie Buck on the seventy-fifth anniversary of the Supreme Court decision in 2002.

Oklahoma and Virginia were not alone. Thirty-two states have had sterilizations programs, many supported with federal funding, that have targeted individuals with developmental disabilities, those of low socioeconomic status, racial and ethnic minorities, unmarried women, and prisoners. California had the unfortunate distinction of being a "pioneer" in sterilization programs at the beginning of the twentieth century, and in modern times we see this legacy in the state's prisons. California has come under scrutiny for coerced and unlawful sterilization of its women prisoners. As recently as 2014, California's state auditor produced a report revealing important ethical and legal lapses by California corrections officials and other medical personnel. These include failing to ensure that the physician and staff follow protocols to obtain a woman's informed consent prior to sterilization and failing to follow protocols designed to ensure that sterilization is medically necessary. The protocols include heightened informed consent protection, such as having a physician certify that the required waiting period has been satisfied, that the patient appears mentally competent and understands the lasting effects of sterilization, and that the patient has been given one final opportunity to change her mind. See California State Auditor, Sterilization of Female Inmates: Report 2013–120 (Jun. 2014). Such protocols were established in response to complaints by women prisoners alleging they had been sterilized without their knowledge or consent and that medical staff encouraged women to get sterilized for birth control purposes.

In response to the report, the Governor of California signed a bill with even greater restrictions on sterilization in state prisons. The law prohibits "sterilization for the purpose of birth control" and prohibits sterilization by any means except when "required for the immediate preservation of the individual's life in an emergency medical situation" or when "medically necessary, as determined by contemporary standards of evidence-based medicine, to treat a diagnosed condition. . . ." Cal. Penal Code § 3440(a) & (b). Additional protections, such as heightened informed consent requirements, must also be met. If a sterilization is performed, the law requires psychological consultation and medical follow up. And the law requires the state to publish data related to the number of sterilizations it performs, disaggregated by race, age, medical justification, and method of sterilization. Id.

Federal law also makes it a crime for government officials and others receiving federal financial assistance to "coerce[ ] or endeavor[ ] to coerce any person to undergo an abortion or sterilization procedure by threatening such person with the loss of, or disqualification for the receipt of, any benefit or service" under a federal program. Violation is punishable by $1000, up to one year in jail, or both. 42 U.S.C.A. § 300a–8.

### Forced Sterilization or Right to Care?

More complex legal and ethical challenges have arisen where guardians or family members of permanently disabled individuals seek permission to authorize sterilization based on the belief that it would be in that person's best interest, as in the following case below.

# CONSERVATORSHIP OF VALERIE N.

Supreme Court of California, 1985.
40 Cal.3d 143, 219 Cal.Rptr. 387, 707 P.2d 760, S.F. No. 24745.

\* \* \*

## I.

Valerie was born on July 13, 1955, apparently a victim of Downs Syndrome as a result of which she is severely retarded. Her IQ is estimated to be 30. She is now 29 years old. She lives with her mother and stepfather. Although she has no comprehension of the nature of these proceedings, she has expressed her wish to continue to have her parents care for her. Her parents' long range plan for Valerie is that she will move to a residential home should they become mentally or physically unable to care for her. She has received therapy and training for behavior modification which was not successful in eliminating her aggressive sexual advances toward men. Her parents are attempting to prepare her for the time when they can no longer care for her, and to broaden her social activities as an aspect of this preparation. They have concluded that other methods of birth control are inadequate in Valerie's case.

On September 5, 1980, appellants [Valerie's mother and stepfather] filed their petition to be named conservators of Valerie's person in the Santa Clara County Superior Court pursuant to section 1820. In the same petition they sought the additional power to authorize "a Salpingectomy or any other operation that will permanently sterilize" Valerie. The petition was supported by the declaration of Valerie's personal physician who stated that the tubal ligation procedure is "advisable and medically appropriate."

[A]ppellants submitted a declaration by a physician who had treated Valerie from the time she was 10 years old. He stated that in his opinion a tubal litigation procedure was "advisable and medically appropriate in that a potential pregnancy would cause psychiatric harm to Valerie." A second declaration [ ] by a licensed marriage, family and child counselor having a master's degree in developmental psychology, was also submitted. This declarant had worked with Valerie on a weekly basis for a year during 1977–1978. She believed that a tubal ligation was "an appropriate means of guarding against pregnancy," and had observed that Valerie acted "affectionately" toward adult men and made "inappropriate" sexual advances toward them. This declarant was of the opinion that because Valerie's parents had found it necessary to be overly restrictive in order to avoid a possible pregnancy which would have "severe psychologically damaging consequences" to Valerie, close monitoring had severely hampered Valerie's ability to form social relationships. She also believed that the level of Valerie's retardation meant that no alternative birth control methods were available that would ensure against pregnancy.

Valerie's mother testified that Valerie had not been sexually active, apart from masturbation, because she had been closely supervised. She was aggressive and affectionate toward boys. On the street she approached men, hugged and kissed them, climbed on them, and wanted to sit on their laps. Valerie had been given birth control pills in her early teens, but she rejected them and became ill. Her doctor then recommended the tubal ligation. Valerie was unable to apply other methods of birth control such as a diaphragm, and would not cooperate in a pelvic examination for an intrauterine device which the witness believed was unsafe in any event.

\* \* \*

The parties agree that [the state statutory scheme] bars nontherapeutic sterilization of conservatees.

### III. *Constitutional Rights of the Developmentally Disabled*

Our conclusion regarding the present legislative scheme requires that we confront appellants' contention that the scheme is unconstitutional. Both appellants and counsel for Valerie pose the constitutional question in terms of the right of procreative choice. Appellants argue that [the statute] deprives Valerie of that right by precluding the only means of contraception realistically available to her, while counsel for Valerie contends that the legislation furthers that right by protecting her against sterilization forced upon her by the will of others. The sad but irrefutable truth, however, is that Valerie is not now nor will she ever be competent to choose between bearing or not bearing children, or among methods of contraception. The question is whether she has a constitutional right to have these decisions made for her, in this case by her parents as conservators, in order to protect her interests in living the fullest and most rewarding life of which she is capable. At present her conservators may, on Valerie's behalf, elect that she not bear or rear children. As means of avoiding the severe psychological harm which assertedly would result from pregnancy, they may choose abortion should she become pregnant; they may arrange for any child Valerie might bear to be removed from her custody; and they may impose on her other methods of contraception, including isolation from members of the opposite sex. They are precluded from making, and Valerie from obtaining the advantage of, the one choice that may be best for her, and which is available to all women competent to choose—contraception through sterilization. We conclude that the present legislative scheme, which absolutely precludes the sterilization option, impermissibly deprives developmentally disabled persons of privacy and liberty interests protected by the Fourteenth Amendment to the United States Constitution [ ].

The right to marriage and procreation are now recognized as fundamental, constitutionally protected interests.[ ] So too, is the right of a woman to choose not to bear children, and to implement that choice by use of contraceptive devices or medication, and, subject to reasonable restrictions, to terminate a pregnancy. These rights are aspects of the right of privacy which exists within the penumbra of the First Amendment to the United States Constitution[ ]. They are also within the concept of liberty protected against arbitrary restrictions by the Fourteenth Amendment.

Although the Supreme Court has not considered the precise question of the right to contraception in the context of an assertion that the right includes sterilization, that sterilization is encompassed within the right to privacy has been acknowledged in this state. * * *

[T]he Legislature has denied incompetent women the procreative choice that is recognized as a fundamental, constitutionally protected right of all other adult women. We realize that election of the method of contraception to be utilized, or indeed whether to choose contraception at all, cannot realistically be deemed a "choice" available to an incompetent since any election must of necessity be made on behalf of the incompetent by others. The interests of the incompetent which mandate recognition of procreative choice as an aspect of the fundamental right to privacy and liberty do not differ from the interests of women able to give voluntary consent to this procedure, however. That these interests include the individual's right to personal growth and development is implicit in decisions of both the United States Supreme Court and this court.

* * *

An incompetent developmentally disabled woman has no less interest in a satisfying or fulfilling life free from the burdens of an unwanted pregnancy than does her competent sister. Her interest in maximizing her opportunities for such a life through habilitation is recognized and given statutory protection by [other state laws that have recognized that many developmentally disabled persons lead self-sufficient, fulfilling lives, and become loving, competent, and caring marriage partners and parents, as well as laws creating social supports to assist these individuals in achieving their maximum developmental potential.] If the state withholds from her the only safe and reliable method of contraception suitable to her condition, it necessarily limits her opportunity for habilitation and thereby her freedom to pursue a fulfilling life. Therefore, whether approached as an infringement of the right of privacy under the First Amendment or the privacy right that is found within the liberty protected by the Fourteenth Amendment, and whether analyzed under due process or equal protection principles, the issue is whether withholding the option of sterilization as a method of contraception to this class of women is constitutionally permissible. Because the rights involved are fundamental the permissibility of the restriction must be justified by a "compelling state interest," and may be no broader than necessary to protect that interest. [ ]

* * *

The state interest [ ] must be in precluding the option of sterilization because it is in most cases an irreversible procedure. Necessarily implicit in the interest asserted by the state is an assumption that the conservatee may at some future time elect to bear children. While the prohibition of sterilization may be a reasonable means by which to protect some conservatees' right to procreative choice, here it sweeps too broadly for it extends to individuals who cannot make that choice and will not be able to do so in the future. [ ]

Respondent argues that the ban is, nonetheless, necessary because past experience demonstrates that when the power to authorize sterilization of incompetents has been conferred on the judiciary it has been subject to abuse. Again, however, the rationale fails since less restrictive alternatives to total prohibition are available in statutory and procedural safeguards as yet untried in this state. [ ]

## NOTES AND QUESTIONS

1. *Lessons of the Past.* One justice in the *Valerie N.* case wrote a particularly strong dissent:

> Today's holding will permit the state, through the legal fiction of substituted consent, to deprive many women permanently of the right to conceive and bear children. The majority run roughshod over this fundamental constitutional right in a misguided attempt to guarantee a procreative choice for one they assume has never been capable of choice and never will be. * * *

> The majority opinion opens the door to abusive sterilization practices which will serve the convenience of conservators, parents, and service providers rather than incompetent conservatees. The ugly history of sterilization abuse against developmentally disabled persons in the name of seemingly enlightened social policies counsels a different choice.

Do you share the dissent's concern? Is there a process we could use to ensure that decisions are truly being made in the person's best interest, as opposed to what is more convenient for parents or conservators? How do we ensure that discriminatory or uninformed assumptions about people with developmental disabilities are not seeping into the decision-making process and leading to decisions that devalue their autonomy and right to equal treatment?

Despite finding the sterilization ban unconstitutional, the majority ultimately affirmed the trial court's denial of the parents' request to authorize sterilization, based on insufficient evidence that sterilization was necessary and that no less intrusive means were available. The affirmance was without prejudice, though, which meant the plaintiffs could renew their application for the power to consent to Valerie's sterilization once they had supporting evidence.

2.   *Judicial Safeguards Against Abuse.* The majority opinion went on to discuss the kind of procedural safeguards that have been used in other states to avoid abuse in these circumstances. The framework it referenced (and commonly used by other states) was established by the case In re Guardianship of Hayes, 93 Wash.2d 228, 608 P.2d 635 (1980):

> The decision [to authorize sterilization] can only be made in a superior court proceeding in which (1) the incompetent individual is represented by a disinterested guardian ad litem, (2) the court has received independent advice based upon a comprehensive medical, psychological, and social evaluation of the individual, and (3) to the greatest extent possible, the court has elicited and taken into account the view of the incompetent individual.

> Within this framework, the judge must first find [ ] the individual is (1) incapable of making his or her own decision about sterilization, and (2) unlikely to develop sufficiently to make an informed judgment about sterilization in the foreseeable future.

> Next it must be proved [ ] that there is a need for contraception. The judge must find that the individual is (1) physically capable of procreation, and (2) likely to engage in sexual activity at the present or in the near future under circumstances likely to result in pregnancy, and must find in addition that (3) the nature and extent of the individual's disability, as determined by empirical evidence and not solely on the basis of standardized tests, renders him or her permanently incapable of caring for a child, even with reasonable assistance.

> Finally, there must be no alternatives to sterilization. The judge must find that (1) all less drastic contraceptive methods, including supervision, education and training, have been proved unworkable or inapplicable, and (2) the proposed method of sterilization entails the least invasion of the body of the individual. In addition, it must be shown [ ] that (3) the current state of scientific and medical knowledge does not suggest either (a) that a reversible sterilization procedure or other less drastic contraceptive method will shortly be available or (b) that science is on the threshold of an advance in the treatment of the individual's disability.

The court also noted that the standard of proof for the above requirements was "clear, cogent and convincing evidence." Do you think this framework adequately safeguards against abuse? Some have read the *Hayes* requirements as effectively removing the possibility of the sterilization of the developmentally disabled. Can you imagine a case that would meet these requirements?

## VI.  MATERNAL-FETAL DECISION MAKING

The topics covered so far in this chapter have dealt with either government restrictions on women's right to prevent or terminate pregnancy, or government's interference with one's ability to procreate. But when a woman is pregnant and wants to carry the fetus to term, can the government compel medical intervention when the woman either does not or cannot consent, on the grounds that such intervention is necessary to protect fetal life? When an apparent conflict arises between the mother's choices and the health of the fetus, how is that conflict resolved? The case below presents this conflict in extreme circumstances—where both the mother's and fetus's lives are at stake. Consider whether the majority and dissent's contrasting approaches are helpful for resolving such conflicts in less extreme circumstances.

## IN RE A.C.
District of Columbia Court of Appeals, 1990.
573 A.2d 1235.

TERRY, ASSOCIATE JUDGE:

\* \* \*

We are confronted here with two profoundly difficult and complex issues. First, we must determine who has the right to decide the course of medical treatment for a patient who, although near death, is pregnant with a viable fetus. Second, we must establish how that decision should be made if the patient cannot make it for herself—more specifically, how a court should proceed when faced with a pregnant patient, *in extremis,* who is apparently incapable of making an informed decision regarding medical care for herself and her fetus. We hold that in virtually all cases the question of what is to be done is to be decided by the patient—the pregnant woman—on behalf of herself and the fetus. If the patient is incompetent or otherwise unable to give an informed consent to a proposed course of medical treatment, then her decision must be ascertained through the procedure known as substituted judgment. \* \* \*

### I

This case came before the trial court when George Washington University Hospital petitioned the emergency judge in chambers for declaratory relief as to how it should treat its patient, A.C., who was close to death from cancer and was twenty-six and one-half weeks pregnant with a viable fetus. After a hearing lasting approximately three hours, which was held at the hospital (though not in A.C.'s room), the court ordered that a caesarean section be performed on A.C. to deliver the fetus. \* \* \* The caesarean was performed, and a baby girl, L.M.C., was delivered. Tragically, the child died within two and one-half hours, and the mother died two days later.

\* \* \*

## II

A.C. was first diagnosed as suffering from cancer at the age of thirteen. In the ensuing years she underwent major surgery several times, together with multiple radiation treatments and chemotherapy. A.C. married when she was twenty-seven, during a period of remission, and soon thereafter she became pregnant. She was excited about her pregnancy and very much wanted the child. Because of her medical history, she was referred in her fifteenth week of pregnancy to the high-risk pregnancy clinic at George Washington University Hospital.

On Tuesday, June 9, 1987, when A.C. was approximately twenty-five weeks pregnant, she went to the hospital for a scheduled check-up. Because she was experiencing pain in her back and shortness of breath, an x-ray was taken, revealing an apparently inoperable tumor which nearly filled her right lung. On Thursday, June 11, A.C. was admitted to the hospital as a patient. By Friday her condition had temporarily improved, and when asked if she really wanted to have her baby, she replied that she did.

Over the weekend, A.C.'s condition worsened considerably. Accordingly, on Monday, June 15, members of the medical staff treating A.C. assembled, along with her family, in A.C.'s room. The doctors then informed her that her illness was terminal, and A.C. agreed to palliative treatment designed to extend her life until at least her twenty-eighth week of pregnancy. The "potential outcome [for] the fetus," according to the doctors, would be much better at twenty-eight weeks than at twenty-six weeks if it were necessary to "intervene." A.C. knew that the palliative treatment she had chosen presented some increased risk to the fetus, but she opted for this course both to prolong her life for at least another two weeks and to maintain her own comfort. When asked if she still wanted to have the baby, A.C. was somewhat equivocal, saying "something to the effect of 'I don't know, I think so.' " As the day moved toward evening, A.C.'s condition grew still worse, and at about 7:00 or 8:00 p.m. she consented to intubation to facilitate her breathing.

The next morning, June 16, the trial court convened a hearing at the hospital in response to the hospital's request for a declaratory judgment. The court appointed counsel for both A.C. and the fetus, and the District of Columbia was permitted to intervene for the fetus as *parens patriae.* * * *

* * *

There was no evidence before the court showing that A.C. consented to, or even contemplated, a caesarean section before her twenty-eighth week of pregnancy. There was, in fact, considerable dispute as to whether she would have consented to an immediate caesarean delivery at the time the hearing was held. A.C.'s mother opposed surgical intervention, testifying that A.C. wanted "to live long enough to hold that baby" and that she expected to do so, "even though she knew she was terminal." Dr. Hamner [a treating obstetrician] testified that, given A.C.'s medical problems, he did not think she would have chosen to deliver a child with a substantial degree of impairment. * * *

After hearing this testimony and the arguments of counsel, the trial court made oral findings of fact. It found, first, that A.C. would probably die, according to uncontroverted medical testimony, "within the next twenty-four to forty-eight hours;" second, that A.C. was "pregnant with a twenty-six and a half week viable fetus who, based upon uncontroverted medical testimony, has approximately a fifty to sixty percent chance to survive if a caesarean section is performed as soon as possible;" third, that because the fetus was viable, "the state has [an] important and legitimate interest in protecting the potentiality of human life;" and fourth, that there had been some testimony that the operation "may very well hasten the death of [A.C.]," but that there had also been testimony that delay would greatly increase the risk to the fetus and that "the prognosis is not great for the fetus to be delivered post-mortem * * *." Most significantly, the court found:

> The court is of the view that it does not clearly know what [A.C.'s] present views are with respect to the issue of whether or not the child should live or die. She's presently unconscious. As late as Friday of last week, she wanted the baby to live. As late as yesterday, she did not know for sure.

Having made these findings of fact and conclusions of law, * * * the court ordered that a caesarean section be performed to deliver A.C.'s child.

The court's decision was then relayed to A.C., who had regained consciousness. [When the court reconvened later in the day, Dr. Hamner testified that A.C. then consented to the procedure.] When the court suggested moving the hearing to A.C.'s bedside, Dr. Hamner discouraged the court from doing so, but he and Dr. Weingold, together with A.C.'s mother and husband, went to A.C.'s room to confirm her consent to the procedure. What happened then was recounted to the court a few minutes later:

* * *

> Dr. Weingold: She does not make sounds because of the tube in her windpipe. She nods and she mouths words. One can see what she's saying rather readily. She asked whether she would survive the operation. She asked [Dr.] Hamner if he would perform the operation. He told her he would only perform it if she authorized it but it would be done in any case. She understood that. She then seemed to pause for a few moments and then very clearly mouthed words several times, *I don't want it done, I don't want it done.* Quite clear to me.

I would obviously state the obvious and that is this is an environment in which, from my perspective as a physician, this would not be an informed consent one way or the other. She's under tremendous stress with the family on both sides, but I'm satisfied that I heard clearly what she said. * * *

Dr. Weingold later qualified his opinion as to A.C.'s ability to give an informed consent, stating that he thought the environment for an informed consent was non-existent because A.C. was in intensive care, flanked by a weeping husband and mother. He added:

I think she's in contact with reality, clearly understood who Dr. Hamner was. Because of her attachment to him [she] wanted him to perform the surgery. Understood he would not unless she consented and did not consent.

That is, in my mind, very clear evidence that she is responding, understanding, and is capable of making such decisions. * * *

After hearing this new evidence, the court found that it was "still not clear what her intent is" and again ordered that a caesarean section be performed. * * * The operation took place, but the baby lived for only a few hours, and A.C. succumbed to cancer two days later.

* * *

## IV

* * *

### A.   Informed Consent and Bodily Integrity

* * *

* * * [O]ur analysis of this case begins with the tenet common to all medical treatment cases: that any person has the right to make an informed choice, if competent to do so, to accept or forgo medical treatment. * * *

In the same vein, courts do not compel one person to permit a significant intrusion upon his or her bodily integrity for the benefit of another person's health. See, e.g., McFall v. Shimp, 10 Pa.D. & C.3d 90 (Allegheny County Ct.1978). In McFall the court refused to order Shimp to donate bone marrow which was necessary to save the life of his cousin, McFall:

The common law has consistently held to a rule which provides that one human being is under no legal compulsion to give aid or to take action to save another human being or to rescue. * * *

* * * Even though Shimp's refusal would mean death for McFall, the court would not order Shimp to allow his body to be invaded. It has been

suggested that fetal cases are different because a woman who "has chosen to lend her body to bring [a] child into the world" has an enhanced duty to assure the welfare of the fetus, sufficient even to require her to undergo caesarean surgery.[ ] Surely, however, a fetus cannot have rights in this respect superior to those of a person who has already been born.[8]

\* \* \*

There are two additional arguments against overriding A.C.'s objections to caesarean surgery. First, as the American Public Health Association cogently states in its *amicus curiae* brief:

> Rather than protecting the health of women and children, court-ordered caesareans erode the element of trust that permits a pregnant woman to communicate to her physician—without fear of reprisal—all information relevant to her proper diagnosis and treatment. An even more serious consequence of court-ordered intervention is that it drives women at high risk of complications during pregnancy and childbirth out of the health care system to avoid coerced treatment.

Second, and even more compellingly, any judicial proceeding in a case such as this will ordinarily take place—like the one before us here—under time constraints so pressing that it is difficult or impossible for the mother to communicate adequately with counsel, or for counsel to organize an effective factual and legal presentation in defense of her liberty and privacy interests and bodily integrity. \* \* \*

\* \* \*

### B.    Substituted Judgment

\* \* \* Sometimes, however, as our analysis presupposes here, a once competent patient will be unable to render an informed decision. In such a case, we hold that the court must make a substituted judgment on behalf of the patient, based on all the evidence. This means that the duty of the court, "as surrogate for the incompetent, is to determine as best it can what choice that individual, if competent, would make with respect to medical procedures."[ ]

\* \* \*

We have found no reported opinion applying the substituted judgment procedure to the case of an incompetent pregnant patient whose own life may be shortened by a caesarean section, and whose unborn child's chances of survival may hang on the court's decision. Despite this precedential void,

---

8    There are also practical consequences to consider. What if A.C. had refused to comply with a court order that she submit to a caesarean? Enforcement could be accomplished only through physical force or its equivalent. A.C. would have to be fastened with restraints to the operating table, or perhaps involuntarily rendered unconscious by forcibly injecting her with an anesthetic, and then subjected to unwanted major surgery. Such actions would surely give one pause in a civilized society, especially when A.C. had done no wrong.

we conclude that substituted judgment is the best procedure to follow in such a case because it most clearly respects the right of the patient to bodily integrity. * * *

* * *

Because it is the patient's decisional rights which the substituted judgment inquiry seeks to protect, courts are in accord that the greatest weight should be given to the previously expressed wishes of the patient. This includes prior statements, either written or oral, even though the treatment alternatives at hand may not have been addressed. * * *

Courts in substituted judgment cases have also acknowledged the importance of probing the patient's value system as an aid in discerning what the patient would choose. We agree with this approach. [Ed. note: The court then discussed the ways in which it could determine the substituted judgment of the patient. For a fuller discussion of this issue, see Chapter 5.]

### C.   The Trial Court's Ruling

* * * The [trial] court did not * * * make a finding as to what A.C. would have chosen to do if she were competent. Instead, the court undertook to balance the state's and [the fetus's] interests in surgical intervention against A.C.'s perceived interest in not having the caesarean performed.

* * *

What a trial court must do in a case such as this is to determine, if possible, whether the patient is capable of making an informed decision about the course of her medical treatment. If she is, and if she makes such a decision, her wishes will control in virtually all cases. If the court finds that the patient is incapable of making an informed consent (and thus incompetent), then the court must make a substituted judgment. * * *

Having said that, we go no further. We need not decide whether, or in what circumstances, the state's interests can ever prevail over the interests of a pregnant patient. * * * Indeed, some may doubt that there could ever be a situation extraordinary or compelling enough to justify a massive intrusion into a person's body, such as a caesarean section, against that person's will. Whether such a situation may someday present itself is a question that we need not strive to answer here. * * *

* * *

BELSON, ASSOCIATE JUDGE, concurring in part and dissenting in part:

* * *

I think it appropriate * * * to state my disagreement with the very limited view the majority opinion takes of the circumstances in which the interests of a viable unborn child can afford such compelling reasons. The state's interest in preserving human life and the viable unborn child's interest in survival are entitled, I think, to more weight than I find them assigned by the majority when it states that "in virtually all cases the decision of the patient * * * will control." I would hold that in those instances, fortunately rare, in which the viable unborn child's interest in living and the state's parallel interest in protecting human life come into conflict with the mother's decision to forgo a procedure such as a caesarean section, a balancing should be struck in which the unborn child's and the state's interest are entitled to substantial weight.

* * *

The balancing test should be applied in instances in which women become pregnant and carry an unborn child to the point of viability. This is not an unreasonable classification because, I submit, a woman who carries a child to viability is in fact a member of a unique category of persons. Her circumstances differ fundamentally from those of other potential patients for medical procedures that will aid another person, for example, a potential donor of bone marrow for transplant. This is so because she has undertaken to bear another human being, and has carried an unborn child to viability. Another unique feature of the situation we address arises from the singular nature of the dependency of the unborn child upon the mother. A woman carrying a viable unborn child is not in the same category as a relative, friend, or stranger called upon to donate bone marrow or an organ for transplant. Rather, the expectant mother has placed herself in a special class of persons who are bringing another person into existence, and upon whom that other person's life is totally dependent. Also, uniquely, the viable unborn child is literally captive within the mother's body. No other potential beneficiary of a surgical procedure on another is in that position.

* * *

I next address the sensitive question of how to balance the competing rights and interests of the viable unborn child and the state against those of the rare expectant mother who elects not to have a caesarean section necessary to save the life of her child. The indisputable view that a woman carrying a viable child has an extremely strong interest in her own life, health, bodily integrity, privacy, and religious beliefs necessarily requires that her election be given correspondingly great weight in the balancing process. In a case, however, where the court in an exercise of a substituted judgment has concluded that the patient would probably opt against a caesarean section, the court should vary the weight to be given this factor in proportion to the confidence the court has in the accuracy of its conclusion. Thus, in a case where the indicia of the incompetent patient's judgment are equivocal, the court should accord this factor correspondingly less weight. The appropriate weight to be given other factors will have to be worked out by the development of law in this area, and cannot be prescribed in a single court opinion. Some considerations obviously merit special attention in the balancing process. One such consideration is any danger to the mother's life or health, physical or mental, including the relatively small but still significant danger that necessarily inheres in any caesarean delivery, and including especially any danger that exceeds that level. The mother's religious beliefs as they relate to the operation would appear to deserve inclusion in the balancing process.

On the other side of the analysis, it is appropriate to look to the relative likelihood of the unborn child's survival. * * * The child's interest in being born with as little impairment as possible should also be considered. This may weigh in favor of a delivery sooner rather than later. The most important factor on this side of the scale, however, is life itself, because the viable unborn child that dies because of the mother's refusal to have a caesarean delivery is deprived, entirely and irrevocably, of the life on which the child was about to embark.

* * *

## NOTES AND QUESTIONS

1.   *Balancing of Interests?* As the opinions in *A.C.* suggest, decisions made by or on behalf of the mother to best serve her health or other interests may conflict with protection of the fetus; this conflict forces courts to answer two questions. First, should the court balance the interests of the fetus (or the interests of the state in protecting the fetus) with the interests of the mother? If the answer to that question is "no," as it was for the majority in *A.C.,* the issue becomes the comparatively simple one of determining the wishes of the mother. See In re Baby Boy Doe, 260 Ill.App.3d 392, 198 Ill.Dec. 267, 632 N.E.2d 326 (Ill.App.1994), where the court refused to balance the interests of a fetus (or the interests of the state in protecting a fetus) against the interests of a competent pregnant woman who refused a caesarean section, even though doctors believed her decision put the life of her fetus at risk.

If there is a decision to balance the interests, however, as the dissenting opinion suggests, the court must also face the question of what standards to apply. Are the interests of the fetus or the state as strong as the interests of the mother? Can the relative strengths of these different interests vary from case to case, depending upon the stage of development of the fetus, the consequences of the decision to be made, or other factors? How might those interests be balanced if the woman objects to recommended medical care on religious grounds? See, e.g., Raleigh Fitkin-Paul Morgan Memorial Hospital v. Anderson, 42 N.J. 421, 201 A.2d 537 (N.J. 1964) (ordering blood transfusions to save an "unborn child" over the objections of a woman who refused the transfusion due to her religious convictions as a Jehovah's Witness); In re Application of Jamaica Hospital, 128 Misc.2d 1006, 491 N.Y.S.2d 898

(Sup.Ct.1985) (ordering blood transfusion to save fetus pre-viability); Jefferson v. Griffin Spalding County Hospital Authority, 247 Ga. 86, 274 S.E.2d 457 (1981) (ordering a caesarean section against the religiously motivated wishes of the mother when physicians argued that failure to do so would result in the death of both the mother and the fetus, noting the "duty of the state to protect a living, unborn human being from meeting [ ]death before being given the opportunity to live.").

2. *Assessing Risk to Fetal Health.* One reason that many commentators have opposed judicial intervention to require pregnant women to undergo medical care for the benefit of their fetuses is the fact that medical diagnosis in this area can be wrong. Doctors seem willing to testify that intervention is necessary to save the fetus even when the prognosis following nonintervention is quite uncertain. There is a series of cases suggesting that when doctors testify that a caesarean is necessary for the health of the fetus, if the mother "escapes" and attempts a normal vaginal birth, there is a good chance the child will be born without complication. J. Fletcher, Drawing Moral Lines in Fetal Therapy, 29 Clin. Obstetrics & Gynecology 595 (1986). Fletcher summarizes his review of six cases:

> First, inaccuracies and possible misdiagnosis appear to be involved in half of the cases * * * since babies were born healthy after vaginal delivery. If precedents flow from examples flawed by faulty assumptions or mistaken evaluations, errors may be replicated. These outcomes also should remind all concerned of the possibility of misdiagnosis before fetal therapy. Forced fetal therapy on the basis of misdiagnosis would constitute an ethical megadisaster.

29 Clin. Obstetrics and Gynecology at 599. See also In re Baby Boy Doe, supra (mother delivered a "normal and healthy" baby despite predictions of disaster). How closely should the court scrutinize medical assertions about what is necessary for fetal health?

3. *Using the Criminal System to Compel Medical Treatment.* Medical treatment has also been coerced by threatening criminal punishment or confinement. In 1989, the Medical University of South Carolina, along with other state and local law enforcement and social service agencies, hatched a plan to deal with what they saw as the pernicious effects of drug use by pregnant women. The program targeted women who met certain guidelines, for example, those with little or incomplete prenatal care. This meant the women who were targeted were also low-income and dependent on public health care providers, such as the Medical University of South Carolina. The women were also predominantly African American.

The women were tested for cocaine use when they arrived at the hospital to deliver their babies. Those who tested positive were given a "choice" between enrolling in a substance abuse program and being arrested for their drug use. Those who chose the treatment option were not prosecuted unless they failed to adhere to the treatment plan or failed a subsequent drug test; the others were reported to, and subsequently arrested by, the police. No other hospital in Charleston chose to participate in the program.

Ten of the arrested mothers brought suit against the hospital and others. In 2001 the Supreme Court, in a 6–3 opinion, determined that the Charleston process constituted an illegal warrantless search and seizure prohibited by the Fourth Amendment. Ferguson v. City of Charleston, 532 U.S. 67, 121 S.Ct. 1281, 149 L.Ed.2d 205 (2001). Justice Stevens, for the Court, pointed out that the "direct and primary purpose" of the test was to aid the police in enforcing a criminal law, and that the Fourth Amendment was implicated even if the ultimate goal of the hospital was to encourage women to get treatment. Justice Kennedy, concurring, pointed out that the case did not prohibit a state from punishing women who put their fetuses at risk, and Justice Scalia, dissenting, said that the majority "proves once again that no good deed goes unpunished."

Indeed, some criminal prosecutions for maternal substance use, based on asserted harm to the fetus, have been successful. For example, two years after the *Ferguson* decision, a woman in South Carolina was convicted of homicide by child abuse for using cocaine during pregnancy that resulted in a stillbirth and she was sentenced to 20 years imprisonment. State v. McKnight, 352 S.C. 635, 576 S.E.2d 168 (2003). See also Ex Parte Ankrom, 152 So.3d 397 (Ala. 2013) (upholding convictions of two women for chemical endangerment of child because they ingested illegal substances during pregnancy). Most state courts have rejected the use of traditional child endangerment or abuse laws for such prosecutions. See, e.g., State v. Wade, 232 S.W.3d 663 (Mo. App. 2007); State v. Martinez, 139 N.M. 741, 137 P.3d 1195 (App.2006); State v. Aiwohi, 109 Hawai'i 115, 123 P.3d 1210 (2005); Reinesto v. Superior Court, 182 Ariz. 190, 894 P.2d 733 (Ariz.App.1995); Johnson v. State, 602 So.2d 1288 (Fla.1992) (reversing a conviction for delivery of a controlled substance from a mother to her child after birth, but before the umbilical cord was severed). Nonetheless, thirty-eight states have enacted statutes specifically prohibiting feticide or harm to unborn children, and some of these have been used as authority for arresting pregnant women. See Lynn M. Paltrow and Jeanne Flavin, Arrests of and Forced Interventions on Pregnant Women in the United States, 1973–2005: Implications for Women's Legal Status and Public Health, 38 J. of Health Pol., Pol'y, & L. 299 (2013). Even states that reject such criminal prosecutions may be willing to allow other government action against women who ingest drugs or alcohol during pregnancy. For example, in State v. Louk, 237 W.Va. 200, 786 S.E.2d 219 (2016), the Supreme Court of Appeals of West Virginia held that an unborn fetus was not a "child" within the meaning of a statute imposing criminal penalty for child neglect resulting in death. But just one year later, the same court found that the presence of illegal drugs in a child's system at birth, in light of mother's admitted use of illegal drugs during pregnancy, was sufficient evidence that the child was abused and/or neglected for purposes of a civil petition by the state Department of Health and Human Resources. In re ALCM, 239 W.Va. 382, 801 S.E.2d 260 (2017).

4.    *Civil Confinement.* The remedy of civil commitment or court ordered protective custody may be used as an alternative to criminal law to prevent

pregnant mothers from engaging in certain behavior. Some states have promulgated statutes that provide explicitly that women who put their fetuses at risk may be restrained from doing so by the court. Is the use of the civil commitment or protective custody remedy any less concerning than the use of the criminal sanction? Are fetuses (and mothers) better protected because of the existence of the possibility of civil commitment?

5.    *Connection Between the State's Action and Fetal Health.* A balancing test to determine whether the state can compel intervention depends upon the state's ability to show that its action is justified by its interest in protecting fetal health. In prosecutions of maternal drug use, however, this assertion has been challenged by health care providers and public health officials. They agree that fetal exposure to drugs and alcohol is an important public health concern because of the risk it poses to the child's development, but they argue that a treatment-focused approach that is supportive and respects patient autonomy, rather than a punitive approach, is more effective for the health of the child and woman. See American Society of Addiction Medicine, Public Policy Statement on Women, Alcohol and Other Drugs, and Pregnancy (Jul. 11, 2011) (noting that women who are pregnant or capable of becoming pregnant are "especially important candidate[s] for intervention, education, and treatment," but that incarceration as a means of preventing fetal exposure "may compromise both maternal and fetal health and inhibit the pregnant woman's opportunity to receive effective treatments to address her long-term recovery from her substance-related disorder"); American College of Obstetricians and Gynecologists Committee on Health Care for Underserved Women, Substance Abuse Reporting and Pregnancy: The Role of Obstetrician-Gynecologist, 117 Obstetrics Gynecology 200 (2011) (reaffirmed 2014) ("incarceration and the threat of incarceration have proved to be ineffective in reducing the incidence of alcohol or drug abuse" and providers are "encouraged to work with state legislators to retract legislation that punishes women for substance abuse during pregnancy"); American Academy of Pediatrics (AAP), Policy Statement: A Public Health Response to Opioid Use in Pregnancy, 139 Pediatrics 1 (Mar. 2017) (noting that punitive measures "are not in the best interest of the health of the mother-infant dyad," and recommending treatment programs that provide "nonjudgmental, trauma-informed services").

A study of drug treatment programs has shown that many pregnant women have trouble accessing them voluntarily, either because the programs will not take them or because of limited slots. See Rebecca Stone, Pregnant Women and Substance Use: Fear, Stigma, and Barriers to Care, 3 Health and Justice (2015). From a public health perspective, it seems counterproductive for states to use threats of criminal enforcement to force women into treatment, given the dearth of resources for women who want to access such programs voluntarily. In addition, some have argued that the state's poor treatment of pregnant women once imprisoned actually undermines the state's purported interests in maternal and fetal health. Examples of this include shackling women during childbirth and preventing incarcerated women from caring for their newborns in ways that are important for child health. See Priscilla Ocen,

Punishing Pregnancy: Race, Incarceration and the Shackling of Pregnant Prisoners, 100 Cal. L. Rev. 1239 (2012).

Forced medical interventions, in combination with criminal or civil confinement, have even been used in cases where there was no evidence of conduct that created a risk of harm to the fetus. Consider an example described in a recent news article: A women who was 14 weeks pregnant voluntarily disclosed at a prenatal checkup that she had been addicted to Percocet the year before. She was not still using drugs and only mentioned it to her doctor because she thought her doctor should know. A urine test confirmed that she was not using drugs, but her doctor and a social worker insisted that she start an anti-addiction drug anyway. The patient refused, and some weeks later county sheriffs came to her home and took her to court, where her doctor accused her of endangering her fetus and she was ordered to attend a mandatory 78-day stay at a drug treatment facility or risk going to jail. Erik Eckholm, Case Explores Rights of Fetus Versus Mother, N.Y. Times (Oct. 23, 2013).

6.    *Punishing Pregnancy and Other Status?* Criminal and civil actions against pregnant women in the name of protecting fetal health have led some scholars to suggest such programs constitute a status-based system of punishment implicating reproductive justice concerns. See, e.g., Priscilla A. Ocen, Birthing Injustice: Pregnancy as a Status Offense, 85 Geo. Wash. L. Rev. 1163 (2017). If a mother is imprisoned for the term of her pregnancy *in order to protect her fetus,* is she being punished for the crime she committed, or for her pregnancy? What if the behavior the woman is punished for would otherwise be lawful if she weren't pregnant? There is tension between the various characteristics of addiction that simultaneously cause society to classify it as behavior deserving of punishment and as an illness deserving treatment. Much has been made about the growing understanding of, and empathy for, people who struggle with substance use disorder (SUD), especially with the national spotlight on opioid addiction. How are the pregnant women who suffer from SUD treated in this public discourse?

Consider also that the testing and surveillance of pregnant women for drug use effectively targets *poor* pregnant women who depend on public resources, as well as those more likely to have interactions with the criminal justice system, such as *racial and ethnic minorities*. South Carolina did not have a similar program targeting mothers who delivered their babies at private hospitals in affluent communities. The study by Lynn Paltrow and Jeanne Flavin, supra, documented over four hundred cases of medical and criminal interventions targeting pregnant women, finding that arrests or deprivations of physical liberty disproportionately impacted minorities and low income individuals. This is despite evidence that drug use is comparable among whites and non-whites. Some scholars have argued that uneven criminal enforcement against certain groups reflects troubling assumptions that parenting by these women—namely poor women and racial or ethnic minorities— is "inherently risky"—a view that harkens back to earlier sterilization programs targeting these same groups. See, e.g., Khiara Bridges, The Poverty of Privacy Rights

(2017); Michele Goodwin, Fetal Protection Laws: Moral Panic and the New Constitutional Battlefront, 102 Calif. L. Rev. 781 (2014).

The role of poverty in these cases presents another complicating factor. There is growing recognition of the outsized role of social determinants of health: food insecurity, housing insecurity, exposure to violence, trauma, environmental hazards, discrimination, and other poverty-related factors can contribute to poor physical and mental health, which in turn pose risks to maternal and fetal health. See, e.g., Z. Mahmoodi et al., Association of Maternal Working Condition with Low Birth Weight: The Social Determinants of Health Approach, 5 Ann. Med. Health Sci. Res. 385 (2015); N.N. Sarkar et al., The Impact of Intimate Partner Violence on Women's Reproductive Health and Pregnancy Outcome, 28 J. of Obstetrics and Gynaecology 266 (2008). How do we determine whether poor fetal outcomes are due to a specific act like drug or alcohol use, to some other behavioral, social, or environmental factor, or to some combination of factors? If causation cannot be proved, is it fair to use criminal or civil sanctions against pregnant women to prevent certain behavior? How effective will the government's efforts be as a health matter, if it only addresses substance use temporarily with confinement or imprisonment, but does not address the other social factors shaping fetal and child health?

7. *Pregnancy, Employment & Sex Discrimination.* As noted above, environmental hazards may pose a risk to fetal health, and some employment environments that are safe for workers may not be safe for workers' fetuses. Even in cases where there may be some risk to fetal health, the question of whether such employment is "good" or "bad" for the fetus may not be simple to answer. For example, employees may not have a choice of where to work, and the job may provide financial resources essential for securing basic needs for the child's well-being. Even if one has a choice, certain jobs may provide greater financial security, independence, and personal fulfillment to the parent, promoting greater psychological health and enhancing the family's resources in ways that may have a significant positive effect on pregnancy outcomes and long-term well-being.

Employers have sought to exclude pregnant women (or even women who may become pregnant) from jobs that could put fetuses at risk—either because the employers wish to protect the fetuses, or because the employers wish to protect themselves from adverse publicity, increased health insurance costs and potential tort liability. Should an employer be able to refuse to assign people to certain jobs based on their capacity to get pregnant because of the possible risk of future harm? This issue has received attention almost exclusively where the employee is a woman (i.e., a potential mother) rather than a man (i.e., a potential father) even though occupational hazards to men may affect the health of the fetus as well.

The United States Supreme Court considered this issue under Title VII of the Civil Rights Act of 1964 in International Union, United Automobile Workers v. Johnson Controls, Inc., 499 U.S. 187, 111 S.Ct. 1196, 113 L.Ed.2d

158 (1991). Johnson Controls excluded women of child-bearing age from its battery manufacturing operation unless they had been sterilized, because workers in that process sometimes developed very high levels of lead in their blood. The United States Supreme Court determined that this policy constituted disparate treatment by sex, under Title VII as amended by the Pregnancy Discrimination Act, which could be justified only if sex was a bona fide occupational qualification. The Court concluded:

> It is no more appropriate for the courts than it is for individual employers to decide whether a woman's reproductive role is more important to herself and her family than her economic role. Congress has left this choice to the woman as hers to make.

# VII.  ASSISTED REPRODUCTIVE TECHNOLOGIES (ART)

## A.  INTRODUCTION

### 1.  The Process of Human Reproduction

Those seeking medical help in facilitating reproduction do so because they want a child. The birth of a child requires the growth of a fetus in a woman's uterus. This, in turn, requires the implantation of a fertilized ovum (also called an egg or an oocyte) in the uterine wall. At least until the cloning of human beings is perfected, the ovum can implant in the uterine wall only if it has been fertilized by a sperm, a process which generally takes place in the fallopian tube.

Within a day of an ovum being fertilized by a sperm, it has divided twice, into a two- and then a four-celled "embryo" (sometimes called a "preembryo") and it is here that we must pause to consider the impact that our language has on our conceptualization and therefore our law. The terminology of early pregnancy is rife with alternative phraseology. For example, a fertilized ovum/egg/oocyte is also called a "zygote," or a cluster of dividing "blastomeres" which eventually divide into a "blastocyst" or hollow cellular ball. Some will argue that because there is no differentiated living matter generated in forming the blastocyst (i.e., there are no fetal or placental cells yet), this division of cell material is not a constructive development of living substance. It is a process which does nothing to distribute particular developmental qualities to particular parts of a resulting fetus. On the other hand, it is the preliminary stage which makes it possible for the blastocyst cell ball to implant and use materials from the uterine wall to grow and develop into a fetus. Obviously, the fertilization of the ovum by the sperm begins the embryonic process, although some use the term "embryo" only to apply to later stages of development.

At any rate, whether it is called an embryo, a preembryo or something else, the fertilized ovum continues its migration through the fallopian tube toward the uterus. The fertilized and subdividing ovum arrives at the lower end of the fallopian tube, hesitating for about two days before being expelled into the uterus. This delay allows the uterine lining to build up for successful implantation. The implantation of this cell cluster is a complicated biological process that takes several days.

Even when all other conditions are met, not all fertilized ova actually do implant and not all implanted ova survive until birth. About 50% of fertilized ova are expelled from the body before the woman has any reason to know that she is pregnant. Some of these spontaneous expulsions occur before implantation, and some occur during the first few days after the commencement of the implantation process.

There are several reasons that those who wish to raise children may not conceive them through this natural process. First, some are unable to participate in coital sexual relations, or choose not to participate in such relations. Others are infertile—that is, normal coitus does not result in a fertilized ovum that implants in the uterine wall and grows into a fetus and then a child. Although estimates vary, at least 10% of American couples are infertile. There are a variety of reasons for infertility. Some men do not produce sperm capable of fertilizing the ovum. Some women are unable to produce ova, for example, and others have fallopian tubes that cannot adequately accept ova to be fertilized, or do not permit the travel of fertilized ova to the uterus. In some cases, the "shell" around the ovum may not admit any sperm at all. In other cases, the ovum is successfully fertilized but the uterus is incapable of allowing for implantation of the fertilized ovum or of maintaining the implanted embryo through the pregnancy. In all of these cases, some form of intervention may allow those who could not become parents through unassisted coitus to achieve parenthood nonetheless.

## 2.   ART Interventions

The range of problems that prevent conception and child-bearing give rise to a wide variety of alternative interventions to facilitate reproduction:

- AIH (artificial insemination-homologous): artificial insemination of a woman with the sperm of the person who is intended to be the biological and nurturing father, often the husband;

- AID (artificial insemination-donor): artificial insemination of the woman with the sperm of someone who is presumed to have no continuing relationship with the child;

- IVF (*in vitro* fertilization): fertilizing an ovum outside of the uterus and then implanting it;

- embryo or egg transfer;

- genetic surrogacy: a woman who is not an intended parent agrees to become pregnant through assisted reproduction using her own gamete; and

- gestational surrogacy: a woman who is not an intended parent agrees to become pregnant through assisted reproduction using gametes that are not her own.

In many cases ART requires the involvement of a host of other people. A sperm source (who is not necessarily a sperm donor—but is usually a sperm vendor) is necessary where the problem is the lack of a man or a man's inability to produce physiologically adequate sperm; an ovum source is necessary where the problem is lack of a woman or a woman's inability to provide a potentially fertile ovum; and a uterus source (originally called a "surrogate mother," now more generally described as a "gestational mother") is necessary because of the lack of a woman or where the intended parent is unable or unwilling to carry the fertilized ovum through the pregnancy in her own uterus. The interventions may also vary in complexity, depending on the specific infertility program. Medical treatment of an ovum may allow it to be fertilized, and treatment of a fertilized ovum may allow it to be implanted. And sometimes a combination of these needs requires that there be a series of interventions to produce a pregnancy and a child. For example, a woman may be unable to produce ova and unable to carry a fertilized ovum in her uterus. There may be several ART options available to allow her to obtain both an ovum that can be fertilized (from an ovum source) and a uterus for the gestation of that fertilized ovum (from a surrogate).

## 3.   The Role of the Law

The law is often required to help parties sort out the formal relationships of those who undertake processes designed to facilitate reproduction. Legal rights and responsibilities arising out of ART may include obligations of support, decision making authority, inheritance, contractual duties, and so on. It is not hard to imagine the variety of unusual legal relationships which can develop as a consequence of medical and non-medical reproductive techniques. It is possible to have a child who is the product of sperm from one source (whose sperm may be mixed with sperm from several sources), an ovum extracted from one woman, implanted in another, and carried for the benefit of yet another set of parents who intend to nurture the child from the time of its birth. Such a child would have two genetic parents, a gestational mother, and two (or more?) intended (or contractual or nurturing) parents.

This implicates social and cultural norms about family, which has changed over time, due in part to ART's ability to facilitate nontraditional family structures. In the face of this change, the law has consistently been forced to answer questions about who *ought* to be treated as the legal parents. Should others involved in the process have any rights whatsoever? In addition, certain forms of ART result in the production of embryos that may never be used for procreative purposes. For what other purposes can they be used? What legal principles should guide our regulation of these embryos? And how might different theories of personhood or definitions of the beginning of life be relevant to these legal principles? This remainder of this section considers these questions.

## B. ART & PARENTAGE LAW

### IN THE INTEREST OF K.M.H.

Supreme Court of Kansas, 2007.
285 Kan. 53, 169 P.3d 1025.

BEIER, J.: This appeal from a consolidated child in need of care (CINC) case and a paternity action arises out of an artificial insemination leading to the birth of twins K.M.H. and K.C.H. We are called upon to decide the existence and extent of the parental rights of the known sperm donor, who alleges he had an agreement with the children's mother to act as the twins' father.

The twins' mother filed a CINC petition to establish that the donor had no parental rights under Kansas law. The donor sued for determination of his paternity. The district court sustained the mother's motion to dismiss, ruling that [the Kansas version of the 1973 Uniform Parentage Act (UPA)] was controlling and constitutional. That statute provides:

"The donor of semen provided to a licensed physician for use in artificial insemination of a woman other than the donor's wife is treated in law as if he were not the birth father of a child thereby conceived, unless agreed to in writing by the donor and the woman." K.S.A. 38–1114(f).

*Factual and Procedural Background*

* * * The mother, S.H., is an unmarried female lawyer who wanted to become a parent through artificial insemination from a known donor. She was a friend of the donor, D.H., an unmarried male nonlawyer, who agreed to provide sperm for the insemination. Both S.H. and D.H. are Kansas residents, and their oral arrangements for the donation occurred in Kansas, but S.H. underwent two inseminations with D.H.'s sperm in Missouri. [After the second, she became pregnant and ultimately gave birth to twins.]

* * *

There was no formal written contract between S.H. and D.H. concerning the donation of sperm, the artificial insemination, or the expectations of the parties with regard to D.H.'s parental rights or lack thereof.

* * *

The district judge ruled that Kansas law governed, that [the Kansas Version of the 1973 UPA] was constitutional and applicable * * *. The [trial court judge concluded] as a matter of law that D.H. had no legal rights or responsibilities regarding K.M.H. and K.C.H.

### Constitutionality of [the Kansas Version of the 1973 UPA]

In his brief, D.H. makes a general allegation that [the Kansas version of the 1973 UPA] offends the [equal protection and due process clauses of the] Constitution. [At oral argument D.H.] acknowledged that he no longer challenges the statute as unconstitutional on its face; rather, he argues it cannot be constitutionally applied to him, as a known sperm donor who alleges he had an oral agreement with the twins' mother that granted him parental rights. * * *

* * *

Given the relative newness of the medical procedure of artificial insemination, and thus the newness of [the Kansas version of the 1973 UPA's] attempt to regulate the relationships arising from it, it is not surprising that the issue raised by D.H. is one of first impression, not only in Kansas but nationally. We therefore begin our discussion of the constitutionality of the statute by surveying the landscape of various states' laws governing the rights of sperm donors for artificial insemination. This landscape and its ongoing evolution provide helpful context for our analysis of [the Kansas version of the 1973 UPA].

The majority of states that have enacted statutes concerning artificial insemination state that the husband of a married woman bears all rights and obligations of paternity as to any child conceived by artificial insemination, whether the sperm used was his own or a donor's.[ ] The 1973 Uniform Parentage Act * * * provided the model for many of the state artificial insemination statutes * * *. Section 5 of the original uniform Act provided:

(a) If, under the supervision of a licensed physician and with the consent of her husband, a wife is inseminated artificially with semen donated by a man not her husband, the husband is treated in law as if he were the natural father of a child thereby conceived. The husband's consent must be in writing and signed by him and his wife. The physician shall certify their signatures and the date of the insemination, and file the husband's consent with the [State Department of Health], where it shall be kept confidential and in a sealed file. However, the physician's failure to do so does not affect the father and child relationship. All papers and records pertaining to the insemination, whether part of the permanent record of a court or of a file held by the supervising physician or elsewhere, are subject to inspection only upon an order of the court for good cause shown.

(b)  The donor of semen provided to a licensed physician for use in artificial insemination of a *married* woman other than the donor's wife is treated in law as if he were not the natural father of a child thereby conceived." (Emphasis added.) Uniform Parentage Act (1973) § 5; 9B U.L.A. at 407–08.

The wording of this original Act and statutes that imitated it did not address the determination of a sperm donor's paternity when an *unmarried* woman conceived a child through artificial insemination. * * *

Certain states [ ] either anticipated the need for their original statutes to govern the relationship of a sperm donor to the child of an unmarried recipient as well as a married recipient or modified their original Uniform Act-patterned statutes to remove the word "married" from the § 5 (b) language. This meant these states' statutes contained complete bars to paternity for any sperm donor not married to the recipient, regardless of whether the recipient was married to someone else and regardless of whether the donor was known or anonymous. An example of such a provision reads: "The donor of semen provided to a licensed physician for use in artificial insemination of a woman other than the donor's wife is treated in law as if he were not the natural father of a child thereby conceived." See, e.g., Cal. Fam. Code § 7613(b) (West 2004) [ ].

* * *

In 1985, Kansas became one of the states that adopted portions of the Uniform Parentage Act of 1973 regarding presumptions of paternity, but it did not adopt any provision relating to artificial insemination.[ ]

In 1994, Kansas amended its statute to incorporate the 1973 Uniform Act's § 5(b) * * *.[ ] It did not differentiate between known and unknown or anonymous donors, but it did make two notable changes in the uniform language.

As discussed above, although the 1973 Uniform Act governed the paternity of children born only to married women as a result of artificial insemination with donor sperm, the version adopted by Kansas omitted the word "married."[ ] This drafting decision demonstrates the legislature's intent that the bar to donor paternity apply regardless of whether the recipient was married or unmarried.

The other alteration in the 1973 Uniform Act's language is directly at issue here. The Kansas Legislature provided that a sperm donor and recipient could choose to opt out of the donor paternity bar by written agreement.[ ] * * *

This second drafting decision is critical and sets this case apart from [the approach taken by other states]. * * *

Ultimately, in view of the requirement that we accept as true D.H.'s evidence supporting existence of an oral agreement, we are faced with a very precise question: Does our statute's requirement that any opt-out agreement between an unmarried mother and a known sperm donor be "in writing" result in an equal protection or due process violation? * * *

### Equal Protection

[The Kansas version of the 1973 UPA] draws a gender-based line between a necessarily female sperm recipient and a necessarily male sperm donor for an artificial insemination. By operation of the statute, the female is a potential parent or actual parent under all circumstances; by operation of the same statute, the male will never be a potential parent or actual parent unless there is a written agreement to that effect with the female. [T]he male's ability to insist on father status effectively disappears once he donates sperm. Until that point, he can unilaterally refuse to participate unless a written agreement on his terms exists. After donation, the male cannot force the fatherhood issue. The female can unilaterally decide if and when to use the donation for artificial insemination and can unilaterally deny any wish of the male for parental rights by refusing to enter into a written agreement.

The guiding principle of equal protection analysis is that similarly situated individuals should be treated alike. * * * In order to pass muster under the federal and state equal protection provisions, a classification that treats otherwise similarly situated individuals differently based solely on the individuals' genders must substantially further a legitimate legislative purpose; the government's objective must be important, and the classification substantially related to achievement of it.[ ]

Given the biological differences between females and males and the immutable role those differences play in conceiving and bearing a child, regardless of whether conception is achieved through sexual intercourse or artificial insemination, we are skeptical that S.H. and D.H. are truly similarly situated. However, assuming for purposes of argument that they are, we perceive several legitimate legislative purposes or important governmental objectives underlying [the Kansas version of the 1973 UPA].

[The Kansas version of the 1973 UPA] envisions that both married and unmarried women may become parents without engaging in sexual intercourse, either because of personal choice or because a husband or partner is infertile, impotent, or ill. It encourages men who are able and willing to donate sperm to such women by protecting the men from later unwanted claims for support from the mothers or the children. It protects women recipients as well, preventing potential claims of donors to parental rights and responsibilities, in the absence of an agreement. Its requirement that any such agreement be in writing enhances predictability, clarity, and enforceability. Although the timing of entry into a written agreement is not set out explicitly, the design of the statute implicitly encourages early resolution of the elemental question of whether a donor will have parental rights. Effectively, the parties must decide whether they will enter into a written agreement before any donation is made, while there is still balanced bargaining power on both sides of the parenting equation.

In our view, the statute's gender classification substantially furthers and is thus substantially related to these legitimate legislative purposes and important governmental objectives. [The Kansas version of the 1973 UPA] establishes the clear default positions of parties to artificial insemination. If these parties desire an arrangement different from the statutory norm, they are free to provide for it, as long as they do so in writing. * * *

### Due Process

* * *

We simply are not persuaded that the requirement of a writing transforms what is an otherwise constitutional statute into one that violates D.H.'s substantive due process rights. Although we agree * * * that one goal of the Kansas Parentage Act as a whole is to encourage fathers to voluntarily acknowledge paternity and child support obligations, the obvious impact of the plain language of this particular provision in the Act is to prevent the creation of parental status where it is not desired or expected. To a certain extent, D.H. * * * evidently misunderstand[s] the statute's mechanism. It ensures no *attachment* of parental rights to sperm donors in the absence of a written agreement to the contrary; it does not *cut off* rights that have already arisen and attached.

* * *

We also reject the argument from D.H. * * * that the statute inevitably makes the female the sole arbiter of whether a male can be a father to a child his sperm helps to conceive. This may be true, as we discussed above, once a donation is made, a recipient who becomes pregnant through artificial insemination using that donation can refuse to enter into an agreement to provide for donor paternity. This does not make the requirement of written agreement unconstitutional. Indeed, it is consistent with United States Supreme Court precedent making even a married pregnant woman the sole arbiter, regardless of her husband's wishes, of whether she continues a pregnancy to term. * * *

All of this being said, we cannot close our discussion of the constitutionality of [the Kansas version of the 1973 UPA] without observing that all that is constitutional is not necessarily wise. We are mindful of, and moved by, the Center's advocacy for public policy to maximize the chance of the availability of two parents—and two parents' resources—to Kansas children. We are also aware of continued evolution in regulation of artificial insemination in this and other countries. In particular, Britain and The Netherlands now ban anonymous sperm donations, near-perfect analogs to donations from known donors who will have no role beyond facilitating artificial insemination. These shifts formally recognize the understandable desires of at least some children conceived through artificial insemination to know the males from whom they have received half of their genes. The Human Fertilisation and Embryology Authority Act of 1990, as amended by Disclosure of Donor Information, Regulations 2004 No. 1511 (requiring, effective April 2005, British donors' identities to be made available to donor-conceived children when children become 18); Netherlands Embryos Bill, Article 3 Dutch Ministry of Health, Welfare, and Sport (2004) www.minvws.nl/en (effective June 2004, child born using donated sperm has right to obtain information about biological father at age 16). As one such child recently wrote,

> "[t]hose of us created with donated sperm won't stay bubbly babies forever. We're all going to grow into adults, and form opinions about the decision to bring us into the world in a way that deprives us of the basic right to know where we came from, what our history is and who both our parents are."

[ ] We sympathize. However, weighing of the interests of all involved in these procedures as well as the public policies that are furthered by favoring one or another in certain circumstances, is the charge of the Kansas Legislature, not of this court.

\* \* \*

*Equity*

D.H. asserts that the district court must be reversed because S.H. has "unclean hands." In essence, he argues that he, a nonlawyer, was tricked by lawyer S.H., who failed to inform him of the statute and failed to explain how the absence of independent legal advice or a written agreement could affect his legal rights. He asserts that he asked S.H. about whether he needed a lawyer or whether they should put their arrangement in writing and was told neither was necessary. This behavior, he alleges, may have constituted a violation of S.H.'s ethical duties as a licensed lawyer.

\* \* \*

Generally speaking, mere ignorance of the law is no excuse for failing to abide by it.[ ] There may be a case in the future in which a donor can prove that the existence of [the Kansas version of the 1973 UPA] was concealed, or that he was fraudulently induced *not* to obtain independent legal advice or *not* to enter into a written agreement to ensure creation and preservation of his parental rights to a child conceived through artificial insemination. This is not such a case.

Affirmed.

CAPLINGER, J., dissenting: I respectfully disagree with the majority's analysis of the constitutionality of [the Kansas version of the 1973 UPA] as applied to D.H. I would hold the statute unconstitutional as applied to D.H. for the reason that it violates his fundamental right to parent his children without due process of law.

\* \* \*

*Requirement that donor take affirmative action to protect his parental rights*

In concluding that the opt-out provision in [the Kansas version of the 1973 UPA] satisfies due process requirements, the majority states that D.H.'s "own *inaction* before donating his sperm" left him unable to meet the statute's requirements of a written agreement.[ ] Therein lies the constitutional problem with the statute. Fundamental rights must be actively waived, rather than passively lost due to inaction.

Initially, before analyzing this issue, I would note that the terminology employed by the majority, i.e., that D.H. failed to "opt out" of the statute, is a misnomer. In effect, the statute requires a known sperm donor, regardless of any agreement or understanding the donor may have as to his role in parenting a child conceived from his sperm, to *opt in* to parenthood or forever waive his right to parent.

\* \* \*

*Effect of "ignorance of the law" on an individual's fundamental right to parent*

Nor can I agree with the majority's conclusion that D.H.'s ignorance of the statute's writing requirement has no effect on the statute's application.

\* \* \*

I would urge the majority to consider the *complete* rationale of *Lehr*: "When an unwed father demonstrates a full commitment to the responsibilities of parenthood by 'com[ing] forward to participate in the rearing of his child,' his interest in personal contact with his child acquires substantial protection under the Due Process Clause."[ ]

That is the scenario with which this court is faced. A putative father has come forward to participate in the rearing of his children, emotionally and financially; consequently, his interest in doing so is entitled to full protection under the Due Process Clause. Instead of being given this protection and an opportunity to prove that he intended to actively parent his children, D.H. has been subjected to the workings of a statute of which he was unaware, that required him to "opt in" to fatherhood before ever donating his sperm, or be forever barred from parenting his children.

* * * Because the rights to parent are fundamental, those rights may be waived only through an intentional, free, and meaningful choice. Here, the record indicates D.H. was not even aware of [the Kansas version of the 1973 UPA], much less its requirement that he must enter into a written agreement formalizing his intent to parent his child before he provided his sperm to S.H.

* * *

HILL, J., dissenting: I must respectfully join with Judge Caplinger in her dissent. I too agree that as applied in this case, [the Kansas version of the 1973 UPA] is unconstitutional when applied to a known donor.

But I raise my hand and ask a different question. Who speaks for the children in these proceedings? As applied by the majority in this case, this generative statute of frauds slices away half of their heritage. A man who was once considered a "putative father" in the initial child in need of care proceeding is now branded a mere "semen donor." The majority offers the children sympathy. But is this in their best interests? The trial court never got to the point of deciding the best interests of the children because it was convinced that such a consideration was barred by the operation of [the Kansas version of the 1973 UPA] to a known donor.

None of the elaborate and meticulous safeguards our Kansas laws afford parents *and children* in proceedings before our courts when confronted with questions of parentage have been extended to these children. * * *

I agree with the Ohio Court of Common Pleas when it said:

"A father's voluntary assumption of fiscal responsibility for his child should be endorsed as a socially responsible action. A statute which absolutely extinguishes a father's efforts to assert the rights and responsibility of being a father, in a case with such facts as those *sub judice,* runs contrary to due process safeguards.[ ]"

I think the same can be said about our statute.

### *NOTE: THE 2017 UNIFORM PARENTAGE ACT*

Most states adopted some version of the 1973 Uniform Parentage Act (UPA). In 2000, the original (1973) UPA and the Uniform Status of Children of Assisted Conception Act were combined and rewritten in the form of a new (2000) UPA, which was amended in 2002. The 2002 UPA was designed to address some of the uncertainty around parentage in assisted conception cases, but those portions of the statute proved controversial and were not embraced by many states. In addition, the 2002 statute continued to reflect certain gendered assumptions about parentage, such as the assumption that children would be born to couples with one man and one woman, which impacted legal presumptions and rights determining parentage. The Uniform Law Commission determined that the UPA needed updating in light of the growth of non-traditional family structures facilitated by ART, as well as the Supreme Court case Obergefell v. Hodges, 135 S.Ct. 2584 (2015), holding laws barring marriage of same sex couples unconstitutional. This ruling was widely understood as implicating parentage laws' differential treatment of same-sex couples versus different-sex couples, and raising questions about the constitutionality of gendered provisions of prior versions of the UPA. To address these infirmities, and to modernize parentage laws in other ways, the Uniform Parentage Act was updated again in 2017. Select provisions are reproduced below.

## UNIFORM PARENTAGE ACT (2017)

\* \* \*

## [ARTICLE 1—GENERAL PROVISIONS]

## § 102.    DEFINITIONS.

(4)   "Assisted reproduction" means a method of causing pregnancy other than sexual intercourse. The term includes:

     (A)   intrauterine insemination;

     (B)   donation of gametes;

     (C)   donation of embryos;

     (D)   in-vitro fertilization and transfer of embryos; and

     (E)   intracytoplasmic sperm injection.

\* \* \*

(8)   "Donor" means an individual who provides gametes intended for use in assisted reproduction, whether or not for consideration. The term does not include:

     (A)   a woman who gives birth to a child by means of assisted reproduction [, except as otherwise provided in [Article] 8]; or

     (B)   a parent under Article 7 [or an intended parent under Article 8].

\* \* \*

(10) "Gamete" means sperm, egg, or any part of a sperm or egg.

\* \* \*

## [ARTICLE 2—PARENT-CHILD RELATIONSHIP]

### § 201.    ESTABLISHMENT OF PARENT-CHILD RELATIONSHIP.

A parent-child relationship is established between an individual and a child if:

(1)  the individual gives birth to the child [, except as otherwise provided in [Article] 8, concerning surrogacy agreements];

(2)  there is a presumption under Section 204 of the individual's parentage of the child, unless the presumption is overcome in a judicial proceeding or a valid denial of parentage is made [pursuant to the rules established elsewhere in this Act];

(3)  the individual is adjudicated a parent of the child * * *;

(4)  the individual adopts the child;

(5)  the individual acknowledges parentage of the child under [the section of the Act establishing the process for voluntary acknowledgment of parentage], unless [such] acknowledgment is rescinded [ ] or successfully challenged [under other provisions of this Act];

(6)  the individual's parentage of the child is established under [Article] 7 [concerning assisted reproduction] [;or

(7)  the individual's parentage of the child is established under [Article] 8]

* * *

### § 202.    NO DISCRIMINATION BASED ON MARITAL STATUS. A parent-child relationship extends equally to every child and parent, regardless of the marital status of the parent.

* * *

### § 204.    PRESUMPTION OF PARENTAGE.

(a)  An individual is presumed to be a parent of a child if:

(1)  except as otherwise provided [in this act]:

(A)  the individual and the woman who gave birth to the child are married to each other and the child is born during the marriage * * *;

(B)  the individual and the woman who gave birth to the child were married to each other and the child is born not later than 300 days after the marriage is terminated by death, [divorce, dissolution, annulment, or declaration of invalidity, or after a decree of separation or separate maintenance]* * *; or

(C)  the individual and the woman who gave birth to the child married each other after the birth of the child * * *, the individual at any time asserted parentage of the child, and [the assertion is in a [state birth] record or on the child's birth certificate]; or

(2)  the individual resided in the same household with the child for the first two years of the life of the child, including any period of temporary absence, and openly held out the child as the individual's child. * * *

* * *

## [ARTICLE 7—ASSISTED REPRODUCTION]

### § 701.    SCOPE OF [ARTICLE].

This [article] does not apply to the birth of a child conceived by means of sexual intercourse[, or assisted reproduction under a surrogacy agreement under [Article] 8]. [For a discussion of article 8, see the Note on Gestational Surrogacy and the UPA after *Johnson v. Calvert*.]

### § 702.    PARENTAL STATUS OF DONOR.

A donor is not a parent of a child conceived by means of assisted reproduction.

### § 703.    PARENTAGE OF CHILD OF ASSISTED REPRODUCTION.

An individual who consents under Section 704 to assisted reproduction by a woman with the intent to be a parent of a child conceived by the assisted reproduction is a parent of the child.

### § 704.    CONSENT TO ASSISTED REPRODUCTION.

(a)  Except as otherwise provided in subsection (b), the consent described in Section 703 must be in a record signed by a woman giving birth to a child conceived by assisted reproduction and an individual who intends to be a parent of the child.

(b)  Failure to consent in a record as required by subsection (a), before, on, or after birth of the child, does not preclude the court from finding consent to parentage if: (1) the woman or the individual proves by clear-and-convincing evidence the existence of an express agreement entered into before conception that the individual and the woman intended they both would be parents of the child; or (2) the woman and the individual for the first two years of the child's life, including any period of temporary absence, resided together in the same household with the child and both openly held out the child as the individual's child * * *.

* * *

### NOTES AND QUESTIONS

1.    *UPA 1973 vs. UPA 2017.* K.M.H. applied the Kansas version of the original UPA. Would the outcome have been different under the 1973 UPA (excerpts cited in *K.M.H.*)? What about the 2017 UPA? Are there children who would have no fathers under the 1973 Act or the Kansas statute but who would

have a father under the 2017 UPA? If we reject genetic essentialism (i.e., that the source of the genetic contribution is the parent), where should we look to decide if a sperm source ought to be the legal father of the child? Should we look to the intent of the parties? Should we look to the best interest of the child, as the dissent in *K.M.H.* suggests?

2.    *Parentage Under Common Law.* The 1973 version of the UPA applies only if the woman who is inseminated is a wife (i.e., is married), if she proceeds with the consent of her husband and the procedure is carried out under the supervision of a licensed physician. If any of these conditions is not met, the statute is inapplicable. See, e.g., Marriage of Witbeck-Wildhagen, 281 Ill.App.3d 502, 217 Ill.Dec. 329, 667 N.E.2d 122 (1996) (lack of husband's consent to wife's insemination precluded statutory or equitable basis for recognition of paternity); Patton v. Vanterpool, 302 Ga. 253, 806 S.E.2d 493 (2017) (statute creating an irrebutable presumption of paternity with respect to children born during marriage who were conceived through artificial insemination did not apply to children conceived by IVF therapy). The third requirement may not be met because artificial insemination need not be done as a medical procedure by a physician. A syringe can be used to place "fresh" semen in the cervical canal or uterus directly into the woman who intends to become pregnant, which can be done successfully at home by anyone who understands the underlying biological principles. When the statute does not apply, the common law has had to define the rights and interests of all of the parties. In a part of the opinion not reproduced in this casebook, the *K.M.H.* case noted that some common law cases have treated the source of the sperm to be the father, with all of the rights (including visitation) and obligations (including child support) that come with such a designation; others have not.

3.    *State Statutes & Donor Paternity.* The *K.M.H.* opinion noted that in adopting their own versions of the 1973 UPA, some states added explicit bars to donor paternity, regardless of whether the recipient was married to someone else and regardless of whether the donor was known or anonymous. Some courts have found that such a bar, while constitutional on its face, could be an unconstitutional violation of a donor's due process rights under certain conditions. See, e.g., McIntyre v. Crouch, 98 Or.App. 462, 780 P.2d 239 (1989) (statute unconstitutional as applied if the donor can prove that he had an agreement with the mother to share the rights and responsibilities of parenthood); accord C.O. v. W.S., 64 Ohio Misc.2d 9, 639 N.E.2d 523 (1994). See also, L.F. v. Breit, 285 Va. 163, 736 S.E. 2d. 711 (2013) (noting that the assisted conception statute did not contemplate situations where unmarried donors have long-term relationships, as well as biological ties, where the donor and birth mother have entered into a written agreement of paternity, and where the donor has voluntarily assumed parental responsibilities; and finding that a bar to donor paternity in this case would violate the donor's due process rights). But see Steven S. v. Deborah D., 127 Cal.App.4th 319, 25 Cal.Rptr.3d 482 (2005) (applying the absolute bar despite the donor's attempt to present evidence of an agreement to share parental rights).

Although earlier versions of the UPA focused on donor *paternity*, the 2017 Act focuses more broadly on donors' *parentage* rights, in ways that eschew earlier gender assumptions. For example, Section 703 in the 2017 UPA (reproduced above) is titled "*Parentage* of Child of Assisted Reproduction" and addresses the rights of "an individual" who intends to parent; but in the 2002 version, this section was titled "*Paternity* of Child Assisted Reproduction." Section 705 in the 2002 UPA addresses limitations on *husband's dispute of paternity*, while the corresponding section in the 2017 UPA refers to limitations on *spouse's dispute of parentage*. Such changes reflect an acknowledgement of the reality that children are not necessarily born to couples with one man and one woman. See the Note on ART & Changing Norms later in this chapter.

4.   *Objections to Artificial Insemination.* Virtually no legal questions have arisen surrounding the use of the sperm of a husband to inseminate his wife. Such a process may be used within a marriage to allow for processing of the semen to overcome low sperm count. In these cases, there is no question about the identity of the mother and the father of the child. While religious objections have been raised to masturbation (which is required) and to any process that alters the "natural" procreative process, artificial insemination-homologous (AIH) of a married woman with sperm from her husband has been well accepted as a social and medical matter. Artificial insemination by a donor (AID), however, has generated greater objections, based on religious beliefs for some and more general social mores for others. For example, in the case of married couples who need to use a donor, some believe that AID constitutes adultery. Some have also expressed concern that the availability of AID will undermine traditional assumptions about appropriate family structure. For others, however, the possibility that ART facilitates new and different family combinations is viewed as empowering for individuals who want to have children and as reshaping society's assumptions about what constitutes a strong and moral family unit in positive ways.

Other objections are focused on the anonymity of the process, in light of the fact that donation of sperm often occurs anonymously in the U.S. Some are concerned that the uncertainty of the screening of the sperm source in AID can provide for uncertainty in the health of the child, and that anonymity of the sperm source may have unforeseen emotional consequences. There is also an argument that AID is inappropriate because if there is no limit on the number of times one man may donate sperm there may be a genetically unacceptably large number of children who unknowingly have the same genetic father, which may lead to the dilution of the genetic pool of some communities.

5.   *Donor Anonymity.* The debate over whether donor anonymity should be protected has historically centered around sperm donation. The question of whether a prospective mother (and, ultimately, the child) should know the identity of the sperm source were seen as having important legal and practical implications for donation. An anonymous (or, at least, unknown) sperm source would have a more difficult time establishing fatherhood rights than one who is known or identifiable, which may encourage prospective mothers to choose unknown sperm sources. That, in turn, may encourage women seeking

artificial insemination to seek the help of cryobanks, run as medical institutions with medical control over the processing of the gametes. In the case of both sperm and egg donations, those who seek anonymous donors typically still want to know something about those donors. Gamete banks provide profiles of their various donors, and some issue catalogs of these profiles allowing their consumers to choose the profile that seems most appropriate. A "donor catalog" may provide information on ethnicity, hair color and texture, eye color, height, weight, blood type, skin tone, years of education, and occupation (or major in college). Some catalogs provide such detailed information as the appearance of teeth, the presence of freckles, the location of dimples, and the donor's favorite movies and songs. Some provide brief health histories of the donor's family members. Short (2-page) profiles, and longer (10-page) descriptions are available on all donors, and audio and video tapes, pictures, and other information may be available for some. In addition to relevant health information, what kind of information, if any, about the gamete source ought to be provided to the intended parents?

6.    *Obligations Concerning Donor Identity*. UPA 2017 requires gamete banks and fertility clinics ("ART clinics") to collect and store certain identifying information and medical history of donors. UPA 2017 also allows donors to maintain anonymity by signing a declaration stating that the donor does not agree to have the donor's identity disclosed. Even in these cases, though, upon request from the child, the ART clinics must make a good-faith effort to notify the donor, who may then elect to withdraw the earlier nondisclosure declaration. The clinic must also make a good-faith effort to provide nonidentifying medical history if requested. The American legal preference for unknown or anonymous donors is not reflected elsewhere in the world, and, especially in Europe, the trend is toward a legal requirement that the source be made known to the child when the child becomes an adult. Which approach is better—the American protection for anonymity, or the preference elsewhere for release of this information? In the United States over the past few years there has been an increase in the number of "directed donations" of gametes—i.e., donations made by identifiable persons for use by identified persons.

At the very least, should a child be informed that he or she was the product of ART, and that there may be a gamete source other than the parents? The most recent recommendations by the American Society of Reproductive Medicine (ASRM) encourage disclosure:

- Disclosure to donor-conceived persons of the use of donor gametes or embryos in their conception is strongly encouraged, while ultimately the choice of recipient parents.

- Counseling and informed consent about disclosure and information sharing are essential for donors and recipients.

- [ART and donation programs and facilities] should expect inquiries from donor-conceived persons about their genetic background and should develop written policies to respond to these inquiries.

- [ART and donation programs and facilities] should gather, maintain, and permanently store medical and genetic information about donors.

- Donors and recipient parents should be informed in advance about how and when ART programs; sperm, oocyte, and embryo banks; and oocyte and embryo donation programs will release donor information to recipients and offspring. Donors and recipients also should be counseled that later changes in the law may affect any agreements.

Informing Offspring of Their Conception by Gamete or Embryo Donation: An Ethics Committee Opinion. American Society for Reproductive Medicine, Fertil. Steril. 2018; 109:601–5.

7. *Timing.* Cryopreservation—the ability to freeze and thaw with viability retention—is beneficial for many reasons. For example, cryopreservation permits testing for the presence of any latent contaminant (such as HIV), and it provides greater flexibility in family planning. This flexibility can have legal and ethical implications, however, because it gives rise to the possibility that the parent of a child conceived through ART could have died years before that child's birth. The Social Security Administration faced this issue in a number of cases where claimants have sought survivor's benefits from fathers who had died before they were born (or even conceived). Their eligibility depends on whether they are recognized as heirs by the states where they reside. In some states a child may be an heir to a parent who died pre-conception; in some states a child may not be. The Uniform Status of Children of Assisted Conception Act explicitly provided that one who died before implantation of his or her genetic contribution was not a parent of the "resulting child." In the 2017 version of the Uniform Parentage Act, Section 708 provides that "if an individual who consented . . . to assisted reproduction by a woman who agreed to give birth to a child dies before a transfer of gametes or embryos, the deceased individual is only a parent if: (1) either[ ] the individual consented in a record that if assisted reproduction were to occur after the death of the individual, the individual would be a parent of the child [or such intent is proved by clear-and-convincing evidence]; and (2) either [ ] the embryo is in utero not later [36] months after the individual's death or [ ] the child is born not later than [45] months after the individual's death." See also Section C below, discussing the legal and ethical implications of IVF and the disposition of frozen gametes.

## JOHNSON V. CALVERT

Supreme Court of California, 1993.
5 Cal.4th 84, 19 Cal.Rptr.2d 494, 851 P.2d 776.

PANELLI, J.:

\* \* \*

Mark and Crispina Calvert are a married couple who desired to have a child. Crispina was forced to undergo a hysterectomy in 1984. Her ovaries remained capable of producing eggs, however, and the couple eventually considered surrogacy. In 1989 Anna Johnson heard about Crispina's plight from a coworker and offered to serve as a surrogate for the Calverts.

On January 15, 1990, Mark, Crispina, and Anna signed a contract providing that an embryo created by the sperm of Mark and the egg of Crispina would be implanted in Anna and the child born would be taken into Mark and Crispina's home "as their child." Anna agreed she would relinquish "all parental rights" to the child in favor of Mark and Crispina. In return, Mark and Crispina would pay Anna $10,000 in a series of installments, the last to be paid six weeks after the child's birth. Mark and Crispina were also to pay for a $200,000 life insurance policy on Anna's life.

The zygote was implanted on January 19, 1990. Less than a month later, an ultrasound test confirmed Anna was pregnant.

Unfortunately, relations deteriorated between the two sides. Mark learned that Anna had not disclosed she had suffered several stillbirths and miscarriages. Anna felt Mark and Crispina did not do enough to obtain the required insurance policy. She also felt abandoned during an onset of premature labor in June.

In July 1990, Anna sent Mark and Crispina a letter demanding the balance of the payments due her or else she would refuse to give up the child. The following month, Mark and Crispina responded with a lawsuit, seeking a declaration they were the legal parents of the unborn child. Anna filed her own action to be declared the mother of the child, and the two cases were eventually consolidated. The parties agreed to an independent guardian ad litem for the purposes of the suit.

The child was born on September 19, 1990, and blood samples were obtained from both Anna and the child for analysis. The blood test results excluded Anna as the genetic mother. The parties agreed to a court order providing that the child would remain with Mark and Crispina on a temporary basis with visits by Anna.

Discussion

*Determining Maternity Under the Uniform
Parentage Act [of 1973]*

* * * [W]e are left with the undisputed evidence that Anna, not Crispina, gave birth to the child and that Crispina, not Anna, is genetically related to him. Both women thus have adduced evidence of a mother and child relationship as contemplated by the [Uniform Parentage] Act [1973].[ ] Yet for any child California law recognizes only one natural mother, despite advances in reproductive technology rendering a different outcome biologically possible.

We decline to accept the contention of amicus curiae * * * that we should find the child has two mothers. Even though rising divorce rates have made multiple parent arrangements common in our society, we see no compelling reason to recognize such a situation here. The Calverts are the genetic and intending parents of their son and have provided him, by all accounts, with a stable, intact, and nurturing home. To recognize parental rights in a third party with whom the Calvert family has had little contact since shortly after the child's birth would diminish Crispina's role as mother.

We see no clear legislative preference in [the statutory law] as between blood testing evidence and proof of having given birth.

* * *

Because two women each have presented acceptable proof of maternity, we do not believe this case can be decided without enquiring into the parties' intentions as manifested in the surrogacy agreement. Mark and Crispina are a couple who desired to have a child of their own genes but are physically unable to do so without the help of reproductive technology. They affirmatively intended the birth of the child, and took the steps necessary to effect in vitro fertilization. But for their acted-on intention, the child would not exist. Anna agreed to facilitate the procreation of Mark's and Crispina's child. The parties' aim was to bring Mark's and Crispina's child into the world, not for Mark and Crispina to donate a zygote to Anna. Crispina from the outset intended to be the child's mother. Although the gestative function Anna performed was necessary to bring about the child's birth, it is safe to say that Anna would not have been given the opportunity to gestate or deliver the child had she, prior to implantation of the zygote, manifested her own intent to be the child's mother. No reason appears why Anna's later change of heart should vitiate the determination that Crispina is the child's natural mother.

We conclude that although the Act recognizes both genetic consanguinity and giving birth as means of establishing a mother and child relationship, when the two means do not coincide in one woman, she who intended to procreate the child—that is, she who intended to bring about the birth of a child that she intended to raise as her own—is the natural mother under California law.[10]

---

[10] Thus, under our analysis, in a true "egg donation" situation, where a woman gestates and gives birth to a child formed from the egg of another woman with the intent to raise the child as her own, the birth mother is the natural mother under California law.

The dissent would decide parentage based on the best interests of the child. Such an approach raises the repugnant specter of governmental interference in matters implicating our most fundamental notions of privacy, and confuses concepts of parentage and custody. Logically, the determination of parentage must precede, and should not be dictated by, eventual custody decisions. The implicit assumption of the dissent is that a recognition of the genetic intending mother as the natural mother may sometimes harm the child. This assumption overlooks California's dependency laws, which are designed to protect all children irrespective of the manner

* * *

Anna urges that surrogacy contracts violate several social policies. Relying on her contention that she is the child's legal, natural mother, she cites the public policy embodied in [the] Penal Code[ ], prohibiting the payment for consent to adoption of a child. She argues further that the policies underlying the adoption laws of this state are violated by the surrogacy contract because it in effect constitutes a prebirth waiver of her parental rights.

We disagree. Gestational surrogacy differs in crucial respects from adoption and so is not subject to the adoption statutes. The parties voluntarily agreed to participate in in vitro fertilization and related medical procedures before the child was conceived; at the time when Anna entered into the contract, therefore, she was not vulnerable to financial inducements to part with her own expected offspring. As discussed above, Anna was not the genetic mother of the child. The payments to Anna under the contract were meant to compensate her for her services in gestating the fetus and undergoing labor, rather than for giving up "parental" rights to the child. Payments were due both during the pregnancy and after the child's birth.

* * *

Finally, Anna and some commentators have expressed concern that surrogacy contracts tend to exploit or dehumanize women, especially women of lower economic status. Anna's objections center around the psychological harm she asserts may result from the gestator's relinquishing the child to whom she has given birth. Some have also cautioned that the practice of surrogacy may encourage society to view children as commodities, subject to trade at their parents' will.

We are unpersuaded that gestational surrogacy arrangements are so likely to cause the untoward results Anna cites as to demand their invalidation on public policy grounds. Although common sense suggests that women of lesser means serve as surrogate mothers more often than do wealthy women, there has been no proof that surrogacy contracts exploit poor women to any greater degree than economic necessity in general exploits them by inducing them to accept lower-paid or otherwise undesirable employment. We are likewise unpersuaded by the claim that surrogacy will foster the attitude that children are mere commodities; no evidence is offered to support it.

---

of birth or conception. Moreover, the best interests standard poorly serves the child in the present situation: it fosters instability during litigation and, if applied to recognize the gestator as the natural mother, results in a split of custody between the natural father and the gestator, an outcome not likely to benefit the child. Further, it may be argued that, by voluntarily contracting away any rights to the child, the gestator has, in effect, conceded the best interests of the child are not with her.

The argument that a woman cannot knowingly and intelligently agree to gestate and deliver a baby for intending parents carries overtones of the reasoning that for centuries prevented women from attaining equal economic rights and professional status under the law. To resurrect this view is both to foreclose a personal and economic choice on the part of the surrogate mother, and to deny intending parents what may be their only means of procreating a child of their own genes.

\* \* \*

The judgment of the Court of Appeal is affirmed.

[ARABIAN, J., concurred with the majority's Uniform Parentage Act analysis, but would leave the issue of whether surrogacy contracts could be consistent with public policy to the legislature.]

KENNARD, J., dissenting.

When a woman who wants to have a child provides her fertilized ovum to another woman who carries it through pregnancy and gives birth to a child, who is the child's legal mother? Unlike the majority, I do not agree that the determinative consideration should be the intent to have the child that originated with the woman who contributed the ovum. In my view, the woman who provided the fertilized ovum and the woman who gave birth to the child both have substantial claims to legal motherhood. Pregnancy entails a unique commitment, both psychological and emotional, to an unborn child. No less substantial, however, is the contribution of the woman from whose egg the child developed and without whose desire the child would not exist.

For each child, California law accords the legal rights and responsibilities of parenthood to only one "natural mother." When, as here, the female reproductive role is divided between two women, California law requires courts to make a decision as to which woman is the child's natural mother, but provides no standards by which to make that decision. The majority's resort to "intent" to break the "tie" between the genetic and gestational mothers is unsupported by statute, and, in the absence of appropriate protections in the law to guard against abuse of surrogacy arrangements, it is ill-advised. To determine who is the legal mother of a child born of a gestational surrogacy arrangement, I would apply the standard most protective of child welfare—the best interests of the child.

\* \* \*

*Analysis of the Majority's "Intent" Test*

\* \* \*

The majority offers four arguments in support of its conclusion to rely on the intent of the genetic mother as the exclusive determinant for deciding who is the natural mother of a child born of gestational surrogacy.

Careful examination, however, demonstrates that none of the arguments mandates the majority's conclusion.

The first argument that the majority uses in support of its conclusion that the intent of the genetic mother to bear a child should be dispositive of the question of motherhood is "but-for" causation. Specifically, the majority relies on a commentator who writes that in a gestational surrogacy arrangement, " 'the child would not have been born but for the efforts of the intended parents.' "[ ] [But the resort to the "but-for" test derived from tort law is unprecedented and unjustified here.]

\* \* \*

Behind the majority's reliance on "but-for" causation as justification for its intent test is a second, closely related argument. The majority draws its second rationale from a student note: " 'The mental concept of the child is a controlling factor of its creation, and the originators of that concept merit full credit as conceivers.' "[ ]

\* \* \*

[This concept is taken from the law of intellectual property.] The problem with this argument, of course, is that children are not property. Unlike songs or inventions, rights in children cannot be sold for consideration, or made freely available to the general public.

Next, the majority offers as its third rationale the notion that bargained-for expectations support its conclusion regarding the dispositive significance of the genetic mother's intent. Specifically, the majority states that " 'intentions that are voluntarily chosen, deliberate, express and bargained-for ought presumptively to determine legal parenthood.' "

\* \* \* But the courts will not compel performance of all contract obligations.[ ] The unsuitability of applying the notion that, because contract intentions are "voluntarily chosen, deliberate, express and bargained-for," their performance ought to be compelled by the courts is even more clear when the concept of specific performance is used to determine the course of the life of a child. Just as children are not the intellectual property of their parents, neither are they the personal property of anyone, and their delivery cannot be ordered as a contract remedy on the same terms that a court would, for example, order a breaching party to deliver a truckload of nuts and bolts.

\* \* \*

The majority's final argument in support of using the intent of the genetic mother as the exclusive determinant of the outcome in gestational surrogacy cases is that preferring the intending mother serves the child's interests, which are " '[u]nlikely to run contrary to those of adults who choose to bring [the child] into being.' "[ ]

I agree with the majority that the best interests of the child is an important goal * * *. The problem with the majority's rule of intent is that application of this inflexible rule will not serve the child's best interests in every case.

* * *

### The Best Interests of the Child

* * *

In the absence of legislation that is designed to address the unique problems of gestational surrogacy, this court should look not to tort, property or contract law, but to family law, as the governing paradigm and source of a rule of decision. The allocation of parental rights and responsibilities necessarily impacts the welfare of a minor child. And in issues of child welfare, the standard that courts frequently apply is the best interests of the child.[ ] This "best interests" standard serves to assure that in the judicial resolution of disputes affecting a child's well-being, protection of the minor child is the foremost consideration. Consequently, I would apply "the best interests of the child" standard to determine who can best assume the social and legal responsibilities of motherhood for a child born of a gestational surrogacy arrangement.

* * *

Factors that are pertinent to good parenting, and thus that are in a child's best interests, include the ability to nurture the child physically and psychologically[ ] and to provide ethical and intellectual guidance.[ ] Also crucial to a child's best interests is the "well recognized right" of every child "to stability and continuity."[ ] The intent of the genetic mother to procreate a child is certainly relevant to the question of the child's best interests; alone, however, it should not be dispositive.

* * *

In this opinion, I do not purport to offer a perfect solution to the difficult questions posed by gestational surrogacy; perhaps there can be no perfect solution. But in the absence of legislation specifically designed to address the complex issues of gestational surrogacy and to protect against potential abuses, I cannot join the majority's uncritical validation of gestational surrogacy.

I would reverse the judgment of the Court of Appeal, and remand the case to the trial court for a determination of disputed parentage on the basis of the best interests of the child.

## NOTES AND QUESTIONS

1.    *Objections to Surrogacy.* Five years earlier, in In the Matter of Baby M, 109 N.J. 396 (1988), the Supreme Court of New Jersey invalidated a surrogacy contract under facts similar to *Johnson v. Calvert.* In both cases, the surrogate and the commissioning parents developed palpable animosity for each other and the surrogate sought to invalidate the surrogacy contract. The court in *Baby M* invalidated the contract as inconsistent with the prohibition on the use of money in adoption, requirements concerning parental fitness in custody determinations, and public policy. The *Baby M* decision reflected many of the objections raised to surrogacy agreements at that time. These objections generally fall into three categories—those related to the contracting parties; those related to the child; and those related to the effect of the process on society as a whole.

The first argument generally advanced against surrogacy is that it exploits women who are willing to give or rent their bodies as vessels to carry other people's children. Could the inducement of payment for pregnancy cause a woman to consent to something that otherwise would be an unthinkable intrusion upon her body? Will the development of commercial surrogacy lead to a class of poor women who will become child-bearers for wealthy women who do not want to spend the time or energy on pregnancy? Does the relationship between ethnicity and the distribution of wealth in this society mean it is likely that we will develop separate childbearing races and child-raising races? For an interesting discussion of American women who "outsource" pregnancy to women in India, where the service is far cheaper than it is in the United States, see Judith Warner, Outsourced Wombs (Domestic Disturbances), N.Y. Times (Jan. 3, 2008).

Feminists are divided on this issue. Some are deeply offended by the use of the woman's body in this way; others believe this is misguided paternalism that leads courts (and others) to conclude that women are incapable of deciding for themselves whether they should enter surrogacy contracts. There are echoes of this paternalism concern in *Johnson*, when Justice Panelli points out that "there is no proof that surrogacy contracts exploit poor women to any greater degree than economic necessity in general exploits them by inducing them to accept lower-paid or otherwise undesirable employment." Some economists argue that making surrogacy contracts unenforceable will merely lower the amount that is paid to surrogates. Thus, they suggest, making surrogacy contracts unenforceable is just another in a long history of allegedly protectionist regulations that restrict what a woman may choose to do with her body. See Debra Satz, Feminist Perspectives on Reproduction and the Family, Stanford Encyclopedia of Philosophy (rev. 2013).

Another argument is that surrogacy contracts ought to be prohibited or discouraged because they advance only the best interests of the contracting parties, not the best interest of the child. Normally in a custody dispute between those with claims as parents, the court will look to the best interest of the child in determining the appropriate placement. Enforcing a surrogacy contract seems inconsistent with this principle. How does Justice Kennard say this concern should be addressed in his dissent in *Johnson?* In addition, some believe that children who find out that they were carried by a surrogate will be injured by that discovery; others argue that surrogacy contracts render children instruments for the use of parents, not ends in themselves, and that this is necessarily harmful for children.

Finally, some believe that the fabric of society as a whole is weakened by surrogacy arrangements, at least commercial ones. In *Baby M*, Chief Justice Wilentz compared the surrogacy contract to the sale of a child and noted that "[a]lmost every evil that prompted the prohibition of the payment of money in connection with adoptions exists here." Surrogacy contracts are often condemned on the ground that they constitute baby selling, which is illegal in every state. There is confusion over the purpose of statutes that prohibit baby selling, though: they may be intended to protect parents from financial inducements to give up their children, or they may be intended to protect children from being reduced to the status of an ordinary commodity. Should surrogacy arrangements be governed by baby selling statutes? For a good debate on baby selling and its logical consequences, see E. Landes & R. Posner, The Economics of the Baby Shortage, 7 J. Legal. Stud. 323 (1978); J.R.S. Prichard, A Market for Babies?, 34 U. Toronto L.J. 341 (1984); and Michele Goodwin, The Free-Market Approach to Adoption: The Value of a Baby, 26 B.C. Third World L.J. 61 (2006).

2.    *The Role of Parentage Law*. Compare the different approaches taken by the majority and dissent in *Johnson*. What do they reveal about the judges' understanding of the role of parentage law and the interests it should advance? As the *Johnson* and *Baby M* cases illustrate, courts have taken different approaches to these questions. Compare McDonald v. McDonald, 196 A.D.2d 7, 608 N.Y.S.2d 477 (1994) (a "true 'egg donation'" case, in which the court determined that a woman who gestated a child produced through the fertilization of another woman's ovum with her husband's sperm was to be considered the mother of the child that resulted, relying heavily on the reasoning of *Johnson v. Calvert*) with Belsito v. Clark, 67 Ohio Misc.2d 54, 644 N.E.2d 760 (1994) (rejecting *Johnson's* reasoning and holding that parentage was to be determined by genetic contribution, not by the intent-to-procreate of the parties to the original surrogacy agreement). But see S.N. v. M.B., 188 Ohio App.3d 324, 935 N.E.2d 463 rev. dismissed 126 Ohio St. 3d 1525, 931 N.E.2d 126 (2010) (relying on intent to enforce a surrogacy contract).

Uncertainty about the enforceability of surrogacy arrangements motivated amendments to the original UPA. The 2002 UPA included an article recognizing and regulating surrogacy contracts, but these provisions were not popular with states. Almost half of the states had not addressed surrogacy by statute, and states that did tended to craft different approaches. In response, updates to surrogacy provisions of the UPA were made in the 2017 UPA, with the goal of making them more consistent with current surrogacy practice and recently adopted statutes in several states. Consider how the 2017 UPA addresses surrogacy in the excerpts below.

## UNIFORM PARENTAGE ACT (2017)
## [ARTICLE 8—SURROGACY AGREEMENT]

§ 801.   DEFINITIONS. In this [article]:

(1) "Genetic surrogate" means a woman who is not an intended parent and who agrees to become pregnant through assisted reproduction using her own gamete, under a genetic surrogacy agreement as provided in this [article].

(2) "Gestational surrogate" means a woman who is not an intended parent and who agrees to become pregnant through assisted reproduction using gametes that are not her own, under a gestational surrogacy agreement as provided in this [article].

(3) "Surrogacy agreement" means an agreement between one or more intended parents and a woman who is not an intended parent in which the woman agrees to become pregnant through assisted reproduction and which provides that each intended parent is a parent of a child conceived under the agreement. Unless otherwise specified, the term refers to both a gestational surrogacy agreement and a genetic surrogacy agreement.

§ 802.   ELIGIBILITY TO ENTER GESTATIONAL OR GENETIC SURROGACY AGREEMENT.

(a)   To execute an agreement to act as a gestational or genetic surrogate, a woman must: (1) have attained 21 years of age; (2) previously have given birth to at least one child; (3) complete a medical evaluation related to the surrogacy arrangement by a licensed medical doctor; (4) complete a mental-health consultation by a licensed mental-health professional; and (5) have independent legal representation of her choice throughout the surrogacy arrangement regarding the terms of the surrogacy agreement and the potential legal consequences of the agreement.

(b)   To execute a surrogacy agreement, each intended parent, whether or not genetically related to the child, must: (1) have attained 21 years of age; (2) complete a medical evaluation related to the surrogacy arrangement by a licensed medical doctor; (3) complete a mental-health consultation by a licensed mental health professional; and (4) have independent legal representation of the intended parent's choice throughout the surrogacy arrangement regarding the terms of the surrogacy agreement and the potential legal consequences of the agreement.

* * *

§ 804.   REQUIREMENTS OF GESTATIONAL OR GENETIC SURROGACY AGREEMENT: CONTENT.

(a)   A surrogacy agreement must comply with the following requirements:

(1) A surrogate agrees to attempt to become pregnant by means of assisted reproduction.

(2) Except as otherwise provided [in this Act], the surrogate and the surrogate's spouse or former spouse, if any, have no claim to parentage of a child conceived by assisted reproduction under the agreement.

(3) The surrogate's spouse, if any, must acknowledge and agree to comply with the obligations imposed on the surrogate by the agreement.

(4) Except as otherwise provided [in this Act], the intended parent or, if there are two intended parents, each one [ ] will be the exclusive parent or parents of the child, regardless of number of children born or gender or mental or physical condition of each child.

(5) Except as otherwise provided [in this Act], [the intended parents] immediately on birth will assume responsibility for the financial support of the child, regardless of number of children born or gender or mental or physical condition of each child.

* * *

(7) The agreement must permit the surrogate to make all health and welfare decisions regarding herself and her pregnancy. This [Act] does not enlarge or diminish the surrogate's right to terminate her pregnancy.

(8) The agreement must include information about each party's right under this [article] to terminate the surrogacy agreement.

(b) A surrogacy agreement may provide for: (1) payment of consideration and reasonable expenses; and (2) reimbursement of specific expenses if the agreement is terminated under this [Article].* * *

* * *

## § 808. TERMINATION OF GESTATIONAL SURROGACY AGREEMENT.

(a) A party to a gestational surrogacy agreement may terminate the agreement, at any time before an embryo transfer, by giving notice of termination in a record to all other parties. If an embryo transfer does not result in a pregnancy, a party may terminate the agreement at any time before a subsequent embryo transfer.

(b) Unless a gestational surrogacy agreement provides otherwise, on termination of the agreement under subsection (a), the parties are released from the agreement, except that each intended parent remains responsible for expenses that are reimbursable under the agreement and incurred by the gestational surrogate through the date of termination.

(c) Except in a case involving fraud, neither a gestational surrogate nor the surrogate's spouse or former spouse, if any, is liable to the intended parent or parents for a penalty or liquidated damages, for terminating a gestational surrogacy agreement under this section.

## § 809.   PARENTAGE UNDER GESTATIONAL SURROGACY AGREEMENT.

(a)   Except as otherwise provided in [this Act], on birth of a child conceived by assisted reproduction under a gestational surrogacy agreement, each intended parent is, by operation of law, a parent of the child.

(b)   Except as otherwise provided in [this Act], neither a gestational surrogate nor the surrogate's spouse or former spouse, if any, is a parent of the child.

* * *

(d)   Except as otherwise provided in [this Act], if, due to a clinical or laboratory error, a child conceived by assisted reproduction under a gestational surrogacy agreement is not genetically related to an intended parent or a donor who donated to the intended parent or parents, each intended parent, and not the gestational surrogate and the surrogate's spouse or former spouse, if any, is a parent of the child, subject to any other claim of parentage.

* * *

## § 812.   EFFECT OF GESTATIONAL SURROGACY AGREEMENT.

(a)   A gestational surrogacy agreement that [complies with §§ 802–804] is enforceable.

(b)   If a child was conceived by assisted reproduction under a gestational surrogacy agreement that does not comply [with the above requirements], the court shall determine the rights and duties of the parties to the agreement consistent with the intent of the parties at the time of execution of the agreement. * * *

* * *

## § 813.   REQUIREMENT TO VALIDATE GENETIC SURROGACY AGREEMENT.

(a)   Except as otherwise provided in Section 816, to be enforceable, a genetic surrogacy agreement must be validated by [designate court] [prior to commencement of the assisted reproduction].

## § 814.   TERMINATION OF GENETIC SURROGACY AGREEMENT.

(a)   A party to a genetic surrogacy agreement may terminate the agreement as follows:

* * *

(2) A genetic surrogate . . . may withdraw consent to the agreement any time before 72 hours after the birth of a child conceived by assisted reproduction under the agreement. * * *

[Ed. note: The other provisions of this section follow the rules for termination of gestational surrogacy in § 808.]

## § 815. PARENTAGE UNDER VALIDATED GENETIC SURROGACY.

(a) Unless a genetic surrogate exercises the right under Section 814 to terminate a genetic surrogacy agreement, each intended parent is a parent of a child conceived by assisted reproduction under an agreement validated under Section 813.

    * * *

## § 816. EFFECT OF NONVALIDATED GENETIC SURROGACY AGREEMENT.

    * * *

(b) If all parties agree, a court may validate a genetic surrogacy agreement after assisted reproduction has occurred but before the birth of a child conceived by assisted reproduction. * * *

(d) If . . . a genetic surrogate [withdraws] her consent to the agreement [after 72 hours after the birth of child], the court shall adjudicate parentage of the child based on the best interest of the child, taking into account . . . the intent of the parties * * *.

### NOTES AND QUESTIONS

1. *Relaxing Surrogacy Rules.* Is the legal standard in Article 8 of the Uniform Parentage Act (2017) different from the test applied by the court in *Johnson v. Calvert*? Would the case have been decided differently under the 2017 UPA? As noted above, one of the goals of the drafters of the 2017 UPA was to update the surrogacy provisions to make them more consistent with current practice and law, including liberalizing the rules governing gestational surrogacy agreements. For example, the 2002 UPA requires procedures similar to those for adoption: parties to a surrogacy agreement must obtain court approval of the agreement before seeking medical procedures relating to the agreement, and the court's approval must be based, in part, on a home study by the relevant child-welfare agency (unless waived by the court). The 2017 version eliminates the requirement of pre-pregnancy court validation for gestational surrogacy agreements, but retains this requirement for genetic surrogacy contracts. The 2017 UPA also eliminates the home study requirement. The 2017 version contains other procedural protections for surrogacy agreements, such as requiring the intended legal parents to pay for independent legal representation for the surrogate, requiring the surrogate's spouse to be a party to the agreement, and requiring execution of the

agreement before any medical procedure is performed. Importantly, the 2017 UPA provides guidance for how parentage may be determined in cases where the surrogacy agreement does not comply with the law.

2. *Gestational vs. Genetic Surrogacy.* Another difference between the 2017 UPA and the prior version is how it regulates genetic vs. gestational surrogacy agreements. The 2017 UPA permits both, but it imposes additional safeguards or requirements on genetic surrogacy agreements. As noted above, court approval is required for genetic surrogacy contracts only. In addition, while gestational surrogacy agreements are binding once successful transfer has occurred, genetic surrogates are allowed to withdraw their consent any time up to 72 hours after birth. The comments explain that "[t]his differentiation . . . is intended to reflect both the factual differences between the two types of surrogacy as well as the reality that policy makers view these two forms of surrogacy as being quite different." What are those differences?

## *NOTE: ART & CHANGING NORMS*

The technology for facilitating reproduction is of special interest to single men and women, and same sex couples. The use of a surrogate is the only way that a single man or same sex male couple could expect to have a genetically-related child. Similarly, the use of artificial insemination may be an attractive option for a single woman or lesbian couple to have a child. In some circumstances, a family may include three people who help to parent the child, but may not have formal recognition. These scenarios have challenged social and legal decisions based on assumptions of traditional family models. They have also highlighted justice concerns arising out of the disparate treatment certain groups face under parentage laws and in trying to access to fertility care.

1. *Application of Parentage Laws to Same Sex Couples.* Same sex couples have had difficulty establishing parentage for a couple of reasons. First, as the previous cases demonstrate, parentage laws have reflected certain heteronormative assumptions about who could be considered parents. Recall that in *Johnson v. Calvert*, the court noted that "for any child California law recognizes only one natural mother, despite advances in reproductive technology rendering a different outcome biologically possible." Consider the implications for a same sex lesbian couple in which one person contributes the ovum and the other carries the child to term. A Florida court confronted this issue in T.M.H. v. D.M.T., 79 So.2d 787 (Fla. App. 2011). In *T.M.H.*, the ovum source and the birth mother planned to raise the child together, paid for the infertility treatment together, and did raise the child together after the child's birth. When the relationship went bad, though, the birth mother absconded with the child to Australia. The genetic mother sought an order that she was a parent of the child and entitled to parental rights. The birth mother disagreed and argued that under the relevant Florida statute an egg donor could not be mother at all:

The donor of any egg, sperm, or preembryo, other than the commissioning couple or a father who has executed a preplanned adoption agreement [ ], shall relinquish all maternal or paternal rights and obligations with respect to the donation or the resulting children. * * *

Fla. Stat. sec. 742.14. The trial court judge reluctantly agreed that the ovum source could not be a parent under the statute, but the decision was appealed. The State Supreme Court ultimately held the application of the statute to preclude assertion of parental rights unconstitutional for two reasons. First, it deprived the biological mother of parental rights where she was an intended parent and actually established a parental relationship with the child. Second, to the extent the statutory exception to relinquishment of rights provided for a "commissioning couple" was applied to opposite sex, but not same sex, couples, this violated state and federal equal protection law. D.M.T. v. T.M.H., 129 So.3d 320 (Fla. 2013).

Same sex couples have also faced barriers as a result of parentage assumptions that rely on marriage status, in states where same sex couples have been denied the right to marry. This issue arose in Miller-Jenkins v. Miller-Jenkins, 180 Vt. 441, 912 A.2d 951 (2006), where Lisa and Janet, a lesbian couple from Virginia, traveled to Vermont to enter a civil union permitted under Vermont law, but not recognized by Virginia law.

After establishing their civil union, Lisa and Janet decided to start a family, and together they chose an anonymous sperm donor. Lisa became pregnant by artificial insemination and gave birth to Isabella in Virginia, and a few months later Lisa, Janet and their child moved to Vermont. After a year in Vermont, Lisa and Janet decided to separate. Lisa and her child moved back to Virginia, and Lisa filed an action to dissolve the civil union in the Vermont family court. That court found that both Lisa and Janet were parents of the child, and gave Lisa primary custody while Janet was given very substantial visitation rights. Lisa objected and filed an action in Virginia seeking a new parentage determination.

The Vermont court held Lisa in contempt for failing to allow Janet's visitation, but the following week, a Virginia court entered an order finding that Lisa was the only mother of the child, and that Janet had no parentage rights. The Virginia court determined that Janet's rights had been established through Vermont's civil union law, which was not recognized in Virginia. Lisa argued that the Virginia court did not have to give full faith and credit to the Vermont family court order because of the language of the Federal Defense of Marriage Act (DOMA), 28 U.S.C. section 1738(C), which read:

No state, territory or possession of the United States, or Indian tribe, shall be required to give effect to any public act, record or judicial proceeding of any other state, territory, possession, or tribe respecting a relationship between persons of the same sex that is treated as a marriage under the laws of such other State, territory, possession, or tribe, or a right or claim arising from such a relationship.

That argument was rejected by the Vermont court, which upheld the family court ruling. The Virginia Court of Appeals ultimately agreed with the position taken by the Vermont court, Miller-Jenkins v. Miller-Jenkins, 49 Va.App. 88, 637 S.E.2d 330 (2006), and, in an unreported opinion, the Virginia court subsequently granted an order allowing Janet to register the Vermont order in Virginia, and thus to enforce it there. The Miller-Jenkins case demonstrates the special legal risks that gay and lesbian couples have had to face in having a child. Even if their own state recognized the status of the parents, other states may not have enforced these rights.

Such discrimination appears to be unconstitutional after Obergefell v. Hodges, 135 S.Ct. 2584 (2015). In a five-to-four decision, *Obergefell* held that denying the right to marry to same sex couples violated the Fourteenth Amendment. *Obergefell* provides that a state cannot treat married couples differently because of the sexual identity or preference of the spouses. The Court also expressly noted that the right to marry protects not only romantic relationships, but "safeguards children and families" as well. *Obergefell* is understood as establishing the parenting rights of same sex couples. For example, before *Obergefell* a dozen states limited the opportunity of same sex couples to adopt or foster children. In 2016, Mississippi, the last state to maintain such a statutory or regulatory limitation, saw it overturned by judicial decision in Campaign for S. Equal. v. Mississippi Dep't. of Human Servs., 175 F.Supp.3d 691 (S.D. Miss. 2016):

> In sum, the majority opinion [in Obergefell] foreclosed litigation over laws interfering with the right to marry and "rights and responsibilities intertwined with marriage." [ ] It also seems highly unlikely that the same court that held a state cannot ban gay marriage because it would deny benefits—expressly including the right to adopt—would then conclude that married gay couples can be denied that very same benefit.

Nonetheless, according to one scholar's comprehensive survey of contemporary regulation of parental recognition in the context of ART, even after *Obergefell* those departing from traditional norms of gender and sexuality have continued to have their parent-child relationships discounted. See Douglas NeJaime, The Nature of Parenthood, 126 Yale L.J. 2260 (2017). Indeed, the 2017 revisions to the UPA were in part an attempt to remedy apparent constitutional deficiencies of state parentage laws in light of *Obergefell*.

2.    *State Recognition of Multiple Parents.* Parentage law has undergone a significant shift since the court's observation in *Johnson v. Calvert* that a child could not have two mothers under California law. Since 2014, California law has allowed legal recognition that a child has more than two parents, but only where such a finding "is necessary to protect the child from the detriment of being separated from one of his or her parents." Cal. Fam. Code § 7612(c) provides:

> In determining detriment to the child, the court shall consider all relevant factors, including, but not limited to, the harm of removing the child from a stable placement with a parent who has fulfilled the child's physical

needs and the child's psychological needs for care and affection, and who has assumed that role for a substantial period of time. A finding of detriment to the child does not require a finding of unfitness of any of the parents or persons with a claim to parentage.

Families with more than two parents are permitted but not preferred, it seems, under the judicial considerations required by the statute. A handful of other states have also recognized more-than-two-parent families, either by statute or by judicial determination.

3. *Refusal to Provide Fertility Treatment.* Despite greater social and legal recognition of non-traditional family structures, some physicians and hospitals are reluctant to provide the full range of infertility services to single people or those who may not conform to traditional norms of gender and sexuality. The California Supreme Court confronted this issue in North Coast Women's Care Medical Group v. Superior Court, 44 Cal. 4th 1145, 189 P.3d 959 (2008), where a lesbian woman alleged that a health care provider refused to provide her with necessary infertility treatment because it was inconsistent with the physician's moral and religious beliefs. The patient filed an action alleging that such refusal violated California's Unruh Civil Rights Act, which provides:

> All persons within the jurisdiction of this state are free and equal, and no matter what their sex, race, color, religion, ancestry, national origin, disability, medical condition, genetic information, marital status, or sexual orientation are entitled to the full and equal accommodations, advantages, facilities, privileges, or services in all business establishments of every kind whatsoever.

Cal. Civ. Code § 51. The patient argued that she was the victim of discrimination because of her sexual orientation, although the Unruh Act would also prohibit a physician from refusing to provide otherwise appropriate treatment because a patient was unmarried.

The physician argued that, to the extent it prohibited this action, the Unruh Civil Rights Act violated the speech and free exercise of religion clauses of the First Amendment of the U.S. Constitution and the analogous California constitutional provisions. The California Supreme Court determined that the Unruh Civil Rights Act was a valid and neutral law of general applicability, and thus met the relatively undemanding test of the federal free exercise clause. Although the court did not determine the appropriate level of scrutiny required for the state free exercise clause, the court upheld the Unruh Act under the state constitution, finding that even if strict scrutiny applied, the state had a compelling state interest in avoiding discrimination on the basis of sexual orientation. Not all states contain similar antidiscrimination protections, however.

This raises a broader question about the gatekeeping role of physicians generally in the area of ART. May physicians refuse to help someone have a child because that person is unmarried (and with no partner), considered psychologically immature, welfare dependent, has a history of a serious genetic disorder, or is HIV positive? Historically, such rejections were commonplace. Office of Technology Assessment, Artificial Insemination Practice in the United States (1988). A 2005 survey of assisted reproductive technology programs revealed that ART providers screened out people for a whole host of reasons. For example, among those surveyed: 81% were very or extremely likely to turn away a couple where the man had been physically abusive to his existing child; 59%—a woman who was HIV+; 55%—a woman who had severe diabetes with a 10% chance that pregnancy would lead to her death; 48%—a gay couple wanting to use a surrogate (yet only 17% were likely to turn away a lesbian couple wanting to use a sperm donor); 38%—a couple dependent on welfare; 20%—a woman with no partner. Andrea D. Gurmankin et al., Screening Practices and Beliefs of Assisted Reproductive Technology Programs, 83 Fertility and Sterility 61 (2005). Are some of these categories of refusals more troubling than others on ethical grounds? Do the underlying reasons for refusal matter? Should ART practitioners be able to consider parental fitness at all? If so, how would fitness be determined and might this trigger the kind of reproductive justice concerns identified earlier in this chapter. For example, there is evidence that some providers assume unfitness among people with certain kinds of disabilities. See Kimberly M. Mitcherson, Disabling Dreams of Parenthood: The Fertility Industry, Anti-discrimination, and Parents with Disabilities, 27 Law & Ineq. 311 (2009). Would any of the above refusals implicate antidiscrimination law, such as the Americans with Disabilities Act or Section 1557 of the ACA? (See Chapter 2).

The Ethics Committee of the American Society of Reproductive Medicine (ASRM) has issued several relevant ethics opinions concerning provider refusals to treat. See Ethics Committee Opinions and Webinars at the ASRM website at ASRM.org. In one opinion, the Committee explains that "fertility programs may withhold services from prospective patients on the basis of well-substantiated judgments that those patients will be unable to provide minimally adequate or safe care for offspring." ASRM, Child-Rearing Ability and the Provision of Fertility Services, 100 Fertil. & Steril., 50 (Jul. 2013). But it goes on to advise programs to develop written policies and procedures for making such determinations, and in a series of opinions the Committee says providers should not deny care solely on the basis of disability, sexual orientation, marital status, gender identity, or HIV status. The Committee grounds its opinions in the view that "[c]reation of family is a basic human right." It describes how social and legal developments have highlighted the harms of discrimination and emphasizes that refusals based on offspring well-being should be supported by reliable evidence rather than stereotypes and scientifically unfounded assumptions about parental fitness based on identity. Id. For example, in the opinion titled Human Immunodeficiency Virus (HIV) and Infertility Treatment, the Committee emphasized that HIV is a manageable disease, and that certain ART and other medical treatments have proven highly effective in avoiding newborn infection in the case of HIV+ men and women. 104 Fertil. & Steril. e1 (Jul. 2015). In the case of requests for treatment by gay men, lesbians, or unmarried persons, the Committee took the position that "[m]oral objection . . . itself is not an acceptable basis for limiting childrearing or reproduction" by single individuals or same-sex couples. Access to Fertility Treatment by Gays, Lesbians, and Unmarried Persons, 100 Fertil. & Steril. 1514 (Dec. 2013).

## C.  *IN VITRO* FERTILIZATION, EGG TRANSFER, AND EMBRYO TRANSFER

*In vitro* (literally, "in glass") fertilization is a highly technical medical intervention. In the normal *in vitro* case, an ovum that is ready to be released from the ovary is identified through laparoscopy or ultrasound and removed from the ovary by surgery or aspiration through a hollow needle. The ovum is placed in a container with the appropriate amount of semen containing fertile sperm. The fertilized ovum is then placed in the woman's uterus, where it is permitted to implant and develop. But in the course of this process, circumstances may change that affect the parties' intent to use the embryos for their original procreative purposes. How do courts decide what happens to the embryos in these instances?

### DAVIS V. DAVIS
Supreme Court of Tennessee, 1992.
842 S.W.2d 588.

DAUGHTREY, J.:

This appeal presents a question of first impression, involving the disposition of the cryogenically-preserved product of in vitro fertilization (IVF), commonly referred to in the popular press and the legal journals as "frozen embryos." The case began as a divorce action, filed by the appellee, Junior Lewis Davis, against his then wife, appellant Mary Sue Davis. The parties were able to agree upon all terms of dissolution, except one: who was to have "custody" of the seven "frozen embryos" stored in a Knoxville fertility clinic that had attempted to assist the Davises in achieving a much-wanted pregnancy during a happier period in their relationship.

### I. Introduction

Mary Sue Davis originally asked for control of the "frozen embryos" with the intent to have them transferred to her own uterus, in a post-divorce effort to become pregnant. Junior Davis objected, saying that he preferred to leave the embryos in their frozen state until he decided whether or not he wanted to become a parent outside the bounds of marriage.

Based on its determination that the embryos were "human beings" from the moment of fertilization, the trial court awarded "custody" to Mary Sue Davis and directed that she "be permitted the opportunity to bring these children to term through implantation." The Court of Appeals reversed, finding that Junior Davis has a "constitutionally protected right not to beget a child where no pregnancy has taken place" and holding that "there is no compelling state interest to justify[ ] ordering implantation against the will of either party." The Court of Appeals further held that "the parties share an interest in the seven fertilized ova" and remanded the case to the trial court for entry of an order vesting them with "joint control . . . and equal voice over their disposition."

Mary Sue Davis then sought review in this Court, contesting the validity of the constitutional basis for the Court of Appeals decision. We granted review, not because we disagree with the basic legal analysis utilized by the intermediate court, but because of the obvious importance of the case in terms of the development of law regarding the new reproductive technologies, and because the decision of the Court of Appeals does not give adequate guidance to the trial court in the event the parties cannot agree.

We note, in this latter regard, that their positions have already shifted: both have remarried and Mary Sue Davis (now Mary Sue Stowe) has moved out of state. She no longer wishes to utilize the "frozen embryos" herself, but wants authority to donate them to a childless couple. Junior Davis is adamantly opposed to such donation and would prefer to see the "frozen embryos" discarded. The result is, once again, an impasse, but the parties' current legal position does have an effect on the probable outcome of the case, as discussed below.

If we have no statutory authority or common law precedents to guide us [in this case], we do have the benefit of extensive comment and analysis in the legal journals. In those articles, medical-legal scholars and ethicists have proposed various models for the disposition of "frozen embryos" when unanticipated contingencies arise, such as divorce, death of one or both of the parties, financial reversals, or simple disenchantment with the IVF process. Those models range from a rule requiring, at one extreme, that all embryos be used by the gamete-providers or donated for uterine transfer, and, at the other extreme, that any unused embryos be automatically discarded. Other formulations would vest control in the female gamete-provider—in every case, because of her greater physical and emotional contribution to the IVF process, or perhaps only in the event that she wishes to use them herself. There are also two "implied contract" models: one would infer from enrollment in an IVF program that the IVF clinic has authority to decide in the event of an impasse whether to donate, discard, or use the "frozen embryos" for research; the other would infer from the parties' participation in the creation of the embryos that they had made an irrevocable commitment to reproduction and would require transfer either to the female provider or to a donee. There are also the so-called "equity models": one would avoid the conflict altogether by dividing the "frozen embryos" equally between the parties, to do with as they wish; the other would award veto power to the party wishing to avoid parenthood, whether it be the female or the male progenitor.

Each of these possible models has the virtue of ease of application. Adoption of any of them would establish a bright-line test that would dispose of disputes like the one we have before us in a clear and predictable manner. As appealing as that possibility might seem, we conclude that given the relevant principles of constitutional law, the existing public policy of Tennessee with regard to unborn life, the current state of scientific knowledge giving rise to the emerging reproductive technologies, and the ethical considerations that have developed in response to that scientific knowledge, there can be no easy answer to the question we now face. We conclude, instead, that we must weigh the interests of each party to the dispute, in terms of the facts and analysis set out below, in order to resolve that dispute in a fair and responsible manner.

\* \* \*

### IV. The "Person" vs. "Property" Dichotomy

One of the fundamental issues the inquiry poses is whether the preembryos in this case should be considered "persons" or "property" in the contemplation of the law. The Court of Appeals held, correctly, that they cannot be considered "persons" under Tennessee law \* \* \*.

Nor do preembryos enjoy protection as "persons" under federal law. \* \* \*

Left undisturbed, the trial court's ruling would have afforded preembryos the legal status of "persons" and vested them with legally cognizable interests separate from those of their progenitors. Such a decision would doubtless have had the effect of outlawing IVF programs in the state of Tennessee. But in setting aside the trial court's judgment, the Court of Appeals, at least by implication, may have swung too far in the opposite direction.

To our way of thinking, the most helpful discussion on this point is found not in the minuscule number of legal opinions that have involved "frozen embryos," but in the ethical standards set by The American Fertility Society, as follows:

> Three major ethical positions have been articulated in the debate over preembryo status. At one extreme is the view of the preembryo as a human subject after fertilization, which requires that it be accorded the rights of a person. This position entails an obligation to provide an opportunity for implantation to occur and tends to ban any action before transfer that might harm the preembryo or that is not immediately therapeutic, such as freezing and some preembryo research.

At the opposite extreme is the view that the preembryo has a status no different from any other human tissue. With the consent of those who have decision-making authority over the preembryo, no limits should be imposed on actions taken with preembryos.

A third view—one that is most widely held—takes an intermediate position between the other two. It holds that the preembryo deserves respect greater than that accorded to human tissue but not the respect accorded to actual persons. The preembryo is due greater respect than other human tissue because of its potential to become a person and because of its symbolic meaning for many people. Yet, it should not be treated as a person, because it has not yet developed the features of personhood, is not yet established as developmentally individual, and may never realize its biologic potential.

\* \* \*

In its report, the Ethics Committee then calls upon those in charge of IVF programs to establish policies in keeping with the "special respect" due preembryos and suggests:

> Within the limits set by institutional policies, decision-making authority regarding preembryos should reside with the persons who have provided the gametes. . . . As a matter of law, it is reasonable to assume that the gamete providers have primary decision-making authority regarding preembryos in the absence of specific legislation on the subject. A person's liberty to procreate or to avoid procreation is directly involved in most decisions involving preembryos.[ ]

We conclude that preembryos are not, strictly speaking, either "persons" or "property," but occupy an interim category that entitles them to special respect because of their potential for human life. It follows that any interest that Mary Sue Davis and Junior Davis have in the preembryos in this case is not a true property interest. However, they do have an interest in the nature of ownership, to the extent that they have decision-making authority concerning disposition of the preembryos, within the scope of policy set by law.

## V. The Enforceability of Contract

\* \* \*

We believe, as a starting point, that an agreement regarding disposition of any untransferred preembryos in the event of contingencies (such as the death of one or more of the parties, divorce, financial reversals, or abandonment of the program) should be presumed valid and should be enforced as between the progenitors. This conclusion is in keeping with the proposition that the progenitors, having provided the gametic material giving rise to the preembryos, retain decision-making authority as to their disposition.

At the same time, we recognize that life is not static, and that human emotions run particularly high when a married couple is attempting to overcome infertility problems. It follows that the parties' initial "informed consent" to IVF procedures will often not be truly informed because of the near impossibility of anticipating, emotionally and psychologically, all the turns that events may take as the IVF process unfolds. Providing that the initial agreements may later be modified by agreement will, we think, protect the parties against some of the risks they face in this regard. But, in the absence of such agreed modification, we conclude that their prior agreements should be considered binding.

\* \* \*

[In this case,] we are \* \* \* left with this situation: there was initially no agreement between the parties concerning disposition of the preembryos under the circumstances of this case; there has been no agreement since; and there is no formula in the Court of Appeals opinion for determining the outcome if the parties cannot reach an agreement in the future.

\* \* \*

## VI. The Right of Procreational Autonomy

Although an understanding of the legal status of preembryos is necessary in order to determine the enforceability of agreements about their disposition, asking whether or not they constitute "property" is not an altogether helpful question. As the appellee points out in his brief, "[as] two or eight cell tiny lumps of complex protein, the embryos have no [intrinsic] value to either party." Their value lies in the "potential to become, after implantation, growth and birth, children." Thus, the essential dispute here is not where or how or how long to store the preembryos, but whether the parties will become parents. The Court of Appeals held in effect that they will become parents if they both agree to become parents. The Court did not say what will happen if they fail to agree. We conclude that the answer to this dilemma turns on the parties' exercise of their constitutional right to privacy.

\* \* \*

[The Court found there was a right to individual privacy in both Federal and Tennessee State law, and that this right to individual privacy encompassed the right of procreational autonomy.]

For the purposes of this litigation it is sufficient to note that, whatever its ultimate constitutional boundaries, the right of procreational autonomy is composed of two rights of equal significance—the right to procreate and the right to avoid procreation. Undoubtedly, both are subject to protections and limitations.

The equivalence of and inherent tension between these two interests are nowhere more evident than in the context of in vitro fertilization. None of the concerns about a woman's bodily integrity that have previously precluded men from controlling abortion decisions is applicable here. We are not unmindful of the fact that the trauma (including both emotional stress and physical discomfort) to which women are subjected in the IVF process is more severe than is the impact of the procedure on men. In this sense, it is fair to say that women contribute more to the IVF process than men. Their experience, however, must be viewed in light of the joys of parenthood that is desired or the relative anguish of a lifetime of unwanted parenthood. As they stand on the brink of potential parenthood, Mary Sue Davis and Junior Lewis Davis must be seen as entirely equivalent gamete-providers.

It is further evident that, however far the protection of procreational autonomy extends, the existence of the right itself dictates that decisional authority rests in the gamete-providers alone, at least to the extent that their decisions have an impact upon their individual reproductive status. * * * [N]o other person or entity has an interest sufficient to permit interference with the gamete-providers' decision to continue or terminate the IVF process, because no one else bears the consequences of these decisions in the way that the gamete-providers do.

Further, at least with respect to Tennessee's public policy and its constitutional right of privacy, the state's interest in potential human life is insufficient to justify an infringement on the gamete-providers' procreational autonomy.

Certainly, if the state's interests do not become sufficiently compelling in the abortion context until the end of the first trimester, after very significant developmental stages have passed, then surely there is no state interest in these preembryos which could suffice to overcome the interests of the gamete-providers. The [Tennessee] abortion statute reveals that the increase in the state's interest is marked by each successive developmental stage such that, toward the end of a pregnancy, this interest is so compelling that abortion is almost strictly forbidden. This scheme supports the conclusion that the state's interest in the potential life embodied by these four-to eight-cell preembryos (which may or may not be able to achieve implantation in a uterine wall and which, if implanted, may or may not begin to develop into fetuses, subject to possible miscarriage) is at best slight. When weighed against the interests of the individuals and the burdens inherent in parenthood, the state's interest in the potential life of these preembryos is not sufficient to justify any infringement upon the freedom of these individuals to make their own decisions as to whether to allow a process to continue that may result in such a dramatic change in their lives as becoming parents. The unique nature of this case requires us to note that the interests of these parties in parenthood are different in scope than the parental interests considered in other cases. Previously, courts have dealt with the childbearing and child-rearing aspects of parenthood. Abortion cases have dealt with gestational parenthood. In this case, the Court must deal with the question of genetic parenthood. We conclude, moreover, that an interest in avoiding genetic parenthood can be significant enough to trigger the protections afforded to all other aspects of parenthood. The technological fact that someone unknown to these parties could gestate these preembryos does not alter the fact that these parties, the gamete-providers, would become parents in that event, at least in the genetic sense. The profound impact this would have on them supports their right to sole decisional authority as to whether the process of attempting to gestate these preembryos should continue. This brings us directly to the question of how to resolve the dispute that arises when one party wishes to continue the IVF process and the other does not.

### VII.  Balancing the Parties' Interests

Resolving disputes over conflicting interests of constitutional import is a task familiar to the courts. One way of resolving these disputes is to consider the positions of the parties, the significance of their interests, and the relative burdens that will be imposed by differing resolutions. In this case, the issue centers on the two aspects of procreational autonomy—the right to procreate and the right to avoid procreation. We start by considering the burdens imposed on the parties by solutions that would have the effect of disallowing the exercise of individual procreational autonomy with respect to these particular preembryos.

Beginning with the burden imposed on Junior Davis, we note that the consequences are obvious. Any disposition which results in the gestation of the preembryos would impose unwanted parenthood on him, with all of its possible financial and psychological consequences. The impact that this unwanted parenthood would have on Junior Davis can only be understood by considering his particular circumstances, as revealed in the record.

Junior Davis testified that he was the fifth youngest of six children. When he was five years old, his parents divorced, his mother had a nervous break-down, and he and three of his brothers went to live at a home for boys run by the Lutheran Church. Another brother was taken in by an aunt, and his sister stayed with their mother. From that day forward, he had monthly visits with his mother but saw his father only three more times before he died in 1976. Junior Davis testified that, as a boy, he had severe problems caused by separation from his parents. He said that it was especially hard to leave his mother after each monthly visit. He clearly feels that he has suffered because of his lack of opportunity to establish a relationship with his parents and particularly because of the absence of his father.

In light of his boyhood experiences, Junior Davis is vehemently opposed to fathering a child that would not live with both parents. Regardless of whether he or Mary Sue had custody, he feels that the child's bond with the non-custodial parent would not be satisfactory. He testified very clearly that his concern was for the psychological obstacles a child in such a situation would face, as well as the burdens it would impose on him. Likewise, he is opposed to donation because the recipient couple might divorce, leaving the child (which he definitely would consider his own) in a single-parent setting.

Balanced against Junior Davis's interest in avoiding parenthood is Mary Sue Davis's interest in donating the preembryos to another couple for implantation. Refusal to permit donation of the preembryos would impose on her the burden of knowing that the lengthy IVF procedures she underwent were futile, and that the preembryos to which she contributed genetic material would never become children. While this is not an insubstantial emotional burden, we can only conclude that Mary Sue Davis's interest in donation is not as significant as the interest Junior Davis has in avoiding parenthood. If she were allowed to donate these preembryos, he would face a lifetime of either wondering about his parental status or knowing about his parental status but having no control over it. He testified quite clearly that if these preembryos were brought to term he would fight for custody of his child or children. Donation, if a child came of it, would rob him twice—his procreational autonomy would be defeated and his relationship with his offspring would be prohibited.

The case would be closer if Mary Sue Davis were seeking to use the preembryos herself, but only if she could not achieve parenthood by any other reasonable means. We recognize the trauma that Mary Sue has already experienced and the additional discomfort to which she would be subjected if she opts to attempt IVF again. Still, she would have a reasonable opportunity, through IVF, to try once again to achieve parenthood in all its aspects—genetic, gestational, bearing, and rearing.

Further, we note that if Mary Sue Davis were unable to undergo another round of IVF, or opted not to try, she could still achieve the child-rearing aspects of parenthood through adoption. The fact that she and Junior Davis pursued adoption indicates that, at least at one time, she was willing to forego genetic parenthood and would have been satisfied by the child-rearing aspects of parenthood alone.

## VIII. Conclusion

In summary, we hold that disputes involving the disposition of preembryos produced by in vitro fertilization should be resolved, first, by looking to the preferences of the progenitors. If their wishes cannot be ascertained, or if there is dispute, then their prior agreement concerning disposition should be carried out. If no prior agreement exists, then the relative interests of the parties in using or not using the preembryos must be weighed. Ordinarily, the party wishing to avoid procreation should prevail, assuming that the other party has a reasonable possibility of achieving parenthood by means other than use of the preembryos in question. If no other reasonable alternatives exist, then the argument in favor of using the preembryos to achieve pregnancy should be considered. However, if the party seeking control of the preembryos intends merely to donate them to another couple, the objecting party obviously has the greater interest and should prevail.

But the rule does not contemplate the creation of an automatic veto, and in affirming the judgment of the Court of Appeals, we would not wish to be interpreted as so holding.

For the reasons set out above, the judgment of the Court of Appeals is affirmed, in the appellee's favor. This ruling means that the Knoxville Fertility Clinic is free to follow its normal procedure in dealing with unused preembryos, as long as that procedure is not in conflict with this opinion.

## NOTES AND QUESTIONS

1. *Davis Aftermath.* The Knoxville Fertility Clinic could not "follow its normal procedure in dealing with unused pre-embryos" because its normal procedure was to provide those pre-embryos to infertile couples—a procedure that would have been in conflict with the opinion. On rehearing directed to this issue, the Tennessee court looked to the report of the American Fertility Society's Ethics Committee, which authorizes the pre-embryos to be donated for research purposes (which would require the consent of both of the Davises) or to be discarded. See Davis v. Davis, Order on Petitions to Rehear (Sup.Ct.Tenn., Nov. 23, 1992).

2. *The Relevance of Abortion Law.* The court suggests that the state interest in assuring that the embryo is implanted and allowed to develop cannot be sufficiently compelling to overcome a gamete-provider's right to avoid parenthood because, by analogy, "the state's interest does not become sufficiently compelling in the abortion context until the end of the first trimester, after very significant developmental stages have passed * * *." Is the analogy to the abortion context a persuasive one? In the same year in which this case was decided, the U.S. Supreme Court reconsidered the value of drawing trimester lines and pointed out that the "State has legitimate interests from the outset of the pregnancy in protecting * * * the life of a fetus that may become a child." Planned Parenthood of Southeastern Pennsylvania v. Casey, *supra* Section III.B. Could the interest of the state in protecting the fetus extend back to before a fertilized ovum is even introduced into the mother's body, back to the pre-embryo in the laboratory? As a constitutional matter, could a state have an interest in protecting fertilized ova that would be sufficiently compelling to overcome the interests of one or both of the gamete providers?

3.   *Property vs. Custody Theories.* The court describes several different rules that could be applied in disputes over the status and control of extracorporeal fertilized ova or pre-embryos. One of the alternatives is to treat the pre-embryos as personal property and apply the common law of property to them; another would be to treat those pre-embryos as if they were children entitled to protection of the state law. Each view has some legal support. See York v. Jones, 717 F.Supp. 421 (E.D.Va.1989) (treating frozen embryos prepared in the course of infertility treatment as property that would be subject to the ordinary law of bailment). See also La. Rev. Stat. § 9:131 (applying the "best interest of the in vitro fertilized ovum" standard).

4.   *Enforceability of Contract.* Several courts have followed a path close to that taken in *Davis.* See Kass v. Kass, 91 N.Y.2d 554, 673 N.Y.S.2d 350, 696 N.E.2d 174 (1998) (enforcing informed consent document declaring that the clinic would use any frozen pre-embryos for research in the event that the progenitors could not agree on their disposition); Roman v. Roman, 193 S.W.3d 40 (Tex.Civ.App.2006, rev. den. 2007) (reversing a divorce court order that granted half of the six pre-embryos to the husband and half to the wife, and allowed each to dispose of them as that one felt appropriate, and instead enforcing the prior agreement allowing the clinic to destroy the embryos); Dahl v. Angle, 222 Or. App. 572, 194 P.3d 834 (2008) (enforcing prior agreement).

Two courts to confront this issue expressly rejected the notion that the prior agreement of the progenitors should always govern the disposition of frozen embryos. See A.Z. v. B.Z., 431 Mass. 150, 725 N.E.2d 1051 (2000) (refusing to enforce agreement that provided that if the intended parents were to become separated, the frozen embryos then available would be given to one of the parents for implantation, because it forced the former husband to become a parent against his will and was thus contrary to public policy); J.B. v. M.B., 170 N.J. 9, 783 A.2d 707 (2001) (holding the parties would not normally be bound by a prior IVF agreement that would now require one of those parties to become a parent against that person's will).

Notably, in *Davis*, *Kass*, *Roman*, and *Dahl*, the enforceable prior agreements provided for the destruction of frozen embryos rather than their implantation; but in *A.Z.* and *J.B.*, the agreements would have resulted in the creation of a child (and, of course, parents) against one of the parties' wishes. How important might that distinction have been to explain the different outcomes? Compare A.Z. and J.B., supra, with Szafranski v. Dunston, 34 N.E.3d 1132, 393 Ill.Dec. 604 (2015) (enforcing prior agreement allowing woman to use cryopreserved pre-embryos created with ex-boyfriend, despite his desire to avoid becoming a parent). See also, Judith Daar, Litowitz v. Litowitz: Feuding over Frozen Embryos and Forecasting the Future of Reproductive Medicine in Sandra Johnson, et al. (eds), Health Law and Bioethics Cases in Context (2009), describing the backstory of an embryo disposition case that involved a battle over which of several agreements signed by the parties should prevail and providing a catalog of frozen embryo cases.

5.    *Other Relevant Factors?* In the United States, clinics conducting *in vitro* fertilization generally try to remove several eggs so that at least a few will be fertilized *in vitro* and can be replaced in the uterus. In some cases there is no fertilization or inadequate fertilization *in vitro,* and, thus, no return to the uterus, although fertilization occurs in most of the ova in which it is attempted. ART success rates can vary based on treatment factors, such as number of embryos transferred and type of ART procedure, as well as patient characteristics, such as age, infertility diagnosis, and history of prior births or miscarriages. In 2015, about 30% of all fresh-nondonor ART cycles led to pregnancy, and only 24% resulted in a live birth. (Some patients undergo multiple cycles.) See CDC, 2015 Assisted Reproductive Technology: Fertility Clinic Success Rates Report (2017). The data also show that "percentages of transfers resulting in pregnancies, live births, and single-infant live births were higher for frozen nondonor embryos than for fresh nondonor embryos." CDC, 2015 Assisted Reproductive Technology: National Summary Report (2017).

Because the chances of success are substantially increased if several fertilized ova are returned to the uterus, and because of the high cost and physical burden of repeating the egg retrieval procedure, women undergoing *in vitro* fertilization are generally given drugs to increase the number of ova that become ripe and ready for release and fertilization in one cycle. While this "superovulation" increases the chances of successful fertilization and implantation, inducing ovulation itself may have adverse side effects. In addition, the simultaneous placement of multiple fertilized ova results in a higher rate of multiple births than in the rest of the population, increasing health risks for the woman and child.

Given the difference in the burden of retrieval processes, should the ovum source (who went through an invasive surgical procedure, following sometimes debilitating hormone therapy) have greater say in the disposition of the frozen embryo than the sperm source (who went into the next room with a cup)? Would this approach violate principles of equal protection?

Most of the cases suggest that the result in a frozen embryo disposition case might be different if the party who wished to bring the frozen embryo to life were otherwise infertile, and would have no other way to become a parent. In fact, this seemed to be an important factor in the court's decision in Szafranski v. Dunston, supra Note 4. Justice Verniero, concurring in the *J.B.* case, also described in note 4, pointed out that "the same principles that compel the outcome in this case would permit an infertile party to assert his or her right to use a preembryo against the objections of the other party, if such use were the only means of procreation. In that instance, the balance arguably would weigh in favor of the infertile party absent countervailing factors of greater weight." What might count as "countervailing factors of greater weight"? The *J.B.* majority didn't seem convinced the result would be different if the one seeking to use the embryo were otherwise infertile, saying, "[w]e express no opinion in respect of a case in which a party who has become infertile seeks use of stored preembryos against the wishes of his or her partner, noting only that the possibility of adoption also may be a consideration, among others, in the court's assessment."

6. *Poor Quality Care & Other Harms.* Reproductive technologies, such as *in vitro* fertilization and embryo cryopreservation, can give rise to a host of different kinds of liability. Of course, the physician and medical institution would be liable as in an ordinary medical malpractice case for negligently performing the medical procedure. Would the duty of due care extend to the fetus as well as the parents? Negligently freezing an ovum or embryo, or negligently thawing it and thus destroying or damaging it, would also subject the appropriate professionals to malpractice liability. For an example of a case based on both intentional and negligent infliction of emotional distress against a provider who destroyed tissue that was cryogenically frozen to allow for later conception, see Witt v. Yale-New Haven Hosp, 51 Conn. Supp. 155, 977 A.2d 779 (2008). But see Miller v. American Fertility Group of Illinois, 386 Ill.App. 3d 141, 897 N.E.2d 837 (2009) (no wrongful death action allowed on behalf of mistakenly destroyed pre-embryo before its implantation in the mother).

The value of cryogenically preserved fertilized pre-embryos (or ova) may also make them targets for theft; clinic employees (or others) may be tempted to provide excess genetic material to those who need it without seeking consent from the original progenitors. Indeed, during the late 1990s that kind of redirection of ova apparently became fairly common at the University of California-Irvine's fertility clinic, where at least fifteen children were born as a result of the use of ova from women who had not consented to their transfer. It also creates the opportunity for mistakes to occur. Consider the case of Prato-Morrison v. Doe, 103 Cal.App.4th 222, 126 Cal.Rptr.2d 509 (2002). The court described the events leading up to the case:

> Donna Prato-Morrison and Robert Morrison engaged the services of a fertility clinic, to no avail, and ultimately abandoned their efforts to conceive, believing their unused genetic materials would be destroyed. When the clinic later became the target of an investigation into its widespread misuse of genetic materials, the Morrisons (along with many others) sued the clinic and later settled their claims for an undisclosed amount of money. The Morrisons, "wondering whether [they have] a genetic child or children in the world," then embarked on a campaign to intrude into the lives of another fertility clinic family (Judith and Jacob Doe) who might have innocently received Donna Morrison's genetic material. The Morrisons filed a complaint in which they asked the court to determine whether they are the genetic parents of the Does' twin daughters (now almost 14 years old) and, if so, to grant custody of the children (who know nothing about this claim and who have no reason to question their parentage) to the Morrisons. Although the Morrisons later withdrew their request for custody, they continued their efforts to compel blood tests and obtain the right to visit the twins."

In rejecting the Morrisons' claims, the court held that plaintiffs failed to introduce admissible evidence that defendant wife had received eggs supplied by plaintiff wife. More significantly, however, the court held that plaintiffs' rights as alleged biological parents did not overcome defendants' rights as presumed parents, so as to entitle plaintiffs to discover whether the twins were born as a result of the theft of their genetic materials. The court further held that even had plaintiffs presented proof of a genetic link to the twins sufficient to establish their standing to pursue a parentage action, it would not be in the best interests of the twins to have plaintiffs intrude into their lives, or to be subjected to the blood tests and mental health evaluation suggested by plaintiffs. But in Robert B. v. Susan B., 109 Cal.App.4th 1109, 135 Cal.Rptr.2d 785 (2003), the husband of a couple subject to an unintentional mix-up was able to establish parentage. In that case, a husband and wife brought a parentage action against a single woman who had given birth to the genetic brother of a child borne to the couple, as the result of the placement of the wrong embryo in the single woman's uterus by a fertility clinic. The husband and wife had sought ova from an anonymous donor for fertilization with the husband's sperm, and the single woman had sought an embryo created from anonymously donated ova and sperm; but after receiving the results of genetic testing of the husband, the single woman learned that she had received ova from an anonymous donor fertilized by the husband's sperm. The Court of Appeal affirmed the trial court's determination that the husband was the child's father, but that the single woman was the child's mother. The husband's wife had no standing because she was biologically unrelated to the child.

7. *Selective Reduction.* One consequence of the implantation of several embryos fertilized *in vitro* is that many of the embryos may continue to develop *in vivo*. While most multiple births pose no substantial problems to the mother or the neonatal siblings, sometimes the life or health of the mother (or some of the developing fetuses) can be preserved only if the number of fetuses that the mother is carrying is reduced. Is the case of such selective reduction governed by the more general law applying to abortion, described earlier in the chapter? Are there any ethical or legal concerns present in cases of selective reduction that are not present in other situations that might give rise to abortion? What legal or ethical considerations, if any, should guide the mother (or the family, or the doctor, or the court) in choosing which of two or more fetuses should be aborted to save the life or health of that fetus's mother or the well-being of the potential siblings?

8. *Genetic Screening.* One consequence of the ability to freeze an embryo is that it permits evaluation of the genetic structure of the embryo before it is thawed and implanted. This allows for pre-implantation genetic screening or diagnosis (PIGD), which allows for a determination of several genetic attributes of the pre-embryo. This screening (for a wide range of conditions or attributes) or diagnosis (for a particular genetic disease) is increasingly available, as a practical matter, for more conditions, and for a lower cost. Some particularly thoughtful legal analysts believe that we will face a host of very difficult social questions soon, as prenatal genetic testing of various forms becomes widely available. See Jaime S. King, And Genetic Testing for All . . .

The Coming Revolution in Non-Invasive Prenatal Genetic Testing, 42 Rutgers L.J. 599 (2011).

9.    *ART Regulation.* Other than questions of parentage, ART is still relatively unregulated. Why are state legislatures, many of which have been active in restricting access to abortion, not banning IVF, especially to the extent that it may involve selective reduction? Why might state legislatures and the federal government be less interested in setting standards for care in this area as compared to other areas, such as nursing home care?

# D.  REPRODUCTIVE CLONING AND STEM CELL RESEARCH

## 1.   Reproductive Cloning

In 1997 the world was stunned by the revelation that a Scottish laboratory had cloned a mammal—to be precise, a Finn Dorset sheep. Scientists achieved this by removing the nucleus from a sheep ovum, replacing it with the genetic material from the sheep to be cloned, and then reimplanting the genetically changed ovum back into the surrogate mother sheep. In fact, the one cloned sheep was the only success in almost 300 attempts. Other mammals have been cloned using the same process, but scientists warned that the likelihood that this technology would be available for human beings remained, for the present, a few years away. Despite this, the bioethics community began a world-wide discussion on the consequences of cloning as a form of human reproduction.

Is it possible to talk about the creation of human beings through cloning in the same terms as we talk about the creation of human beings through other processes of assisted reproduction? How are the questions raised by the existence of cloned human beings truly different from the questions raised by human beings created by other technically driven medical processes? Cloning requires in vitro manipulation (like in vitro fertilization) and then implantation in a womb (like surrogacy). Is it different from either of those two forms of assisted reproduction? Is cloning really a form of reproduction at all, or is it something different—perhaps, merely replication? Who counts as the parents of the cloned individual? Does it make sense to speak of a "parent" or must we limit ourselves to speaking of the cloned person's "antecedent" or "precursor" or "genetic source"?

For generations, science fiction has raised fears of totalitarian regimes that can clone human beings for enslavement for the benefit of the regime. Should this present a genuine worry to this society? Could cloning be appropriated by the state in support of a totalitarian eugenics policy? A related worry is that a society could treat a newly cloned person as nothing more than the continuation of the source of its genetic material—or as a body parts source for the person who provided the genetic material. But wouldn't a cloned person have all of the rights of any other person? As some bioethicists argue, if our society were to treat cloned human beings as enslaved persons or spare parts warehouses, the existence of cloning would be the least of our problems.

Would cloned people have the same relationship to each other that identical twins maintain? Identical twins have a common genetic make-up, as a clone and his source would, yet we treat those twins as separate human beings with separate lives and we have identified no social dislocation that arises out of their existence. Why should we be more worried about cloned human beings than about identical twins? In fact, because a cloned person and his source would be different ages, they would be likely to be raised in different environments, and thus to be less similar than identical twins. On the other hand, the number of identical twins is naturally limited, and there are very few identical triplets. We could, through cloning, create a much larger number of identical "siblings."

In any case, is there any justifiable reason for cloning a full human being? A few have been suggested. Suppose a child were dying of a disease that could be treated with a bone marrow transplant from a genetically identical donor, but such a donor could not be found. Might it be acceptable to clone the patient, and then, independently, determine if the newly replicated person ought to be a donor for his "brother"? Alternatively, suppose a couple has an infertility problem which makes it impossible for either of them to become a parent in the ordinary course of events. Should they be able to opt for cloning so that their child will be related to one of them? What if only one of the parents is infertile, and they want a child that does not require the potentially interfering involvement of a third party?

The issue has become more complicated because human reproduction is not the only goal of cloning. Cloning of human stem cells may also be useful in developing therapies for medical conditions that are now untreatable. Many view cloning with the intent of creating a new human being—*reproductive cloning*—as posing far more ethical and legal difficulty than cloning human stem cells with the intent to research or create a medical treatment—*therapeutic cloning*.

Both forms of cloning generally require somatic cell nuclear transfer, a process in which the nucleus of an unfertilized human ovum is removed and replaced with the nucleus from an adult cell. The resulting ovum cell, which has the full complement of human genetic material, is then stimulated so that it will divide and form a pre-embryo. In *therapeutic cloning*, some cells from the pre-embryo are removed for purposes of medical research or treatment. These stem cells have the potential to develop into almost any human cells, and they may be useful in repairing almost any human tissue, but once those cells are removed, the pre-embryo cannot develop into a human being. In *reproductive cloning*, the pre-embryo would be placed in a uterus to develop into a human being.

The National Bioethics Advisory Commission published a comprehensive and thoughtful report on the cloning of human beings within months of the revelation that it had been successfully performed on sheep. The report includes a useful description of the relevant scientific procedures as well as a fully annotated analysis of the ethical, theological, legal and policy issues, and it was careful to distinguish between reproductive cloning (which it considered medically risky) and therapeutic cloning (which, it thought, held great scientific promise).

## RECOMMENDATIONS OF THE NATIONAL BIOETHICS ADVISORY COMMISSION (NBAC) WITH REGARD TO CLONING
(1997).

\* \* \*

As somatic cell nuclear transfer cloning could represent a means of human reproduction for some people, limitations on that choice must be made only when the societal benefits of prohibition clearly outweigh the value of maintaining the private nature of such highly personal decisions. Especially in light of some arguably compelling cases for attempting to clone a human being using somatic cell nuclear transfer, the ethics of policy making must strike a balance between the values society wishes to reflect and issues of privacy and the freedom of individual choice.

\* \* \*

\* \* \* At present, the use of this technique to create a child would be a premature experiment that exposes the developing child to unacceptable risks. This in itself is sufficient to justify a prohibition on cloning human beings at this time, even if such efforts were to be characterized as the exercise of a fundamental right to attempt to procreate. More speculative psychological harms to the child, and effects on the moral, religious, and cultural values of society may be enough to justify continued prohibitions in the future, but more time is needed for discussion and evaluation of these concerns.

\* \* \*

Within this overall framework the Commission came to the following conclusions and recommendations:

I.    The Commission concludes that at this time it is morally unacceptable for anyone in the public or private sector, whether in a research or clinical setting, to attempt to create a child using somatic cell nuclear transfer cloning. We have reached a consensus on this point because current scientific information indicates that this technique is not safe to use in humans at this time. * * *

II. Federal legislation should be enacted to prohibit anyone from attempting, whether in a research or clinical setting, to create a child through somatic cell nuclear transfer cloning. It is critical, however, that such legislation include a sunset clause to ensure that Congress will review the issue after a specified time period (three to five years) in order to decide whether the prohibition continues to be needed. * * *

III. Any regulatory or legislative actions undertaken to effect the foregoing prohibition on creating a child by somatic cell nuclear transfer should be carefully written so as not to interfere with other important areas of scientific research. In particular, no new regulations are required regarding the cloning of human DNA sequences and cell lines, since neither activity raises the scientific and ethical issues that arise from the attempt to create children through somatic cell nuclear transfer, and these fields of research have already provided important scientific and biomedical advances.

* * *

This was not the last federal bioethics panel to consider the issue. The President's Council on Bioethics, which effectively replaced NBAC, issued a series of reports, including Human Cloning and Human Dignity (2002), Monitoring Stem Cell Research (2004), and Reproduction and Responsibility (2004), which supported a ban on reproductive cloning and both a moratorium and then careful regulation of all other cloning. Although disagreements between those who opposed reproductive cloning and those who supported therapeutic cloning (and disagreements among those on each side, too) made it difficult for Congress to legislate with regard to reproductive cloning, many state legislatures have done so. Several have outlawed reproductive cloning, some have outlawed cloning of any kind, and some have outlawed reproductive cloning while at the same time authorizing state funding for stem cell research (which is thought to be both scientifically and economically promising).

## 2. Stem Cell Research

Because of the scientific promise shown by stem cell research, many people who support legislation banning reproductive cloning vigorously oppose placing any limitation upon therapeutic cloning that is, many scientists believe, necessary to effective stem cell research. The ethical issues which have given rise to the legal argument are a bit more subtle than you might have expected.

## JUDITH JOHNSON AND ERIN WILLIAMS, CRS REPORT FOR CONGRESS: STEM CELL RESEARCH (2006)

\* \* \*

Stem cell research is controversial not because of its goals, but rather because of the means of obtaining some of the cells. Research involving most types of stem cells, such as those derived from adult tissues and umbilical cord blood, is uncontroversial, except when its effectiveness as an alternative to embryonic stem cells is debated. The crux of the debate centers around embryonic stem cells, which enable research that may facilitate the development of medical treatments and cures, but which require the destruction of an embryo to derive. In addition, because cloning is one method of producing embryos for research, the ethical issues surrounding cloning are also relevant.

\* \* \*

Most positions on embryonic stem cell research rest at least in part on the relative moral weight accorded to embryos and that accorded to the prospect of saving, prolonging, or improving others' lives. \* \* \*

Some groups explore the moral standing of human embryos, and also consider the "duty to relieve the pain and suffering of others." Others take the position that embryos do not have the same moral status as persons. They acknowledge that embryos are genetically human, but hold that they do not have the same moral relevance because they lack specific capacities, including consciousness, reasoning and sentience. They also argue that viewing embryos as persons would "rule out all fertility treatments that involve the creation and discarding of excess embryos," and further assert that we do not have the same "moral or religious" response to the natural loss of embryos (through miscarriage) that we do to the death of infants. \* \* \* They conclude that performing research to benefit persons justifies the destruction of embryos. Acceptance of the notion that the destruction of embryos can be justified in some circumstances forms the basis of pro-stem cell research opinions, and is usually modified with some combination of the distinctions and limitations that follow.

\* \* \*

Some proponents of embryonic stem cell research base their support on the question of whether an embryo is viable. The relevance of the viability distinction rests on the premise that it is morally preferable for embryos that will not grow or develop beyond a certain stage and/or those that would otherwise be discarded to be used for the purpose of alleviating human suffering.

\* \* \*

A separate distinction that often leads to the same conclusions as viability is the purpose for which embryos are created. This distinction draws an ethical line based upon the intent of the people creating embryos. In the view of some, it is permissible to create an embryo for reproductive purposes (such as IVF), but impermissible to create one with the intention of destroying it for research.

* * *

A further distinction has been drawn based upon the timing of the creation of embryonic stem cell lines. Here, the premise is that it is unacceptable to induce the destruction of embryos for the creation of new lines. However, in cases in which embryos have already been destroyed and the lines already exist, it is morally preferable to use those lines for research to improve the human condition. This was one central distinction drawn in the 2001 Bush policy, which limited the use of federal funding to research on lines derived on or before the date of the policy. Supporters of the Bush policy on both sides of the issue favor this distinction as a compromise.

* * *

One factual distinction that has been used to support competing ethical viewpoints is the efficacy of alternatives to embryonic stem cell research. The promise of stem cell therapies derived from adult tissue and umbilical cord blood have buttressed opposition to embryonic stem cell research. * * * These opponents argue that therapies and cures can be developed without the morally undesirable destruction of embryos.

* * *

Some division over the support for and opposition to embryonic stem cell research focuses on the question of whether the use of federal funding is appropriate. Those who oppose federal funding argue that the government should not be associated with embryo destruction. They point out that embryo destruction violates the "deeply held moral beliefs of some citizens," and suggest that "funding alternative research is morally preferable." Proponents of federal funding argue that it is immoral to discourage life-saving research by withholding federal funding. They point out that consensus support is not required for many federal spending policies, as it "does not violate democratic principles or infringe on the rights of dissent of those in the minority." They argue that the efforts of both federally supported and privately supported researchers are necessary to keep the United States at the forefront of what they believe is a very important, cutting edge area of science. Furthermore, supporters believe that the oversight that comes with federal dollars will result in better and more ethically controlled research in the field.

* * *

## 42 U.S.C. § 289g

(Dickey-Wicker Amendment, 2006).

(a)  None of the funds made available [in appropriations for the Departments of Labor, Education, and Health and Human Services] may be used for—

(1)  the creation of a human embryo or embryos for research purposes; or

(2)  research in which a human embryo or embryos are destroyed, discarded, or knowingly subjected to risk of injury or death greater than that allowed for research on fetuses in utero * * *.

(b)  For purposes of this section, the term "human embryo or embryos" includes any organism, not protected as a human subject * * * that is derived by fertilization, parthenogenesis, cloning, or any other means from one or more human gametes or human diploid cells.

When the first Dickey-Wicker Amendment was passed, scientists had no access to stem cells derived from fertilized ova ("embryonic stem cells"), but in 1998 a laboratory at the University of Wisconsin stabilized such stem cells so that they could be used in research. In 1999 the Department of Health and Human Services determined that the Dickey-Wicker Amendment did not apply to embryonic stem cell research because the stem cells were not embryos under the statute. Despite this, no federal research grants were made for stem cell research during the Clinton administration. In 2001, President Bush issued an executive order providing that federal funding could be made available for research involving embryonic stem cell lines that were already available for research, but that no new stem cell lines could be used in federally-funded research. He reasoned that the damage had already been done to the embryos that were destroyed to create the stem cell lines that were already available, but that federal funding agencies should act to assure that no new embryos would be destroyed for use in federally funded research.

In 2009, President Obama greatly expanded the class of embryonic stem cells that could be used in federally-funded research. He determined that the Dickey-Wicker Amendment permitted the use of embryonic stem cells in federally funded research, but that it did not permit federal funds to be used in deriving the stem cell from the embryo. That is, private resources would have to be expended to obtain the embryonic stem cells, an act which requires destroying the embryo, but federal funds could be used for the subsequent research upon the stem cells derived from the embryo. The Obama regulations provided that the stem cells used in federally funded research could only come from leftover fertilized ova created by infertility laboratories for patients engaged in infertility treatment, and only when the progenitors approved of the use of their cells for this purpose in writing. See 74 Fed.Reg. 32, 170–32, 175 (July 7, 2009). Two scientists tried, unsuccessfully, to challenge these regulations as a violation of the Dickey-Wicker Amendment. Sherley v. Sebelius, 689 F.3d 776 (D.C. Cir. 2012), cert. den. 133 S.Ct. 847 (2013). At the time of this writing, President Trump's policy on embryonic stem cell research is not yet clear, though Vice President Pence has consistently opposed such research.

There have been several other bills introduced in Congress to deal with stem cell research. Some would appropriate large amounts for this research; some would ban it altogether. Because of the deadlock over the propriety of this process, no other significant federal legislation has been signed into law—yet. State legislatures have produced far more legislation on the use of stem cells than has Congress. Some states have sought to outlaw all cloning, and thus most stem cell research, while others have encouraged stem cell research by appropriating funding for stem cell research within the state. California, for example, which is one of a dozen states to outlaw reproductive cloning, has also established the California Institute of Regenerative Medicine, originally funded by the authorization of $3 billion in state bonds, to stimulate the scientific and economic benefits many believe will follow in the wake of this research. For a good (but early) account of the debate over the role of the state in dealing with cloning, see Report of the California Advisory Committee on Human Cloning, 53 Hastings L.J. 1143 (2002). For a discussion of the sale of human tissue, see Chapter 7. The international debate on cloning has largely paralleled the debate in the United States. In 2005, the United Nations General Assembly faced conflicting conventions that would ban either reproductive cloning or all cloning. Ultimately, the General Assembly adopted a resolution encouraging member nations to ban cloning that is "incompatible with human dignity and the protection of human life." Countries have taken different approaches to the regulation of stem cell research. See Report of the U.N. International Bioethics Committee on Human Cloning and International Governance (Jun. 9, 2009).

# CHAPTER 4

# ORGAN TRANSPLANTATION AND THE DETERMINATION OF DEATH

▪ ▪ ▪

## I.  ORGAN TRANSPLANTATION

### A.  RATIONING SCARCE ORGANS

Is it moral, or good public policy, to ration medical care by ability to pay? And, in the case of scarce resources such as human organs or certain technologies, if not by ability to pay, then how?

Many argue that health care is distinct from ordinary consumer goods—such as iPads and cars—which we distribute entirely by ability to pay. The argument that health care is distinct rests on the dignity of persons (and what is required for human flourishing); the moral duty to relieve human suffering; and the communal benefits of fostering good health (in terms of public health and a robust economy). Counterarguments in favor of treating health care, even life-saving medical treatment, as an ordinary consumer good, have been prominent during the debates over the Affordable Care Act (ACA). Some argue that placing responsibility, with consequences, upon the individual to pay for medical care incentivizes work, savings, and fitness while guaranteeing health care rewards irresponsibility. Others argue that public guarantees of health care force an involuntary transfer of earnings from one person to another. See Chapter 1.

Most arguments in favor of providing health care to those who cannot pay reference a "basic" package of health care services. See Chapter 3 discussion of preventive health care in the ACA. What are the relevant considerations in deciding whether particular medical treatments, like organ transplants, fit within the basic package? Survival rates? Quality of life post-transplant, and if so, how should that be measured? Global budgets that trade off some health care interventions (e.g., transplants v. preventive care) in order to spread limited funds most effectively? Compare Gil Siegal & Richard Bonnie, Closing the Organ Gap: A Reciprocity-based Social Contract Approach, 34 J. L. Med. & Ethics 415 (2006), calling organ transplantation a "remarkable achievement" that saves lives, improves quality of life, and reduces costs (for kidney transplants as compared to hemodialysis, for example) with Albert R. Jonsen, The God Squad and the

Origins of Transplantation Ethics and Policy, 35 J. L. Med. & Ethics 238 (2007), arguing that the looming problem behind transplantation policy is the "incessant . . . demand that life must be salvaged at all costs."

Organ transplantation raises a second issue of allocation: the supply simply does not satisfy the need or demand and rationing follows. A rather famous example of explicit rationing occurred in the 1960s when the Admissions and Policy Committee (sometimes known as the "God Squad") of the Seattle Artificial Kidney Center decided which patients would receive the life-saving "artificial kidney" (i.e., hemodialysis). The God Squad was reported to have selected patients partly on the basis of age, gender, marital status, number of dependents, emotional stability, education, and occupation, among other characteristics. Media exposure of the work of the God Squad contributed to the decision to have Medicare cover dialysis for all individuals with end-stage renal disease (ESRD), even those not otherwise eligible for Medicare, which in turn led to Medicare's decision to cover kidney transplants. Richard A. Rettig, Special Treatment—The Story of Medicare's ESRD Entitlement, 364 NEJM 596 (2011).

Ability to pay actually is one factor that determines who gets an organ transplant. A candidate generally is not placed on the active waiting list unless there is a source of payment for the transplant and the expensive lifelong post-transplant care. Even with the ACA, private insurance, Medicaid, and Medicare will not cover all medically possible transplants or necessary aftercare.

While ability to pay is the gateway to being listed for a transplant, one cannot buy an organ from a willing seller. Instead, we use other criteria to ration scarce organs. Consider the following Problem.

### PROBLEM: SELECTING AN ORGAN TRANSPLANT RECIPIENT

For the last few weeks, two patients have been under treatment at General Hospital for acute liver failure. One, James Patterson, is a 65-year-old retired CEO of a major computer software company. He has two children, a 40-year-old daughter with a child of her own and a 24-year-old son. Patterson is active in his church and is a financial supporter of the local university athletics department. He was exposed to hepatitis B, which has destroyed most of his liver. The second patient is Antonia Friedman, a 30-year-old attorney with two children, ages 2 and 4. She is an active member of the local city council and has contributed generously in the past year to the hospital's building fund. Friedman is a recovering alcoholic and has been through rehabilitation programs several times. This time, though, she has abstained from alcohol for six months and so meets common minimum criteria for former alcoholics for liver transplant. Within the last week, both patients have taken a turn for the worse; and both will die within the next few weeks if they do not receive a liver transplant.

A few hours ago, a patient was admitted to the hospital with massive head trauma caused by an automobile accident. The patient is brain dead but is being kept on support systems to preserve his organs for transplantation. The liver is undamaged. Tissue matching shows that it is an equally acceptable organ for either Patterson or Friedman. Circumstances make it impossible for the liver to be divided between the two patients. Patterson's physician was the first to list his patient on the transplant list, which he did three days earlier than did Friedman's physician. Who should receive the single available organ?

Is this decision essentially a medical decision to be made by the physician? Would you prefer that a committee decide? Who should be on the committee? Should your hospital establish a procedure in which patients are notified that listing is being considered and given an opportunity to advocate for themselves? Should the hospital keep a record documenting the reasons a patient wasn't listed or selected? Should the government set the criteria for deciding who gets the organ? See Section I. B, below.

Would you prefer to use a lottery system in which a recipient is selected from among all qualified candidates by drawing lots? What advantages and disadvantages would a pure "first come-first served" policy present? Should time on the waiting list make any difference? What if you knew that Patterson's doctor was more aggressive in listing patients than was Friedman's? What if you knew that other doctors at that hospital simply refuse to list recovering alcoholics for a transplant? Is considering Friedman's alcoholism inappropriate or is it morally required? See, e.g., Robert S. Brown, Transplantation for Alcoholic Hepatitis—Time to Rethink the 6-Month "Rule," 365 NEJM 1836 (2011), discussing a study demonstrating the effectiveness of transplantation, in terms of survival and post-transplant abstinence from alcohol, even without a 6-month pre-transplant abstinence period; Erin Minelli & Bryan Liang, Transplant Candidates and Substance Use: Adopting Rational Health Policy for Resource Allocation, 44 U. Mich. J. L. Reform 667 (2011).

How important is the risk of graft failure; i.e., that the organ itself will fail due to rejection? Will that always outweigh other concerns? Consider that under current national kidney allocation policies, patients who have previously received a kidney that failed within a short time after transplant receive priority even though the presensitization caused by the earlier transplant increases the risk of graft failure. In addition, a person who has donated specific organs as a living donor receives priority in receiving an organ should the need arise in the future.

Projected lifespan of the patient is not the same as the risk of graft failure. Should younger always have precedence over older patients in the same medical situation? See Alan B. Leichtman et al., Improving the Allocation System for Deceased-Donor Kidneys, 364 NEJM 1287 (2011); Benjamin E. Hippen et al., Risk, Prognosis, and Unintended Consequences in Kidney Allocation, 364 NEJM 1285 (2011). Aside from age, are there any other characteristics that are more important than others? Or suspect? Should the post-transplant coverage provided by each patient's insurance or, alternatively, the net worth of each be considered?

# B. REGULATING ORGAN DISTRIBUTION

The National Organ Transplant Act of 1984 (NOTA) requires the Department of Health and Human Services (HHS) to establish an Organ Procurement and Transplantation Network (OPTN) to organize the retrieval, distribution, and transplantation of human organs. OPTN is the primary vehicle for federal regulation of the organ transplant system in the United States (42 C.F.R. Pt. 121). HHS contracts with the United Network for Organ Sharing (UNOS), a private nonprofit organization, for management of the federal OPTN. OPTN/UNOS manages procedures and standards for listing patients, retrieval and testing of organs, distribution to transplant hospitals, and the national waiting list and standards for selection of recipients from that list, among other issues. OPTN/UNOS policies are being constantly revised and can be found on the OPTN and UNOS websites. The Centers for Medicare & Medicaid Services also sets quality and policy standards as conditions for federal payments to transplant hospitals and other facilities involved in organ retrieval and transplantation.

*Access to the Transplant Waiting List*

Individual doctors and hospitals decide who gets on the transplant waiting list and when. Patient listing practices vary substantially among transplant centers around the country. Psychosocial factors, including anticipated compliance with medical recommendations; absence of a reliable support system; availability of alternative therapies; and the cause of original organ failure, influence physician listing decisions. Denise M. Dudzinski, Shifting to Other Justice Issues: Examining Listing Practices, 4 Am. J. Bioethics 35 (2004), reviewing studies of listing practices that conclude that standards and procedures tend to be informal and disadvantage racial minorities and women; Geert Verleden et al., Recipient Selection Processes and Listing for Lung Transplantation, 9 J. Thoracic Disease 3372 (2017); C.K. Argo et al., Regional Variability in Symptom-Based MELD Exceptions: A Response to Organ Shortage? 11 Am J. Transplant. 2353 (2011). For a compelling narrative of the effect of race on listing decisions, see Vanessa Grubbs, Good for Harvest, Bad for Planting, 26 Health Affairs 232 (2007). These factors have also excluded adults and children with cognitive disabilities. Lenny Bernstein, Persons with Autism, Intellectual Disabilities Fight Bias in Transplants, Wash. Post (Mar. 4, 2017).

Hospitals doing transplants have an incentive to engage in listing practices that increase volume. Federal investigations revealed that physicians at some transplant hospitals exaggerated their patients' medical condition to move them up higher on the list so the hospital would be able to perform more transplants. The charged hospitals settled with the government without admitting guilt, with one facility paying $1 million. A Man of Principle, Chicago Tribune Magazine, Jan. 25, 2004. Several studies have found that transplant centers located in high-competition areas listed a higher percentage of patients for transplant than areas with less competition. See, e.g., P.S. Cho et al, Competitive Market Analysis of Transplant Centers and Discrepancy of Wait-Listing of Recipients for Kidney Transplantation, 6 Int'l J. Organ Transplant Med. 141 (2015); E. Haavi Morreim, Another Kind of End-run: Status Upgrades, 5 Am. J. Bioethics 11 (2005).

When you are lining up for tickets to Disney World, you naturally try to seek out the shortest line even though there is very little at stake. When you are lining up for a life-saving transplant, finding the shortest line can be a life-or-death matter. In fact, median waiting times for particular organs have varied significantly among geographic regions despite a federal regulation requiring that organs be distributed "over as broad a geographic region as feasible" consistent with assuring that organs are not damaged. The reasons for these variations are many: all organs are limited in the distance they can safely be transported so distribution favors closer rather than farther and some organs (such as hearts) are particularly vulnerable in transport; some regions have higher rates of organ donation and others, higher rates of medical need; and some localities have hospitals with more aggressive listing practices thereby drawing in a higher share of available organs. David L. Weimer, Public and Private Regulation of Organ Transplantation: Liver Allocation and the Final Rule, 32 J. Health Pol. Pol'y & L. 9 (2007). One potential cause of persisting regional variation may be that transplant centers in different regions vary in their assessment of and requests for symptom-based exceptions (SBE) to move patients up in line. See Argo et al., above, pointing out that Medicaid patients are least likely to receive SBEs.

The persistent difference in regional wait times for organs encourages the practice of "multiple listing," in which patients with the means to travel at a moment's notice get listed in more than one region. Several websites provide transplant candidates with the wait time for specific organs in specific localities along with the travel time require to get there from their home. OPTN policy allows multiple listing, but the AMA holds that physicians should "refrain" from multiple listing and instead place candidates on a "single waiting list for each type of organ." Code of Medical Ethics Opinion E-6.2.1(g).

*Selecting the Recipient*

Federal regulations require that OPTN organ allocation policies be "equitable" and rely on "objective and measurable medical criteria" that are "based on sound medical judgment," "seek to achieve the best use of donated organs," and "avoid wasting organs." 42 C.F.R. § 121.8. Indeed, OPTN policies governing selection of a recipient from among listed patients use "objective and measurable medical criteria," quantifying medical urgency, measuring how good a match the organ and recipient are, and so on. But these apparently scientific criteria have measurable effects on access to organs for specific populations (minority, ethnic, age) and most obviously upon individuals. Kidney allocation policies provide an illustration of apparently neutral criteria that have had an adverse racial impact. For years, UNOS kidney allocation policies used very granular levels of antigen matching to select recipients from the transplant list even though the difference in graft failure was miniscule between each level. Before UNOS revised these criteria, whites received double the number of kidney transplants as compared to African Americans. The two populations were equally represented on the transplant waiting list (even though African Americans suffer a higher rate of total kidney failure) but in raw numbers more whites donated organs. OPTN, Annual Report 2003. Revised matching criteria have significantly increased the proportion of organs allocated to African Americans. A. Hart et al., OPTN/SRTR 2015 Annual Data Report: Early Effects of the New Kidney Allocation System, 17 Am. J. Transplant. 543 (2015).

Should courts get involved in deciding whether an individual patient receives an available organ? In Murnaghan v. HHS, Civ. Action No. 13-3083 (E.D. Pa. Jan. 5 and 13, 2013), the judge enjoined application of the OPTN "Under 12 Rule," so that Sarah Murnaghan, a 10-year-old girl facing imminent death, could have access to an adult lung rather than waiting for a pediatric lung. OPTN policy at the time allocated pediatric lungs to children and adult lungs to individuals over the age of 12 unless no appropriate adult recipient was on the list in which case the lungs would be allocated to a younger child. The judge's order calls the policy discriminatory, arbitrary, and capricious. The order required OPTN to consider Sarah as a candidate without applying the "Under 12 Rule." The Secretary of HHS refused to set aside the policy on her own for this case, commenting that making a decision on "who lives and who dies" without following policies that applied to all was inappropriate. She noted that 40 other children in Pennsylvania were awaiting lung transplants at that time. Paige Cunningham, Sibelius Won't Intervene on Transplant, Politico, June 5, 2013. See also, Daniel Bruggebrew, The Administrative Law Implications of Quasi-Governmental Organ Allocation, 41 Seton Hall Legis. J. 1 (2016). Sarah's first lung transplant, received within several days of the judge's order, failed, but a second transplant has sustained her since that time.

## C. LEGAL FRAMEWORK FOR THE PROCUREMENT OF ORGANS AND TISSUE

NOTA defers to state law on most questions related to organ donation, and most states have adopted the Uniform Anatomical Gift Act (UAGA), with some few variations, to govern donation of organs that will be retrieved post-mortem. Donation of non-life-sustaining organs by living donors is governed by familiar informed consent principles and by policies issued by OPTN. Legal restraints on the collection of human organs for transplantation contribute to the current shortage by requiring that there be consent for organ retrieval and that organs be donated instead of purchased.

### 1. The Uniform Anatomical Gift Act (UAGA)

### § 4. Who May Make Anatomical Gift Before Donor's Death.

(1) [T]he donor, if the donor is an adult or if the donor is a minor and is:

(A) emancipated; or

(B) authorized under state law to apply for a driver's license . . . :

(2) the agent of the donor unless the power or attorney for health care or other record prohibits the agent from making an anatomical gift;

(3) a parent of the donor, if the donor is an unemancipated minor . . .; or

(4) the donor's guardian.

### § 5. Manner of Making Anatomical Gift Before Donor's Death.

[This section provides that a donor may make an anatomical gift by indicating so on the driver's license, in a will, on a donor card, through a donor registry, or by any means of communication if terminally ill or fatally injured.]

### § 8. Preclusive Effect of Anatomical Gift, Amendment, or Revocation.

(a) Except as otherwise provided in subsection (g) . . . , in the absence of an express, contrary indication by the donor, a person other than the donor is barred from making, amending, or revoking an anatomical gift of a donor's body or part if the donor made an anatomical gift of the donor's body or part under Section 5. . . .

(g) If a donor who is an unemancipated minor dies, a parent of the donor who is reasonably available may revoke or amend an anatomical gift of the donor's body or part.

(h)   If an unemancipated minor who signed a refusal dies, a parent of the minor who is reasonably available may revoke the minor's refusal.

## § 9.  Who May Make Anatomical Gift of Decedent's Body or Part.

(a)   [A]n anatomical gift of a decedent's body or part for purpose of transplantation, therapy, research, or education may be made by any member of the following classes of persons who is reasonably available, in the order of priority listed:

(1)   an agent [appointed by the decedent prior to death];

(2)   the spouse of the decedent;

(3)   adult children of the decedent;

(4)   parents of the decedent;

(5)   adult siblings of the decedent;

(6)   adult grandchildren of the decedent;

(7)   grandparents of the decedent;

(8)   an adult who exhibited special care and concern for the decedent;

(9)   the persons who were acting as the [guardians] of the person of the decedent at the time of death; and

(10) any other person having the authority to dispose of the decedent's body.

## § 14.  Rights and Duties of Procurement Organization and Others.

(a)   When a hospital refers an individual at or near death to a procurement organization, the organization shall make a reasonable search of the records of the [state department of motor vehicles] and any donor registry . . . to ascertain whether the individual has made an anatomical gift.

* * *

(c)   When a hospital refers an individual at or near death to a procurement organization, the organization may conduct any reasonable examination necessary to ensure the medical suitability of a part that is or could be the subject of an anatomical gift . . . from a donor or a prospective donor. During the examination period, measures necessary to ensure the medical suitability of the part may not be withdrawn unless the hospital or procurement organization knows that the individual expressed a contrary intent.

* * *

(f)   Upon the death of a minor who was a donor or had signed a refusal, unless a procurement organization knows the minor is emancipated, the procurement organization shall conduct a reasonable search for the parents of the minor and provide the parents with an opportunity to revoke or amend the anatomical gift or revoke the refusal.

(g) Upon referral by a hospital . . ., a procurement organization shall make a reasonable search for any person listed in Section 9 having priority to make an anatomical gift on behalf of a prospective donor. . . .

\* \* \*

(i) Neither the physician who attends the decedent at death nor the physician who determines the time of the decedent's death may participate in the procedures for removing or transplanting a part from the decedent.

### § 18. Immunity.

A person that acts in accordance with this [Act] or with the applicable anatomical gift law of another state, or attempts in good faith to do so, is not liable for the act in a civil action, criminal prosecution, or administrative proceeding.

### PROBLEM: ORGAN DONATION AND THE UAGA

Laurel Singer, age 16, her sister Rebecca, age 22, and Rebecca's friend Peter Klaus, also age 22, were brought to General Hospital after an extremely serious car accident. Although they were alive when treated by the emergency medical technicians at the scene, Laurel, Rebecca, and Peter have died. Physicians have initiated standard procedures to maintain respiration and circulation in their bodies and preserve their organs for transplantation, including administering certain drugs and inserting a catheter into an artery to provide profusion. Time is critical as organs deteriorate quickly. The Singer sisters' parents have arrived at the hospital, but Peter's parents are on vacation somewhere in Asia. Peter's friends and the hospital continue to try to contact his parents but without success.

Laurel and Rebecca each signed the organ donor card on the back of their driver's licenses; however, their parents have told the hospital to discontinue the organ maintenance procedures and objected to removal of their organs. Peter didn't have a driver's license or donor card and hadn't enrolled on the state's donor registry, but his friends all agree that he was clear about his intentions to be an organ donor.

May surgeons remove Laurel's, Rebecca's, and Peter's transplantable organs? Under the UAGA, what must the hospital do in order to proceed? Do the Singer parents have the right to stop the removal of their daughters' organs? Should the hospital abide by their wishes? If Peter's parents arrive after the surgery has been completed and object to the removal of their son's organs, would they have any action against the physicians or the hospital? Why would Peter not have signed a donor card or signed up with his state's online donor registry?

## NOTES AND QUESTIONS

1.   The UAGA speaks in terms of a "gift" made by the decedent prior to death or by authorized decision makers after the death. It does not require that there be informed consent for organ donation. What information would be required for the donor or surrogate to give informed consent for the retrieval of organs? Should they be informed of the exact medical procedures that will be performed to preserve the organs prior to death, as they would if they were consenting to medical treatment; the criteria that will be used to determine that the patient has died; or the nature of the procedures that will be used to remove the organs (or bones or skin)? See Section II.C, below. Why is informed consent not required? See Ana Iltis, Organ Donation, Brain Death and the Family: Valid Informed Consent, 43 J.L.Med. & Ethics 369 (2015); Leili Monfared & Lois Shepherd, Organ Procurement Now: Does the United States Still "Opt In?", 2017 U. Ill. L. Rev. 1003.  See Section I.C.2, below, as to whether donor's permission ought to be required at all.

2.   Although the UAGA provides immunity for "good faith" attempts at compliance (§ 18, above), courts have interpreted good faith as a question of fact, which allows the case to go to the jury. See, for example, Cooper v. Louisiana Organ Procurement, 146 So.3d 908 (La.App. 2014); Siegel v. LifeCenter Organ Donor Network, 969 N.E.2d 1271 (Ohio App. 2011); Schembre v. Mid-America Transplant Assn., 135 S.W.3d 527 (Mo. Ct. App. 2004), in which plaintiff claimed nurse was negligent in describing procedures used to harvest bones.

3.   Hospitals receiving Medicare or Medicaid are required to contact the appropriate organ procurement organization whenever they have a patient whose death is imminent or who has died. The procurement organization is to evaluate the viability of organs and tissue and speak with the family about the option of donation. 42 C.F.R. § 482.45. Under the UAGA, interventions to preserve the organs are continued without permission unless the patient had earlier expressed a "contrary intent." § 14, above. See Section II.C, below.

## NOTE: ORGAN TRANSPLANTATION FROM LIVING DONORS

Individuals who have decisional capacity may donate non-life-sustaining organs for transplantation, supplying about 6,000 donations annually. Most frequently, the recipients are family members or friends but, increasingly, strangers in need. The possibility of donation from a stranger has led patients and families to campaign publicly to recruit a donor. Several organizations offer matching services as well.

A willing donor's organ may not be a match for the intended recipient, however. Transplant centers have overcome the problem of incompatibility in kidney transplantation by arranging for kidney paired donations (KPD). In KPD, a mismatched donor and recipient are matched with another pair in the same situation and the kidneys are exchanged, with the surgeries occurring simultaneously. Some transplant centers arrange kidney chains that result in a long series of transplantation surgeries as kidneys incompatible with a designated recipient proceed down a chain of possibly dozens of persons. Evelyn Tenenbaum, Bartering for a Compatible Kidney Using Your Incompatible, Live Kidney Donor: Legal and Ethical Issues Related to Kidney Chains, 42 Am J. L. & Med. 129 (2016); Kimberly Krawiec et al., Contract Development in a Matching Market: The Case of Kidney Exchange, 80 L. & Contemp. Probs. 11 (2017).

Concerns over safety and outcomes for living donors are significant. The Renal and Lung Living Donors Evaluation Study (RELIVE), a multiyear study of long-term outcomes for living lung and kidney donors, produced data on several measures including long-term health effects, emotional well-being, and satisfaction. See, e.g., C.R. Gross et al., Health Related Quality of Life in Kidney Donors from the Last Five Decades: Results from the RELIVE Study, 13 Am. J. Transplant. 2924 (Nov. 2013), reporting health status roughly equivalent to general population but identifying pre-surgical conditions that predict negative health outcomes for donors. How much risk should a potential donor be allowed to undertake, and does it matter whether the potential donor has the legal capacity to make health care decisions?

Legal issues relating to consent can arise in any inter vivos transplant (see Green v. Buell, 215 So.3d 715 (La.App. 2017), but they are more common when the donor is legally incapacitated. The principles relied on in such cases are the same as those that govern other medical treatment decisions for incompetent patients, relying on either the donor's best interests or substituted judgment criterion for decision making. See Chapter 5. See also, Macey Henderson and Jed Gross, Living Organ Donation and Informed Consent in the United States: Strategies to Improve the Process, 45 J. L. Med. & Ethics 66 (2017); Michael T. Morley, Proxy Consent to Organ Donation by Incompetents, 111 Yale L.J. 1215 (2002). Ethical concerns relating to coercion of living donors are not easily accounted for in a legal framework, however.

Advances in reproductive technologies, particularly preimplantation genetic diagnosis (see Chapter 3), create the capacity for parents of a child in need of a transplant to conceive and birth a child (a so-called "savior sibling") that is certain to be a match for the older sibling. The practice raises serious ethical and legal concerns at the intersection of reproductive rights and organ transplants. See, e.g., Amy Lai, To Be or Not to Be My Sister's Keeper, 32 J. Legal Med. 261 (2011).

## 2. Presumed Consent and Property Rights

### NEWMAN V. SATHYAVAGLSWARAN

United States Court of Appeals, Ninth Circuit, 2002.
287 F.3d 786.

Parents, whose deceased children's corneas were removed by the Los Angeles County Coroner's office without notice or consent, brought this 42 U.S.C. § 1983 action alleging a taking of their property without due process of law. The complaint was dismissed by the district court for a failure to state a claim upon which relief could be granted. We must decide whether the longstanding recognition in the law of California, paralleled by our national common law, that next of kin have the exclusive right to possess the bodies of their deceased family members creates a property interest, the deprivation of which must be accorded due process of law under the Fourteenth Amendment of the United States Constitution. We hold that it does. . . .

\* \* \*

Robert Newman and Barbara Obarski (the parents) each had children, Richard Newman and Kenneth Obarski respectively, who died in Los Angeles County in October 1997. Following their deaths, the Office of the Coroner for the County of Los Angeles (the coroner) obtained possession of the bodies of the children and, under procedures adopted pursuant to California Government Code § 27492.47 as it then existed, removed the corneas from those bodies without the knowledge of the parents and without an attempt to notify them and request consent. The parents became aware of the coroner's actions in September 1999 and subsequently filed this § 1983 action alleging a deprivation of their property without due process of law in violation of the Fourteenth Amendment.

## II.   Property Interests in Dead Bodies

[T]he Supreme Court repeatedly has affirmed that "the right of every individual to the possession and control of his own person, free from all restraint or interference of others," [ ] is "so rooted in the traditions and conscience of our people," [ ] as to be ranked as one of the fundamental liberties protected by the "substantive" component of the Due Process Clause. [ ] This liberty, the Court has "strongly suggested," extends to the personal decisions about "how to best protect dignity and independence at the end of life." [ ] The Court has not had occasion to address whether the rights of possession and control of one's own body, the most "sacred" and "carefully guarded" of all rights in the common law, [ ] are property interests protected by the Due Process Clause. Nor has it addressed what Due Process protections are applicable to the rights of next of kin to possess and control the bodies of their deceased relatives.

### A.   History of Common Law Interests in Dead Bodies

\* \* \*

Many early American courts adopted Blackstone's description of the common law, holding that "a dead body is not the subject of property right." [ ] The duty to protect the body by providing a burial was often described as flowing from the "universal . . . right of sepulture," rather than from a concept of property law. [ ] As cases involving unauthorized mutilation and disposition of bodies increased toward the end of the 19th century, paralleling the rise in demand for human cadavers in medical science and use of cremation as an alternative to burial, [ ] courts began to recognize an exclusive right of the next of kin to possess and control the disposition of the bodies of their dead relatives, the violation of which was actionable at law. Thus, in holding that a city council could not "seize upon existing private burial grounds, make them public, and exclude the proprietors from their management," the Supreme Court of Indiana commented that "the burial of the dead can [not] . . . be taken out of the hands of the relatives thereof" because "we lay down the proposition, that the bodies of the dead belong to the surviving relations, in the order of inheritance, as property, and that they have the right to dispose of them as such, within restrictions analogous to those by which the disposition of other property may be regulated." [ ] . . .

### B.   Interests in Dead Bodies in California Law

[The court traces the history of California law concerning the disposition of dead bodies. California courts referred to "quasi-property" rights in cases disputing the handling of cadavers, including cases in which the courts held that civil litigants had no right to demand an autopsy; next-of-kin could exclude the decedent's friends from the funeral; and permitted an action for retaining organs after autopsy.]

### C.   The Right to Transfer Body Parts

The first successful transplantation of a kidney in 1954 led to an expansion of the rights of next of kin to the bodies of the dead. In 1968, the National Conference of Commissioners on Uniform State Laws approved the Uniform Anatomical Gift Act (UAGA), adopted by California the same year, which grants next of kin the right to transfer the parts of bodies in their possession to others for medical or research purposes. [ ] The right to transfer is limited. . . .

In the 1970s and 1980s, medical science improvements and the related demand for transplant organs prompted governments to search for new ways to increase the supply of organs for donation. [ ] Many perceived as a hindrance to the supply of needed organs the rule implicit in the UAGA that donations could be effected only if consent was received from the decedent or next of kin. [ ] In response, some states passed "presumed consent" laws that allow the taking and transfer of body parts by a coroner without the consent of next of kin as long as no objection to the removal is known. [ ] California Government Code § 27491.47, enacted in 1983, was such a law.

### III.  Due Process Analysis

"[T]o provide California non-profit eye banks with an adequate supply of corneal tissue," S. Com. Rep. SB 21 (Cal.1983), § 27491.47(a) authorized the coroner to "remove and release or authorize the removal and release of corneal eye tissue from a body within the coroner's custody" without any effort to notify and obtain the consent of next of kin "if . . . [t]he coroner has no knowledge of objection to the removal." The law also provided that the coroner or any person acting upon his or her request "shall [not] incur civil liability for such removal in an action brought by any person who did not object prior to the removal . . . nor be subject to criminal prosecution." § 27491.47(b).[11]

\* \* \*

In two decisions the Sixth Circuit, the only federal circuit to address the issue until now, held that the interests of next of kin in dead bodies recognized in Michigan and Ohio allowed next of kin to bring § 1983 actions challenging implementation of cornea removal statutes similar to California's. [ ] . . .

The supreme courts of Florida and Georgia, however, have held that similar legal interests of next of kin in the possession of the body of a deceased family member, recognized as "quasi property" rights in each state, are "not . . . of constitutional dimension." *Georgia Lions Eye Bank, Inc. v. Lavant,* 255 Ga. 60, 335 S.E.2d 127, 128 (1985); *State v. Powell,* 497 So.2d 1188, 1191 (Fla. 1986) (commenting that "[a]ll authorities generally agree that the next of kin have no property right in the remains of a decedent"). The Florida Supreme Court recently rejected the broad implications of the reasoning in *Powell* distinguishing that decision as turning on a balance between the public health interest in cornea donation and the " 'infinitesimally small intrusion' " of their removal. *Crocker v. Pleasant,* 778 So.2d 978, 985, 988 (Fla. 2001) (allowing a § 1983 action to go forward for interference with the right of next of kin to possess the body of their son because "in Florida there is a legitimate claim of entitlement by the next of kin to possession of the remains of a decedent for burial or other lawful disposition").

We agree with the reasoning of the Sixth Circuit and believe that reasoning is applicable here. Under traditional common law principles, serving a duty to protect the dignity of the human body in its final disposition that is deeply rooted in our legal history and social traditions, the parents had exclusive and legitimate claims of entitlement to possess, control, dispose and prevent the violation of the corneas and other parts of the bodies of their deceased children. With California's adoption of the UAGA, [ ], it statutorily recognized other important rights of the parents in relation to the bodies of their deceased children the right to transfer body parts and refuse to allow their transfer. These are all important components of the group of rights by which property is defined, each of

---

[11] For body parts other than corneas, California adopted the 1987 version of the UAGA authorizing transfer when no knowledge of objection is known and after "[a] reasonable effort has been made to locate and inform [next of kin] of their option to make, or object to making, an anatomical gift." Cal. Health & Safety Code § 7151.5(a)(2).

which carried with it the power to exclude others from its exercise, "traditionally . . . one of the most treasured strands in an owner's bundle of property rights." [ ]

\* \* \*

Nor does the fact that California forbids the trade of body parts for profit mean that next of kin lack a property interest in them. The Supreme Court has "never held that a physical item is not 'property' simply because it lacks a positive economic or market value." [ ]

We need not . . . decide whether California has transgressed basic property principles [ ] because that statute did not extinguish California's legal recognition of the property interests of the parents to the corneas of their deceased children. It allowed the removal of corneas only if "the coroner has no knowledge of objection," a provision that implicitly acknowledges the ongoing property interests of next of kin.

\* \* \*

. . . The property rights that California affords to next of kin to the body of their deceased relatives serve the premium value our society has historically placed on protecting the dignity of the human body in its final disposition. California infringed the dignity of the bodies of the children when it extracted the corneas from those bodies without the consent of the parents. The process of law was due the parents for this deprivation of their rights.

\* \* \*

The scope of the process of law that was due the parents is not a question that we can answer based on the pleadings alone. This question must be addressed in future proceedings.

\* \* \*

We do not hold that California lacks significant interests in obtaining corneas or other organs of the deceased in order to contribute to the lives of the living. Courts are required to evaluate carefully the state's interests in deciding what process must be due the holders of property interests for their deprivation. [ ] An interest so central to the state's core police powers as improving the health of its citizens is certainly one that must be considered seriously in determining what process the parents were due. [ ] But our Constitution requires the government to assert its interests and subject them to scrutiny when it invades the rights of its subjects. Accordingly, we reverse the district court's dismissal of the parents' complaint and remand for proceedings in which the government's justification for its deprivation of parents' interests may be fully aired and appropriately scrutinized.

## NOTES AND QUESTIONS

1.    As noted in *Newman*, the California statute departed from the UAGA provision of the time which required a "reasonable effort" to contact persons authorized to permit donation before tissue or organs could be removed by the coroner. The Ninth Circuit leaves open the possibility that the State could structure the coroner's removal of tissue in a way that would satisfy due process concerns. Would requiring that there be a reasonable attempt to contact next-of-kin satisfy due process requirements? Would the existence of an easily accessible system for registering objections (an opt out system) satisfy the court? The UAGA provision was removed in 2006 in response to this litigation and now provides that no tissue or organ can be removed unless there is an anatomical gift (although in an uncommon scenario, the coroner can gift a decedent's tissue under the authority provided for in § 9(a)(10), above).

2.    The California statute may be seen as relying on "presumed consent," long advocated as a tool for increasing the supply of organs and tissue for transplant. Presumed consent relies on the assumption, grounded in repeated surveys, that most people intend to donate when the opportunity arises but simply fail to do so. Presumed consent shifts the responsibility for objecting to the individual. Before the decision in *Newman*, a series of news articles demonstrated that the practice of coroner harvesting of tissue had a disproportionate impact on people of color. At the time, 80% of coroner autopsies were performed on African American or Latino individuals and only 16% on whites. Is the assumption that the individual would consent if asked a persuasive claim in this situation? See Michele Goodwin, *Newman v. Sathyavaglswaran: Unbundling Property in the Dead*, in Health Law and Bioethics Cases in Context (Sandra Johnson et al. eds. 2009); Gil Siegel & Richard Bonnie, Closing the Organ Gap: A Reciprocity-Based Social Contract Approach, 34 J. L. Med. & Ethics 415 (2006). Almost all states have followed the lead of the 2006 UAGA in repealing presumed consent provisions. But see, e.g., Mo.Stat. § 58–770, which allows for the removal of the pituitary gland without attempting to notify the family when there is no known objection. See also, David Orentlicher, Presumed Consent to Organ Donation: Its Rise and Fall in the United States, 61 Rutgers L. Rev. 295 (2009).

3.    Several cases have focused attention on the robust commercial market for human cadaveric tissue. In Adams v. King County, 192 P.3d 891 (Wash. 2008), for example, the Washington Supreme Court held that the adult decedent's parents may have a cause of action under Washington law where their son's brain was removed by the medical examiner and given to the Stanley Medical Research Institute (SMRI). SMRI funded a position in the examiner's office in exchange for the examiner providing brains to SMRI for research. The decedent had signed a donor card donating "any organ," but the court held that Washington's anatomical gift statute provided that only hospitals could receive undesignated gifts and so the pre-mortem donation document did not apply. See also, Geary v. Stanley Medical Research Institute, 939 A.2d 86 (Me. 2008), in which multiple plaintiffs alleged that an agent who was paid $1,000 per brain falsified consent forms; Commonwealth v.

Mastromarino, 2 A.3d 581 (Super. Ct. Pa. 2010), reviewing prison sentence of 25–58 years for tissue procurer who had taken cadaver tissue and bones without consent, earning over $1 million from tissue banks. See also Michele Goodwin, Empires of the Flesh: Tissue and Organ Taboos, 60 Ala. L. Rev. 1219 (2009).

4.    The context for the question of the right to tissue determines the outcome. See, e.g., Shelley v. County of San Joaquin, 996 F.Supp.2d 921 (E.D. Cal. 2014), distinguishing *Newman* as applying only to anatomical gifts and holding that loss of decedent's remains by the sheriff's office did not violate family's Constitutional rights. See also, ownership of tissue in research in Chapter 7.

## 3.    Paying "Donors" for Organs and Tissue

### FLYNN V. HOLDER
United States Court of Appeals, Ninth Circuit, 2012.
684 F.3d 852.

\* \* \*

The complaint challenges the constitutionality of the ban on compensation for human organs in the National Organ Transplant Act, as applied to bone marrow transplants. . . .

Some plaintiffs are parents of sick children who have diseases such as leukemia and a rare type of anemia, which can be fatal without bone marrow transplants. Another plaintiff is a physician and medical school professor, and an expert in bone marrow transplantation. He says that at least one out of five of his patients dies because no matching bone marrow donor can be found, and many others have complications when scarcity of matching donors compels him to use imperfectly matched donors. One plaintiff is a parent of mixed race children, for whom sufficiently matched donors are especially scarce, because mixed race persons typically have the rarest marrow cell types. . . .

Another plaintiff is a California nonprofit corporation that seeks to operate a program incentivizing bone marrow donations. The corporation proposes to offer $3,000 awards in the form of scholarships, housing allowances, or gifts to charities selected by donors, initially to minority and mixed race donors of bone marrow cells, who are likely to have the rarest marrow cell type. The corporation, MoreMarrowDonors.org, alleges that it cannot launch this program because the National Organ Transplant Act criminalizes payment of compensation for organs, and classifies bone marrow as an organ.

\* \* \*

Until about twenty years ago, bone marrow was extracted from donors' bones by "aspiration." Long needles, thick enough to suck out the soft, fatty marrow, were inserted into the cavities of the anesthetized donor's hip bones. These are large bones with big central cavities full of marrow. Aspiration is a painful, unpleasant procedure for the donor. It requires hospitalization and general or local anesthesia, and involves commensurate risks.

. . . With [a] new technique, now used for at least two-thirds of bone marrow transplants, none of the soft, fatty marrow is actually donated. Patients who need bone marrow transplants do not need everything that the soft, fatty substance from bone cavities contains, just some of the marrow's "hematopoietic stem cells." These stem cells are seeds from which white blood cells, red blood cells, and platelets grow.

These are not the embryonic stem cells often the subject of controversy. Those stem cells, taken from human embryos, are "pluripotent," that is, they can turn into any kind of cell—brain, blood, retina, toenail, whatever. The stem cells at issue in this case are "hematopoietic stem cells." . . . Hematopoietic stem cells turn into blood cells and nothing else. Humans and other large mammals produce these blood stem cells constantly in vast numbers, because our blood cells die within a few months and need continual replacement. . . . [N]ew ones are made in the bone marrow, as long as we live.

[S]ome blood stem cells flow into and circulate in the bloodstream before they mature [into blood cells]. These are called "peripheral" blood stem cells. . . . The new bone marrow donation technique, developed during the past twenty years, is called "peripheral blood stem cell apheresis." . . . This procedure begins with five days of injections of a medication called a "granulocyte colony-stimulating factor" into the donor's blood. The medication accelerates blood stem cell production in the marrow, so that more stem cells go into the bloodstream. . . .

The main difference between an ordinary blood donation and apheresis is that instead of just filling up a plastic bag with whole blood, the donor sits for some hours in a recliner while the blood passes through the apheresis machine. This same apheresis technique is sometimes used for purposes other than bone marrow donations, such as when the machine is set up to collect plasma or platelets, rather than stem cells, from a donor's blood. When it is used for these other purposes, the identical technique is called a "blood donation" or "blood plasma donation." When used to separate out and collect hematopoietic stem cells from the donor's bloodstream, apheresis is called "peripheral blood stem cell apheresis" or a "bone marrow donation."

* * *

[E]ven with [the National Marrow Donor Program registry, funded by the federal government], good [marrow] matches often cannot be found. And even when a good match is found in the registry, tracking down the potential donor from what may be an outdated address may be impossible to accomplish in time to save the patient's life—assuming the potential donor is willing to go through with the process when found.

The plaintiff nonprofit proposes to mitigate this matching problem by using a financial incentive [which plaintiff concedes constitutes "valuable consideration" under NOTA]. The idea is that the financial incentive will induce more potential donors to sign up, stay in touch so that they can be located when necessary, and go through with the donations. . . .

Plaintiffs argue that the National Organ Transplant Act, as applied to MoreMarrowDonors.org's planned pilot program, violates the Equal Protection Clause. They claim that blood stem cell harvesting is not materially different from blood, sperm, and egg harvesting, which are not included under the statutory or regulatory definitions of "human organ." Like donors of blood and sperm, a bone marrow donor undergoing apheresis suffers no permanent harm, experiences no significant risk, and quickly regenerates what is donated. Plaintiffs also argue that any rational basis that Congress had when it passed the statute no longer exists with respect to the pilot program, because of the subsequent development of the apheresis method. Plaintiffs seek declaratory and injunctive relief so that MoreMarrowDonors.org can proceed with the initiative.

\* \* \*

. . . [NOTA] makes it a felony "to knowingly acquire, receive, or otherwise transfer any human organ for valuable consideration for use in human transplantation." And it defines the term "human organ" to include "bone marrow." Ergo, the statute expressly prohibits compensating bone marrow donors. According to the government's brief, Congress took the view that "human body parts should not be viewed as commodities," [citing a Senate Report] and had several policy reasons for disallowing compensation to donors, which suffice to serve as a rational basis for the prohibition.

[T]he government argues that because it is much harder to find a match for patients who need bone marrow transplants than for patients who need blood transfusions, exploitative market forces could be triggered if bone marrow could be bought. The government also asserts that peripheral blood stem cell apheresis poses greater health risks for the donor than blood donations do, because of the side effects of the medicine used to increase stem cell secretion. [The court holds that the question of risk is one for trial or summary judgment rather than motion to dismiss, but notes that "there are significant risks from egg donations, but the government concedes that the statute allows them."]

. . . To the extent that plaintiffs challenge the constitutionality of the compensation ban on bone marrow donation by the old aspiration method . . . the challenge must fail.

. . . It is irrelevant that the legislative history indicates that Congress viewed certain types of regenerable tissue, such as blood, as falling outside the statutory definition of "human organ." It may be that senators themselves, their staffs, or lobbyists for blood banks argued for an exception for body substances that can regenerate, and persuaded committee staffers to put that reason in the legislative history. But the statute does not say that compensation is permitted for organs or body parts that regenerate and prohibited for those that do not. Nor is the statute consistent with such a construction. The statute defines the liver "or any subpart thereof" as an organ for which compensation is prohibited. The drafters doubtless knew that a partial resection of a liver can yield a donation that will save the recipient's life, and that the donor's liver will grow back. So the statute does expressly prohibit compensation for at least one explicitly denoted "human organ" that will regenerate.

. . . Congress may have been concerned that if donors could be paid, rich patients or the medical industry might induce poor people to sell their organs, even when the transplant would create excessive medical risk, pain, or disability for the donor. Or, looking from the other end, Congress might have been concerned that every last cent could be extracted from sick patients needful of transplants, by well-matched potential donors making "your money or your life" offers. The existing commerce in organs extracted by force or fraud by organ thieves might be stimulated by paying for donations. Compensation to donors might also degrade the quality of the organ supply, by inducing potential donors to lie about their medical histories in order to make their organs marketable. Plaintiffs argue that a $3,000 housing subsidy, scholarship, or charitable donation is too small an amount to create a risk of any of these evils, but for a lot of people that could amount to three to six months' rent.

Congress may have had philosophical as well as policy reasons for prohibiting compensation. People tend to have an instinctive revulsion at denial of bodily integrity, particularly removal of flesh from a human being for use by another, and most particularly "commodification" of such conduct, that is, the sale of one's bodily tissue. While there is reportedly a large international market for the buying and selling of human organs, in the United States, such a market is criminal and the commerce is generally seen as revolting. Leon Kass [observes]:

> [A]lthough we allow no commerce in organs, transplant surgeons and hospitals are making handsome profits from the organ-trading business, and even the not-for-profit transplant registries and procurement agencies glean for their employees a middleman's

livelihood. Why . . . should everyone be making money from this business except the person whose organ makes it possible? Could it be that [the] real uneasiness [lies] with organ donation or with transplantation itself, for if not, what would be objectionable about its turning a profit? [Leon R. Kass, *Life, Liberty and the Defense of Dignity: The Challenge for Bioethics* 177 (2002).]

. . . Kass points to the idea of "psychophysical unity, a position that regards a human being as largely, if not wholly, self-identical with his enlivened body," so that, as [Immanuel] Kant put it, to " 'dispose of oneself as a mere means to some end of one's own liking is to degrade the humanity in one's person.' " . . .

[T]here are strong arguments for contrary views. But these policy and philosophical choices are for Congress to make, not us. The distinctions made by Congress must have a rational basis, but do not need to fit perfectly with that rational basis, and the basis need merely be rational, not persuasive to all. Here, Congress made a distinction between body material that is compensable and body material that is not. The distinction has a rational basis, so the prohibition on compensation for bone marrow donations by the aspiration method does not violate the Equal Protection Clause.

The focus, though, of plaintiffs' arguments is compensation for "bone marrow donations" by the peripheral blood stem cell apheresis method. For this, we need not answer any constitutional question, because the statute contains no prohibition. Such donations of cells drawn from blood flowing through the veins may sometimes anachronistically be called "bone marrow donations," but none of the soft, fatty marrow is donated, just cells found outside the marrow, outside the bones, flowing through the veins.

Congress could not have had an intent to address the apheresis method when it passed the statute, because the method did not exist at that time. We must construe the words of the statute to see what they imply about extraction of hematopoietic stem cells by this method. . . .

Since payment for blood donations has long been common, the silence in [NOTA] on compensating blood donors is loud. . . . The government concedes that the common practice of compensating blood donors is not prohibited by the statute.

The government argues that hematopoietic stem cells in the veins should be treated as "bone marrow" because "bone marrow" is a statutory organ, and the statute prohibits compensation not only for donation of an organ, but also "any subpart thereof." . . .

We reject this argument. . . . If the government's argument that what comes from the marrow is a subpart of the marrow were correct, then the statute would prohibit compensating blood donors. . . .

[E]very blood draw includes some hematopoietic stem cells. . . . Once the stem cells are in the bloodstream, they are a "subpart" of the blood, not the bone marrow. The word "subpart" refers to the organ from which the material is taken, not the organ in which it was created. . . .

* * *

We construe "bone marrow" to mean the soft, fatty substance in bone cavities, as opposed to blood, which means the red liquid that flows through the blood vessels. The statute does not prohibit compensation for donations of blood and the substances in it, which include peripheral blood stem cells. The Secretary of Health and Human Services has not exercised regulatory authority to define blood or peripheral blood stem cells as organs. We therefore need not decide whether prohibiting compensation for such donations would be unconstitutional.

### NOTES AND QUESTIONS

1.    *Flynn* relies on the specific type of tissue involved and the method for removing it from the body to hold that payment is not prohibited under NOTA. Should tissue, such as corneas, be treated differently than solid organs for purposes of payment? For purposes of consent? (See *Newman* and notes following, above.) See also Emily Largent, NOTA: Not a Good Act for Tissues to Follow, 19 Quinnipiac Health L. J. 179 (2016), arguing that tissue generally should be subject to a different regulatory regime than are organs but that the post-retrieval market should be regulated.

2.    The AMA recommends that payment for organs be studied with the following limitations: incentives are modest and set at the lowest level that can reasonably be expected to increase donations and payment should be limited to "voluntary donation" of cadaveric organs only with "an explicit prohibition against the selling of organs." AMA Code of Medical Ethics Opinion E-6.1.3. Do these limits respond persuasively to objections to payment for human body parts or not? How would you separate the act of payment from the act of "selling"? See, e.g., Glenn Cohen, Regulating the Organ Market: Normative Foundations for Market Regulation, 77 L. & Contemp. Probs. 71 (2014); Radhika Rao, A Small Price to Pay: Incentivizing Cadaveric Organ Donation with Posthumous Payments, 18 Minn. J. L. Sci. & Tech. 273 (2017); Michele Goodwin, Black Markets: The Supply and Demand of Body Parts (2006), arguing in favor of payment. But see Institute of Medicine, Organ Donation: Opportunities for Action (2006), rejecting market exchanges.

3.    The incentives proposed in *Flynn* did not include payments of cash to the donor. Does the form the financial transfer takes make a difference to legal, ethical, or public policy issues in providing financial incentives for donors? NOTA provides that "valuable consideration" does not include "reasonable payments associated with the removal, transportation, implantation, processing, preservation, quality control, and storage of a human organ or the expenses of travel, housing, and lost wages incurred by the donor of a human

organ in connection with the donation . . . ". 42 U.S.C.A. § 274(e). (The UAGA, which unlike NOTA applies only to cadaveric organs and tissue, has a similar provision. § 16.) "Reasonable payments" allows profit for the firms involved in transplantation. See discussion following *Newman*, above. Some states compensate donors within these restrictions. Pennsylvania, for example, has established a public trust fund for families of decedents who donate organs. The statute limits payments to $3,000 per donor (although the program currently pays only $300) to be used to cover funeral expenses and incidental expenses (lodging, food) borne by the family in relation to the donation. 20 Pa.C.S.A. § 8621. Other states have state income tax incentives allowing living donors to deduct expenses related to donation, including lost wages. Wis. Stat.Ann. § 71.05(10)(i). The federal Organ Donation and Recovery Improvement Act of 2004 provides grants to procurement organizations (and other groups) for reimbursing living donors for travel and certain living expenses. 42 U.S.C. § 274f. NOTA was amended in 2007 (42 U.S.C. § 274e) to specifically exclude paired exchanges from the Act's prohibition of the payment of "valuable consideration" for organ donation even though each organ is donated for the purpose of procuring another organ for a designated recipient. See Note on Living Donors, above.

4.    Organ procurement and transplantation operates on a global scale. Persons of means in need of transplants can go where the organs are. While there had once been significant concern that transplant tourism was bringing foreign nationals to the United States to receive one of "our" scarce organs, the issue has shifted dramatically. Now a primary concern is United States citizens who avoid the waiting list here by travelling abroad to receive transplants. There are concerns for public safety and quality as these patients return to the United States for post-transplant care. See, e.g., A.J. Polcari et al., Transplant Tourism—A Dangerous Journey? 25 Clin. Transplant. 633 (2011). The most dramatic concern, however, is that transplant tourism may have created a global black market in which organs are bought and sold or retrieved from persons under even more extreme circumstances. See, e.g., Robert Ainley, Organ Transploitation: A Model Law Approach to Combat Human Trafficking and Transplant Tourism, 13 Or. R. Int'l L. 427 (2011). But see F. Ambagtsheer et al., On Patients Who Purchase Organ Transplants Abroad, 10 Am J. Transplant. 2800 (2016), arguing that data do not support claims of this abuse. One nation allows legal payment to living donors of kidneys while retaining the concept of donation. Hooman Movassagh, Human Organ Donations under the "Iranian Model:" A Rewarding Scheme for U.S. Regulatory Reform?, 13 Ind. Health L. Rev. 82 (2016).

# II.  THE DETERMINATION OF DEATH

## A.  THE UNIFORM DETERMINATION OF DEATH ACT

Determining that a person has died used to be simple. If the heart and lungs had stopped functioning, eventually other less observable processes stopped as well. The cessation of cardiopulmonary function signaled death without the need for testing whether other processes, such as neurological activity, continued.

The first well accepted definition of death to include what has become known as "brain death" came in 1968 from the Ad Hoc Committee of the Harvard Medical School to Examine the Definition of Brain Death. The Committee identified two developments that required an expansion of the traditional heart-lung definition of death. First, the Committee pointed out that "resuscitative and support measures" had improved and were being used more frequently though often unsuccessfully, leaving patents with serious brain injuries and burdening patients, families, and society in unacceptable ways. These technological advances could "restore 'life' as judged by the ancient standards of persistent respiration and continuing heart beat" even when "there is not the remotest possibility of an individual recovering consciousness following massive brain damage." Second, the Committee explained that the uncertainty that "brain death" was real death was hindering the ability to recover life-sustaining organs that would be used for transplantation. The full report of the Committee is available at 205 JAMA 85 (1968).

The Committee listed characteristics of brain death (which the Committee called "irreversible coma") as unreceptivity and unresponsivity, no autonomous movements or breathing, no reflexes, and flat electroencephalogram. The Committee recommended that death be declared before the respirator is turned off ("in our judgment it will provide a greater degree of legal protection to those involved"); that the physician in charge consult with other physicians before the declaration of death is made; that the physician (rather than the family) determine death; and that the decision to declare death be made by physicians who are not involved "in any later effort to transplant organs or tissue from the deceased individual."

The Ad Hoc Committee suggested that "no statutory change in the law should be necessary [to accommodate brain death] since the law treats this question essentially as one of fact to be determined by physicians." Nevertheless, brain death statutes began appearing shortly after the publication of the Committee's report. In 1980, the Uniform Determination of Death Act (UDDA) ultimately was developed with the cooperation of both the AMA and the ABA.

## UNIFORM DETERMINATION OF DEATH ACT (1980)

§ 1. An individual who has sustained either (1) irreversible cessation of circulatory and respiratory functions, or (2) irreversible cessation of all functions of the entire brain, including the brain stem, is dead. A determination of death must be made in accordance with accepted medical standards.

### *PROBLEM: WHEN DOES DEATH OCCUR?*

Alberto Arcturus was lying face down by the side of the road, apparently after being run down by a hit-and-run driver. A passing motorist called the local emergency medical services, and an ambulance arrived on the scene about fifteen minutes after the call. The two EMTs found that Mr. Arcturus was not breathing and had no pulse. They also discovered that a substantial portion of his head (including his forehead and forebrain) was crushed. One paramedic looked at the other and said, "He's dead; let's call the morgue." The second, less experienced paramedic insisted on trying to resuscitate Mr. Arcturus, as was required by the emergency medical services manual for paramedics. They placed him in the ambulance and administered cardiopulmonary resuscitation throughout the fifteen minute ride to the nearest hospital emergency room.

At the emergency room, physicians confirmed that Mr. Arcturus did not breathe spontaneously and had no spontaneous cardiac activity. One doctor told the charge nurse that he was dead, and that "dead on arrival" should be marked on his chart. A young intern balked at this, however, because the hospital emergency room protocol required more before a brain injured patient could be declared dead. The physicians then administered drugs and used paddles that sent an electric current through Mr. Arcturus's chest in an effort to start his heart. After some time they managed to get a weak pulse, and they placed Mr. Arcturus on a ventilator and moved him to the intensive care unit. A neurology consult revealed that Mr. Arcturus's neocortex was completely and irreversibly destroyed—most of it was literally gone, left on the highway—although his brain stem remained intact. With the help of a ventilator, Mr. Arcturus's body could continue functioning indefinitely. If the ventilator were to be removed, Mr. Arcturus's heart and lung function would cease within some minutes as repeated trials proved that he could not breathe on his own.

After considerable investigation, police have captured the hit-and-run driver. They want to know whether to charge him with vehicular homicide or something else. The doctors and Mr. Arcturus's family want to know whether he is dead or alive. Further, if he is dead, the family wants to know when he died—at the roadside, in the hospital emergency room, in the intensive care unit, or somewhere else. Mr. Arcturus's health insurer is involved because insurance ordinarily won't cover medical services to a dead patient. Finally, the regional Organ Procurement Organization has been notified that there is a potential donor, and the transplant team at the hospital wants to know if Mr. Arcturus's healthy organs (including his kidneys and liver) are available for transplantation to save the life of patients on the transplant waiting list.

Is Mr. Arcturus dead? If so, when did he die?

## B.  VARIATION IN MEDICAL AND LEGAL STANDARDS

Although the Ad Hoc Committee advocated the adoption of neurological determination of death over 50 years ago and "brain death" has been adopted as a legal standard for death by all of the states for several decades, controversy has persisted. Cases in which families refuse to accept that their loved one is dead garner headlines because they touch a nerve. Although these cases are often dismissed as instances where laypersons are in denial or do not trust physicians and hospitals or are incapable of understanding that the condition of the body supported by mechanical ventilation is not evidence of life or are relying on religious exceptionalism, a deeper look reveals more. In addition, there are fissures in the medical community itself in terms of the standards and procedures used to determine brain death and, for some, even whether the legal standard requiring the cessation of *all* brain activity aligns with current medical practice in determining death. See Thaddeus Pope, Brain Death Forsaken: Growing Conflict and New Legal Challenges, 37 J. Leg. Med. 265 (2017). See also Rachel Aviv, The Death Debate, New Yorker 30 (Feb. 5, 2018), describing the complexities arising in the dispute over the status of Jahi McMath. The Nevada Supreme Court considered a similar situation in *Hailu*, below.

## IN RE GUARDIANSHIP OF HAILU

Supreme Court of Nevada, 2015.
361 P.3d 524.

PICKERING, J.:

"For legal and medical purposes, a person is dead if the person has sustained an irreversible cessation of . . . [a]ll functions of the person's entire brain, including his or her brain stem." NRS 451.007(1). The determination of death "must be made in accordance with accepted medical standards." NRS 451.007(2). Here, we are asked to decide whether the American Association of Neurology [AAN] guidelines are considered "accepted medical standards" that satisfy the definition of brain death in NRS 451.007. We conclude that the district court failed to properly consider whether the [AAN] guidelines adequately measure all functions of the entire brain, including the brain stem, . . . and are considered accepted medical standards by states that have adopted the Uniform Determination of Death Act. Accordingly, we reverse the district court's order denying a petition for temporary restraining order and remand.

*FACTS*

*Medical history*

On April 1, 2015, 20-year-old university student Aden Hailu went to St. Mary's Regional Medical Center (St. Mary's) after experiencing abdominal pain. Medical staff could not determine the cause of her pain and decided to perform an exploratory laparotomy and remove her appendix. During the laparotomy, Hailu's blood pressure was low and she suffered "severe, catastrophic anoxic, or lack of brain oxygen damage," and she never woke up. After her surgery, Hailu was transferred to the St.

Mary's Intensive Care Unit (ICU), under the care of Dr. Anthony Floreani. Within the first two weeks of April, three different electroencephalogram (EEG) tests were conducted, all of which showed brain functioning.

On April 13, 2015, Dr. Aaron Heide, the Director of Neurology and Stroke at St. Mary's, first examined Hailu. Dr. Heide concluded that Hailu was not brain dead at that time but was "rapidly declining." To make that determination, Dr. Heide conducted an examination of Hailu's neurological functions; her left eye was minimally responsive, she was chewing on the ventilator tube, and she moved her arms with stimulation. The next day, April 14, 2015, Hailu did not exhibit these same indicia of neurological functioning.

On May 28, 2015, St. Mary's performed an apnea test, which involved taking Hailu off ventilation support for ten minutes to see if she could breathe on her own; Hailu failed the apnea test, leading St. Mary's to conclude that "[t]his test result confirms Brain Death unequivocally." Based on Hailu's condition, Dr. Jeffrey Bacon wrote the following in his notes: "Awaiting administration and hospital lawyers for direction re care—withdrawal of Ventilator support indicated NOW in my opinion as brain death unequivocally confirmed." On June 2, 2015, St. Mary's notified Hailu's father and guardian, Fanuel Gebreyes, that it intended to discontinue Hailu's ventilator and other life support. Gebreyes opposed taking Hailu off life support and sought judicial relief.

*Procedural history*

Gebreyes filed an emergency motion for temporary restraining order to enjoin St. Mary's from removing Hailu from life-sustaining services. On June 18, 2015, the district court held a hearing on the matter. The parties stipulated that St. Mary's would continue life-sustaining services until July 2, 2015, at 5:00 p.m. to allow Gebreyes to have an independent neurologist examine Hailu. They further stipulated that if, after the independent examination, Gebreyes wished St. Mary's to continue life support, he would need to request it through guardianship court. However, "if on July 2, 2015, it is determined that Aden Hailu is legally and clinically deceased, the hospital shall proceed as they see fit." Based on the stipulation, the district court dismissed the complaint for a temporary restraining order.

For reasons unknown, Gebreyes was unable to obtain the services of a neurologist before the stipulated July 2, 2015, deadline. Consequently, on July 1, 2015, Gebreyes filed an "Emergency Petition for Order Authorizing Medical Care, Restraining Order and Permanent Injunction." In the petition, he alleged that the doctors at St. Mary's had prematurely determined that Hailu had experienced brain death and sought to prevent the hospital from removing Hailu from the ventilator. St. Mary's opposed the emergency petition on July 2, 2015, and the district court held a hearing that same day.

At the July 2, 2015, hearing, the district court heard from four witnesses. First, Gebreyes testified that he wanted Hailu to get a tracheostomy and feeding tube to prepare her for transport; he hoped to take her home or relocate her to Las Vegas, where he resides. When asked why he did not obtain the services of another doctor to perform the tracheostomy, he stated that it was something he thought St. Mary's had to do because Hailu is at St. Mary's. Second, Gebreyes obtained the services of Dr. Paul Byrne—a known opponent of brain-death declarations who is unlicensed in Nevada—to testify that Hailu is still alive. Dr. Byrne complained that Hailu was never treated for thyroid problems and testified that this treatment will help her improve.

Third, Dr. Aaron Heide testified on behalf of St. Mary's. Dr. Heide applied the [AAN] guidelines to Hailu to determine if she was brain dead. He testified that the AAN guidelines are the accepted medical standard in Nevada. The AAN guidelines call for three determinations: (1) whether there is a coma and unresponsiveness; (2) whether there is brainstem activity (determined by conducting a clinical examination of reflexes, eyes, ears, etc.); and (3) whether the patient can breathe on her own (determined by conducting an apnea test). Although another doctor conducted the apnea test one month after Dr. Heide's last examination of Hailu, Dr. Heide believed that Hailu "had zero percent chance of any form of functional neurological outcome." Further, Dr. Heide also administered a Transcranial Doppler test, which is a test that measures blood flow to the brain. While there was still some blood flow to Hailu's brain, the lack of blood flow was consistent with brain death.

Last, Helen Lidholm, the CEO of St. Mary's, testified that the hospital is in favor of allowing Hailu to be transported to Las Vegas, where her father lives. Lidholm stated that St. Mary's "could make that happen" as long as Gebreyes arranges the proper medical equipment and transportation for Hailu and ensures a transfer location that can care for her. St. Mary's would allow the family to retain the services of any neurologist to come in and test Hailu as long as the physician is licensed in the State of Nevada; St. Mary's also offered to pay for the physician's examination fee. On cross-examination, Lidholm clarified that if the family has a licensed neurologist examine Hailu and determine that she is still alive, the physician can then order treatment for Hailu. Gebreyes said that he never received this offer before the hearing.

After Gebreyes said that he wanted to take advantage of the opportunity to bring in his own neurologist, the parties stipulated to extend the hearing until July 21, 2015, to give Gebreyes time to retain the services of a neurologist. . . . [T]he district court stated that Gebreyes needs a neurological expert because the matter involves "primarily neurological issues." . . .

On July 21, 2015, Gebreyes presented a plan to transport Hailu to Las Vegas based on the testimony of two physicians. First, Gebreyes called Dr. Brian Callister to testify. Dr. Callister is not a neurologist, but specializes in internal medicine and hospitalist medicine. He examined Hailu the day of his testimony and reviewed her medical records. Based on his examination of Hailu and review of her records, Dr. Callister testified: "I believe that her status is quite grim. I think that her chance of survival, her chance of awakening from her current state is a long shot. However, I do not think that the chance is zero." Dr. Callister stated that all three EEG tests did show brainwaves, albeit abnormal and slow. In Dr. Callister's opinion, the EEG tests are "something that should give you just enough pause to say you can't say with certainty that her chances are zero." Although Dr. Callister admitted that under the AAN guidelines Hailu's condition looks irreversible, Dr. Callister pointed to other factors that demonstrate improvement is a possibility. As examples, Dr. Callister cites Hailu's young age, her health, her skin, her ability to make urine and pass bowel movements, and the fact that the general functioning of the rest of her body is good. . . .

. . . [O]n cross-examination, Dr. Callister conceded that under "a strict definition" of the AAN guidelines, Hailu "would meet their category [of brain death]." On redirect, Dr. Callister concluded that "there's enough variables and enough questions based on the condition of her physical body, the EEG's and the fact that no further neurological testing has been done in several months, and the fact that no outside third party neurologist has looked at her that I would have pause."

[Gebreyes also called a doctor who was willing to perform the tracheostomy but not to take Hailu into his care for other purposes.]

* * *

Next, St. Mary's called Dr. Anthony Floreani to testify. Dr. Floreani took care of Hailu in the ICU since the night following her surgery. Dr. Floreani is a pulmonary doctor, not a neurologist. Dr. Floreani agreed with the conclusions of Dr. Heide that Hailu is brain dead. . . . Dr. Floreani testified that the St. Mary's doctors did the tests "by the book exactly how you should do it." Based on all of the evidence from the July 2 hearing and the July 21 hearing, the district court ruled in favor of St. Mary's. The district court stated that a restraining order should not be granted because the medical evidence from Dr. Heide and Dr. Floreani suggested that the AAN guidelines were followed, and thus, "medical standards were met, the outcome and criteria were satisfied in terms of the statute, the [AAN] protocol was followed, the outcome of the various three step tests under the [AAN] protocol all direct certification of death, and I agree." . . .

*DISCUSSION*

\* \* \*

The district court focused exclusively on whether St. Mary's physicians satisfied the AAN guidelines, without discussing whether the AAN guidelines satisfy NRS 451.007. Although St. Mary's presented testimony that the AAN guidelines are the accepted medical standard in Nevada—albeit a simple "yes" to the question of whether the AAN guidelines are the accepted medical standard in Nevada—the district court and St. Mary's failed to demonstrate that the AAN guidelines are considered "accepted medical standards" that are applied uniformly throughout states that have enacted the UDDA . . . . The district court did not reach this issue at all, while St. Mary's has only cited one source to support its argument that the AAN guidelines are the nationally accepted medical standard.

St. Mary's cites the New Jersey Law Revision Commission's Report relating to the Declaration of Death Act. However, the report actually supports the opposite conclusion for which St. Mary's argues. . . . *See* N.J. Law Revision Comm'n, Final Report Relating to New Jersey Declaration of Death Act, at 14 (Jan. 18, 2013). [T]he report cited to multiple studies suggesting that "the AAN guidelines need more research" and "there is still a great variety of practice in U.S. hospitals" even though the AAN guidelines were published in 1995. Despite recognizing the AAN as guidelines "upon which most hospitals and physicians rely," the report concluded that the AAN guidelines were not so broadly adopted and utilized as to have become *the* accepted medical standard for determining brain death. Based on the foregoing, and the record before us, we are not convinced that the AAN guidelines are considered the accepted medical standard that can be applied in a way to make Nevada's Determination of Death Act uniform with states that have adopted [the UDDA]. . . .

\* \* \*

It appears from a layperson's review of the Harvard criteria versus the AAN guidelines that the AAN guidelines incorporated many of the clinical tests used in the Harvard criteria. [ ] However, the AAN guidelines do not require confirmatory/ancillary testing, such as EEGs. Although the AAN guidelines state that ancillary testing should be ordered "only if clinical examination cannot be fully performed due to patient factors, or if apnea testing is inconclusive or aborted," the AAN's own study recognized that a decade after publication of the guidelines, 84 percent of brain death determinations still included EEG testing. [ ]

\* \* \*

[T]he briefing and record before us do not answer two key questions. First, the briefing and testimony do not establish whether the AAN guidelines are considered accepted medical standards among states that have enacted the UDDA. . . . Second, whatever their medical acceptance generally, the briefing and testimony do not establish whether the AAN guidelines adequately measure the extraordinarily broad standard laid out by NRS 451.007, which requires, before brain death can be declared under the UDDA, an "irreversible cessation" of "[a]*ll functions* of the person's *entire* brain, including his or her brain stem." [ ] Emphasis added. Though courts defer to the medical community to determine the applicable criteria to measure brain functioning, it is the duty of the law to establish the applicable standard that said criteria must meet. . . .

* * *

We concur: HARDESTY, C.J., and PARRAGUIRRE, DOUGLAS, CHERRY, SAITTA, and GIBBONS, JJ.

## NOTES AND QUESTIONS

1.    The position that dead is dead (whether measured by the irreversible cessation of cardiopulmonary function or total brain function) forms the foundation for legal standards and medical practice in relation to the determination that death has occurred. It certainly can be difficult for laypersons to accept that someone who has been declared brain dead, currently often referred to as "neurological determination of death," is dead. The person who is being supported by a ventilator but who is declared dead by neurological criteria still looks so alive—warm to the touch and with a steady rhythm of breath due to the ventilator. The irreversible cessation of brain function, even including the brain stem, does not mean that the body is not functioning in some parts. The body maintained with the support of a ventilator can continue to function for some time, producing hormones, urine, and so on, even though there is no brain activity measurable under common medical protocols used in brain death. Even health care professionals may experience cognitive dissonance in "caring for" persons who are brain dead while preparing the body for retrieval of organs for transplantation or maintaining the body on support while family matters are settled. Robert D. Truog, Brain Death—Too Flawed to Endure, Too Ingrained to Abandon, 35 J. L. Med. & Ethics 273 (2007). It should not be surprising, then, that conflicts between families and hospitals regarding the determination of death by neurological criteria occur and sometimes reach the courts.

2.    Cases like *Hailu* always raise questions about whether there were steps that could have been taken to avoid the conflict and lead to acceptance of the determination of death. Do you see any opportunities in *Hailu*? Both Aden Hailu and Jahi McMath, the subject of the New Yorker piece cited above, were young women of color. What impact might the gender and race of the patients or their next of kin make in this context? Both Ms. Hailu and Ms. McMath suffered severe injuries during surgery. As is routine, the declaration of death in each case was made by physicians affiliated with that hospital. Should hospitals establish different default procedures when the patient has been

injured during the course of treatment in the hospital? If a patient is not declared to be dead, life-sustaining treatment may still be withdrawn. See Chapter 5. Is it possible that approaching the situation from that direction could produce a different result in some cases? The Ad Hoc Committee (see Section II.A, above) rejected involving the family in the determination of death and allocated the process entirely to the physician. Does a hard-edge boundary protect families or does it create alienation in the process?

3.    After the Law Revision Commission's report cited in the court's opinion, the New Jersey legislature amended the state's determination of death statute to require that the determination of brain death be "based upon the exercise of the physician's best medical judgment and in accordance with currently accepted medical standards that are based upon nationally recognized sources of practice guidelines, including, but not limited to, those adopted by the American Academy of Neurology." After *Hailu*, the Nevada legislature went even further by requiring that the determination of brain death in adults "must be made" in compliance with the 2010 AAN Guidelines and subsequent revisions adopted by the AAN. Nev. Rev. Stat. § 451.007(2)(b)(1). Compare Fonseca v. Karen Smith, 2017 WL 4237865 (E.D. Cal.), holding that California's determination of death statute does not set a specific protocol but defers to physicians to determine that death has occurred. In fact, there is significant variability in the protocols doctors and hospitals use to determine whether brain death has occurred. See D.M. Greer et al., Variability of Brain Death Policies in the U.S., 73 JAMA Neurology 213 (2016). Should legislatures select the specific medical protocol to be used, or is that a question for medicine? Should the determination of death be treated differently than other medical decisions in that regard?

4.    The court is careful to note that it is not concluding that the AAN criteria are not the generally accepted medical standard for determining death, but only that the issue was not addressed in the court below. The court, however, states that the brain death statute requires that it must be determined that there is absolutely no function in the brain at all. In fact, some extremely minimal activity continues in the brain (such as the secretion of hormones regulating salts and fluids) that can continue certain bodily functions in some patients who are accurately determined to be brain dead under current medical standards. See, e.g., Seema K. Shah, Piercing the Veil: The Limits of Brain Death as a Legal Fiction, 48 Mich. J. L. Reform 301 (2015). See also President's Council on Bioethics, Controversies in the Determination of Death (2008), recognizing the persistence of some activity but recommending continuation of the current standards as applied although shifting the term to "total brain failure." Must state statutes be revised to account for the persistence of some brain activity if the whole brain death standard is to be retained? (See *T.A.C.P.*, below.) Or, should the statutes remain the same, and the interpretation of "all functions of the entire brain" be understood to tolerate the incidental activity that remains? Cases like *Hailu* reveal some level of resistance to brain death and probe the weak spots in state statutes and medical standards. Such cases, and the practice of DCD described in Section

II.C. below, stimulate debate. But see Fonseca v. Kaiser Permanente Medical Ctr. Roseville, 222 F.Supp. 3d 850 (E.D. Cal. 2016), "a professional doubt surrounding brain death as death, legally or medically, represents a minority position."

5.    Should state statutes provide for individual choice as between cardiopulmonary or neurological determination of death? Several states have formally adopted exemptions from the application of the brain death standard for determination of death for patients who reject brain death on specific grounds, as has New Jersey:

> The death of an individual shall not be declared upon the basis of neurological criteria . . . when the licensed physician authorized to declare death, has reason to believe, on the basis of information in the individual's available medical records, or information provided by a member of the individual's family or any other person knowledgeable about the individual's personal religious beliefs that such a declaration would violate the personal religious beliefs of the individual. In these cases, death shall be declared, and the time of death fixed, solely upon the basis of cardio-respiratory criteria. . . . N.J. Stat. § 26:6A–5.

The New York State Department of Health requires that hospitals provide reasonable accommodations for those with "religious or moral objections" to brain death; but explicitly does not require accommodation for persons with objections based "solely on the psychological denial that death has occurred or on an alleged inadequacy of the brain death determination." The Department's guidelines advise sensitivity in the latter case. N.Y. State Dept. of Health, Guidelines for Determining Brain Death (2011). Would either the New Jersey or New York provisions apply to the situation in *Hailu*? Compare Cal. Health & Safety Code § 1254.4, encompassing a broader range of objections but providing only for a reasonable time to allow the family to adjust to the diagnosis and, in the case of cultural or religious objections, some reasonable efforts to accommodate those "religious or cultural practices or concerns."

6.    After remand, the hospital asked the trial court for permission to perform additional testing, including an EEG, over the father's objection, and the court allowed two EEGs to be performed. It's not clear whether that testing took place. Shortly before the date set for the hearing on the issue of the remand, Aden Hailu suffered cardiopulmonary arrest. The death certificate listed the date of death as January 4, 2016, the date of the arrest. Siobhan McAndres, The Contested Death of Aden Hailu, Reno-Gazette-Journal, Mar. 25, 2016.

## IN RE T.A.C.P.

Supreme Court of Florida, 1992.
609 So.2d 588.

We have for review an order of the trial court certified by the Fourth District Court of Appeal as touching on a matter of great public importance requiring immediate resolution by this Court. We frame the issue as follows:

Is an anencephalic newborn considered "dead" for purposes of organ donation solely by reason of its congenital deformity?

\* \* \*

## I.    Facts

At or about the eighth month of pregnancy, the parents of the child T.A.C.P. were informed that she would be born with anencephaly. . . .

In this case, T.A.C.P. actually survived only a few days after birth. The medical evidence in the record shows that the child T.A.C.P. was incapable of developing any sort of cognitive process, may have been unable to feel pain or experience sensation due to the absence of the upper brain, and at least for part of the time was placed on a mechanical ventilator to assist her breathing. . . .

On the advice of physicians, the parents continued the pregnancy to term and agreed that the mother would undergo caesarean section during birth. The parents agreed to the caesarean procedure with the express hope that the infant's organs would be less damaged and could be used for transplant in other sick children. Although T.A.C.P. had no hope of life herself, the parents both testified in court that they wanted to use this opportunity to give life to others. However, when the parents requested that T.A.C.P. be declared legally dead for this purpose, her health care providers refused out of concern that they thereby might incur civil or criminal liability. . . .

## II.    The Medical Nature of Anencephaly

Although appellate courts appear never to have confronted the issue, there already is an impressive body of published medical scholarship on anencephaly. From our review of this material, we find that anencephaly is a variable but fairly well defined medical condition. Experts in the field have written that anencephaly is the most common severe birth defect of the central nervous system seen in the United States, although it apparently has existed throughout human history.

A statement by the Medical Task Force on Anencephaly ("Task Force") printed in the New England Journal of Medicine generally described "anencephaly" as "a congenital absence of major portions of the brain, skull, and scalp, with its genesis in the first month of gestation." David A. Stumpf et al., *The Infant with Anencephaly*, 322 New Eng.J.Med. 669, 669 (1990). The large opening in the skull accompanied by the absence or severe congenital disruption of the cerebral hemispheres is the characteristic feature of the condition. *Id.*

The Task Force defined anencephaly as diagnosable only when all of the following four criteria are present:

(1) A large portion of the skull is absent. (2) The scalp, which extends to the margin of the bone, is absent over the skull defect. (3) Hemorrhagic, fibrotic tissue is exposed because of defects in the skull and scalp. (4) Recognizable cerebral hemispheres are absent.

\* \* \*

Thus, it is clear that anencephaly is distinguishable from some other congenital conditions because its extremity renders it uniformly lethal. . . .

The Task Force stated that most reported anencephalic children die within the first few days after birth, with survival any longer being rare. . . . The Task Force reported, however, that these survival rates are confounded somewhat by the variable degrees of medical care afforded to anencephalics. Some such infants may be given considerable life support while others may be given much less care.

The Task Force reported that the medical consequences of anencephaly can be established with some certainty. All anencephalics by definition are permanently unconscious because they lack the cerebral cortex necessary for conscious thought. Their condition thus is quite similar to that of persons in a persistent vegetative state. Where the brain stem is functioning, as it was here, spontaneous breathing and heartbeat can occur. In addition, such infants may show spontaneous movements of the extremities, "startle" reflexes, and pupils that respond to light. Some may show feeding reflexes, may cough, hiccup, or exhibit eye movements, and may produce facial expressions.

\* \* \*

There appears to be general agreement that anencephalics usually have ceased to be suitable organ donors by the time they meet all the criteria for "whole brain death," i.e., the complete absence of brainstem function. . . . There also is no doubt that a need exists for infant organs for transplantation. Nationally, between thirty and fifty percent of children under two years of age who need transplants die while waiting for organs to become available. . . .

### III.  Legal Definitions of "Death" & "Life"

[The court considers Florida's statute:]

For legal and medical purposes, *where respiratory and circulatory functions are maintained by artificial means of support* so as to preclude a determination that these functions have ceased, the occurrence of death *may* be determined where there is the irreversible cessation of the functioning of the entire brain, including the brain stem, determined in accordance with this section.

§ 382.009(1), Fla.Stat. (1991) (emphasis added). A later subsection goes on to declare:

> Except for a diagnosis of brain death, the standard set forth in this section is not the exclusive standard for determining death or for the withdrawal of life-support systems.

§ 382.009(4), Fla.Stat. (1991). This language is highly significant for two reasons.

First, the statute does not purport to codify the common law standard applied in some other jurisdictions, as does the uniform act. The use of the permissive word "may" in the statute in tandem with the savings clause of section 382.009(4) buttresses the conclusion that the legislature envisioned other ways of defining "death." Second, the statutory framers clearly did not intend to apply the statute's language to the anencephalic infant not being kept alive by life support. To the contrary, the framers expressly limited the statute to that situation in which "respiratory and circulatory functions are maintained by artificial means of support."

\* \* \*

IV.  Common Law & Policy

\* \* \*

The question remaining is whether there is good reason in public policy for this Court to create an additional common law standard applicable [only] to anencephalics. Alterations of the common law, while rarely entertained or allowed, are within this Court's prerogative. . . . We believe, for example, that our adoption of the cardiopulmonary definition of death today is required by public necessity and, in any event, merely formalizes what has been the common practice in this state for well over a century.

Such is not the case with petitioners' request. Our review of the medical, ethical, and legal literature on anencephaly discloses absolutely no consensus that public necessity or fundamental rights will be better served by granting this request.

We are not persuaded that a public necessity exists to justify this action, in light of the other factors in this case—although we acknowledge much ambivalence about this particular question. We have been deeply touched by the altruism and unquestioned motives of the parents of T.A.C.P. The parents have shown great humanity, compassion, and concern for others. The problem we as a Court must face, however, is that the medical literature shows unresolved controversy over the extent to which anencephalic organs can or should be used in transplants.

\* \* \*

We express no opinion today about who is right and who is wrong on these issues—if any "right" or "wrong" can be found here. The salient point is that no consensus exists as to: (a) the utility of organ transplants of the type at issue here; (b) the ethical issues involved; or (c) the legal and constitutional problems implicated.

### V.   Conclusions

Accordingly, we find no basis to expand the common law to equate anencephaly with death. We acknowledge the possibility that some infants' lives might be saved by using organs from anencephalics who do not meet the traditional definition of "death" we reaffirm today. But weighed against this is the utter lack of consensus, and the questions about the overall utility of such organ donations. The scales clearly tip in favor of not extending the common law in this instance.

To summarize: We hold that Florida common law recognizes the cardiopulmonary definition of death as stated above; and Florida statutes create a "whole-brain death" exception applicable whenever cardiopulmonary function is being maintained artificially. There are no other legal standards for determining death under present Florida law.

Because no Florida statute applies to the present case, the determination of death in this instance must be judged against the common law cardiopulmonary standard. The evidence shows that T.A.C.P.'s heart was beating and she was breathing at the times in question. Accordingly, she was not dead under Florida law, and no donation of her organs would have been legal.

### NOTES AND QUESTIONS

1.   Despite the UDDA, there is significant variation among state statutes recognizing irreversible cessation of all brain function as a legal standard for the determination of death. These can be significant as illustrated in the court's discussion of the Florida statute in *T.A.C.P.* In fact, only about one-third of the states have adopted the UDDA as written; about one-third with variations; and about one-third crafted their own statutes. Several states have accepted brain death for the determination of death in case law rather than by statute. In departing from the UDDA, some states adopted definitions for "irreversible," which the UDDA leaves undefined; and some provide that brain function is relevant for the determination of death *only* where cardiopulmonary function is maintained by mechanical means. Some statutes provide that a person *may* (instead of *shall*) be considered dead in the presence of irreversible cessation of cardiopulmonary or all brain function. Jason Goldsmith, Wanted! Dead and/or Alive: Choosing Among the Not-So-Uniform Statutory Definitions of Death, 61 U. Miami L. Rev. 871 (2007).

2.   If the Florida court had declared that anencephaly was acceptable as a legal standard for the determination of death, what implications would that

have for medical treatment of individuals with the same medical condition? In *T.A.C.P.*, the court asks whether the newborn should be declared dead "for the purposes of organ donation." Should the standard for determination of death depend on the purpose or consequences of doing so? Shortly after, the *T.A.C.P.* opinion was issued, a mother successfully fought a hospital refusal to repeatedly resuscitate her infant who had anencephaly with the court ultimately holding that a federal statute requiring that hospitals provide emergency care covered the child. In re Baby K, 16 F. 3d 590 (4th Cir. 1994). The hospital in *Baby K* claimed that continued treatment was futile, not that Baby K met a legal standard for death. See Chapter 5. Some states already allow individual choice in the application of the neurological determination of death. See discussion after *Hailu*, above.

    3.    Does it matter whether the question is presented as whether a person is alive rather than whether the person is dead? Some have argued that the legal standard for death should be expanded to embrace the irreversible cessation of so-called "higher brain" functions related to cognition, identity, and personality. Proponents argue that neocortical function is essential to being human; that without it humans cannot function as a whole; and that counting this as life is a base and animalistic view of the nature of being human. Ben Sarbey, Definition of Death: Brain Death and What Matters in a Person, 3 J. L. & Biosciences 745 (2016). Objections to this expansion range from practical to metaphysical concerns. These include that death would be pronounced while the body is breathing on its own; diagnosis of conditions producing persistent unconsciousness or minimal consciousness continues to be challenging; newer knowledge about higher brain injuries continues to emerge; declaring a person to be dead when there is still brain function violates the sanctity of human life; and reliance on cognitive function as a measure of personhood leads inevitably to a slippery slope and devaluation of persons with cognitive disabilities. See, e.g., James Bernat et al., Defining Death in Theory and Practice, 12 Hastings Ctr. Rep. 5 (1982).

## C.  CARDIOPULMONARY DEATH REVIVED IN ORGAN RETRIEVAL

    The adoption of neurological determination of death, or brain death, was designed in part to increase the retrieval of life-sustaining organs for transplant. In the face of continuing shortages of organs for transplant, an Institute of Medicine report (Organ Donation: Opportunities for Action 2006) advocated the widespread adoption of the then emerging practice of donation after cardiopulmonary (or circulatory or cardiac) death (DCD), also known as donation after circulatory determination of death (DCDD). (The literature and hospital policies have used a variety of terms over time to describe this process, including "non-heart-beating donors," "donors without a heartbeat," or "asystolic donors.") The volume of organs retrieved through DCD has increased dramatically. In 2006, there were 642 donors through DCD, representing 8% of donated cadaveric organs; and in 2015, 1494, totaling 16.5%.

In a way, DCD appears to return to the older, common law standard as it relies on the cessation of cardiopulmonary function as the indicator that death has occurred. Although DCD at first glance appears to bring us full circle, the procedures differ quite substantially from the procedures used to determine cardiopulmonary death in earlier times and in contexts other than organ donation. The practice of DCD is now a mainstream practice, but it continues to raise significant ethical and legal controversies, including challenges to legal standards for the determination of death and the continued viability of the "dead donor rule," i.e., that a person's life-sustaining organs may be removed only after death. See, e.g., Robert D. Truog, Defining Death: Getting it Wrong for All the Right Reasons, 93 Tex. L. Rev. 1885 (2015).

## PROBLEM: CENTRAL CITY HOSPITAL'S PROPOSAL FOR DONATION AFTER CIRCULATORY DEATH

Central City Hospital (CCH) is a large teaching hospital. The hospital has decided to increase the volume of its organ procurement and transplant program in an effort to develop programs that produce a substantial net revenue stream, to meet the need of desperate patients, to realize the improved outcomes that a higher volume of transplants produces, and to develop a source of pride for hospital staff. CCH hired a new medical director for its transplant program, Dr. Joshua Niblet, who had been directing a very successful program at a hospital in another state.

Until now, all cadaveric organs donated at CCH have come from patients who have been declared brain dead while they are on mechanical cardiopulmonary support. Dr. Niblet is recommending that the hospital engage in organ recovery in controlled DCD. "Controlled DCD" occurs when "death is anticipated and occurs after medical supportive therapy is withdrawn, usually in an operating room, or hospital intensive care unit, or within a closely monitored time frame." IOM Report 2006. "Uncontrolled DCD" (or unexpected, unplanned, or unanticipated cardiac death) occurs when cardiopulmonary function has stopped spontaneously and usually unexpectedly. The IOM report recognizes that organ retrieval in uncontrolled cardiac death presents special challenges. Dr. Niblet is not seeking implementation of uncontrolled DCD at this time.

As a newly minted health lawyer and newly appointed assistant hospital counsel, you have been assigned to work with Dr. Niblet to help him institute the new program. You are being asked to assist in drafting the substance of the hospital's policies for DCD. Identify the issues you see in the following plan and how you would resolve them. Assume that your state has adopted the UDDA without revision. As a guide for your work, use the following federal regulation:

### 42 C.F.R. § 486.344(f)

If an [Organ Procurement Organization] recovers organs from donors after cardiac death, the OPO must have protocols that address the following: (1) Criteria for evaluating patients for donation after cardiac death; (2) Withdrawal of support, including the relationship between the time of consent to donation and the withdrawal of support; (3) Use of medications and interventions not related to withdrawal of support; (4) Involvement of family members prior to organ recovery; (5) Criteria for declaration of death and the time period that must elapse prior to organ recovery.

### Potential DCD Donors

The federal policy governing organ transplantation currently provides that potential DCD donors include "persons who have died, or whose death is imminent, whose medical treatment no longer offers medical benefit to the patient as determined by the patient, the patient's authorized surrogate, or the patient's advance directive, if applicable." OPTN Policy 2.16. (See Chapter 5 on treatment decision making at the end of life.) OPTN policy specifies that the decision to withdraw life-sustaining treatment be made before organ donation is discussed. If the patient who is the potential donor is making the donation decision, the patient's capacity to make that decision must be assessed. If the patient is incompetent but had earlier executed a document indicating intent to donate organs, that document (which typically does not include specific directions concerning DCD) controls. Failing those first two options, the individual identified in state law decides whether to donate organs. See Section I.C., above.

### Declaration of Death

The determination of death must be made in compliance with state law. Once the decision to withdraw treatment is made, medical interventions to preserve the organs are begun, and the patient is taken to the operating room. Mechanical support sustaining cardiac function is removed; and the patient is observed to see whether the heart will begin to function on its own, before death is declared and the surgeon makes the incision and removes the organs. Although an uncommon occurrence, the hospital must be ready to treat the patient if the heart begins beating spontaneously.

Hospital protocols concerning the period to watch for spontaneous breathing vary significantly, but typically range from two to five minutes. The OPTN policy does not adopt a specific wait time. It is generally recognized that measurable brain activity continues for a significant time, perhaps up to 15 minutes after cessation of cardiopulmonary function. See James DuBois, Is Organ Procurement Causing the Death of Patients?, 18 Issues L. & Med. 21 (2002); Jerry Menikoff, The Importance of Being Dead: Non-Heart-Beating Organ Donation, 18 Issues L. & Med. 3 (2002).

Dr. Niblet wants to set the shortest time possible, as the organs begin to deteriorate quickly once circulation stops.

*Medical Interventions Prior to DCD*

Medications to thin the blood, expand the blood vessels, cool down the body, and preserve the organs are administered before the patient is declared dead. Where the patient does not have decisional capacity, the decision to withdraw treatment is made by a surrogate or pursuant to the patient's advance directive (such as a living will or durable power of attorney). Most advance directives do not include instructions concerning medical treatment provided for pre-mortem organ preservation in DCD and instead only specify that medical treatment is to be stopped if certain medical conditions are met. The Uniform Anatomical Gift Act (see Section I.C.1) provides that during the time in which a potential donor is being evaluated, "measures necessary to ensure the medical suitability of the [organs] may not be withdrawn unless the hospital . . . knows that the individual expressed a contrary intent." (§ 14(c), above) As to whether the typical advance directive evidences contrary intent, the Act provides that interventions required for successful organ recovery continue until the apparent conflict between the two instructions (the advance directive and the document for organ donation) is resolved, unless the interventions to preserve the organs are contraindicated for end-of-life care. (§ 21). See Richard Bonnie, Stephanie Wright, & Kelly Dineen, Legal Authority to Preserve Organs in Cases of Uncontrolled Cardiac Death, 36 J. L. Med. & Ethics 741 (2008).

Some protocols use extracorporeal membrane oxygenation (ECMO) to provide oxygenated blood to preserve organs after the death. Because there is a concern that oxygenated blood flowing through the heart after mechanical support has been withdrawn would be evidence of spontaneous cardiac function, physicians may block blood flow above the diaphragm so that only the abdominal organs receive oxygenated blood. See A.L. Dalle Ave et al., Ethical Issues in the Use of ECMO in Controlled Donation after Circulatory Determination of Death, 16 Am J. Transplant. 2293 (Aug. 2016). The demand for heart transplantation, however, is driving increasing retrievals from DCD donors. Aravinda Page et al., Heart Transplantation from Donation after Circulatory Determined Death, 7 Annals of Cardiothoracic Surgery 75 (2018).

Dr. Niblet wants full discretion to employ the most effective organ preservation interventions as needed.

*Questions for Hospital Policy Development*

When patients or families are considering decisions relating to treatment at the end of life, when should the possibility of organ donation be raised? Who should present the option?

If the patient no longer has the capacity to make decisions but has executed a document for donation of organs upon death by signing up with the state's donor registry, signifying so on the driver's license, or signing a donor card, does that indicate consent to donation after DCD? These documents ordinarily do not provide information concerning DCD or measures that must be taken to preserve the organs. If the patient lacks decisional capacity, would you treat the organ donation document as determinative or would you require that the consent of the surviving next-of-kin be secured? Under the UAGA, pre-mortem documents of gift are binding on family members and others (see Section I.C, above). Would you recommend that the hospital secure informed consent from the surrogate for the specific interventions required to preserve organs, or would you structure the consent to donate organs to include permission to perform "all procedures necessary to retrieve the organs?" If the patient left an advance directive declining all medical treatment, would that preclude donation upon DCD?

What would you recommend as to wait time for the CCH policy? How does the wait time relate to whether the donor is dead under the UDDA? Could the precise language of your state's determination of death statute make a difference to your legal analysis? See *T.A.C.P.* and the notes following, above. Would you prefer that the state legislature amend its statute to specifically allow DCD, or are you satisfied that it falls within the UDDA?

# CHAPTER 5

# LIFE AND DEATH DECISIONS

∎ ∎ ∎

## I.  INTRODUCTION

Over the last few decades, the law has been invoked regularly by physicians and other health care providers concerned about the ethical, legal, and medical propriety of discontinuing what is now generally referred to as "life-sustaining treatment." A number of questions taken to the courts and legislatures arguably are outside the competence of the law. For example, consider what might constitute a "terminal illness," a concept that some have considered relevant in bioethical decision-making. While there surely is a medical element to a determination that a patient is "terminally ill," reflection upon the suggestion that there could be a lab test for this condition indicates that it is more than that. Classifying a patient as "terminally ill" depends on a combination of the patient's medical condition and the social, ethical, and legal consequences of the classification. If such a classification triggers a provision in an advance directive, or if it allows a physician to participate in aid in dying, for example, it might be treated differently than if it triggers the patient's relocation from one room to another within a hospital.

If a determination of terminal illness is not solely a medical decision, but rather a hybrid medical, ethical, social, political, and legal determination, where is the locus of appropriate decision-making? Should the decision be made by health care professionals alone? By a patient and his family? By a hospital committee? By some external committee? By a court appointed guardian? By the court itself? By the state legislature? By Congress? Should the decision be based upon principles and rules that emerge from medicine, ethics, religion, litigation, or legislative social policy making? Finally, what substantive principles ought to govern the decision-maker?

The difficulties in allocating decision-making authority and developing appropriate substantive principles are not limited to the "terminal illness" classification. They extend to such defining terms as "irreversible coma," "life-sustaining treatment," "death prolonging," "maintenance medical care," "extraordinary means," "heroic efforts," "intractable pain," "suffering," "persistent vegetative state," and even breathing and feeding.

For almost every question that arises within bioethics, we must make two determinations: (1) a procedural determination—who should be authorized to resolve the problem, and (2) a substantive determination—what substantive principles should apply. As one might expect, the substantive questions are often hidden in apparently procedural inquiries.

As these issues have come before the courts over the past few decades, the courts have looked both to the traditions of the common law and the traditions of ethics and medicine to discover principles for decision-making. In turn, judicial decisions have often formed the basis for new ethical and medical approaches. In fact, the debate over appropriate ethical policy in determining when life-sustaining treatment should be initiated or discontinued, and over whether physicians should be permitted to aid in the death of a patient, now involve lawyers as much as bioethics scholars, and the public debates on these issues have centered on the judicial resolution of cases and the promulgation of statutes as much as on any other source of formal principles. The law is not merely looking to ethics for potential methods of analysis, it is supplanting (some would say usurping) ethics in debate on these issues.

The law is not developed only through rationally justified and formally articulated judicial opinions. The law also comes out of political compromises in legislative action and public perceptions of well-publicized bioethical cases. Congress's decision to fund kidney dialysis through an expansion of the Medicare program for all those who need it, for example, had a substantial effect on determining who would live and who would die. See Chapter 4. Infants have names, and cry, and can be cuddled, while fetuses do none of these things; not surprisingly, we are willing to spend a great deal more to treat seriously ill newborns than we are to provide prenatal care. Of course, there may be other political values at play here, too.

Finally, the increasingly overtly political nature of some questions—such as whether physicians may aid in their patients' deaths—has brought formerly nonpolitical, personal questions into the political sphere. Is this society spending too much to extend the life of the very ill? Forty years ago Governor Lamm of Colorado was considered outrageous when he suggested that the elderly may have an obligation to die; today the social consequences of health care decisions have become a matter of real concern to those who realize that all of a family's assets easily could be consumed by a final illness. There is real controversy over whether there is any truth to the public perception that medical resources are being used (much less, wasted) to prolong the dying process.

The starting point for caselaw concerning end-of-life treatment decision-making is generally the law of informed consent, which is discussed in Chapter 1. The law of informed consent is bolstered by state administrative regulations (often from the state health department or its equivalent), state statutes (for example, patients' rights provisions in some states), state constitutional provisions (including the sometimes state-protected rights of privacy and dignity), federal statutes and regulations (like HIPAA and those assuring the privacy and security of medical records, and those governing research involving human subjects), and the United States Constitution. A second starting point for end-of-life treatment decisions is drawn from cases involving persons who are incapacitated and cannot make decisions for themselves. In such cases, the courts have often referenced the traditional law of guardianship in which the state assumes a parens patriae role to protect the incompetent person. While at times the two approaches work in harmony, at other times they lead to conflicting results. In this chapter you will face primarily cases that implicate and vindicate the doctrine of informed consent and its application to competent adults or those adults who had been competent. Legal rights for persons who have never been competent are discussed in the materials on the application of disability law in Chapter 2.

This chapter begins with a discussion of the Constitutional foundation upon which health care decision-making is based. This chapter addresses "life and death decisions," but the principles that arise out of these cases are extended to other health care contexts as well. In the *Cruzan* case, which you will be reading in this chapter, and in the *Glucksberg* case, which you will be reading in the next chapter, the United States Supreme Court was called upon to apply the Constitution to end-of-life care, but the principles it established in those cases have ramifications throughout the health care system. The United States Constitution sets the basic ground rules for recognizing health care decision-making authority, but it leaves a great deal of room for state regulation.

After examining the constitutional framework, this chapter examines the authority of an adult who has decisional capacity—a competent adult— to make his or her own health care decisions. We then move on to review the decision-making rules for adults who lack that capacity. We review advance directives like individual instructions (previously called living wills) and durable powers of attorney as tools for deciding for a now-incapacitated individual. The chapter concludes with a discussion of whether the decision that the proposed treatment is "futile" affects the nature of the decision-making surrounding it.

In reading this chapter, consider what role individuals, families, hospitals, institutional ethics committees, health care professionals, courts, legislatures, advocacy organizations and others ought to play in dealing with the ethical, medical, legal, social and political questions that often arise out of our new found technical ability to maintain life. As you review the way courts and others have considered individual cases, attempt to distill reasoned principles from their judgments. Is your analysis a procedural or substantive one? Who ought to be involved in the decision-making at each point? What principles are relevant to your analysis at each point?

## II. MAKING HEALTH CARE DECISIONS ABOUT DEATH AND DYING: THE CONSTITUTIONAL FOUNDATION

### CRUZAN V. DIRECTOR, MISSOURI DEPARTMENT OF HEALTH

Supreme Court of the United States, 1990.
497 U.S. 261, 110 S.Ct. 2841, 111 L.Ed.2d 224.

CHIEF JUSTICE REHNQUIST delivered the opinion of the Court.

Petitioner Nancy Beth Cruzan was rendered incompetent as a result of severe injuries sustained during an automobile accident. Co-petitioners Lester and Joyce Cruzan, Nancy's parents and co-guardians, sought a court order directing the withdrawal of their daughter's artificial feeding and hydration equipment after it became apparent that she had virtually no chance of recovering her cognitive faculties. The Supreme Court of Missouri held that because there was no clear and convincing evidence of Nancy's desire to have life-sustaining treatment withdrawn under such circumstances, her parents lacked authority to effectuate such a request. We granted certiorari and now affirm.

On the night of January 11, 1983, Nancy Cruzan lost control of her car as she traveled down Elm Road in Jasper County, Missouri. The vehicle overturned, and Cruzan was discovered lying face down in a ditch without detectable respiratory or cardiac function. Paramedics were able to restore her breathing and heartbeat at the accident site, and she was transported to a hospital in an unconscious state. An attending neurosurgeon diagnosed her as having sustained probable cerebral contusions compounded by significant anoxia (lack of oxygen). The Missouri trial court in this case found that permanent brain damage generally results after 6 minutes in an anoxic state; it was estimated that Cruzan was deprived of oxygen from 12 to 14 minutes. She remained in a coma for approximately three weeks and then progressed to an unconscious state in which she was able to orally ingest some nutrition. In order to ease feeding and further the recovery, surgeons implanted a gastrostomy feeding and hydration tube in Cruzan with the consent of her then husband. Subsequent rehabilitative efforts proved unavailing. She now lies in a Missouri state hospital in what is commonly referred to as a persistent vegetative state: generally, a condition in which a person exhibits motor reflexes but evinces no indications of significant cognitive function. The State of Missouri is bearing the cost of her care.

After it had become apparent that Nancy Cruzan had virtually no chance of regaining her mental faculties her parents asked hospital employees to terminate the artificial nutrition and hydration procedures. All agree that such a removal would cause her death. The employees refused to honor the request without court approval. The parents then sought and received authorization from the state trial court for termination. The court found that a person in Nancy's condition had a fundamental right under the State and Federal Constitutions to refuse or direct the withdrawal of "death prolonging procedures." The court also found that Nancy's "expressed thoughts at age twenty-five in somewhat serious conversation with a housemate friend that if sick or injured she would not wish to continue her life unless she could live at least halfway normally suggests that given her present condition she would not wish to continue on with her nutrition and hydration."

The Supreme Court of Missouri reversed by a divided vote. * * *

We granted certiorari to consider the question of whether Cruzan has a right under the United States Constitution which would require the hospital to withdraw life-sustaining treatment from her under these circumstances.

* * *

State courts have available to them for decision a number of sources—state constitutions, statutes, and common law—which are not available to us. In this Court, the question is simply and starkly whether the United States Constitution prohibits Missouri from choosing the rule of decision which it did. This is the first case in which we have been squarely presented with the issue of whether the United States Constitution grants what is in common parlance referred to as a "right to die."

* * *

The Fourteenth Amendment provides that no State shall "deprive any person of life, liberty, or property, without due process of law." The principle that a competent person has a constitutionally protected liberty interest in refusing unwanted medical treatment may be inferred from our prior decisions. * * *

But determining that a person has a "liberty interest" under the Due Process Clause does not end the inquiry;[7] "whether respondent's constitutional rights have been violated must be determined by balancing his liberty interests against the relevant state interests." [ ]

---

[7]    Although many state courts have held that a right to refuse treatment is encompassed by a generalized constitutional right of privacy, we have never so held. We believe this issue is more properly analyzed in terms of a Fourteenth Amendment liberty interest. See *Bowers v. Hardwick,* 478 U.S. 186, 194–195 (1986).

Petitioners insist that under the general holdings of our cases, the forced administration of life-sustaining medical treatment, and even of artificially-delivered food and water essential to life, would implicate a competent person's liberty interest. Although we think the logic of the cases discussed above would embrace such a liberty interest, the dramatic consequences involved in refusal of such treatment would inform the inquiry as to whether the deprivation of that interest is constitutionally permissible. But for purposes of this case, we assume that the United States Constitution would grant a competent person a constitutionally protected right to refuse lifesaving hydration and nutrition.

Petitioners go on to assert that an incompetent person should possess the same right in this respect as is possessed by a competent person. * * *

The difficulty with petitioners' claim is that in a sense it begs the question: an incompetent person is not able to make an informed and voluntary choice to exercise a hypothetical right to refuse treatment or any other right. Such a "right" must be exercised for her, if at all, by some sort of surrogate. Here, Missouri has in effect recognized that under certain circumstances a surrogate may act for the patient in electing to have hydration and nutrition withdrawn in such a way as to cause death, but it has established a procedural safeguard to assure that the action of the surrogate conforms as best it may to the wishes expressed by the patient while competent. Missouri requires that evidence of the incompetent's wishes as to the withdrawal of treatment be proved by clear and convincing evidence. The question, then, is whether the United States Constitution forbids the establishment of this procedural requirement by the State. We hold that it does not.

Whether or not Missouri's clear and convincing evidence requirement comports with the United States Constitution depends in part on what interests the State may properly seek to protect in this situation. Missouri relies on its interest in the protection and preservation of human life, and there can be no gainsaying this interest. As a general matter, the States— indeed, all civilized nations—demonstrate their commitment to life by treating homicide as serious crime. Moreover, the majority of States in this country have laws imposing criminal penalties on one who assists another to commit suicide. We do not think a State is required to remain neutral in the face of an informed and voluntary decision by a physically-able adult to starve to death.

But in the context presented here, a State has more particular interests at stake. The choice between life and death is a deeply personal decision of obvious and overwhelming finality. We believe Missouri may legitimately seek to safeguard the personal element of this choice through the imposition of heightened evidentiary requirements. It cannot be disputed that the Due Process Clause protects an interest in life as well as an interest in refusing life-sustaining medical treatment. Not all incompetent patients will have loved ones available to serve as surrogate decisionmakers. * * * A State is entitled to guard against potential abuses in such situations. Similarly, a State is entitled to consider that a judicial proceeding to make a determination regarding an incompetent's wishes may very well not be an adversarial one, with the added guarantee of accurate factfinding that the adversary process brings with it. [ ] Finally, we think a State may properly decline to make judgments about the "quality" of life that a particular individual may enjoy, and simply assert an unqualified interest in the preservation of human life to be weighed against the constitutionally protected interests of the individual.

In our view, Missouri has permissibly sought to advance these interests through the adoption of a "clear and convincing" standard of proof to govern such proceedings.

* * *

We think it self-evident that the interests at stake in the instant proceedings are more substantial, both on an individual and societal level, than those involved in a run-of-the-mine civil dispute. But not only does the standard of proof reflect the importance of a particular adjudication, it also serves as "a societal judgment about how the risk of error should be distributed between the litigants." [ ] The more stringent the burden of proof a party must bear, the more that party bears the risk of an erroneous decision. We believe that Missouri may permissibly place an increased risk of an erroneous decision on those seeking to terminate an incompetent individual's life-sustaining treatment. An erroneous decision not to terminate results in a maintenance of the status quo; the possibility of subsequent developments such as advancements in medical science, the discovery of new evidence regarding the patient's intent, changes in the law, or simply the unexpected death of the patient despite the administration of life-sustaining treatment, at least create the potential that a wrong decision will eventually be corrected or its impact mitigated. An erroneous decision to withdraw life-sustaining treatment, however, is not susceptible of correction.

* * *

In sum, we conclude that a State may apply a clear and convincing evidence standard in proceedings where a guardian seeks to discontinue nutrition and hydration of a person diagnosed to be in a persistent vegetative state. * * *

The Supreme Court of Missouri held that in this case the testimony adduced at trial did not amount to clear and convincing proof of the patient's desire to have hydration and nutrition withdrawn. * * * The testimony adduced at trial consisted primarily of Nancy Cruzan's statements made to a housemate about a year before her accident that she would not want to live should she face life as a "vegetable," and other observations to the same effect. The observations did not deal in terms with withdrawal of medical treatment or of hydration and nutrition. We cannot say that the Supreme Court of Missouri committed constitutional error in reaching the conclusion that it did.

* * *

JUSTICE O'CONNOR, concurring.

I agree that a protected liberty interest in refusing unwanted medical treatment may be inferred from our prior decisions, and that the refusal of artificially delivered food and water is encompassed within that liberty interest. I write separately to clarify why I believe this to be so.

As the Court notes, the liberty interest in refusing medical treatment flows from decisions involving the State's invasions into the body. Because our notions of liberty are inextricably entwined with our idea of physical freedom and self-determination, the Court has often deemed state incursions into the body repugnant to the interests protected by the Due Process Clause. [ ] The State's imposition of medical treatment on an unwilling competent adult necessarily involves some form of restraint and intrusion. A seriously ill or dying patient whose wishes are not honored may feel a captive of the machinery required for life-sustaining measures or other medical interventions. Such forced treatment may burden that individual's liberty interests as much as any state coercion. [ ]

The State's artificial provision of nutrition and hydration implicates identical concerns. Artificial feeding cannot readily be distinguished from other forms of medical treatment. * * * Whether or not the techniques used to pass food and water into the patient's alimentary tract are termed "medical treatment," it is clear they all involve some degree of intrusion and restraint. Feeding a patient by means of a nasogastric tube requires a physician to pass a long flexible tube through the patient's nose, throat and esophagus and into the stomach. Because of the discomfort such a tube causes, "[m]any patients need to be restrained forcibly and their hands put into large mittens to prevent them from removing the tube." * * * A gastrostomy tube (as was used to provide food and water to Nancy Cruzan), or jejunostomy tube must be surgically implanted into the stomach or small intestine. * * * Requiring a competent adult to endure such procedures against her will burdens the patient's liberty, dignity, and freedom to determine the course of her own treatment. Accordingly, the liberty guaranteed by the Due Process Clause must protect, if it protects anything, an individual's deeply personal decision to reject medical treatment, including the artificial delivery of food and water.

I also write separately to emphasize that the Court does not today decide the issue whether a State must also give effect to the decisions of a surrogate decisionmaker. In my view, such a duty may well be constitutionally required to protect the patient's liberty interest in refusing medical treatment. Few individuals provide explicit oral or written instructions regarding their intent to refuse medical treatment should they become incompetent. States which decline to consider any evidence other than such instructions may frequently fail to honor a patient's intent. Such failures might be avoided if the State considered an equally probative source of evidence: the patient's appointment of a proxy to make health care decisions on her behalf.

\* \* \*

Today's decision, holding only that the Constitution permits a State to require clear and convincing evidence of Nancy Cruzan's desire to have artificial hydration and nutrition withdrawn, does not preclude a future determination that the Constitution requires the States to implement the decisions of a patient's duly appointed surrogate. Nor does it prevent States from developing other approaches for protecting an incompetent individual's liberty interest in refusing medical treatment. \* \* \* Today we decide only that one State's practice does not violate the Constitution; the more challenging task of crafting appropriate procedures for safeguarding incompetents' liberty interests is entrusted to the "laboratory" of the States, in the first instance.

JUSTICE SCALIA, concurring.

\* \* \*

While I agree with the Court's analysis today, and therefore join in its opinion, I would have preferred that we announce, clearly and promptly, that the federal courts have no business in this field; that American law has always accorded the State the power to prevent, by force if necessary, suicide—including suicide by refusing to take appropriate measures necessary to preserve one's life; that the point at which life becomes "worthless," and the point at which the means necessary to preserve it become "extraordinary" or "inappropriate," are neither set forth in the Constitution nor known to the nine Justices of this Court any better than they are known to nine people picked at random from the Kansas City telephone directory; and hence, that even when it *is* demonstrated by clear and convincing evidence that a patient no longer wishes certain measures to be taken to preserve her life, it is up to the citizens of Missouri to decide, through their elected representatives, whether that wish will be honored. It is quite impossible (because the Constitution says nothing about the matter) that those citizens will decide upon a line less lawful than the one we would choose; and it is unlikely (because we know no more about "life-and-death" than they do) that they will decide upon a line less reasonable.

The text of the Due Process Clause does not protect individuals against deprivations of liberty *simpliciter*. It protects them against deprivations of liberty "without due process of law." To determine that such a deprivation would not occur if Nancy Cruzan were forced to take nourishment against her will, it is unnecessary to reopen the historically recurrent debate over whether "due process" includes substantive restrictions. [ ] It is at least true that no "substantive due process" claim can be maintained unless the claimant demonstrates that the State has deprived him of a right historically and traditionally protected against State interference. [ ] That cannot possibly be established here.

* * * "[T]here is no significant support for the claim that a right to suicide is so rooted in our tradition that it may be deemed 'fundamental' or 'implicit in the concept of ordered liberty.' "[ ]

Petitioners rely on three distinctions to separate Nancy Cruzan's case from ordinary suicide: (1) that she is permanently incapacitated and in pain; (2) that she would bring on her death not by any affirmative act but by merely declining treatment that provides nourishment; and (3) that preventing her from effectuating her presumed wish to die requires violation of her bodily integrity. None of these suffices.

[Scalia points out (1) that pain and incapacity have never constituted legal defenses to a charge of suicide, (2) that the distinction between "action" and "inaction" is logically and legally meaningless, and (3) that preventing suicide often (or always) requires the violation of bodily integrity, and it begs the question of whether the refusal of treatment is itself suicide.]

* * *

Are there, then, no reasonable and humane limits that ought not to be exceeded in requiring an individual to preserve his own life? There obviously are, but they are not set forth in the Due Process Clause. What assures us that those limits will not be exceeded is the same constitutional guarantee that is the source of most of our protection—what protects us, for example, from being assessed a tax of 100% of our income above the subsistence level, from being forbidden to drive cars, or from being required to send our children to school for 10 hours a day, none of which horribles is categorically prohibited by the Constitution. Our salvation is the Equal Protection Clause, which requires the democratic majority to accept for themselves and their loved ones what they impose on you and me. This Court need not, and has no authority to, inject itself into every field of human activity where irrationality and oppression may theoretically occur, and if it tries to do so it will destroy itself.

JUSTICE BRENNAN, with whom JUSTICE MARSHALL and JUSTICE BLACKMUN join, dissenting.

\* \* \*

Today the Court, while tentatively accepting that there is some degree of constitutionally protected liberty interest in avoiding unwanted medical treatment, including life-sustaining medical treatment such as artificial nutrition and hydration, affirms the decision of the Missouri Supreme Court. The majority opinion, as I read it, would affirm that decision on the ground that a State may require "clear and convincing" evidence of Nancy Cruzan's prior decision to forgo life-sustaining treatment under circumstances such as hers in order to ensure that her actual wishes are honored. Because I believe that Nancy Cruzan has a fundamental right to be free of unwanted artificial nutrition and hydration, which right is not outweighed by any interests of the State, and because I find that the improperly biased procedural obstacles imposed by the Missouri Supreme Court impermissibly burden that right, I respectfully dissent. Nancy Cruzan is entitled to choose to die with dignity.

\* \* \*

The right to be free from unwanted medical attention is a right to evaluate the potential benefit of treatment and its possible consequences according to one's own values and to make a personal decision whether to subject oneself to the intrusion. For a patient like Nancy Cruzan, the sole benefit of medical treatment is being kept metabolically alive. Neither artificial nutrition nor any other form of medical treatment available today can cure or in any way ameliorate her condition. Irreversibly vegetative patients are devoid of thought, emotion and sensation; they are permanently and completely unconscious. As the President's Commission concluded in approving the withdrawal of life support equipment from irreversibly vegetative patients:

> "[T]reatment ordinarily aims to benefit a patient through preserving life, relieving pain and suffering, protecting against disability, and returning maximally effective functioning. If a prognosis of permanent unconsciousness is correct, however, continued treatment cannot confer such benefits. Pain and suffering are absent, as are joy, satisfaction, and pleasure. Disability is total and no return to an even minimal level of social or human functioning is possible." [ ]

There are also affirmative reasons why someone like Nancy might choose to forgo artificial nutrition and hydration under these circumstances. Dying is personal. And it is profound. For many, the thought of an ignoble end, steeped in decay, is abhorrent. A quiet, proud death, bodily integrity intact, is a matter of extreme consequence. "In certain, thankfully rare, circumstances the burden of maintaining the

corporeal existence degrades the very humanity it was meant to serve."
* * *

Such conditions are, for many, humiliating to contemplate, as is visiting a prolonged and anguished vigil on one's parents, spouse, and children. A long, drawn-out death can have a debilitating effect on family members. [ ] For some, the idea of being remembered in their persistent vegetative states rather than as they were before their illness or accident may be very disturbing.

* * *

The only state interest asserted here is a general interest in the preservation of life. But the State has no legitimate general interest in someone's life, completely abstracted from the interest of the person living that life, that could outweigh the person's choice to avoid medical treatment. * * * [T]he State's general interest in life must accede to Nancy Cruzan's particularized and intense interest in self-determination in her choice of medical treatment. There is simply nothing legitimately within the State's purview to be gained by superseding her decision.

* * *

As the majority recognizes Missouri has a *parens patriae* interest in providing Nancy Cruzan, now incompetent, with as accurate as possible a determination of how she would exercise her rights under these circumstances. * * *

Accuracy, therefore, must be our touchstone. Missouri may constitutionally impose only those procedural requirements that serve to enhance the accuracy of a determination of Nancy Cruzan's wishes or are at least consistent with an accurate determination. The Missouri "safeguard" that the Court upholds today does not meet that standard. The determination needed in this context is whether the incompetent person would choose to live in a persistent vegetative state on life-support or to avoid this medical treatment. Missouri's rule of decision imposes a markedly asymmetrical evidentiary burden. Only evidence of specific statements of treatment choice made by the patient when competent is admissible to support a finding that the patient, now in a persistent vegetative state, would wish to avoid further medical treatment. Moreover, this evidence must be clear and convincing. No proof is required to support a finding that the incompetent person would wish to continue treatment.

Even more than its heightened evidentiary standard, the Missouri court's categorical exclusion of relevant evidence dispenses with any semblance of accurate factfinding. The court adverted to no evidence supporting its decision, but held that no clear and convincing, inherently reliable evidence had been presented to show that Nancy would want to avoid further treatment. * * * The court did not specifically define what kind of evidence it would consider clear and convincing, but its general discussion suggests that only a living will or equivalently formal directive from the patient when competent would meet this standard.

* * *

Finally, I cannot agree with the majority that where it is not possible to determine what choice an incompetent patient would make, a State's role as *parens patriae* permits the State automatically to make that choice itself. [ ] Under fair rules of evidence, it is improbable that a court could not determine what the patient's choice would be. Under the rule of decision adopted by Missouri and upheld today by this Court, such occasions might be numerous. But in neither case does it follow that it is constitutionally acceptable for the State invariably to assume the role of deciding for the patient. A State's legitimate interest in safeguarding a patient's choice cannot be furthered by simply appropriating it.

* * *

JUSTICE STEVENS, dissenting.

* * *

Choices about death touch the core of liberty. Our duty, and the concomitant freedom, to come to terms with the conditions of our own mortality are undoubtedly "so rooted in the traditions and conscience of our people as to be ranked as fundamental," [ ] and indeed are essential incidents of the unalienable rights to life and liberty endowed us by our Creator. [ ]

The more precise constitutional significance of death is difficult to describe; not much may be said with confidence about death unless it is said from faith, and that alone is reason enough to protect the freedom to conform choices about death to individual conscience. We may also, however, justly assume that death is not life's simple opposite, or its necessary terminus, but rather its completion. Our ethical tradition has long regarded an appreciation of mortality as essential to understanding life's significance. It may, in fact, be impossible to live for anything without being prepared to die for something. * * *

These considerations cast into stark relief the injustice, and unconstitutionality, of Missouri's treatment of Nancy Beth Cruzan. Nancy Cruzan's death, when it comes, cannot be an historic act of heroism; it will inevitably be the consequence of her tragic accident. But Nancy Cruzan's interest in life, no less than that of any other person, includes an interest in how she will be thought of after her death by those whose opinions mattered to her. There can be no doubt that her life made her dear to her family, and to others. How she dies will affect how that life is remembered. The trial court's order authorizing Nancy's parents to cease their daughter's treatment would have permitted the family that cares for Nancy to bring to a close her tragedy and her death. Missouri's objection to that order subordinates Nancy's body, her family, and the lasting significance of her life to the State's own interests. The decision we review thereby interferes with constitutional interests of the highest order.

To be constitutionally permissible, Missouri's intrusion upon these fundamental liberties must, at a minimum, bear a reasonable relationship to a legitimate state end. [ ] Missouri asserts that its policy is related to a state interest in the protection of life. In my view, however, it is an effort to define life, rather than to protect it, that is the heart of Missouri's policy.

* * *

Life, particularly human life, is not commonly thought of as a merely physiological condition or function. Its sanctity is often thought to derive from the impossibility of any such reduction. When people speak of life, they often mean to describe the experiences that comprise a person's history, as when it is said that somebody "led a good life."[20] They may also mean to refer to the practical manifestation of the human spirit, a meaning captured by the familiar observation that somebody "added life" to an assembly. If there is a shared thread among the various opinions on this subject, it may be that life is an activity which is at once the matrix for and an integration of a person's interests. In any event, absent some theological abstraction, the idea of life is not conceived separately from the idea of a living person. Yet, it is by precisely such a separation that Missouri asserts an interest in Nancy Cruzan's life in opposition to Nancy Cruzan's own interests.

* * *

Only because Missouri has arrogated to itself the power to define life, and only because the Court permits this usurpation, are Nancy Cruzan's life and liberty put into disquieting conflict. If Nancy Cruzan's life were defined by reference to her own interests, so that her life expired when her biological existence ceased serving *any* of her own interests, then her constitutionally protected interest in freedom from unwanted treatment would not come into conflict with her constitutionally protected interest in life. Conversely, if there were *any* evidence that Nancy Cruzan herself defined life to encompass every form of biological persistence by a human being, so that the continuation of treatment would serve Nancy's own liberty, then once again there would be no conflict between life and liberty. The opposition of life and liberty in this case are thus not the result of Nancy Cruzan's tragic accident, but are instead the artificial consequence

---

[20] It is this sense of the word that explains its use to describe a biography: for example, Boswell's Life of Johnson or Beveridge's The Life of John Marshall. The reader of a book so titled would be surprised to find that it contained a compilation of biological data.

of Missouri's effort, and this Court's willingness, to abstract Nancy Cruzan's life from Nancy Cruzan's person.

* * *

The Cruzan family's continuing concern provides a concrete reminder that Nancy Cruzan's interests did not disappear with her vitality or her consciousness. However commendable may be the State's interest in human life, it cannot pursue that interest by appropriating Nancy Cruzan's life as a symbol for its own purposes. Lives do not exist in abstraction from persons, and to pretend otherwise is not to honor but to desecrate the State's responsibility for protecting life. A State that seeks to demonstrate its commitment to life may do so by aiding those who are actively struggling for life and health. In this endeavor, unfortunately, no State can lack for opportunities: there can be no need to make an example of tragic cases like that of Nancy Cruzan.

## NOTES AND QUESTIONS

1.    Subsequent to this judgment the Missouri trial court heard additional evidence, provided by Nancy Cruzan's friends and colleagues, that she had made explicit and unambiguous statements that demonstrated, clearly and convincingly, that she would not want continued the treatment that she was receiving. Without opposition from the Attorney General of Missouri, the trial court authorized Ms. Cruzan's guardians to terminate her nutrition and hydration. See Sandra H. Johnson, Quinlan and Cruzan: Beyond the Symbols, in Health Law: Cases in Context (Sandra H. Johnson et al., eds. 2009).

2.    There are many ethical approaches to health care decision-making. The approach that has most influenced judicial decision-making is one that relies on the identification and application of particular principles, often called the "principlist approach." Tom Beauchamp and James Childress, Principles of Biomedical Ethics (7th ed. 2013). There are three primary substantive principles that operate here: autonomy, beneficence, and social justice. Autonomy and beneficence have been the principles most often relied upon in bioethics caselaw, which has largely ignored questions of cost (and allocation and rationing) and health disparities that implicate social justice. The principle of autonomy declares that each person is in control of his own person, including his body and mind. This principle, in its purest form, presumes that no other person or social institution ought to overrule a person's choice, whether or not that choice is "right" from an external perspective. Essentially, it is a libertarian principle. The principle of beneficence declares that what is best for each person should be done. The principle incorporates both the negative obligation of nonmaleficence ("primum non nocere"—"first of all, do no harm"—the foundation of the Hippocratic Oath) and the positive obligation to do that which is good. Thus, a physician is obliged to provide the highest quality of medical care for her patients. Similarly, a physician ought to treat a seriously ill newborn, or incapacitated adult child, in a way that best serves

that patient, whatever she may think her patient "wants" and whatever the parents of the patient may desire.

When a person does not desire what others determine to be in her best interests, the principles of autonomy and beneficence conflict. For example, if we consider the continued life of a healthy person to be in that person's interest, the values of autonomy and beneficence conflict when a healthy competent adult decides to take his own life. You can see that there can be serious conflict over what is in any individual's self interest and that values other than autonomy and beneficence will come into play in some of these cases. Did the *Cruzan* opinions address autonomy and beneficence? Did they imply any other values?

3.     Does the Opinion of the Court recognize a Constitutional right to die? Many authoritative sources presumed that the opinion did recognize a Constitutionally protected liberty interest in a competent person to refuse unwanted medical treatment. Indeed, the syllabus prepared for the Court says just that, and the case was hailed by the New York Times as the first to recognize a right to die. On the other hand, the Chief Justice's language does not support such a conclusion. While the majority agrees that "[t]he principle that a competent person has a Constitutionally protected liberty interest in refusing unwanted medical treatment *may* be inferred from our prior decisions," (emphasis added) the Court never makes the inference itself. In fact, the opinion says explicitly that "*for purposes of this case,* we assume that the United States Constitution would grant a competent person a Constitutionally protected right to refuse life saving nutrition and hydration." (emphasis added)

Why is this assumption limited to the "purposes of this case"? Does the Court question (1) whether there is a Constitutionally protected liberty interest in refusing unwanted medical treatment, (2) whether the right extends to life-sustaining treatment, or (3) whether it covers hydration and nutrition?

It must have been difficult for the Chief Justice to craft an opinion that would be joined by a majority of the court. Justice Scalia clearly did not believe that there was any Constitutional right implicated. If the Chief Justice were to formally recognize a Constitutional right, he might have lost Justice Scalia's signature—and thus lost an opportunity for there to be any majority opinion.

The dissents filed in this case are long and obviously heartfelt. Do the dissenters, all of whom would recognize a Constitutionally protected right to refuse life-sustaining treatment, and Justice O'Connor, who would also do so, create a majority in support of this Constitutional position?

4.     The majority opinion permits a state to limit its consideration to those wishes previously expressed by the patient and to ignore the decisions of another person acting on behalf of the patient. In fact, the Court explicitly does not address the question of whether a state must defer to an appropriately nominated surrogate acting on behalf of the patient. On the other hand, the

dissenting justices would recognize the decisions of a surrogate under appropriate circumstances, and Justice O'Connor suggests that the duty to give effect to those decisions "may well be constitutionally required." What is the Constitutional status of surrogate decision-making after *Cruzan*?

5.     Note that none of the opinions refers to the "right of privacy," a term which had caused the Court such tremendous grief in the abortion context. The Chief Justice analyzes this issue in the more general terms of a Fourteenth Amendment liberty interest, and none of the counsel argued the case in terms of the right to privacy. Apparently the Court just did not wish to entangle itself any further with the "P" word. See Chapter 3.

6.     Seven years after *Cruzan* was decided, the Supreme Court again considered end-of-life medical decision-making in Washington v. Glucksberg, in Chapter 6, below, which addressed the Constitutional status of medically assisted dying. Chief Justice Rehnquist, writing for the Court, announced in *Glucksberg* that "We have * * * assumed, and strongly suggested, that the Due Process Clause protects the traditional right to refuse unwanted lifesaving medical treatment." Is that an accurate description of the holding in *Cruzan*? A few pages later, in the same opinion, Chief Justice Rehnquist describes the *Cruzan* case slightly differently: "[A]lthough Cruzan is often described as a 'right to die' case [ ], we were, in fact, more precise: we assumed that the Constitution granted competent persons a 'constitutionally protected right to refuse lifesaving hydration and nutrition.'" Is that a more accurate account of what the Court decided in *Cruzan*?

Justice O'Connor, concurring in *Glucksberg*, says that "there is no need to address the question whether suffering patients have a constitutionally cognizable interest in obtaining relief from the suffering that they may experience in the last days of their lives." This issue, according to Justice O'Connor, was decided by *Cruzan*. Is she right? Justice Stevens also commented on the *Cruzan* case in the course of his concurring opinion in *Glucksberg*. He explained that "Cruzan did give recognition * * * to the more specific interest in making decisions about how to confront an imminent death. * * * Cruzan makes it clear that some individuals who no longer have the option of deciding whether to live or to die because they are already on the threshold of death have a constitutionally protected interest [in deciding how they will die] that may outweigh the State's interest in preserving life at all costs." Is this an accurate description of *Cruzan*? If the Justices who participated in both the *Cruzan* and *Glucksberg* cases cannot agree on just what the case really means, how can your health law teacher expect you to do so?

7.     Constitutional arguments are not limited to those who want to forgo treatment; they can be asserted by seriously ill patients who want access to treatment, too. In Abigail Alliance v. von Eschenbach, 495 F.3d 695 (D.C. Cir. 2007), the D.C. Circuit, *en banc*, addressed the argument that a terminally ill patient had a Constitutional right to access drugs that had not yet been approved by the FDA. The Abigail Alliance, named for a 21-year-old student

who died of cancer after being denied drugs in the earliest stages of testing, argued that *Cruzan* and *Glucksberg* paved the way for the recognition of a Constitutional right to access these not-yet-approved treatments, at least when those treatments provided the only hope of survival for the patient. The Court found, 8–2, that there was no such right, reversing the decision of the original three judge panel, Abigail Alliance v. von Eschenbach, 445 F.3d 470 (D.C. Cir. 2006), in part because of the longstanding tradition of governmental drug safety efforts in our legal system. The majority and the spirited dissenters disagreed about the way to articulate the right that Abigail Alliance sought to have recognized in this case. Was the right asserted the right "to access experimental and unproven drugs," as the majority suggested, or the right to "try to save one's life," as the dissent argued? As you have seen in *Cruzan*, and as you will recognize in *Glucksberg*, below, the due process arguments often depend upon the precise articulation of the right sought to be protected. Do you think the *Cruzan* case provides support for the position that an otherwise terminally ill cancer patient has access to drugs that have not yet been found to be safe or effective through the government's required administrative process? From a Constitutional perspective, is the argument that a patient is entitled to forgo treatment any different from the argument that a patient is entitled to have access to treatment? In any case, the notion that a terminally ill person for whom no established treatment is effective should be able to try other, unapproved, treatments is a powerful one. In 2017 and 2018 several states passed "Right to Try" laws to permit such otherwise unauthorized experimentation with unproven treatment.

8.    Except for a glancing reference by Justice Stevens in his dissent, the opinions do not consider the cost of providing care to Nancy Cruzan. Should the cost be relevant? Should the Constitutional right (to liberty or to life) vary depending on who bears the cost, or how great the cost actually is to keep a patient alive under particular circumstances? Would your analysis of this case be any different if the costs were being paid by an insurance company, by Ms. Cruzan's parents, by a gofundme.com account or by community fund raising in Nancy Cruzan's neighborhood, rather than by the state of Missouri? Should the one who pays the bills get to do the health care decision-making?

Judge Blackmar's dissent to the Missouri Supreme Court's opinion in *Cruzan* addresses the inconsistency of requiring some patients to be kept alive, at great expense, while the state is unable (or unwilling) to provide adequate care to others who actually want that care. He points out:

> The absolutist position is also infirm because the state does not stand prepared to finance the preservation of life, without regard to the cost, in very many cases. In this particular case the state has Nancy in its possession, and is litigating its right to keep her. Yet, several years ago, a respected judge needed extraordinary treatment which the hospital in which he was a patient was not willing to furnish without a huge advance deposit and the state apparently had no desire to help out. Many people die because of the unavailability of heroic medical treatment. It simply

cannot be said that the state's interest in preserving and prolonging life is absolute.

760 S.W.2d at 429. Judge Blackmar also points out, in a footnote, that "an absolutist would undoubtedly be offended by an inquiry as to whether the state, by prolonging Nancy's life at its own expense, is disabling itself from [providing] needed treatment to others who do not have such dire prognosis." 760 S.W.2d at 429 n. 4.

9.    The result of the *Cruzan* case (confirmed in *Glucksberg*) is that most law regarding health care decision-making has continued to be established on a state-by-state basis; there seems to be very little, if any, United States Constitutional limit on what states may do. *Cruzan* may have deflected the "right to die" debate to the political decision-making process in the same way that several abortion decisions have done. See Chapter 3, above.

10.    The decision of the United States Supreme Court to opt out of providing much Constitutional guidance to the states may allow a crazy quilt of state laws to persist such that a patient who would have a right to forgo life-sustaining treatment that could be exercised by his family in California or New Jersey would not have that right (or would not have a right that could be exercised by his family) in Missouri or Michigan. Indeed, the conditions and extent of, and the restrictions and exceptions to, any right to forgo life-sustaining treatment might be different in each state. State policies will thus require different results in factually identical cases. Is there anything wrong with this?

What would happen if Nancy Cruzan's family had decided to move her to the Yale Medical Center "because of the more favorable medical facilities" there? Could they have moved her from Missouri to Connecticut, where removal of the gastrostomy tube clearly would be legally permitted, just for the purpose of removing the gastrostomy tube? If they could not, then Nancy Cruzan could have become a prisoner of a state that rejects her family's values—values that have been incorporated into official state policies in other jurisdictions. If they could move her, however, Missouri would have allowed the family to undercut the important policy objectives of the state law and imperil the very life the law was designed to protect. Would it violate any criminal statute to move someone across state lines for the purpose of avoiding the laws governing termination of life support in the first state? Could a state make such an action a crime?

In early 1991 the father and guardian of Christine Busalacchi sought to have his daughter moved from Missouri to Minnesota for medical consultation with a nationally known neurologist who had consulted on several leading cases that resulted in the withdrawal of life-sustaining treatment. Ms. Busalacchi, who had been living in the same nursing home that had housed Nancy Cruzan, was arguably in a persistent vegetative state. The state of Missouri sought (and obtained) an order forbidding the move because of the fear that her father wanted only to find some place where his daughter could die. A divided Missouri Court of Appeals determined that the trial court was required to commence a new hearing on whether the move could be justified by other medical objectives. In deciding the case, the majority made it clear that " * * * we will not permit [the] guardian to forum shop in an effort to control whether Christine lives or dies." The dissent argued that "Minnesota is not a medical or ethical wasteland * * *. There is a parochial arrogance in suggesting, as the state does, that only in Missouri can Christine's medical, physical, and legal well being be protected and only here will her best interests be considered." Matter of Busalacchi, 1991 WL 26851 (Mo.App.1991). Ultimately, the State decided not to pursue the case, and Busalacchi died in Missouri. See also Mack v. Mack, 329 Md. 188, 618 A.2d 744 (1993) (Maryland Court denies full faith and credit to Florida judgment appointing the Florida-resident wife of a Maryland patient in persistent vegetative state as guardian so that patient could be moved to Florida, where life-sustaining treatment could be withdrawn.)

11. Missouri is not the only state to adopt the strict standard approved by the majority and decried by the dissenters; that standard was also adopted in Michigan in In re Martin, 450 Mich. 204, 538 N.W.2d 399 (1995). Arguably, the same standard has also been adopted in California, Conservatorship of Wendland, 26 Cal.4th 519, 110 Cal.Rptr.2d 412, 28 P.3d 151 (2001), at least when a patient is in a minimally conscious state. The strict Missouri "clear and convincing evidence" rule was also applied in New York, see In re Westchester County Medical Center on Behalf of O'Connor, 72 N.Y.2d 517, 534 N.Y.S.2d 886, 531 N.E.2d 607 (1988), until the Legislature adopted the Family Health Care Decisions Act, N.Y. Pub. Health Sec. 2994–d in 2010.

## NOTE: STATE LAW BASES FOR A "RIGHT TO DIE"

Although some courts have found the right to forgo life-sustaining treatment in the United States Constitution, *Cruzan*'s interpretation of the Fourteenth Amendment has encouraged state courts to look for other bases for this right, too. State courts find this right in state common law, state statutes, or state constitutions.

The vast majority of state courts recognizing a right to refuse life-sustaining treatment have found that right in state common law, usually in the law of informed consent, often applied even after the patient has lost the capacity to make decisions. As the Chief Justice recognized in *Cruzan*, the informed consent doctrine has become firmly entrenched in American tort law and "* * * the logical corollary of the doctrine of informed consent is that the patient generally possesses the right not to consent, that is, to refuse treatment. * * *" Once a court finds a common law right, it is not necessary to determine whether the right is also conferred by statute or by the United States or a state Constitution. See, e.g., In re Storar, 52 N.Y.2d 363, 438 N.Y.S.2d 266, 420 N.E.2d 64 (1981).

Some courts, however, bolster their common law basis for a "right to die" with references to the state and federal Constitutions. See In the Matter of Tavel, 661 A.2d 1061 (Del.1995). While the New Jersey court initially recognized a Constitutional "right to die" in In re Quinlan, 70 N.J. 10, 355 A.2d 647, 664 (N.J. 1976), it later recognized that the Constitutional determination was unnecessary and retrenched:

> While the right of privacy might apply in a case such as this, we need not decide that since the right to decline medical treatment is, in any event, embraced within the common law right to self determination. In re Conroy, 98 N.J. 321, 486 A.2d 1209, 1223 (1985).

Some courts have found the right to refuse life-sustaining treatment in state statutes. Generally, courts that rely on a statutory "right to die" also find a consistent common law right. See, e.g., McConnell v. Beverly Enterprises-Connecticut, 209 Conn. 692, 553 A.2d 596, 601–602 (1989). The Illinois Supreme Court, for example, explicitly rejected state and federal constitutional justifications for a "right to die" because of the existence of both state common law and state statutory remedies. In re Estate of Longeway, 133 Ill.2d 33, 139 Ill.Dec. 780, 549 N.E.2d 292, 297 (1989).

Several state courts have found the "right to die" in their state constitutions. A decision based on the state constitution may be the strongest kind of support such a right can ever find, because it is not subject to review by the United States Supreme Court (absent an improbable argument that a state created right would itself violate the United States Constitution) and it is not subject to change by the state legislature (except through the generally cumbersome state constitutional amendment process). Relevant state constitutional provisions take different forms. For example, the Florida Constitution provides that "[e]very natural person has the right to be let alone and free from governmental intrusion into his private life except as otherwise provided herein. * * * " Fla. Const., art. 1, section 23. The Arizona Constitution provides that "[n]o person shall be disturbed in his private affairs or his home invaded, without authority of law." Arizona Const., art. 2, section 8. Both of these constitutional provisions have given rise to state court recognized rights to forgo life-sustaining treatment. See In re Guardianship of Barry, 445 So.2d 365 (Fla.App.1984) and Rasmussen v. Fleming, 154 Ariz. 207, 741 P.2d 674 (1987). See also DeGrella v. Elston, 858 S.W.2d 698 (Ky.1993) and Lenz v. L.E. Phillips Career Dev. Ctr., 167 Wis.2d 53, 482 N.W.2d 60 (Wis. 1992). The California Court of Appeal also found that such a right for competent patients could be found in the California Constitution. See Bouvia v. Superior Court, 179 Cal. App. 3d 1127, 225 Cal. Rptr. 297 (1986), reprinted below following the next problem. In 2009 the Montana Supreme Court hinted that the Montana Constitution's "dignity" clause might be interpreted to give competent terminally ill individuals a right to seek and receive a prescription for a lethal dose in some circumstances. It seems likely that the same substantive constitutional source of law would guarantee the right to remove life-sustaining medical care. See Baxter v. Montana, 354 Mont. 234, 224 P.3d 1211 (2009).

# III. HEALTH CARE DECISION-MAKING BY ADULTS WITH DECISIONAL CAPACITY

## PROBLEM: THE CHRISTIAN SCIENTIST IN THE EMERGENCY ROOM

Shortly after Ms. Elizabeth Boroff was hit by a drunk driver who went through a red light and directly into her Volkswagen bus, she found herself being attended by paramedics and loaded into an ambulance for a trip to the Big County General Hospital emergency room. Although she was briefly unconscious at the scene of the accident, and although she suffered a very substantial blood loss, several broken bones and a partially crushed skull, she had regained consciousness by her arrival at the hospital. The doctors explained to her that her life was at risk and that she needed a blood transfusion and brain surgery immediately. She explained that she was a Christian Scientist, that she believed in the healing power of prayer, that she rejected medical care, and that she wished to be discharged immediately so that she could consult a Christian Science healer.

A quick conference of emergency room staff revealed a consensus that failure to relieve the pressure caused by her intracranial bleed would result in loss of consciousness within a few hours, and, possibly, her death. When this information was provided to her she remained unmoved. The hospital staff asked her to identify her next of kin, and she explained that she was a widow with no living relatives except for her seven minor children, ages 1 through 9. Further inquiries revealed that she was the sole support for these children, that she had no life insurance, that she had an elementary school education, and that she had been employed as a clerk since her husband, a self-employed maintenance man, was himself killed in an automobile accident a year ago. Uncertain of what to do, the emergency room staff called you, the hospital legal counsel, for advice. What advice should you give? Should they discharge Ms. Boroff, as she requests? Should you commence a legal action to keep her in the hospital and institute treatment? If you were to file a legal action, what relief would you seek, and what would be the substantive basis of your claim?

## BOUVIA v. SUPERIOR COURT

California Court of Appeal, Second District, 1986.
179 Cal.App.3d 1127, 225 Cal.Rptr. 297.

BEACH, ASSOCIATE JUSTICE.

Petitioner, Elizabeth Bouvia, a patient in a public hospital, seeks the removal from her body of a nasogastric tube inserted and maintained against her will and without her consent by physicians who so placed it for the purpose of keeping her alive through involuntary forced feeding.

\* \* \*

Petitioner is a 28-year-old woman. Since birth she has been afflicted with and suffered from severe cerebral palsy. She is quadriplegic. She is now a patient at a public hospital maintained by one of the real parties in interest, the County of Los Angeles. Other parties are physicians, nurses and the medical and support staff employed by the County of Los Angeles. Petitioner's physical handicaps of palsy and quadriplegia have progressed to the point where she is completely bedridden. Except for a few fingers of one hand and some slight head and facial movements, she is immobile. She is physically helpless and wholly unable to care for herself. * * * She suffers also from degenerative and severely crippling arthritis. She is in continual pain. * * *

She is intelligent, very mentally competent. She earned a college degree. She was married but her husband has left her. She suffered a miscarriage. She lived with her parents until her father told her that they could no longer care for her. She has stayed intermittently with friends and at public facilities. A search for a permanent place to live where she might receive the constant care which she needs has been unsuccessful. She is without financial means to support herself and, therefore, must accept public assistance for medical and other care.

She has on several occasions expressed the desire to die. In 1983 she sought the right to be cared for in a public hospital in Riverside County while she intentionally "starved herself to death." A court in that county denied her judicial assistance to accomplish that goal. * * * Thereafter, friends took her to several different facilities, both public and private, arriving finally at her present location. Efforts by * * * social workers to find her an apartment of her own with publicly paid live-in help or regular visiting nurses to care for her, or some other suitable facility have proved fruitless.

Petitioner must be spoon fed in order to eat. Her present medical and dietary staff have determined that she is not consuming a sufficient amount of nutrients. Petitioner stops eating when she feels she cannot orally swallow more, without nausea and vomiting. As she cannot now retain solids, she is fed soft liquid-like food. Because of her previously announced resolve to starve herself, the medical staff feared her weight loss might reach a life-threatening level. Her weight since admission to real parties' facility seems to hover between 65 and 70 pounds. Accordingly, they inserted the subject tube against her will and contrary to her express written instructions.[2]

Petitioner's counsel argue that her weight loss was not such as to be life threatening and therefore the tube is unnecessary. However, the trial court found to the contrary as a matter of fact, a finding which we must

---

[2]  Her instructions were dictated to her lawyers, written by them and signed by her by means of her making a feeble "x" on the paper with a pen which she held in her mouth.

accept. Nonetheless, the point is immaterial, for, as we will explain, a patient has the right to refuse any medical treatment or medical service, even when such treatment is labeled "furnishing nourishment and hydration." This right exists even if its exercise creates a "life threatening condition."

### The Right to Refuse Medical Treatment

"[A] person of adult years and in sound mind has the right, in the exercise of control over his own body, to determine whether or not to submit to lawful medical treatment." [ ] It follows that such a patient has the right to refuse *any* medical treatment, even that which may save or prolong her life. [ ]

* * *

A recent Presidential Commission for the Study of Ethical Problems in Medicine and Biomedical and Behavioral Research concluded in part: "The voluntary choice of a competent and informed patient should determine whether or not life-sustaining therapy will be undertaken, just as such choices provide the basis for other decisions about medical treatment. Health care institutions and professionals should try to enhance patients' abilities to make decisions on their own behalf and to promote understanding of the available treatment options * * *. Health care professionals serve patients best by maintaining a presumption in favor of sustaining life, while recognizing that competent patients are entitled to choose to forgo any treatments, including those that sustain life."

* * *

The American Hospital Association Policy and Statement of Patients' Choices of Treatment Options, approved by the American Hospital Association in February of 1985 discusses the value of a collaborative relationship between the patient and the physician and states in pertinent part: "Whenever possible, however, the authority to determine the course of treatment, if any, should rest with the patient" and "the right to choose treatment includes the right to refuse a specific treatment *or all treatment* * * *."

* * *

Significant also is the statement adopted on March 15, 1986, by the Council on Ethical and Judicial Affairs of the American Medical Association. It is entitled "Withholding or Withdrawing Life Prolonging Medical Treatment." In pertinent part, it declares: "The social commitment of the physician is to sustain life and relieve suffering. Where the performance of one duty conflicts with the other, the choice of the patient, or his family or legal representative if the patient is incompetent to act in his own behalf, should prevail."

\* \* \*

It is indisputable that petitioner is mentally competent. She is not comatose. She is quite intelligent, alert and understands the risks involved.

### The Claimed Exceptions to the Patient's
### Right to Choose Are Inapplicable

\* \* \* The real parties in interest, a county hospital, its physicians and administrators, urge that the interests of the State should prevail over the rights of Elizabeth Bouvia to refuse treatment. Advanced by real parties under this argument are the State's interests in (1) preserving life, (2) preventing suicide, (3) protecting innocent third parties, and (4) maintaining the ethical standards of the medical profession, including the right of physicians to effectively render necessary and appropriate medical service and to refuse treatment to an uncooperative and disruptive patient. Included, whether as part of the above or as separate and additional arguments, are what real parties assert as distinctive facts not present in other cases, i.e., (1) petitioner is a patient in a public facility, thereby making the State a party to the result of her conduct, (2) she is not comatose, nor incurably, nor terminally ill, nor in a vegetative state, all conditions which have justified the termination of life-support system in other instances, (3) she has asked for medical treatment, therefore, she cannot accept a part of it while cutting off the part that would be effective, and (4) she is, in truth, trying to starve herself to death and the State will not be a party to a suicide.

\* \* \*

At bench the trial court concluded that with sufficient feeding petitioner could live an additional 15 to 20 years; therefore, the preservation of petitioner's life for that period outweighed her right to decide. In so holding the trial court mistakenly attached undue importance to the *amount of time* possibly available to petitioner, and failed to give equal weight and consideration for the *quality* of that life; an equal, if not more significant, consideration.

All decisions permitting cessation of medical treatment or life-support procedures to some degree hastened the arrival of death. In part, at least, this was permitted because the quality of life during the time remaining in those cases had been terribly diminished. In Elizabeth Bouvia's view, the quality of her life has been diminished to the point of hopelessness, uselessness, unenjoyability and frustration. She, as the patient, lying helplessly in bed, unable to care for herself, may consider her existence meaningless. She cannot be faulted for so concluding. If her right to choose may not be exercised because there remains to her, in the opinion of a court, a physician or some committee, a certain arbitrary number of years, months, or days, her right will have lost its value and meaning.

Who shall say what the minimum amount of available life must be? Does it matter if it be 15 to 20 years, 15 to 20 months, or 15 to 20 days, if such life has been physically destroyed and its quality, dignity and purpose gone? As in all matters lines must be drawn at some point, somewhere, but that decision must ultimately belong to the one whose life is in issue.

Here Elizabeth Bouvia's decision to forgo medical treatment or life-support through a mechanical means belongs to her. It is not a medical decision for her physicians to make. Neither is it a legal question whose soundness is to be resolved by lawyers or judges. It is not a conditional right subject to approval by ethics committees or courts of law. It is a moral and philosophical decision that, being a competent adult, is hers alone.

* * *

Here, if force fed, petitioner faces 15 to 20 years of a painful existence, endurable only by the constant administrations of morphine. Her condition is irreversible. There is no cure for her palsy or arthritis. Petitioner would have to be fed, cleaned, turned, bedded, toileted by others for 15 to 20 years! Although alert, bright, sensitive, perhaps even brave and feisty, she must lie immobile, unable to exist except through physical acts of others. Her mind and spirit may be free to take great flights but she herself is imprisoned and must lie physically helpless subject to the ignominy, embarrassment, humiliation and dehumanizing aspects created by her helplessness. We do not believe it is the policy of this State that all and every life must be preserved against the will of the sufferer. It is incongruous, if not monstrous, for medical practitioners to assert their right to preserve a life that someone else must live, or, more accurately, endure, for "15 to 20 years." We cannot conceive it to be the policy of this State to inflict such an ordeal upon anyone.

* * * Being competent she has the right to live out the remainder of her natural life in dignity and peace. It is precisely the aim and purpose of the many decisions upholding the withdrawal of life-support systems to accord and provide as large a measure of dignity, respect and comfort as possible to every patient for the remainder of his days, whatever be their number. This goal is not to hasten death, though its earlier arrival may be an expected and understood likelihood.

* * *

Moreover, the trial court seriously erred by basing its decision on the "motives" behind Elizabeth Bouvia's decision to exercise her rights. If a right exists, it matters not what "motivates" its exercise. We find nothing in the law to suggest the right to refuse medical treatment may be exercised only if the patient's *motives* meet someone else's approval. It certainly is not illegal or immoral to prefer a natural, albeit sooner, death than a drugged life attached to a mechanical device.

* * *

We do not purport to establish what will constitute proper medical practice in all other cases or even other aspects of the care to be provided petitioner. We hold only that her right to refuse medical treatment even of the life-sustaining variety, entitles her to the immediate removal of the nasogastric tube that has been involuntarily inserted into her body. The hospital and medical staff are still free to perform a substantial, if not the greater part of their duty, i.e., that of trying to alleviate Bouvia's pain and suffering.

Petitioner is without means to go to a private hospital and, apparently, real parties' hospital as a public facility was required to accept her. Having done so it may not deny her relief from pain and suffering merely because she has chosen to exercise her fundamental right to protect what little privacy remains to her.

Personal dignity is a part of one's right of privacy. * * *

## NOTES AND QUESTIONS

1.    The *Bouvia* court depended, in large part, upon Bartling v. Superior Court, 163 Cal.App.3d 186, 209 Cal.Rptr. 220 (1984), the first case to confirm a competent patient's right to make decisions to forgo life-sustaining treatment. Mr. Bartling was a competent adult suffering from depression (the original reason for his hospitalization), a tumor on his lung, and emphysema. He had a living will, a separate declaration asking that treatment be discontinued, and a durable power of attorney appointing his wife to make his health care decisions. He and his wife continuously asked that the ventilator that was preserving his life be removed, and he, his wife, and his daughter all executed documents releasing the hospital from any liability claims arising out of honoring Mr. Bartling's request. Still, the hospital, which was a Christian hospital established and operated on pro-life principles, opposed discontinuation of Mr. Bartling's ventilator on ethical grounds. The California Court of Appeal found that the trial court should have granted Mr. Bartling's request for an injunction against the hospital, concluding that, "if the right to patient self-determination as to his own medical treatment means anything at all, it must be paramount to the interests of the patient's hospital and doctors. The right of a competent adult to refuse medical treatment is a constitutionally guaranteed right which must not be abridged."

2.    The court describes the quality of Elizabeth Bouvia's life in startling terms. Are they also offensive terms? Does the court describe her life as useless, meaningless, and embarrassing solely because that was her view of her own life, or does the court agree that this must be the case? *Bouvia* is viewed by disabilities rights advocates as a case which denigrated the value of the lives of persons who were dependent and disabled and in which a disabled person was driven to desperate measures for lack of the support she needed to live to her fullest capacity. See, e.g., Paul K. Longmore, Elizabeth Bouvia, Assisted

Suicide and Social Prejudice, 3 Issues L. & Med. 141 (1987). For a wonderful attempt to reconcile the principles of bioethics (and especially the principle of autonomy) with the principles of protection (and beneficence) that underlie the disabilities rights movement, see Alicia Ouellette, Bioethics and Disability: Toward a Disability-Conscious Bioethics (2011). The disabilities rights movement has become a key player in controversies over end-of-life decision-making, generally seeking to assure that those who seek to justify ending life by terminating life-sustaining treatment or by medically assisted dying have not equated the worth or dignity of an individual with the absence of any disability or abnormality.

3.     Do you agree that the hospital had an obligation to accept Ms. Bouvia and provide her with medical relief from her pain and suffering, even though the physicians and hospital found her conduct immoral and her request an abuse of the medical profession? Is the obligation anything more than to provide adequate end-of-life care, even when the patient refuses a particular course of treatment? Cf. Brophy v. New England Sinai Hospital, Inc., 398 Mass. 417, 497 N.E.2d 626 (1986), where the Massachusetts Supreme Judicial Court found that a patient in a persistent vegetative state could, through his family, deny consent to feeding through a gastric tube, but that the hospital need not remove or clamp the tube if it found it to be contrary to the ethical dictates of the medical profession. The *Brophy* decision required that the family move the patient to another medical institution more receptive to his apparent desires for his feeding tube to be removed. The New Jersey Supreme Court took a middle ground in In re Jobes, 108 N.J. 394, 529 A.2d 434, 450 (1987):

> The trial court held that the nursing home could refuse to participate in the withdrawal of the j-tube by keeping Mrs. Jobes connected to it until she is transferred out of that facility. Under the circumstances of this case, we disagree, and we reverse that portion of the trial court's order.

> Mrs. Jobes' family had no reason to believe that they were surrendering the right to choose among medical alternatives when they placed her in the nursing home. [ ] The nursing home apparently did not inform Mrs. Jobes' family about its policy toward artificial feeding until May of 1985 when they requested that the j-tube be withdrawn. In fact there is no indication that this policy has ever been formalized. Under these circumstances Mrs. Jobes and her family were entitled to rely on the nursing home's willingness to defer to their choice among courses of medical treatment. * * *

> We do not decide the case in which a nursing home gave notice of its policy not to participate in the withdrawal or withholding of artificial feeding at the time of a patient's admission. Thus, we do not hold that such a policy is never enforceable. But we are confident in this case that it would be wrong to allow the nursing home to discharge Mrs. Jobes. The evidence indicates that at this point it would be extremely difficult, perhaps impossible, to find another facility that would accept Mrs. Jobes as a

patient. Therefore, to allow the nursing home to discharge Mrs. Jobes if her family does not consent to continued artificial feeding would essentially frustrate Mrs. Jobes' right of self-determination.

Some state statutes governing end-of-life decision-making include specific provisions for situations in which health care professionals or facilities object to the decisions of patients (or their surrogates). See, e.g., Uniform Health-Care Decisions Act, below. The option to inform patients in advance of particular policies and then seek transfer is the most common compromise. Many states also have enacted statutes allowing such conscience-based actions by health care professionals in particular contexts, such as abortion and medically assisted dying. For a thorough discussion of this issue in the context of the pharmacist's obligation to dispense some controversial kinds of contraceptive medication, see Chapter 3.

4.    If we take seriously the *Bouvia* suggestion that hospitals have an obligation to provide comfort to patients who choose to forgo treatment and thus die, do physicians have an obligation to inform patients of the various ways of dying that are available to them, and the consequences of choosing any one of them?

Consider Margaret Battin, The Least Worst Death, 13 Hastings Ctr. Rep. 13–16 (April 1983):

> In the face of irreversible, terminal illness, a patient may wish to die sooner but "naturally," without artificial prolongation of any kind. By doing so, the patient may believe he is choosing a death that is, as a contributor to the *New England Journal of Medicine* has put it, "comfortable, decent, and peaceful". "[N]atural death," the patient may assume, means a death that is easier than a medically prolonged one.

> [II]e may assume that it will allow time for reviewing life and saying farewell to family and loved ones, for last rites or final words, for passing on hopes, wisdom, confessions, and blessings to the next generation. These ideas are of course heavily stereotyped * * *: Even the very term "natural" may have stereotyped connotations for the patient: something close to nature, uncontrived, and appropriate. As a result of these notions, the patient often takes "natural death" to be a painless, conscious, dignified, culminative slipping-away.

> Now consider what sorts of death actually occur under the rubric of "natural death." A patient suffers a cardiac arrest and is not resuscitated. Result: sudden unconsciousness, without pain, and death within a number of seconds. Or a patient has an infection that is not treated. Result: * * * fever, delirium, rigor or shaking, and lightheadedness; death usually takes one or two days, depending on the organism involved.

> * * *

> What the patient who rejects active euthanasia or assisted suicide may realistically hope for is this: the least worst death among those that could

naturally occur. Not all unavoidable surrenders need involve rout: in the face of inevitable death, the physician becomes strategist, the deviser of plans for how to meet death most favorably.

\* \* \*

To recognize the patient's right to autonomous choice in matters concerning the treatment of his own body, the physician must provide information about all the legal options open to him, not just information sufficient to choose between accepting or rejecting a single proposed procedure.

In the current enthusiasm for "natural death" it is not patient autonomy that dismays physicians. What does dismay them is the way in which respect for patient autonomy can lead to cruel results. The cure for that dismay lies in the realization that the physician can contribute to the *genuine* honoring of the patient's autonomy and rights, assuring him of "natural death" in the way in which the patient understands it, and still remain within the confines of good medical practice and the law.

    5.      Growing concerns that patients are provided more treatment at the end of life than they really want gave rise to the promulgation of the Right to Know End of Life Options Act in California in 2009 and the stronger Palliative Care Information Act in New York in 2010. Both statutes are designed to assure that patients are given all of the information they request (in California) or need (in New York) once they have been diagnosed as terminally ill. In California the Right to Know End of Life Options Act was opposed by Right to Life organizations and medical professional groups, which generally object to all statutory intrusion on the doctor-patient relationship. The stronger New York statute was opposed only by medical professional organizations, and it passed by large margins in both houses of the legislature. The New York statute is a simple statement of principle, more hortatory than enforceable:

## Palliative Care Patient Information

## New York Pub. Health Law § 2997–c

1.      Definitions. \* \* \*

(a)   "Appropriate" means consistent with applicable legal, health and professional standards; the patient's clinical and other circumstances; and the patient's reasonably known wishes and beliefs.

\* \* \*

(c)   "Palliative care" means health care treatment, including interdisciplinary end-of-life care, and consultation with patients and family members, to prevent or relieve pain and suffering and to enhance the patient's quality of life, including hospice care \* \* \*.

(d) "Terminal illness or condition" means an illness or condition which can reasonably be expected to cause death within six months, whether or not treatment is provided.

2. If a patient is diagnosed with a terminal illness or condition, the patient's attending health care practitioner shall offer to provide the patient with information and counseling regarding palliative care and end-of-life options appropriate to the patient, including but not limited to: the range of options appropriate to the patient; the prognosis, risks and benefits of the various options; and the patient's legal rights to comprehensive pain and symptom management at the end of life. The information and counseling may be provided orally or in writing. Where the patient lacks capacity to reasonably understand and make informed choices relating to palliative care, the attending health care practitioner shall provide information and counseling under this section to a person with authority to make health care decisions for the patient. The attending health care practitioner may arrange for information and counseling under this section to be provided by another professionally qualified individual.

Is this kind of a statute a good idea? Should other states follow the lead of California and New York? Writing in The New England Journal of Medicine just three months after the statute became effective, two New York physicians argue that legislation is the wrong way to address problems with care at the end of life:

> What is needed in such cases is not simply information, but an appreciation for the profound anxiety everyone feels at the border between life and death. In asserting power over the way in which deep and troubling human questions should be addressed—and showing so little interest in or understanding of the physician's experience—the New York legislature seems likely only to generate cynicism at the times when critically ill patients and their families are most in need of honesty, kindness, and engagement.

Alan Astrow and Beth Propp, Perspective: The Palliative Care Information Act in Real Life, (Topics: Public Health, NEJM, May 18, 2011). Are they right? Should the underlying question be one about patients' and families' experiences, physicians' experiences, or both? The original Right to Know End of Life Options bill introduced in California explicitly mentioned some alternatives about which patients should be informed in appropriate circumstances—for example, palliative sedation (described in the *Cruzan* case) and the voluntary stopping of eating and drinking. Political compromise required that mention of those specific alternatives be deleted from the bill. Would general language, like that in the New York statute, require that a patient be told of those end-of-life alternatives? Under what circumstances?

6. After the California Supreme Court confirmed Ms. Bouvia's right to choose to die, she decided to accept the medical care necessary to treat her pain and to keep her alive. She appeared on television (on "60 Minutes") in 1998,

where she expressed the hope that she would die soon. Why would someone seek judicial confirmation of a "right to die" and then not act upon it? Does it indicate that people waver on this issue? Does it suggest that knowing that one has the choice—when it becomes necessary—contributes to that person's well being? Are those who seek a judicially confirmed "right to die" really seeking control over their destiny, not their death? Ironically, the existence of a right to die may be the reason that some people choose to live, just as the existence of medically assisted dying may be a reason that many people choose not to ingest the lethal dose of medication they have been legally prescribed. See Chapter 6, below. For a discussion of related issues, see L.M. Cohen, M.J. Germain and D.M. Poppel, Practical Considerations in Dialysis Withdrawal: "To Have That Option is a Blessing," 289 JAMA 2113 (2002).

7.     Is it surprising that the fundamental principle that competent adults can make all of their own health care decisions has made it into the statutes of only a very few states? For an exception to this general rule, see N.M. Stat. Ann. Section 24–7A–2. Especially after the concern shown for this issue in *Bouvia*, one might expect more legislatures to have confirmed this right. Have they failed to do so because the law is so clear that legislative confirmation is unnecessary, or because there is a real dispute about the substance of the principle?

8.     It is not always easy to determine the wishes of a competent patient. In order to express a wish, the patient must be fully informed, but the very information that is most useful to a patient in deciding whether to forgo life-sustaining medical treatment may not be available, or the health care providers may not realize that it is relevant to the patient making the decision. One study set out to determine what kind of information is significant to patients making decisions about the removal of life-sustaining medical care:

> The provision of care at the end of life should honor patients' preferences. If these preferences are to be honored, they must first be understood. Our results suggest than an understanding of patients' preferences depends on an assessment of [1] how they view the burden of treatment [2] in relation to their possible outcomes and [3] their likelihood. The possibility of functional or cognitive impairment has a particularly important role in patients' preferences and thus merits explicit consideration in advance care planning.

Terri R. Fried et al., Understanding the Treatment Preferences of Seriously Ill Patients, 346 NEJM 1061 (2002). What information would be relevant to you in making decisions about end-of-life care? Do you think that this study was correct in determining the significance of possible functional or cognitive impairments? For an interesting approach to this issue, see D.E. Meier & R.S. Morrison, Autonomy Reconsidered, 346 NEJM 1087 (2002). For evaluations of these issues within particular medical specialties, A.K. Simonds, Ethics and Decision-making in End Stage Lung Disease, 58 Thorax 272 (2003) and C.O. Granai, What Matters Matter?, 102 Obstetrics & Gynecology 393 (2003).

### NOTE: COUNTERVAILING STATE INTERESTS USED TO JUSTIFY THE STATE'S DETERMINATION THAT PATIENTS MAY NOT REJECT LIFE-SUSTAINING TREATMENT

The right to choose to forgo life-sustaining treatment is not absolute, even for competent adults. In Superintendent of Belchertown State School v. Saikewicz, 373 Mass. 728, 370 N.E.2d 417 (1977), the Massachusetts Supreme Judicial Court first identified the four "countervailing State interests" that could overcome a patient's choice: (1) preservation of life; (2) protection of the interests of innocent third parties; (3) prevention of suicide; and (4) maintenance of the ethical integrity of the medical profession.

Although *Saikewicz* involved an incompetent patient who was born with significant intellectual deficits and had never been competent, the mantra of those four interests has also been applied in later cases involving competent patients—including *Bouvia*—but they have never been found to be sufficient to overcome the choice of a *competent* patient. You will see the state's interests discussed in almost every case in this chapter.

In *Saikewicz* the Massachusetts Supreme Judicial Court explored the significance of these four state interests and their limitations:

It is clear that the most significant of the asserted State interests is that of the preservation of human life. Recognition of such an interest, however, does not necessarily resolve the problem where the affliction or disease clearly indicates that life will end soon, and inevitably be extinguished. The interest of the State in prolonging a life must be reconciled with the interest of an individual to reject the traumatic cost of that prolongation. There is a substantial distinction in the State's insistence that human life be saved where the affliction is curable, as opposed to the State interest where, as here, the issue is not whether but when, for how long, and at what cost to the individual that life may be briefly extended. Even if we assume that the State has an additional interest in seeing to it that individual decisions on the prolongation of life do not in any way tend to "cheapen" the value which is placed on the concept of living, we believe it is not inconsistent to recognize a right to decline medical treatment in a situation of incurable illness. The constitutional right to privacy, as we conceive it, is an expression of the sanctity of individual free choice and self-determination as fundamental constituents of life. The value of life as so perceived is lessened not by a decision to refuse treatment, but by the failure to allow a competent human being the right of a choice.

A second interest of considerable magnitude, which the State may have some interest in asserting, is that of protecting third parties, particularly minor children, from the emotional and financial damage which may occur as a result of the decision of a competent adult to refuse life-saving or life-prolonging treatment. Thus, even when the State's interest in preserving an individual's life was not sufficient, by itself, to outweigh the individual's interest in the exercise of free choice, the possible impact on minor children would be a factor which might have a critical effect on the outcome of the balancing process.

\* \* \*

The last State interest requiring discussion[11] is that of the maintenance of the ethical integrity of the medical profession as well as allowing hospitals the full opportunity to care for people under their control. The force and impact of this interest is lessened by the prevailing medical ethical standards. Prevailing medical ethical practice does not, without exception, demand that all efforts toward life prolongation be made in all circumstances. Rather, the prevailing ethical practice seems to be to recognize that the dying are more often in need of comfort than treatment. Recognition of the right to refuse necessary treatment in appropriate circumstances is consistent with existing medical mores; such a doctrine does not threaten either the integrity of the medical profession, the proper role of hospitals in caring for such patients or the State's interest in protecting the same. It is not necessary to deny a right of self-determination to a patient in order to recognize the interest of doctors, hospitals, and medical personnel in attendance on the patient. Also, if the doctrines of informed consent and right of privacy have as their foundations in the right to bodily integrity, and control of one's own fate, then those rights are superior to the institutional considerations. 370 N.E.2d at 425–427.

In fact, these four interests raise issues beyond those discussed in Saikewicz:

(1) *Preservation of life.* If the value of the preservation of life is the very question faced by the court in right-to-die cases, does it make sense to define it, *a priori,* as a value that is countervailing to the patient's desire to discontinue treatment?

The nature of the state's interest in the preservation of life was discussed in the *Cruzan* case, in which it was the only interest advanced by the state of Missouri. The Chief Justice said that

> a state may properly decline to make judgments about the 'quality' of life that a particular individual may enjoy, and simply assert an unqualified interest in the preservation of human life to be weighed against the constitutionally protected interests of the individual.

---

[11] The interest in protecting against suicide seems to require little if any discussion. In the case of the competent adult's refusing medical treatment such an act does not necessarily constitute suicide since (1) in refusing treatment the patient may not have the specific intent to die, and (2) even if he did, to the extent that the cause of death was from natural causes, the patient did not set the death producing agent in motion with the intent of causing his own death. Furthermore, the underlying State interest in this area lies in the prevention of irrational self-destruction. What we consider here is a competent, rational decision to refuse treatment when death is inevitable, and the treatment offers no hope of cure or preservation of life. There is no connection between the conduct here in issue and any State concern to prevent suicide.

Not surprisingly, the dissenters viewed the state's interest in the preservation of life very differently. Justice Stevens objected to Missouri's policy of "equating [Cruzan's] life with the biological persistence of her bodily functions." He pointed out that,

> [l]ife, particularly human life, is not commonly thought of as a merely physiological condition or function. Its sanctity is often thought to derive from the impossibility of any such reduction. When people speak of life, they often mean to describe the experiences that comprise a person's history. * * *

Justice Brennan was especially offended by the notion that the generalized state interest in life could overcome the liberty interest to forgo life-sustaining treatment. One's rights, he argued, may not be sacrificed just to make society feel good:

> If Missouri were correct that its interests outweigh Nancy's interests in avoiding medical procedures as long as she is free of pain and physical discomfort, [ ] it is not apparent why a state could not choose to remove one of her kidneys without consent on the ground that society would be better off if the recipient of that kidney were saved from renal poisoning * * *, patches of her skin could also be removed to provide grafts for burn victims, and scrapings of bone marrow to provide grafts for someone with leukemia. * * *. Indeed, why could the state not perform medical experiments on her body, experiments that might save countless lives, and would cause her no greater burden than she already bears by being fed through her gastrostomy tube? This would be too brave a new world for me and, I submit, for our constitution.

497 U.S. 261, 312–14 n. 13, 110 S.Ct. 2841, 2869–70 n. 13, 111 L.Ed.2d 224. Chief Justice Rehnquist states in *Glucksberg*, Chapter 6, below, that *Cruzan* had decided that states may choose to act to protect the sanctity of all life, independent of any inquiry into quality of life, and independent of the value of that life to the one living it.

(2) *Protection of innocent third parties.* Does the protection of the interests of innocent third parties have any meaning if courts are not willing to force people to stop pursuing their own interests and to serve some undefined communal goal? Is it merely a make-weight argument in a society as individualistic as ours? On the other hand, might children, for example, have a claim on the lives of their parents? Under what circumstances would such a claim be strongest?

(3) *Prevention of suicide.* Although *Glucksberg* confirmed that a state could make assisting suicide a crime, committing suicide is no longer a crime in any state. Is there still a consensus behind Justice Nolan's position, dissenting in Brophy v. New England Sinai Hosp., 398 Mass. 417, 497 N.E.2d 626, 640 (1986), that "suicide is direct self-destruction and is intrinsically evil. No set of circumstances can make it moral * * *."?

(4) *Protecting the ethical integrity of the medical profession.* Finally, there is no longer any reason to believe that the ethics of the medical profession do not permit discontinuation of medical treatment to a competent patient who refuses it. See AMA Code of Medical Ethics Opinion 5.3, Withholding or Withdrawing Life-Prolonging Medical Treatment (2016). Even if there were, though, should the protection of the "ethical integrity of the medical profession" overcome an otherwise proper decision to forgo some form of treatment? If all other analyses point to allowing a patient to deny consent to some form of treatment, in what cases, if any, should the medical profession be able to require the treatment in the interest of its own self-defined integrity?

Are there special circumstances in which the interest of the patient ought not to be recognized or the interest of the state is especially important? Can the state require a criminal defendant to submit to medical treatment to make him competent to stand trial? See Sell v. U.S., 539 U.S. 166, 123 S.Ct. 2174, 156 L.Ed.2d 197 (2003), holding that forced medication may violate Due Process rights. Does the national interest allow the military to require its soldiers to undergo life saving (or other) medical care so that they can be returned to the front? Can a prisoner refuse kidney dialysis that is necessary to save his life unless the prison administration moves him from a medium to minimum security prison? See Commissioner of Correction v. Myers, 379 Mass. 255, 399 N.E.2d 452 (1979) (interest in "orderly prison administration" outweighs any privacy right of the prisoner to refuse dialysis unless he were moved to another site); People ex rel. Illinois Department of Corrections v. Millard, 335 Ill.App.3d 1066, 270 Ill.Dec. 407, 782 N.E.2d 966 (2003) (force feeding of prisoner allowed). For a general discussion of several courts' approaches to balancing a patient's right to refuse treatment with these countervailing state interests, see Alan Meisel & Kathy L. Cerminara, The Right to Die, 3rd ed. (2004, and, with Thaddeus Pope, the 2017 Supplement).

## PROBLEM: MEDICAL AND CULTURAL UNCERTAINTY

Mrs. Ayood, clearly pregnant, enters the emergency room wearing a traditional Niqab showing only her eyes. She appears distressed, breathing heavily, visibly sweating and clutching her belly. The receptionist is able to glean some basic information from Mrs. Ayood's husband despite the language barrier. There is no one else who speaks Arabic in the emergency room, while Mr. and Mrs. Ayood speak only Arabic and a very little bit of English. Mrs. Ayood is 41-years-old and has 4 other children at home. An interpreter should be arriving shortly, but it's clear that Mrs. Ayood's labor is already underway.

Her water broke, yet she and her husband remain seated in the waiting room, refusing to be admitted or otherwise move. They both seem scared. Mrs. Ayood begins to shift around uncomfortably and appears increasingly panicked, although she remains seated. Mr. Ayood will not allow any of the male staff to address his wife. A new receptionist, the only woman currently on staff, is able to approach Mrs. Ayood, and extends her arm as if to guide Mrs. Ayood into a nearby wheelchair. Mrs. Ayood holds on to the nurse's arm, but Mr. Ayood physically intervenes and prevents Mrs. Ayood from standing.

Security has been called and has just arrived, and the new receptionist is growing increasingly hostile to Mr. Ayood.

Once the translator arrives, Mr. Ayood explains that his religion forbids inter-gender medical treatment, although it's permitted under compulsion of necessity. Mr. Ayood is concerned for his wife, but he is a very religious man. He insists that his wife be attended to by a female doctor, but believes the hospital is obligated to save his wife in an emergency in any case. "I do not consent, but you have obligations," Mr. Ayood says through his translator. Mrs. Ayood continues to be verbally non-responsive and relies on Mr. Ayood to communicate for her, answering only him and speaking very quietly. It's nearly 3 a.m. and the only on-call doctor qualified to deliver the child is Dr. Chuck Robinson, a 45-year-old male doctor who responded to the emergency page, and dutifully reported to the hospital in under 30 minutes. Mr. Ayood becomes very concerned when Dr. Robinson came to the waiting room and approached Mrs. Ayood to care for her. Mrs. Ayood remains by her husband's side, apparently not willing to go to an examining room with Dr. Robinson, but her age and other risk factors warrant immediate medical assistance. The absence of such immediate assistance could pose a risk to the health and life of both Mrs. Ayood and her baby. Dr. Robinson calls you, the hospital legal counsel, because he is concerned with obtaining consent to administer care to Mrs. Ayood and with the potential liability facing the hospital for failure to act or provide Ms. Ayood and her baby with adequate access to reasonable care. What advice do you give him?

## APPLICATION OF THE PRESIDENT AND DIRECTORS OF GEORGETOWN COLLEGE

United States Court of Appeals, District of Columbia Circuit, 1964.
331 F.2d 1000, 9 A.L.R.3d 1367.

J. SKELLY WRIGHT, CIRCUIT JUDGE.

Mrs. Jones was brought to the hospital by her husband for emergency care, having lost two thirds of her body's blood supply from a ruptured ulcer. She had no personal physician, and relied solely on the hospital staff. She was a total hospital responsibility. It appeared that the patient, age 25, mother of a seven-month-old child, and her husband were both Jehovah's Witnesses, the teachings of which sect, according to their interpretation, prohibited the injection of blood into the body. When death without blood became imminent, the hospital sought the advice of counsel, who applied to the District Court in the name of the hospital for permission to administer blood. Judge Tamm of the District Court denied the application, and counsel immediately applied to me, as a member of the Court of Appeals, for an appropriate writ.

* * *

Mr. Jones, the husband of the patient * * * [s]aid, that if the court ordered the transfusion, the responsibility was not his.

* * *

I tried to communicate with her, advising her again as to what the doctors had said. The only audible reply I could hear was "Against my will." It was obvious that the woman was not in a mental condition to make a decision. I was reluctant [t]o press her because of the seriousness of her condition and because I felt that to suggest repeatedly the imminence of death without blood might place a strain on her religious convictions. I asked her whether she would oppose the blood transfusion if the court allowed it. She indicated, as best I could make out, that it would not then be her responsibility.

* * *

I thereupon signed the order allowing the hospital to administer such transfusions as the doctors should determine were necessary to save her life.

It has been firmly established that the courts can order compulsory medical treatment of children for any serious illness or injury, and that adults, sick or well, can be required to submit to compulsory treatment or prophylaxis, at least for contagious diseases, *e.g.,* Jacobson v. Massachusetts. [ ] And there are no religious exemptions from these orders * * *.

The right to practice religion freely does not include liberty to expose the community or the child to communicable disease or the latter to ill health or death. [ ]

Of course, there is here no sick child or contagious disease. However, the sick child cases may provide persuasive analogies because she was as little able competently to decide for herself as any child would be. Under the circumstances, it may well be the duty of a court of general jurisdiction, such as the United States District Court for the District of Columbia, to assume the responsibility of guardianship for her, as for a child, at least to the extent of authorizing treatment to save her life. And if, as shown above, a parent has no power to forbid the saving of his child's life, *a fortiori* the husband of the patient here had no right to order the doctors to treat his wife in a way so that she would die. * * *

[Another] set of considerations involved the position of the doctors and the hospital. Mrs. Jones was their responsibility to treat. The hospital doctors had the choice of administering the proper treatment or letting Mrs. Jones die in the hospital bed, thus exposing themselves, and the hospital, to the risk of civil and criminal liability in either case. * * *

[N]either the principle that life and liberty are inalienable rights, nor the principle of liberty of religion, provides an easy answer to the question whether the state can prevent martyrdom. Moreover, Mrs. Jones had no wish to be a martyr. And her religion merely prevented her consent to a transfusion. If the law undertook the responsibility of authorizing the transfusion without her consent, no problem would be raised with respect to her religious practice. Thus, the effect of the order was to preserve for Mrs. Jones the life she wanted without sacrifice of her religious beliefs.

The final, and compelling, reason for granting the emergency writ was that a life hung in the balance. There was no time for research and reflection. Death could have mooted the cause in a matter of minutes, if action were not taken to preserve the *status quo*. To refuse to act, only to find later that the law required action, was a risk I was unwilling to accept. I determined to act on the side of life.

## NOTES AND QUESTIONS

1.     The right to choose to forgo life-sustaining treatment is usually based upon the premise that a person rationally may decide that death is preferable to the pain, expense, and inconvenience of life. Given that the process of weighing the value of life and death is necessarily based in personal history, religious and moral values, and individual sensitivity to a number of different factors, and given that it finds its philosophical basis in the principle of autonomy, is there any justification for independent judicial evaluation of whether the balancing was properly, or even rationally, performed by the patient? In fact, the most difficult cases have arisen over decisions based upon the dictates of religious principles. For example, Christian Scientists generally accept the healing power of prayer to the exclusion of medical assistance—most Christian Scientists refuse most traditional medical care. Jehovah's Witnesses, on the other hand, accept most medical care, but they do not accept blood transfusions, which they perceive to be a violation of the biblical prohibition on the ingestion of blood. Should a court treat a Christian Scientist or Jehovah's Witness who chooses for religious reasons to forgo necessary care any differently than it treats Elizabeth Bouvia? Is it relevant that others consider the religious ban on the ingestion of blood or the rejection of all medical treatment to be irrational?

Because courts were less able to empathize with patients who had unusual religious beliefs than with others, for many years courts were less willing to entertain the right to forgo life-sustaining treatment on religious grounds than on other grounds. Are the arguments used to justify judicial intervention to require blood transfusions for Jehovah's Witnesses when such transfusions are necessary to preserve life persuasive examples of the social value of law and medicine, or are they unconvincing examples of the paternalistic heritage of both professions?

2.     The Jehovah's Witness belief that the ingestion of blood is prohibited finds its source in a number of Biblical passages. See Leviticus 17:10 ("As for any man * * * who eats any sort of blood, I shall certainly set my face against the soul that is eating the blood * * * "), Leviticus 17:14 ("You must not eat the blood of any sort of flesh * * * "), Acts 15:10 and Genesis 9:4. These passages cause Witnesses to believe that receiving blood products will render them

unable to obtain resurrection and eternal life. Is the fact that Biblical and religious scholars of other faiths reject the Witness reading of these passages significant? Should the courts ever engage in Biblical exegesis? Should the courts ever attempt to decide whether an interpretation of the Bible is correct, or even just reasonable?

Christian Scientists may be less likely than Jehovah's Witnesses to find themselves in litigation over their refusal of medical treatment because they are less likely to be at the hospital seeking medical care. Jehovah's Witnesses do believe in medicine, remember—outside of the use of blood; many Christian Scientists reject all medical intervention. For an account of the Christian Science position, see Mary Baker Eddy, Manual of the Mother Church, 17–19 (1935). Given the ability of eighteenth century medicine, it was likely that in its early days the Christian Science faith saved more lives than it cost by discouraging its adherents from seeing doctors. More recent literature suggests that today Christian Scientists do not live quite as long as others. See W. Simpson, Comparative Longevity in a College Cohort of Christian Scientists, 262 JAMA 1657 (1989).

Many other sects also believe that God will provide any cure that is appropriate for each sick person, and their actions pose the same legal and ethical problems as do those of the Christian Scientists and the Jehovah's Witnesses. In England, for example, the "Peculiar People" presented the British courts with this issue long before the first case arose on this side of the Atlantic. See R v. Senior, All ER 511 (1895–9).

3.    In *Georgetown College*, Judge Wright concluded that Jehovah's Witnesses were not required by their religious code to forgo blood transfusions; they were merely required to refuse consent to those transfusions. Thus, a weak denial was taken as a plea for medical intervention against the patient's stated, but misleading, request to be left without adequate care. Would the decision, based on this reasoning, vindicate the principle of autonomy? Is it appropriate for Judge Wright, in his role as a federal judge, to determine that the Jehovah's Witness faith requires only that an adherent deny consent to a transfusion, not that she avoid actually having one? Is it relevant that Jehovah's Witness religious authorities reject this position?

The other reasons for the court's decision in *Georgetown College* seem equally fragile. The hospital could hardly claim that the risk of civil or criminal liability would require the transfusion after the hospital went to court to determine its legal responsibility. This claim is better understood as one asking for resolution of the liability issues should the hospital follow or override refusals of transfusions in future cases. Finally, the presumption that anyone so ill as to need a blood transfusion to save her life is likely to be incompetent is simply unsupported by fact. The need for a blood transfusion is hardly sufficient to justify the literal infantalization of a patient like Mrs. Jones. These bases for the decision demonstrate why this opinion by one of the great federal judges of the last century has come to be seen as one of the most painful examples of judicial rationalization.

4.    Most of the cases that have considered this issue have concluded that competent adult Jehovah's Witnesses may choose to forgo medical treatment, whatever the results of those decisions may be, because the patient bears the consequences of choosing to forgo life-sustaining treatment. See, for example, Norwood Hosp. v. Munoz, 409 Mass. 116, 564 N.E.2d 1017 (1991), In re Brooks' Estate, 32 Ill.2d 361, 205 N.E.2d 435 (1965), In re Osborne, 294 A.2d 372 (D.C.App.1972). Compare Fosmire v. Nicoleau, 75 N.Y.2d 218, 551 N.Y.S.2d 876, 551 N.E.2d 77 (1990) (Jehovah's Witness mother permitted to forgo a blood transfusion during child birth even though her life was thus put at risk) and Raleigh Fitkin-Paul Morgan Mem. Hosp v. Anderson, 42 N.J. 421, 201 A.2d 537 (1964), cert. denied, 377 U.S. 985, 84 S.Ct. 1894, 12 L.Ed.2d 1032 (1964) (pregnant Jehovah's Witness not permitted to refuse a necessary transfusion).

Courts may be more disposed to recognize religious beliefs that prohibit forms of medical treatment when the courts are familiar with the beliefs (as in the case of Jehovah's Witnesses) and where there are a large number of believers who share the limitation. In In the Matter of J.M., 416 N.J.Super. 222, 3 A.3d 651 (Super. Ct. 2010) the Chancery Division of the New Jersey Superior Court was faced with an arguably incompetent patient who decided, inconsistently with the medical advice she received, that she did not need dialysis because "Jesus would save her." The psychiatrists split on her competence, but the court decided that her views were not based on her religion because there was no tenet of her religion that explicitly rejected dialysis and her evangelical pastor had attempted to talk her into accepting the dialysis. Her dependence on her view that Jesus would save her was thus not a religious view upon which a competent person could base a decision; rather, it was part of her delusional thought process. The court thus found her incompetent, transferred decision-making authority to a special medical guardian, and ordered that she undergo dialysis. Was that the proper analysis of that case?

Even when others (such as children) are indirectly affected, the courts now tend to recognize the competent adult's right to forgo treatment:

## PUBLIC HEALTH TRUST OF DADE COUNTY V. WONS
Supreme Court of Florida, 1989.
541 So.2d 96.

\* \* \*

The Court of Appeal has certified the following question as one of great public importance:

WHETHER A COMPETENT ADULT HAS A LAWFUL RIGHT TO REFUSE A BLOOD TRANSFUSION WITHOUT WHICH SHE MAY WELL DIE.

\* \* \*

The issues presented by this difficult case challenge us to balance the right of an individual to practice her religion and protect her right of privacy against the state's interest in maintaining life and protecting innocent third parties.

Norma Wons entered * * * a medical facility operated by the Public Health Trust of Dade County, with a condition known as dysfunctional uterine bleeding. Doctors informed Mrs. Wons that she would require treatment in the form of a blood transfusion or she would, in all probability, die. Mrs. Wons, a practicing Jehovah's Witness and mother of two minor children, declined the treatment on ground that it violated her religious principles to receive blood from outside her own body. At the time she refused consent Mrs. Wons was conscious and able to reach an informed decision concerning her treatment.

The Health Trust petitioned the Circuit Court to force Mrs. Wons to undergo a blood transfusion. * * * [T]he court granted the petition, ordering the hospital doctors to administer the blood transfusion, which was done while Mrs. Wons was unconscious. The trial judge reasoned that minor children have a right to be reared by two loving parents, a right which overrides the mother's rights of free religious exercise and privacy. Upon regaining consciousness, Mrs. Wons appealed to the Third District which reversed the order. After holding that the case was not moot due to the recurring nature of Mrs. Wons condition * * *, the district court held that Mrs. Wons' constitutional rights of religion and privacy could not be overridden by the state's purported interests.

* * *

The Health Trust asserts that the children's right to be reared by two loving parents is sufficient to trigger the compelling state interest [in protection of innocent third parties]. While we agree that the nurturing and support by two parents is important in the development of any child, it is not sufficient to override fundamental constitutional rights. * * * As the district court noted in its highly articulate opinion below:

Surely nothing, in the last analysis, is more private or more sacred than one's religion or view of life, and here the courts, quite properly, have given great deference to the individual's right to make decisions vitally affecting his private life according to his own conscience. It is difficult to overstate this right because it is, without exaggeration, the very bedrock upon which this country was founded.

## NOTES AND QUESTIONS

1.    A concurring opinion in *Wons* depends in part upon the fact that the children would be cared for by relatives even if Mrs. Wons were to die. In that opinion the Chief Justice points out:

The medical profession may consider a blood transfusion a rather ordinary or routine procedure, but, given Mrs. Wons' religious beliefs, that procedure for her is extraordinary. * * * [W]e must not assume from her choice that Mrs. Wons was not considering the best interests of her children. She knows they will be well cared for by her family. As a parent, however, she also must consider the example she sets for her children, how to teach them to follow what she believes is God's law if she herself does not. The choice for her can not be an easy one, but it is hers to make. It is not for this court to judge the reasonableness or validity of her beliefs. Absent a truly compelling state interest to the contrary, the law must protect her right to make that choice.

2.    The dissent in *Wons* depended in part upon another portion of *Georgetown College, supra*, where Judge Wright concluded that

[t]he state, as parens patriae, will not allow a parent to abandon a child, and so it should not allow this most ultimate of voluntary abandonments. The patient had a responsibility to the community to care for her infant. Thus the people had an interest in preserving the life of this mother.

Would this rationale support state intervention and an injunction to stop a mother (or a father) who had decided to take up hang-gliding, bronco-riding, working as a firefighter, or some other dangerous occupation? Why do you think it is applied in the case of a Jehovah's Witness, and not in any of these other cases?

3.    The rule allowing patients to adhere to their religious faiths, even if that means that they choose to forgo life-sustaining treatment, is different for children. The courts have always held that children are not permitted to become martyrs to their parents' (or their own) religious beliefs. Where the refused treatment is not highly invasive, and where it is likely to return the child to full health—as in the case of a blood transfusion for a Jehovah's Witnesses child—courts universally order the treatment. On the other hand, where the chance of success is lower—as in the case of certain kinds of chemotherapy for some childhood cancers—the courts are less likely to overrule the parents and the child. See section V of this chapter, below.

## IV.  HEALTH CARE DECISIONS FOR ADULTS WITHOUT DECISION-MAKING CAPACITY

### A.  DECISIONAL CAPACITY

#### PROBLEM: DETERMINING THE DECISIONAL CAPACITY OF A DYING PATIENT

Theodore Flores is a 27 year old who has been quadriplegic since a serious auto accident (in which he was driving while intoxicated) about a year ago. His spinal injury was so high and so substantial that he requires intermittent ventilator support, and he is fed through a gastrostomy tube that has been inserted through his abdominal wall and directly into his stomach. Although he has not worked since his accident, he had been employed as a pharmacist. He now communicates with others by winking his eyes or blowing through a straw connected to an alphabet board. The accident appears to have had no effect on his intellectual abilities, although he is now unable to concentrate for more than a few minutes, and he sometimes refuses to communicate to outsiders for days at a time.

Mr. Flores has now informed his physician that he wishes to have the ventilator disconnected and the feeding tube removed. His physician has informed him of the certainty that death will follow from either of these acts. Mr. Flores refuses to respond to such information, except to repeat his request. Mr. Flores has read most of the important recent medical journal articles about his condition, and his physician believes that Mr. Flores understands the risks, benefits, and alternatives more thoroughly than most similarly situated patients. Despite this, though, the physician is concerned about whether Mr. Flores has the capacity to decide to forgo ventilator support and nutrition and hydration. His concern grows out of several circumstances, including Mr. Flores's limited concentration span, his occasional unwillingness to communicate with anyone, and the following three factors:

(1)   A psychiatrist who has been seeing Mr. Flores regularly has informed his physician that Mr. Flores became seriously depressed about three weeks ago, when he began to realize that there would never be any improvement in his physical condition. As the psychiatrist pointed out, of course, most reasonable people would become depressed upon such a realization. The psychiatrist has recommended antidepressants for Mr. Flores, but he refuses to take them.

(2)   Since the accident, Mr. Flores has become a devoted follower of August Marsh, a religious leader who preaches that self-abnegation (and, particularly, self-abnegation leading to death) is the only way to gain salvation. In particular, Rev. Marsh believes that the self-discipline of starvation (he usually recommends a period of a week) can bring substantial and, perhaps, eternal joy.

(3)   Mr. Flores has always desperately wanted to father a child. His ability to contribute gametes to create a fertilized ovum is not precluded by his current condition. While the doctors have explained to Mr. Flores that his reproductive system is intact and unaffected by the accident, he insists that there is no way that he will be able to have children. No matter what the medical staff does, and despite Mr. Flores's generally sophisticated understanding of his medical condition, he does not understand how he will be able to become a father.

Does Mr. Flores possess sufficient decisional capacity to make the choice to forgo nutrition and hydration and ventilator support? What other information would you want to have before you make this determination? Remember, you are looking only for information relevant to a determination of decisional capacity, you are not looking for information that is relevant to the substantive decision. What process should be employed to make this determination? Is a court order required to confirm Mr. Flores's capacity? Incapacity? What kind of evidence should be introduced in the hearing that would lead to an appropriate court order?

---

To determine whether a patient can choose to undergo (or forgo) medical care, someone must determine whether the patient has the capacity to make that choice. Because the theory behind decisional capacity serves the social principle of autonomy, capacity determinations should not be entirely medical; social, philosophical, and political factors should also be considered.

Until recently, most courts that addressed this issue referred to the "competency" of the patient. In other areas of law, such as those concerned with guardianships and conservatorships, "competency" was often employed as a term with all-or-nothing consequences. A person was either competent for all purposes and at all times, or incompetent for all purposes and at all times. When we evaluate the ability of a patient to make a health care decision, though, we are dealing with something far more subtle. A patient may have the capacity to make some simple health care decisions, and not to make other more complex decisions. Similarly, a patient may be able to make certain decisions at some times but not at others. To recognize these potential variabilities in competency, many courts and legislatures use the term "decisional capacity"—a term which focuses on the actual decision to be made—rather than "competency"—a term which focuses on the status of the patient. The change has been recognized in the law of guardianship and conservatorship in many states, too. In this text, the terms "decisional capacity" and "competency" are used interchangeably.

Courts have been reluctant to articulate a standard for decisional capacity. There are few reported opinions in which courts state and apply any formal principle. Courts have been much more likely to finesse the issue out of the law and back into medicine by inviting physicians, especially psychiatrists, to testify about the mental state and, thus, capacity of a patient. Ironically, medical textbooks point out that the standard for capacity is a legal, not a medical, one.

For many years, physicians were likely to find that a patient had decisional capacity to make a serious medical decision whenever that patient agreed with the physician. When the patient disagreed with the physician—especially if that the patient's choice would lead to the death of the patient—the physician, and subsequently the court, would be likely to find that the patient lacked capacity and then seek out some surrogate decision maker more likely to agree with the physician. In reaction to this, and as a consequence of the frustration of attempting to develop any consistent and practical definition of competence, consumerist attorneys and physicians in the 1970s suggested that any patient who could indicate an affirmative or negative ought to be considered to have decisional capacity. Of course, this reactionary view is no more satisfactory than the previously prevailing view. Neither serves the purpose of protecting the individual personality of the patient and the authority of the patient to control his own life in a way that is consistent with his own values.

Despite the extremes described above, some scholars have attempted to categorize the possible tests for decisional capacity (or competency) that could be applied to patients of questionable capacity. Five different kinds of tests of competency were described in an early and influential article prepared by a psychiatrist, a lawyer, and a sociologist with extensive expertise in psychiatry. In Loren H. Roth, Alan Meisel, and Charles W. Lidz, Tests of Competency to Consent to Treatment, 134 Am.J.Psychiatry 279 (1977), the authors review the legal and medical literature and conclude that there are five different tests applied to determine if a patient is competent:

(1) Does the patient evidence a choice? This test sets the lowest standard for competency. If the patient can communicate a choice, the patient is competent.

(2) Is the outcome of the patient's choice reasonable (or "right" or "responsible")?

(3) Whether or not the outcome is "reasonable," was the choice based on "rational" reasons?

(4) Does the patient have the ability to understand the information that must be communicated as a matter of informed consent—the risks, benefits, and alternatives of treatment?

(5) Does the patient actually understand that information?

Would you find any one of these tests for competency to be satisfactory? Which one? Might you apply different tests under different circumstances?

Roth, Meisel, and Lidz suggest that each of their tests is influenced by the evaluator's analysis of whether the treatment would succeed—that is, whether the evaluator would consent for herself under the same circumstances. The authors conclude that where the benefit of treatment is likely to far outweigh the risk (i.e., the evaluator would choose to undergo it), there is likely to be a low standard for competency when the patient consents and a high standard for competency when the patient refuses. Analogously, where the risk greatly outweighs the benefit (again, of course, in the evaluator's mind), a low standard for competency will be applied if the patient refuses treatment, but a high standard will be applied when the patient consents. The authors point out:

The search for a single test of competency is a search for a Holy Grail. * * * In practice, judgments of competency go beyond semantics or straightforward applications of legal rules; such judgments reflect social considerations and societal biases as much as they reflect matters of law and medicine.

134 Am.J.Psych. at 283.

In what might have been the most successful endeavor to unpack the theoretical basis of decision-making capacity, in 1980 the President's Commission for the Study of Ethical Problems in Medicine and Biomedical and Behavioral Research articulated the three elements of capacity:

(1)  Possession of a set of values and goals,

(2)  The ability to communicate and to understand information, and

(3)  The ability to reason and to deliberate about one's choices.

President's Commission, 1 Making Health Care Decisions 57–60 (1980). Is this a complete list of the elements of capacity? Does the President's Commission approach serve the purposes that we require a patient to have capacity before we allow that patient to make health care decisions? As a practical matter, how easy is it to apply the President's Commission's test?

One case that squarely faced the question of whether a patient had the capacity to refuse life-sustaining treatment involved Robert Quakenbush, a seventy-two-year-old recluse whose gangrenous leg would have to be amputated to avoid a certain, quick death. He was rambunctious, belligerent, and "a conscientious objector to medical therapy" who had shunned medical care for 40 years. In deciding that the patient was competent, the court depended on the testimony of two psychiatrists and the judge's own visit with Mr. Quackenbush.

> The testimony concerning Quackenbush's mental condition was elicited from two psychiatrists. The first, appearing for the hospital, was Dr. Michael Giuliano. Dr. Giuliano * * * saw Quackenbush once on January 6. The doctor's conclusions are that Quackenbush is suffering from an organic brain syndrome with psychotic elements. He asserts that the organic brain syndrome is acute—i.e., subject to change—and could be induced by the septicemia * * *. [Dr. Giuliano] concluded that Quackenbush's mental condition was not sufficient to make an informed decision concerning the operation.

> * * *

> Dr. [Abraham] Lenzner [a specialist in geriatric psychiatry testifying at the request of the court] is of the opinion, based upon reasonable medical certainty, that Quackenbush has the mental capacity to make decisions, to understand the nature and extent of his physical condition, to understand the nature and extent of the operations, to

understand the risks involved if he consents to the operation, and to understand the risks involved if he refuses the operation * * *.

I visited with Quackenbush for about ten minutes on January 12. During that period he did not hallucinate, his answers to my questions were responsive and he seemed reasonably alert. His conversation did wander occasionally but to no greater extent than would be expected of a 72-year-old man in his circumstances. He spoke somewhat philosophically about his circumstances and desires. He hopes for a miracle but realizes there is no great likelihood of its occurrence. He indicates a desire—plebian, as he described it—to return to his trailer and live out his life. He is not experiencing any pain and indicates that if he does, he could change his mind about having the operation.

* * *

* * * My findings * * * are that Robert Quackenbush is competent and capable of exercising informed consent on whether or not to have the operation. I do not question the events and conditions described by Dr. Giuliano but find they were of a temporary, curative, fluctuating nature, and whatever their cause the patient's lucidity is sufficient for him to make an informed choice.

* * *

In re Quackenbush, 156 N.J.Super. 282, 383 A.2d 785, 788 (1978).

Did the court merely chose the more credible of the two psychiatrists, or did the court depend upon some intuitive conclusions that followed the judge's ten-minute visit with the patient? Which would be the more satisfying basis for the court's determination of competency?

To what extent do value judgments and prejudices enter into decisions regarding competency? Would the *Quackenbush* case have been a simpler one if Mr. Quackenbush were a retired lawyer leading a middle class life rather than a belligerent hermit? One fascinating review of "right to die" cases suggests that gender may be an important factor, and that the legal system takes the expressed wishes of men more seriously than those of women. Steven Miles & Allison August, Courts, Gender, and "The Right to Die," 18 L. Med. & Health Care 85 (1990). Stereotypes about the elderly and about dementia may also have an effect on evaluations of capacity by family members and doctors. For a discussion of evaluating capacity for these groups, see Jennifer Moye, Evaluating the Capacity of Older Adults: Psychological Models and Tools, 17 Nat'l Acad. Elder L. Attys 3 (2004).

How significant is it that terminally ill patients who seek a right to die are often depressed, or perceived to be so? Isn't it natural for someone dying of an incurable disease to be depressed? Two psychiatrists have suggested that physicians should attempt to treat depression in the seriously ill and those facing imminent death, but that psychiatrists also should recognize that some depression in terminally ill patients is not treatable, and that "[g]ravely ill medical patients should not lose their right to refuse medical treatment simply because they have been transferred to a medical-psychiatric unit. Just as internists must at some point decide 'enough is enough,' so might psychiatrists at some point appropriately stop trying to intervene and let the dying process proceed." Mark Sullivan & Stuart Youngner, Depression, Competence, and the Right to Refuse Lifesaving Medical Treatment, 151 Am.J. Psych. 971, 977 (1994). Do any of the suggested tests help you decide when depression renders a person incapable of making a health care decision? For a discussion of whether the decision of a terminally ill patient to hasten his death ought to be characterized as "suicide," see Chapter 6.

# B. ADVANCE DIRECTIVES

It is very difficult to serve the underlying goal of autonomy, if that goal is defined as personal choice, in patients who no longer have decisional capacity. One way to serve this principle is through the application of the doctrine of substituted judgment. Under this doctrine, a person, committee, institution or other substitute decision maker attempts to determine what the patient would do if the patient had decisional capacity. It may be possible to review the values of a formerly competent patient to determine whether that patient would choose to undergo or forgo proposed medical care. This can be done through a thoughtful analysis of the patient's values during life or through review of formal statements made by the patient when the patient had capacity. The most relevant considerations may be statements made by the patient about the proposed treatment itself. Indeed, such statements may provide the only *Constitutionally* relevant information about an incompetent patient's wishes with regard to life-sustaining medical treatment after *Cruzan*.

Of course, there is no way to know with certainty what the now-incompetent patient would do under the precise circumstances at the time the decision must be made. Some have argued that the doctrine of substituted judgment is too speculative to be applied reliably and that there is simply no way to protect the autonomy of a patient without decisional capacity. Where there is no possible method for establishing what the autonomous patient would do, bioethicists (and increasingly, courts) move to the second principle of bioethical decision-making, beneficence. In these circumstances, the alternative to serving autonomy is serving beneficence, and the alternative to the doctrine of substituted judgment is the doctrine of the "best interest" of the patient. As we shall see, the more difficult it becomes to decide what the patient would do if that patient had decisional capacity, the more likely it is that the court will apply the principle of beneficence rather than the principle of autonomy.

Although there are several kinds of statutes that allow competent individual patients to control some element of their health care when they lose decisional capacity, the most influential model statute within the United States is probably the Uniform Health-Care Decisions Act, which was adopted by the Uniform Law Commissioners in the early 1990s. Although it has not been fully adopted by most states, it forms the basis of several states' laws with regard to advance directives.

## UNIFORM HEALTH-CARE DECISIONS ACT

Uniform Law Commissioners, 1993.

**SECTION 1.    DEFINITIONS.** In this [Act]:

(1)  "Advance health-care directive" means an individual instruction or a power of attorney for health care.

(2)  "Agent" means an individual designated in a power of attorney for health care to make a health-care decision for the individual granting the power.

(3)  "Capacity" means an individual's ability to understand the significant benefits, risks, and alternatives to proposed health care and to make and communicate a health-care decision.

\* \* \*

(5)  "Health care" means any care, treatment, service, or procedure to maintain, diagnose, or otherwise affect an individual's physical or mental condition.

(6)  "Health-care decision" means a decision made by an individual or the individual's agent, guardian, or surrogate, regarding the individual's health care, including:

> (i)    selection and discharge of health-care providers and institutions;

> (ii)   approval or disapproval of diagnostic tests, surgical procedures, programs of medication, and orders not to resuscitate; and

> (iii)  directions to provide, withhold, or withdraw artificial nutrition and hydration and all other forms of health care.

\* \* \*

(9)  "Individual instruction" means an individual's direction concerning a health-care decision for the individual.

\* \* \*

(12) "Power of attorney for health care" means the designation of an agent to make health-care decisions for the individual granting the power.

\* \* \*

(16) "Supervising health-care provider" means the primary physician or, if there is no primary physician or the primary physician is not reasonably available, the health-care provider who has undertaken primary responsibility for an individual's health care.

(17) "Surrogate" means an individual, other than a patient's agent or guardian, authorized under this [Act] to make a health-care decision for the patient.

## SECTION 2. ADVANCE HEALTH-CARE DIRECTIVES.

(a) An adult or emancipated minor may give an individual instruction. The instruction may be oral or written. The instruction may be limited to take effect only if a specified condition arises.

(b) An adult or emancipated minor may execute a power of attorney for health care, which may authorize the agent to make any health-care decision the principal could have made while having capacity. The power must be in writing and signed by the principal. The power remains in effect notwithstanding the principal's later incapacity and may include individual instructions. * * *

(c) Unless otherwise specified in a power of attorney for health care, the authority of an agent becomes effective only upon a determination that the principal lacks capacity, and ceases to be effective upon a determination that the principal has recovered capacity.

(d) Unless otherwise specified in a written advance health-care directive, a determination that an individual lacks or has recovered capacity, or that another condition exists that affects an individual instruction or the authority of an agent, must be made by the primary physician.

(e) An agent shall make a health-care decision in accordance with the principal's individual instructions, if any, and other wishes to the extent known to the agent. Otherwise, the agent shall make the decision in accordance with the agent's determination of the principal's best interest. In determining the principal's best interest, the agent shall consider the principal's personal values to the extent known to the agent.

* * *

## SECTION 4. OPTIONAL FORM. The [form included in this Act] may, but need not, be used to create an advance health-care directive.

* * *

## SECTION 5. DECISIONS BY SURROGATE.

(a) A surrogate may make a health-care decision for a patient who is an adult or emancipated minor if the patient has been determined by the primary physician to lack capacity and no agent or guardian has been appointed or the agent or guardian is not reasonably available.

(b)  An adult or emancipated minor may designate any individual to act as surrogate by personally informing the supervising health-care provider. In the absence of a designation, or if the designee is not reasonably available, any member of the following classes of the patient's family who is reasonably available, in descending order of priority, may act as surrogate:

(1)  the spouse, unless legally separated;

(2)  an adult child;

(3)  a parent; or

(4)  an adult brother or sister.

(c)  If none of the individuals eligible to act as surrogate under subsection (b) is reasonably available, an adult who has exhibited special care and concern for the patient, who is familiar with the patient's personal values, and who is reasonably available may act as surrogate.

* * *

(e)  If more than one member of a class assumes authority to act as surrogate, and they do not agree on a health-care decision and the supervising health-care provider is so informed, the supervising health-care provider shall comply with the decision of a majority of the members of that class who have communicated their views to the provider. If the class is evenly divided concerning the health-care decision and the supervising health-care provider is so informed, that class and all individuals having lower priority are disqualified from making the decision.

(f)  A surrogate shall make a health-care decision in accordance with the patient's individual instructions, if any, and other wishes to the extent known to the surrogate. Otherwise, the surrogate shall make the decision in accordance with the surrogate's determination of the patient's best interest. In determining the patient's best interest, the surrogate shall consider the patient's personal values to the extent known to the surrogate.

* * *

## SECTION 7.   OBLIGATIONS OF HEALTH-CARE PROVIDER.

* * *

(e)  A health-care provider may decline to comply with an individual instruction or health-care decision for reasons of conscience. A health-care institution may decline to comply with an individual instruction or health-care decision if the instruction or decision is contrary to a policy of the institution which is expressly based on reasons of conscience and if the policy was timely communicated to the patient or to a person then authorized to make health-care decisions for the patient.

(f)   A health-care provider or institution may decline to comply with an individual instruction or health-care decision that requires medically ineffective health care or health care contrary to generally accepted health-care standards applicable to the health-care provider or institution.

(g)   A health-care provider or institution that declines to comply with an individual instruction or health-care decision shall:

(1)   promptly so inform the patient, if possible, and any person then authorized to make health-care decisions for the patient;

(2)   provide continuing care to the patient until a transfer can be effected; and

(3)   unless the patient or person then authorized to make health-care decisions for the patient refuses assistance, immediately make all reasonable efforts to assist in the transfer of the patient to another health-care provider or institution that is willing to comply with the instruction or decision.

(h)   A health-care provider or institution may not require or prohibit the execution or revocation of an advance health-care directive as a condition for providing health care.

* * *

## SECTION 11.   CAPACITY.

(a)   This [Act] does not affect the right of an individual to make health-care decisions while having capacity to do so.

(b)   An individual is presumed to have capacity to make a health-care decision, to give or revoke an advance health-care directive, and to designate or disqualify a surrogate.

* * *

**SECTION 14.   JUDICIAL RELIEF.** On petition of a patient, the patient's agent, guardian, or surrogate, a health-care provider or institution involved with the patient's care, or an individual described in Section 5(b) or (c), the [appropriate] court may enjoin or direct a health-care decision or order other equitable relief.

### NOTES AND QUESTIONS ON THE UNIFORM
### HEALTH-CARE DECISIONS ACT

1.     Should decisions to terminate life-sustaining medical treatment be treated differently from other kinds of health care decisions? The Uniform Health Care Decisions Act does not distinguish between life-sustaining medical treatment and other forms of treatment. Should it make that distinction and treat decisions that may lead to the patient's death differently from decisions that will not?

2. The Uniform Health Care Decisions Act does not defer to institutional ethics committees under any circumstances. Should it have been written to recognize and defer to an "ethics review committee," as the more recent New York statute does, at least in the most serious of cases? See Family Health Care Decisions Act, NY Pub. Health sec. 2994–d. Might the fact that these committees now have formal statutory authority enhance the status of hospital and nursing home ethics committees? Does it make sense to look to the courts as an alternative to a determination of institutional ethics committees?

## NOTE ON THE HISTORY OF ADVANCE DIRECTIVES AND SURROGATE CONSENT LAWS

*The Starting Point: Family Consent Laws.* Over the past century, it became standard medical practice to seek consent to any medical procedure from close family members of an incompetent patient. There is no common law authority for this practice; it is an example of medical practice (and good common sense) being subtly absorbed by the law. The President's Commission suggests five reasons for this deference to family members:

(1) The family is generally most concerned about the good of the patient.

(2) The family will also usually be most knowledgeable about the patient's goals, preferences, and values.

(3) The family deserves recognition as an important social unit that ought to be treated, within limits, as a responsible decision maker in matters that intimately affect its members.

(4) Especially in a society in which many other traditional forms of community have eroded, participation in a family is often an important dimension of personal fulfillment.

(5) Since a protected sphere of privacy and autonomy is required for the flourishing of this interpersonal union, institutions and the state should be reluctant to intrude, particularly regarding matters that are personal and on which there is a wide range of opinion in society.

President's Commission, Deciding to Forego Life-Sustaining Treatment, 127 (1983). It is difficult to determine whether the resort to close relatives to give consent is merely a procedural device to discover what the patient, if competent, would choose, or whether it is based in an independent substantive doctrine. Although it seems essentially procedural—the family is most likely to know what the patient would choose—many courts are willing to accept most decisions of family members even when there is little support for the position that these family members are actually choosing what the patient would choose. Of course, the assumptions about family relationships are quite optimistic. Consulting with family members also neutralizes potential malpractice plaintiffs; this factor accounts for part of the longstanding popularity of this decision-making process among health care providers.

Over the past twenty-five years some states have enacted formal family consent laws that authorize statutorily designated family members to make health care decisions for their relatives in circumscribed situations. These statutes often apply to a wide range of health care decisions (including, in most cases, decisions to forgo life-sustaining treatment), although sometimes they apply only when there has been a physician's certification of the patient's inability to make the health care decision. Sometimes they are limited to particular kinds of treatment (e.g., cardiopulmonary resuscitation) or exclude particular decisions (like discontinuing nutrition and hydration). In addition, family consent laws often provide immunity from liability for family members and physicians acting in good faith and judicial authority to resolve disputes about the authority of the family members under the statutes. The definition of "family member" and the position of each family member in the hierarchy vary from state to state. In some states those in a long term spouse-like relationship with the patient are included in the list of family members who can make decisions for the incompetent patient; in some states they are not. Some lists include a residuary class of anyone who knows the values, interest, and wishes of the patient; some states list the physician as the residuary decision maker; some provide for no residuary decision maker. Some states give a general guardian top priority; some states place surrogates actually appointed by the patient (whether family members or not) ahead of the general guardian.

***The Rise of Living Wills.*** Nearly two decades before the Uniform Health-Care Decisions Act was proposed, many people first became concerned about the potential abuses of powerful new forms of life-sustaining medical treatment. Frightened by the "treatment" provided to Karen Quinlan, whose life was thought to be sustained by a ventilator but who was given no chance of regaining consciousness, people began to search for a way to avoid a similar fate. Within two years of the first press reports of the *Quinlan* case, several states had adopted statutes that formally recognized certain forms of written statements requesting that some kinds of medical care be discontinued. These statutes, generally referred to as "living will" statutes, "right to die" legislation, or "natural death" acts, provided a political outlet for the frustration that accompanied the empathy for Ms. Quinlan.

The statutes, which still provide the only statutory advance directive in some jurisdictions, vary among the states in several respects. In some states living wills may be executed by any person, at any time (and in some states they may be executed on behalf of minors), while in other states they require a waiting period, and may not be executed during a terminal illness. In most states they are of indefinite duration, although in some states they expire after a determined number of years.

Some statutes address only the terminally ill, others include those in "irreversible coma" or persistent vegetative state, and still others provide for different conditions to trigger the substantive provisions of the document. In many states, living wills are not effective while the patient is pregnant. Some states require the formalities of a will for the living will to be recognized by statute, while other states require different formalities. Living will statutes that do not apply to those in persistent vegetative state, irreversible coma, or any other medical condition that may not be considered "terminal" are of no assistance to people in the position of Nancy Cruzan. Is there a reason to limit legislation to terminal conditions, or should such statutes be extended to other conditions where there is broad social consensus that patients should have the right to forgo life-sustaining treatment?

The statutes generally relieve physicians and other health care providers of any civil or criminal liability for withdrawal of treatment if they properly follow the requirements of the statute. A living will is always relevant as evidence of a patient's intent, although immunity does not apply unless the statute is followed.

Some of the statutes require that any physician who cannot, in good conscience, carry out those provisions, transfer the patient to a physician who can. The statutes also provide that carrying out the provisions of a properly executed living will does not constitute homicide or suicide for any legal purpose. It is hard to know whether the absence of litigation over the terms of living wills means that these documents are working well or that they are not working at all. Because health care providers were not used to seeing these documents and were used to making these decisions on their own, many were reluctant to accept and follow the instructions in living wills. Some health care professionals are still reluctant to carry out advance directives, even when they are clearly legally authorized.

Many living will statutes specifically exclude "the performance of any procedure to provide nutrition or hydration" from the definition of death-prolonging or life-sustaining procedures, and thus do not extend any statutory protection to those who remove nutrition or hydration from a patient. For the most famous example, see Vernon's Ann.Mo.Stat. § 459.010(3). After the United States Supreme Court decision in *Cruzan,* are such exceptions legally meaningful? Are they Constitutional? For an example of judicial avoidance of the unwelcome consequences of a nutrition and hydration exception to a living will statute, see McConnell v. Beverly Enterprises-Connecticut, 209 Conn. 692, 553 A.2d 596 (1989). See also In re Guardianship of Browning, 568 So.2d 4 (Fla.1990).

***The Next Step: Durable Powers of Attorney for Health Care.*** Another means of identifying who should speak for the patient when the patient is incompetent is to allow the competent individuals to designate a spokesperson or agent to act if the patient becomes incompetent. This may be accomplished through the patient's execution of a durable power of attorney, the most common form of advance directive available today.

Powers of attorney have been available over the past several centuries to allow for financial transactions to be consummated by agents of a principal. A power of attorney may be executed by any competent person. It provides that the agent designated shall have the right to act on behalf of the principal for purposes that are described and limited in the document itself. Thus, a principal may give an agent a power of attorney to enter into a particular contract, a particular kind of contract, or all contracts. The power may be limited by time, by geographic area, or in any other way. It may be granted to any person, who, upon appointment, becomes the agent and "attorney-in-fact" for the principal. At common law, a power of attorney expired upon the "incapacity" of the principal. This was necessary to assure that the principal could maintain adequate authority over his agent. As long as a power of attorney expired upon the incapacity of the principal, the power of attorney had no value in making medical decisions. After all, a competent patient could decide for himself; there was no reason for him to delegate authority to an agent.

In the mid-1970s it became clear that the value of the power of attorney could be increased if it could extend beyond the incapacity of the principal. For example, as an increasing number of very elderly people depended upon their children and others to handle their financial affairs, it became important that there be some device by which they could delegate their authority to these agents. For such principals it was most important that the authority remain with their agents when they did become incapacitated. The Uniform Probate Code was amended to provide for a durable power of attorney; that is, a power of attorney that would remain in effect (or even become effective) upon the incapacity of the principal if the document clearly stated that. There is no reported judicial opinion formally holding that the authority of a durable power of attorney executed under the Uniform Probate Code extends to health care decision-making. The President's Commission assumed, without any discussion, that it could be used for this purpose. See President's Commission, Deciding to Forego Life-Sustaining Treatment, 145–149 (1983). The vast majority of states have now adopted statutes that formally authorize the execution of durable powers of attorney for health care decisions.

Health care providers, who were uncertain about how to deal with living wills that were often ambiguous and rarely written with knowledge of the patient's eventual diagnosis and prognosis, were more accepting of the durable power of attorney for health care, at least in theory. Providers need a sure decision by a clear decision maker when they cannot get informed consent from a patient, and the durable powers allowed clearly identified decision makers to make exactly the decision that confronted the patient at any given moment. Durable powers, then, protected patients, who could appoint trusted family members and friends to make decisions, and physicians, who needed someone they could rely upon to be present and actually make the decisions.

Some state statutes now allow an agent authorized by a durable power of attorney to make health care decisions for a principal even if the principal has capacity—as long as that is the explicit desire of the principal. Why should an agent make a decision for a principal *with* capacity? Doesn't that undermine the principle of autonomy? Such a provision gives health care providers a surrogate decision maker to turn to in the case of a patient with capacity that is highly variable. Some argue that, in such cases, health care providers ought to be able to depend upon the consent of a patient-designated surrogate without doing a full competency analysis each time a health care decision is to be made. Of course, the decision of the surrogate can always be overruled by the patient herself if she has capacity.

The legal significance of a durable power of attorney for health care is defined by each state's durable power statute. In her concurring opinion in *Cruzan*, though, Justice O'Connor suggested that there may also be constitutional significance to a properly executed durable power of attorney:

> I also write separately to emphasize that the Court does not today decide the issue whether a state must also give effect to the decisions of a surrogate decision-maker. In my view, such a duty may well be Constitutionally required to protect the patient's liberty interest in refusing medical treatment.

497 U.S. at 289, 110 S.Ct. at 2857. She commends those several states that have recognized "the practical wisdom of such a procedure by enacting durable power of attorney statutes"; and she suggests that a written appointment of a proxy "may be a valuable additional safeguard of the patient's interest in directing his medical care." In the final paragraph of her opinion she points out that "[t]oday's decision * * * does not preclude a future determination that the Constitution requires the states to implement the decisions of a patient's duly appointed surrogate."

***The Development of the Uniform Health-Care Decisions Act.*** The Uniform Health-Care Decisions Act (UHCDA), excerpted above, takes a comprehensive approach to the issue by combining the living will (which is retitled the "individual instruction"), the durable power of attorney (now called the "power of attorney for health care"), a family consent law, and some provisions concerning organ donation together in one statute. Further, the statute integrates the current living will and durable power (and statement of desire to donate organs) into a single document. The UHCDA provides a statutory form, but it also explicitly declares that the form is not a mandatory one, and that individuals may draft their own form that includes only some of the kinds of instructions permitted in the unified form.

The new "individual instruction" can apply to virtually any health care decision, not just the end of life decisions to which living wills are typically applicable. Further, "health care decision" is defined very broadly.

The uniform act also makes the execution of the unified document very easy. It has no witness requirement, and it does not require that the document be notarized. The drafters of the proposed act concluded that the formalities often associated with living wills and durable powers served to discourage their execution more than to deter fraud. Despite this approach of the uniform act, most adopting states have added some execution formalities. Do you think that executing these documents ought to require witnesses, an oath, a seal, a notary, or some other formalizing act?

The residual decision-making portion of the Act is very much like the family consent statutes that have now been adopted in some states and this section of the act applies only if there is no applicable individual instruction or appointed agent. While it provides for a common family hierarchy of decisionmakers for decisionally incapacitated patients, it also provides that the family can be trumped by an "orally designated surrogate," who may be appointed by a patient informing her "supervising physician" that the surrogate is entitled to make health care decisions on her behalf. Thus, patients can effectively orally appoint decision-making agents who previously could only be appointed in a writing signed pursuant to a rigorous process. Thus, under the Uniform Act, a health care decision will be made by the first available in this hierarchy:

(1)   the patient, if the patient has decisional capacity,

(2)   the patient, through an individual instruction,

(3)   an agent appointed by the patient in a written power of attorney for health care, unless a court has given this authority explicitly to a guardian,

(4)   a guardian appointed by the court,

(5)   a surrogate appointed orally by the patient,

(6)   a surrogate selected from the list of family members and others who can make health care decisions on behalf of the patient.

The drafters of the Uniform Act make it clear in their comments that one purpose of the statute is to assure that these intimate health care decisions remain within the realm of the patient, the patient's family and close friends, and the health care providers, and that others not be permitted to disrupt that process. The court would very rarely have a role in any decision-making under this statute, and outsiders (including outside organizations) who do not think a patient is adequately protected have no standing to seek judicial intervention. See Protection and Advocacy System, Inc. v. Presbyterian Healthcare Services, 128 N.M. 73, 989 P.2d 890 (1999).

The Uniform Act explicitly provides that the decision maker (whether an agent, guardian or surrogate) should make a decision based on the principle of substituted judgment rather than the best interest principle. If it is impossible to apply the substituted judgment principle, the statute would allow the substitute decision maker to apply the best interests principle.

The Uniform Act includes the normal raft of recordkeeping provisions, limitations on the reach of the criminal law, assurances regarding the insurance rights of those who execute the documents, and restrictions on the liability of those who act under the statute in good faith. A provision for $500 in liquidated damages in actions for breach of the act may not encourage litigation when the statute is ignored, but the provision for attorney's fees in those cases might provide an incentive for lawyers to bring those cases. The act applies only to adults.

*The Values History and the "Five Wishes" Form.* Because it is almost impossible to predict exactly what kinds of medical care one might need and what kind of medical condition one will suffer, some courts and scholars have suggested that the most helpful kind of advance directive would be one that appoints a substitute decision maker (through a durable power of attorney) and then describes generally the principal's interests and values that are likely to be significant in subsequent decision-making over medical treatment.

One particularly good device for encouraging such discussion (and for recording the results) is the "Values History Form," which asks prospective patients about their general values, their medical values, their relationships with family members, friends, and health care providers, their wishes in particular cases, and a host of other issues likely to become relevant if they become incompetent and health care decisions must be made on their behalf. There is no doubt that the existence of such a document would be of great value to a substitute decision maker and to any court called upon to confirm that substitute's decision even though it doesn't carry the immunity provision or requirement of compliance that a living will does. See Joan McIver Gibson, Reflecting on Values, 51 Ohio St.L.J. 451 (1990).

In addition, over the past several years the "Five Wishes" document, a simple and easy to use advance directive that is arguably legally effective under the laws of most states, has become popular. The Five Wishes document, developed by the advocacy group Aging with Dignity, tells your family and doctors:

1.   Which person you want to make health care decisions for you when you can't make them,

2.   The kind of medical treatment you want or don't want,

3.   How comfortable you want to be,

4.   How you want people to treat you,

5.   What you want your loved ones to know.

Finally, over the past few years there has been considerable research on the efficacy of advanced directives generally and their value in particular circumstances—for example, when a patient is likely to suffer from dementia, or a patient's current mild dementia is likely to become increasingly severe. Several research and advocacy groups now offer particular advance directive language that might be useful to those dementia patients, as long as that language is also consistent with other state statutory requirements. See Paula Span, The New Old Age: One Day Your Mind May Fade. But You Can Plan Ahead, NY Times, January 23, 2018, at D5.

***Physicians' Orders Regarding End-of-Life Care.*** Health care providers remain inconsistent in their recognition and implementation of advance directives, even when there is no doubt about the authenticity or legality of the advance directive under local law. By custom, health care institutions and health care workers caring for patients rely on orders given by the health care professional responsible for the patient's treatment, not on documents signed outside of the health care system. Recognizing the strength of this custom, some patient advocates argue that the best way to protect a patient's interests at the end of life is to incorporate the patient's health care decisions into a physician's order. One particularly effective way of doing this is to incorporate those decisions into a Physician Order for Life Sustaining Treatment (POLST). A POLST (which goes by a variety of other names with other acronyms in other states—MOST, MOLST, SMOST, TPOP, or, in the Veteran's Administration hospitals, SAPO) may include information about a patient's decisions with regard to resuscitation orders, the extent of appropriate medical intervention, the use of antibiotics and other pharmaceuticals, the provision of nutrition and hydration, the desired place of treatment (home, hospital or nursing home), the identity of the authorized health care decision maker, and other relevant issues likely to arise in each case. Modeled on emergency medical services' DNR or DNAR ("do not resuscitate," or, more recently, "do not attempt resuscitation") orders, the POLST is a real medical order, signed by a health care provider—in some states it must be a physician, but in others it can be signed by other providers— with authority to issue that order. As a result, it is more likely to be implemented across health care settings: in the emergency room, at the rehabilitation hospital, in the nursing home, and in the field. It is designed to travel with the patient as the patient moves among these health care settings. An example of a POLST—this one called a "MOST" (for "Medical Orders for Scope of Treatment") and used by providers in Colorado—is reprinted below. For discussion of the development of this MOST and a useful discussion of the utility of the document, see http://coloradoadvancedirectives.com/most-in-colorado/.

**SEND ORIGINAL FORM WITH PERSON WHENEVER TRANSFERRED OR DISCHARGED**

### Colorado Medical Orders for Scope of Treatment (MOST)

- **FIRST** follow these orders, **THEN** contact Physician, Advanced Practice Nurse (APN), or Physician Assistant (PA) for further orders if indicated.
- These Medical Orders are based on the person's medical condition & wishes.
- If Section A or B is not completed, full treatment for that section is implied.
- May only be completed by, or on behalf of, a person 18 years of age or older.
- Everyone shall be treated with dignity and respect.

| Legal Last Name | | |
|---|---|---|
| Legal First Name/Middle Name | | |
| Date of Birth | | Sex |
| Hair Color | Eye Color | Race/Ethnicity |

*In preparing these orders, please inquire whether patient has executed a living will or other advance directive.*
*If yes and available, review for consistency with these orders and update as needed. (See additional instructions on page 2.)*

| **A** Check one box only | **CARDIOPULMONARY RESUSCITATION (CPR)**     ***Person has no pulse and is not breathing.***<br><br>☐ **Yes CPR:** Attempt Resuscitation     ☐ **No CPR:** Do Not Attempt Resuscitation<br>*NOTE: Selecting 'Yes CPR' requires choosing "Full Treatment" in Section B.*<br>*When not in cardiopulmonary arrest, follow orders in Section B.* |
|---|---|

| **B** Check one box only | **MEDICAL INTERVENTIONS**     ***Person has pulse and/or is breathing.***<br><br>☐ **Full Treatment**—primary goal to prolong life by all medically effective means:<br>  In addition to treatment described in Selective Treatment and Comfort-focused Treatment, use intubation, advanced airway interventions, mechanical ventilation, and cardioversion as indicated. Transfer to hospital if indicated. Includes intensive care.<br><br>☐ **Selective Treatment**—goal to treat medical conditions while avoiding burdensome measures:<br>  In addition to treatment described in Comfort-focused Treatment below, use IV antibiotics and IV fluids as indicated. <u>Do not intubate.</u> May use noninvasive positive airway pressure. Transfer to hospital if indicated. <u>Avoid intensive care.</u><br><br>☐ **Comfort-focused Treatment**—primary goal to maximize comfort:<br>  Relieve pain and suffering with medication by any route as needed; use oxygen, suctioning, and manual treatment of airway obstruction. Do not use treatments listed in Full and Selective Treatment unless consistent with comfort goal. <u>Do not transfer to hospital for life-sustaining treatment. Transfer only if comfort needs cannot be met in current location.</u><br><br>*Additional Orders:* _____ |
|---|---|

| **C** Check one box only | **ARTIFICIALLY ADMINISTERED NUTRITION**     *Always offer food & water by mouth if feasible.*<br><br>Any surrogate legal decision maker (Medical Durable Power of Attorney [MDPOA], Proxy-by-Statute, guardian, or other) must follow directions in the patient's living will, if any. Not completing this section *does not* imply any one of the choices—further discussion is required. *NOTE: <u>Special rules for Proxy-by-Statute apply;</u> see reverse side ("Completing the MOST form") for details.*<br><br>☐ Artificial nutrition by tube long term/permanent if indicated.<br>☐ Artificial nutrition by tube short term/temporary only. (May state term & goal in "Additional Orders")<br>☐ No artificial nutrition by tube.<br>*Additional Orders:* _____ |
|---|---|

| **D** | **DISCUSSED WITH** (check all that apply):<br>☐ Patient<br>☐ Agent under Medical Durable Power of Attorney | ☐ Proxy-by-Statute (per C.R.S. 15-18.5-103(6))<br>☐ Legal guardian<br>☐ Other:_____ |
|---|---|---|

**SIGNATURES OF PROVIDER AND PATIENT, AGENT, GUARDIAN, OR PROXY-BY-STATUTE AND DATE (*MANDATORY*)**

Significant thought has been given to these instructions. Preferences have been discussed and expressed to a healthcare professional. This document reflects those treatment preferences, which may also be documented in a Medical Durable Power OA, CPR Directive, living will, or other advance directive (attached if available). To the extent that previously completed advance directives do not conflict with these *Medical Orders for Scope of Treatment*, they shall remain in full force and effect.

*If signed by surrogate legal decision maker, preferences expressed must reflect patient's wishes as best understood by surrogate.*

| Patient/Legal Decision Maker Signature *(Mandatory)* | Name *(Print)* | Relationship/ Decision maker status *(Write "self" if patient)* | Date Signed *(Mandatory; Revokes all previous MOST forms)* |
|---|---|---|---|
| | | | |

| Physician / APN / PA Signature *(Mandatory)*<br><br>Colorado License #: | Print Physician / APN / PA Name, Address, and Phone Number | Date Signed *(Mandatory)* |
|---|---|---|

**HIPAA PERMITS DISCLOSURE OF THIS INFORMATION TO OTHER HEALTHCARE PROFESSIONALS AS NECESSARY**

Authority for this form and process is granted by C.R.S. 15-18.7: Directives Concerning Medical Orders for Scope of Treatment, enacted 2010.

| SEND ORIGINAL FORM WITH PERSON WHENEVER TRANSFERRED OR DISCHARGED | | | |
|---|---|---|---|
| **ADDITIONAL INFORMATION:** *Please provide contact information below, in case follow up or more information needed.* | | | |
| *Patient Legal Last Name* | *Patient Legal First Name* | *Patient Middle Name (if any)* | *Patient Date of Birth* |
| | | | |
| *Primary Contact Person for the Patient* | *Relationship and/or MDPOA, Proxy, Guardian* | *Phone Number/email/Other contact information* | |
| | | | |
| *Healthcare Professional Preparing Form* | *Preparer Title* | *Phone Number/Email* | *Date Prepared* |
| | | | |
| *Patient Primary Diagnosis* | *Hospice Program (if applicable) /Address* | *Hospice Phone Number* | |

## DIRECTIONS FOR HEALTH CARE PROFESSIONALS
### For more information, please refer to the "Getting the MOST Out of the Medical Orders for Scope of Treatment: Guidelines for Healthcare Professionals," www.ColoradoMOST.com

*Completing the MOST form:*

- MOST form master may be downloaded from www.ColoradoMOST.com and photocopied onto **Astrobrights® "Vulcan Green"** or **"Terra Green"** 60lb paper. This special paper is strongly encouraged but not required. Visit www.ColoradoMOST.com for a link to paper suppliers.
- The form must be signed by a physician, advanced practice nurse, or physician assistant to be valid as medical orders. Physician assistants must include physician name and contact information. In the absence of a provider signature, however, the patient selections should be considered as valid, documented patient preferences for treatment.
- Verbal orders are acceptable with follow-up signature by physician, advanced practice nurse, or physician assistant in accordance with facility policy, but not to exceed 30 days.
- **Completion of the MOST form is _not_ mandatory.** "A healthcare facility shall not require a person to have executed a MOST form as a condition of being admitted to, or receiving medical treatment from, the healthcare facility" per C.R.S. 15-18.7-108.
- Patient preferences and medical indications shall guide the healthcare professional in completing the MOST form.
- Patients with capacity should participate in the discussion and sign these orders; a healthcare agent, Proxy-by-Statute, or guardian may complete these orders on behalf of an incapacitated patient, *making selections according to patient preferences, if known.*
- "Proxy-by-Statute" is a decision maker selected through a proxy process, per C.R.S. 15-18.5-103(6). Such a decision maker may not decline artificial nutrition or hydration (ANH) for an incapacitated patient without an attending physician and a second physician trained in neurology certifying that "the provision of ANH is merely prolonging the act of dying and is unlikely to result in the restoration of the patient to independent neurological functioning."
- **Photocopy, fax, and electronic images of signed MOST forms are legal and valid.**

*Following the Medical Orders:*

- Per C.R.S. 15-18.7-104: **Emergency medical personnel, a healthcare provider, or healthcare facility _shall_ comply with an adult's properly executed MOST form that has been executed in this state or another state and is apparent and immediately available.** The fact that the signing physician, advanced practice nurse, or physician assistant does not have admitting privileges in the facility where the adult is receiving care does not remove the duty to comply with these orders. Providers who comply with the orders are immune from civil and criminal prosecution in connection with any outcome of complying with the orders.
- If a healthcare provider considers these orders *medically* inappropriate, she or he should discuss concerns with the patient or surrogate legal decision maker and revise orders only after obtaining the patient or surrogate consent.
- If Section A or B is not completed, full treatment is implied for that section.
- **Comfort care is never optional.** Among other comfort measures, oral fluids and nutrition must be offered if tolerated.
- When "Comfort-focused Treatment" is checked in Section B, hospice or palliative care referral is strongly recommended.
- If a healthcare provider or facility cannot comply with these orders due to policy or ethical/religious objections, the provider or facility must arrange to transfer the patient to another provider or facility and provide appropriate care until transfer.

*Reviewing the Medical Orders:*

- These medical orders should be reviewed
  - ○ regularly by the person's attending physician or facility staff with the patient and/or patient's legal decision maker;
  - ○ on admission to or discharge from any facility or on transfer between care settings or levels;
  - ○ at any substantial change in the person's health status or treatment preferences; and
  - ○ when legal decision maker or contact information changes.
- If substantive changes are made, please complete a new form and void the replaced one.
- **To void the form, draw a line across Sections A through C and write "VOID" in large letters. Sign and date.**

### REVIEW OF THIS COLORADO MOST FORM

| Review Date | Reviewer | Location of Review | Review Outcome |
|---|---|---|---|
| | | | ☐ No Change  ☐ New Form Completed |
| | | | ☐ No Change  ☐ New Form Completed |
| | | | ☐ No Change  ☐ New Form Completed |
| | | | ☐ No Change  ☐ New Form Completed |

HIPAA PERMITS DISCLOSURE OF THIS INFORMATION TO OTHER HEALTHCARE PROFESSIONALS AS NECESSARY

Colorado Advance Directives Consortium, www.ColoradoMOST.com                    2015

**WHO HAS LEGAL AUTHORITY TO MAKE A HEALTH-CARE DECISION FOR AN ADULT PATIENT?**

1. **THE PATIENT.** As long as an adult patient is competent (i.e., maintains decisional capacity to make the particular health-care decision in question), that patient has the authority to make her own health care decisions.

2. **THE AGENT.** If an adult patient with decisional capacity loses that capacity with regard to a particular health care decision, the agent appointed by that patient to make health care decisions when that patient was competent has the authority to make decisions on behalf of the patient. *(Note: an **agent** is a person specifically appointed, usually in writing, to exercise the authority of the patient. Under the Uniform Health Care Decisions Act, an agent has priority over a judicially appointed general guardian and any other **surrogate**.)*

3. **THE GUARDIAN.** If an adult patient has not appointed an agent, a guardian appointed by a court and generally authorized to make personal decisions for the patient is authorized to make health care decisions for that patient. *(Note: historically, and still in many states, the guardian's authority trumps the agent's authority)*

4. **THE SURROGATE.** If an adult patient has not appointed an agent, and no guardian has been appointed by a court, the patient's surrogate has the authority to make the decision on behalf of the patient. *(Note: a **surrogate** is a person appointed by operation of law – not directly by the patient – or, in some states, a person orally appointed by the patient when competent.)*
   **Who is legally authorized to act as a surrogate for a patient who needs one to make a health care decision?**
     a. The person orally appointed by the patient (by telling the "supervising" health-care provider under the Uniform Health Care Decisions Act).
     b. The patient's spouse *(This is universal, at least within the United States)*
     c. A spouse-like person *(In some states – language varies by state in pre-Obergefell statutes.)*
     d. Adult child
     e. Parent
     f. Adult sibling
       *(Note: There is some variation in this list by state, but very little.)*
     g. A residual decision-maker. *(This person varies by jurisdiction, but it may include the physician or institutional provider, the patient's spiritual advisor, and, most commonly, anyone the provider can find who knows the wishes and values of the patient and is available to make the decision.)*

   **What happens if there is no agent, guardian or surrogate authorized to make a particular decision?**
   If there is no agent, guardian or surrogate for an adult patient without decisional capacity, as a legal matter no one is authorized to make decisions and someone with legal authority must be created. This can be done by asking a court to appoint a guardian, by finding a relative close enough to appear on the surrogate list, or by creating a residual decision-maker. This last alternative can be achieved by finding a volunteer who is available and who agrees to learn the values and interests of the patient.

   **Does everyone really follow these rules?**
   No, but they should. Health care decision-making is often guided by formal policy, unstated and informal policy, the immediate needs of the patient or provider, and whim. In any case, there are other relevant principles that guide decisions in an emergency (see chapter 4), when research is being conducted (see chapter 21), and when the proposed treatment would be futile.

POLST forms are generally entered in the patient's medical record after the provider has discussed all of the relevant issues with the patient, the patient's family, the agent or surrogate authorized to make health care decisions, and others. The POLST form may include a summary of the values and goals of the patient that form the basis of the order, and the nature of the discussions that gave rise to the order. The patient or the patient's decision maker is often asked to countersign the order, so it is clear that it represents the agreed view of the patient and the provider. Sometimes the patient's (or the patient's representative's) signature is required; sometimes it is not. In some jurisdictions there is no place for the countersignature at all. In order to assure that these forms are not lost in the patient's chart, they are often printed on distinctively colored (usually bright pink or bright green) paper. Such orders can be recognized by state law (as they are in a many states), or by institutional or community policy.

The process of entering a POLST requires discussion among all of the relevant parties, and it provides a way of integrating a patient's advance directive and the physician's order. It does not trump a legally authorized advance directive, but it may make it easier for succeeding health care providers to be aware of advance directives made earlier by the patient; and it eliminates a provider's concern over the obligation to carry out an advance directive that appears to be inconsistent with an order of a physician. The POLST is usually filled out when the need for end-of-life care is imminent by those familiar with the current medical needs of the patient, and those factors may also account for the very high level of implementation of these documents.

Some people are concerned that the development of the POLST paradigm marks a return to the days of paternalistic medicine when it was the physician, not the patient, who decided the treatment to be applied in each case. Here, the provider's signature on the POLST effectively supplants the patient's signature on an advance directive, although the effect is ameliorated by the fact that the entry of a POLST requires a discussion with the patient or the substitute decision maker, and, often, that person's signature as well. Does the POLST require a patient to give up some level of autonomy that the patient might have had when making decisions through other forms of advance directives? Is the fact that the POLST really will be honored enough to get in return to justify giving up that autonomy? For a good account of the state of POLSTs in the United States (and Canada, and Australia, where similar concepts have developed) see Thaddeus Mason Pope and Melinda Hexum, Legal Briefing: POLST: Physicians Order for Life-Sustaining Treatment, 36 J. Clinical Ethics 353 (2012). See also, Keith Sonderling, POLST: A Cure for the Common Advance Directive—It's Just What the Doctor Ordered, 33 Nova L. Rev. 451 (2009) and Susan Hickman et al., Hope for the Future: Achieving the Original Intent of Advance Directives, 35 Hastings Ctr. Rep. (6) Supp. 26–30 (2005).

***Religious Objections to Some Provisions of Advance Directives.*** Some religious denominations have principled objections to facilitating certain decisions that might be made in advance directives. These objections are reflected in a range of state statutes because those statutes are products of political compromise. For example, as this note suggests, many states limit the applicability of advance directives when the patient is pregnant or when the patient wishes to reject some forms of nutrition or hydration. These limitations are consistent with the tenets of particular religious groups (although there are secular arguments to support them as well). Advance directive laws without these explicit limitations often include other "conscience" provisions which serve to relieve health care institutions and individual providers from taking actions which violate their own values. See section 7(e) of the Uniform Health-Care Decisions Act, above.

What should happen when a patient with particular values makes a decision that is protected by law in that jurisdiction but inconsistent with the religious values of a health care institution? What if the legally authorized decision maker (through a durable power of attorney) or the patient (through an individual instruction) requests that all artificial nutrition and hydration be terminated if the patient is in a persistent vegetative state, but the patient finds himself in a religious hospital that refuses to honor that decision? What if a patient seeking palliative sedation finds himself at a religious hospital that, as a matter of religious and ethical principle, will not provide that form of treatment? What if the family of a religious person seeks the continuation of nutrition and hydration as long as the patient remains in a persistent vegetative state, treatment arguably required by the patient's faith, in an institution that considers it to be a medically useless and futile form of treatment? Several advocacy groups now provide sample language that individuals can include in their advance directives to request that, if the patient must be hospitalized, the hospitalization take place—for example—in a Catholic hospital bound by the Ethical and Religious Directives (ERDs) of the Catholic Church, or alternatively, that the patient *not* be hospitalized in a Catholic hospital bound by the ERDs. Should providers be bound by that kind of request, on either side? Under the California Right to Know End of Life Options Act and the New York Palliative Care Information Act, must hospitalized patients be told of legal alternatives that might not be available at the hospital because they are not permitted by religious doctrine? Is it a violation of the First Amendment to require that those institutions provide care (or information about care) to which they have strong moral objection?

***The Patient Self-Determination Act and Advance Directives.*** The federal Patient Self-Determination Act applies to hospitals, skilled nursing facilities, home health agencies, hospice programs, and HMOs that receive Medicaid or Medicare funding. It requires each of those covered by the Act to provide each patient with written information concerning:

(i)   an individual's rights under State law (whether statutory or as recognized by the courts of the State) to make decisions concerning * * * medical care, including the right to accept or refuse medical or surgical treatment and the right to formulate advance directives * * * and

(ii)   the written policies of the provider or organization respecting the implementation of such rights.

42 U.S.C.A. § 1395cc(a)(1)(f)(1)(A). In addition, those covered must document in each patient's record whether that patient has signed an advance directive, assure that the state law is followed in the institution, and provide for education of both the staff and the public concerning living wills and durable powers of attorney.

A few states have also taken action to increase the utility of advance directives. For example, some states have central registries of advance directives, and a handful of states provide for drivers' licenses to show if a patient has an advance directive. At least one statute requires managed health care providers to discuss advance directives with their patients/enrollees. There has also been some attention given to how to make advance directives of various stripes enforced across state and provincial borders.

---

### DOCTORS HOSPITAL OF AUGUSTA V. ALICEA

Supreme Court of Georgia, 2016.
299 Ga. 315, 788 S.E.2d 392.

NAHMIAS, JUSTICE.

In March 2012, Jacqueline Alicea's 91-year-old grandmother, Bucilla Stephenson, died at the end of a two-week stay at Doctors Hospital of Augusta, LLC * * *. In May 2013, Alicea, acting as the administratix of her grandmother's estate, sued the Hospital and Dr. Phillip Catalano * * *. Alicea alleged among other things that they intubated her grandmother and put her on a mechanical ventilator, which prolonged her life when she was in a terminal condition and caused her unnecessary pain and suffering, contrary to her advance directive for health care and the specific directions of Alicea, her designated health care agent. The Defendants filed a motion for summary judgment, arguing among other things that the Georgia Advance Directive for Health Care Act ("Advance Directive Act" or "Act") [ ] provided them immunity from liability.

* * *

On November 12, 2009, Stephenson, who was then 89 years old, executed an advance directive for health care ("Advance Directive"), designating as her health care agent Alicea, the granddaughter with whom she lived. The Advance Directive specified that Alicea was "authorized to make all health-care decisions for me, including decisions to provide, withhold, or withdraw artificial nutrition and hydration, and all other forms of health care to keep me alive." The Advance Directive also said:

> My agent shall make health-care decisions for me in accordance with this power of attorney for health care, any instructions I give in this form, and my other wishes to the extent known to my agent. * * *.

Stephenson repeatedly told her family members that "she was ready to go when the good Lord called her," and said "when it's my time, it's my time, don't prolong it." She told Alicea specifically that "[s]he did not want . . . to rely on a machine to have to live," including a ventilator to breathe for her. In 2007, Alicea's 80-year-old father had died at the Hospital after entering it with pneumonia and without an advance directive or other document concerning end-of-life decisions. Because Alicea's mother had Alzheimer's disease, Alicea ultimately had to make the decision to take her father off a ventilator. Stephenson did not want Alicea to have to make that kind of decision about her. In the paragraph of the Advance Directive addressing "end-of-life decisions," Stephenson initialed the option that said:

> Choice NOT to Prolong Life.

> I do not want my life to be prolonged if (1) I have an incurable[ ] and irreversible condition that will result in my death within a relatively short time, (2) I become unconscious and, to a reasonable degree of medical certainty, I will not regain consciousness, or (3) the likely risks and burdens of treatment would outweigh the expected benefits.

[ ] Two years passed. Then, around February 28, 2012, Stephenson developed a persistent cough. On Saturday, March 3, she woke up lethargic; she was minimally responsive and had urinated on herself. After Alicea and her husband assisted Stephenson in sitting up, she became more aware, and they helped her to the bathroom to clean up. As Alicea was bathing her, Stephenson lost control of her bowels, and her eyes rolled toward the back of her head. Alicea and her husband feared that Stephenson was having a stroke and drove her to the Hospital's emergency room; Alicea brought the Advance Directive with her.

Blood tests and a chest x-ray showed that Stephenson was suffering from pneumonia, sepsis, and acute renal failure, and she was admitted to the Hospital. Alicea gave the Hospital the Advance Directive, which was placed in Stephenson's medical record, but not in the front behind the admission tab as required by hospital policy to ensure its ready availability to all doctors and hospital staff. Alicea also gave the Hospital her contact information, including her home, work, and cell phone numbers and her husband's cell phone number, so that she could be reached whenever she was away from the Hospital. Alicea has presented evidence showing that from the time Stephenson arrived at the Hospital, she was unable or chose not to make significant health care decisions for herself, triggering Alicea's authority to make those decisions pursuant to the Advance Directive.

Around 9:00 a.m. the next day, Dr. Catalano, a surgeon with staff privileges at the Hospital, called Alicea to tell her that he was taking care of Stephenson and that she was being moved to the intensive care unit ("ICU"). Dr. Catalano said that he planned to perform a computed tomography ("CT") scan to better assess her condition. Alicea did not object to the CT scan, but she told Dr. Catalano about Stephenson's Advance Directive and specifically instructed that "by no means was CPR [cardio-pulmonary resuscitation] to ever be administered" and that "no heroic measures were to be used" to prolong Stephenson's life.

[Another physician at the hospital] asked Alicea about ventilation specifically, and Alicea directed him to call her before intubating

Stephenson and putting her on a ventilator. [That physician] wrote twice in his progress note that Stephenson was "no CPR" and that Alicea had to be called "before patient is intubated."

On Monday morning, March 5, Dr. Catalano called Alicea and requested her verbal consent for a "surgical" thoracentesis to drain more fluid from Stephenson's lung cavity. * * * Dr. Catalano had not read the Advance Directive or the progress notes in Stephenson's medical chart; he did not tell Alicea, and she did not know, that this procedure would require intubation and the use of a ventilator. Had Alicea known that intubation was required, she would not have consented to the surgery. During the surgery, Dr. Catalano found that much of Stephenson's right lung was necrotic (dead tissue), and he removed two-thirds of the lung. Stephenson was extubated in the recovery room, and Alicea was not told that she had been intubated and put on a ventilator.

Two days later, on March 7, Stephenson was experiencing respiratory distress in the early morning hours * * *. Around 4:00 a.m., the nursing staff called Dr. Catalano at home. Dr. Catalano decided to have Stephenson intubated and put on a ventilator to prevent her from going into respiratory or cardiac arrest. A nurse asked Dr. Catalano if he wanted to call Alicea before ordering the life-prolonging intubation, but he rebuffed her, saying, "I'm not going to call her at six o'clock in the morning and scare the hell out of her. I'll wait till, you know, she wakes up and then I'm going to call her and tell her what happened." Dr. Catalano then spoke to the on-duty doctor and directed him to intubate Stephenson, telling the doctor, "I don't want her to die."[3] The on-duty doctor arrived at Stephenson's bedside * * *, performed the intubation, and hooked Stephenson up to a ventilator. No effort was made to contact Alicea before or after Stephenson was intubated.

When Alicea's husband stopped by the Hospital that morning around 8:00 a.m. to check on Stephenson, he was surprised to see her on a ventilator. He called Alicea, who was shocked by the news, and told her that the nursing staff could not find the Advance Directive. * * * It took the nursing staff 15 to 20 minutes of searching to locate the Hospital's copy of the Advance Directive, and one nurse remarked to Alicea's husband, "Boy, somebody has really messed up. I found it."

When Alicea got to the Hospital, she * * * held up the Advance Directive and told the doctor that her grandmother had expressed her

---

[3]    In his deposition, Dr. Catalano explained his thought process at the time as follows:

I'm thinking, well, I mean what's the worst. If the family does not want her on the respirator, well, we can just pull the tube out. And, you know, we've wasted an hour or two of her staying in the hospital ICU but, on the other hand, if we try to make calls she'd be dead. I mean I can't call the family. . . . I said, well, let's just do what's right for the patient. My God, we can always undo it. But . . . if the patient dies, you know, that's my ultimate loss. There's no way I can get her back. So when this happened I really didn't go into any of the code/no code/do not intubate/resuscitate. Save the patient's life first and then we'll do whatever it takes to make the family and that patient whatever, but we can't undo death. So that's what I was thinking.

wishes, which were contrary to what had happened, and that Alicea had specifically said to call her before putting Stephenson on a ventilator. * * *

Alicea asked [the director of the ICU] about possible next steps. He told her that she could decide to have Stephenson taken off the ventilator and extubated, which would cause her grandmother to suffocate and die (as had happened with Alicea's father), and that the only other option was to perform another surgery to clean out Stephenson's lung cavity more. Had Stephenson been allowed to die that morning, Alicea "would have understood that it was her time and God took her." Having been deprived of the opportunity to let nature take its course, Alicea consented to the surgical procedure and others recommended by Dr. Catalano and the Hospital staff over the next week, including the placement of a feeding tube, a bronchoscopy to remove pus from Stephenson's airway, and a tracheostomy to provide an alternate airway and to remove secretions.

On March 14, Alicea was informed that Stephenson's kidneys were shutting down and that she needed dialysis, and Alicea gathered the family at the Hospital to discuss the situation. * * * Alicea then authorized the removal of the ventilator and the provision of comfort measures only, and three days later, on March 17, 2012, Stephenson died.

[ ] On May 14, 2013, Alicea, acting as the administratrix of Stephenson's estate, filed a complaint against the Hospital and Dr. Catalano, raising claims of breach of agreement, professional and ordinary negligence, medical battery, intentional infliction of emotional distress, and breach of fiduciary duty. The Hospital's alleged liability was based on respondeat superior for the actions of its agents and employees. The complaint alleged that Dr. Catalano and other medical personnel associated with the Hospital had subjected the terminally ill Stephenson to unnecessary medical procedures, in particular her intubation and placement on a ventilator on * * * in violation of her Advance Directive and the directions of Alicea as her designated health care agent.

In support of her claims, Alicea relied on an expert on gerontology, geriatrics, and palliative care. The expert concluded that when Stephenson arrived at the Hospital on March 4, she already "had an incurable and irreversible condition that was likely to result in her death within a relatively short period of time thereafter," and that "her condition was such that the likely risk and burdens of any invasive procedures and treatment outweighed any expected benefits." Consequently, the expert opined that the Defendants were required under the standard of care to refrain from taking steps to prolong her life in accordance with her Advance Directive as well as the instructions of Alicea, her designated health care agent. According to Alicea's expert, Dr. Catalano breached the standard of care by, among other things, failing to review Stephenson's Advance Directive and the progress notes in her medical chart to determine if Alicea had given any directions for Stephenson's care and by failing to obtain basic consent from Alicea before the March 7 intubation. The expert further opined that the nurses employed by the Hospital had violated the standard of care by failing to contact Alicea before the March 7 intubation and failing to call Dr. Catalano's attention to Stephenson's Advance Directive and the notation in the progress notes regarding intubation.

[T]he Defendants filed a motion for summary judgment, contending among other things that they were immune from liability based on the March 7 surgical procedure under [the provisions of the Georgia Advance Directive Act].

* * *

[ ] The Defendants argue that the Court of Appeals misconstrued the Advance Directive Act as requiring health care providers to act in "good faith reliance" on the designated health care agent's directions and decisions in order to qualify for the immunity from civil liability [ ]. Our rejection of this argument depends in part on our understanding of the Act's overall purpose and operation, so we will [first] outline those features before turning to a detailed examination of [the statute].

(a)  In 2007, the General Assembly enacted the statute * * *. As the uncodified first section of the 2007 statute explained:

> The General Assembly has long recognized the right of the individual to control all aspects of his or her personal care and medical treatment, including the right to insist upon medical treatment, decline medical treatment, or direct that medical treatment be withdrawn.

[ ] Thus,

> the clear expression of an individual's decisions regarding health care, whether made by the individual or an agent appointed by the individual, is of critical importance not only to citizens but also to the health care and legal communities, third parties, and families.

* * * Thus, a clear objective of the Act is to ensure that in making decisions about a patient's health care, it is the will of the patient or her designated agent, and not the will of the health care provider, that controls.

* * *

The Act * * * sets forth several rules for how decisions are to be made in caring for a patient with an advance directive. If the patient's attending physician determines in good faith that the patient is able to understand the general nature of the health care procedure being consented to or refused, the patient's own decision about that procedure prevails over contrary instructions by a health care agent. * * * However,

[w]henever a health care provider believes a declarant is unable to understand the general nature of the health care procedure which the provider deems necessary, the health care provider shall consult with any available health care agent known to the health care provider who then has power to act for the declarant under an advance directive for health care.

\* \* \*

The health care decision now at issue in this case is the decision that needed to be made on March 7, 2012, about whether Stephenson should be intubated and put on a ventilator to prolong her life. Stephenson was unable to, and clearly did not, make that decision for herself, so Alicea had the authority to make that decision for Stephenson under her Advance Directive, which Alicea had given to the Hospital's staff and had discussed with them and with Dr. Catalano. With respect to the duties of "[e]ach health care provider and each other person with whom a health care agent interacts under an advance directive for health care" in this situation, the Act says the following [ ]:

> A health care decision made by a health care agent in accordance with the terms of an advance directive for health care shall be complied with by every health care provider to whom the decision is communicated, subject to the health care provider's right to administer treatment for the [patient's] comfort or alleviation of pain; provided, however, that if the health care provider is unwilling to comply with the health care agent's decision, the health care provider shall promptly inform the health care agent who shall then be responsible for arranging for the [patient's] transfer to another health care provider. A health care provider who is unwilling to comply with the health care agent's decision shall provide reasonably necessary consultation and care in connection with the pending transfer.

Thus, a health care provider in this situation generally must comply with the health care agent's decision, with two exceptions. The first, not pertinent here, is as to pain treatment. The second recognizes that the provider may be "unwilling" to comply with the agent's decision, on medical, moral, or other grounds. But the unwilling provider is not entitled to then make the health care decision for the patient himself, or to just walk away. The Act requires such a provider to "promptly inform" the agent of his unwillingness to comply and also to "provide reasonably necessary consultation and care" in connection with the transfer of the patient to another care-giver as arranged by the agent—presumably a transfer to a provider (who may be in the same facility) who will comply with the agent's decision.

The Advance Directive Act then includes a series of immunity provisions [ ]. The Defendants seek to rely [first, on] a general release of liability for

> [e]ach health care provider, health care facility, and any other person who acts in good faith reliance on any direction or decision by the health care agent . . . to the same extent as though such person had interacted directly with the declarant as a fully competent person.

The Act then says:

> Without limiting the generality of the foregoing, the following specific provisions shall also govern, protect, and validate the acts of the health care agent and each such health care provider, health care facility, and any other person acting in good faith reliance on such direction or decision: . . . .

After the colon come five specific immunity provisions.[ ]

The first three of these statutory immunity provisions, it is important to recognize, mirror the statutory duties imposed on health care providers by [the statute]. Corresponding to the first clause [ ] which requires that "[a] health care decision made by a health care agent in accordance with the terms of an advance directive for health care shall be complied with by every health care provider to whom the decision is communicated," [the statute] grants providers immunity from civil or criminal liability or professional discipline "solely for complying with any direction or decision by the health care agent, even if death or injury to the declarant ensues." And corresponding to the proviso [ ] for health care providers who are "unwilling to comply with the health care agent's decision," [the statute] give such providers similarly broad immunity—so long as they promptly inform the agent of the "refusal or failure" to comply with the agent's direction or decision and assist with the patient's continued care to the extent of continuing to provide reasonably necessary consultation and care in connection with a pending transfer of the patient, acting substantially in accord with reasonable medical standards, and cooperating in any transfer of the patient as authorized by [the statute itself].

\* \* \*

[O]nly health care providers who act in good faith reliance on the agent's directions are entitled to immunity [ ], the introductory clause speaks of "each such health care provider . . . acting in good faith reliance on such direction or decision"—the "such" referring back to the providers discussed in the preceding general-release sentence, that is, "[e]ach health care provider who acts in good faith reliance on any direction or decision by the health care agent."

\* \* \*

The [statute] plainly authorizes a health care provider to make no effort to comply with an agent's direction—to refuse or fail entirely to comply—so long as the provider promptly informs the agent of that choice and takes the other steps of care and cooperation that the Act requires. * * * What is critical, in our view, is that a provider claiming to have acted in "good faith reliance" on the agent's direction or decision can show that he acted in dependence on that direction or decision, not without reference to the agent's wishes. * * *

Recall that a primary purpose of the Advance Directive Act is to ensure that in making decisions about a patient's health care, it is the will of the patient or her designated agent, rather than the will of the health care provider, that controls. OCGA § 31–32–8 (1) enforces this purpose by declaring that a health care provider who

> believes a declarant is unable to understand the general nature of the health care procedure which the provider deems necessary . . . shall consult with any available health care agent known to the health care provider who then has power to act for the declarant under an advance directive for health care.

If a provider is aware of what the agent has decided, and then proceeds as the statute mandates [ ]—either by complying with that decision or by taking the steps required when he is unwilling to comply with the decision—then he may look to the immunity provisions [ ] for protection. But a provider cannot claim this immunity when his action was not based in good faith on the agent's direction, just because the decision he made for the patient happens to be one that arguably complied or failed to comply with what the agent would have decided. * * *

* * * The health care decision in question is the decision to intubate Stephenson and put her on a ventilator as a life-prolonging measure around 4:00 a.m. on the morning of March 7, 2012. Although there is evidence to the contrary, there is ample evidence that in ordering that procedure, Dr. Catalano was not acting in good faith reliance—in honest dependence—on any decision Alicea had made as Stephenson's health care agent, either to comply with it or to refuse or fail to comply with it and then promptly inform Alicea of his unwillingness. Instead, the evidence would support a finding that Dr. Catalano made the health care decision himself, in the exercise of his own medical and personal judgment. * * *

[T]he Advance Directive Act is all about letting patients and their health care agents, rather than the health care provider, control such decisions. * * *

Because there is at least a disputed issue of fact as to whether Dr. Catalano acted with good faith reliance on any decision made by his patient's health care agent, Dr. Catalano cannot on motion for summary judgment claim the immunity that [is available] to providers who honestly depend on such a decision to either comply with it or promptly inform the patient that they are unwilling to comply with it. Likewise, the Hospital points to no evidence that its staff acted based on a decision by Alicea with respect to the March 7 intubation; when Dr. Catalano made the decision himself, the staff simply proceeded based on his directive.

## NOTES AND QUESTIONS

1.     In this case, the matter was settled just before the trial was scheduled to begin in 2017. One report suggests the plaintiff originally sought $200,000 to compensate for additional medical expenses, and also punitive damages and attorneys' fees. In fact, the case settled for about $1,000,000. While normally the settlement figure itself would be kept confidential by agreement of the parties, in this case the plaintiffs insisted that the amount be made public so that it would serve as a warning to other physicians and institutions in Georgia who might be tempted to ignore agents and advance directives. See S. Hodson, Hospital Settles Lawsuit Failing to Honor Patient's Wishes on Extending Life, Augusta Chronicle, May 25, 2017 . See also Paula Span, The New Old Age: The Patient was Saved. That's Why the Families Are Suing, New York Times, April 10, 2017. While the *Alicea* case is one of the rare reported cases suggesting damages are available to improperly "saved" patients, there are several other cases that have recognized wrongful prolongation of life claims.

2.     Should damages that are accrued because physicians ignore agents be assessed in the same way as damages that are accrued because physicians ignore patients themselves? Should damages that accrue from the failure of a hospital to follow a POLST be treated just like damages that accrue because physicians ignore agents and patients? See Paula Span, supra note 2.

The Georgia statute authorizing agents to make decisions for incompetent patients in this case is based on the Uniform Health Care Decisions Act, supra in this chapter. Would you expect the same rule on damages to apply in other states that have adopted this form of that Uniform Act? Should the Uniform Act be amended to explicitly provide that damages are available under these circumstances?

3.     The Georgia Supreme Court suggests that the hospital is liable in this case because it is vicariously liable for the acts of the physicians. Is that always true? Are the physicians here agents of the hospital? Apparent or ostensible agents of the hospital? Might the hospital be directly liable for not enforcing its policy on the placement of advance directives at the front of the patient chart? Might the hospital be liable for not having an adequate policy recognizing the decision-making authority of agents and surrogate?

4.     When a physician or an institution ignores the request of a patient, agent or surrogate, does that automatically create an informed consent action on behalf of the patient? Are informed consent damages different from other damages (like ordinary tort damages or medical malpractice damages) that might be awarded to a patient under these circumstances?

5.     This case focused on the meaning of the immunity provision in the statute. Is that provision necessary? Why do you think it was included in the statute? If there is no liability in any case, why would a provider have to worry about immunity?

## C. DECISION-MAKING IN THE ABSENCE OF ADVANCE DIRECTIVES OR STATUTORILY DESIGNATED SURROGATES

### IN RE EICHNER
New York Court of Appeals, 1981.
52 N.Y.2d 363, 438 N.Y.S.2d 266, 420 N.E.2d 64.

WACHTLER, JUDGE.

For over 66 years Brother Joseph Fox was a member of the Society of Mary, a Catholic religious order which, among other things, operates Chaminade High School in Mineola. * * *

While [an] operation was being performed * * * he suffered cardiac arrest, with resulting loss of oxygen to the brain and substantial brain damage. He lost the ability to breathe spontaneously and was placed on a respirator which maintained him in a vegetative state. The attending physicians informed Father Philip Eichner, who was the president of Chaminade and the director of the society at the school, that there was no reasonable chance of recovery and that Brother Fox would die in that state.

After retaining two neurosurgeons who confirmed the diagnosis, Father Eichner requested the hospital to remove the respirator. The hospital, however, refused to do so without court authorization. Father Eichner then applied * * * to be appointed committee of the person and property of Brother Fox, with authority to direct removal of the respirator. The application was supported by the patient's 10 nieces and nephews, his only surviving relatives. The court appointed a guardian ad litem and directed that notice be served on various parties, including the District Attorney.

At the hearing the District Attorney opposed the application and called medical experts to show that there might be some improvement in the patient's condition. All the experts agreed, however, that there was no reasonable likelihood that Brother Fox would ever emerge from the vegetative coma or recover his cognitive powers.

There was also evidence, submitted by the petitioner, that before the operation rendered him incompetent the patient had made it known that under these circumstances he would want a respirator removed. Brother Fox had first expressed this view in 1976 when the Chaminade community discussed the moral implications of the celebrated *Karen Ann Quinlan* case, in which the parents of a 19-year-old New Jersey girl who was in a vegetative coma requested the hospital to remove the respirator [ ]. These were formal discussions prompted by Chaminade's mission to teach and promulgate Catholic moral principles. At that time it was noted that the Pope had stated that Catholic principles permitted the termination of extraordinary life support systems when there is no reasonable hope for the patient's recovery and that church officials in New Jersey had concluded that use of the respirator in the *Quinlan* case constituted an extraordinary measure under the circumstances. Brother Fox expressed agreement with those views and stated that he would not want any of this "extraordinary business" done for him under those circumstances. Several years later, and only a couple of months before his final hospitalization, Brother Fox again stated that he would not want his life prolonged by such measures if his condition were hopeless.

\* \* \*

In this case the proof was compelling. There was no suggestion that the witnesses who testified for the petitioner had any motive other than to see that Brother Fox' stated wishes were respected. The finding that he carefully reflected on the subject, expressed his views and concluded not to have his life prolonged by medical means if there were no hope of recovery is supported by his religious beliefs and is not inconsistent with his life of unselfish religious devotion. These were obviously solemn pronouncements and not casual remarks made at some social gathering, nor can it be said that he was too young to realize or feel the consequences of his statements [ ]. That this was a persistent commitment is evidenced by the fact that he reiterated the decision but two months before his final hospitalization. There was, of course, no need to speculate as to whether he would want this particular medical procedure to be discontinued under these circumstances. What occurred to him was identical to what happened in the *Karen Ann Quinlan* case, which had originally prompted his decision. In sum, the evidence clearly and convincingly shows that Brother Fox did not want to be maintained in a vegetative coma by use of a respirator.

\* \* \*

## NOTES AND QUESTIONS

1. The Illinois Supreme Court described the principle of substituted judgment clearly and simply:

> Under substituted judgment, a surrogate decisionmaker attempts to establish, with as much accuracy as possible, what decision the patient would make if he were competent to do so. Employing this theory, the surrogate first tries to determine if the patient had expressed explicit intent regarding this type of medical treatment prior to becoming

incompetent. [ ] Where no clear intent exists, the patient's personal value system must guide the surrogate. * * *

In re Estate of Longeway, 133 Ill.2d 33, 139 Ill.Dec. 780, 549 N.E.2d 292, 299 (1989).

2.     In applying the principle of substituted judgment, most courts look wherever they can to determine the patient's wishes. In Brophy v. New England Sinai Hosp., Inc., 398 Mass. 417, 497 N.E.2d 626 (1986), the Massachusetts Supreme Court based its conclusion that food and hydration could be withheld from a comatose adult on the substituted judgment analysis done by the lower court.

> [After full hearing] the judge found on the basis of ample evidence which no one disputes, that Brophy's judgment would be to decline the provision of food and water and to terminate his life. In reaching that conclusion, the judge considered various factors including the following: (1) Brophy's expressed preferences; (2) his religious convictions and their relation to refusal of treatment; (3) the impact on his family; (4) the probability of adverse side effects; and (5) the prognosis, both with and without treatment. The judge also considered present and future incompetency as an element which Brophy would consider in his decision-making process. The judge relied on several statements made by Brophy prior to the onset of his illness. Although he never had discussed specifically whether a G-tube or feeding tube should be withdrawn in the event that he was diagnosed as being in a persistent vegetative state following his surgery, the judge inferred that, if presently competent, Brophy would choose to forgo artificial nutrition and hydration by means of a G-tube. The judge found that Brophy would not likely view his own religion as a barrier to that choice.

3.     Other factors that have been considered include the patient's diagnosis, life history, ability to knowingly participate in treatment, potential quality of life, and, more generally, the patient's values and attitude toward health care. See, e.g., Mack v. Mack, 329 Md. 188, 618 A.2d 744 (1993) (focusing on the "moral views, life goals, and values" of the patient, and her "attitudes toward sickness, medical procedures, suffering and death"), and DeGrella v. Elston, 858 S.W.2d 698 (Ky.1993). For a thorough and well annotated list of relevant factors that have been considered by the courts see Alan Meisel & Kathy L. Cerminara, The Right to Die, 3rd ed. (2004, and 2017 Supplement).

4.     How difficult is it for a surrogate decision maker to distinguish what the patient would really want from what that decision maker would want if she were in the position of that patient? Is it really possible to clearly distinguish the subjective "substituted judgment" standard from an objective standard that asks what a reasonable person would do under the circumstances? Courts do struggle to distinguish the "substituted judgment" and "best interest" principles, and even those who appear to adopt the "best interest" approach may qualify it by requiring that the best interest of the patient be defined in terms of the wishes, values and desires of the patient.

Some state courts appear to adopt the best interest test while they actually take the "substituted judgment" approach. See Conservatorship of Drabick, 200 Cal.App.3d 185, 245 Cal.Rptr. 840 (1988) and In re Gordy, 658 A.2d 613 (Del.Ch.1994).

### NOTE ON DISTINCTIONS AS TO TREATMENT: "ACTIVE" AND "PASSIVE" CONDUCT, "WITHHOLDING" AND "WITHDRAWING" TREATMENT, AND "ORDINARY" AND "EXTRAORDINARY" TREATMENT

Distinctions between "active" and "passive" conduct and between "withholding" and "withdrawing" treatment are anachronistic distinctions which have not found a safe harbor in the law, just as they have been increasingly recognized as meaningless in ethics. An early New Jersey case, *In re Conroy*, 98 N.J. 321, 486 A.2d 1209 (N.J. 1985) considered each of these distinctions, and summarized the ethical and legal literature and the reasons for rejecting the distinctions. As to the distinction between active and passive conduct, the *Conroy* court announced:

> We emphasize that in making decisions whether to administer life-sustaining treatment to patients such as Claire Conroy, the primary focus should be the patient's desires and experience of pain and enjoyment—not the type of treatment involved. Thus, we reject the distinction that some have made between actively hastening death by terminating treatment and passively allowing a person to die of a disease as one of limited use in a legal analysis of such a decision-making situation.

> Characterizing conduct as active or passive is often an elusive notion, even outside the context of medical decision-making * * *. The distinction is particularly nebulous, however, in the context of decisions whether to withhold or withdraw life-sustaining treatment. In a case like that of Claire Conroy, for example, would a physician who discontinued nasogastric feeding be actively causing her death by removing her primary source of nutrients; or would he merely be omitting to continue the artificial form of treatment, thus passively allowing her medical condition, which includes her inability to swallow, to take its natural course? [ ] The ambiguity inherent in this distinction is further heightened when one performs an act within an over-all plan of non-intervention, such as when a doctor writes an order not to resuscitate a patient. * * *

> For a similar reason, we also reject any distinction between withholding and withdrawing life-sustaining treatment. Some commentators have suggested that discontinuing life-sustaining treatment once it has been commenced is morally more problematic than merely failing to begin the treatment. Discontinuing life-sustaining treatment, to some, is an "active" taking of life, as opposed to the more "passive" act of omitting the treatment in the first instance.

This distinction is more psychologically compelling than logically sound. As mentioned above, the line between active and passive conduct in the context of medical decisions is far too nebulous to constitute a principled basis for decision-making. Whether necessary treatment is withheld at the outset or withdrawn later on, the consequence—the patient's death—is the same. Moreover, from a policy standpoint, it might well be unwise to forbid persons from discontinuing a treatment under circumstances in which the treatment could permissibly be withheld. Such a rule could discourage families and doctors from even attempting certain types of care and could thereby force them into hasty and premature decisions to allow a patient to die. [ ]

486 A.2d at 1233–1234.

As to the distinction between "ordinary" and "extraordinary" treatment, *Conroy* pointed out:

We also find unpersuasive the distinction relied upon by some courts, commentators, and theologians between "ordinary" treatment, which they would always require, and "extraordinary" treatment, which they deem optional. * * * The terms "ordinary" and "extraordinary" have assumed too many conflicting meanings to remain useful. To draw a line on this basis for determining whether treatment should be given leads to a semantical milieu that does not advance the analysis.

The distinction between ordinary and extraordinary treatment is frequently phrased as one between common and unusual, or simple and complex, treatment [ ]; "extraordinary" treatment also has been equated with elaborate, artificial, heroic, aggressive, expensive, or highly involved or invasive forms of medical intervention [ ]. Depending on the definitions applied, a particular treatment for a given patient may be considered both ordinary and extraordinary. [ ] Further, since the common/unusual and simple/complex distinctions among medical treatments "exist on continuums with no precise dividing line," [ ] and the continuum is constantly shifting due to progress in medical care, disagreement will often exist about whether a particular treatment is ordinary or extraordinary. In addition, the competent patient generally could refuse even ordinary treatment; therefore, an incompetent patient theoretically should also be able to make such a choice when the surrogate decision-making is effectuating the patient's subjective intent. In such cases, the ordinary/extraordinary distinction is irrelevant except insofar as the particular patient would have made the distinction.

The ordinary/extraordinary distinction has also been discussed in terms of the benefits and burdens of treatment for the patient. If the benefits of the treatment outweigh the burdens it imposes on the patient, it is characterized as ordinary and therefore ethically required; if not, it is characterized as extraordinary and therefore optional. [ ] This formulation is extremely fact-sensitive and would lead to different classifications of the same treatment in different situations.

\* \* \* Moreover, while the analysis may be useful in weighing the implications of the specific treatment for the patient, essentially it merely restates the question: whether the burdens of a treatment so clearly outweigh its benefits to the patient that continued treatment would be inhumane.

468 A.2d at 1234–1235. See also Brophy v. New England Sinai Hosp., Inc., 398 Mass. 417, 497 N.E.2d 626 (1986) ("while we believe that the distinction between extraordinary and ordinary care is a factor to be considered, the use of such a distinction as the sole, or major, factor of decision tends \* \* \* to create a distinction without meaning.")

## NOTE: THE SPECIAL STATUS OF NUTRITION AND HYDRATION

The issue of withdrawing nutrition and hydration has become an especially contentious one. Medical sources generally recognize the irrelevancy of distinguishing between nutrition and hydration and other forms of medical treatment. Generally, courts also have concluded that the termination of nutrition and hydration is no different from the termination of other forms of mechanical support. For example, *Conroy* suggested:

> Some commentators, \* \* \* have made yet [another] distinction, between the termination of artificial feedings and the termination of other forms of life-sustaining medical treatment. \* \* \* According to the Appellate Division:
>
> > If, as here, the patient is not comatose and does not face imminent and inevitable death, nourishment accomplishes the substantial benefit of sustaining life until the illness takes its natural course. Under such circumstances nourishment always will be an essential element of ordinary care which physicians are ethically obligated to provide. [ ]

> Certainly, feeding has an emotional significance. As infants we could breathe without assistance, but we were dependent on others for our lifeline of nourishment. Even more, feeding is an expression of nurturing and caring, certainly for infants and children, and in many cases for adults as well.

> Once one enters the realm of complex, high-technology medical care, it is hard to shed the "emotional symbolism" of food. \* \* \* Analytically, artificial feeding by means of a nasogastric tube or intravenous infusion can be seen as equivalent to artificial breathing by means of a respirator. Both prolong life through mechanical means when the body is no longer able to perform a vital bodily function on its own.

> Furthermore, while nasogastric feeding and other medical procedures to ensure nutrition and hydration are usually well tolerated, they are not free from risks or burdens; they have complications that are sometimes serious and distressing to the patient.

Finally, dehydration may well not be distressing or painful to a dying patient. For patients who are unable to sense hunger and thirst, withholding of feeding devices such as nasogastric tubes may not result in more pain than the termination of any other medical treatment. * * * Thus, it cannot be assumed that it will always be beneficial for an incompetent patient to receive artificial feeding or harmful for him not to receive it. * * *

Under the analysis articulated above, withdrawal or withholding of artificial feeding, like any other medical treatment, would be permissible [under some circumstances]. A competent patient has the right to decline any medical treatment, including artificial feeding, and should retain that right when and if he becomes incompetent. In addition, in the case of an incompetent patient who has given little or no trustworthy indication of an intent to decline treatment * * * the pain and invasiveness of an artificial feeding device, and the pain of withdrawing that device, should be treated just like the results of administering or withholding any other medical treatment.

98 N.J. 321, 486 A.2d 1209, 1235–1237.

In McConnell v. Beverly Enterprises-Connecticut, 209 Conn. 692, 553 A.2d 596 (1989), the court authorized the withdrawal of feeding by a gastrostomy tube despite a statute that appeared to say that under such circumstances "nutrition and hydration must be provided." The court reasoned that the nutrition and hydration that was implicated in the statute was that provided by "a spoon or a straw," and that feeding by gastrostomy tube was no different than any other mechanical or electronic medical intervention.

In 1990, at least, a majority of the Supreme Court (the four dissenters and concurring Justice O'Connor in *Cruzan*) viewed nutrition and hydration as another form of medical care. As Justice O'Connor pointed out, "artificial feeding cannot readily be distinguished from other forms of medical treatment. Whether or not the techniques used to pass food and water into the patient's alimentary tract are termed 'medical treatment,' it is clear they all involve some degree of intrusion and restraint." She concluded that "the liberty guaranteed by the due process clause must protect, if it protects anything, an individual's deeply personal decision to reject medical treatment, including the artificial delivery of food and water."

In his dissent, Justice Brennan reached the same conclusion, vividly describing the medical processes involved:

The artificial delivery of nutrition and hydration is undoubtedly medical treatment. The technique to which Nancy Cruzan is subject—artificial feeding through a gastrostomy tube—involves a tube implanted surgically into her stomach through incisions in her abdominal wall. It may obstruct the intestinal tract, erode and pierce the stomach wall, or cause leakage of the stomach's contents into the abdominal cavity. [ ] The tube can cause pneumonia from reflux of the stomach's contents into the lung. [ ]

Typically, and in this case, commercially prepared formulas are used, rather than fresh food. [ ] The type of formula and method of administration must be experimented with to avoid gastrointestinal problems. [ ] The patient must be monitored daily by medical personnel as to weight, fluid intake and fluid output; blood tests must be done weekly.

Artificial delivery of food and water is regarded as medical treatment by the medical profession and the federal government. * * * The federal government permits the cost of the medical devices and formulas used in enteral feeding to be reimbursed under Medicare. [ ] The formulas are regulated by the Federal Drug Administration as "medical foods," [ ] and the feeding tubes are regulated as medical devices [ ].

497 U.S. at 306–308, 110 S.Ct. at 2866–67.

To many, nutrition and hydration remain symbols of the bonds between human beings; the care we provide to the ones we love includes, at the very least, food and water. For others, the provision of artificial nutrition and hydration has religious and moral significance. Consider the following documents defining the Catholic position on this issue.

## UNITED STATES CONFERENCE OF CATHOLIC BISHOPS, ETHICAL AND RELIGIOUS DIRECTIVES FOR CATHOLIC HEALTH CARE SERVICES
### (5th ed. 2009).

* * *

The Church's teaching authority has addressed the moral issues concerning medically assisted nutrition and hydration. We are guided on this issue by Catholic teaching against euthanasia, which is "an action or an omission which of itself or by intention causes death, in order that all suffering may in this way be eliminated."[ ] While medically assisted nutrition and hydration are not morally obligatory in certain cases, these forms of basic care should in principle be provided to all patients who need them, including patients diagnosed as being in a "persistent vegetative state" (PVS), because even the most severely debilitated and helpless patient retains the full dignity of a human person and must receive ordinary and proportionate care.

* * *

[DIRECTIVE 58] In principle, there is an obligation to provide patients with food and water, including medically assisted nutrition and hydration for those who cannot take food orally. This obligation extends to patients in chronic and presumably irreversible conditions (e.g., the "persistent vegetative state") who can reasonably be expected to live indefinitely if given such care. [ ] Medically assisted nutrition and hydration become morally optional when they cannot reasonably be expected to prolong life or when they would be "excessively burdensome for the patient or [would] cause significant physical discomfort, for example resulting from complications in the use of the means employed."[ ] For instance, as a patient draws close to inevitable death from an underlying progressive and fatal condition, certain measures to provide nutrition and hydration may become excessively burdensome and therefore not obligatory in light of their very limited ability to prolong life or provide comfort.

* * *

## CONGREGATION FOR THE DOCTRINE OF THE FAITH, RESPONSES TO CERTAIN QUESTIONS OF THE UNITED STATES CONFERENCE OF CATHOLIC BISHOPS CONCERNING ARTIFICIAL NUTRITION AND HYDRATION

(2007)

***First question:*** *Is the administration of food and water (whether by natural or artificial means) to a patient in a "vegetative state" morally obligatory except when they cannot be assimilated by the patient's body or cannot be administered to the patient without causing significant physical discomfort?*

**Response:** Yes. The administration of food and water even by artificial means is, in principle, an ordinary and proportionate means of preserving life. It is therefore obligatory to the extent to which, and for as long as, it is shown to accomplish its proper finality, which is the hydration and nourishment of the patient. In this way suffering and death by starvation and dehydration are prevented.

***Second question:*** *When nutrition and hydration are being supplied by artificial means to a patient in a "permanent vegetative state", may they be discontinued when competent physicians judge with moral certainty that the patient will never recover consciousness?*

**Response:** No. A patient in a "permanent vegetative state" is a person with fundamental human dignity and must, therefore, receive ordinary and proportionate care which includes, in principle, the administration of water and food even by artificial means.

For interpretations of the content and application of this statement within the Roman Catholic tradition, see John Hardt & Kevin O'Rourke, Nutrition and Hydration: The [Congregation for the Doctrine of Faith], In Perspective, 88 Health Progress 1 (2007), arguing, inter alia, that Catholic Canon Law requires that the statement be interpreted strictly as it restricts rights; that the form of the statement has less force than other vehicles for establishing directives; that the use of the term "in principle" indicates that there are exceptions. In particular, in contrast to earlier statements on nutrition and hydration, this statement is specifically confined to circumstances of confirmed diagnosis of PVS and addresses only nutrition and hydration and not other medical interventions. See also Daniel Sulmasy, Preserving Life? The Vatican and PVS, 134 Commonweal (No. 21) 16 (Dec. 7, 2007).

## PROBLEM: NOT QUITE PERSISTENT VEGETATIVE STATE

When unhelmeted 57-year-old Tad Gonzales ran his motorcycle into a bridge support post on an interstate highway, he was revived at the scene and rushed to Big Central Hospital. There he underwent several hours of emergency surgery designed to preserve his life and repair the very substantial head injuries he sustained. A few days after the surgery, he began to regain consciousness, and a week later he was able to be removed from the ventilator which was supporting his breathing, although he still needs ventilator assistance from time to time. During his first two weeks in the hospital, Tad showed little improvement. He was not in a coma, but he was only occasionally responsive, and he demonstrated no awareness of Ralph, his partner of twenty-two years, or his two brothers and his parents, even though Tad had always shared a close relationship with all of them.

After two weeks, Big City Hospital transferred Tad to Commercial Affiliated Nursing Home, where he began receiving physical and occupational therapy. After a year of care there, he has shown little improvement. He still does not seem to recognize Ralph, who visits daily, or anyone else. He is able to sit up and his eyes sometimes seem to be following images on a screen. He grunts when he is hungry or uncomfortable. He cannot eat or drink, and he is fed through a feeding tube in his abdomen. He cannot control his bowels or bladder. He has regularly suffered from urinary tract infections and asthma during his nursing home stay, although his need for the ventilator is becoming rarer. On a few, increasingly rare, occasions, his heart stopped beating, but he was resuscitated immediately. Doctors believe that there is little chance of substantial improvement in his condition (although, in the words of one doctor, "Who knows? Anything can happen.") Tad's doctors estimate that his life expectancy could be another twenty years or more.

Tad's doctor and Ralph have developed a good working relationship, and the doctor has called upon Ralph to approve any change in Tad's treatment regimen even though Tad never signed any kind of advance directive. Ralph has now informed the doctor that he believes that Tad would want the use of the feeding tube (and the occasional use of the ventilator) discontinued, and that he would not want to be resuscitated (i.e., if his heart were to stop beating, he would not want health care providers to try to start it again). When the doctor challenged him on this, Ralph respectfully ordered the doctor to terminate feeding, and to note that Tad was not to be mechanically ventilated or resuscitated. Ralph explained that he had spoken with Tad often about "this kind of thing," and that Tad had said that the indignity of being fed, or wearing diapers, or being bed-bound, was not worth the value of life to him. In particular, Ralph remembers Tad describing one of their friends, another motorcyclist who became a quadriplegic and suffered some intellectual impairment after an accident, as "better off dead." Tad and Ralph promised each other that neither would ever let that happen to the other. Tad's parents and one of his brothers agree that there is no doubt that Tad would want all treatment terminated under these circumstances. Tad's other brother disagrees. As he has articulated it, "How can we know what he would want? He could never have imagined himself in this situation, and we shouldn't read anything in to what he said about other people. Maybe he thought those other people could feel more pain than he can."

Tad's doctor has approached you, the hospital counsel, to ask you what she should do. Should she discontinue feeding? The use of the ventilator? Should the hospital pursue an action in court? What position should the hospital take if Ralph, or Tad's dissenting brother, pursues an action in court? How should that action be resolved?

### NOTE: THE ROLE OF THE COURT IN RESOLVING DISPUTES ABOUT THE PROVISION OF LIFE-SUSTAINING MEDICAL CARE

1.     Whether the courts have any role at all in these matters has been the subject of some debate. On the one hand, there is a fear that the absence of judicial oversight will lead to arbitrary decisions and, thus, arbitrary deaths. On the other hand, any attempt to bring every case that could result in the termination of life-sustaining treatment to the courts would yield an intolerable caseload and delay the deaths of many patients who desperately seek that relief. In addition, there is little reason to believe that courts have any wisdom that will make them better than a patient's family at making these decisions. The Massachusetts Supreme Judicial Court changed its view of the necessity of judicial confirmation of a guardian's decision that a patient should forgo life-sustaining treatment. See In re Spring, 380 Mass. 629, 405 N.E.2d 115 (1980) (no review required in most circumstances; reversing prior position requiring judicial review).

Should judicial review of all decisions to terminate life-sustaining treatment be required? Should such judicial review be required in some cases? In cases in which there is no written advance directive? In which there is no agreement among family members? In which the patients disagree with the health care providers? In which the health care providers disagree among themselves? In which the decision maker is self interested? In which there is an ambiguity in the previous statements of the patient? Is there any way to adequately categorize those cases in which judicial review ought to be required? If judicial review is not required, should some other form of review— by an ethics committee, for example—be required in its stead? Is the choice of the Uniform Health-Care Decisions Act, which would rarely countenance judicial involvement in any health care decision, the best choice? Why?

2.     When resort to a court is required, what procedure ought to be employed by the court? Should the court's involvement be limited to the appointment of a decision maker, should the court make the decision itself, or

should the court review every decision (or some decisions) made by an appointed decision maker? Should the action be a special statutory action, an injunction action, a guardianship, or does the form of the action really make much difference? Should the court always appoint a guardian ad litem for the patient? What would the role of such a guardian be? Is the role of the guardian ad litem to represent what that person believes the patient would want, or what that person believes is in the best interest of the patient? Alternatively, should the guardian ad litem always oppose the petitioner (who is usually seeking the termination of the treatment)? Every state has a nursing home ombudsman. Should the ombudsman be notified whenever discontinuation of treatment of a nursing home patient is requested? Should the ombudsman participate in every such case?

In In re Guardianship of Hamlin, 102 Wash.2d 810, 689 P.2d 1372 (1984), the Washington Supreme Court announced two entirely separate processes— one to be followed where there is "total agreement among the patient's family, treating physicians and prognosis committee as to the course of medical treatment," and one to be followed where there is "an incompetent with no known family, who has never made his wishes known." No judicial process and no formal guardianship is required in the first case where "the incompetent patient is in * * * a persistent vegetative state with no reasonable chance of recovery and * * * the patient's life is being maintained by life support systems." In the second situation a guardian must be appointed by the court, but that guardian need not obtain judicial confirmation of any particular decision "if the treating physicians and prognosis committee are unanimous that life-sustaining efforts should be withheld or withdrawn and the guardian concurs." Of course, most cases fall between the two extremes discussed in Hamlin.

3.    Who should have standing to commence a judicial action seeking to review a decision to terminate life-sustaining medical treatment? All relatives? Health care providers? Health care institutions? Patient advocacy groups? Right-to-Life or Right-to-Die or disability advocacy groups? Who should be able to join such litigation as a party? Is the Uniform-Health Care Decisions Act approach to this issue—that there will be no judicial hearing unless a relative or health care provider is willing to file an action—the best way of dealing with this issue? See Protection and Advocacy System, Inc. v. Presbyterian Healthcare Services, 128 N.M. 73, 989 P.2d 890 (1999) (no standing in advocacy group to challenge unanimous decision of family members and health care providers).

4.    If there is to be a judicial process, should it be an adversary process? While Chief Justice Rehnquist appeared to think that the adversary process would be helpful in these cases (see Cruzan, above), that part of the opinion gave Justice Stevens pause:

The Court recognizes that "the state has been involved as an adversary from the beginning" in this case only because Nancy Cruzan "was a patient at a state hospital when this litigation commenced." * * * It seems to me, however, that the Court draws precisely the wrong conclusion from this insight. The Court apparently believes that the absence of the state from the litigation would have created a problem, because agreement among the family and the independent guardian *ad litem* as to Nancy Cruzan's best interests might have prevented her treatment from becoming the focus of a "truly adversarial" proceeding. [ ] It may reasonably be debated whether some judicial process should be required before life-sustaining treatment is discontinued; this issue has divided the state courts. [ ] * * * I tend, however, to agree * * * that the intervention of the state in these proceedings as an *adversary* is not so much a cure as it is part of the disease.

Cruzan v. Director, Missouri Dept. of Health, 497 U.S. 261, 341, n.13, 110 S.Ct. 2841, 2884, n.13, 111 L.Ed.2d 224 (1990) (Stevens, J., dissenting). A decade earlier the Florida Supreme Court had expressed the same reservations:

> Because the issue with its ramifications is fraught with complexity and encompasses the interests of the law, both civil and criminal, medical ethics and social morality, it is not one which is well suited for a solution in an adversary judicial proceeding.

Satz v. Perlmutter, 379 So.2d 359, 360 (Fla.1980). See also *Protection and Advocacy System, supra* note 3. Are the "advantages" of an adversary proceeding truly advantageous in these agonizing cases? See Nancy Dubler, Conflict and Consensus at the End of Life, Hastings Ctr. Spec. Rep. on Improving End of Life Care (Jennings, et al., eds. 2005); Alan Meisel, The Role of Litigation in End of Life Care: A Reappraisal, Hastings Ctr. Spec. Rep. on Improving End of Life Care (Jennings, et al., eds. 2005).

5.    "Right to die" cases seeking damages to vindicate the federal privacy rights of patients against state entities (like state hospitals) may be based on 42 U.S.C.A. § 1983. When one successfully raises a federal civil rights claim under that statute, the prevailing party is entitled to attorney's fees under 42 U.S.C.A. § 1988. While most such attempts to collect attorney's fees have failed, some have been successful. The Uniform Health-Care Decisions Act explicitly provides for attorney's fees in cases where there has been an "intentional" violation of the Act. Is this an appropriate standard?

### NOTE ON MAKING DECISIONS FOR ADULTS WHO HAVE NEVER BEEN COMPETENT

Where the patient has never been competent—where the patient has been severely developmentally disabled from birth, for example—the courts still make an attempt to determine what the patient's choice would be when deciding what treatment would be legally appropriate. Of course, it is exceptionally difficult to imagine what an incompetent person, who has never been competent, would want to do if that person were suddenly competent. Should the courts treat such patients as it treats infants, who have not yet had an opportunity to develop and manifest values? Are you concerned about the courts infantilizing those with mental disabilities by treating them as infants for this purpose? See Alicia Ouellette, Bioethics and Disability: Toward a Disability-Conscious Bioethics (2011).

Might our society be more willing to err on the side of removing life-sustaining treatment when the patient has cognitive deficits? Is this simply an example of social prejudice against such people, and is the resulting analysis yet another example of discrimination against the developmentally delayed? Perhaps the courts should review all decisions to remove life-sustaining medical treatment from patients in this class, even if the courts need not be involved in similar cases with previously competent patients. See *Protection and Advocacy System, supra.* See also Kathy Cerminara, Critical Essay: Musings on the Need to Convince Some People With Disabilities that End-of-Life Decision Making Advocates Are Not Out to Get Them, 37 Loy.U.Chi. L.J. 343 (2006); Adrienne Asch, Recognizing Death While Affirming Life: Can End of Life Reform Uphold a Disabled Person's Interest in Continued Life?, Hastings Ctr. Spec. Rep. on Improving End of Life Care (Jennings, et al., eds. 2005).

For a more complete analysis of the elements of discrimination that are present when there is a decision to terminate life-sustaining medical treatment for a patient with serious intellectual impairment from birth, see Chapter 2.

# V.  HEALTH CARE DECISION-MAKING FOR CHILDREN

### PROBLEM: CHOOSING TO FORGO CANCER TREATMENT

Jack Armstrong was a healthy, socially well adjusted intelligent fourteen-year-old when he discovered that he had testicular cancer which had also produced a mass in his liver. The prognosis was not terribly optimistic: with intensive intervention he would have about a 50% chance of surviving for 2 years, and a 25% chance of a "cure" (i.e., of surviving five years). "Intensive intervention" would include several months of painful and debilitating chemotherapy, surgery to remove part of his liver and his testes, and a substantial amount of radiation therapy. Without treatment, Jack would probably die within six months.

Jack has informed his oncologist that he has decided to forgo the proposed surgery, even though he recognizes that this will result in his death. He explained that he reached this conclusion after reading everything accessible to him about his cancer and the proposed treatment, after praying with his religious advisor and mentor (a Presbyterian minister), and after discussing the issue with his family, friends, and two patients (names provided by the oncologist) who had previously undergone the same surgery and chemotherapy. He also admits that the playground razzing he has taken over the primary location of his disease, and his consequent extreme embarrassment, were not irrelevant factors in his decision.

Jack's parents, who are divorced and have joint legal and physical custody, are split on this issue. His father believes that it is Jack's decision to make, and he supports Jack's decision. His mother insists that the oncologist and the hospital provide the proposed treatment. In addition, a social worker in the local child protective services office (which was informed about the case by one of Jack's teachers) has informed all of the parties that, in her opinion, Jack would be a neglected child if the treatment were not administered.

Jack's parents have now filed cross petitions seeking to vindicate their positions. Jack has filed a petition as well. The oncologist and the hospital have filed a declaratory judgment action seeking an order of the court before taking any action, and the child protective services agency has filed a neglect petition against the father. All of these actions have been consolidated and all assigned to the same trial court judge to resolve. How should the judge proceed? What kind of hearing, if any, should the judge hold? How should she rule?

## NEWMARK V. WILLIAMS
Supreme Court of Delaware, 1991.
588 A.2d 1108.

MOORE, JUSTICE.

Colin Newmark, a three year old child, faced death from a deadly aggressive and advanced form of pediatric cancer known as Burkitt's Lymphoma. We were presented with a clash of interests between medical science, Colin's tragic plight, the unquestioned sincerity of his parents' religious beliefs as Christian Scientists, and the legal right of the State to protect dependent children from perceived neglect when medical treatment is withheld on religious grounds. The Delaware Division of Child Protective Services ("DCPS") petitioned the Family Court for temporary custody of Colin to authorize the Alfred I. DuPont Institute ("DuPont Institute"), a nationally recognized children's hospital, to treat Colin's condition with chemotherapy. His parents, Morris and Kara Newmark, are well educated and economically prosperous. As members of the First Church of Christ, Scientist ("Christian Science") they rejected medical treatment proposed for Colin, preferring instead a course of spiritual aid and prayer. The parents rely upon provisions of Delaware law, which exempt those who treat their children's illnesses "solely by spiritual means" from the abuse and neglect statutes. Thus, they opposed the State's petition. [ ] The Newmarks also claimed that removing Colin from their custody would violate their First Amendment right, guaranteed under the United States Constitution, to freely exercise their religion.

* * *

[The Court explained how the Newmarks discovered that Colin suffered from Burkitt's Lymphoma, an extremely fast growing and dangerous form of pediatric cancer, when they took him to the doctor "out of concern for their potential criminal liability * * *."]

We have concluded that Colin was not an abused or neglected child under Delaware law. Parents enjoy a well established legal right to make important decisions for their children. Although this right is not absolute, the State has the burden of proving by clear and convincing evidence that intervening in the parent-child relationship is necessary to ensure the safety or health of the child, or to protect the public at large. DCPS did not meet this heavy burden. This is especially true where the purpose of the custody petition was to administer, over the objections of Colin's parents, an extremely risky, toxic and dangerously life threatening medical treatment offering less than a 40% chance for "success".

* * *

Dr. Meek [an attending physician and board certified pediatric hematologist—oncologist] opined that chemotherapy offered a 40% chance of "curing" Colin's illness. She concluded that he would die within six to eight months without treatment. The Newmarks * * * advised Dr. Meek that they would place him under the care of a Christian Science practitioner and reject all medical treatment for their son. Accordingly, they refused to authorize the chemotherapy. There was no doubt that the Newmarks sincerely believed, as part of their religious beliefs, that the tenets of their faith provided an effective treatment.

## II.

We start with an overview of the relevant Delaware statutory provisions. Delaware law defines a neglected child as:

[A] child whose physical, mental or emotional health and well-being is threatened or impaired because of inadequate care and protection by the child's custodian, who has the ability and financial means to provide for the care but does not or will not provide adequate care; or a child who has been abused or neglected * * *

[The statute] further defines abuse and neglect as:

Physical injury by other than accidental means, injury resulting in a mental or emotional condition which is a result of abuse or neglect, negligent treatment, sexual abuse, maltreatment, mistreatment, nontreatment, exploitation or abandonment, of a child under the age of 18. (Emphasis added).

Sections of the Delaware Code, however, contain spiritual treatment exemptions which directly affect Christian Scientists. Specifically, the exemptions state:

No child who in good faith is under treatment solely by spiritual means through prayer in accordance with the tenets and practices of a recognized church or religious denomination by a duly accredited practitioner thereof shall for that reason alone be considered a neglected child for purposes of this chapter.

[ ] These exceptions reflect the intention of the Delaware General Assembly to provide a "safe harbor" for parents, like the Newmarks, to pursue their own religious beliefs. [We recognize] that the spiritual treatment exemptions reflect, in part, "the policy of this State with respect to the quality of life" a desperately ill child might have in the caring and loving atmosphere of his or her family, versus the sterile hospital environment demanded by physicians seeking to prescribe excruciating, and life threatening, treatments of doubtful efficacy.

    * * * [W]e recognize the possibility that the spiritual treatment exemptions may violate the ban against the establishment of an official State religion guaranteed under both the Federal and Delaware Constitutions. Clearly, in both reality and practical effect, the language providing an exemption only to those individuals practicing "in accordance" with the "practices of a recognized church or religious denomination by a duly accredited practitioner thereof" is intended for the principal benefit of Christian Scientists. Our concern is that it possibly forces us to impermissibly determine the validity of an individual's own religious beliefs.

    Neither party challenged the constitutionality of the spiritual treatment exemptions in either the Family Court or on appeal. Thus, except to recognize that the issue is far more complicated than was originally presented to us, we must leave such questions for another day.

### III.

    Addressing the facts of this case, we turn to the novel legal question whether, under any circumstances, Colin was a neglected child when his parents refused to accede to medical demands that he receive a radical form of chemotherapy having only a forty percent chance of success. [The court then explained that it would apply a balancing test to answer this question.]

* * *

### A.

    Any balancing test must begin with the parental interest. The primacy of the familial unit is a bedrock principle of law. [ ] We have repeatedly emphasized that the parental right is sacred which can be invaded for only the most compelling reasons.

* * *

    Courts have also recognized that the essential element of preserving the integrity of the family is maintaining the autonomy of the parent-child relationship. [ ] In Prince v. Commonwealth of Massachusetts, [ ] the United States Supreme Court announced:

> It is cardinal with us that the custody, care and nurture of the child reside first in the parents, whose primary function and freedom include preparation for obligations the state can neither supply nor hinder. [ ]

Parental autonomy to care for children free from government interference therefore satisfies a child's need for continuity and thus ensures his or her psychological and physical well-being. [ ]

Parental authority to make fundamental decisions for minor children is also a recognized common law principle. A doctor commits the tort of battery if he or she performs an operation under normal circumstances without the informed consent of the patient. [ ] Tort law also assumes that a child does not have the capacity to consent to an operation in most situations. [ ] Thus, the common law recognizes that the only party capable of authorizing medical treatment for a minor in "normal" circumstances is usually his parent or guardian. [ ]

Courts, therefore, give great deference to parental decisions involving minor children. In many circumstances the State simply is not an adequate surrogate for the judgment of a loving, nurturing parent. [ ] As one commentator aptly recognized, the "law does not have the capacity to supervise the delicately complex interpersonal bonds between parent and child." [ ]

## B.

We also recognize that parental autonomy over minor children is not an absolute right. Clearly, the State can intervene in the parent-child relationship where the health and safety of the child and the public at large are in jeopardy. [ ] Accordingly, the State, under the doctrine of parens patriae, has a special duty to protect its youngest and most helpless citizens.

The parens patriae doctrine is a derivation of the common law giving the State the right to act on behalf of minor children in certain property and marital disputes. [ ] More recently, courts have accepted the doctrine of parens patriae to justify State intervention in cases of parental religious objections to medical treatment of minor children's life threatening conditions. [ ] The Supreme Court of the United States [pointed out] that parental autonomy, under the guise of the parents' religious freedom, was not unlimited. [ ] Rather, the Court held:

> Parents may be free to become martyrs themselves. But it does not follow they are free, in identical circumstances, to make martyrs of their children before they have reached the age of full and legal discretion when they can make that choice for themselves. [ ]

The basic principle underlying the parens patriae doctrine is the State's interest in preserving human life. [ ] Yet this interest and the parens patriae doctrine are not unlimited. In its recent Cruzan opinion, the Supreme Court of the United States announced that the state's interest in preserving life must "be weighed against the constitutionally protected interests of the individual." [ ]

The individual interests at stake here include both the Newmarks' right to decide what is best for Colin and Colin's own right to life. We have already considered the Newmarks' stake in this case and its relationship to the parens patriae doctrine. The resolution of the issues here, however, is incomplete without a discussion of Colin's interests.

C.

All children indisputably have the right to enjoy a full and healthy life. Colin, a three year old boy, unfortunately lacked the ability to reach a detached, informed decision regarding his own medical care. This Court must therefore substitute its own objective judgment to determine what is in Colin's "best interests." [ ]

There are two basic inquiries when a dispute involves chemotherapy treatment over parents' religious objections. The court must first consider the effectiveness of the treatment and determine the child's chances of survival with and without medical care. [ ] The court must then consider the nature of the treatments and their effect on the child. [ ]

The "best interests" analysis is hardly unique or novel. Federal and State courts have unhesitatingly authorized medical treatment over a parent's religious objection when the treatment is relatively innocuous in comparison to the dangers of withholding medical care. [ ] Accordingly, courts are reluctant to authorize medical care over parental objection when the child is not suffering a life threatening or potential life threatening illness. [ ]

The linchpin in all cases discussing the "best interests of a child," when a parent refuses to authorize medical care, is an evaluation of the risk of the procedure compared to its potential success. This analysis is consistent with the principle that State intervention in the parent-child relationship is only justifiable under compelling conditions. [ ] The State's interest in forcing a minor to undergo medical care diminishes as the risks of treatment increase and its benefits decrease.

* * *

Applying the foregoing considerations to the "best interests standard" here, the State's petition must be denied. The egregious facts of this case indicate that Colin's proposed medical treatment was highly invasive, painful, involved terrible temporary and potentially permanent side effects, posed an unacceptably low chance of success, and a high risk that the treatment itself would cause his death. The State's authority to intervene in this case, therefore, cannot outweigh the Newmarks' parental prerogative and Colin's inherent right to enjoy at least a modicum of human dignity in the short time that was left to him.

### IV.

Dr. Meek originally diagnosed Colin's condition as Burkitt's Lymphoma. She testified that the cancer was "a very bad tumor" in an advanced disseminated state and not localized to only one section of the body. She accordingly recommended that the hospital begin an "extremely intensive" chemotherapy program scheduled to extend for at least six months.

[The court then explained how intensive such a chemotherapy program would be, and how such a treatment program would itself threaten Colin's life.]

Dr. Meek prescribed "maximum" doses of at least six different types of cancer-fighting drugs during Colin's chemotherapy. This proposed "maximum" treatment represented the most aggressive form of cancer therapy short of a bone marrow transplant. The side effects would include hair loss, reduced immunological function creating a high risk of infection in the patient, and certain neurological problems. The drugs also are toxic to bone marrow.

The record demonstrates that this form of chemotherapy also would adversely affect other parts of Colin's body.

* * *

The physicians planned to administer the chemotherapy in cycles, each of which would bring Colin near death. Then they would wait until Colin's body recovered sufficiently before introducing more drugs.

* * *

Dr. Meek also wanted the State to place Colin in a foster home after the initial phases of hospital treatment. Children require intensive home monitoring during chemotherapy. For example, Dr. Meek testified that a usually low grade fever for a healthy child could indicate the presence of a potentially deadly infection in a child cancer patient. She believed that the Newmarks, although well educated and financially responsible, were incapable of providing this intensive care because of their firm religious objections to medical treatment.

Dr. Meek ultimately admitted that there was a real possibility that the chemotherapy could kill Colin. In fact, assuming the treatment did not itself prove fatal, she offered Colin at "best" a 40% chance that he would "survive."[12] Dr. Meek additionally could not accurately predict whether, if Colin completed the therapy, he would subsequently suffer additional tumors.

### A.

No American court, even in the most egregious case, has ever authorized the State to remove a child from the loving, nurturing care of his parents and subject him, over parental objection, to an invasive regimen of treatment which offered, as Dr. Meek defined the term, only a forty percent chance of "survival."

\* \* \*

### B.

The aggressive form of chemotherapy that Dr. Meek prescribed for Colin was more likely to fail than succeed. The proposed treatment was also highly invasive and could have independently caused Colin's death. Dr. Meek also wanted to take Colin away from his parents and family during the treatment phase and place the boy in a foster home. This certainly would have caused Colin severe emotional difficulties given his medical condition, tender age, and the unquestioned close bond between Colin and his family.

In sum, Colin's best interests were served by permitting the Newmarks to retain custody of their child. Parents must have the right at some point to reject medical treatment for their child. Under all of the circumstances here, this clearly is such a case. The State's important and legitimate role in safeguarding the interests of minor children diminishes in the face of this egregious record.

Parents undertake an awesome responsibility in raising and caring for their children. No doubt a parent's decision to withhold medical care is both deeply personal and soul wrenching. It need not be made worse by the invasions which both the State and medical profession sought on this record. Colin's ultimate fate therefore rested with his parents and their faith.

### NOTES AND QUESTIONS

1.  Most judicial encounters with parents' rights to refuse medical treatment for their children follow the pattern established in *Newmark*. The court first announces the legal presumption that parents can make important decisions, including health care decisions, for their children. This is a common law right in every state, and it is protected by the United States Constitution

---

[12] Dr. Meek testified that there was no available medical data to conclude that Colin could survive to adulthood. Rather, she stated that the term "survival", as applied to victims of leukemia or lymphoma, refers only to the probability that the patient will live two years after chemotherapy without a recurrence of cancer.

as well. See Troxel v. Granville, 528 U.S. 1151; 120 S. Ct. 1225; 145 L. Ed. 2d 1068 (2000), Parham v. J.R., 442 U.S. 584, 99 S.Ct. 2493, 61 L.Ed.2d 101 (1979), and Santosky v. Kramer, 455 U.S. 745, 102 S.Ct. 1388, 71 L.Ed.2d 599 (1982). However, this presumption can be overcome if the conditions of the state's child protective services statute are met. Most state child abuse and neglect statutes are similar to the Delaware statute discussed in *Newmark*, and they provide—with greater or lesser specificity—that the parents' failure to provide adequate health care for their children constitutes neglect. If parents neglect their children, the state may commence a legal process (as the state did in *Newmark*) to obtain legal custody of the child to assure that the child is no longer medically neglected. The state need not take physical custody of the child, and the child can (as a technical legal matter) remain in the physical custody of the parents even while receiving the medical care to which the parents object.

2.    What is the legal test that the court applied to determine that Colin Newmark should not be ordered to undergo the proposed chemotherapy? Did the court determine that it was in Colin's best interests not to undergo this treatment, or did the court apply a balancing test and determine that the parents' interest in maintaining custody of their child (and in making health care decisions for their child) outweighed the state's interest in providing Colin with potentially life saving treatment? The choice between these two alternative forms of analysis may make no difference in this particular case, but can you think of a case in which the choice between these two legal positions would be dispositive?

3.    As a general matter, courts reviewing young children's decisions to forgo life-sustaining treatment apply the "best interests" test (with a substantial bow to the articulated desires of the parents, who are deemed to have the best interests of their children in mind). While the application of the "substituted judgment" standard seems appropriate as the children approach majority, a few states attempt to apply the "substituted judgment" theory to very young children, too. Compare, e.g., Care and Protection of Beth, 412 Mass. 188, 587 N.E.2d 1377 (1992) and Custody of a Minor, 385 Mass. 697, 434 N.E.2d 601 (1982) (applying the substituted judgement test) with In re K.I., B.I. and D.M., 735 A.2d 448 (D.C.1999) (applying the best interests test). See In re Christopher I., 106 Cal.App.4th 533, 131 Cal.Rptr.2d 122 (2003) (applying the best interest test to a child in the custody of the state). Does the "substituted judgment" standard make any sense when it is applied to infants or very young children? Although it may be absurd to search for the values, interests, desires, and expectancies of a newborn or a 3-month old, or even a four-year old, might not a seven- or eight-year old child's parents be able to talk about all of those attributes? Of course, it is hard to imagine anyone other than the parents (or their legal substitutes) being able to evaluate such factors. Does that mean that a court's decision to apply a substituted judgment standard to small children amounts to a *de facto* decision to defer to the parent's wishes?

In Matter of AB, 196 Misc.2d 940, 768 N.Y.S.2d 256 (Sup. Ct. 2003), a New York trial court confirmed the right of a mother of a child in persistent vegetative state to discontinue life-sustaining medical treatment—but only because the best interests test had been met:

> Thus, this Court holds that it is [the mother's] right, as a parent and natural guardian of AB, to exercise her responsibility and prerogative to make this decision to withhold extraordinary life-prolonging measures, with the assistance of treating physicians. CD's parental choice, made in the best interest of her child, to allow her daughter to pass away peacefully and with dignity are to be honored. This decision respects the values of family privacy without compromising a patient's rights or overstepping the State's legitimate interests.
>
> Having sought judicial intervention, CD has proven by clear and convincing evidence that it is in the best interest of her child to remove the mechanical ventilator. As CD sought intervention, this Court has employed the best interest standard, weighing whether the burdens of prolonged life outweigh any physical pleasure, emotional enjoyment, or intellectual satisfaction that the child may still be able to derive from life.

768 N.Y.S.2d at 271–272. In that case, AB's mother had sought a court order only because the hospital refused to permit the removal of treatment unless a court order supported that decision. Is the mother free to make health care decisions for her child—but only if the court agrees that the decisions are in the best interest of the child? Who is the real decision maker in this case?

In a subsequent case, ethics consultants, a guardian ad litem appointed for the child by the court, the institution's ethics committee, and the parents all agreed that the termination of treatment was proper. Because one board eligible doctor and one nurse at the institution thought that the treatment would not constitute an "extraordinary burden" on the patient, though, the trial judge determined that the consensus determination of all other interested parties did not rise to the level of clear and convincing evidence that removal of the treatment was in the best interest of this teenager. See In re D.H., 15 Misc.3d 565, 834 N.Y.S.2d 623 (Sup. 2007).

4.    How is a court to determine what is in the best interest of a child? Does the court look to its own values, to values derived from community sources, to values held by the child's family, or elsewhere? For example, in the case of a neurologically devastated child with no cognitive facilities and no hope of regaining any—a child who is entirely insensate and can not feel pleasure or pain—is the terminal removal of a feeding tube or a ventilator *always* in the child's best interest, *never* in the child's best interest, or *sometimes* in the child's best interest? If you chose "sometimes," what other factors are relevant? In *Matter of AB*, the court depended on standards provided by the New York Health Care Decisions for Mentally Retarded Persons Act and AMA guidelines. The AMA best interests guidelines, which are designed to address decision-making for newborns, are available at American Medical Association, Code of Medical Ethics, Opinion 2.2.4, *Treatment Decisions for Seriously Ill Newborns*

*(2016)*. In In re Christopher I., 106 Cal. App. 4th 533, 131 Cal. Rptr. 2d 122 (Cal. App. 2003), the court announced an exhaustive list of factors, drawn from local and national state court guidelines:

> We conclude that a court making the decision of whether to withhold or withdraw life-sustaining medical treatment from a dependent child should consider the following factors: (1) the child's present levels of physical, sensory, emotional and cognitive functioning; (2) the quality of life, life expectancy and prognosis for recovery with and without treatment, including the futility of continued treatment; (3) the various treatment options, and the risks, side effects, and benefits of each; (4) the nature and degree of physical pain or suffering resulting from the medical condition; (5) whether the medical treatment being provided is causing or may cause pain, suffering, or serious complications; (6) the pain or suffering to the child if the medical treatment is withdrawn; (7) whether any particular treatment would be proportionate or disproportionate in terms of the benefits to be gained by the child versus the burdens caused to the child; (8) the likelihood that pain or suffering resulting from withholding or withdrawal of treatment could be avoided or minimized; (9) the degree of humiliation, dependence and loss of dignity resulting from the condition and treatment; (10) the opinions of the family, the reasons behind those opinions, and the reasons why the family either has no opinion or cannot agree on a course of treatment; (11) the motivations of the family in advocating a particular course of treatment; and (12) the child's preference, if it can be ascertained, for treatment.

131 Cal. Rptr. at 551, 552. How helpful are these lists of factors? What factors do you believe a court should employ in determining if the removal of life-sustaining medical care is in the best interest of a child?

5.    Parental rights to make health care decisions for their children are terminated when the child reaches majority. Those rights may be diminished or terminated earlier if the child is a "mature minor," a condition governed by statute (in some states) or the common law (in other states) or both. At the very least, a child is a mature minor when he can "present clear and convincing evidence that he [is] mature enough to exercise an adult's judgment and [understand] the consequences of his decision." *Newmark*, at 1116 n. 9. See In re E.G., 133 Ill.2d 98, 139 Ill.Dec. 810, 549 N.E.2d 322 (1989), where a Jehovah's Witness child "just months shy of her eighteenth birthday" was found to be sufficiently mature to choose to forgo a blood transfusion in a case with a rather dim chance of long-term survival. See also Belcher v. Charleston Area Med. Ctr., 188 W.Va. 105, 422 S.E.2d 827 (1992) (17-year-old may have been mature enough to demand a DNR order; the issue is for the jury in a subsequent informed consent action). But see In re Application of Long Island Jewish Med. Ctr., 147 Misc.2d 724, 557 N.Y.S.2d 239 (Sup.1990). In Commonwealth v. Nixon, 563 Pa. 425, 761 A.2d 1151 (2000), this issue arose in the context of a defense in a criminal action. The Pennsylvania Supreme Court unanimously rejected the parents' appeal of their involuntary manslaughter and child endangerment convictions (and their consequent 2 1/2

to 5 year sentences) after their sixteen-year-old daughter died at home as a result of the religiously based decision not to seek diabetes treatment. The parents had argued that their daughter had decided, on her own, against seeking treatment, and that she was a "mature minor" under Pennsylvania law and thus entitled to make that decision, but the court concluded that she didn't meet the narrow definition of a "mature minor" under Pennsylvania law. For a discussion of the propriety of statutory recognition of the decision-making authority of teenagers, see Rhonda Hartman, Coming of Age: Devising Legislation for Adolescent Medical Decision-Making, 28 Am.J.L. & Med. 409 (2002).

Courts may give some weight to the statements of older children even if those courts are reluctant to declare those children "emancipated" or "mature minors." Although children under 16 typically are not found sufficiently mature to independently choose to forgo life-sustaining treatment, many courts have given considerable weight to the statements made by children considerably younger than that. See, e.g., In re Guardianship of Crum, 61 Ohio Misc.2d 596, 580 N.E.2d 876 (Prob.Ct., Franklin Co. 1991). Also see discussion of children's assent to participation in research in Chapter 7.

6.   At least one state explicitly authorizes children who understand the relevant health care factors to make their own decisions with regard to end-of-life care, even if they have not been emancipated and are not authorized to make other health care decisions. See N.M. Stat. Ann. § 24–7A–6.1(C), providing:

> [I]f an unemancipated minor has capacity sufficient to understand the nature of that unemancipated minor's medical condition, the risks and benefits of treatment and the contemplated decision to withhold or withdraw life-sustaining treatment, that unemancipated minor shall have the authority to withhold or withdraw life-sustaining treatment.

Should a child who cannot consent to an appendectomy under state law have the authority to consent to removal of life-sustaining treatment? Are children who are most likely to meet the statutory standard—those teenagers who have spent years suffering from a degenerative disease, for example—more likely than others to be able to recognize and apply their own life values to these important decisions? For a particularly interesting account of the roles of parents and children in consenting to body-reshaping medical care, see Alicia Ouellette, Shaping Parental Authority over Children's Bodies, 85 Ind. L.J. 955 (2010).

7.   As the *Newmark* court explained, courts have "unhesitatingly authorized medical treatment over a parent's religious objection when the treatment is relatively innocuous in comparison with the dangers of withholding medical care." Of course, what constitutes an innocuous treatment for most of us might constitute a very serious intrusion for others. Most people are not terribly concerned by the prospect of a blood transfusion; for others, it may eliminate a possibility of eternal salvation. Despite this, courts have not flinched when they have been presented with requests for treatment that is

"medically necessary"—i.e., when the child will surely die if the treatment is not provided, and just as surely will live if the treatment is provided. Courts routinely and consistently order blood transfusions for children of objecting Jehovah's Witness parents, at least when they meet this requirement of medical necessity; in this sense the courts treat Jehovah's Witness children very differently from Jehovah's Witness adults. On the other hand, courts generally do not order treatment for children who do not face life threatening conditions. The hardest cases, like the *Newmark* case, are those cases in which the proposed treatment is highly invasive, but the child faces a life threatening condition. As the chance of temporary remission and long term cure increases, the courts are more likely to order the treatment. Is this consistent with evaluation under the factors listed in note 4, above?

8.    While courts regularly face parental decisions that their children not receive treatment, they are sometimes confronted with the reverse situation. In In re K.I., B.I. and D.M., 735 A.2d 448 (D.C.1999) the District of Columbia Court of Appeals approved a DNR order for a neglected, comatose two-year-old child who was born "neurologically devastated." The child was taken from his drunken mother after he had been left alone for days without his necessary heart and lung medication. The mother opposed the hospital's request that the child be given DNR status. Applying the best interests (rather than the substituted judgment) standard, the court recognized that the mother might be criminally liable for homicide if the child were to die, and it thus disregarded her request that there be aggressive attempts at resuscitation. See also Care and Protection of Sharlene, 445 Mass. 756, 840 N.E.2d 915 (2006).

Can you imagine other circumstances in which a parent might inappropriately demand treatment for her child? Should these cases be treated any differently from those in which the parent denies consent for (rather than demands) the recommended care? See also *In re Christopher I*, above, in which the father, whose abuse had resulted in the child's serious neurological injury, argued that the child's life should be maintained, and J.N. v. Superior Court, 156 Cal.App.4th 523, 67 Cal.Rptr.3d 384 (Cal. App. 2007), where the court ultimately permitted the withdrawal of a breathing tube but not the entry of a "do not attempt resuscitation" order in an abuse and neglect case involving an arguably criminally "shaken baby." A family court also allowed for the de-escalation of treatment of an allegedly "shaken baby" in Division of Family Services v. Truselo, 846 A.2d 256 (Del. Fam. Ct. 2000).

9.    Like Delaware, most states have promulgated statutes that provide that "spiritual healing" *per se* cannot constitute child abuse or neglect for purposes of the state's criminal or child protective services statutes. In fact, for some time the existence of such protections were required as a condition of receiving some forms of federal funding. These spiritual healing statutes were the consequence of lobbying by the Christian Science church, and they were written using terms (e.g., "accredited practitioner") that have well defined meanings within that church. Are such statutes Constitutional? Might they violate the Establishment Clause of the First Amendment because they give a preference to Christian Scientists, and protect them in ways that they do not

protect others? Is it relevant that the statute only protects members of "recognized" religions, and that the state is called upon to determine which religions it will "recognize"? Might they violate the Establishment Clause because they disfavor children within certain religious communities? Most commentators who have considered the issue have determined that these statutes are not constitutional (at least as they are applied to civil abuse and neglect proceedings) because they violate either the Establishment Clause or the Equal Protection Clause of the Fourteenth Amendment. For a good account of the best arguments on this issue, see Ann MacLean Massie, The Religion Clauses and Parental Health Care Decision-making for Children: Suggestions for a New Approach, 21 Hastings Const. L. Q. 725 (1994). Also see State v. Miskimens, 22 Ohio Misc.2d 43, 490 N.E.2d 931 (Com.Pl.1984) and Walker v. Superior Court, 222 Cal.Rptr. 87 (Cal.App.1986) aff'd 47 Cal.3d 112, 253 Cal.Rptr. 1, 763 P.2d 852 (1988).

10. The law generally views decision-making for newborns as a separate inquiry from decision-making for other children, and questions about the propriety of discontinuing treatment for newborns and infants often revolve around whether such treatment would be futile, and whether denying such treatment would constitute discrimination based on the newborn's medical condition. The questions of how life and death decisions should be made for newborns, and how federal statutes and rules apply under such circumstances, are discussed in Chapter 3, which focuses on discrimination based on medical condition.

### PROBLEM: CONJOINED TWINS

After a woman was diagnosed as carrying conjoined (i.e., "Siamese") twins, she left her home village of Xaghra on the Mediterranean island of Gozo to seek medical care at a hospital in the United Kingdom well known for its care of such birth anomalies. At the birth it was clear that one baby's heart and lungs were providing for the circulation in both babies. That baby, Jodie, was generally healthy, while her conjoined sibling, Mary, suffered from severe brain damage as well as other substantial disabilities. The doctors concluded that Jodie could lead a fairly normal life if she were separated from her sister and provided a series of reconstructive surgeries. Of course, the separation would result in Mary's immediate death. Alternatively, the failure to separate the twins would result in both of their deaths within the next several months.

The devout Catholic parents denied consent for the surgery, saying "[w]e cannot begin to accept or contemplate that one of our children should die to enable the other one to survive." Others also pointed out that the decision to allow Mary to die during the separation surgery could be met with horror in Xaghra, and make it very difficult for the family to return home. The physicians, however, were distressed that both children would be allowed to die when one could be saved, and they sought an order from the court to authorize the separation surgery.

Would it be homicide to do the surgery with the certain knowledge that it would result in Mary's death? Is it medical neglect to deny consent to surgery which will save one child but result in the death of the second? Should the decision be left to the parents, or should the state intervene and exercise its *parens patriae* authority? What would you do if you were (1) a parent of these children? (2) the primary care physician for these children? (3) the judge before whom the case was presented? The court was well briefed in this case. In addition to counsel retained by the parents and the public health service, a guardian ad litem was appointed for each child. What position should each of those guardians ad litem take?

For a description of this case (and how it came out), see Jacob Appel, Recent Developments in Health Law, 28 J. L. Med. & Ethics 312 (2000); Alexander MacLeod, Medical, Religious Values Clash Over Conjoined Twins, Christian Science Monitor, September 29, 2000, page 7.

# VI. "FUTILE" TREATMENT

## BETANCOURT V. TRINITAS HOSPITAL
Superior Court of New Jersey, Appellate Division, 2010.
415 N.J.Super. 301, 1 A.3d 823.

PER CURIAM.

\* \* \*

On January 22, 2008, Rueben [Betancourt] underwent surgery at defendant to remove a malignant tumor from his thymus gland. \* \* \* [T]he surgery went well, but while Rueben was recovering in the post-operative intensive care unit, the ventilation tube that was supplying him with oxygen somehow became dislodged. As a result, his brain was deprived of oxygen, and he developed anoxic encephalopathy, a condition that left him in a persistent vegetative state.

Rueben was subsequently discharged from defendant and admitted to other facilities that attempted rehabilitative treatments. He was readmitted to defendant on July 3, 2008, however, with a diagnosis of renal failure. Further attempts at placement in another facility proved fruitless, and he remained at defendant until his death on May 29, 2009.

At the time of his death, Rueben had not executed an advanced directive under the New Jersey Advanced Directives for Health Care Act. [ ] He had neither designated a health care representative nor memorialized "specific wishes regarding the provision, withholding or withdrawal of any form of health care, including life-sustaining treatment." [ ]

Witnesses for both parties to the dispute presented disparate views of Rueben's condition, the impact of treatment and prognosis. At the hearing,

Rueben's attending physician, Dr. Arthur E. Millman, indicated that Rueben was a seventy-three-year-old man who was suffering from multi-system organ failure; his kidneys had failed, his lungs had failed, he was intermittently septic, he had hypertensive heart disease and congestive heart disease, and his skin was breaking down. He had "truly horrific decubitus ulcers" that had progressed to the bone, developing into osteomyelitis. Rueben was on a ventilator and received renal dialysis three times per week; he was fed through a tube into his stomach, given antibiotics and was turned frequently in his bed.

Millman stated that Rueben's most overwhelming problem was his permanent anoxic encephalopathy. He described Rueben's neurological state as "non-cognitive" with no higher mental functioning. He did believe, however, that Rueben was responsive to pain because he had personally witnessed Rueben's reactions to it. There had been no change in Rueben's neurological condition since he was admitted in July 2008, and Millman believed that the likelihood of his return to cognizant function was "virtually zero."

Dr. Bernard Schanzer, Chief of Neurology at defendant, corroborated most of Millman's views concerning Rueben's neurological condition. He explained that the cortical part of Rueben's brain had been irreversibly damaged. As a result, Rueben was in a permanent vegetative state, unable to speak or respond to verbal cues, and although Rueben's eyes were open and he appeared awake, he was not alert or aware of his environment. Schanzer disagreed with Millman, however, concerning Rueben's ability to experience pain. He believed that Rueben did not feel pain, and Rueben's responses to stimuli were due to basic reflexes of the brain stem and spinal cord. He opined that there was no chance that Rueben would ever regain a cognitive state.

Dr. Maria Silva Khazaei, a nephrologist, concluded that Rueben was suffering from end-stage renal disease, and there was no likelihood of improvement. She opined that it was contrary to accepted standards of medical care to continue dialysis treatments because they only prolonged Rueben's dying process.

Not surprisingly, plaintiff's consulting nephrologist had a different opinion. Dr. Carl Goldstein, a nephrologist retained by plaintiff, stated that Rueben's current plan of dialysis "comports in every way with the prevailing standards of care." He explained that the dialysis had been effective in removing excess fluid and waste products from Rueben's body. Rueben was tolerating the treatment well, and it was not harmful or dangerous to him.

Dr. William J. McHugh, Medical Director at defendant, was a member of the hospital's prognosis committee. The committee had been consulted concerning the efficacy of continuing Rueben's treatment; as a result,

McHugh reviewed many, but not all, of the relevant medical records. He concluded that Rueben had "no outlook" because no affirmative treatment would improve his condition. As opposed to Millman, who believed that Rueben would probably die within a matter of months regardless of continued treatment, McHugh stated that Rueben's death "may take some time." In fact, he opined that if treatment were continued at the present level, Rueben "could go on for quite a while." On cross-examination, McHugh admitted that Rueben's present medical treatment was harmful only in the sense that the doctors were continuing to treat a hopeless situation.

Other members of the hospital's prognosis committee weighed in as well. Dr. Paul Veiana, president of the defendant's medical staff, examined Rueben the day before the hearing while Rueben was "wheeling" down to dialysis. Based on his review, he concluded that the doctors were not treating Rueben—they were just treating a body. He stated that the everyday drawing of blood and injections violated Rueben's body, and as a Christian, he believed that a body should not be so desecrated.

On several occasions, the hospital administration sought agreement from Rueben's family to place a DNR order and cease dialysis treatment, but they staunchly refused. It also made "exhaustive efforts" to transfer Rueben to another facility, but no other facility was willing to accept him. Ultimately, defendant acted unilaterally, placing the DNR order in Rueben's chart as well as surgically removing a dialysis port from Rueben's body.

At the hearing, plaintiff provided information about Rueben. Before his illness, Rueben lived with his wife and his two adult sons. Plaintiff resided next door and saw her father every day. The family had always been very close, and Rueben was "dedicated" to his wife and children.

Plaintiff described Rueben's history of medical treatment at the hospital, asserting that it was the hospital's fault that he suffered a brain injury. She visited her father in the hospital almost daily and saw him make movements and gestures that led her to believe that he was awake and alert. She did not, however, believe that he was suffering. The family determined that they did not want a DNR order placed in Rueben's chart and did not want the dialysis treatment to be stopped. Rather, they wanted to make the decision as to whether Rueben was "ready to go." Plaintiff explained: "[M]y father is a fighter. He will not give up."

Robin, Rueben's thirty-six-year-old son, offered that his father was his "only * * * real friend" and that he loved him very much. He recalled, anecdotally, that he and his father had discussed the Terri Schiavo case when it was in the news, and his father had said that it was the right of Schiavo's parents—not her doctors—to decide what to do. Robin stated that his father reacted to him during hospital visits, and that those reactions were not simply reflexes. He described how his father had different facial expressions depending on what was happening around him and how his father's pulse would slow down when family members spoke to him or played music. He said the family did not trust the doctors to make the decision as to when to terminate his father's life.

Maria, Rueben's wife of thirty-seven years, was convinced that her husband reacted positively when she spoke to him or touched him. She believed that he would want "to continue living until God wished."

Nonetheless, the trial judge acknowledged that the temporary restraining order procedure should rarely be used to direct affirmative relief, but he found that the matter presented an "extreme situation" in which he needed to move quickly in order to maintain the status quo. The judge ordered defendant to re-establish the level of treatment that had been provided to Rueben prior to the discontinuation of dialysis and also to remove a DNR order that had been placed in his chart. He then ordered a hearing, which was held approximately two weeks later.

Following the hearing, Judge Malone issued a written opinion in which he concluded that decisions concerning the proper course of treatment for Rueben could not be made by the hospital; rather, such decisions should be made by a surrogate who could take Rueben's personal value systems into account when determining what medical treatment was appropriate. He granted plaintiff's application, appointed plaintiff as her father's guardian and permanently restrained the hospital from discontinuing treatment to Rueben. This was memorialized in a March 20, 2009 order. This appeal followed.

On May 29, 2009, Rueben died. Plaintiff filed a motion to dismiss the appeal as moot, and we reserved decision on the motion pending consideration of the merits of the appeal. We now grant the motion and dismiss the appeal.

[The portion of the opinion discussing mootness is omitted. The court determined that the sparse record and the unique circumstances of the case—the plaintiff thought that Reuben's death was caused by the defendant's negligence, and they thought that the hospital's conduct was generated by the fact that they owed so much for the care provided by defendant—made it appropriate to dismiss on mootness grounds even though the case presented a matter of substantial public importance that would likely to arise again and could easily evade judicial review. The Supreme Court of New Jersey denied review. If you are disappointed that the court provided no legal analysis on the substantive issue, you should treat this case as a "problem" and supply your own analysis!]

## TEX. HEALTH & SAFETY CODE § 166.046; § 166.052; § 166.053 [THE "TEXAS FUTILITY STATUTE," A PART OF THE TEXAS ADVANCE DIRECTIVES ACT]

\* \* \*

### § 166.046—Procedure if Not Effectuating a Directive or Treatment Decision

(a)   If an attending physician refuses to honor a patient's advance directive or a health care or treatment decision made by or on behalf of a patient, the physician's refusal shall be reviewed by an ethics or medical committee. The attending physician may not be a member of that committee. The patient shall be given life-sustaining treatment during the review.

(b)   The patient or the person responsible for the health care decisions of the individual who has made the decision regarding the directive or treatment decision:

(1)   may be given a written description of the ethics or medical committee review process and any other policies and procedures related to this section adopted by the health care facility;

(2)   shall be informed of the committee review process not less than 48 hours before the meeting called to discuss the patient's directive, unless the time period is waived by mutual agreement;

(3)   at the time of being so informed, shall be provided:

(A)   a copy of the appropriate statement [describing this process]; and

(B)   a copy of the registry list of health care providers and referral groups that have volunteered their readiness to consider accepting transfer or to assist in locating a provider willing to accept transfer \* \* \*; and

(4)   is entitled to:

(A)   attend the meeting;

(B)   receive a written explanation of the decision reached during the review process;

(C)   receive a copy of the portion of the patient's medical record related to the treatment received by the patient in the facility for the lesser of:

(i)   the period of the patient's current admission to the facility; or

(ii)   the preceding 30 calendar days; and

(D) receive a copy of all of the patient's reasonably available diagnostic results and reports related to the medical record provided under Paragraph (C).

(c)   The written explanation * * * must be included in the patient's medical record.

(d)   If the attending physician, the patient, or the person responsible for the health care decisions of the individual does not agree with the decision reached during the review process under Subsection (b), the physician shall make a reasonable effort to transfer the patient to a physician who is willing to comply with the directive. If the patient is a patient in a health care facility, the facility's personnel shall assist the physician in arranging the patient's transfer to:

(1)   another physician;

(2)   an alternative care setting within that facility; or

(3)   another facility.

(e)   If the patient or the person responsible for the health care decisions of the patient is requesting life-sustaining treatment that the attending physician has decided and the ethics or medical committee has affirmed is medically inappropriate treatment, the patient shall be given available life-sustaining treatment pending transfer under Subsection (d). This subsection does not authorize withholding or withdrawing pain management medication, medical procedures necessary to provide comfort, or any other health care provided to alleviate a patient's pain. The patient is responsible for any costs incurred in transferring the patient to another facility. The attending physician, any other physician responsible for the care of the patient, and the health care facility are not obligated to provide life-sustaining treatment after the 10th day after both the written decision and the patient's medical record required under Subsection (b) are provided to the patient or the person responsible for the health care decisions of the patient unless ordered to do so under Subsection (g), except that artificially administered nutrition and hydration must be provided unless, based on reasonable medical judgment, providing artificially administered nutrition and hydration would:

(1)   hasten the patient's death;

(2)   be medically contraindicated such that the provision of the treatment seriously exacerbates life-threatening medical problems not outweighed by the benefits of the provision of the treatment;

(3)   result in substantial irremediable physical pain not outweighed by the benefit of the provision of the treatment;

(4)   be medically ineffective in prolonging life; or

(5) be contrary to the patient's or surrogate's clearly documented desire not to receive artificially administered nutrition or hydration.

(e–1) If during a previous admission to a facility a patient's attending physician and the review process * * * have determined that life-sustaining treatment is inappropriate, and the patient is readmitted to the same facility within six months from the date of the decision reached during the review process conducted upon the previous admission, Subsections (b) through (e) need not be followed if the patient's attending physician and a consulting physician who is a member of the ethics or medical committee of the facility document on the patient's readmission that the patient's condition either has not improved or has deteriorated since the review process was conducted.

(f) Life-sustaining treatment under this section may not be entered in the patient's medical record as medically unnecessary treatment until the time period provided under Subsection (e) has expired.

(g) At the request of the patient or the person responsible for the health care decisions of the patient, the appropriate district or county court shall extend the time period provided under Subsection (e) only if the court finds, by a preponderance of the evidence, that there is a reasonable expectation that a physician or health care facility that will honor the patient's directive will be found if the time extension is granted.

(h) * * * This section does not apply to hospice services provided by a home and community support services agency * * *.

* * *

## § 166.052—Statements Explaining Patient's Right to Transfer

(a) In cases in which the attending physician refuses to honor an advance directive or health care or treatment decision requesting the provision of life-sustaining treatment, the statement required * * * shall be in substantially the following form:

> **When There Is A Disagreement About Medical Treatment: The Physician Recommends Against Certain Life-Sustaining Treatment That You Wish To Continue**
>
> You have been given this information because you have requested life-sustaining treatment* for yourself as the patient or on behalf of the patient, as applicable, which the attending physician believes is not

---

\* "Life-sustaining treatment" means treatment that, based on reasonable medical judgment, sustains the life of a patient and without which the patient will die. The term includes both life-sustaining medications and artificial life support, such as mechanical breathing machines, kidney dialysis treatment, and artificially administered nutrition and hydration. The term does not include the administration of pain management medication or the performance of a medical procedure considered to be necessary to provide comfort care, or any other medical care provided to alleviate a patient's pain.

medically appropriate. This information is being provided to help you understand state law, your rights, and the resources available to you in such circumstances. It outlines the process for resolving disagreements about treatment among patients, families, and physicians. It is based upon [this section].

When an attending physician refuses to comply with an advance directive or other request for life-sustaining treatment because of the physician's judgment that the treatment would be medically inappropriate, the case will be reviewed by an ethics or medical committee. Life-sustaining treatment will be provided through the review.

You will receive notification of this review at least 48 hours before a meeting of the committee related to your case. You are entitled to attend the meeting. With your agreement, the meeting may be held sooner than 48 hours, if possible.

You are entitled to receive a written explanation of the decision reached during the review process.

If after this review process both the attending physician and the ethics or medical committee conclude that life-sustaining treatment is medically inappropriate and yet you continue to request such treatment, then the following procedure will occur:

1.     The physician, with the help of the health care facility, will assist you in trying to find a physician and facility willing to provide the requested treatment.

2.     You are being given a list of health care providers, licensed physicians, health care facilities, and referral groups that have volunteered their readiness to consider accepting transfer, or to assist in locating a provider willing to accept transfer* * *. You may wish to contact providers, facilities, or referral groups on the list or others of your choice to get help in arranging a transfer.

3.     The patient will continue to be given life-sustaining treatment until the patient can be transferred to a willing provider for up to 10 days from the time you were given both the committee's written decision that life-sustaining treatment is not appropriate and the patient's medical record. The patient will continue to be given after the 10-day period treatment to enhance pain management and reduce suffering, including artificially administered nutrition and hydration, unless, based on reasonable medical judgment, providing artificially administered nutrition and hydration would hasten the patient's death, be medically contraindicated such that the provision of the treatment seriously exacerbates life-threatening medical problems not outweighed by the benefit of the provision of the treatment, result in

substantial irremediable physical pain not outweighed by the benefit of the provision of the treatment, be medically ineffective in prolonging life, or be contrary to the patient's or surrogate's clearly documented desires.

4.   If a transfer can be arranged, the patient will be responsible for the costs of the transfer.

5.   If a provider cannot be found willing to give the requested treatment within 10 days, life-sustaining treatment may be withdrawn unless a court of law has granted an extension.

6.   You may ask the appropriate district or county court to extend the 10-day period if the court finds that there is a reasonable expectation that you may find a physician or health care facility willing to provide life-sustaining treatment if the extension is granted. Patient medical records will be provided to the patient or surrogate in accordance with [the] Texas Health and Safety Code.

\* \* \*

(c)   An attending physician or health care facility may, if it chooses, include any additional information concerning the physician's or facility's policy, perspective, experience, or review procedure.

### § 166.053—Registry to Assist Transfers

(a)   The [Texas Department of State Health Services] shall maintain a registry listing the identity of and contact information for health care providers and referral groups \* \* \* that have voluntarily notified the department they may consider accepting or may assist in locating a provider willing to accept transfer of a patient under [this statute].

(b)   The listing of a provider or referral group in the registry described in this section does not obligate the provider or group to accept transfer of or provide services to any particular patient.

\* \* \*

## FROEDTERT HOSPITAL—MEDICAL COLLEGE OF WISCONSIN, FUTILITY POLICY
(revised, 2018 version).

\* \* \*

A.   If, in the judgment of the attending physician and a staff physician consultant, life-sustaining medical treatment would be futile, the attending physician may write an order withholding or withdrawing the treatment after notifying the patient or patient's surrogate(s). Appropriate palliative care measures should be instituted.

B.   A life-sustaining medical intervention should be considered "futile" if it cannot be expected to restore or maintain vital organ function or to achieve the expressed goals of the patient when decisional.

C.   Life-sustaining medical treatment includes cardiopulmonary resuscitation, mechanical ventilation, artificial nutrition and hydration, blood products, renal dialysis, vasopressors, or any other treatment that prolongs dying.

D.   Consultation with Palliative Medicine, Social Services, and Chaplaincy, as appropriate, is strongly encouraged. If there are remaining questions, the physician should consult the Ethics Committee. If the patient (or surrogate) disagrees, the attending physician should consider whether transfer to another attending physician, or another health care facility willing to accept the patient, is feasible. If transfer to a physician or facility willing to accept the patient is not feasible, further life-sustaining medical treatment may be withdrawn.

\* \* \*

F.   The attending physician must inform the Office of the Chief Medical Officer verbally when this policy is invoked and document the notice in the patient's legal health record \* \* \*.

## NOTES AND QUESTIONS

1.   The *Betancourt* case was never resolved on its merits. Should the court have decided it on the merits even though it was moot? How should it have been decided? You have been presented with the factual portion of the opinion; how would you write the substantive legal analysis? How would this issue have been resolved if the hospital had a policy like the Froedtert policy?

2.   Who has the final authority to make that decision under the Texas statute and the two hospital policies? Who would you allow to be the final arbiter of whether a proposed treatment is futile?

3.   When is requested care truly "futile"? Under the Froedtert Hospital Policy, how is futility defined? Who has the authority to make that decision? Under the Texas statute, how is futility defined? Which definition makes the most sense, given the purposes of futility laws and policies? How would you define futility? Meir Katz, When Is Medical Care Futile? The Institutional Competence of the Medical Profession Regarding the Provision of Life-Sustaining Medical Care, 90 Neb.L.Rev.1 (2011).

4.   The term futility is subject to a variety of interpretations. Treatment is *scientifically futile* (or *medically futile*) when it cannot achieve the medical result that is expected by the patient (or by the family) making the request. As a general matter, scientifically futile treatment need not be offered or provided to a patient. A seriously ill cancer patient need not be provided with laetrile, a useless drug that has been popularized by those who would prey upon

desperate patients and their families, even if that treatment is requested. A child with a viral illness need not be prescribed an antibiotic, even if the child's parents request one, because, as a matter of science, the antibiotic will not be effective in treating that illness. Doctors need not do a CAT scan on a patient with a cold, even if that is what the patient wants, because there is no reason to believe that there will be any connection between what can be discovered on the scan and the appropriate treatment of the cold. As a general matter healthcare providers, who are trained in the science of medicine, are entitled to determine which treatments are scientifically futile.

A harder question arises when a patient requests treatment that is not scientifically futile, but that is, in the opinion of the health care provider, *ethically futile*. Treatment is ethically futile if it will not serve the underlying interests of the patient. For example, some providers believe that it is ethically futile to keep a patient's body aerated and nourished when that patient is in persistent vegetative state. These healthcare providers believe that it is beyond the scope of medicine to sustain mere corporeal existence. Some healthcare providers believe that it would be ethically futile to engage in CPR under circumstances in which the most that can be accomplished through that intervention would be to prolong the patient's life by a few hours. Families may disagree with physicians over what constitutes ethically futile treatment. Is there any reason to adopt the provider's perspective, rather than the family's, as the ethically "correct" one?

The Council on Ethical and Judicial Affairs of the AMA has determined that:

> Physicians are not required to offer or provide interventions that, in their best medical judgment, cannot reasonably be expected to yield the intended clinical benefit or achieve agreed-on goals for care. Respecting patient autonomy does not mean that patients should receive specific interventions simply because they (or their surrogates) request them.

Code of Medical Ethics Opinion 5.5, *Medically Ineffective Interventions (2016)*.

Is the Council's position a convincing one, or is it merely a device to transfer the authority to make ethically charged decisions from patients to physicians? See Patrick Moore, An End-of-Life Quandry in Need of a Statutory Response: When Patients Demand Life-Sustaining Treatment That Physicians Are Unwilling to Provide, 48 B.C.L.Rev. 433 (2007).

5. Under the Texas statute, what process must be followed before a patient seeking futile care is discharged from the hospital? You might prepare a flow chart including all of the steps required by the statute. Do these requirements seem reasonable? Is ten days enough to find an alternative placement for one who is about to have futile treatment removed?

6. The Texas statute has given rise to litigation. In one celebrated case the mother of Sun Hudson, an infant, sought judicial intervention to avoid the discontinuation of treatment that physicians believed to be futile. In another case involving an adult, Spiro Nikolouzos had been transferred once after

ventilator support was found to be futile. When the receiving institution reached the same conclusion and began to prepare for his discharge, his family sought more time to arrange for yet a second transfer. Both cases were decided on procedural grounds largely unrelated to the substantive provisions of the statute, but each ultimately recognized the authority of the health care provider to make futility determinations. See Hudson v. Texas Children's Hosp., 177 S.W.3d 232 (Tex. Ct. App. 2005) and Nikolouzos v. St. Luke's Episcopal Hosp., 162 S.W.3d 678 (Tex. Ct. App. 2005). Several other litigated cases have resulted in a great deal of press coverage but no significant reported opinions.

7.    Some states with statutes modeled on the Uniform Health-Care Decisions Act, reprinted in Section IV above, provide that physicians need not give futile care. Recall that section 7(f) of that UHCDA provides that "[a] health-care provider or institution may decline to comply with an individual instruction or health-care decision that requires medically ineffective health care or health care contrary to generally accepted health-care standards applicable to the health-care provider or institution." See also Md. Code Ann., Health-Gen. section 5–611 and Va. Code Ann. section 54.1–2990. The Texas statute differs from these earlier statutes by providing an authoritative and conclusive endpoint for disputes. Thaddeus Pope, Medical Futility Statutes: No Safe Harbor to Unilaterally Refuse Life-sustaining Treatment, 51 Tenn. L. Rev. 1 (2007), arguing in part that the failure to provide conclusive procedures diminishes the utility of earlier statutes.

8.    In 2012 Froedtert Hospital was cited by a CMS inspector for not telling a patient about the existence of the hospital's futility policy. In that case a dying patient had been hospitalized 21 times in the past year and was in such failing health that the physicians concluded that any further life-sustaining treatment would be futile under the hospital policy. The family objected and continued to insist that all available treatment, including near daily blood transfusions, be continued. The patient was given DNR status without the agreement of the family.

The CMS inspector did not find that the Froedtert futility policy violated any law, but, rather, that the hospital violated the Patient Self Determination Act, described earlier in this chapter, by not telling the patient and his family of the existence of the futility policy. Ultimately the patient's family requested the transfer of the patient to another facility, and Froedtert cooperated in arranging for that transfer.

9.    Robert Truog, a thoughtful physician and bioethicist, writes that medical futility issues are based in "power, trust, hope, money, and suffering." Robert Truog, Medical Futility, 25 Ga. St. U.L. Rev. 985, 986 (2009). Is he right? If he is right, is this fact helpful in figuring out how to resolve disputes over medical futility? Mediation is often employed to help resolve these disputes in health care institutions. How helpful is mediation in dealing with conflict based in power, trust, hope, money and suffering?

10. There is a great deal of good writing on the proper legal approach to arguably futile treatment. The Summer, 2008 issue of Health Matrix has an excellent symposium on futility in health care and the legal response. For a good account of the fundamental issues at stake, see Lawrence Schneiderman & Nancy Jecker, Wrong Medicine (1995). See also Robert Truog, Medical Futility, 25 Ga. St. U.L. Rev. 985 (2009)(focus on the Sun Hudson case), Jerry Menikoff, Demanded Medical Care, 30 Ariz. St. L. J. 1091 (1998), and Judith Daar, Medical Futility and Implications for Physician Autonomy, 21 Am. J. L. & Med. 221 (1995). For a useful account of issues related to physicians' willingness to accept decisions to continue futile care, see M. Fetters et al., Conflict Resolution at the End of Life, 29 Critical Care Med. 921 (2001).

# CHAPTER 6

# MEDICALLY ASSISTED DYING

■ ■ ■

## I.  INTRODUCTION

There has been a significant debate in the United States and elsewhere over the past quarter of a century over the propriety of medically assisted death; that is, medical care designed to help a patient die how and when the patient wants to die. As the last chapter established, every state allows a physician to assist a patient who wishes to discontinue life-sustaining medical care, at least under most circumstances. May a health care provider also provide affirmative intervention that will hasten the patient's death? Under what circumstances?

The language we use to discuss these questions has become especially divisive over the past few years, and we must be careful how we use words that have become laden with political and philosophical meaning. "Euthanasia," for example, generally refers to an affirmative act that directly and immediately causes the death of a patient for the benefit of that patient. "Involuntary euthanasia" is sometimes used to describe euthanasia against the will of the patient, although sometimes it means euthanasia without the formal and expressed consent of the patient. "Voluntary euthanasia" is sometimes used to refer to euthanasia upon request of the patient, although most careful thinkers avoid using that term altogether. "Active euthanasia" sometimes refers to some affirmative act of euthanasia, while "passive euthanasia" generally refers, technically incorrectly, to withholding or withdrawing life-sustaining treatment.

"Suicide" can refer to any act taken by a person to intentionally end his life (including the act of a patient taking a prescribed lethal dose of medication), but sometimes it refers only to an act taken by someone acting irrationally, or under the influence of extraordinary emotional distress or mental disease (and not, for example, to the act of a terminally ill, competent patient who knowingly takes a prescribed lethal dose to end his suffering). Both "euthanasia" and "suicide" have highly negative connotations, and the people who use those terms generally oppose the propriety of the act. The words "death" and "killing" in this context also have strong negative connotations, and those terms are used to describe medically assisted dying primarily by those who oppose its legality.

On the other hand, "Death with Dignity," which often refers to these same acts, has a positive connotation. Is anyone opposed to death with dignity? That is why advocates of the practice now made legal in Oregon and Washington placed the "Death with Dignity" title on the initiatives that were ultimately approved by the voters in each of those states. Similarly, "Right to Die" is generally a popular concept, and that term is used almost exclusively by those who approve of the use of this practice. For years, however, the phrase was used to describe the withdrawal of life-sustaining treatment. Using the same phrase in this context implicitly argues that there is no difference between the two. Although earlier editions of this casebook used the term "physician assisted suicide" or "physician assisted death," both have been abandoned in this edition because these terms are now used primarily by those who oppose this role for physicians.

As you read the materials that follow, make sure that you identify with specificity exactly what practice is being considered. While there are a few countries that permit euthanasia under certain limited circumstances, that has never been an option available in the United States and it is rarely part of the legal debate. In this country, the debate has centered on the propriety (and legality) of a medically prescribed lethal dose designed to be ingested by the competent, fully informed patient who originally requested a prescription for it from a physician. It is that practice that forms the core of the discussion in this chapter. While, increasingly, physicians, judges and scholars are calling this assistance "Aid in Dying," the authors have chosen to call it "Medically Assisted Dying" because this term does not reflect the values of those who support it or oppose it.

## II. THE CONSTITUTIONAL FRAMEWORK

### WASHINGTON V. GLUCKSBERG
Supreme Court of the United States, 1997.
521 U.S. 702, 117 S.Ct. 2258, 138 L.Ed.2d 772.

REHNQUIST, C. J., delivered the opinion of the Court, in which O'CONNOR, SCALIA, KENNEDY, and THOMAS, JJ., joined. O'CONNOR, J., filed a concurring opinion, in which GINSBURG and BREYER, JJ., joined in part. STEVENS, J., SOUTER, J., GINSBURG, J., and BREYER, J., filed opinions concurring in the judgment.

CHIEF JUSTICE REHNQUIST delivered the opinion of the Court.

The question presented in this case is whether Washington's prohibition against "causing" or "aiding" a suicide offends the Fourteenth Amendment to the United States Constitution. We hold that it does not.

\* \* \*

The plaintiffs assert [ ] "the existence of a liberty interest protected by the Fourteenth Amendment which extends to a personal choice by a mentally competent, terminally ill adult to commit physician-assisted suicide." [ ] Relying primarily on Planned Parenthood v. Casey, [ ] and Cruzan v. Director, Missouri Dept. of Health, [ ] the District Court agreed, [ ] and concluded that Washington's assisted-suicide ban is unconstitutional because it "places an undue burden on the exercise of [that] constitutionally protected liberty interest." [ ] The District Court also decided that the Washington statute violated the Equal Protection Clause's requirement that " 'all persons similarly situated . . . be treated alike.' "[ ]

A panel of the Court of Appeals for the Ninth Circuit reversed, emphasizing that "in the two hundred and five years of our existence no constitutional right to aid in killing oneself has ever been asserted and upheld by a court of final jurisdiction." [ ] The Ninth Circuit reheard the case en banc, reversed the panel's decision, and affirmed the District Court. [ ] Like the District Court, the en banc Court of Appeals emphasized our Casey and Cruzan decisions. [ ] The court also discussed what it described as "historical" and "current societal attitudes" toward suicide and assisted suicide, [ ] and concluded that "the Constitution encompasses a due process liberty interest in controlling the time and manner of one's death—that there is, in short, a constitutionally-recognized 'right to die.' "[ ] After "weighing and then balancing" this interest against Washington's various interests, the court held that the State's assisted-suicide ban was unconstitutional "as applied to terminally ill competent [ ] adults who wish to hasten their deaths with medication prescribed by their physicians." [ ] We granted certiorari [ ] and now reverse.

## I

We begin, as we do in all due-process cases, by examining our Nation's history, legal traditions, and practices. [ ] In almost every State—indeed, in almost every western democracy—it is a crime to assist a suicide. The States' assisted-suicide bans are not innovations. Rather, they are longstanding expressions of the States' commitment to the protection and preservation of all human life. [ ] Indeed, opposition to and condemnation of suicide—and, therefore, of assisting suicide—are consistent and enduring themes of our philosophical, legal, and cultural heritages. [ ]

More specifically, for over 700 years, the Anglo—American common-law tradition has punished or otherwise disapproved of both suicide and assisting suicide. . . . [The Chief Justice then reviews the common law of England and the American colonies and states with regards to suicide, from the 13th century to the present.]

\* \* \*

Attitudes toward suicide itself have changed since [the 13th Century prohibitions on suicide] . . . but our laws have consistently condemned, and continue to prohibit, assisting suicide. Despite changes in medical technology and notwithstanding an increased emphasis on the importance of end-of-life decisionmaking, we have not retreated from this prohibition. Against this backdrop of history, tradition, and practice, we now turn to respondents' constitutional claim.

## II

The Due Process Clause guarantees more than fair process, and the "liberty" it protects includes more than the absence of physical restraint. [ ] The Clause also provides heightened protection against government interference with certain fundamental rights and liberty interests. [ ] In a long line of cases, we have held that, in addition to the specific freedoms protected by the Bill of Rights, the "liberty" specially protected by the Due Process Clause includes the rights to marry, [ ]; to have children, [ ]; to direct the education and upbringing of one's children, [ ]; to marital privacy, [ ]; to use contraception, [ ]; to bodily integrity, [ ] and to abortion, [ ]. We have also assumed, and strongly suggested, that the Due Process Clause protects the traditional right to refuse unwanted lifesaving medical treatment. [ ]

But we "have always been reluctant to expand the concept of substantive due process because guideposts for responsible decisionmaking in this unchartered area are scarce and open-ended." [ ] By extending constitutional protection to an asserted right or liberty interest, we, to a great extent, place the matter outside the arena of public debate and legislative action. We must therefore "exercise the utmost care whenever we are asked to break new ground in this field" [ ] lest the liberty protected by the Due Process Clause be subtly transformed into the policy preferences of the members of this Court [ ].

Our established method of substantive-due-process analysis has two primary features: First, we have regularly observed that the Due Process Clause specially protects those fundamental rights and liberties which are, objectively, "deeply rooted in this Nation's history and tradition" [ ] and "implicit in the concept of ordered liberty," such that "neither liberty nor justice would exist if they were sacrificed" [ ]. Second, we have required in substantive-due-process cases a "careful description" of the asserted fundamental liberty interest. [ ] Cruzan, supra, at 277–278. Our Nation's history, legal traditions, and practices thus provide the crucial "guideposts for responsible decisionmaking" [ ] that direct and restrain our exposition of the Due Process Clause. As we stated recently in Flores, the Fourteenth Amendment "forbids the government to infringe . . . 'fundamental' liberty interests at all, no matter what process is provided, unless the infringement is narrowly tailored to serve a compelling state interest." [ ]

* * *

Turning to the claim at issue here, the Court of Appeals stated that "properly analyzed, the first issue to be resolved is whether there is a liberty interest in determining the time and manner of one's death" [ ] or, in other words, "is there a right to die?" [ ]. Similarly, respondents assert a "liberty to choose how to die" and a right to "control of one's final days," [ ] and describe the asserted liberty as "the right to choose a humane, dignified death" [ ] and "the liberty to shape death" [ ]. As noted above, we have a tradition of carefully formulating the interest at stake in substantive-due-process cases. For example, although Cruzan is often described as a "right to die" case [ ] we were, in fact, more precise: we assumed that the Constitution granted competent persons a "constitutionally protected right to refuse lifesaving hydration and nutrition." [ ] The Washington statute at issue in this case prohibits "aiding another person to attempt suicide," [ ] and, thus, the question before us is whether the "liberty" specially protected by the Due Process Clause includes a right to commit suicide which itself includes a right to assistance in doing so.

. . . With this "careful description" of respondents' claim in mind, we turn to Casey and Cruzan.

[The Chief Justice next discusses the Cruzan case, where, he says,] "we assumed that the United States Constitution would grant a competent person a constitutionally protected right to refuse lifesaving hydration and nutrition."

* * *

The right assumed in Cruzan, however, was not simply deduced from abstract concepts of personal autonomy. Given the common-law rule that forced medication was a battery, and the long legal tradition protecting the decision to refuse unwanted medical treatment, our assumption was entirely consistent with this Nation's history and constitutional traditions. The decision to commit suicide with the assistance of another may be just as personal and profound as the decision to refuse unwanted medical treatment, but it has never enjoyed similar legal protection. Indeed, the two acts are widely and reasonably regarded as quite distinct. [ ] In Cruzan itself, we recognized that most States outlawed assisted suicide—and even more do today—and we certainly gave no intimation that the right to refuse unwanted medical treatment could be somehow transmuted into a right to assistance in committing suicide. [ ]

Respondents also rely on Casey. There, the Court's opinion concluded that "the essential holding of Roe v. Wade should be retained and once again reaffirmed." [ ] We held, first, that a woman has a right, before her fetus is viable, to an abortion "without undue interference from the State"; second, that States may restrict post-viability abortions, so long as exceptions are made to protect a woman's life and health; and third, that the State has legitimate interests throughout a pregnancy in protecting the health of the woman and the life of the unborn child. [ ] In reaching this conclusion, the opinion discussed in some detail this Court's substantive-due-process tradition of interpreting the Due Process Clause to protect certain fundamental rights and "personal decisions relating to marriage, procreation, contraception, family relationships, child rearing, and education," and noted that many of those rights and liberties "involve the most intimate and personal choices a person may make in a lifetime." [ ]

\* \* \*

That many of the rights and liberties protected by the Due Process Clause sound in personal autonomy does not warrant the sweeping conclusion that any and all important, intimate, and personal decisions are so protected, [ ] and Casey did not suggest otherwise.

The history of the law's treatment of assisted suicide in this country has been and continues to be one of the rejection of nearly all efforts to permit it. That being the case, our decisions lead us to conclude that the asserted "right" to assistance in committing suicide is not a fundamental liberty interest protected by the Due Process Clause. The Constitution also requires, however, that Washington's assisted-suicide ban be rationally related to legitimate government interests. [ ] This requirement is unquestionably met here. As the court below recognized, [ ] Washington's assisted-suicide ban implicates a number of state interests. [ ]

First, Washington has an "unqualified interest in the preservation of human life."

\* \* \*

Relatedly, all admit that suicide is a serious public-health problem, especially among persons in otherwise vulnerable groups. [ ] The State has an interest in preventing suicide, and in studying, identifying, and treating its causes. [ ]

\* \* \*

The State also has an interest in protecting the integrity and ethics of the medical profession. . . . [T]he American Medical Association, like many other medical and physicians' groups, has concluded that "physician-assisted suicide is fundamentally incompatible with the physician's role as healer." [ ] And physician-assisted suicide could, it is argued, undermine the trust that is essential to the doctor-patient relationship by blurring the time-honored line between healing and harming. [ ]

Next, the State has an interest in protecting vulnerable groups—including the poor, the elderly, and disabled persons—from abuse, neglect, and mistakes. . . . [One respected state task force] warned that "legalizing physician-assisted suicide would pose profound risks to many individuals who are ill and vulnerable. . . . The risk of harm is greatest for the many individuals in our society whose autonomy and well-being are already compromised by poverty, lack of access to good medical care, advanced age, or membership in a stigmatized social group." [ ] If physician-assisted suicide were permitted, many might resort to it to spare their families the substantial financial burden of end-of-life health-care costs.

. . . The State's assisted-suicide ban reflects and reinforces its policy that the lives of terminally ill, disabled, and elderly people must be no less valued than the lives of the young and healthy, and that a seriously disabled person's suicidal impulses should be interpreted and treated the same way as anyone else's. [ ]

Finally, the State may fear that permitting assisted suicide will start it down the path to voluntary and perhaps even involuntary euthanasia. . . . [Justice Rehnquist then discussed how this fear could arise out of the practice in the Netherlands.]

We need not weigh exactingly the relative strengths of these various interests. They are unquestionably important and legitimate, and Washington's ban on assisted suicide is at least reasonably related to their promotion and protection. We therefore hold that [the Washington ban on assisting suicide] does not violate the Fourteenth Amendment, either on its face or "as applied to competent, terminally ill adults who wish to hasten their deaths by obtaining medication prescribed by their doctors."[24] [ ]

* * *

Throughout the Nation, Americans are engaged in an earnest and profound debate about the morality, legality, and practicality of physician-assisted suicide. Our holding permits this debate to continue, as it should in a democratic society. The decision of the en banc Court of Appeals is reversed, and the case is remanded for further proceedings consistent with this opinion.

It is so ordered.

JUSTICE O'CONNOR, concurring [in both Glucksberg and Vacco].*

---

[24] Justice Stevens states that "the Court does conceive of respondents' claim as a facial challenge—addressing not the application of the statute to a particular set of plaintiffs before it, but the constitutionality of the statute's categorical prohibition. . . . "[ ] We emphasize that we today reject the Court of Appeals' specific holding that the statute is unconstitutional "as applied" to a particular class. [ ] Justice Stevens agrees with this holding, [ ] but would not "foreclose the possibility that an individual plaintiff seeking to hasten her death, or a doctor whose assistance was sought, could prevail in a more particularized challenge," ibid. Our opinion does not absolutely foreclose such a claim. However, given our holding that the Due Process Clause of the Fourteenth Amendment does not provide heightened protection to the asserted liberty interest in ending one's life with a physician's assistance, such a claim would have to be quite different from the ones advanced by respondents here.

* Justice Ginsburg concurs in the Court's judgments substantially for the reasons stated in this opinion. Justice Breyer joins this opinion except insofar as it joins the opinions of the Court.

Death will be different for each of us. For many, the last days will be spent in physical pain and perhaps the despair that accompanies physical deterioration and a loss of control of basic bodily and mental functions. Some will seek medication to alleviate that pain and other symptoms.

The Court frames the issue in this case as whether the Due Process Clause of the Constitution protects a "right to commit suicide which itself includes a right to assistance in doing so," [ ] and concludes that our Nation's history, legal traditions, and practices do not support the existence of such a right. I join the Court's opinions because I agree that there is no generalized right to "commit suicide." But respondents urge us to address the narrower question whether a mentally competent person who is experiencing great suffering has a constitutionally cognizable interest in controlling the circumstances of his or her imminent death. I see no need to reach that question in the context of the facial challenges to the New York and Washington laws at issue here. [ ] The parties and amici agree that in these States a patient who is suffering from a terminal illness and who is experiencing great pain has no legal barriers to obtaining medication, from qualified physicians, to alleviate that suffering, even to the point of causing unconsciousness and hastening death. [ ] In this light, even assuming that we would recognize such an interest, I agree that the State's interests in protecting those who are not truly competent or facing imminent death, or those whose decisions to hasten death would not truly be voluntary, are sufficiently weighty to justify a prohibition against physician-assisted suicide. [ ]

Every one of us at some point may be affected by our own or a family member's terminal illness. There is no reason to think the democratic process will not strike the proper balance between the interests of terminally ill, mentally competent individuals who would seek to end their suffering and the State's interests in protecting those who might seek to end life mistakenly or under pressure. As the Court recognizes, States are presently undertaking extensive and serious evaluation of physician-assisted suicide and other related issues. [ ] In such circumstances, "the . . . challenging task of crafting appropriate procedures for safeguarding . . . liberty interests is entrusted to the 'laboratory' of the States . . . in the first instance." [ ]

In sum, there is no need to address the question whether suffering patients have a constitutionally cognizable interest in obtaining relief from the suffering that they may experience in the last days of their lives. There is no dispute that dying patients in Washington and New York can obtain palliative care, even when doing so would hasten their deaths. The difficulty in defining terminal illness and the risk that a dying patient's request for assistance in ending his or her life might not be truly voluntary justifies the prohibitions on assisted suicide we uphold here.

JUSTICE STEVENS, concurring in the judgments [in both Glucksberg and Vacco].

The Court ends its opinion with the important observation that our holding today is fully consistent with a continuation of the vigorous debate about the "morality, legality, and practicality of physician-assisted suicide" in a democratic society. [ ] I write separately to make it clear that there is also room for further debate about the limits that the Constitution places on the power of the States to punish the practice.

## I

The morality, legality, and practicality of capital punishment have been the subject of debate for many years. In 1976, this Court upheld the constitutionality of the practice in cases coming to us from Georgia, Florida, and Texas. In those cases we concluded that a State does have the power to place a lesser value on some lives than on others; there is no absolute requirement that a State treat all human life as having an equal right to preservation. Because the state legislatures had sufficiently narrowed the category of lives that the State could terminate, and had enacted special procedures to ensure that the defendant belonged in that limited category, we concluded that the statutes were not unconstitutional on their face. In later cases coming to us from each of those States, however, we found that some applications of the statutes were unconstitutional.

Today, the Court decides that Washington's statute prohibiting assisted suicide is not invalid "on its face," that is to say, in all or most cases in which it might be applied. That holding, however, does not foreclose the possibility that some applications of the statute might well be invalid.

* * *

History and tradition provide ample support for refusing to recognize an open-ended constitutional right to commit suicide. Much more than the State's paternalistic interest in protecting the individual from the irrevocable consequences of an ill-advised decision motivated by temporary concerns is at stake. There is truth in John Donne's observation that "No man is an island." The State has an interest in preserving and fostering the benefits that every human being may provide to the community—a community that thrives on the exchange of ideas, expressions of affection, shared memories and humorous incidents as well as on the material contributions that its members create and support. The value to others of a person's life is far too precious to allow the individual to claim a constitutional entitlement to complete autonomy in making a decision to end that life. Thus, I fully agree with the Court that the "liberty" protected by the Due Process Clause does not include a categorical "right to commit suicide which itself includes a right to assistance in doing so." [ ]

But just as our conclusion that capital punishment is not always unconstitutional did not preclude later decisions holding that it is sometimes impermissibly cruel, so is it equally clear that a decision upholding a general statutory prohibition of assisted suicide does not mean that every possible application of the statute would be valid. A State, like Washington, that has authorized the death penalty and thereby has concluded that the sanctity of human life does not require that it always be preserved, must acknowledge that there are situations in which an interest in hastening death is legitimate. Indeed, not only is that interest sometimes legitimate, I am also convinced that there are times when it is entitled to constitutional protection.

## II

In Cruzan [ ] the Court assumed that the interest in liberty protected by the Fourteenth Amendment encompassed the right of a terminally ill patient to direct the withdrawal of life-sustaining treatment. As the Court correctly observes today, that assumption "was not simply deduced from abstract concepts of personal autonomy." [ ] Instead, it was supported by the common-law tradition protecting the individual's general right to refuse unwanted medical treatment. [ ] We have recognized, however, that this common-law right to refuse treatment is neither absolute nor always sufficiently weighty to overcome valid countervailing state interests. . . .

Cruzan, however, was not the normal case. Given the irreversible nature of her illness and the progressive character of her suffering, Nancy Cruzan's interest in refusing medical care was incidental to her more basic interest in controlling the manner and timing of her death. In finding that her best interests would be served by cutting off the nourishment that kept her alive, the trial court did more than simply vindicate Cruzan's interest in refusing medical treatment; the court, in essence, authorized affirmative conduct that would hasten her death. When this Court reviewed the case and upheld Missouri's requirement that there be clear and convincing evidence establishing Nancy Cruzan's intent to have life-sustaining nourishment withdrawn, it made two important assumptions: (1) that there was a "liberty interest" in refusing unwanted treatment protected by the Due Process Clause; and (2) that this liberty interest did not "end the inquiry" because it might be outweighed by relevant state interests. [ ] I agree with both of those assumptions, but I insist that the source of Nancy Cruzan's right to refuse treatment was not just a common-law rule. Rather, this right is an aspect of a far broader and more basic concept of freedom that is even older than the common law. This freedom embraces, not merely a person's right to refuse a particular kind of unwanted treatment, but also her interest in dignity, and in determining the character of the memories that will survive long after her death. In recognizing that the State's interests did not outweigh Nancy Cruzan's liberty interest in refusing medical treatment, Cruzan rested not simply on the common-law right to refuse medical treatment, but—at least implicitly—on the even more fundamental right to make this "deeply personal decision," [ ].

\* \* \*

While I agree with the Court that Cruzan does not decide the issue presented by these cases, Cruzan did give recognition, not just to vague, unbridled notions of autonomy, but to the more specific interest in making decisions about how to confront an imminent death. Although there is no absolute right to physician-assisted suicide, Cruzan makes it clear that some individuals who no longer have the option of deciding whether to live or to die because they are already on the threshold of death have a constitutionally protected interest that may outweigh the State's interest in preserving life at all costs. The liberty interest at stake in a case like this differs from, and is stronger than, both the common-law right to refuse medical treatment and the unbridled interest in deciding whether to live or die. It is an interest in deciding how, rather than whether, a critical threshold shall be crossed.

### III

The state interests supporting a general rule banning the practice of physician-assisted suicide do not have the same force in all cases. First and foremost of these interests is the " 'unqualified interest in the preservation of human life' "[ ].

... Although as a general matter the State's interest in the contributions each person may make to society outweighs the person's interest in ending her life, this interest does not have the same force for a terminally ill patient faced not with the choice of whether to live, only of how to die. . . .

Similarly, the State's legitimate interests in preventing suicide, protecting the vulnerable from coercion and abuse, and preventing euthanasia are less significant in this context. I agree that the State has a compelling interest in preventing persons from committing suicide because of depression, or coercion by third parties. But the State's legitimate interest in preventing abuse does not apply to an individual who is not victimized by abuse, who is not suffering from depression, and who makes a rational and voluntary decision to seek assistance in dying.

\* \* \*

The final major interest asserted by the State is its interest in preserving the traditional integrity of the medical profession. The fear is that a rule permitting physicians to assist in suicide is inconsistent with the perception that they serve their patients solely as healers. But for some patients, it would be a physician's refusal to dispense medication to ease their suffering and make their death tolerable and dignified that would be inconsistent with the healing role . . . .

. . . I do not . . . foreclose the possibility that an individual plaintiff seeking to hasten her death, or a doctor whose assistance was sought, could prevail in a more particularized challenge. Future cases will determine whether such a challenge may succeed.

IV

* * *

There may be little distinction between the intent of a terminally-ill patient who decides to remove her life-support and one who seeks the assistance of a doctor in ending her life; in both situations, the patient is seeking to hasten a certain, impending death. The doctor's intent might also be the same in prescribing lethal medication as it is in terminating life support. . . .

Thus, although the differences the majority notes in causation and intent between terminating life-support and assisting in suicide support the Court's rejection of the respondents' facial challenge, these distinctions may be inapplicable to particular terminally ill patients and their doctors. Our holding today in Vacco v. Quill that the Equal Protection Clause is not violated by New York's classification, just like our holding in Washington v. Glucksberg that the Washington statute is not invalid on its face, does not foreclose the possibility that some applications of the New York statute may impose an intolerable intrusion on the patient's freedom.

There remains room for vigorous debate about the outcome of particular cases that are not necessarily resolved by the opinions announced today. How such cases may be decided will depend on their specific facts. In my judgment, however, it is clear that the so-called "unqualified interest in the preservation of human life," [ ] is not itself sufficient to outweigh the interest in liberty that may justify the only possible means of preserving a dying patient's dignity and alleviating her intolerable suffering.

JUSTICE SOUTER, concurring in the judgment.

* * *

When the physicians claim that the Washington law deprives them of a right falling within the scope of liberty that the Fourteenth Amendment guarantees against denial without due process of law, they are not claiming some sort of procedural defect in the process through which the statute has been enacted or is administered. Their claim, rather, is that the State has no substantively adequate justification for barring the assistance sought by the patient and sought to be offered by the physician. Thus, we are dealing with a claim to one of those rights sometimes described as rights of substantive due process and sometimes as unenumerated rights, in view of the breadth and indeterminacy of the "due process" serving as the claim's textual basis. The doctors accordingly arouse the skepticism of those who find the Due Process Clause an unduly vague or oxymoronic warrant for judicial review of substantive state law, just as they also invoke two centuries of American constitutional practice in recognizing unenumerated, substantive limits on governmental action. . . .

\* \* \*

[Justice Souter explained that he was adopting Justice Harlan's approach to the Constitutional evaluation and protection of unenumerated rights under the Due Process Clause, as articulated in his dissent in Poe v. Ullman.] My understanding of unenumerated rights in the wake of the Poe dissent and subsequent cases avoids the absolutist failing of many older cases without embracing the opposite pole of equating reasonableness with past practice described at a very specific level. [ ] That understanding begins with a concept of "ordered liberty," [ ] comprising a continuum of rights to be free from "arbitrary impositions and purposeless restraints" [ ].

\* \* \*

This approach calls for a court to assess the relative "weights" or dignities of the contending interests, and to this extent the judicial method is familiar to the common law. Common law method is subject, however, to two important constraints in the hands of a court engaged in substantive due process review. First, such a court is bound to confine the values that it recognizes to those truly deserving constitutional stature, either to those expressed in constitutional text, or those exemplified by "the traditions from which [the Nation] developed," or revealed by contrast with "the traditions from which it broke." [ ]

The second constraint, again, simply reflects the fact that constitutional review, not judicial lawmaking, is a court's business here. The weighing or valuing of contending interests in this sphere is only the first step, forming the basis for determining whether the statute in question falls inside or outside the zone of what is reasonable in the way it resolves the conflict between the interests of state and individual.

\* \* \*

The State has put forward several interests to justify the Washington law as applied to physicians treating terminally ill patients, even those competent to make responsible choices: protecting life generally [ ], discouraging suicide even if knowing and voluntary [ ], and protecting terminally ill patients from involuntary suicide and euthanasia, both voluntary and nonvoluntary [ ].

It is not necessary to discuss the exact strengths of the first two claims of justification in the present circumstances, for the third is dispositive for me. . . . [Justice Souter then explained why the Washington State Legislature, on the basis of information now available, could have reasonably decided that a statute forbidding assisting suicide might protect terminally ill patients.]

\* \* \*

The Court should accordingly stay its hand to allow reasonable legislative consideration. While I do not decide for all time that respondents' claim should not be recognized, I acknowledge the legislative institutional competence as the better one to deal with that claim at this time.

JUSTICE BREYER, concurring in the judgments [in both Glucksberg and Vacco].

I believe that Justice O'Connor's views, which I share, have greater legal significance than the Court's opinion suggests. I join her separate opinion, except insofar as it joins the majority. . . .

I agree with the Court in Vacco v. Quill [ ] that the articulated state interests justify the distinction drawn between physician assisted suicide and withdrawal of life-support. I also agree with the Court that the critical question in both of the cases before us is whether "the 'liberty' specially protected by the Due Process Clause includes a right" of the sort that the respondents assert. [ ] I do not agree, however, with the Court's formulation of that claimed "liberty" interest. The Court describes it as a "right to commit suicide with another's assistance." [ ] But I would not reject the respondents' claim without considering a different formulation, for which our legal tradition may provide greater support. That formulation would use words roughly like a "right to die with dignity." But irrespective of the exact words used, at its core would lie personal control over the manner of death, professional medical assistance, and the avoidance of unnecessary and severe physical suffering—combined.

\* \* \*

I do not believe, however, that this Court need or now should decide whether or a not . . . [a right to die with dignity] is "fundamental." That is because, in my view, the avoidance of severe physical pain (connected with death) would have to comprise an essential part of any successful claim and because . . . the laws before us do not force a dying person to undergo that kind of pain. [ ] Rather, the laws of New York and of Washington do not prohibit doctors from providing patients with drugs sufficient to control pain despite the risk that those drugs themselves will kill. [ ] And under these circumstances the laws of New York and Washington would overcome any remaining significant interests and would be justified, regardless.

\* \* \*

Were the legal circumstances different—for example, were state law to prevent the provision of palliative care, including the administration of drugs as needed to avoid pain at the end of life—then the law's impact upon serious and otherwise unavoidable physical pain (and accompanying death) would be more directly at issue. And as JUSTICE O'CONNOR suggests, the Court might have to revisit its conclusions in these cases.

\* \* \*

## VACCO V. QUILL
Supreme Court of the United States, 1997.
521 U.S. 793, 117 S.Ct. 2293, 138 L.Ed.2d 834.

CHIEF JUSTICE REHNQUIST delivered the opinion of the Court.

In New York, as in most States, it is a crime to aid another to commit or attempt suicide, but patients may refuse even lifesaving medical treatment. The question presented by this case is whether New York's prohibition on assisting suicide therefore violates the Equal Protection Clause of the Fourteenth Amendment. We hold that it does not.

. . . Respondents, and three gravely ill patients who have since died, sued the State's Attorney General in the United States District Court. They urged that because New York permits a competent person to refuse life-sustaining medical treatment, and because the refusal of such treatment is "essentially the same thing" as physician-assisted suicide, New York's assisted-suicide ban violates the Equal Protection Clause. [ ]

The District Court disagreed . . . .

The Court of Appeals for the Second Circuit reversed. [ ] The court determined that, despite the assisted-suicide ban's apparent general applicability, "New York law does not treat equally all competent persons who are in the final stages of fatal illness and wish to hasten their deaths," because "those in the final stages of terminal illness who are on life-support systems are allowed to hasten their deaths by directing the removal of such systems; but those who are similarly situated, except for the previous attachment of life-sustaining equipment, are not allowed to hasten death by self-administering prescribed drugs." [ ] The Court of Appeals then examined whether this supposed unequal treatment was rationally related to any legitimate state interests, and concluded that "to the extent that [New York's statutes] prohibit a physician from prescribing medications to be self-administered by a mentally competent, terminally-ill person in the final stages of his terminal illness, they are not rationally related to any legitimate state interest." [ ] We granted certiorari [ ] and now reverse.

The Equal Protection Clause commands that no State shall "deny to any person within its jurisdiction the equal protection of the laws." This provision creates no substantive rights. [ ] Instead, it embodies a general rule that States must treat like cases alike but may treat unlike cases accordingly. [ ] If a legislative classification or distinction "neither burdens a fundamental right nor targets a suspect class, we will uphold [it] so long as it bears a rational relation to some legitimate end." [ ]

New York's statutes outlawing assisting suicide affect and address matters of profound significance to all New Yorkers alike. They neither infringe fundamental rights nor involve suspect classifications. [ ] These laws are therefore entitled to a "strong presumption of validity." [ ]

On their faces, neither New York's ban on assisting suicide nor its statutes permitting patients to refuse medical treatment treat anyone differently than anyone else or draw any distinctions between persons. Everyone, regardless of physical condition, is entitled, if competent, to refuse unwanted lifesaving medical treatment; no one is permitted to assist a suicide. Generally speaking, laws that apply evenhandedly to all "unquestionably comply" with the Equal Protection Clause. [ ]

The Court of Appeals, however, concluded that some terminally ill people—those who are on life-support systems—are treated differently than those who are not, in that the former may "hasten death" by ending treatment, but the latter may not "hasten death" through physician-assisted suicide. [ ] This conclusion depends on the submission that ending or refusing lifesaving medical treatment "is nothing more nor less than assisted suicide." [ ] Unlike the Court of Appeals, we think the distinction between assisting suicide and withdrawing life-sustaining treatment, a distinction widely recognized and endorsed in the medical profession and in our legal traditions, is both important and logical; it is certainly rational. [ ]

The distinction comports with fundamental legal principles of causation and intent. First, when a patient refuses life-sustaining medical treatment, he dies from an underlying fatal disease or pathology; but if a patient ingests lethal medication prescribed by a physician, he is killed by that medication. [ ]

Furthermore, a physician who withdraws, or honors a patient's refusal to begin, life-sustaining medical treatment purposefully intends, or may so intend, only to respect his patient's wishes and "to cease doing useless and futile or degrading things to the patient when [the patient] no longer stands to benefit from them." [ ] The same is true when a doctor provides aggressive palliative care; in some cases, painkilling drugs may hasten a patient's death, but the physician's purpose and intent is, or may be, only to ease his patient's pain. A doctor who assists a suicide, however, "must, necessarily and indubitably, intend primarily that the patient be made dead." [ ] Similarly, a patient who commits suicide with a doctor's aid necessarily has the specific intent to end his or her own life, while a patient who refuses or discontinues treatment might not. [ ]

The law has long used actors' intent or purpose to distinguish between two acts that may have the same result. [ ] Put differently, the law distinguishes actions taken "because of" a given end from actions taken "in spite of" their unintended but foreseen consequences. [ ]

Given these general principles, it is not surprising that many courts, including New York courts, have carefully distinguished refusing life-sustaining treatment from suicide. . . .

Similarly, the overwhelming majority of state legislatures have drawn a clear line between assisting suicide and withdrawing or permitting the refusal of unwanted lifesaving medical treatment by prohibiting the former and permitting the latter. [ ] And "nearly all states expressly disapprove of suicide and assisted suicide either in statutes dealing with durable powers of attorney in health-care situations, or in 'living will' statutes." [ ] Thus, even as the States move to protect and promote patients' dignity at the end of life, they remain opposed to physician-assisted suicide.

\* \* \*

This Court has also recognized, at least implicitly, the distinction between letting a patient die and making that patient die. In Cruzan [ ] we concluded that "the principle that a competent person has a constitutionally protected liberty interest in refusing unwanted medical treatment may be inferred from our prior decisions," and we assumed the existence of such a right for purposes of that case [ ]. But our assumption of a right to refuse treatment was grounded not, as the Court of Appeals supposed, on the proposition that patients have a general and abstract "right to hasten death," [ ] but on well established, traditional rights to bodily integrity and freedom from unwanted touching [ ]. In fact, we observed that "the majority of States in this country have laws imposing criminal penalties on one who assists another to commit suicide." [ ] Cruzan therefore provides no support for the notion that refusing life-sustaining medical treatment is "nothing more nor less than suicide."

For all these reasons, we disagree with respondents' claim that the distinction between refusing lifesaving medical treatment and assisted suicide is "arbitrary" and "irrational.[11] Granted, in some cases, the line between the two may not be clear, but certainty is not required, even were it possible. Logic and contemporary practice support New York's judgment that the two acts are different, and New York may therefore, consistent

---

[11] Respondents also argue that the State irrationally distinguishes between physician-assisted suicide and "terminal sedation," a process respondents characterize as "inducing barbiturate coma and then starving the person to death." [ ] Petitioners insist, however, that "'although proponents of physician-assisted suicide and euthanasia contend that terminal sedation is covert physician-assisted suicide or euthanasia, the concept of sedating pharmacotherapy is based on informed consent and the principle of double effect.'"[ ] Just as a State may prohibit assisting suicide while permitting patients to refuse unwanted lifesaving treatment, it may permit palliative care related to that refusal, which may have the foreseen but unintended "double effect" of hastening the patient's death. [ ]

with the Constitution, treat them differently. By permitting everyone to refuse unwanted medical treatment while prohibiting anyone from assisting a suicide, New York law follows a longstanding and rational distinction.

New York's reasons for recognizing and acting on this distinction—including prohibiting intentional killing and preserving life; preventing suicide; maintaining physicians' role as their patients' healers; protecting vulnerable people from indifference, prejudice, and psychological and financial pressure to end their lives; and avoiding a possible slide towards euthanasia—are discussed in greater detail in our opinion in Glucksberg, ante. These valid and important public interests easily satisfy the constitutional requirement that a legislative classification bear a rational relation to some legitimate end.

The judgment of the Court of Appeals is reversed.

\* \* \*

JUSTICE SOUTER, concurring in the judgment.

Even though I do not conclude that assisted suicide is a fundamental right entitled to recognition at this time, I accord the claims raised by the patients and physicians in this case and Washington v. Glucksberg a high degree of importance, requiring a commensurate justification. [ ] The reasons that lead me to conclude in Glucksberg that the prohibition on assisted suicide is not arbitrary under the due process standard also support the distinction between assistance to suicide, which is banned, and practices such as termination of artificial life support and death-hastening pain medication, which are permitted. I accordingly concur in the judgment of the Court.

\* \* \*

## NOTES AND QUESTIONS

1.    The Ninth Circuit's en banc decision and an extraordinarily diverse and thoughtful set of opinions in *Glucksberg* can be found at Compassion in Dying v. Washington, 79 F.3d 790 (9th Cir.1996). The en banc court reversed a 2–1 decision of the original panel, which also included an impassioned opinion on each side of the issue. See 49 F.3d 586 (9th Cir.1995). The meticulously organized district court opinion in the Compassion in Dying case is reported at 850 F.Supp. 1454 (W.D.Wash.1994). The Second Circuit's opinion in Quill v. Vacco can be found at 80 F.3d 716 (2d Cir.1996).

2.    These cases generated many highly emotional responses. Although the Supreme Court's unanimous decision brought a semblance of propriety back to the discussion of these issues, supporters and opponents of medically assisted dying continue to attack the arguments of their opponents—and, as in the case of the abortion debate—they continue to attack their opponents,

too. Some of the commentary on the Ninth Circuit opinions was especially personal. Judge Reinhardt (who wrote the primary decision finding the Washington law to be unconstitutional) was roundly criticized for his ACLU connections, which, some said, made it impossible for him to fairly decide the case. On the other hand, Judge Noonan (who would have upheld the statute for the first panel) had been criticized for his Right to Life connections and his Catholic faith which, others argued, made it impossible for him to be impartial. Should judges recuse themselves from cases involving these difficult and controversial bioethics issues if they have deeply held personal beliefs about the underlying practice—here medically assisted dying? Does it make a difference if they were members (or officers, or high ranking employees) of organizations which have taken explicit positions on the underlying issues? On the particular case in litigation? Should they recuse themselves if the issue is one on which the religion to which they subscribe has taken a formal position? Should Catholic judges recuse themselves from abortion and medically assisted dying cases? Should judges who belong to the United Church of Christ (which has been strongly pro-choice for decades) recuse themselves from abortion cases? Should the member of a congregation whose rabbi helped organize a march to support access to contraception through the ACA recuse herself from all contraception rights cases? Is their obligation any different from the obligation of a judge who is a dedicated ACLU (or American Family Association or Republican Party) member and who confronts a case upon which the ACLU (or the American Family Association, or the Republican Party) has taken a firm position?

3.        Judge Calabresi concurred in the Second Circuit decision in *Quill* but on entirely different grounds. Depending on the theory of statutory construction that he had explained fifteen years earlier in his text, A Common Law for the Age of Statutes (1982), he concluded that the history of the New York manslaughter statute suggested that there was no reason to believe that its framers ever intended it to apply to cases of competent terminally ill patients seeking aid in dying from physicians. Still, as he pointed out, "neither *Cruzan,* nor *Casey,* nor the language of our Constitution, nor our constitutional tradition clearly makes these laws invalid."

So, what should the court do with a "highly suspect" but "not clearly invalid" statute that may no longer serve the purposes for which it was originally promulgated? The answer, according to Judge Calabresi, is the "constitutional remand."

> I contend that when a law is neither plainly unconstitutional . . . nor plainly constitutional, the courts ought not to decide the ultimate validity of that law without current and clearly expressed statements by the people or their elected officials of the state involved. It is my further contention, that, absent such statements, the courts have frequently struck down such laws, while leaving open the possibility of reconsideration if appropriate statements were subsequently made.

Thus, Judge Calabresi finds the New York statute unconstitutional, but he "takes no position" on whether verbatim identical statutes would be constitutional "were New York to reenact them while articulating the reasons for the distinctions it makes. . . . " Is this a reasonable way to deal with ancient statutes effectively criminalizing medically assisted dying? Is this argument still available to those challenging state statutes that forbid assisting suicide?

4.    Why has medically assisted dying engendered such passion over the last several decades? Daniel Callahan has a suggestion:

> The power of medicine to extend life under poor circumstances is now widely and increasingly feared. The combined powers of a quasi-religious tradition of respect for individual life and a secular tradition of relentless medical progress creates a bias toward aggressive, often unremitting treatment that appears unstoppable.

> How is control to be gained? For many the answer seems obvious and unavoidable: active euthanasia and assisted suicide.

19 Hastings Ctr. Rep., Special Supplement, 4 (1989). Dr. Callahan goes on to suggest that those who strongly oppose euthanasia, as he does, ought to focus on "dampening . . . the push for medical progress, a return to older traditions of caring as an alternative to curing, and a willingness to accept decline and death as part of the human condition (not a notable feature of American medicine)." Is he right? It used to be that people were afraid that if they went to the hospital they would die there. Now people are afraid that if they go to the hospital they will be kept alive there. Is it this fear that gives rise to our current interest in euthanasia?

5.    Medically assisted dying may constitute murder, manslaughter, some other form of homicide, or no crime at all, depending on the language of the state statute and the nature of the physician's act. While most states criminalize assisting suicide, it is not always easy to determine what conduct is prohibited by those statutes. Consider one representative statute:

> Every person who deliberately aids, or advises, or encourages another to commit suicide, is guilty of a felony. Cal. Pen. Code § 401.

Would this statute apply to a physician who clamps a feeding tube? To a physician who withholds antibiotics? To a physician who prescribes morphine to a patient in persistent pain, provides enough morphine to constitute a lethal dose? To a physician who prescribes that same morphine and tells the patient what would constitute a lethal dose? To those who publish instructions on how to commit suicide for the use of those who are terminally ill or in excruciating pain? To those who make generally available information about how to commit suicide at home? See McCollum v. CBS, Inc., 202 Cal.App.3d 989, 249 Cal.Rptr. 187 (1988), rejecting on free speech grounds application of the statute to those who play rock music with lyrics that suggest that suicide is acceptable.

6.    Might women, specifically, be put at risk in a society that permits medically assisted dying? That argument is made by Susan Wolf, who regularly has argued that women's requests should be better respected by the

health care system and that requests to remove life-sustaining treatment should be heeded.

> As I have argued, there is a strong right to be free of unwanted bodily invasion. Indeed, for women, a long history of being harmed specifically through unwanted bodily invasion such as rape presents particularly compelling reasons for honoring a woman's refusal of invasion and effort to maintain bodily intactness. When it comes to the question of whether women's suicides should be aided, however, or whether women should be actively killed, there is no right to command physician assistance, the dangers of permitting assistance are immense, and the history of women's subordination cuts the other way. Women have historically been seen as fit objects for bodily invasion, self-sacrifice, and death at the hands of others. The task before us is to challenge all three.

> Certainly some women, including some feminists, will see this problem differently. That may be especially true of women who feel in control of their lives, are less subject to subordination by age or race or wealth, and seek yet another option to add to their many. I am not arguing that women should lose control of their lives and selves. Instead, I am arguing that when women request to be put to death or ask help in taking their own lives, they become part of a broader social dynamic of which we have properly learned to be extremely wary. These are fatal practices. We can no longer ignore questions of gender or insights of feminist argument.

Susan Wolf, Gender, Feminism and Death: Physician Assisted Suicide and Euthanasia, in S. Wolf, Feminism and Bioethics: Beyond Reproduction 308 (1996). For an account of Professor Wolf's thoughtful approach to death and dying, see Daniel Bergner, Death in the Family, New York Times Magazine (December 2, 2007), reporting that 72% of the 75 individuals assisted by euthanasia advocate Kervorkian were women.

Susan Wolf also wrote a moving account of her own father's death, including her own response when he inquired whether it could be "accelerated" beyond withdrawing treatment. Her answer to her father was no, and she explains why in her essay; but she doesn't romanticize his dying and the great difficulties he and his family faced in getting the end-of-life care he needed. Confronting Physician-Assisted Suicide and Euthanasia: My Father's Death, 38 Hastings Ctr. Rept. 23 (2008).

7.   Organized   medical   groups   generally   oppose   any   medical participation in euthanasia or assisted death. As to euthanasia, the AMA Council on Ethical and Judicial Affairs provides:

### Code of Medical Ethics Opinion 5.8, Euthanasia (2016)

Euthanasia is the administration of a lethal agent by another person to a patient for the purpose of relieving the patient's intolerable and incurable suffering.

It is understandable, though tragic, that some patients in extreme duress—such as those suffering from a terminal, painful, debilitating illness—may come to decide that death is preferable to life.

However, permitting physicians to engage in euthanasia would ultimately cause more harm than good.

Euthanasia is fundamentally incompatible with the physician's role as healer, would be difficult or impossible to control, and would pose serious societal risks. Euthanasia could readily be extended to incompetent patients and other vulnerable populations.

The involvement of physicians in euthanasia heightens the significance of its ethical prohibition. The physician who performs euthanasia assumes unique responsibility for the act of ending the patient's life.

Instead of engaging in euthanasia, physicians must aggressively respond to the needs of patients at the end of life.

Patients

(a)    Should not be abandoned once it is determined that cure is impossible.

(b)    Must respect patient autonomy.

(c)    Must provide good communication and emotional support.

(d)    Must provide appropriate comfort care and adequate pain control. As to Physician Assisted Suicide, the Council has adopted this position:

## Code of Medical Ethics Opinion 5.7, Physician Assisted Suicide (2016)

Physician-assisted suicide occurs when a physician facilitates a patient's death by providing the necessary means and/or information to enable the patient to perform the life-ending act (eg, the physician provides sleeping pills and information about the lethal dose, while aware that the patient may commit suicide).

It is understandable, though tragic, that some patients in extreme duress—such as those suffering from a terminal, painful, debilitating illness—may come to decide that death is preferable to life. However, allowing physicians to participate in assisted suicide would cause more harm than good.

Physician-assisted suicide is fundamentally incompatible with the physician's role as healer, would be difficult or impossible to control, and would pose serious societal risks.

Instead of engaging in assisted suicide, physicians must aggressively respond to the needs of patients at the end of life. Physicians:

(a)    Should not abandon a patient once it is determined that cure is impossible.

(b)   Must respect patient autonomy.

(c)   Must provide good communication and emotional support.

(d)   Must provide appropriate comfort care and adequate pain control.

Does the AMA oppose both of these kinds of medically assisted dying because they are equally morally reprehensible, or because they are too morally complicated?

> A strict proscription against aiding in death may betray a limited conceptual framework that seeks the safety of ironclad rules and principles to protect the physician from the true complexity of individual cases. Patients seeking comfort in their dying should not be held hostage to our inability or unwillingness to be responsible for knowing right from wrong in each specific situation. Christine Cassel and Diane Meier, Morals and Moralism in the Debate Over Euthanasia and Assisted Suicide, 323 NEJM 750, 751 (1990).

8.   In a footnote in *Vacco*, Justice Rehnquist raises the issue of the legal status of "terminal sedation," which is sometimes described as "palliative sedation" because it is employed to provide palliation both in patients who are quickly approaching death and in those who are suffering but not yet otherwise terminal. Patients whose suffering cannot be ameliorated in any other way can be sedated with enough medication so that they are put into a medication-induced coma. This sedation may be accompanied by the withdrawal of other forms of treatment, including artificial nutrition and hydration. This withdrawal may (and, with the withdrawal of nutrition and hydration, will) lead to the patient's death. Justice Rehnquist suggests that terminal sedation, which has not given rise to the ethical objections that have come with medically assisted dying, is distinguishable from an affirmative act intended to bring about death, applying the principle of "double effect." Do you agree? Under *Vacco*, whether palliative sedation is treated like the withdrawal of life-sustaining treatment or like an affirmative act causing death makes all the legal difference. As an ethical and legal matter, should terminal sedation be treated like the withdrawal of treatment or like medically assisted dying? See J.A. Rietjens et al., Terminal Sedation and Euthanasia: A Comparison of Clinical Practices, 166 Archives Internal Med. 749 (2006). T. Morita et al., Terminal Sedation for Existential Distress, 17 Am. J. Hospital Palliation 189 (2000).

In 2008, over a decade after *Glucksberg* was decided, the AMA adopted a policy providing that it is ethically appropriate for physicians to offer palliative sedation, which the AMA called "sedation to unconsciousness in end-of-life care" at least to some terminally ill patients. The relevant opinion was amended in 2016:

### Code of Medical Ethics Opinion 5.6, Sedation to Unconsciousness in End-of-Life Care (2016):

The duty to relieve pain and suffering is central to the physician's role as healer and is an obligation physicians have to their patients. When a terminally ill patient experiences severe pain or other distressing clinical symptoms that do not respond to aggressive, symptom-specific palliation it can be appropriate to offer sedation to unconsciousness as an intervention of last resort.

Sedation to unconsciousness must never be used to intentionally cause a patient's death.

When considering whether to offer palliative sedation to unconsciousness, physicians should:

(a)   Restrict palliative sedation to unconsciousness to patients in the final stages of terminal illness.

(b)   Consult with a multi-disciplinary team (if available), including an expert in the field of palliative care, to ensure that symptom-specific treatments have been sufficiently employed and that palliative sedation to unconsciousness is now the most appropriate course of treatment.

(c)   Document the rationale for all symptom management interventions in the medical record.

(d)   Obtain the informed consent of the patient (or the authorized surrogate when the patient lacks decision-making capacity).

(e)   Discuss with the patient (or surrogate) the plan of care relative to:

(1)   Degree and length of sedation

(2)   Specific expectations for continuing, withdrawing, or withholding future life-sustaining treatments

(f)   Monitor care once palliative sedation to unconsciousness is initiated.

The 2016 revision of this Ethical Opinion made a couple of notable changes to the earlier version of the opinion. First, the following paragraph, part of the 2008 version of the Ethical Opinion, was omitted from the more recent version:

Palliative sedation is not an appropriate response to suffering that is primarily existential, defined as the experience of agony and distress that may arise from such issues as death anxiety, isolation and loss of control. Existential suffering is better addressed by other interventions. For example, palliative sedation is not the way to address suffering created by social isolation and loneliness; such suffering should be addressed by providing the patient with needed social support.

Is this suggestion that sedation to unconsciousness is appropriate for existential suffering under some circumstances? Is it? Can all suffering (except physical pain) be treated through the provision of social support? Should palliative sedation be reserved for those with physical, not psychic, pain? See A. de Graeff and M. Dean,. Palliative Sedation Therapy in the Last Weeks of Life: A Literature Review and Recommendations for Standards, 10 J. Palliat Mcd. 67 (2007). At least one study suggests that palliative sedation does not actually shorten the lives of cancer patients. M. Maltoni et al., Palliative Sedation in End-of-Life Care and Survival: a Systematic Review, 30 J. Clin.Oncology 1378 (2012).

Second, in 2016 the following portion of the Ethical Opinion was removed:

> When symptoms cannot be diminished through all other means of palliation, including symptom-specific treatments, it is the ethical obligation of a physician to offer palliative sedation to unconsciousness as an option for the relief of intractable symptoms.

Why was this sentence removed? Is it no longer an ethical obligation to offer palliative sedation to a patient? Should there be such an obligation if the physician believes that it is unethical to provide that form of care?

## III. STATE LEGISLATION AND LITIGATION TO SUPPORT MEDICALLY ASSISTED DYING

The debate over the proper role of physicians in assisting their patients in death has been carried on through the legislative and citizen initiative processes as well as through litigation. "Death with Dignity" initiatives were narrowly defeated in California in 1991 and in Washington in 1992. However, Oregon's "Death with Dignity" initiative was approved by voters in the November 1994 election, and it thus became part of the statute law of Oregon.

### DEATH WITH DIGNITY ACT
Or.Rev.Stat. §§ 127.800–.897.

**127.800. Definitions.**

The following words and phrases, whenever used in ORS 127.800 to 127.897, have the following meanings:

(1) "Adult" means an individual who is 18 years of age or older.

(2) "Attending physician" means the physician who has primary responsibility for the care of the patient and treatment of the patient's terminal disease.

(3) "Capable" means that in the opinion of a court or in the opinion of the patient's attending physician or consulting physician, psychiatrist or psychologist, a patient has the ability to make and communicate health care decisions to health care providers, including communication through persons familiar with the patient's manner of communicating if those persons are available.

(4) "Consulting physician" means a physician who is qualified by specialty or experience to make a professional diagnosis and prognosis regarding the patient's disease.

(5) "Counseling" means one or more consultations as necessary between a state licensed psychiatrist or psychologist and a patient for the purpose of determining that the patient is capable and not suffering from a psychiatric or psychological disorder or depression causing impaired judgment.

(6) "Health care provider" means a person licensed, certified or otherwise authorized or permitted by the law of this state to administer health care or dispense medication in the ordinary course of business or practice of a profession, and includes a health care facility.

(7) "Informed decision" means a decision by a qualified patient, to request and obtain a prescription to end his or her life in a humane and dignified manner, that is based on an appreciation of the relevant facts and after being fully informed by the attending physician of:

(a) His or her medical diagnosis;

(b) His or her prognosis;

(c) The potential risks associated with taking the medication to be prescribed;

(d) The probable result of taking the medication to be prescribed; and

(e) The feasible alternatives, including, but not limited to, comfort care, hospice care and pain control.

(8) "Medically confirmed" means the medical opinion of the attending physician has been confirmed by a consulting physician who has examined the patient and the patient's relevant medical records.

(9) "Patient" means a person who is under the care of a physician.

(10) "Physician" means a doctor licensed to practice medicine * * *

(11) "Qualified patient" means a capable adult who is a resident of Oregon and has satisfied the requirements of ORS 127.800 to 127.897 in order to obtain a prescription for medication to end his or her life in a humane and dignified manner.

(12) "Terminal disease" means an incurable and irreversible disease that has been medically confirmed and will, within reasonable medical judgment, produce death within six months.

### 127.805. Who may initiate a written request for medication.

(1) An adult who is capable, is a resident of Oregon, and has been determined by the attending physician and consulting physician to be suffering from a terminal disease, and who has voluntarily expressed his or her wish to die, may make a written request for medication for the purpose of ending his or her life in a humane and dignified manner in accordance with ORS 127.800 to 127.897.

(2) No person shall qualify under the provisions of ORS 127.800 to 127.897 solely because of age or disability.

### 127.810. Form of the written request.

(1) A valid request for medication under ORS 127.800 to 127.897 shall be in substantially the form described in ORS 127.897, signed and dated by the patient and witnessed by at least two individuals who, in the presence of the patient, attest that to the best of their knowledge and belief the patient is capable, acting voluntarily, and is not being coerced to sign the request.

(2) One of the witnesses shall be a person who is not:

(a) A relative of the patient by blood, marriage or adoption;

(b) A person who at the time the request is signed would be entitled to any portion of the estate of the qualified patient upon death under any will or by operation of law; or

(c) An owner, operator or employee of a health care facility where the qualified patient is receiving medical treatment or is a resident.

(3) The patient's attending physician at the time the request is signed shall not be a witness.

(4) If the patient is a patient in a long term care facility at the time the written request is made, one of the witnesses shall be an individual designated by the facility and having the qualifications specified by the Department of Human Services by rule.

### 127.815. Attending physician responsibilities.

(1) The attending physician shall:

(a) Make the initial determination of whether a patient has a terminal disease, is capable, and has made the request voluntarily;

(b) Request that the patient demonstrate Oregon residency pursuant to ORS 127.860;

(c) To ensure that the patient is making an informed decision, inform the patient of:

(A) His or her medical diagnosis;

(B) His or her prognosis;

(C) The potential risks associated with taking the medication to be prescribed;

(D) The probable result of taking the medication to be prescribed; and

(E) The feasible alternatives, including, but not limited to, comfort care, hospice care and pain control;

(d) Refer the patient to a consulting physician for medical confirmation of the diagnosis, and for a determination that the patient is capable and acting voluntarily;

(e) Refer the patient for counseling if appropriate pursuant to ORS 127.825;

(f) Recommend that the patient notify next of kin;

(g) Counsel the patient about the importance of having another person present when the patient takes the medication prescribed pursuant to ORS 127.800 to 127.897 and of not taking the medication in a public place;

(h) Inform the patient that he or she has an opportunity to rescind the request at any time and in any manner, and offer the patient an opportunity to rescind at the end of the 15 day waiting period pursuant to ORS 127.840;

(i) Verify, immediately prior to writing the prescription for medication under ORS 127.800 to 127.897, that the patient is making an informed decision;

(j) Fulfill the medical record documentation requirements of ORS 127.855;

(k) Ensure that all appropriate steps are carried out in accordance with ORS 127.800 to 127.897 prior to writing a prescription for medication to enable a qualified patient to end his or her life in a humane and dignified manner; and

(A) Dispense medications directly . . . or [(B) through a pharmacist].

(2) Notwithstanding any other provision of law, the attending physician may sign the patient's report of death.

## 127.820. Consulting physician confirmation.

Before a patient is qualified under ORS 127.800 to 127.897, a consulting physician shall examine the patient and his or her relevant medical records and confirm, in writing, the attending physician's diagnosis that the patient is suffering from a terminal disease, and verify that the patient is capable, is acting voluntarily and has made an informed decision.

## 127.825. Counseling referral.

If in the opinion of the attending physician or the consulting physician a patient may be suffering from a psychiatric or psychological disorder or depression causing impaired judgment, either physician shall refer the patient for counseling. No medication to end a patient's life in a humane and dignified manner shall be prescribed until the person performing the counseling determines that the patient is not suffering from a psychiatric or psychological disorder or depression causing impaired judgment.

### 127.830. Informed decision.

No person shall receive a prescription for medication to end his or her life in a humane and dignified manner unless he or she has made an informed decision as defined in ORS 127.800 (7). Immediately prior to writing a prescription for medication under ORS 127.800 to 127.897, the attending physician shall verify that the patient is making an informed decision.

### 127.835. Family notification.

The attending physician shall recommend that the patient notify the next of kin of his or her request for medication pursuant to ORS 127.800 to 127.897. A patient who declines or is unable to notify next of kin shall not have his or her request denied for that reason.

### 127.840. Written and oral requests.

In order to receive a prescription for medication to end his or her life in a humane and dignified manner, a qualified patient shall have made an oral request and a written request, and reiterate the oral request to his or her attending physician no less than fifteen (15) days after making the initial oral request. At the time the qualified patient makes his or her second oral request, the attending physician shall offer the patient an opportunity to rescind the request.

### 127.845. Right to rescind request.

A patient may rescind his or her request at any time and in any manner without regard to his or her mental state. No prescription for medication under ORS 127.800 to 127.897 may be written without the attending physician offering the qualified patient an opportunity to rescind the request.

### 127.850. Waiting periods.

No less than fifteen (15) days shall elapse between the patient's initial oral request and the writing of a prescription under ORS 127.800 to 127.897. No less than 48 hours shall elapse between the patient's written request and the writing of a prescription under ORS 127.800 to 127.897.

\* \* \*

### 127.860. Residency requirement.

Only requests made by Oregon residents under ORS 127.800 to 127.897 shall be granted. Factors demonstrating Oregon residency include but are not limited to [being licensed to drive, registering to vote, owning property, and paying taxes in Oregon.]

\* \* \*

### 127.880. Construction of Act.

Nothing in ORS 127.800 to 127.897 shall be construed to authorize a physician or any other person to end a patient's life by lethal injection, mercy killing or active euthanasia. Actions taken in accordance with ORS 127.800 to 127.897 shall not, for any purpose, constitute suicide, assisted suicide, mercy killing or homicide, under the law.

\* \* \*

### 127.897. Form of the request.

A request for a medication as authorized by ORS 127.800 to 127.897 shall be in substantially the following form:

#### REQUEST FOR MEDICATION TO END MY LIFE IN A HUMANE AND DIGNIFIED MANNER

I, _____, am an adult of sound mind.

I am suffering from _____, which my attending physician has determined is a terminal disease and which has been medically confirmed by a consulting physician.

I have been fully informed of my diagnosis, prognosis, the nature of medication to be prescribed and potential associated risks, the expected result, and the feasible alternatives, including comfort care, hospice care and pain control.

I request that my attending physician prescribe medication that will end my life in a humane and dignified manner.

INITIAL ONE:

_____ I have informed my family of my decision and taken their opinions into consideration.

_____ I have decided not to inform my family of my decision.

_____ I have no family to inform of my decision.

I understand that I have the right to rescind this request at any time.

I understand the full import of this request and I expect to die when I take the medication to be prescribed. I further understand that although most deaths occur within three hours, my death may take longer and my physician has counseled me about this possibility.

I make this request voluntarily and without reservation, and I accept full moral responsibility for my actions.

[SIGNATURE LINE; WITNESS LINES]

\* \* \*

Early in 1999 the Oregon Department of Health issued its first annual report, which collected data on those who received lethal prescriptions under the Act during its first year of operation. Each year for eight years the Oregon Department of Health issued a comprehensive annual report describing activity under the Death with Dignity Act. Starting with the report for the ninth year of the operation of the statute, reflecting activity in 2006 and released in 2007, the Department of Health made available a brief summary of activity under the statute and other charts and tables. All of the annual reports, and the summaries (starting in 2007), are available at the Oregon Department of Health website. The Summary released in 2013 provides detailed information on the first fifteen years of operation under the statute, with a focus on activity over the most recent year.

## OREGON DEPARTMENT OF HUMAN SERVICES, OREGON'S DEATH WITH DIGNITY ACT—2017

(released February, 2018).

# Introduction

The Oregon Death with Dignity Act (DWDA) allows terminally ill Oregonians who meet specific qualifications to end their lives through the voluntary self-administration of a lethal dose of medications, expressly prescribed by a physician for that purpose. The Act requires the Oregon Health Authority (OHA), Public Health Division, to collect information about the patients and physicians who participate in the Act and to publish an annual statistical report.

The DWDA outlines specific patient requirements to participate. A patient must be: 1) 18 years of age or older, 2) a resident of Oregon, 3) capable of making and communicating health care decisions for him/herself, and 4) diagnosed with a terminal illness that will lead to death within six (6) months. It is up to the attending and consulting physicians to determine whether these requirements have been met, and to report that fact to OHA at the time a prescription is written. If OHA identifies any issues of noncompliance with the statutory requirements, that fact is reported to the appropriate licensing board.

Data presented in this summary, including the number of people for whom DWDA prescriptions were written (DWDA prescription recipients) and the resulting deaths from the ingestion of the medications (DWDA deaths), are based on required reporting forms and death certificates received by OHA as of January 19, 2018. More information on the reporting process, required forms, and annual reports is available at: http://www.healthoregon.org/dwd.

Figure 1: DWDA prescription recipients and deaths*, by year, Oregon, 1998-2017

*As of January 19, 2018
See Table 2 for detailed information

# Participation summary and trends

During 2017, 218 people received prescriptions for lethal medications under the provisions of the Oregon DWDA, compared to 204 during 2016 (Figure 1 and Table 2). As of January 19, 2018, OHA had received reports of 143 people who had died during 2017 from ingesting the medications prescribed under DWDA, compared to 138 during 2016.

Since the law was passed in 1997, a total of 1,967 people have had prescriptions written under the DWDA, and 1,275 patients have died from ingesting the medications. During 2017, the estimated rate of DWDA deaths was 39.9 per 10,000 total deaths.

A summary of DWDA prescriptions written and medications ingested is shown in Figure 2. Of the 218 patients for whom prescriptions were written during 2017, 130 (59.6%) ingested the medication; 129 died from ingesting the medication, and one patient ingested the medication but regained consciousness before dying from the underlying illness and is therefore not counted as a DWDA death. An additional 44 patients (20.2%) did not take the medications and subsequently died of other causes.

Ingestion status is unknown for 44 patients prescribed DWDA medications in 2017. Twenty-three of these patients died, but follow up information is not yet available. For the remaining 21 patients, both death and ingestion status are pending (Figure 2).

**Figure 2: Summary of DWDA prescriptions written and medications ingested in 2017, as of January 19, 2018**

# Patient characteristics

Of the 143 DWDA deaths during 2017, most patients (80.4%) were aged 65 years or older. The median age at death was 74 years. As in previous years, decedents were commonly white (94.4%) and well educated (48.9% had a least a baccalaureate degree).

Patients' underlying illnesses were similar to those of previous years. Most patients had cancer (76.9%), followed by amyotrophic lateral sclerosis (ALS) (7.0%) and heart/circulatory disease (6.3%). The majority of patients (90.2%) died at home, and most (90.9%) were enrolled in hospice care. Excluding unknown cases, most (99.1%) had some form of health care insurance. The percent of patients who had private insurance (31.3%) and Medicare or Medicaid insurance (67.8%) in 2017 was similar to last year (29.7% and 69.5%, respectively).

Similar to previous years, the three most frequently reported end-of-life concerns were decreasing ability to participate in activities that made life enjoyable (88.1%), loss of autonomy (87.4%), and loss of dignity (67.1%).

# DWDA process

A total of 92 physicians wrote 218 prescriptions during 2017 (1–29 prescriptions per physician). Five patients were referred for psychological or psychiatric evaluation. During 2017, no referrals were made to the Oregon Medical Board for failure to comply with DWDA requirements.

A procedure revision was made in 2010 to standardize reporting on the follow-up questionnaire. The new procedure accepts information about the time of death and circumstances surrounding death only when the physician or another health care provider was present at the time of death. For 42 patients, either the prescribing physician or another healthcare provider was present at the time of death. Prescribing physicians were present at time of death for 23 patients (16.1%); 19 additional cases had other health care providers present (e.g., hospice nurse). Data on time from ingestion to death are available for only 40 DWDA deaths during 2017. Among those 40 patients, time from ingestion until death ranged from ten minutes to 21 hours.

Table 1. Characteristics and end-of-life care of 1,275 DWDA patients who have died from ingesting a lethal dose of medication as of January 19, 2018, by year, Oregon, 1998–2017

| Characteristics | 2017 (N=143) | | 1998–2016 (N=1,132) | | Total (N=1,275) | |
|---|---|---|---|---|---|---|
| | N | (%)[1] | N | (%)[1] | N | (%)[1] |
| **Sex** | | | | | | |
| Male (%) | 83 | (58.0) | 585 | (51.7) | 668 | (52.4) |
| Female (%) | 60 | (42.0) | 547 | (48.3) | 607 | (47.6) |
| **Age** | | | | | | |
| 18-34 (%) | 0 | (0.0) | 9 | (0.8) | 9 | (0.7) |
| 35-44 (%) | 2 | (1.4) | 24 | (2.1) | 26 | (2.0) |
| 45-54 (%) | 3 | (2.1) | 70 | (6.2) | 73 | (5.7) |
| 55-64 (%) | 23 | (16.1) | 225 | (19.9) | 248 | (19.5) |
| 65-74 (%) | 46 | (32.2) | 342 | (30.2) | 388 | (30.4) |
| 75-84 (%) | 43 | (30.1) | 292 | (25.8) | 335 | (26.3) |
| 85+ (%) | 26 | (18.2) | 170 | (15.0) | 196 | (15.4) |
| Median years (range) | 74 | (41-99) | 72 | (25-102) | 72 | (25-102) |
| **Race** | | | | | | |
| White (%) | 135 | (94.4) | 1,088 | (96.5) | 1,223 | (96.3) |
| African American (%) | 0 | (0.0) | 1 | (0.1) | 1 | (0.1) |
| American Indian (%) | 0 | (0.0) | 2 | (0.2) | 2 | (0.2) |
| Asian (%) | 4 | (2.8) | 15 | (1.3) | 19 | (1.5) |
| Pacific Islander (%) | 0 | (0.0) | 1 | (0.1) | 1 | (0.1) |
| Other (%) | 0 | (0.0) | 3 | (0.3) | 3 | (0.2) |
| Two or more races (%) | 1 | (0.7) | 5 | (0.4) | 6 | (0.5) |
| Hispanic (%) | 3 | (2.1) | 12 | (1.1) | 15 | (1.2) |
| *Unknown* | *0* | | *5* | | *5* | |
| **Marital status** | | | | | | |
| Married (including Registered Domestic Partner) (%) | 75 | (52.4) | 514 | (45.7) | 589 | (46.5) |
| Widowed (%) | 26 | (18.2) | 258 | (22.9) | 284 | (22.4) |
| Never married (%) | 6 | (4.2) | 86 | (7.6) | 92 | (7.3) |
| Divorced (%) | 36 | (25.2) | 267 | (23.7) | 303 | (23.9) |
| *Unknown* | *0* | | *7* | | *7* | |
| **Education** | | | | | | |
| Less than high school (%) | 7 | (5.0) | 63 | (5.6) | 70 | (5.5) |
| High school graduate (%) | 36 | (25.5) | 242 | (21.6) | 278 | (22.0) |
| Some college (%) | 29 | (20.6) | 299 | (26.6) | 328 | (26.0) |
| Baccalaureate or higher (%) | 69 | (48.9) | 518 | (46.2) | 587 | (46.5) |
| *Unknown* | *2* | | *10* | | *12* | |

| Characteristics | 2017 (N=143) | | 1998–2016 (N=1,132) | | Total (N=1,275) | |
|---|---|---|---|---|---|---|
| **Residence** | | | | | | |
| Metro counties (Clackamas, Multnomah, Washington) (%) | 55 | (38.5) | 484 | (43.1) | 539 | (42.6) |
| Coastal counties (%) | 12 | (8.4) | 80 | (7.1) | 92 | (7.3) |
| Other western counties (%) | 65 | (45.5) | 471 | (41.9) | 536 | (42.3) |
| East of the Cascades (%) | 11 | (7.7) | 88 | (7.8) | 99 | (7.8) |
| *Unknown* | *0* | | *9* | | *9* | |
| **End of life care** | | | | | | |
| **Hospice** | | | | | | |
| Enrolled (%) | 130 | (90.9) | 989 | (90.1) | 1119 | (90.2) |
| Not enrolled (%) | 13 | (9.1) | 109 | (9.9) | 122 | (9.8) |
| *Unknown* | *0* | | *34* | | *34* | |
| **Insurance** | | | | | | |
| Private (%) | 36 | (31.3) | 569 | (53.8) | 605 | (51.6) |
| Medicare, Medicaid or other governmental (%) | 78 | (67.8) | 474 | (44.8) | 552 | (47.1) |
| None (%) | 1 | (0.9) | 14 | (1.3) | 15 | (1.3) |
| Unknown | 28 | | 75 | | 103 | |
| **Underlying illness** | | | | | | |
| Cancer (%) | 110 | (76.9) | 883 | (78.0) | 993 | (77.9) |
| Lung and bronchus (%) | 23 | (16.1) | 193 | (17.0) | 216 | (16.9) |
| Breast (%) | 6 | (4.2) | 86 | (7.6) | 92 | (7.2) |
| Colon (%) | 6 | (4.2) | 73 | (6.4) | 79 | (6.2) |
| Pancreas (%) | 15 | (10.5) | 74 | (6.5) | 89 | (7.0) |
| Prostate (%) | 10 | (7.0) | 48 | (4.2) | 58 | (4.5) |
| Ovary (%) | 4 | (2.8) | 41 | (3.6) | 45 | (3.5) |
| Other cancers (%) | 46 | (32.2) | 368 | (32.5) | 414 | (32.5) |
| Neurological disease (%) | 20 | (14.0) | 114 | (10.1) | 134 | (10.5) |
| Amyotrophic lateral sclerosis (%) | 10 | (7.0) | 90 | (8.0) | 100 | (7.8) |
| Other neurological disease (%) | 10 | (7.0) | 24 | (2.1) | 34 | (2.7) |
| Respiratory disease [e.g., COPD] (%) | 2 | (1.4) | 59 | (5.2) | 61 | (4.8) |
| Heart/circulatory disease (%) | 9 | (6.3) | 40 | (3.5) | 49 | (3.8) |
| Infectious disease [e.g., HIV/AIDS] (%)) | 0 | (0.0) | 13 | (1.1) | 13 | (1.0) |
| Gastrointestinal disease [e.g., liver disease] (%) | 0 | (0.0) | 8 | (0.7) | 8 | (0.6) |
| Endocrine/metabolic disease [e.g., diabetes](%) | 1 | (0.7) | 7 | (0.6) | 8 | (0.6) |
| Other illnesses (%)[2] | 1 | (0.7) | 8 | (0.7) | 9 | (0.7) |

| Characteristics | 2017 (N=143) | | 1998–2016 (N=1,132) | | Total (N=1,275) | |
|---|---|---|---|---|---|---|
| **DWDA process** | | | | | | |
| Referred for psychiatric evaluation (%) | 5 | (3.5) | 57 | (5.1) | 62 | (4.9) |
| Patient informed family of decision (%)[3] | 139 | (97.9) | 982 | (93.1) | 1,121 | (93.7) |
| **Patient died at** | | | | | | |
| Home (patient, family or friend) (%) | 129 | (90.2) | 1,052 | (93.4) | 1,181 | (93.1) |
| Long term care, assisted living or foster care facility (%) | 13 | (9.1) | 55 | (4.9) | 68 | (5.4) |
| Hospital (%) | 0 | (0.0) | 4 | (0.4) | 4 | (0.3) |
| Other (%) | 1 | (0.7) | 15 | (1.3) | 16 | (1.3) |
| *Unknown* | *0* | | *6* | | *6* | |
| **Lethal medication** | | | | | | |
| Secobarbital (%) | 71 | (49.7) | 676 | (59.7) | 747 | (58.6) |
| Pentobarbital (%) | 0 | (0.0) | 386 | (34.1) | 386 | (30.3) |
| Phenobarbital (%) | 6 | (4.2) | 57 | (5.0) | 63 | (4.9) |
| Morphine sulfate (%) | 66 | (46.2) | 6 | (0.5) | 72 | (5.6) |
| Other (%) | 0 | (0.0) | 7 | (0.6) | 7 | (0.5) |
| **End of life concerns[4]** | **(N=143)** | | **(N=1,132)** | | **(N=1,275)** | |
| Losing autonomy (%) | 125 | (87.4) | 1,029 | (91.4) | 1,154 | (90.9) |
| Less able to engage in activities making life enjoyable (%) | 126 | (88.1) | 1,011 | (89.7) | 1,137 | (89.5) |
| Loss of dignity (%)[5] | 96 | (67.1) | 769 | (76.9) | 865 | (75.7) |
| Losing control of bodily functions (%) | 53 | (37.1) | 526 | (46.8) | 579 | (45.7) |
| Burden on family, friends/caregivers (%) | 79 | (55.2) | 475 | (42.2) | 554 | (43.7) |
| Inadequate pain control or concern about it (%) | 30 | (21.0) | 297 | (26.4) | 327 | (25.8) |
| Financial implications of treatment (%) | 8 | (5.6) | 39 | (3.5) | 47 | (3.7) |
| **Health-care provider present (collected since 2001)** | **(N=143)** | | **(N=1,062)** | | **(N=1,205)** | |
| When medication was ingested[6] | | | | | | |
| Prescribing physician | 24 | | 163 | | 187 | |
| Other provider, prescribing physician not present | 24 | | 270 | | 294 | |
| No provider | 6 | | 91 | | 97 | |
| *Unknown* | *89* | | *538* | | *627* | |
| At time of death | | | | | | |
| Prescribing physician (%) | 23 | (16.1) | 149 | (14.3) | 172 | (14.6) |
| Other provider, prescribing physician not present (%) | 19 | (13.3) | 295 | (28.4) | 314 | (26.6) |
| No provider (%) | 101 | (70.6) | 595 | (57.3) | 606 | (58.9) |
| *Unknown* | *0* | | *23* | | *23* | |
| **Complications[6]** | **(N=143)** | | **(N=1,121)** | | **(N=1,264)** | |
| Difficulty ingesting/regurgitated | 1 | | 24 | | 25 | |
| Seizures | 2 | | 0 | | 2 | |
| Other | 1 | | 6 | | 7 | |
| None | 38 | | 554 | | 592 | |
| *Unknown* | *101* | | *537* | | *638* | |

10 Patient characteristics | Oregon Death with Dignity Act

| Characteristics | 2017 (N=143) | 1998–2016 (N=1,132) | Total (N=1,275) |
|---|---|---|---|
| **Other outcomes** | | | |
| Regained consciousness after ingesting DWDA medications[7] | 1 | 6 | 7 |
| **Timing of DWDA event** | | | |
| Duration (weeks) of patient-physician relationship | | | |
|    Median | 10 | 13 | 13 |
|    Range | 1-2,138 | 0-1,905 | 0-2,138 |
|    *Number of patients with information available* | *140* | *1,128* | *1,268* |
|    *Number of patients with information unknown* | *3* | *4* | *7* |
| Duration (days) between first request and death | | | |
|    Median | 52 | 48 | 48 |
|    Range | 15-603 | 14-1,009 | 14-1,009 |
|    *Number of patients with information available* | *143* | *1,132* | *1,275* |
|    *Number of patients with information unknown* | *0* | *0* | *0* |
| Minutes between ingestion and unconsciousness | | | |
|    Median | 6 | 5 | 5 |
|    Range | 2-240 | 1-60 | 1-240 |
|    *Number of patients with information available* | *38* | *556* | *594* |
|    *Number of patients with information unknown* | *105* | *576* | *681* |
| Minutes between ingestion and death | | | |
|    Median | 31 | 25 | 25 |
|    Range | 10min-21hrs | 1min-104hrs | 1min-104hrs |
|    *Number of patients with information available* | *40* | *562* | *602* |
|    *Number of patients with information unknown* | *103* | *570* | *673* |

1  Unknowns are excluded when calculating percentages.

2  Includes deaths due to arthritis, arteritis, sclerosis, stenosis, kidney failure, and musculoskeletal systems disorders.

3  First recorded in 2001. Since then, 55 patients (4.6%) have chosen not to inform their families, and 21 patients (1.7%) have had no family to inform. There was one unknown case in 2002, two in 2005, one in 2009, three in 2013, and one in 2017.

4  Affirmative answers only ("Don't know" included in negative answers). Categories are not mutually exclusive. Data unavailable for four patients in 2001.

5  First asked in 2003. Data available for 143 patients in 2017, 1,003 patients between 1998 and 2016, and 1,146 patients for all years.

6  A procedure revision was made mid-year in 2010 to standardize reporting on the follow-up questionnaire. The new procedure accepts information about time of death and circumstances surrounding death only when the physician or another health care provider is present at the time of death. This resulted in a larger number of unknowns beginning in 2010.

7  There have been a total of seven patients who regained consciousness after ingesting prescribed lethal medications. These patients are not included in the total number of DWDA deaths. These deaths occurred in 2005 (1 death), 2010 (2 deaths), 2011 (2 deaths), 2012 (1 death), and 2017 (1 death). Please refer to the appropriate years' annual reports on our website (http://www.healthoregon.org/dwd) for more detail on these deaths.

Table 2. Number of DWDA prescription recipients, DWDA deaths, and
attending physicians, 1998-2017

| Year | Prescription recipients | DWDA deaths | Attending physicians |
|------|------|------|------|
| 1998 | 24  | 16  | n/a |
| 1999 | 33  | 27  | n/a |
| 2000 | 39  | 27  | 22 |
| 2001 | 44  | 21  | 33 |
| 2002 | 58  | 38  | 33 |
| 2003 | 68  | 42  | 42 |
| 2004 | 60  | 37  | 40 |
| 2005 | 65  | 38  | 40 |
| 2006 | 65  | 46  | 41 |
| 2007 | 85  | 49  | 46 |
| 2008 | 88  | 60  | 60 |
| 2009 | 95  | 59  | 64 |
| 2010 | 97  | 65  | 59 |
| 2011 | 114 | 71  | 62 |
| 2012 | 116 | 85  | 62 |
| 2013 | 121 | 73  | 62 |
| 2014 | 155 | 105 | 83 |
| 2015 | 218 | 135 | 106 |
| 2016 | 204 | 138 | 102 |
| 2017 | 218 | 143 | 92 |

## NOTES AND QUESTIONS

1.    The Oregon Death with Dignity Act provides that no contract or
statute can affect a person's request for physician assisted suicide, and that no
insurance policy can be conditioned upon, or affected by, a patient's decision to
choose (or reject) physician assisted suicide. The measure includes a section

providing immunity for those who follow the requirements of the statute, and imposing liability on those who violate it.

2. Does the Report address whether the requirements of Section 127.815, or any other section, actually were followed in practice? How would the Department determine the answer to that question? Those who are skeptical about whether the annual report accurately presents the impact of the Act point out that the report can describe only those cases that are reported to the state. They argue that cases that do not comply with the specific requirements of the statute will not be reported. It is in this potential body of unreported cases that evidence for concerns over the effectiveness of the statute's boundaries would be found.

3. As the Summary published in 2018 indicates, most Oregonians who have sought medically assisted dying have done so because of their fear of losing control of their lives (and the concomitant suffering that would follow), not because of physical pain. In 2017, more than three times as many patients listed loss of autonomy as a reason for seeking medically assisted dying (91%) as listed inadequate pain control (26%). An excerpt from Oregon's Second Annual Report, published in 2000, explains this:

> Responses from both physician and family interviews indicate that patient's decisions to request PAS were motivated by multiple interrelated concerns. Physical suffering was discussed by several families as a cause of loss of autonomy, inability to participate in activities that made life enjoyable, or a "non-existent" quality of life. For example, "She would have stuck it out through the pain if she thought she'd get better . . . [but she believed that] when quality of life has no meaning, it's no use hanging around." For another participant, a feeling of being trapped because of ALS contributed to concern about loss of autonomy. Family members frequently commented on loss of control of bodily functions when discussing loss of autonomy. Those reporting patient concern about being a burden on friends and family also reported concern about loss of autonomy and control of bodily functions. Reasons for requesting a prescription were sometimes so interrelated they were difficult to categorize. According to one family member being asked to distinguish reasons for the patient's decision, "It was everything; it was nothing; [he was suffering terribly]."

> Difficulty categorizing and differences in interpreting the nature of the concerns made physician and family member responses hard to compare quantitatively. Nonetheless, family interviews corroborate physician reports from both years that patients are greatly concerned about issues of autonomy and control. In addition, responses of both physicians and family consistently pointed to patient concerns about quality of life and the wish to have a means of controlling the end of life should it become unbearable. As one family member said, "She always thought that if something was terminal, she would [want to] control the end . . . It was not the dying that she dreaded, it was getting to that death."

\* \* \*

Oregonians choosing physician-assisted suicide appeared to want control over how they died. One woman had purchased poison over a decade before her participation, when her cancer was first diagnosed, so that she would never be without the means of controlling the end of her life should it become unbearable. Like many others who participated, she was described as "determined" to have this control. Another woman was described as a "gutsy woman" who was ". . . determined in her lifetime, and determined about [physician-assisted suicide]." Family members expressed profound grief at losing a loved one. However, mixed with this grief was great respect for the patient's determination and choice to use physician-assisted suicide. As one husband said about his wife of almost 50 years, "She was my only girl; I didn't want to lose her . . . but she wanted to do this."

Might a family member have mistaken what motivated a relative's decisions? In any case, could the expressed concerns have been relieved by better medical and nursing care? Should these individuals have toughed it out, or did they choose the better course for themselves? For their families? Are those who do take advantage of the statute brave? Cowardly? Why do you think so?

4.    The Oregon initiative was immediately challenged for a wide range of reasons. Some argued that it discriminated against the disabled, for example, by coercing them into choosing medically assisted dying, and others argued it discriminated against the disabled because those with physical disabilities that made it impossible to take oral medications would not be able to use the statute. The United States District Court in Oregon issued a preliminary injunction against enforcing the initiative shortly after its passage and issued a permanent injunction several months later. Ultimately, the Ninth Circuit reversed the District Court, finding that those challenging the Oregon initiative had no standing to raise the issue in federal court. Lee v. Oregon, 107 F.3d 1382 (9th Cir.1997).

5.    The federal government has not ignored medically assisted dying, either. Even before the Oregon statute became effective, Congress passed the Assisted Suicide Prevention Restriction Act of 1997, which outlawed the use of federal money to aid medically assisted dying, directly or indirectly.

Shortly after the Oregon Death with Dignity Act became effective, some suggested that any physician who prescribed a lethal drug under that statute would be prescribing that drug without a "legitimate medical purpose," and thus would be acting inconsistently with the federal Controlled Substances Act (CSA). A physician's violation of the Act could lead to both the loss of prescribing authority and criminal indictment. In 1998, after the matter had been pending for some time, the United States Department of Justice published a report concluding that use of controlled substances under the Oregon statute would satisfy the "legitimate medical purpose" requirement of the federal Act.

Members of the House and Senate then introduced the Lethal Drug Abuse Prevention Act of 1998, which would have expanded the authority of the Drug Enforcement Agency to investigate lethal use of controlled substances, which could not be used with the intent of causing death. Supporters of medically assisted dying joined many of their staunchest opponents and mainstream medical organizations (including the AMA) to oppose the bill because, they said, it would be likely to chill physicians from providing adequate pain relief at the end of life. Although the bill failed, it was resurrected in slightly milder form in 2000 as the Pain Relief Promotion Act (PRPA), which included a well publicized section announcing that the provision of medication with the intent to manage pain (and not the intent to cause death) was protected. The 2000 version of the bill also provided for the education of health-care professionals on issues related to pain management, and it was supported by the AMA (but opposed by the American Bar Association, the American Cancer Society and most groups advocating for improved pain management). Although the stated purpose of PRPA was to promote adequate pain relief practices, its effect would be (and, some say, its real purpose was) to render it impossible for physicians in Oregon to carry out the provisions of the Death With Dignity Act. The PRPA died when Congress adjourned in late 2000.

In 2001, the Attorney General, John Ashcroft, issued an interpretive rule that reversed the 1998 Department of Justice position on the issue of the application of the CSA and implemented an enforcement action. Within a day of the announcement of this change in the federal position, Oregon sought relief from the Attorney General's decision in the federal court. A private action seeking an injunction against the Ashcroft position was filed shortly thereafter on behalf of an Oregon oncologist. The District Court immediately restrained the United States from enforcing the new interpretation of the CSA, and in 2006 the Supreme Court determined that the Attorney General's interpretive rule was beyond the scope of his authority and was improperly promulgated. Gonzales v. Oregon, 546 U.S. 243, 126 S.Ct. 904, 163 L.Ed.2d 748 (2006). The Court left open the possibility that the Attorney General could properly promulgate a substantive rule that would bar the operation of the Oregon Death with Dignity Act, and that Congress could amend the Controlled Substances Act to achieve this end. Neither has happened, although there is some indication that Attorney General Sessions, who took office in 2017, is a much stronger opponent of aid in dying than his predecessor in the Obama administration.

6. The Oregon statute has been amended, but the changes are not substantial. The legislature added the definition of "capable," added some new language designed to encourage patients to discuss the matter with their families, and provided some factors to be considered in determining residency. The amendments also made clear the broad extent of the institutional conscience exception to the statute, which permits health-care institutions to limit physicians from engaging in assisted death on their premises or in their organizations, and it changed the written consent form to assure that patients

recognize that death will probably, but not always, take place about three hours after taking the medication.

7.    Emboldened by the success in Oregon, many groups have sought state statutes that would accomplish what Oregon's Measure 16 did. A measure similar to the Oregon statute was very narrowly defeated at the polls in Maine in 2000. In part as a result of the narrow defeat of the Maine measure, during the next legislative session both supporters and opponents of medically assisted dying joined to support a number of bills improving the quality of end-of-life care in that state.

8.    Advocates for medically assisted dying in Washington made that state the second to use the initiative process to provide for medically assisted dying with the passage of the Washington Death with Dignity Act, again through the initiative process and a statewise vote, in 2008. Former Washington Governor Booth Gardner, who had Parkinson's disease, became the leading advocate for an Oregon-like statute. For the story of Governor Gardner's "last campaign" from the perspective of someone who opposes medically assisted dying, see Daniel Bergner, Death in the Family, New York Times Magazine (December 2, 2007). The Washington Death with Dignity statute, R.C.W. section 70.245, became effective in 2009. Like Oregon, Washington has published annual reports with substantial detail about the use of the statute within the state. Overall, the Washington data looks very much like that from Oregon. In 2016, 248 Washington patients received prescriptions under the statute, and 192 died from ingesting the medication. Another 36 died without taking the lethal prescription. 94% were from west of the Cascades, 97% were White, 43% were married, and two-thirds had at least some college education. Washington State Department of Health, 2016 Death with Dignity Report (issued September 2017).

9.    After a very hard-fought and expensive initiative battle over a statute almost identical to the Oregon and Washington statutes, in 2012 the voters of Massachusetts rejected any change in the law. In 2013 Vermont became the first state to adopt a statute permitting aid in dying through the regular legislative process (rather than through an initiative) in the Patient Choice and Control at the End of Life Act. California followed with the End of Life Option Act (signed in 2015, effective in mid-2016), and the District of Columbia City Council promulgated a Death with Dignity Act in 2016. Although there were threats of a Congressional veto of that legislation—a remedy available to Congress only with regard to the District, and not with regard to states—attempts to do so failed. Congress could still effectively repeal the D.C. statute through separate legislation, but it has not done so. Voters passed the Colorado End of Life Options Act in 2016, and it became effective at the end of that year. Finally, the Hawai'i Legislature passed an Oregon-like statute in 2018. That means that eight jurisdictions in the United States now formally permit medically assisted dying, at least under some circumstances—Oregon, Washington, and Colorado by initiative, Vermont, California, Hawai'i and the District of Columbia by ordinary legislative action, and, as we shall see in the Note, below, Montana by judicial interpretation of current statutory law.

10. Legislatures in several other states are currently considering legislation that would permit medically assisted dying, and there is likely to be a serious attempt to pass such legislation in 2018 or 2019 in Massachusetts, Delaware, New York, New Jersey, New Mexico and several other jurisdictions.

11. Is there some common ground available to those, on the one hand, who believe that permitting medically assisted dying is necessary for patients to be properly treated at the end of life, and those, on the other hand, who believe that medically assisted dying must be outlawed for patients to be properly treated? Both groups agree that pain is often inadequately treated at the end of life, in part because physicians fear legal action for homicide (if pain relief results in the death of the patient) or distribution of drugs (if the condition of a patient requires a larger dose of narcotic medication than is standard).

In some states advocates on both sides of the medically assisted dying issue have joined together to support intractable pain relief statutes, which are designed to protect health-care providers who deliver adequate pain relief from adverse licensing and criminal actions. These statutes generally provide that a health-care provider will not be liable in a state disciplinary proceeding or a criminal action for the aggressive prescription of pain medication as long as the use of that medication is in accord with accepted guidelines for pain management. Several states have promulgated intractable pain relief acts, and several more are considering them. For a model pain relief act, see 24 J.L., Med. Ethics 317 (1996). See also, Ann Alpers, Criminal Act or Palliative Care? Prosecutions Involving the Care of the Dying, 26 J. L. Med. Ethics 308 (1998), identifying factors that create a risk of prosecution. For a series of articles on the relationship between pain relief and medically assisted dying, with the conclusion that we ought to create a system that provides excellent palliative care in every case and allows for medically assisted dying in the rare cases in which it is necessary, see Timothy Quill and Margaret Battin, eds., Physician-Assisted Dying: the Right to Excellent End-of-Life Care and Patient Choice (2004). See also, Kathleen Foley, The Case Against Assisted Suicide: For the Right to End of Life Care (2002), written by a leading palliative care physician. For an account of the meaning of euthanasia and suicide in our society and others, and a description of how these arguments are likely to be discussed in the future, see Margaret Battin, Ending Life: Ethics and the Way We Die (2005).

12. Federal and state policy may conflict on one kind of palliative care— the use of marijuana. Some cancer patients, patients with glaucoma, AIDS patients, patients with multiple sclerosis, those with migraine headaches and others find that they can obtain relief from some of the symptoms of the disease—or from some of the side effects of the treatments for the disease— through the use of marijuana. In particular, some cancer patients find that marijuana helps them overcome the nausea that follows the use of many chemotherapeutic agents. While several states have now legalized the use of marijuana under such circumstances, the manufacture and distribution of marijuana is still a felony under the Federal Controlled Substances Act (CSA).

In 2001, the Supreme Court determined that there was no medical necessity defense available to those who manufactured or distributed marijuana to patients in violation of the federal law. U.S. v. Oakland Cannabis Buyers' Cooperative, 532 U.S. 483, 121 S.Ct. 1711, 149 L.Ed.2d 722 (2001). Four years later the Supreme Court confirmed that the CSA marijuana prohibition fell within Congress's commerce power. Gonzales v. Raich, 545 U.S. 1, 125 S.Ct. 2195, 162 L.Ed.2d 1 (2005).

Several states now have institutionalized formal programs for distributing marijuana to those who are found to be in medical need (under highly varying state standards). In 2012 the federal government indicated that it would not seek legal redress against those who acted strictly within their state legal limitations in providing patients with medical marijuana through non-commercial enterprises. Despite this, though, the United States has sought to close down several large and otherwise legal medical dispensaries in California and elsewhere. In 2012 the voters in Colorado and Washington approved new regulatory schemes that would allow (and tax) the use of marijuana, even for non-medical purposes, and that has added a measure of additional confusion to the resolution of problems caused by the apparent conflict between federal and state laws. Attorney General Sessions added to this confusion in 2016 by threatening the prosecution of those who violate federal law without regard to state laws and the expectations of those providing marijuana to patients (and others), and by questioning the propriety of the 2012 position of the Department of Justice.

13. The public interest in this issue is not limited to the United States. Medically assisted dying has been tolerated in the Netherlands, as a legal matter, since 1969, and it was formally legalized by the Parliament in 2001 in cases of intractable suffering (not just pain), where the patient has been informed of all of the alternative treatments available, has consulted two physicians, and has followed other requirements established by the national medical association. Belgium recently joined the Netherlands in legalizing medically assisted dying through the legislative process, and the practice is now officially tolerated under some circumstances in Switzerland. The Constitutional Court of Colombia has approved legislation that provides for medically assisted dying, and there has been an active debate over the propriety of permitting medically assisted dying in France, Venezuela and Australia.

Australia's Northern Territory's Parliament passed The Rights of the Terminally Ill Act (1995), which permitted what some have called "voluntary euthanasia" under some circumstances; however, the national Parliament effectively overturned that territorial statute. The national Parliament has no such control over legislation coming from the states (rather than territories) in Australia, and the State of Victoria Parliament in Melbourne has approved a plan for medically assisted dying (including euthanasia, when appropriate) that is currently scheduled to go into effect in that state in 2019.

Canada has allowed for medically assisted dying since the Parliament, encouraged (or, perhaps, compelled) by a decision of the Supreme Court of Canada, permitted it in mid-2016. The governing statute has many of the requirements of the Oregon and Washington statutes, although it is generally more liberal in permitting the practice, and it allows a patient to choose euthanasia (where the final dose is actually delivered by a healthcare provider) rather than taking the medication himself, if that is his desire. The vast majority of Canadian patients given the option to choose medical delivery of the lethal dose (rather than self-administration) have done so. The Canadian statute was encouraged by the 2015 decision in Carter v. Canada (AG), 2015 SCC 5, which found that not allowing a competent adult access to relief from suffering at the end of life by outlawing medically assisted dying violated the Canadian Charter of Rights and Freedoms.

The European Court of Human Rights considered a challenge to the laws of the United Kingdom that outlawed medically assisted dying in Pretty v. United Kingdom, 35 Eur. H. R. Rep. 1 (2002). Applying analysis similar, in many respects, to that in Glucksberg and Vacco, the Court found that the United Kingdom had the authority to enforce its law. An English court again confirmed the legal prohibition against medically assisted dying in 2012. For a brief description of the current state of the law in other countries, see Alan Meisel and Kathy Cerminara, The Right to Die (3d ed. 2005, Supplement 2017).

### *PROBLEM: DRAFTING LEGISLATION*

You are the nonpolitical legislative counsel to a state legislature. Currently that state has a statute prohibiting assisting suicide which, it is assumed, would outlaw any conduct intended to result in the death of another person. You have been asked by several members of the legislature to draft bills relating to medically assisted dying. One member has asked you to draft a bill that would outlaw all medically assisted dying, under all circumstances. A second member wants you to draft a bill that would put as few limitations on medically assisted dying as is possible; this libertarian member believes that the decision should be left to individual doctors and patients. Another member has asked you to draft a statute that would protect health-care providers from potential liability for participating in medically assisted dying, and would give providers an option to avoid participating in medically assisted dying if they chose not to do so. Yet another member has asked you to draft a statute that would prohibit managed care organizations from directly or indirectly giving any incentives to their members to choose medically assisted dying. Finally, one long time incumbent has asked you to draft a consensus statute—one with enough political support across the spectrum that it has a reasonable chance of passing. Presumably, this would be a statute that would permit some narrow form of medically assisted dying under carefully controlled and narrowly defined circumstances.

How would you go about drafting these statutes? How would they be different? What facts (about the legal landscape in this state, about the politics of the current officeholders, about the religious backgrounds of those within the state, about other issues) would you want to have before you started drafting these statutes?

## NOTE: ESTABLISHING A STATE RIGHT TO MEDICALLY ASSISTED DYING THROUGH LITIGATION

1.    As it becomes clear that each state is going to determine the legal status of medically assisted dying within its borders, advocates of legal medically assisted dying have looked to state judiciaries as well as state legislatures to establish such a right. While the issue of the legalization of medically assisted dying has been litigated in a host of different forms over the last few decades, the highest courts of only five states—Florida, Alaska, Montana, New Mexico and New York—have had a chance to directly address the issue in the last few years. State constitutional claims were raised in all five states, and they were rejected in all five cases. One of these courts, in Montana, also did a statutory analysis and found that there was no violation of any statute when a provider wrote a lethal prescription under circumstances similar to those permitted by statute in Oregon. Thus, the Supreme Court of Montana found that current Montana law did not outlaw medically assisted dying, even if the Montana Constitution did not independently protect a person who was seeking that form of treatment. The other state courts to consider the issue—the Florida, Alaska, and New Mexico Supreme Courts and the New York Court of Appeals—found no state constitutional right to medically assisted dying, and, unlike the court in Montana, they also found that there was no statutory right to medically assisted dying within their states because any exercise of medically assisted dying would constitute the crime of aiding or abetting (or assisting) suicide under state statute. See Note 5, below.

2.    The Montana case, Baxter v. Montana, 354 Mont. 234, 224 P.3d 1211 (2009), rejected the argument (which had been accepted at the trial court) that outlawing medically assisted dying would violate the protection of individual dignity guaranteed by Article II, section 4 of the Montana Constitution, which provides that "[t]he dignity of the human being is inviolable." While at least one judge would have found that the individual dignity clause was sufficient to protect medically assisted dying, the majority decided the case on statutory grounds. The court determined that under Montana law consent is a defense, even to homicide crimes, as long as the defendant's conduct is not "against public policy." Here, the court determined, medically assisted dying was not contrary to public policy; indeed, the Legislature had never spoken about it in a way that approved or disapproved of it. Thus, while the Montana Legislature could outlaw medically assisted dying, it had not done so as a matter of statutory law, and no state constitutional analysis was necessary.

3.    At the next plenary Montana legislative session following Baxter, in 2011, the Legislature was squarely confronted with bills that would outlaw medically assisted dying, and with a bill that would formally legalize it and impose the same kinds of restrictions that are imposed in Washington and

Oregon. The bills were carefully followed by the press, and there was a good deal of advocacy by partisans on both sides of the issue. Ultimately, the legislature rejected all of the bills on both sides of the issue, and left the law as it stood the day that Baxter was decided.

In 2013 the Montana state Legislature again faced bills to both institutionalize (on one side) and prohibit (on the other side) aid in dying. It seems like the default position will always be the legislative winner in Montana; whatever the law is today will remain the law indefinitely because there is inadequate legislative support either to make medically assisted death legal (if it is not) or illegal (if it is now legal).

In fact, given the difficulty of pushing legislation through a state legislature and across a Governor's desk, the state "default" position—the law in the absence of any legislation dealing directly with medically assisted dying—will determine whether medically assisted dying is permitted. This "default" position, of course, must be determined by the courts. The Montana Supreme Court described the "default" position as one in which there was no statutory provision outlawing medically assisted dying—so medically assisted dying is permitted in Montana. Other state judiciaries to consider the issue found the "default" position to be that medically assisted dying is outlawed by state statutes criminalizing assisting suicide. Thus, medically assisted dying is not permitted in Florida, Alaska, New Mexico or New York. Because neither side on this issue has the political strength to change the current statutory law on medically assisted dying—whatever that law may be—the status of the state law is really determined by the state courts in determining the "default" position in that state.

4.    Those opposed to medically assisted dying also sought to use the administrative process to reinstate the ban in Montana. An attempt to have the Montana Board of Medical Examiners declare that they would impose professional sanctions against any Montana physician who provided medically assisted dying in accord with the Baxter opinion was met with this response in 2012:

### Physician Aid in Dying

As a result of [Baxter], the Montana Board of Medical Examiners has been asked if it will discipline physicians for participating in such aid-in-dying. This statement reflects the Board's position on this controversial question.

The Board recognizes that its mission is to protect the citizens of Montana against the unprofessional, improper, unauthorized and unqualified practice of medicine by ensuring that its licensees are competent professionals. [ ] In all matters of medical practice, including end-of-life matters, physicians are held to professional standards. If the Board receives a complaint related to physician aid-in-dying, it will evaluate the complaint on its individual merits and will consider, as it would any other medical procedure or intervention, whether the physician engaged in unprofessional conduct as defined by the laws and rules pertinent to the Board.

Mont. Bd. Of Med. Examiners, Position Statement No. 20 (2012). This statement was applauded by those who support aid-in-dying and who believe that it should be treated like any other medical procedure. Montanans Against Assisted Suicide and for Living with Dignity, an advocacy group opposed to aid-in-dying, asked the Board to withdraw the statement, which, those advocates said, was issued without proper notice, without statutory authority, and in violation of the principle of separation of powers. They argued that the Position Statement put doctors and the public at risk.

5.    Litigation to establish the kind of right recognized in *Baxter* has not been successful outside of Montana. In Krischer v. McIver, 697 So.2d 97 (Fla.1997), a terminally ill AIDS patient and his physician sought an injunction against the prosecution of the physician for assisting in his patient's suicide. The Florida Supreme Court rejected a claim that the privacy provision of the Florida Constitution included the right to have a physician assist in one's death. The court announced that a properly drawn statute authorizing physician-assisted suicide would be constitutionally permissible, but that principles of separation of powers left the decision about whether it should be made legal to the legislature. The Chief Justice filed a vigorous dissent, arguing that, " . . . the right of privacy attaches with unusual force at the death bed. . . . What possible interest does society have in saving life when there is nothing of life to save but a final convulsion of agony? The state has no business in this arena." 697 So.2d at 111. See also Sampson v. State, 31 P.3d 88 (Alaska 2001).

The New Mexico Supreme Court faced an argument that its assisting suicide statute was a violation of state constitutional law in Morris v. Brandenburg, S-1-S-35478 (NM 2016). The unanimous Supreme Court affirmed a 2–1 decision of the Court of Appeals, which reversed a judgment for the plaintiffs rendered after a multi-day trial. The New Mexico Supreme Court determined that medically assisted dying would constitute "assisting suicide," a crime in New Mexico, and thus it was illegal unless that criminal statute itself violated a federal or state constitutional provision. The court rejected due process arguments based on both the United States and state constitutions by deferring to the United States Supreme Court's analysis in *Glucksberg*, supra. The court separately rejected the application of the New Mexico constitution's provision which assures that the state will protect such "natural, inherent and inalienable" rights as those of "seeking and obtaining safety and happiness." The court concluded that any right to medically assisted dying would have to come from the Legislature.

The New York Court of Appeals faced the same issue in Myers v. Schneiderman, 2017 NY Slip Op 06412, (New York Court of Appeals 2017)(per curiam). Like the New Mexico court, the New York Court of Appeals deferred to the *Glucksberg* analysis of the due process and equal protection issues and, in addition, found that there was a rational basis for applying the law prohibiting assisted suicide. Like the New Mexico court, the New York Court of Appeals determined that the application of the criminal assisted suicide statute to those offering medically assisted dying is a matter for the New York Legislature, at least given the current state of the record. Although that application of the criminal law is not required by state constitutional law, it is not prohibited by state constitutional law either.

### PROBLEM: MEDICALLY ASSISTED DYING, A LEGAL ISSUE OR A MEDICAL ISSUE?

Our conflict over medically assisted dying has been fought in the arena of law. Is there a right to engage in medically assisted dying? Do homicide and suicide statutes prohibit the practice of medically assisted dying? Those with more libertarian views tend to support finding such a right; those with strongly developed religious views or a more expansive view of criminal law are less likely to find such a right. The battles over legislation and most of the reported litigation reflect this rights-oriented legal battle over this issue.

Instead, should we be asking whether medically assisted dying is within the medical standard of care? If we were to take this approach, we would treat medically assisted dying as one of many end-of-life care possibilities, and we would let providers determine if it is appropriate on a case by case basis. Instead of arguing about the issue to courts, we would leave it to health-care professionals, who could offer to their patients whatever came within the standard of care.

Do you think the issue is best analyzed as one of legal rights and obligations, ultimately to be decided by courts, or is best analyzed as one of good medicine, ultimately to be determined by the physician and her patient in each case?

For an account of an early effort by physicians to establish a standard of care in this area, see T.E. Quill, C.K. Cassel and D.E. Meier, Care of the Hopelessly Ill: Proposed Clinical Criteria for Physician-Assisted Suicide, 327 N.Eng.J.Med. 1380 (1992). For a more recent legal suggestion that physicians should be developing standards of practice in this area, written by an advocate of medically assisted death, see Kathryn Tucker, Aid in Dying: Guidance for an Emerging End-of-Life Practice, 142 Chest 218 (2012).

# CHAPTER 7

## REGULATION OF RESEARCH INVOLVING HUMAN SUBJECTS

■ ■ ■

## I.  INTRODUCTION

Medical research has contributed to relieving great human suffering. It also has been the cause of injustice and misery to individuals and groups who have been treated as grist for the research mill or as conscripts in the war against disease.

The ethical framework for the relationship between researcher and subject differs from that for physician and patient. While the goal of improving the well-being of the individual patient is held as the essential goal in the physician-patient relationship that is simply not the case in medical research. Instead, research has as a primary goal the production of new knowledge for the good of society and requires risk to the individual, although formal ethical principles for medical research require respect for the autonomy and well-being of the individual subject as well. This balance rests on the fulcrum of the prohibition against research without the voluntary consent of the subject, but distrusts that consent alone is up to the task of protecting individuals while benefiting the common good.

Problems are especially likely to arise when subjects are also patients and their physicians are also researchers. In this context, the goals of research and the goals of treatment may become incompatible in ways that are not readily apparent. Research studies, for example, adopt strict protocols to assure validity of results which may differ from the more flexible approach taken in a treatment context. In addition, claims of trust as a basis for the relationship of patient to physician rely on the primacy of the physician's duty to act in the patient's best interest, an underlying assumption that is inapt for the researcher-subject relationship. As a result, modeling the consent process for medical research upon the informed consent process for treatment creates an ill-fitting foundation for judging adequacy of consent. Similarly, applying the legal framework for rights and duties in medical treatment to the context of medical research can produce unsatisfying results.

The regulatory framework for research in the United States reflects that same tension between the gains in knowledge and health promised by research and the value of protecting the individual subject from harm.

Research regulation constantly confronts competing claims about the nature of the research enterprise: Is medical research such a privileged endeavor for the common good that restraints should be minimal; or is competition for accomplishment, reputation, and new products so strong that robust oversight is required?

### Chapter Roadmap

Section II introduces the sources of current standards governing research with human subjects. Section III provides excerpts of the text of the federal regulations that make up the Common Rule. Section IV moves you into the application of the federal regulations to key issues in research using common research scenarios. The chapter closes with a very brief section on U.S. research performed outside the United States.

## II. STANDARDS GOVERNING PROTECTION OF HUMAN SUBJECTS

### A. THE NUREMBERG CODE

The Nuremberg Code is the foundational document for the legal and moral principles that govern research with human subjects. This Code was born of tragedy on an enormous scale. The shocking horrors that could be perpetrated in the name of medical experimentation became apparent to the world through the Nazi war crimes trials. The Medical Trial detailed experiments in which "volunteers," usually concentration camp inmates, were exposed to extremely low atmospheric pressure until they died; were forced to drink seawater or breathe mustard gas; were intentionally infected with malaria and typhus; were placed in ice water until they froze; underwent macabre surgeries often without anesthesia; or were subjected to other tortures. Perpetrators justified their actions as legitimate medical research. Most of the twenty physicians accused of participating in or directing this experimentation were convicted, and some were hanged. A few were acquitted and one, the infamous Dr. Mengele, escaped. In one of the tribunal's most significant actions, the court sitting in Nuremberg promulgated principles for legal and ethical medical research. Perhaps surprisingly, prosecutors at Nuremberg had struggled to find an authoritative formal legal canon governing medical research in either the United States or Germany, and this code emerged from that experience. See Sandra Johnson, *Nazi Experiments, the Nuremberg Code, and the United States*, in Nazi Law: From Nuremberg to Nuremberg (John Michalczyk (ed.), 2018).

### NUREMBERG CODE: PERMISSIBLE MEDICAL EXPERIMENTS

The great weight of the evidence before us is to the effect that certain types of medical experiments on human beings, when kept within reasonably well-defined bounds, conform to the ethics of the medical profession generally. The protagonists of the practice of human experimentation justify their views on the basis that such experiments yield results for the good of society that are unprocurable by other methods or means of study. All agree, however, that certain basic principles must be observed in order to satisfy moral, ethical, and legal concepts:

1.    The voluntary consent of the human subject is absolutely essential.

This means that the person involved should have legal capacity to give consent; should be so situated as to be able to exercise free power of choice, without the intervention of any element of force, fraud, deceit, duress, over-reaching, or other ulterior form of constraint or coercion; and should have sufficient knowledge and comprehension of the elements of the subject matter involved as to enable him to make an understanding and enlightened decision. This latter element requires that before the acceptance of an affirmative decision by the experimental subject there should be made known to him the nature, duration, and purpose of the experiment; the method and means by which it is to be conducted; all inconveniences and hazards reasonably to be expected; and the effects upon his health or person which may possibly come from his participation in the experiment.

The duty and responsibility for ascertaining the quality of the consent rests upon each individual who initiates, directs, or engages in the experiment. It is a personal duty and responsibility which may not be delegated to another with impunity.

2.    The experiment should be such as to yield fruitful results for the good of society, unprocurable by other methods or means of study, and not random and unnecessary in nature.

3.    The experiment should be so designed and based on the results of animal experimentation and a knowledge of the natural history of the disease or other problem under study that the anticipated results will justify the performance of the experiment.

4.    The experiment should be so conducted as to avoid all unnecessary physical and mental suffering and injury.

5.    No experiment should be conducted where there is an *a priori* reason to believe that death or disabling injury will occur; except, perhaps, in those experiments where the experimental physicians also serve as subjects.

6.    The degree of risk to be taken should never exceed that determined by the humanitarian importance of the problem to be solved by the experiment.

7.   Proper preparations should be made and adequate facilities provided to protect the experimental subject against even remote possibilities of injury, disability, or death.

8.   The experiment should be conducted only by scientifically qualified persons. The highest degree of skill and care should be required through all stages of the experiment by those who conduct or engage in the experiment.

9.   During the course of the experiment the human subject should be at liberty to bring the experiment to an end if he has reached the physical or mental state where continuation of the experiment seems to him to be impossible.

10.   During the course of the experiment the scientist in charge must be prepared to terminate the experiment at any stage, if he has probable cause to believe, in the exercise of the good faith, superior skill, and careful judgment required of him, that a continuation of the experiment is likely to result in injury, disability, or death to the experimental subject.

## B.  LEGAL STANDARDS IN THE UNITED STATES

The Nuremberg Code did not have an immediate impact in the United States, perhaps because the Nazi doctors were viewed as monsters separate and apart from ordinary human nature and outside the tradition of medical ethics in the this country. See George Annas, Mengele's Birthmark: The Nuremberg Code in United States Courts, 7 J. Contemp. Health L. and Pol'y 17 (1991). In fact, the United States government was conducting research at the same time that would violate the principles of the Nuremberg Code. In just one example, the government tested the human response to radiation by injecting patients (many of whom were inaccurately described as terminally ill) with plutonium or uranium to observe its physical effect. These subjects were never informed of the nature of the experiments. See Advisory Committee on Human Radiation Experiments, The Human Radiation Experiments (1996); Susan Smith, Mustard Gas and American Race-Based Human Experimentation in World War II, 36 J. L. Med. & Ethics 517 (2008).

It wasn't until the publication of a landmark article detailing abuses of human subjects in the United States that it was recognized that medical research abuse was possible, if not common, in this country. Henry K. Beecher, Ethics and Clinical Research, 274 NEJM 1354 (1966). Just a few years later, in 1972, the most infamous violation of research ethics in twentieth-century America came to light. In the Tuskegee Syphilis Study, begun in 1932, the United States Public Health Service (USPHS) studied the natural course of untreated syphilis in 399 poor African-American men. Even when penicillin, the first effective treatment for syphilis, became available, the USPHS physicians refused to offer that treatment to most of their subjects; and many of these men were expressly and regularly discouraged from seeking treatment. For nearly 40 years, the USPHS condemned these men and their wives, partners, and families to the ravages of untreated syphilis. See James H. Jones, Bad Blood: The Tuskegee Syphilis Experiment (1981); Ruquaiija Yearby, Exploitation in Medical Research: The Enduring Legacy of the Tuskegee Syphilis Study, 67 Case W. Res. L. Rev. 1171 (2017).

The Tuskegee experiment is iconic, but it is only one episode in a long history of exploitation of African Americans in medical research. See Harriet A. Washington, Medical Apartheid: The Dark History of Medical Experimentation on Black Americans from Colonial Times to the Present (2007). Much experimentation with African-American subjects was motivated more by a voyeuristic fascination rather than a scientific research design and routinely relied on the disadvantages produced first by slavery and then by poverty and segregation. See also, Camille A. Nelson, American Husbandry: Legal Norms Impacting the Production of (Re)productivity, 19 Yale J. L. & Fem. 1 (2007), detailing the work of Dr. Marion Sims, the "father of modern gynecology," who developed his surgical techniques through repeated unanesthetized vaginal surgeries on slave women; Section IV.E, below for description of case of Henrietta Lacks. Racialized medicine in the United States permeated these experiments and influenced pre-War Nazi health laws, which in turn laid the foundation for the Nazi experiments. See Johnson, above.

These stories do not stand alone as examples of exploitation in medical research in the United States. Other publicized cases include a study at the Jewish Chronic Disease Hospital, in which live cancer cells were injected into patients without their knowledge, and the Willowbrook State Hospital hepatitis study, in which parents seeking hospital admission for their children were required to allow researchers to infect their child with the disease. See David Rothman, Strangers at the Bedside: A History of How Law and Bioethics Transformed Medical Decisionmaking (1991). These and other episodes, and the patterns of vulnerability and advantage-taking they reveal, influenced the regulatory framework ultimately adopted in the United States to govern research. For a comprehensive treatment of the history of legal standards for research in the United States, see Carl H. Coleman et al., The Ethics and Regulation of Research with Human Subjects (2d ed. 2015).

## 1. Federal Regulation of Research

Congress enacted the National Research Act in 1974, shortly after Congressional hearings on the Tuskegee study. The Act established the National Commission for Protection of Human Subjects of Biomedical and Behavioral Research to identify "basic ethical principles" that should guide the conduct of human subjects research; to develop procedures to assure that the research would be consistent with those principles; and to recommend guidelines for human subjects research funded by the precursor to HHS. The Commission issued several reports between 1975 and 1978, the most significant of which is the Belmont Report. Ethical Principles and Guidelines for the Protection of Human Subjects of Research (1979). This document established an analytical framework that guided subsequent federal regulations; continues to influence research regulation today; and became the primary approach for decision making in bioethics far beyond questions relating to research.

The main federal regulations governing research with human subjects, first adopted jointly by a number of federal agencies in 1991, traditionally have been called the "Common Rule." While the Common Rule forms the core of federal regulation of medical research, other federal statutes, such as HIPAA, apply to a variety of issues that can arise in the research enterprise.

## 2.   State Law

State law also plays an important role in controls on medical research as the Common Rule does not preempt state law that provides additional protections for individuals participating as subjects. A good number of individual states have enacted legislation to govern the conduct of research within their boundaries. Some states, for example, have enacted statutes requiring that all medical research performed in that state be subject to the standards of the federal regulations even if the research is not federally funded. See, e.g., Md. Code, Health-General § 13–2001. A good number of states have enacted legislation setting limits on the use of some types of tissue in research. See, e.g., Mo. Const. Art. 3 § 38d, regarding stem cell research. Most have statutes governing the release of state-held data or tissue for research. See, e.g., 410 Ill. Comp. Stat. § 525/9, N.D. Admin. Code § 33–06–16–05. Some states also regulate research performed on persons with cognitive disabilities. See, e.g., Ala. Code § 22–56–4.

The most influential impact of state law on medical research, however, comes in litigation under state common law. Plaintiffs claiming violation of standards for medical research most often rely on negligence, informed consent, breach of contract, or other state law claims. See Sections IV.C, D, and E, below.

## III.  THE COMMON RULE

After nearly six years of notice and comment, seventeen federal agencies jointly promulgated revised regulations in 2017, accomplishing the first substantial revision of the Common Rule in decades. Significant revisions include changes in the required elements of consent, expanded categories of exempt research, and requirements for research with biospecimens and health information, among others. Jerry Menikoff et al., The Common Rule Updated, 376 NEJM 613 (2017). Although most of the revised requirements were due to be in effect in January, 2018, the agencies jointly issued a notice delaying implementation of most of the revisions until July 19, 2018, because the agencies had not yet developed interpretative guidance and research organizations needed more time to build new procedures and design IT systems to assure compliance. 83 Fed. Reg. 2885 (Jan. 22, 2018). The notice later issued a proposed rule to delay implementation until January 21, 2019. 83 Fed. Reg. 17595 (Apr. 20, 2018).

The FDA, in the most significant exception among federal agencies, abides by regulations on research that continue to depart significantly from the Common Rule in a few respects. 21 CFR § 50.1. All studies funded by or submitted to the FDA for its approval of drugs, devices, or other substances must meet the FDA's standards for research. Where a study is subject to both the FDA and another federal agency (e.g., pharmaceutical research funded by NIH) and the regulations of the two agencies differ, the stricter of the two standards (in terms of protection of subjects) applies. The FDA is working toward harmonizing its requirements with the Common Rule as required by the 21st Century Cures Act, P.L. 114–255, § 3023 (2016).

Take the time to read through this edited version of the Common Rule. It includes the regulations you will need to resolve the Problems presented in the rest of this chapter. (The numbers indicated by the underline are unique to each agency, so for example, the HHS regulations are found at 45 C.F.R. § 46.101 et seq. The regulations presented below include revisions promulgated in 2017. Where the 2017 revisions depart substantially and substantively from the earlier regulations, however, this is noted in the text of Notes and Problems in the rest of this chapter.) In addition to these regulations, federal agencies regulating research issue informal guidance, policy statements, enforcement letters, and so on which provide the agency's interpretation of the requirements of the regulations. These documents are accessible on the agencies' websites. See, e.g., www.hhs.gov/ohrp.

## § __.101 To what does this policy apply?

(a) Except as detailed in § __.104, this policy applies to all research involving human subjects conducted, supported, or otherwise subject to regulation by any Federal department or agency .... It also includes research conducted, supported, or otherwise subject to regulation by the Federal Government outside the United States. ...

\* \* \*

(e) Compliance with this policy requires compliance with pertinent federal laws or regulations that provide additional protections for human subjects.

(f) This policy does not affect any state or local laws or regulations (including tribal law . . .) that may otherwise be applicable and that provide additional protections for human subjects.

(g) This policy does not affect any foreign laws or regulations that may otherwise be applicable and that provide additional protections to human subjects of research.

(h) When research covered by this policy takes place in foreign countries, procedures normally followed in the foreign countries to protect human subjects may differ from those set forth in this policy. In these circumstances, if a department or agency head determines that the procedures prescribed by the institution afford protections that are at least equivalent to those provided in this policy, the department or agency head may approve the substitution of the foreign procedures in lieu of the procedural requirements provided in this policy. . . .

(i) Unless otherwise required by law, department or agency heads may waive the applicability of some or all of the provisions of this policy to specific research activities or classes of research activities otherwise covered by this policy, provided the alternative procedures to be followed are consistent with the principles of the Belmont Report. . . .

* * *

## § __.102 Definitions for purposes of this policy.

* * *

(e)(1) Human subject means a living individual about whom an investigator . . . conducting research: (i) Obtains information or biospecimens through intervention or interaction with the individual, and uses, studies, or analyzes the information or biospecimens; or (ii) Obtains, uses, studies, analyzes, or generates identifiable private information or identifiable biospecimens.

(2) Intervention includes both physical procedures by which information or biospecimens are gathered (e.g., venipuncture) and manipulations of the subject or the subject's environment that are performed for research purposes.

(3) Interaction includes communication or interpersonal contact between investigator and subject.

(4) Private information includes information about behavior that occurs in a context in which an individual can reasonably expect that no observation or recording is taking place, and information that has been

provided for specific purposes by an individual and that the individual can reasonably expect will not be made public (e.g., a medical record).

(5) Identifiable private information is private information for which the identity of the subject is or may readily be ascertained by the investigator or associated with the information.

(6) An identifiable biospecimen is a biospecimen for which the identity of the subject is or may readily be ascertained by the investigator or associated with the biospecimen.

\* \* \*

(j) Minimal risk means that the probability and magnitude of harm or discomfort anticipated in the research are not greater in and of themselves than those ordinarily encountered in daily life or during the performance of routine physical or psychological examinations or tests.

\* \* \*

(l) Research means a systematic investigation, including research development, testing, and evaluation, designed to develop or contribute to generalizable knowledge. . . .

\* \* \*

§ __.104 Exempt research.

(d) [T]he following categories of human subjects research are exempt from this policy:

\* \* \*

(2) Research that only includes interactions involving educational tests . . . , survey procedures, interview procedures, or observation of public behavior . . . [under certain conditions relating to identifiability of the subject, risk of liability, financial or reputational harm to the subject, and protection of confidentiality and privacy. This category of exemption is further limited in the case of child subjects].

\* \* \*

(4) Secondary research for which consent is not required: Secondary research uses of identifiable private information or identifiable biospecimens, if at least one of the following criteria is met:

(i) The identifiable private information or identifiable biospecimens are publicly available;

(ii) Information, which may include information about biospecimens, is recorded by the investigator in such a manner that the identity of the human subjects cannot readily be ascertained directly or through identifiers linked to the subjects, the investigator does not contact the subjects, and the investigator will not re-identify subjects;

(iii) The research involves only information collection and analysis involving the investigator's use of identifiable health information when that use is regulated under [HIPAA], for the purposes of "health care operations" or "research" . . . or for "public health activities and purposes" [as defined in HIPAA]; or

(iv) The research is conducted by, or on behalf of, a Federal department or agency using government-generated or government-collected information obtained for nonresearch activities, if [the data meets certain federal statutory standards for collection and security of identifiable private data.]

\* \* \*

(7)   Storage or maintenance for secondary research for which broad consent is required: Storage or maintenance of identifiable private information or identifiable biospecimens for potential secondary research use if an IRB conducts a limited IRB review [an expedited review by the Chair or a designated member of the IRB] and makes the determinations required by § __.111(a)(8).

(8)   Secondary research for which broad consent is required: Research involving the use of identifiable private information or identifiable biospecimens for secondary research use, if the following criteria are met:

(i)   Broad consent for the storage, maintenance, and secondary research use of the identifiable private information or identifiable biospecimens was obtained in accordance with § __.116(a)(1) through (4), (a)(6), and (d);

(ii)   Documentation of informed consent or waiver of documentation of consent was obtained . . . ;

(iii)   An IRB conducts a limited IRB review [an expedited review by the Chair or a designated member of the IRB] and makes the determination required by § __.111(a)(7) and makes the determination that the research to be conducted is within the scope of the broad consent . . . ; and

(iv)   The investigator does not include returning individual research results to subjects as part of the study plan. This provision does not prevent an investigator from abiding by any legal requirements to return individual research results.

## § __.107  IRB membership.

(a)   Each IRB shall have at least five members, with varying backgrounds to promote complete and adequate review of research activities commonly conducted by the institution. The IRB shall be sufficiently qualified through the experience and expertise of its members (professional competence), and the diversity of its members, including race, gender, and cultural backgrounds and sensitivity to such issues as community attitudes, to promote respect for its advice and counsel in safeguarding the rights and welfare of human subjects. The IRB shall be able to ascertain the acceptability of proposed research in terms of institutional commitments (including policies and resources) and regulations, applicable law, and standards of professional conduct and practice. The IRB shall therefore include persons knowledgeable in these areas. If an IRB regularly reviews research that involves a category of subjects that is vulnerable to coercion or undue influence, such as children, prisoners, individuals with impaired decision-making capacity, or economically or educationally disadvantaged persons, consideration shall be given to the inclusion of one or more individuals who are knowledgeable about and experienced in working with these categories of subjects.

(b)  Each IRB shall include at least one member whose primary concerns are in scientific areas and at least one member whose primary concerns are in nonscientific areas.

(c)  Each IRB shall include at least one member who is not otherwise affiliated with the institution and who is not part of the immediate family of a person who is affiliated with the institution.

(d)  No IRB may have a member participate in the IRB's initial or continuing review of any project in which the member has a conflicting interest, except to provide information requested by the IRB.

(e)  An IRB may, in its discretion, invite individuals with competence in special areas to assist in the review of issues that require expertise beyond or in addition to that available on the IRB. These individuals may not vote with the IRB.

* * *

### § __.109  IRB review of research.

(a)  An IRB shall review and have authority to approve, require modifications in (to secure approval), or disapprove all research activities covered by this policy. . . .

* * *

(e)  An IRB shall conduct continuing review of research . . . at intervals appropriate to the degree of risk, not less than once per year, except [for studies eligible for expedited or limited review or studies that involve only data analysis or "accessing follow-up clinical data from procedures that subjects would undergo as part of clinical care"].

* * *

(g)   An IRB shall have authority to observe or have a third party observe the consent process and the research.

\* \* \*

## § __.111  Criteria for IRB approval of research.

(a)   [T]he IRB shall determine that all of the following requirements are satisfied:

(1)   Risks to subjects are minimized: (i) By using procedures that are consistent with sound research design and that do not unnecessarily expose subjects to risk, and (ii) Whenever appropriate, by using procedures already being performed on the subjects for diagnostic or treatment purposes.

(2)   Risks to subjects are reasonable in relation to anticipated benefits, if any, to subjects, and the importance of the knowledge that may reasonably be expected to result. In evaluating risks and benefits, the IRB should consider only those risks and benefits that may result from the research (as distinguished from risks and benefits of therapies subjects would receive even if not participating in the research). . . .

(3)   Selection of subjects is equitable. In making this assessment the IRB should take into account the purposes of the research and the setting in which the research will be conducted. The IRB should be particularly cognizant of the special problems of research that involves a category of subjects who are vulnerable to coercion or undue influence, such as children, prisoners, individuals with impaired decision-making capacity, or economically or educationally disadvantaged persons.

(4)   Informed consent will be sought from each prospective subject, or the subject's legally authorized representative, in accordance with, and to the extent required by, § __.116.

\* \* \*

(6)   When appropriate, the research plan makes adequate provision for monitoring the data collected to ensure the safety of subjects.

(7)   When appropriate, there are adequate provisions to protect the privacy of subjects and to maintain the confidentiality of data.

(8)   For purposes of conducting the limited IRB review required by § __.104(d)(7)), the IRB need not make the determinations at paragraphs (a)(1) through (7) of this section, and shall make the following determinations: (i) Broad consent for storage, maintenance, and secondary research use of identifiable private information is obtained in accordance with the requirements of § __.116(a)(1)–(4), (a)(6), and (d); (ii) [consent is documented]; and (iii) [if there is a change in the way information or

biospecimens are stored, there are adequate provisions for confidentiality and privacy.]

\* \* \*

(b)   When some or all of the subjects are likely to be vulnerable to coercion or undue influence, such as children, prisoners, individuals with impaired decision-making capacity, or economically or educationally disadvantaged persons, additional safeguards have been included in the study to protect the rights and welfare of these subjects.

## § __.112  Review by institution.

Research covered by this policy that has been approved by an IRB may be subject to further appropriate review and approval or disapproval by officials of the institution. However, those officials may not approve the research if it has not been approved by an IRB.

## § __.113  Suspension or termination of IRB approval of research.

An IRB shall have authority to suspend or terminate approval of research that is not being conducted in accordance with the IRB's requirements or that has been associated with unexpected serious harm to subjects. . . .

\* \* \*

## § __.116  General requirements for informed consent.

(a)   . . . Except as provided elsewhere in this policy:

(1)   Before involving a human subject in research covered by this policy, an investigator shall obtain the legally effective informed consent of the subject or the subject's legally authorized representative.

(2)   An investigator shall seek informed consent only under circumstances that provide the prospective subject . . . sufficient opportunity to discuss and consider whether or not to participate and that minimize the possibility of coercion or undue influence.

(3)   The information that is given to the subject . . . shall be in language understandable to the subject . . . .

(4)   The prospective subject . . . must be provided with the information that a reasonable person would want to have in order to make an informed decision about whether to participate, and an opportunity to discuss that information.

(5)   Except for broad consent obtained in accordance with paragraph (d) of this section:

(i)   Informed consent must begin with a concise and focused presentation of the key information that is most likely to assist a prospective subject . . . in understanding the reasons why one might or might not want to participate in the research. . . .

(ii) Informed consent as a whole must present information in sufficient detail relating to the research, and must be organized and presented in a way that does not merely provide lists of isolated facts, but rather facilitates the prospective subject's . . . understanding of the reasons why one might or might not want to participate.

(6) No informed consent may include any exculpatory language through which the subject . . . is made to waive or appear to waive any of the subject's legal rights, or releases or appears to release the investigator, the sponsor, the institution, or its agents from liability for negligence.

(b) Basic elements of informed consent. Except as provided in paragraph (d), (e), or (f) of this section, in seeking informed consent the following information shall be provided to each subject . . . :

(1) A statement that the study involves research, an explanation of the purposes of the research and the expected duration of the subject's participation, a description of the procedures to be followed, and identification of any procedures that are experimental;

(2) A description of any reasonably foreseeable risks or discomforts to the subject;

(3) A description of any benefits to the subject or to others that may reasonably be expected from the research;

(4) A disclosure of appropriate alternative procedures or courses of treatment, if any, that might be advantageous to the subject;

(5) A statement describing the extent, if any, to which confidentiality of records identifying the subject will be maintained;

(6) For research involving more than minimal risk, an explanation as to whether any compensation and an explanation as to whether any medical treatments are available if injury occurs and, if so, what they consist of, or where further information may be obtained; . . .

(8) A statement that participation is voluntary, refusal to participate will involve no penalty or loss of benefits to which the subject is otherwise entitled, and the subject may discontinue participation at any time without penalty or loss of benefits to which the subject is otherwise entitled; and

(9) One of the following statements about any research that involves the collection of identifiable private information or identifiable biospecimens:

(i) A statement that identifiers might be removed from the identifiable private information or identifiable biospecimens and that, after such removal, the information or biospecimens could be used for future research studies or distributed to another investigator for future research studies without additional informed consent from the subject . . ., if this might be a possibility; or

(ii) A statement that the subject's information or biospecimens collected as part of the research, even if identifiers are removed, will not be used or distributed for future research studies.

(c) Additional elements of informed consent. Except as provided in paragraph (d) . . . or (f) of this section, one or more of the following elements of information, when appropriate, shall also be provided to each subject . . . .

(1) A statement that the particular treatment or procedure may involve risks to the subject (or to the embryo or fetus, if the subject is or may become pregnant) that are currently unforeseeable;

(2) Anticipated circumstances under which the subject's participation may be terminated by the investigator without regard to the subject's . . . consent;

* * *

(4) The consequences of a subject's decision to withdraw from the research and procedures for orderly termination of participation by the subject;

(5) A statement that significant new findings developed during the course of the research that may relate to the subject's willingness to continue participation will be provided to the subject;

(6) The approximate number of subjects involved in the study;

(7) A statement that the subject's biospecimens (even if identifiers are removed) may be used for commercial profit and whether the subject will or will not share in this commercial profit;

(8) A statement regarding whether clinically relevant research results, including individual research results, will be disclosed to subjects, and if so, under what conditions; and

(9) For research involving biospecimens, whether the research will (if known) or might include whole genome sequencing.

(d) Elements of broad consent for the storage, maintenance, and secondary research use of identifiable private information or identifiable biospecimens (collected for either research studies other than the proposed research or nonresearch purposes) is permitted as an alternative to the informed consent requirements in paragraphs (b) and (c) of this section. If the subject . . . is asked to provide broad consent, the following shall be provided to each subject . . . :

(1) The information required in paragraphs (b)(2), (b)(3), (b)(5), and (b)(8) and, when appropriate, (c)(7) and (9) of this section;

(2) A general description of the types of research that may be conducted . . . . This description must include sufficient information such

that a reasonable person would expect that the broad consent would permit the types of research conducted;

(3)   A description of the identifiable private information or identifiable biospecimens that might be used in research, whether sharing of [this material] might occur, and the types of institutions or researchers that might conduct research with [this material];

(4)   A description of the period of time that [this material] may be stored and maintained (which period of time could be indefinite), and a description of the period of time that [this material] may be used for research purposes (which period of time could be indefinite);

(5)   Unless the subject . . . will be provided details about specific research studies, a statement that they will not be informed of the details of any specific research studies that might be conducted using [this material], including the purposes of the research, and that they might have chosen not to consent to some of those specific research studies; [and]

(6)   Unless it is known that clinically relevant research results, including individual research results, will be disclosed to the subject in all circumstances, a statement that such results may not be disclosed to the subject. . . .

\* \* \*

(f) (1) [A]n IRB may waive the requirement to obtain informed consent for research under paragraphs (a) through (c) of this section, provided the IRB satisfies the requirements of paragraph (f)(3) of this section. If an individual was asked to provide broad consent . . . in accordance with the requirements at paragraph (d) of this section, and refused to consent, an IRB cannot waive consent [for those activities].

(2)   Alteration. An IRB may approve a consent procedure that omits some, or alters some or all, of the elements of informed consent set forth in paragraphs (b) and (c) of this section provided the IRB satisfies the requirements of paragraph (f)(3) of this section. An IRB may not omit or alter any of the requirements described in paragraph (a) of this section. If a broad consent procedure is used, an IRB may not omit or alter any of the elements required under paragraph (d) of this section.

(3)   Requirements for waiver and alteration. In order for an IRB to waive or alter consent as described in this subsection, the IRB must find and document that:

(i)   The research involves no more than minimal risk to the subjects;

(ii)  The research could not practicably be carried out without the requested waiver or alteration;

(iii) If the research involves using identifiable private information or identifiable biospecimens, the research could not practically be carried out without using such information or biospecimens in an identifiable format;

(iv) The waiver or alteration will not adversely affect the rights and welfare of the subjects; and

(v) Whenever appropriate, the subjects . . . will be provided with additional pertinent information after participation.

\* \* \*

(i) Preemption. The informed consent requirements in this policy are not intended to preempt any applicable Federal, state, or local laws (including tribal laws . . .) that require additional information to be disclosed in order for informed consent to be legally effective.

\* \* \*

## IV. APPLYING THE COMMON RULE

### A. INSTITUTIONAL REVIEW BOARDS

The Common Rule delegates the frontline enforcement of the federal regulations to institutional review boards (IRBs), which most commonly are committees of the research institution, appointed and managed by the institution itself. What is the rationale for delegating oversight to the research entity itself?

Criticisms of the efficiency and effectiveness of IRB review contributed significantly to momentum for revision of the Common Rule. For a debate over the role of IRBs, see Symposium, Censorship and Institutional Review Boards, 101 Nw. U. L. Rev. 399 (2007); see also *Grimes* in Section IV.D. The revised Common Rule generally left the structure of IRBs unchanged, however, with one exception. For studies conducted at more than one institution after January 20, 2020, the revised regulations require approval by a single IRB rather than the IRBs of each institution involved in the multisite study (called "cooperative research" in the regulations). § __.114. In addition, the revision expands the range of studies that are exempt from the Rule, and therefore from full IRB review. See § __.104(d)(4), (7) and (8), above.

The Office for Human Research Protections (OHRP) enforces the HHS regulations through investigation of complaints and episodic audits of the human subject protection programs (including the IRBs) of organizations conducting research subject to the regulations. The FDA uses similar processes to enforce its regulations. The biggest stick that OHRP carries is the authority to suspend or terminate all HHS funding of research. It suspended funding for twenty universities during 1999–2000, and this extreme remedy is still used but rarely. The Office of Inspector General of HHS also enforces the federal regulations on research through its prosecution of fraud and false claims. Even with this oversight, the reviews performed by an IRB are the most significant tool in assuring compliance with the federal regulations.

## PROBLEM: FORMING AN IRB

Assume that you have been charged with forming the first IRB for a community hospital that has begun to apply for small federal research grants and contracts with pharmaceutical firms to conduct clinical trials. Consider §§ __.107, 109, 111, 112, and 113, above, in forming your recommendations to these questions:

1.     What is the ideal size for your IRB to incorporate the competencies and perspectives described in the regulations? Should hospital counsel be a member? Should nonscientific members of the IRB defer to the scientific members on the questions of risk assessment, research design, or continuing review of the results being produced by the research protocol? Can they do otherwise? What sort of competency should the nonscientific member have?

2.     Assume that your hospital serves a large proportion of economically disadvantaged patients and that research subjects are likely to be recruited from among that population. Does that influence the composition of your IRB?

3.     Assume that your new IRB has already ruffled some feathers with its review process. In particular, it has asked for more information, several times, on research proposed by a prominent physician on the hospital's medical staff. This researcher has approached the hospital's CEO for assistance. What can the CEO do?

4.     Instead of establishing its own IRB, the hospital could contract with and pay a free-standing independent IRB for review of protocols. See Janet Lis and Melinda Murray, The Ins and Outs of Independent IRBs, 2 J. Health & Life Sci. L. 73 (2008). See also Colleen Zern, Is the Customer Always Right? HHS Proposed Regulation Allows IRBs to Place Customer Service Ahead of the Welfare of Research Participants, 32 St. Louis U. Pub. L. Rev. 411 (2013), criticizing independent IRBs. What are the advantages and disadvantages of this approach for the hospital? For researchers? For patients who will be participating in research?

## B. DEFINING "RESEARCH"

The Common Rule applies only to activities that meet its definition of research. Furthermore, the Common Rule does not apply to research that is not conducted by or funded by a federal agency; and the FDA regulations only apply to research that is funded by the FDA or submitted to the FDA for action regarding drugs or devices requiring FDA approval. An organization that conducts research subject to the Common Rule must file a Federalwide Assurance (FWA) every five years. In the FWA, the organization represents that it complies with applicable federal regulations on research covered by the Rule and maps essential components of that compliance. Most academic institutions filing an FWA voluntarily commit to compliance for all their research studies, whether federally funded or not.

## PROBLEM: IS IT RESEARCH?

Use the Common Rule §§ __.101(a), 102(e) and (l), and 104, above, to resolve whether each scenario constitutes research subject to the regulations.

1.     An oncologist treating a patient with colon cancer for whom customary chemotherapy drugs have proven ineffective offers his patient the option of trying another drug. The drug is currently used for other cancers and is being tested for colon cancer, but the research is not yet complete. Although the oncologist is not participating in any of the clinical trials of this drug, preliminary unpublished reports and informal discussions with researchers testing the drug show promise. Once a drug is approved for one purpose, physicians may prescribe it for other purposes, a practice known as off-label prescribing. If the doctor gives his patient this drug, is it research as defined in the Common Rule? See Nancy Kass et al., The Research-Treatment Distinction: A Problematic Approach for Determining Which Activities Should Have Ethical Oversight, 43 Hastings Ctr. Rep. S4 (2013). See also Section IV.C, below.

2.     It can be difficult to intubate seriously overweight adult patients, especially in an emergency. Assume that an experienced nurse anesthetist suggested that physicians use a pediatric tube for a particular patient, with great success. Because of their experience with this approach, the hospital decides to adopt this as a regular practice if a first attempt at intubation fails. The nurse who developed this approach has decided to present the hospital's experience with this practice at a regional anesthesiology conference and has published an article in a professional journal. Is this research? Scenario based on Atul Gawande, "When Doctors Make Mistakes" in Complications: A Surgeon's Notes on an Imperfect Science (2002).

3.     Iatrogenic infections are a significant risk for hospitalized patients. A teaching hospital developed a simple five-step checklist for the insertion of a catheter into an artery for the delivery of medication to assure that proper techniques are used to prevent infection. The hospital reduced the infection rate for this procedure from 4 percent to 0 percent. A consortium of hospitals wants to implement the checklist based on these results. They have also agreed to provide their results to the teaching hospital so that the benefits of the checklist can be documented and published to encourage its wider adoption. Is this research under the Common Rule? Special provisions addressing quality improvement research were considered during the process of revising the Common Rule, but the final version did not adopt significant changes in that direction except for one. The revisions categorize low risk reviews of patient

health information within an organization governed by HIPAA privacy rules and consistent with those rules as exempt. § __.104(d)(4)(iii). See, Joshua Rolnick et al., Ethical Oversight of Quality Improvement and the Research-QI Boundary: A New Common Rule Changes Little, IRB: Ethics and Human Research 39/3 (May-June 2017).

4.    A large multispecialty physician practice group is considering adding medical scribes to their offices. These individuals would be present as the physician works with the patient and would input findings, prescriptions, and directions into the patient's electronic medical record. This should allow physicians to focus on the patient rather than the keyboard. Because of the size of the financial investment required, the practice wants to make sure that adding scribes would be efficient and would improve accuracy and thoroughness of medical records in their particular practice setting. They have hired a small number of scribes and have established a number of variables, requiring examination of patient records and observing physician-patient interaction, which will be analyzed to judge whether further investment will add value. The group will use the results only within their own practice. They have no interest in sharing their findings. Who are the subjects of this study? Is this research subject to the Common Rule?

## C.  RISK AND CONSENT

The Common Rule sets standards for consent to research in §§ __.111 and 116, above. Standardization in consent forms, to improve efficiency and effectiveness, was considered during the revision of the regulations, but that didn't occur. Instead, the regulations add a new requirement that consent forms be posted on a public website once enrollment in the study has closed. § __.116(h). The regulations also significantly altered the consent requirements for "secondary use" of "identifiable private information" and "identifiable biospecimens." See Section IV.F, below.

The issue of risk is intertwined with consent in several ways. First, the federal regulations do not permit research, even with consenting adults, if the risks to the subject are not reasonable. See § __.111(a)(2), above. Assuming a competent adult is acting voluntarily and without coercion, what, if anything, justifies the restrictive federal regulations concerning risk? See Richard A Epstein, Defanging IRBs: Replacing Coercion with Information, 101 Nw. U. L. Rev. 735 (2007), arguing that IRBs should assure only that information to the subject about the risks is accurate and understandable, leaving to the individual the decision to enroll or not. What criteria would you use to decide whether risk is excessive, either for yourself personally or as a matter of applying the regulation? Are these two different questions?

The consent process must communicate the nature and degree of risk (and benefit) presented in the study in an accurate and understandable manner. See *Looney*, below. In some circumstances, however, natural optimism on the part of patients, and even researchers, influences how the information is heard. The term "therapeutic misconception" was coined over thirty years ago to describe the observation that patients tend to believe that clinical trials testing only the safety of a new drug (called Phase I trials) will benefit them directly by providing treatment for their condition despite clear statements to the contrary. See Paul Appelbaum et al., The Therapeutic Misconception: Informed Consent to Psychiatric Research, 5 Int'l J.L. & Psych. 319 (1982); Lynn Jansen, Two Concepts of Therapeutic Optimism, 37 J. Med. Ethics 563 (2011).

The calculus of risk can change over the life of a study. IRBs must perform ongoing risk assessments for certain approved studies (§ __.109(e), above, with exceptions adopted in the 2017 revision) and must suspend research that is "associated with unexpected serious harm to subjects" (§ __.113, above). This monitoring should assure that a study is halted when unanticipated levels of risk or unexpectedly early and strong positive results occur. How does the latter present a risk of harm?

Some research studies include medical tests that will produce results that are "clinically relevant" to individual subjects. In the context of medical treatment, a patient expects that her physician would inform her of significant test results. If this common expectation is carried to the research context, individuals may assume, to their detriment, that if the tests reveal a serious threat to their health, they would be informed. The revised Common Rule addresses this situation as an element of informed consent but does not require disclosure of results. See § __.116(c)(8) and (d)(6), above. See Susan Wolf et al., Returning a Research Participant's Genomic Results to Relatives: Analysis and Recommendations, 43 J. L. Med. & Ethics 440 (2015).

### *PROBLEM: HOW INFORMED? HOW VOLUNTARY?*

Consider the following scenarios under § __.116, above.

1.    A teaching hospital is likely to enroll a large proportion of Medicaid beneficiaries and uninsured individuals in a particular study. The medication being tested has been approved for one use, but not for the one being tested in this study. Sales of the medication overall currently exceed $300 million annually even though Medicaid does not pay for the drug for the use being studied. Does the fact that Medicaid does not cover the medication make the enrollment of Medicaid beneficiaries coercive? If the protocol promises subjects hospital care that some otherwise would not receive for inability to pay, is that coercive? See generally, Ruqaiijah Yearby, Involuntary Consent: Conditioning Access to Health Care on Participation in Clinical Trials, 44 J. L. Med. & Ethics 445 (2016).

2.    To recruit adequate numbers of subjects, an investigator at the same hospital plans on paying subjects $50 per hour for the time the subject spends traveling to and from the office as well as the time spent in undergoing tests

and evaluation. How does payment relate to consent? Is the $50 excessive? Adequate? Fair? Emily Largent and Holly Lynch, Paying Research Participants: Regulatory Uncertainty, Conceptual Confusion, and a Path Forward, 17 Yale J. Health Pol'y & Ethics 61 (2017).

3.    A terminally ill cancer patient is told by her oncologist that "nothing more can be done" to treat the disease in her case. When she contacts a cancer center at a teaching hospital, she is invited to participate in a Phase I trial to test the safety of a new drug. The investigators have some reason to believe that the drug holds promise because of its performance in animal studies, but the drug has not been tested in humans. They plan to randomly assign subjects to receive either the drug or a placebo, and neither the physicians nor the subjects will know which arm they are participating in. What issues do you see in securing informed consent under § __.116? What if the patient tells the researcher that her willingness to continue in the trial depends on whether she is in the placebo arm? On access to investigational drugs, see Abigail Alliance for Better Access to Developmental Drugs v. von Eschenbach, 495 F.3d 695 (D.C. Cir. 2007), cert. denied, 128 S.Ct. 1069 (2008), rejecting plaintiff's claim of a Constitutional right to receive drugs that are in Phase I clinical trials without enrolling in the trial. After *Abigail Alliance*, the FDA increased access to experimental drugs outside of clinical trials. The 21st Century Cures Act, P.L. 114–255 (2016) adopted a number of policies to accelerate drug approval and relax standards for data required in the approval process. See also Rebecca Dresser, The "Right to Try" Investigational Drugs: Science and Stories in the Access Debate, 93 Tex. L. Rev. 1631 (2015).

4.    An individual has read about some promising results in a clinical trial of a new treatment being tested for her serious medical condition and has inquired about enrolling in the study. The medication is not new, but it has not been approved for her particular medical condition. Does the Common Rule require that she be told that her own treating physician could prescribe the medication for her off-label? See, e.g., Jerry Menikoff and Edward Richards, What the Doctor Didn't Say: The Hidden Truth About Medical Research (2006).

## LOONEY V. MOORE
Court of Appeals for the 11th Circuit, 2017.
861 F.3d 1303.

Through their parents, Plaintiffs DreShan Collins, Christian Lewis, and Jaylen Malone, brought claims against Defendants for harms allegedly visited on Plaintiffs when the latter were enrolled in a clinical study while being treated for health issues accompanying their premature births. . . .

Plaintiffs brought claims against the various Defendants for negligence, negligence per se, breach of fiduciary duty, products liability, and lack of informed consent. The district court granted summary judgment on all claims. Like the district court, we conclude that Plaintiffs have failed to establish that participation in the clinical study caused any injuries, which means that the negligence, negligence per se, breach of fiduciary duty, and products liability claims were properly dismissed.

The viability of the claim alleging lack of informed consent, however, is less clear. . . .

## I.    BACKGROUND

The University of Alabama at Birmingham was the lead study site for a national clinical research trial known as the Surfactant, Positive Pressure, and Oxygenation Randomized Trial ("SUPPORT"). Designed by Dr. [Waldemar] Carlo and approved by the IRB Defendants, the SUPPORT study was created to analyze the effects of differing oxygen saturation levels on premature infants. At the time of the study, it was nationally accepted (and neither party contests) that the recognized standard of care was to keep the oxygen saturation levels of low-birth-weight infants at between 85% and 95%. This standard notwithstanding, it was also known that a prolonged period of high oxygen saturation can result in oxygen toxicity which leads to an increased risk of "retinopathy of prematurity". On the other hand, a prolonged period of low oxygen saturation can result in neuro-developmental impairment and death. Given the difficulties of calibrating the optimal oxygen range, the SUPPORT study sought to determine whether, within the accepted standard of care, there was a more precise range of oxygen saturation that would better reduce the risk of exposing an infant to either too much or too little oxygen.

The SUPPORT study randomly divided eligible and enrolled premature infants into two groups. One group was to be kept at an oxygen saturation level between 85–89%, which is the low end of the standard-of-care range, while the other would be kept at an oxygen saturation level between 90–95%, which is the high end of that range. Further, to ensure double-blind data collection, the study would employ specialized oximeters . . . that would "mask" to an onlooker the true oxygen saturation levels of the infants. The oximeters would, however, signal an alarm whenever an infant's oxygen level strayed below 85% or above 95%.

Publishing the results of the study in the New England Journal of Medicine, the study authors concluded that infants in the high-oxygen group were more likely to be diagnosed with retinopathy while infants in the low-oxygen group were more likely to die. There was no statistically significant difference in the incidence of neuro-developmental impairments between the high and low groups.

To enroll in the study, Plaintiffs' guardians had to execute informed consent documents that were drafted and approved by Defendants. After the study's completion, however, the Department of Health and Human Services authored a letter questioning whether these informed consent documents had properly disclosed all of the risks associated with enrollment in the SUPPORT study.

. . . Plaintiffs allege that they suffered serious injuries as a result of their participation in the study. Specifically, Plaintiffs Lewis and Malone were assigned to the low-oxygen group, with prolonged periods of low oxygen saturation being associated with neuro-developmental impairment and death. Fortunately, neither infant died, but they did develop neurological issues. Plaintiff Collins was assigned to the high-oxygen group, with prolonged high-oxygen saturation being associated with retinopathy, which can lead to blindness. Plaintiff Collins did develop retinopathy, but fortunately he did not suffer permanent vision loss. Following discovery, Defendants moved for summary judgment asserting that, based on the undisputed material facts, Plaintiffs had failed to demonstrate that participation in the SUPPORT study had caused the injuries alleged in the Complaint. The district court agreed that Plaintiffs had failed to prove that their injuries were caused by participation in the SUPPORT study, as opposed to being a consequence of their premature births.

## II.  ANALYSIS

We agree that under applicable Alabama law and taking all inferences in the light most favorable to Plaintiffs, Plaintiffs have failed to show that enrollment in the SUPPORT study caused their injuries. What is not clear is whether the absence of an actual physical injury caused by the SUPPORT study dooms Plaintiffs' argument that Defendants are nonetheless liable because they failed to obtain Plaintiffs' informed consent to participate in that study. . . .

. . . As far as we can tell . . . Alabama law has yet to explicitly address the question whether proof of a medical injury is also required before a plaintiff can claim that his consent to a medical procedure was not informed. Specifically, if a plaintiff cannot prove that he suffered any injury as a result of a particular medical procedure, can he still potentially prevail if he shows that the doctor failed to obtain his informed consent to that procedure? In other words, is there a free-standing tort arising from a lack of informed consent, even if there is no injury resulting from the procedure at issue? Assuming that injury is required to sustain an informed consent claim arising out of medical treatment, does that rule still apply if the medical treatment is provided as part of a clinical study?

The answer to the above questions will depend on how an informed consent claim is characterized. If an informed consent claim is considered to be a type of medical malpractice claim [under the Alabama malpractice statute] . . . then it is clear that a plaintiff must show the existence of an actual injury resulting from the procedure before he can raise a viable informed consent claim. If an informed consent claim is not classified as a malpractice type of claim—or if it exits the malpractice arena when the uninformed consent pertains to participation in a medical study administered as part of the medical treatment—then we must search for an answer in Alabama common law. And if, as Plaintiffs argue, an informed consent claim arising out of a medical study is neither a malpractice nor a negligence claim, then we must identify precisely what type of claim it is and determine what Alabama law would prescribe as its elements.

\* \* \*

. . . Because substantial doubt exists here about the answer to a material state law question, we respectfully certify the following question [to the Alabama Supreme Court] for a determination of state law:

Must a patient whose particular medical treatment is dictated by the parameters of a clinical study, and who has not received adequate warnings of the risks of that particular protocol, prove that an injury actually resulted from the medical treatment in order to succeed on a claim that his consent to the procedure was not informed?

## NOTES AND QUESTIONS

1. The Eleventh Circuit certified an intriguing question to the Alabama Supreme Court, but that court declined to answer it. In its subsequent opinion in the case, the Eleventh Circuit makes only a glancing reference to the distinction between medical treatment and medical experimentation, referring to plaintiffs' claim as "an informed consent claim arising out of participation in a medical study administered as part of the medical treatment" provided plaintiffs. There is no other discussion of the issue. The court concludes that, in its interpretation of Alabama law, informed consent claims are a form of negligence claim and require proof of physical injury. 2018 WL 1547260. See also the discussion of the litigation involving Jesse Gelsinger and John Moore in Section IV.E, below.

2. Should the federal regulations be enforceable in litigation by participants in research such as those in *Looney*, or should the government hold exclusive enforcement authority? Almost all of the cases considering the question have held that the federal regulations do not create an implied private right of action. Compare *Grimes*, below. See Valerie Koch, A Private Right of Action for Informed Consent in Research, 45 Seton Hall L. Rev. 173 (2015); Richard S. Saver, Medical Research and Intangible Harm, 74 U. Cinn. L. Rev. 941 (2006). If a private right of action is desirable, should Congress or the state legislature enact legislation providing for statutory damages in the absence of physical harm? See Cal. Health & Safety Code § 24176, providing for fines for violation of state standards for consent for research but only for research not subject to the federal regulations. Actions brought for failure of consent under the FDA's regulations on research may be barred by federal preemption of state products liability law. See Day v. Howmedica Osteonics Corp., 2015 WL 13469348 (D. Colo. 2015); but see Mink v. Smith & Nephew, Inc., 860 F.3d 1319 (11th Cir. 2017), overturning dismissal of claim of misrepresentation.

3.    The written consent for SUPPORT stated that "[s]ometimes higher ranges [of oxygen] are used and sometimes lower ranges are used. All of them are acceptable ranges." Is this statement accurate? Complete? The federal Office for Human Research Protections determined that consent in SUPPORT failed to meet regulatory standards as it did not clearly identify risks and how the study might impact treatment decisions. OHRP noted that, while the entire range of oxygenation was within the current standard of care, treating physicians, including those at some of the research sites, often avoid the extreme poles of the acceptable range to reduce risks. OHRP Determination Letter (June 6, 2013). See also Robert Morse and Robin Wilson, Realizing Informed Consent in Times of Controversy: Lessons from the SUPPORT Study, 44 J. L. Med. & Ethics 402 (2016). The OHRP letter states:

> Doctors are required . . . to do what they view as being best for their individual patients. Researchers do not have the same obligation: Our society relaxes that requirement because of the need to conduct research, the results of which are important to us all. As a modest but crucial trade-off . . . society requires that researchers tell subjects how participating in the study might alter the risks to which they are exposed.

OHRP, however, took no compliance action against research institutions participating in SUPPORT and stated that they would not take any action against studies with a similar design until OHRP developed and posted formal guidance. OHRP has posted Draft Guidance on Disclosing Reasonably Foreseeable Risks in Research Evaluating Standards of Care, 79 Fed. Reg. 63629 (Oct. 24, 2014).

4.    The SUPPORT study is an example of comparative effectiveness research, as the study tested the outcomes of different treatment approaches in common practice at the time. D. Magnus, The SUPPORT Controversy and the Debate over Research within the Standard of Care, 13 Am. J. Bioethics 1 (2013), part of a symposium issue on SUPPORT. The June 2013 OHRP determination letter stated that OHRP "does not and has never questioned whether the design of the SUPPORT study was ethical," but only that consent was inadequate.

5.    Research participants may be injured in the course of research, just as patients may be injured in the course of treatment either through unavoidable adverse effects or through negligence. The Common Rule addresses this issue in §§ __.116(a)(6) and (b)(6), above. See Leslie Henry, Moral Gridlock: Conceptual Barriers to No-Fault Compensation for Injured Research Subjects, 41 J. L. Med. & Ethics 411 (2013).

## D.  EQUITABLE SELECTION OF SUBJECTS AND VULNERABLE POPULATIONS

The Common Rule requires that IRBs assure that the selection of subjects for research be "equitable" and that special attention be paid when subjects are selected from "vulnerable populations," including but not limited to those listed in the regulation. § __.111(a)(3), above. In addition, if research subjects are selected from populations vulnerable to undue influence or coercion, the IRB must assure that "additional safeguards" are put in place to protect these subjects. § __.111(b), above. If an IRB regularly reviews research with vulnerable populations, it is to "give consideration" to the composition of its own membership. (See Section IV.A, above.)

Review these regulations before reading *Grimes*. Develop your own working definition of "equitable" and "vulnerability" to apply to the case. See Ana Iltis, Introduction: Vulnerability in Biomedical Research (Symposium), 37 J. L. Med. & Ethics 6 (2009); Ruqaiijah Yearby, Missing the "Target:" Preventing the Unjust Inclusion of Vulnerable Children for Medical Research Studies, 42 Am. J. Law & Med. 797 (2016).

## GRIMES V. KENNEDY KRIEGER INSTITUTE, INC.
Court of Appeals of Maryland, 2001.
366 Md. 29, 782 A.2d 807.

CATHELL, JUDGE.

\* \* \*

[According to the record before the Court on the motion for summary judgment in] these present cases, [the Kennedy Krieger Institute,] a prestigious research institute associated with Johns Hopkins University ... created a nontherapeutic research program[2] whereby it required certain classes of homes to have only partial lead paint abatement modifications performed, and in at least some instances, including at least one of the cases at bar, arranged for the landlords to receive public funding by way of grants or loans to aid in the modifications. The research institute then encouraged, and in at least one of the cases at bar, required, the landlords to rent the premises to families with young children. In the event young children already resided in one of the study houses, it was contemplated that a child would remain in the premises, and the child was encouraged to remain, in order for his or her blood to be periodically analyzed. In other words, the continuing presence of the children that were the subjects of the study was required in order for the study to be complete. Apparently, the children and their parents involved in the cases *sub judice* were from a lower economic strata and were, at least in one case, minorities.

---

[2] At least to the extent that commercial profit motives are not implicated, therapeutic research's purpose is to directly help or aid a patient who is suffering from a health condition the objectives of the research are designed to address—hopefully by the alleviation, or potential alleviation, of the health condition. Nontherapeutic research generally utilizes subjects who are not known to have the condition the objectives of the research are designed to address, and/or is not designed to directly benefit the subjects utilized in the research, but, rather, is designed to achieve beneficial results for the public at large (or, under some circumstances, for profit).

The purpose of the research was to determine how effective varying degrees of lead paint abatement procedures were. Success was to be determined by periodically, over a two-year period of time, measuring the extent to which lead dust remained in, or returned to, the premises after the varying levels of abatement modifications, and, as most important to our decision, by measuring the extent to which the theretofore healthy children's blood became contaminated with lead, and comparing that contamination with levels of lead dust in the houses over the same periods of time. . . .

* * *

. . . There was no complete and clear explanation in the consent agreements signed by the parents of the children that the research to be conducted was designed, at least in significant part, to measure the success of the abatement procedures by measuring the extent to which the children's blood was being contaminated. It can be argued that the researchers intended that the children be the canaries in the mines but never clearly told the parents. . . .

. . . Institutional Review Boards (IRB) are oversight entities within the institutional family to which an entity conducting research belongs. In research experiments, an IRB can be required in some instances by either federal or state regulation, or sometimes by the conditions attached to governmental grants that are used to fund research projects. Generally, their primary functions are to assess the protocols of the project to determine whether the project itself is appropriate, whether the consent procedures are adequate, whether the methods to be employed meet proper standards, whether reporting requirements are sufficient, and the assessment of various other aspects of a research project. One of the most important objectives of such review is the review of the potential safety and the health hazard impact of a research project on the human subjects of the experiment, especially on vulnerable subjects such as children. Their function is *not* to help researchers seek funding for research projects.

. . . In a letter dated May 11, 1992, [the IRB sent a message to the researcher of this project stating, in part]:

* * *

2.  *Federal guidelines are really quite specific regarding using children as controls in projects in which there is no potential benefit* [to those children]. To call a subject a normal control is to indicate that there is no real benefit to be received [by the child]. . . . So we think it would be much more acceptable to indicate that the "control group" is being studied to determine what exposure outside the home may play in a total lead exposure; thereby, indicating that these control individuals are gaining some benefit, namely learning whether safe

housing alone is sufficient to keep the blood-lead levels in acceptable bounds. We suggest that you modify . . . the consent form[s] . . . accordingly. [Emphasis added [by the court].]

[T]his statement shows two things: (1) that the IRB had a partial misperception of the difference between therapeutic and nontherapeutic research and the IRB's role in the process and (2) that the IRB was willing to aid researchers in getting around federal regulations designed to protect children used as subjects in nontherapeutic research. . . .

* * *

While the validity of the consent agreement and its nature as a contract, the existence or nonexistence of a special relationship, and whether the researchers performed their functions under that agreement pursuant to any special relationships are important issues in these cases that we will address, the very inappropriateness of the research itself cannot be overlooked. It is apparent that the protocols of research are even more important than the method of obtaining parental consent and the extent to which the parents were, or were not, informed. If the research methods, the protocols, are inappropriate then, especially when the IRB is willing to help researchers avoid compliance with applicable safety requirements for using children in nontherapeutic research, the consent of the parents, or of any consent surrogates, in our view, cannot make the research appropriate or the actions of the researchers and the Institutional Review Board proper.

. . . The experiment was simply a "for the greater good" project. The specific children's health was put at risk, in order to develop low-cost abatement measures that would help all children, the landlords, and the general public as well.

* * *

It is clear to this Court that the scientific and medical communities cannot be permitted to assume sole authority to determine ultimately what is right and appropriate in respect to research projects involving young children free of the limitations and consequences of the application of Maryland law. The Institutional Review Boards, IRBs, are, primarily, in-house organs. In our view, they are not designed, generally, to be sufficiently objective in the sense that they are as sufficiently concerned with the ethicality of the experiments they review as they are with the success of the experiments. . . .

The conflicts are inherent. This would be especially so when science and private industry collaborate in search of material gains. Moreover, the special relationship between research entities and human subjects used in the research will almost always impose duties.

. . . It may well be that in the end, the trial courts will determine that no damages have been incurred in the instant cases and thus the actions will fail for that reason. In that regard, we note that there are substantial factual differences [among the] cases. But the actions, themselves, are not defective on the ground that no legal duty can, according to the trial courts, possibly exist. . . .

## I.    The Cases

. . . [Plaintiffs] allege that KKI [Kennedy Krieger Institute] discovered lead hazards in their respective homes and, having a duty to notify them, failed to warn in a timely manner or otherwise act to prevent the children's exposure to the known presence of lead. Additionally, plaintiffs alleged that they were not fully informed of the risks of the research.

[The trial court granted summary judgment on the basis that KKI had no legal duty to warn the subjects of their exposure to lead.]

The trial court was incorrect. Such research programs normally create special relationships and/or can be of a contractual nature that create duties. The breaches of such duties may ultimately result in viable negligence actions. Because, at the very least, there are viable and genuine disputes of material fact concerning whether a special relationship, or other relationships arising out of agreements, giving rise to duties existed between KKI and both sets of appellants, we hold that the Circuit Court erred in granting KKI's motions for summary judgment in both cases before this Court. . . .

## II.    Facts & Procedural Background

In summary, KKI conducted a study of five test groups of twenty-five houses each. The first three groups consisted of houses known to have lead present. The amount of repair and maintenance conducted increased from Group 1 to Group 2 to Group 3. The fourth group consisted of houses, which had at one time lead present but had since allegedly received a complete abatement of lead dust. The fifth group consisted of modern houses, which had never had the presence of lead dust. The twenty-five homes in each of the first three testing levels were then to be compared to the two control groups: the twenty-five homes in Group 4 that had previously been abated and the 25 modern homes in Group 5. The research study was specifically designed to do less than full lead dust abatement in some of the categories of houses in order to study the potential effectiveness, if any, of lesser levels of repair and maintenance.

If the children were to leave the houses upon the first manifestation of lead dust, it would be difficult, if not impossible, to test, over time, the rate of the level of lead accumulation in the blood of the children attributable to the manifestation. . . . Thus, it would benefit the accuracy of the test, and thus KKI, the compensated researcher, if children remained in the houses over the period of the study even after the presence of lead dust in the houses became evident.

* * *

### B.   Case No. 128 [Ms. Viola Hughes and Daughter Ericka Grimes]

* * *

Nowhere in the consent form was it clearly disclosed to the mother that the researchers contemplated that, as a result of the experiment, the child might accumulate lead in her blood, and that in order for the experiment to succeed it was necessary that the child remain in the house as the lead in the child's blood increased or decreased, so that it could be measured. The Consent Form states in relevant part:

"PURPOSE OF STUDY:

As you may know, lead poisoning in children is a problem in Baltimore City and other communities across the country. Lead in paint, house dust and outside soil are major sources of lead exposure for children. Children can also be exposed to lead in drinking water and other sources. We understand that your house is going to have special repairs done in order to reduce exposure to lead in paint and dust. On a random basis, homes will receive one of two levels of repair. We are interested in finding out how well the two levels of repair work. The repairs are not intended, or expected, to completely remove exposure to lead.

We are now doing a study to learn about how well different practices work for reducing exposure to lead in paint and dust. We are asking you and over one hundred other families to allow us to test for lead in and around your homes up to 8 to 9 times over the next two years provided that your house qualifies for the full two years of study. Final eligibility will be determined after the initial testing of your home. We are also doing free blood lead testing of children aged 6 months to 7 years, up to 8 to 9 times over the next two years. We would also like you to respond to a short questionnaire every 6 months. This study is intended to monitor the effects of the repairs and is not intended to replace the regular medical care your family obtains.

* * *

BENEFITS

To compensate you for your time answering questions and allowing us to sketch your home we will mail you a check in the amount of $5.00. In the future we would mail you a check in the amount of $15 each time the full questionnaire is completed. The dust, soil, water, and blood samples would be tested for lead at [KKI] at no charge to you.

*We would provide you with specific blood-lead results. We would contact you to discuss a summary of house test results and steps that you could take to reduce any risks of exposure.* [Emphasis added [by the court].]"

Pursuant to the plans of the research study, KKI collected dust samples [from the Grimes' house] on March 9, 1993, August 23, 1993, March 9, 1994, September 19, 1994, April 18, 1995, and November 13, 1995.[22] The March 9, 1993 dust testing revealed what the researchers referred to as "hot spots" where the level of lead was "higher than might be found in a completely renovated [abated] house." This information about the "hot spots" was not furnished to Ms. Hughes until December 16, 1993, more than nine months after the samples had been collected and, as we discuss, *infra,* not until after Ericka Grimes's blood was found to contain elevated levels of lead.

KKI drew blood from Ericka Grimes for lead content analysis on April, 9, 1993, September 15, 1993, and March 25, 1994. Unlike the lead concentration analysis in dust testing, the results of the blood testing were typically available to KKI in a matter of days. KKI notified Ms. Hughes of the results of the blood tests by letters dated April 9, 1993, September 29, 1993, and March 28, 1994, respectively. The results of the April 9, 1993 test found Ericka Grimes blood to be [within normal range]. * * * However, on two subsequent retests, long after KKI had identified "hot spots," but before KKI informed Ms. Hughes of the "hot spots," Ericka Grimes's blood lead level registered [highly elevated] on March 25, 1994. Ms. Hughes and her daughter vacated the Monroe Street property in the Summer of 1994, and, therefore, no further blood samples were obtained by KKI after March 25, 1994.

* * *

### III. Discussion

* * *

Because of the way the cases *sub judice* have arrived, as appeals from the granting of summary judgments, there is no complete record of the specific compensation of the researchers involved. . . . Neither is there in the record any development of what pressures, if any, were exerted in respect to the researchers obtaining the consents of the parents and conducting the experiment. Nor, for the same reason, is there a sufficient indication as to the extent to which the Institute has joined with commercial interests, if it has, for the purposes of profit, that might potentially impact upon the researcher's motivations and potential

---

[22] For some unexplained reason, processing the dust samples typically took several months. KKI notified Ms. Hughes of the dust sample results via letters dated December 16, 1993, December 17, 1993, May 19, 1994, October 28, 1994, July 19, 1995, and January 18, 1996, respectively.

conflicts of interest—motivations that generally are assumed, in the cases of prestigious entities such as John Hopkins University, to be for the public good rather than a search for profit.

We do note that the institution involved . . . is a highly respected entity, considered to be a leader in the development of treatments, and treatment itself, for children infected with lead poisoning. With reasonable assurance, we can note that its reputation alone might normally suggest that there was no realization or understanding on the Institute's part that the protocols of the experiment were questionable, except for the letter from the IRB requesting that the researchers mischaracterize the study.

\* \* \*

### C. Negligence

\* \* \*

The relationship that existed between KKI and both sets of appellants in the case at bar was that of medical researcher and research study subject. Though not expressly recognized in the Maryland Code or in our prior cases as a type of relationship which creates a duty of care, evidence in the record suggests that such a relationship involving a duty or duties would ordinarily exist, and certainly could exist, based on the facts and circumstances of each of these individual cases. . . .

### IV. The Special Relationships

### A. The Consent Agreement

\* \* \*

By having appellants sign the Consent Form, both KKI and appellants expressly made representations, which, in our view, created a bilateral contract between the parties. At the very least, it suggests that appellants were agreeing with KKI to participate in the research study with the expectation that they would be compensated, albeit, more or less, minimally, be informed of all the information necessary for the subject to freely choose whether to participate, and continue to participate, and receive promptly any information that might bear on their willingness to continue to participate in the study. This includes full, detailed, prompt, and continuing warnings as to all the potential risks and hazards inherent in the research or that arise during the research. KKI, in return, was getting the children to move into the houses and/or to remain there over time, and was given the right to test the children's blood for lead. As consideration to KKI, it got access to the houses and to the blood of children that had been encouraged to live in a "risk" environment. In other words, KKI received a measuring tool—the children's blood. Considerations existed, mainly money, food coupons, trinkets, bilateral promises, blood to be tested in order to measure success. "Informed consent" of the type used here, which imposes obligation and confers consideration on both researcher and subject (in these cases, the parents of the subjects) may differ from the more one-sided "informed consent" normally used in actual medical practice. . . .

### B.   The Sufficiency of the Consent Form

\* \* \*

A reasonable parent would expect to be clearly informed that it was at least contemplated that her child would ingest lead dust particles, and that the degree to which lead dust contaminated the child's blood would be used as one of the ways in which the success of the experiment would be measured. The fact that if such information was furnished, it might be difficult to obtain human subjects for the research, does not affect the need to supply the information, or alter the ethics of failing to provide such information. A human subject is entitled to *all* material information. . . . The "informed" consent was not valid because full material information was not furnished to the subjects or their parents.

\* \* \*

### D.   The Federal Regulations

A duty may be prescribed by a statute, or a special relationship creating duties may arise from the requirement for compliance with statutory provisions. [F]ederal regulations have been enacted that impose standards of care that attach to federally funded or sponsored research projects that use human subjects. [ ] . . . [The court excerpts the Common Rule, 45 C.F.R. § 46.116, which is reproduced, above]

\* \* \*

. . . [T]he risks associated with exposing children to lead-based paint were not only foreseeable, but were well known by KKI . . .. Moreover, in the present cases, the consent forms did not directly inform the parents that it was possible, even contemplated, that some level of lead, a harmful substance depending upon accumulation, might contaminate the blood of the children.

Clearly, KKI, as a research institution, is required to obtain a human participant's fully informed consent, using sound ethical principles. It is clear from the wording of the applicable federal regulations that this requirement of informed consent continues during the duration of the research study and applies to new or changing risks. . . .

\* \* \*

### V. The Ethical Appropriateness of the Research

\* \* \*

Researchers cannot ever be permitted to completely immunize themselves by reliance on consents, especially when the information furnished to the subject, or the party consenting, is incomplete in a material respect. A researcher's duty is not created by, or extinguished by, the consent of a research subject or by IRB approval. The duty to a vulnerable research subject is independent of consent, although the obtaining of consent is one of the duties a researcher must perform. All of this is especially so when the subjects of research are children. Such legal duties, and legal protections, might additionally be warranted because of the likely conflict of interest between the goal of the research experimenter and the health of the human subject, especially, but not exclusively, when such research is commercialized. There is always a potential substantial conflict of interest on the part of researchers as between them and the human subjects used in their research. If participants in the study withdraw from the research study prior to its completion, then the results of the study could be rendered meaningless. There is thus an inherent reason for not conveying information to subjects as it arises, that might cause the subjects to leave the research project. That conflict dictates a stronger reason for full and continuous disclosure.

\* \* \*

. . . Practical inequalities exist between researchers, who have superior knowledge, and participants "who are often poorly placed to protect themselves from risk." [ ] "[G]iven the gap in knowledge between investigators and participants and the inherent conflict of interest faced by investigators, participants cannot and should not be solely responsible for their own protection." [ ]

### VI. Parental Consent for Children to Be Subjects of Potentially Hazardous Nontherapeutic Research

The issue of whether a parent can consent to the participation of her or his child in a nontherapeutic health-related study that is known to be potentially hazardous to the health of the child raises serious questions with profound moral and ethical implications. What right does a parent have to knowingly expose a child not in need of therapy to health risks or otherwise knowingly place a child in danger, even if it can be argued it is for the greater good? . . . We have long stressed that the "best interests of the child" is the overriding concern of this Court in matters relating to children. . . .

To think otherwise, to turn over human and legal ethical concerns solely to the scientific community, is to risk embarking on slippery slopes, that all too often in the past, here and elsewhere, have resulted in practices we, or any community, should be ever unwilling to accept.

\* \* \*

[The court describes several judicial opinions involving the donation of organs or tissue from a minor child or incompetent to a family member.]

What is of primary importance to be gleaned in [these transplantation] cases is not that the parents or guardians consented to the procedures, but that they first sought permission of the courts, and received that permission, before consenting to a nontherapeutic procedure in respect to some of their minor children, but that was therapeutic to other of their children.

*In the case sub judice, no impartial judicial review or oversight was sought by the researchers or by the parents.* [Emphasis in original.] . . .

\* \* \*

### VII. Conclusion

We hold that in Maryland a parent, appropriate relative, or other applicable surrogate, cannot consent to the participation of a child or other person under legal disability in nontherapeutic research or studies in which there is any risk of injury or damage to the health of the subject.

We hold that informed consent agreements in nontherapeutic research projects, under certain circumstances can constitute contracts; and that, under certain circumstances, such research agreements can, as a matter of law, constitute "special relationships" giving rise to duties, out of the breach of which negligence actions may arise. We also hold that, normally, such special relationships are created between researchers and the human subjects used by the researchers. Additionally, we hold that governmental regulations can create duties on the part of researchers towards human subjects out of which "special relationships" can arise. Likewise, such duties and relationships are consistent with the provisions of the Nuremberg Code.

The determination as to whether a "special relationship" actually exists is to be done on a case by case basis. [ ] The determination as to whether a special relationship exists, if properly pled, lies with the trier of fact. We hold that there was ample evidence in the cases at bar to support a fact finder's determination of the existence of duties arising out of contract, or out of a special relationship, or out of regulations and codes, or out of all of them, in each of the cases.

\* \* \*

RAKER, JUDGE, concurring in result only:

* * *

I cannot join in the majority's sweeping factual determinations that the risks associated with exposing children to lead-based paint were foreseeable and well known to appellees and that appellees contemplated lead contamination in participants' blood; that the children's health was put at risk; that there was no complete and clear explanation in the consent agreements that the research to be conducted was designed to measure the success of the abatement procedures by measuring the extent to which the children's blood was being contaminated and that a certain level of lead accumulation was anticipated; that the parental consent was ineffective; that the consent form was insufficient because it lacked certain specific warnings; that the consent agreements did not provide that appellees would provide repairs in the event of lead dust contamination subsequent to the original abatement measures; that the Institutional Review Board involved in these cases abdicated its responsibility to protect the safety of the research subjects by misconstruing the difference between therapeutic and nontherapeutic research and aiding researchers in circumventing federal regulations; that Institutional Review Boards are not sufficiently objective to regulate the ethics of experimental research; that it is never in the best interest of any child to be placed in a nontherapeutic research study that might be hazardous to the child's health; that there was no therapeutic value in the research for the child subjects involved; that the research did not comply with applicable regulations; or that there was more than a minimal risk involved in this study. I do not here condone the conduct of appellee, and it may well be that the majority's conclusions are warranted by the facts of these cases, but the record before us is limited. Indeed, the majority recognizes that the record is "sparse." The critical point is that these are questions for the jury on remand and are not properly before this Court at this time.

. . . I cannot join the majority in holding that, in Maryland, a parent or guardian cannot consent to the participation of a minor child in a nontherapeutic research study in which there is *any* risk of injury or damage to the health of the child without prior judicial approval and oversight. Nor can I join in the majority's holding that the research conducted in these cases was *per se* inappropriate, unethical, and illegal. Such sweeping holdings are far beyond the question presented in these appeals, and their resolution by the Court, at this time, is inappropriate. I also do not join in what I perceive as the majority's wholesale adoption of the Nuremberg Code into Maryland state tort law. . . .

Accordingly, I join the majority only in the judgment to reverse the Circuit Courts' granting of summary judgments to appellees.

## NOTES AND QUESTIONS

1.    HHS regulations on research with children divide that research into three categories based on the level of risk presented: (1) "research not involving greater than the minimal risk;"  (2) "research involving greater than minimal risk but presenting the prospect of direct benefit to the individual subjects;" and (3) "research involving greater than minimal risk and no prospect of direct benefit to individual subjects, but likely to yield generalizable knowledge about the subject's disorder or condition." 45 C.F.R. §§ 46.401–46.409. "Minimal risk" is defined in § __.102(j), above.

Where there is more than minimal risk but the research will also benefit the child, the risk must be justified "by the anticipated benefit to the subjects;" and "[t]he relation of the anticipated benefit to the risk [must be] at least as favorable to the subjects as that presented by available alternative approaches."

Research providing no direct benefit to the individual child subject and involving more than minimal risk is not allowed unless: there is only a "minor" increase over minimal risk; the "experiences" that accompany the research are those that the child-subjects are likely to undergo anyway; and the research is aimed at a disorder or condition actually suffered by the subject. On this point, see Ana Iltis, Justice, Fairness, and Membership in a Class: Conceptual Confusions and Moral Puzzles in the Regulation of Human Subjects Research, 39 J. L. Med. & Ethics 488 (2011).

2.    Was the *Grimes* court correct in its conclusion that federal regulations on research with children prohibited the lead study? See, Loretta Kopelman, Pediatric Research Regulations Under Legal Scrutiny: Grimes Narrows Their Interpretation, 30 J.L. Med. & Ethics 38 (2002), arguing that the key issue in *Grimes* is the interpretation of "risk" as used in the regulations and that *Grimes* was correct in application to the particular protocol. But see, Lainie F. Ross, In Defense of the Hopkins Lead Abatement Studies, 30 J.L. Med. & Ethics, 50 (2002), arguing that the court misinterpreted the regulations, making important research impossible. See also, Diane Hoffmann and Karen Rothenberg, Whose Duty is it Anyway? The Kennedy Krieger Opinion and Its Implications for Public Health Research, 6 J. Health Care L. & Pol'y 109 (2003), criticizing the case for misunderstanding the nature of public health research. How would the regulations on research with children have applied in the SUPPORT study in *Looney*, above?

3.    The Court denied the University's motion for reconsideration, but in doing so, it issued a *per curiam* opinion noting that "the only conclusion we reached as a matter of law was that . . . summary judgment was improperly granted." It went on to state:

> In the Opinion, we said at one point that a parent "cannot consent to the participation of a child . . . in nontherapeutic research or studies in which there is any risk of injury or damage to the health of the subject." [W]e think is clear [that] by "any risk," we meant any articulable risk beyond

the minimal kind of risk that is inherent in any endeavor. The context of the statement was a nontherapeutic study that promises no medical benefit to the child whatever, so that any balance between risk and benefit is necessarily negative. As we indicated, the determination of whether the study in question offered some benefit, and therefore could be regarded as therapeutic in nature, or involved more than that minimal risk is open for further factual development on remand.

Does this statement clarify or confuse the Court's position? Subsequent Maryland cases considered the application of *Grimes*. See, e.g., Partlow v. Kennedy Krieger Institute, 2017 WL 4772626 (Md. Ct. Spec. App. 2017), holding that the duty of researcher to subject identified in *Grimes* extended to the sibling who lived in the same house as a child enrolled as a subject; Smith v. Kennedy Krieger, 2017 WL 1076481 (Md. Ct. Spec. App. 2017), upholding refusal to instruct jury that consent form was a contract and upholding admission of testimony of mayor as to seriousness of lead paint hazards in Baltimore; and White v. Kennedy Krieger, 110 A.3d 724 (Md. Ct. Spec. App. 2015), distinguishing therapeutic trial of treatment for children with moderate lead blood levels from nontherapeutic research in *Grimes* but holding that a duty existed between researcher and subject.

4.    The *Grimes* majority noted that the "breach of obligations imposed on researchers by the Nuremberg Code, might well support actions sounding in negligence in cases such as those at issue here." Compare Washington University v. Catalona, 437 F.Supp.2d 985 (E.D.Mo. 2006), *aff'd on other grounds*, 490 F.3d 667 (8th Cir. 2007), in which the trial court concluded that the Nuremberg Code and the Declaration of Helsinki (see Section V, below) were irrelevant to legal standards for research in the United States.

5.    Does the protection of particular groups always work for good, or can it have undesirable consequences? For example, pregnant women may participate as subjects in research only if the research is therapeutic and the risk to the fetus is minimized, or if the risk to the fetus is minimal. 45 C.F.R. § 46.204–207. Fetal protection practices which raise the cost or inconvenience of including women in research contribute to the exclusion of all women who could be pregnant or become pregnant during the course of a study presenting any fetal risk. As a result, nearly all women, from early adolescence through post-menopause, were excluded from most drug studies. Fetal protection policies were not the only reason women have been excluded from research studies, but these practices contributed to the absence of research examining how life-threatening conditions behave in the female body as compared to the male body and on the effectiveness and safety of pharmaceuticals on other than the male body. See Cynthia Hathaway, A Patent Extension Proposal to End the Underrepresentation of Women in Clinical Trials and Secure Meaningful Drug Guidance for Women, 67 Food & Drug L. J. 143 (2012); Barbara Noah, The Inclusion of Pregnant Women in Clinical Research, 7 St. Louis U. J. Health L. & Pol'y 353 (2014). In this context, can "equitable" selection of subjects be read to require inclusion of certain groups? Several federal statutes, for example, have encouraged and provided significant incentives for

pharmaceutical research with children. (See, e.g., Best Pharmaceuticals for Children Act and the Pediatric Research Equity Act.)

## E.  COMMERCIAL INTERESTS IN RESEARCH

Several developments have worked a revolution in the financial infrastructure for research in the United States. In 1980, Congress enacted the Bayh-Dole Act (35 U.S.C. § 200) and unleashed the entrepreneurial spirit in academic research, transferring property rights in the products of federally funded research to the researchers and their institutions. The Act encouraged researchers to form for-profit companies for the development and marketing of the products of research for quicker translation into clinical use. Universities developed "tech transfer" offices to capitalize on this opportunity, and the number of patents issued to universities increased more than tenfold in the early years after Bayh-Dole. Direct financial support for research also has shifted significantly, with much more research on pharmaceuticals, biologics, testing materials, and devices being supported directly by industry rather than public funds. In fact, industry support for pharmaceutical research dwarfs that available from government sources. See Marc Rodwin, Independent Clinical Trials to Test Drugs: The Neglected Reform, 6 St. Louis U. J. Health L. & Pol'y 113 (2012). The advent of entrepreneurial incentives and a profit-oriented infrastructure has raised serious concerns, however.

Critics of financial incentives in research argue that they can compromise research design; lead to overreaching in enrollment and retention of subjects; and censor research results if they are adverse to the sponsor. Because these financial interests are viewed as conflicting with goals of validity and credibility in research as well as protection of human subjects, they are often called "conflicts of interests." To the extent that a conflict of interest generally requires that there be a fiduciary relationship between the parties—as between a treating physician and patient—using that term to embrace this situation may not be entirely accurate. See, e.g., William M. Sage, Some Principles Require Principals: Why Banning "Conflicts of Interest" Won't Solve Incentive Problems in Biomedical Research, 85 Tex. L. Rev. 1413 (2007). By shorthanding "financial relationships" to "conflicts of interests," the term can be misunderstood to represent an individualized judgment about the personal integrity of the researcher. A financial conflict of interest, however, is identified at the point the financial relationship is established and the research proposed without an assessment of the researcher's personal character and before there is even opportunity for bad conduct. Robert Gatter, Walking the Talk of Trust in Human Subjects Research: The Challenge of Regulating Financial Conflicts of Interest, 52 Emory L.J. 327 (2003); Greg Koski, Research, Regulations, and Responsibility: Confronting the Compliance Myth: A Reaction to Professor Gatter, 52 Emory L.J. 403 (2003); Jesse

Goldner, Regulating Conflicts of Interest in Research: The Paper Tiger Needs Real Teeth, 53 St. Louis U. L. J. 1211 (2009).

Financial payments and ownership interests of researchers and research institutions are not the only incentives in research, and so are not the only source of conflicts of interest. This narrow focus on financial interests alone fails to account for the broader range of incentives (reputational, competitive, etc.) that can influence researcher behavior in directions that may harm research subjects or compromise the validity of results. These incentives are often apparent in scientific misconduct cases where researchers have falsified results rather than under the financial conflicts of interests regulations. See generally, Gary Marx, An Overview of the Research Misconduct Process and an Analysis of the Appropriate Burden of Proof, 42 J.C. & U.L. 311 (2016).

The revised Common Rule addresses the issue of commercial exploitation of research results and products as a matter of consent. See § __.116(c)(7) as to biospecimens. See also Section IV.F, below. Consider the following case:

### GREENBERG v. MIAMI CHILDREN'S HOSPITAL RESEARCH INSTITUTE

United States District Court, S.D. Florida, 2003.
264 F.Supp.2d 1064.

[Ed. Note: Canavan disease is a progressive, neurological genetic condition for which there is no cure. Symptoms usually appear in infancy, and most children with the disease do not live past the age of 10. It is genetic and primarily affects children of eastern and central European Jewish (Ashkenazi) or Saudi Arabian descent.]

\* \* \*

The Complaint alleges a tale of a successful research collaboration gone sour. In 1987, Canavan disease still remained a mystery—there was no way to identify who was a carrier of the disease, nor was there a way to identify a fetus with Canavan disease. Plaintiff Greenberg approached Dr. Matalon, a research physician who was then affiliated with the University of Illinois at Chicago, for assistance. Greenberg requested Matalon's involvement in discovering the genes that were ostensibly responsible for this fatal disease, so that tests could be administered to determine carriers and allow for prenatal testing for the disease.

At the outset of the collaboration, Greenberg and the Chicago Chapter of the National Tay-Sachs and Allied Disease Association, Inc. ("NTSAD") located other Canavan families and convinced them to provide tissue (such as blood, urine, and autopsy samples), financial support, and aid in identifying the location of Canavan families internationally. The other individual Plaintiffs began supplying Matalon with the same types of information and samples beginning in the late 1980s. Greenberg and NTSAD also created a confidential database and compilation—the Canavan registry—with epidemiological, medical and other information about the families.

Defendant Matalon became associated in 1990 with Defendants Miami Children's Hospital Research Institute, Inc. and Variety Children's Hospital d/b/a Miami Children's Hospital. Defendant Matalon continued his relationship with the Plaintiffs after his move, accepting more tissue and blood samples as well as financial support.

The individual Plaintiffs allege that they provided Matalon with these samples and confidential information "with the understanding and expectations that such samples and information would be used for the specific purpose of researching Canavan disease and identifying mutations in the Canavan disease which could lead to carrier detection within their families and benefit the population at large." Plaintiffs further allege that it was their "understanding that any carrier and prenatal testing developed in connection with the research for which they were providing essential support would be provided on an affordable and accessible basis, and that Matalon's research would remain in the public domain to promote the discovery of more effective prevention techniques and treatments and, eventually, to effectuate a cure for Canavan disease." . . .

There was a breakthrough in the research in 1993. Using Plaintiffs' blood and tissue samples, familial pedigree information, contacts, and financial support, Matalon and his research team successfully isolated the gene responsible for Canavan disease. After this key advancement, Plaintiffs allege that they continued to provide Matalon with more tissue and blood in order to learn more about the disease and its precursor gene.

In September 1994, unbeknownst to Plaintiffs, a patent application was submitted for the genetic sequence that Defendants had identified. This application was granted in October 1997, and Dr. Matalon was listed as an inventor on the gene patent and related applications for the Canavan disease. Through patenting, Defendants acquired the ability to restrict any activity related to the Canavan disease gene, including without limitation: carrier and prenatal testing, gene therapy and other treatments for Canavan disease and research involving the gene and its mutations.

Although the Patent was issued in October 1997, Plaintiffs allege that they did not learn of it until November 1998, when MCH revealed their intention to limit Canavan disease testing through a campaign of restrictive licensing of the Patent. Specifically, on November 12, 1998, Plaintiffs allege that Defendants MCH and MCHRI began to "threaten" the centers that offered Canavan testing with possible enforcement actions regarding the recently-issued patent. Defendant MCH also began restricting public accessibility through negotiating exclusive licensing agreements and charging royalty fees.

Plaintiffs allege that at no time were they informed that Defendants intended to seek a patent on the research. Nor were they told of Defendants' intentions to commercialize the fruits of the research and to restrict access to Canavan disease testing.

. . . Plaintiffs generally seek a permanent injunction restraining Defendants from enforcing their patent rights, damages in the form of all royalties Defendants have received on the Patent as well as all financial contributions Plaintiffs made to benefit Defendants' research. Plaintiffs allege that Defendants have earned significant royalties from Canavan disease testing in excess of $75,000 through enforcement of their gene patent, and that Dr. Matalon has personally profited by receiving a recent substantial federal grant to undertake further research on the gene patent.

### Informed Consent

. . . Plaintiffs, who served as research subjects, . . . claim that Defendants owed a duty of informed consent. . . . Defendants breached this duty, Plaintiffs claim, when they did not disclose the intent to patent and enforce for their own economic benefit the Canavan disease gene. . . . Finally, the Plaintiffs allege that if they had known that the Defendants would "commercialize" the results of their contributions, they would not have made the contributions.

\* \* \*

Defendants assert that extending a possible informed consent duty to disclosing economic interests . . . would have pernicious effects over medical research, as it would give each donor complete control over how medical research is used and who benefits from that research. The Court agrees and declines to extend the duty of informed consent to cover a researcher's economic interests in this case.

Plaintiffs cite a variety of authorities in support of their contention that the duty of informed consent mandates that research subjects must be informed of the financial interests of the researcher. They first rely on *Moore v. Regents of the University of California,* where the court held that a physician/researcher had a duty of informed consent to disclose that he was both undertaking research and commercializing it. [ ] . . . Defendants correctly contest Plaintiffs' interpretation of *Moore.* . . . *Moore* involved a physician breaching his duty when he asked his patient to return for follow-up tests after the removal of the patient's spleen because he had research and economic interests. . . . The allegations in the Complaint are clearly distinguishable as Defendants here are solely medical researchers and there was no therapeutic relationship as in *Moore.*

In declining to extend the duty of informed consent to cover economic interests, the Court takes note of the practical implications of retroactively imposing a duty of this nature. First, imposing a duty of the character that Plaintiffs seek would be unworkable and would chill medical research as it would mandate that researchers constantly evaluate whether a discloseable event has occurred. Second, this extra duty would give rise to a type of dead-hand control that research subjects could hold because they would be able to dictate how medical research progresses. Finally, these Plaintiffs are more accurately portrayed as donors rather than objects of human experimentation, and thus the voluntary nature of their submissions warrants different treatment. . . .

\* \* \*

## Unjust Enrichment

. . . Plaintiffs allege that the [researchers' profit from the patent] violates the fundamental principles of justice, equity, and good conscience [as they would not have contributed to the research had they known that this would happen]. While Defendants claim that they have invested significant amounts of time and money in research, with no guarantee of success and are thus entitled to seek reimbursement, the same can be said of Plaintiffs. . . . The Complaint has alleged more than just a donor-donee relationship for the purposes of an unjust enrichment claim. Rather, the facts paint a picture of a continuing research collaboration that involved Plaintiffs also investing time and significant resources in the race to isolate the Canavan gene. Therefore, given the facts as alleged, the Court finds that Plaintiffs have sufficiently pled the requisite elements of an unjust enrichment claim and the motion to dismiss for failure to state a claim is DENIED as to this count.

\* \* \*

## NOTES AND QUESTIONS

1.    The issue of financial interests in research rose to public attention with the death of Jesse Gelsinger and the subsequent lawsuit filed by his father against the University of Pennsylvania, the research physician, and the bioethicist who had consulted with the IRB in its approval of the protocol. Jesse was 18 years old and had a liver disorder that was under control. Under a research protocol and with a signed consent form, physicians inserted a virus, based on the cold virus, to deliver genetic material with the hope that this genetic therapy would cure the disease. An FDA investigation after the death revealed a number of violations of federal regulations including continuing with the protocol after four patients had suffered serious reactions; failing to notify the FDA of the adverse events, contrary to a specific agreement between the University and the FDA; and altering consent forms to eliminate information that monkeys subjected to the intervention had died. Because the

protocol involved genetic therapy it had been subjected to heightened review at the FDA itself as a condition of approval. Financial conflicts of interest on the part of both the researcher and the University attracted the most public attention, however. Although reports vary in details, it appears that the University gave Genovo, a private corporation, the exclusive rights to patent the results from the researcher's laboratory. The University also allowed the researcher to control up to 30% of Genovo stock, a company he founded, in an exception to the University's conflict of interests guidelines. The University would receive $21 million to support research, and it also owned stock in Genovo. The University had received legal advice, covering research regulation issues, from an outside law firm in arranging the tripartite financial relationship. Gelsinger's lawsuit was resolved by a confidential settlement. Informal reports indicate that the settlement was about $5 to $10 million. For a detailed history of the case, see Robin Fretwell Wilson, *Estate of Gelsinger v. Trustees of University of Pennsylvania: Money, Prestige, and Conflicts of Interest in Human Subject Research* in Health Law & Bioethics: Cases in Context (Sandra Johnson et al., eds. 2009). See also Steven Raper, An Artless Tale: Challenges Faced in Clinical Research, 71 Food & Drug L. J. 59 (2016), written by the principle investigator in the Gelsinger protocol. For a description of similar cases, see Gabriela Weigel, Unresolved Conflicts of Interests in University Human Subject Research, 43 J. C. & U. L. 77 (2017).

2.    In *Moore v. Regents of the University of California*, cited by the court in *Greenberg,* a treating physician removed tissue, under allegedly false pretenses, and used that tissue to develop a profitable cell line. The court in *Moore* held that the patient stated a claim for informed consent, subject to the elements required for that claim (see Section IV.C, above), because the actions occurred in a therapeutic relationship. The court rejected plaintiff's claim for conversion, however, which would have allowed the plaintiff to claim some of the profit because the court believed that would significantly harm the research enterprise. Henrietta Lacks was an African-American woman being treated for cancer when tissue removed in the course of treatment was used to produce one of the most widely used and lucrative cell lines without her knowledge or consent. Neither she nor her family or descendants received an acknowledgement, much less compensation, for decades. See Rebecca Skoot, The Immortal Life of Henrietta Lacks (2010), placing the episode in the larger context of race and human experimentation. Both the "HeLa" and "Mo" cell lines survive and continue to be used to this day. On the differences between property claims and informed consent liability, see Jorge Contreras, Genetic Property, 105 Geo. L. J. 1 (2016).

3.    The *Greenberg* parties ultimately settled by agreeing that the defendants would retain their patents but that they would allow the gene to be used without fee in any research relating to Canavan disease. Kevin L. J. Oberdorfer, The Lessons of Greenberg: Informed Consent and the Protection of Tissue Sources' Research Interests, 93 Geo. L.J. 365, 376 (2004).

## PROBLEM: MANAGING FINANCIAL INTERESTS

Several federal agencies have promulgated regulations or policies to address financial interests of researchers. These generally do not prohibit researchers from patenting and licensing their work, investing in research companies, or receiving financial support from industry. Instead, they place obligations on research institutions to manage these relationships.

The HHS regulation, for example, requires that organizations receiving Public Health Service grants have a written policy that defines what financial interests must be reported to the organization and identifies the procedures used by the organization to review and manage those interests. 42 C.F.R. § 50.601 et seq. Financial transactions or relationships that are required to be reported include intellectual property rights; sponsored travel; "any remuneration" in excess of $5,000 (except from the research institution itself); and equity interests in a publicly traded entity in excess of $5,000. The regulation requires the organization to maintain a publicly accessible website with its policies and procedures posted as well as specifics on financial relationships that the organization has identified as a conflict of interest on the part of a researcher. The regulation provides many options, beyond terminating the financial relationship or prohibiting the researcher from conducting the study, for managing financial conflicts of interest. These include, for example, public disclosure of the financial relationship, disclosure to prospective subjects, modifying the research plan, or appointing an independent monitor for the study. See F. Lisa Murtha et al., Conflicts of Interest in Research: Assessing the Effectiveness of COI Disclosure Program, 18 J. Health Care Comp. 5 (July/August 2016).

1. If you decide to require disclosure of a conflict of interest to subjects participating in a study, is the following statement, used in the Gelsinger protocol (see Note 1 following *Greenberg*, above) adequate? If not, how would you change it?

> Please be aware that the University of Pennsylvania, Dr. James M. Wilson, (the Director of the Institute for Human Gene Therapy) and Genovo, Inc. (a gene therapy company in which Dr. Wilson holds an interest) have a financial interest in a successful outcome from the research involved in this study.

Would clearer language resolve the issue? See Kevin Weinfurt et al., Disclosure of Financial Relationships to Participants in Clinical Research, 361 NEJM 916 (2009), describing empirical study of patients' decision making.

2. Should the following protocols be approved by your IRB or should your conflicts policy prohibit the research? If you believe it can go forward but with specific requirements, what would they be?

a. A protocol covers a clinical trial of a new medication. The principal investigator for the protocol is on the speakers' bureau for the pharmaceutical firm that is funding the protocol and receives a fee of $1500 for every presentation she gives at any conference in relation to any research she does. The firm does not require that she submit any information regarding the content of her presentations. Last year, she received $24,000 for such presentations.

b.    A university is courting a biotech firm for a major donation for a new research building. The university's development office has asked researchers whose research is financially supported by the firm to make a presentation on the importance of the new building at the meeting at which the firm will be asked for a donation. The associate provost for research is a member of the fundraising committee and a member of the university's IRB.

c.    An untenured faculty member is in his last year before tenure. He has had difficulty in getting publishable results from his research because he has had problems in enrolling and retaining subjects for his research on early signs of dementia. This research involves a "vulnerable population" and presents significant challenges, including assessment of the subject's capacity to consent. See Section IV.D and §§ __.111(a)(3) and (b) and 109(g), above.

## F.   RESEARCH AND BIOBANKS

The use of human specimens and private health information in research is included within the definition of "human subject" (§ __.102(e), above) whether the research protocol involves the actual removal or collection of tissue or data or whether the research merely uses material that is already stored in some sort of repository. The question of how this "secondary use" of stored specimens and data should be handled was one of the most controversial issues in the revision of the Common Rule and remains so.

There are over 600 biobanks (repositories of human specimens and related data) in the U.S. alone. The number of biobanks continues to grow explosively. The organizational structure of biobanks varies as some are associated with academic institutions or networks and others are industry created and controlled and still others are held by federal and state governments. See Kara Swanson, Body Banking from the Bench to the Bedside (2014). 23andMe, a firm that sells popular DNA screening tests directly to consumers, has built a significant biobank with the information and specimens provided by their customers. The firm's website includes its policies on privacy and consent for research access to this material, which it sells to researchers.

Claims over ownership of biobanked material and resultant products have been litigated among researchers, research organizations, biobanks, and patients whose tissue has been used in research and product development. For example, approximately 6,000 former patients of a surgeon-researcher signed forms, at his request, directing that their tissue, stored by a university hospital, be released to the custody of the surgeon-researcher for his move to another university. Washington University v. Catalona, 490 F.3d 667 (8th Cir. 2007), cert. denied, 128 S.Ct. 1122 (2008). The court ultimately concluded that the earlier consent forms that the patients had signed when their tissue was removed and stored governed and that their later request to remove them did not constitute withdrawal from a research protocol and would not be enforced. See § __.116(b)(8), above. The court held that the university, and not the researcher, owned the specimens. See also Section IV.E, above, and Chapter 4 concerning property rights in tissue removed from cadavers.

Other legal protections for privacy and confidentiality of data have a significant effect on research using human biospecimens and health information. These restrictions emerge from a great number of statutory and common law provisions. See Heather Harrell and Mark Rothstein, Biobanking Research and Privacy Laws in the United States, 44 J. L. Med. & Ethics 106 (2016).

The critical issues facing regulators in the revision of the Common Rule were whether research on stored tissue and data ("secondary use") would continue to be embraced within the definition of "human subject;" and, if yes, whether use of such material requires the consent of the individual from whom the specimen or information was collected. The core value of biobanks is that they create a pool of raw material to be used in research many years down the line, much of which cannot be anticipated when the tissue or data is collected. See Arti K. Rai, Risk Regulation and Innovation: The Case of Rights-Encumbered Biomedical Data Silos, 92 Notre Dame L. Rev. 1641 (2017). Many argue that this material should be treated as a commons from which researchers can draw material without consent. Others argue that individual dignity and respect for persons are at risk when something as intimate as health records and body parts are used without the consent of the individual. See, e.g., Institute of Medicine, Beyond the HIPAA Privacy Rule: Enhancing Privacy, Improving Health through Research (2009), recommending that consent not be required for research on health information; Mark Rothstein, Improve Privacy in Research by Eliminating Informed Consent? IOM Report Misses the Mark, 37 J.L. Med. & Ethics 507 (2009); Sharona Hoffman & Andy Podgurski, Balancing Privacy, Autonomy, and Scientific Needs in Electronic Health Records Research, 65 S.M.U. L. Rev. 85 (2012); Ken Gatter, Biobanks as a Tissue and Information Semicommons: Balancing Interests for Personalized Medicine, Tissue Donors and the Public Health, 15 J. Health Care L. & Pol'y 303 (2012).

Before the revision of the Common Rule in 2017, guidance from OHRP provided researchers using repositories of data or biospecimens with only two options. They could secure consent for their specific research project from each individual whose health information or tissue they wanted to use, or they could follow a mandatory detailed procedure for "deidentifying" the material (which could result in removing relevant health data in an effort to assure that the individual could not be identified and which still presented the risk that the material could be "reidentified").

In its final form, the 2017 revision of the Common Rule appears to have landed on a compromise that retains this research within the definition of human subjects research (§ __.102(e)(1)(ii), above) but places a good deal of research on stored tissue and data within the category of exempt research. Under the revised Rule, consent is not required for studies using identifiable private information or identifiable biospecimens that have been deidentified (as was the case before the revision) or are publicly available or are the subject of a study by or for federal agencies using information generated or collected by the government for nonresearch purposes if the information is maintained in a fashion that meets other federal statutes regarding privacy and security. Research in these categories is considered exempt. § __.104(d)(4), above.

For research that does not fit those categories, the Rule adopts a new concept of "broad consent" that applies to the "storage, maintenance, and secondary use of identifiable private information or identifiable biospecimens." The advantage of broad consent over the prior regime is that it accepts a one-time consent for any research that may be done in the future. For broad consent to be effective, the individual must be provided with the information listed in the regulation, and IRBs are prohibited from waiving those elements. §§ __.116(d) and (f), above. Broad consent allows studies to use identifiable information and biospecimens, without deidentification, for many studies over many years and requires only a limited IRB review to assure merely that broad consent has been secured and documented and that, if there is a change in the way the material is stored, there have been adequate protections for privacy and confidentiality. §§ __.104(d)(7) and (8) and __.116(d), above. The revised Common Rule adopted an additional significant change regarding use of medical records within organizations governed by HIPAA privacy rules for research consistent with HIPAA. Such studies are considered exempt. § __.104(d)(4)(iii).

### PROBLEM: DRAFTING STATE LEGISLATION

The Common Rule does not preempt state law or tribal law that provides additional protections for human subjects or that "require additional information to be disclosed in order for informed consent to be legally effective." §§ __.101(f) and __.116(i), above. States, for example, have regulated research uses of state-held biobanks such as those created by storing bloodspots collected as part of mandated screening of newborns for specific genetic conditions. See, e.g., See, Tufik Shayeb, Informed Consent for the Use and Storage of Residual Dried Blood Samples from State-Mandated Newborn Genetic Screening Programs, 64 Buff. L. Rev. 1017 (2016).

Assume that you are legislative counsel to the state legislature charged with developing proposed legislation for your state. A state senator wants to propose legislation to require consent for research studies on biospecimens or health records that may offend an individual's religious or cultural values or that might stigmatize a particular group. She is also concerned that individuals might object to certain products that may be produced using their stored tissue.

The state senator has brought a particular controversy to your attention. A research team from Arizona State University collected blood samples from members of the Havasupai tribe with a consent form stating that the research would study "the causes of behavioral/medical disorders." After discussions with the researchers, those who provided blood samples thought that they would be used in diabetes and related public health research. The stored blood samples were used in subsequent research studies of schizophrenia, inbreeding, and migration genetics. Tribal members objected when the research turned toward areas that brought unwanted notice to the tribe; that may mark the tribe members as having a propensity toward mental illness; and that would undermine core tribal beliefs about the origins of the tribe. The tribe sued and the University settled the case. See Michelle Mello & Leslie Wolf, The Havasupai Indian Tribe Case: Lessons for Research Involving Stored Biologic Samples, 363 NEJM 204 (2010).

An earlier version of the revisions to the Common Rule proposed that consent to future unspecified research with biospecimens be allowed (as does the "broad consent" in the final Rule) but that individuals be offered the opportunity to refuse consent for use of their health records or tissue for specific categories of research that presented "unique concerns." 76 Fed. Reg. 44512 (July 26, 2011). That option was eliminated in the final version, however. Would you draw on this model for the state legislation the senator desires? Would you restrict certain uses without specific consent, or would you allow the individual to specify what uses would be prohibited? What public policy concerns arise in these proposals, and what stakeholders would be interested in the result? What enforcement tools would you use if you do adopt such a restriction?

# V. INTERNATIONAL RESEARCH

The modern medical research enterprise is a global venture conducted through international academic collaborations or by multinational corporations. In 2010, an OIG report determined that over 80% of applications for FDA approval for drugs and biologics contained information generated abroad. OIG, Challenges to FDA's Ability to Monitor and Inspect Foreign Clinical Trials (June 2010). See also Darby Hall, Reining in the Commercialized Foreign Clinical Trial, 36 J. Leg. Med. 367 (2015).

International research in developing countries in particular presents several distinctive ethical challenges and has engendered considerable controversy. Clinical trials of pharmaceuticals in developing countries often test medications that the country will never be able to afford to provide to the very population from whom research subjects are drawn. Ruqaiijah Yearby, Good Enough to Use for Research, But Not Good Enough to Benefit from the Results of that Research: Are the Clinical HIV Vaccine Trials in Africa Unjust?, 53 DePaul L. Rev. 1127 (2004). Limits on access to needed care may also influence research design in ethically challenging ways. In African trials of AZT, for example, United States agencies and pharmaceutical firms conducted a trial of low-dose AZT for pregnant women with HIV to prevent transmission of the virus to the newborn. The cost of the standard dose of AZT used for this purpose in the United States made its use in impoverished countries impossible unless companies discount. The goal of the AIDS trials in Africa was to test whether a dose of AZT that was very significantly lower and cheaper than that used in the United States would be equally effective. As a control arm, however, the studies used a placebo rather than the higher, and more expensive dose used in the United States. Jerry Menikoff and Edward Richards, What the Doctor Didn't Say: The Hidden Truth About Medical Research 67 (2006); Claire Wendland, Research, Therapy and Bioethical Hegemony, The Controversy over Perinatal AZT Trials in Africa, 51 African Studies Rev. 1 (2008); Sheryl Stolberg, U.S. AIDS Research Abroad Sets Off Outcry Over Ethics, N.Y. Times (Sept. 18, 1997).

In addition to the serious ethical issues involved in studies conducted in developing countries outside of the United States, there are scientific concerns relating to whether specific populations (defined by race, genetics, gender, or age) and specific clinical environments might influence results in a way that would make outcomes in the United States less predictable. See, e.g., FDA, Draft Guidance, Acceptance of Medical Device Clinical Data from Studies Conducted Outside the United States (April 22, 2015), withdrawn as Guidance but still useful for illustrations. See also, Blake Wilson, Clinical Studies Conducted Outside the United States and their Role in the FDA's Drug Marketing Approval Process, 34 U. Pa. J. Int'l L. 641 (2013).

*Sources of Law*

Most nations have established standards and procedures governing medical research conducted within their own boundaries. See, e.g., Obiajulu Nnamuchi, Biobank/Genomic Research in Nigeria: Examining Relevant Privacy and Confidentiality Frameworks, 43 J. L. Med. & Ethics 776 (2015), part of a special issue on comparative approaches to research regulation; Jacob Kolman et al., Conflicts Among Multinational Ethical and Scientific Standards for Clinical Trials of Therapeutic Interventions, 40 J. L. Med. & Ethics 99 (2012).

The Common Rule governs research within the scope of the Rule even if it is performed abroad. The Rule requires that its criteria apply to that research unless the agency head determines that the country's policies provide protections for human subjects that are "at least equivalent" to those in the Common Rule. See § __.101(h), above. This would include provisions related to vulnerable populations. See Section IV.D, above.

The FDA accepts certain investigational drug studies conducted abroad if the study was conducted "in accordance with good clinical practice (GCP)" 21 C.F.R. § 312.120. GCP is defined as a standard that assures that studies are designed, conducted, and reported in a manner that assures that the results are "credible and accurate" and that "the rights, safety and well-being of trial subjects are protected." The regulation specifies that GCP includes review and approval by an independent ethics committee and voluntary consent from the research subject as well as other protections and procedures. GCP is a concept proffered by the International Conference on Harmonisation of Technical Requirements for Registration of Pharmaceuticals for Human Use (ICH), an international organization of the pharmaceutical regulatory agencies and pharmaceutical industry in the United States, Europe, and Japan. Earlier FDA regulations had accepted foreign clinical trials if they followed the laws of the host country or the principles of the Declaration of Helsinki, "whichever represents the greater protection of the individual." The FDA substituted compliance with GCP for drug studies in 2008 (73 Fed.Reg. 22800 (April 28, 2008)) and for device studies in 2018 (83 Fed.Reg. 7366 (Feb. 21, 2018)).

The Declaration of Helsinki, Ethical Principles for Medical Research Involving Human Subjects, is promulgated by the World Medical Association (WMA), an organization consisting of representatives from most of the world's national medical associations. Revisions of the Declaration over the past several years have struggled with issues relating to vulnerable populations. For example, the Declaration states that:

> Medical research involving a disadvantaged or vulnerable population or community is only justified if the research is responsive to the health needs or priorities of this population or community and if there is a reasonable likelihood that this population or community stands to benefit from the results of the research.

A 2000 revision of the Declaration included a statement that "every patient entered into the study should be assured of access to the best proven prophylactic, diagnostic and therapeutic methods identified by the study." This provision attracted strong opposition and may have influenced the action of the FDA to adopt GCP. The most recent revision of the Declaration (2013) modifies that article to provide:

> In advance of a clinical trial, sponsors, researchers and host country governments should make provisions for post-trial access for all

participants who still need an intervention identified as beneficial in the trial.

In contrast, the Common Rule does not require that research subjects, in the United States or elsewhere, continue to receive medication after the clinical trial has ended. See Abney v. Amgen, 443 F.3d 540 (6th Cir. 2006), holding that the company had no fiduciary duty to subjects to provide the drug tested after a study was terminated. See also Michelle M. Mello et al., Compact v. Contract: Industry Sponsors' Obligations to their Research Subjects, 356 NEJM 2738 (2007).

International law may form a basis for claims in U.S. courts by persons injured in clinical trials conducted in foreign countries. In 1996, for example, Pfizer conducted clinical trials of the antibiotic Trovan on children in Kano, Nigeria, during an epidemic of bacterial meningitis. According to news reports, only one child had received Trovan prior to these trials, and animal testing had indicated significant potential for serious adverse effects on children. Parents consenting to administration of the drug reported that they had not been informed that the medication was experimental or that conventional treatment was available to them at no charge at the same site. Parents sued Pfizer in the United States under the Alien Tort Statute (ATS) alleging that the medication caused the deaths of 11 children and paralysis, deafness, and blindness in many others. The Court of Appeals, reversing the trial court, held that nonconsensual medical research violated universal norms of customary international law and, therefore, supported a claim under the ATS. Abdullahi v. Pfizer, 562 F.3d 163 (2d Cir. 2009). Pfizer settled the case through an agreement with the Nigerian government to establish a trust fund of up to $35 million to compensate injured parties; to underwrite several health care initiatives ($30 million over two years) in Nigeria; and to reimburse Nigeria for $10 million in litigation costs. In 2011, Pfizer also settled with the private plaintiffs in an agreement that included them in the compensation trust fund. 10 Med. Res. L. & Pol'y Rep.6 d2 (March 16, 2011). See also, Fazal Khan, The Human Factor: Globalizing Ethical Standards in Drug Trials through Market Exclusion, 57 DePaul L. Rev. 877 (2008).

A medical historian investigating archives relating to the Tuskegee syphilis study (See Section II.B., above) discovered documents revealing that the United States government had conducted similar research in Guatemala in the 1940s. See Kayte Spector-Bagdady & Paul Lombardo, "Something of an Adventure:" Postwar NIH Research Ethos and the Guatemala STD Experiments, 41 J. Law, Med. & Ethics 697 (2013). The Presidential Commission for the Study of Bioethical Issues conducted an investigation of the matter, and subsequently issued a report (Ethically Impossible: STD Research in Guatemala from 1946–1948). Over 5,000 prison inmates, sex workers, soldiers, children, and psychiatric patients were included in the study, and over 1,300 adults were intentionally infected with STDs. The report concluded that the study was unethical and would have been viewed as unethical even under the standards of the mid-1940s. President Obama issued a formal apology for the research, but the federal government claimed sovereign immunity in the suit filed by those who were subjects in the study. The federal district court agreed and dismissed the suit. Garcia v. Sebelius, 867 F.Supp.2d 125 (D.D.C., 2012), vacated in part 919 F.Supp.2d 43 (D.D.C. 2013). In a related case (Estate of Alvarez v. Johns Hopkins Univ., 275 F.Supp.3d 670 (D. Md. 2017), a federal district court considered claims against a number of private parties, including the university and the pharmaceutical company, and refused to dismiss the suit as barred by the statute of limitations, stating that:

> The experimenters allegedly targeted the subjects of the Guatemala Experiments because of their inability to understand, discover, and control what was happening to them. Many of the subjects were young schoolchildren, patients in an asylum, or prisoners without access to proper medical care, education, or resources. These types of persons would have been unlikely to discover his or her exact injury and its cause.

# CHAPTER 8

# POPULATION HEALTH AND PUBLIC HEALTH LAW

■ ■ ■

## I.  INTRODUCTION

Between 1900 and 2000, life expectancy in the United States increased by thirty years. Five of those thirty years are attributable to the individualized health care that is the subject of most of this casebook and the basis of most of our healthcare industry. Twenty-five of those additional years of life, however, are a result of public health interventions. The primary goal of those interventions is population health. The Centers for Disease Control and Prevention (CDC) lists the following as the "Ten Great Public Health Achievements" of the 20th Century (48 MMWR 241):

- Vaccination

- Motor-vehicle safety

- Safer workplaces

- Control of infectious diseases

- Decline in deaths from coronary heart disease and stroke

- Safer and healthier foods

- Healthier mothers and babies

- Family planning

- Fluoridation of drinking water

- Recognition of tobacco use as a health hazard

Public health, then, is what a community, generally through its government, does to establish the conditions that allow members of that community to lead long and healthy lives. As the Institute of Medicine has pointed out, public health generally involves collective action. Because the principle of autonomy and the value of individualism are so important in the United States, and because we tend to be suspect of government and collective action, we are called upon to weigh the benefit of public health interventions with the cost of government-imposed requirements more often than is the case in similar countries. While we do not often think about the way public health interventions protect us, we do when we need public health resources and help—when an epidemic spreads through our schools, for example.

Because public health generally requires collective and sometimes coercive action, law is implicated in most public health interventions. The law may set standards for purity of food and water, for example, or at least designate those with appropriate expertise who will. The law may encourage or require immunization, as we will see, and it may require medical testing for diseases or conditions—either among the general population or subgroups like teachers, students, pilots, food workers, or prisoners. Public health law may also protect the public by placing exceptions on limitations imposed by other laws—in allowing for needle exchanges or opiate replacement therapy to avoid communicable diseases among addicts, for example, when drug laws may otherwise prohibit those actions. Additionally, the law may require the reporting of medical status to government agencies to allow those agencies to determine if there is a public health problem, and then to protect the public health. The application of public health law sometimes breaches some notions of individual privacy. Indeed, the collection of huge amounts of health information, some of it identifiable and some not, is one of the most important tools, and one of the greatest risks, of public health operations. When individually identifiable data is collected, particular follow-up measures—including, for example, tracing the contacts of those who could be transmitting communicable diseases—heighten privacy concerns. In rare circumstances, the law can require patients to receive treatment (or be placed in isolation or quarantine).

What makes an issue a "public health" issue? Is the quality of the gene pool a public health issue? The widespread use of alternative medicines? Tobacco? Gun violence? The availability and use of video games (or just violent video games)? Domestic violence? Restrictive licensure for midwives? What difference does it make whether an issue is characterized as a public health issue? Are we more likely to defer to governmental decisions, and more likely to accept governmental intrusions on individual liberties, where the public health is involved? Article 25 of the Universal Declaration of Human Rights says:

> Everyone has a right to a standard of living adequate for the health and well-being of [oneself] and [one's] family, including food, clothing, housing and medical care and necessary social services, and the right to security in the event of unemployment, sickness, disability, widowhood, old age or other lack of livelihood in circumstances beyond one's control.

Is this a principle of public health?

Public health can endeavor to encourage healthy individual behavior just as it can act to prohibit or discourage risky behavior. For example, while the Affordable Care Act (ACA) was designed to support a private health care system, it also recognizes the value of public health approaches to many issues. The Act provides subsidies for small employers who wish to establish employee wellness programs, and it allows employers of all sizes to give premium discounts to those employees who participate in some kinds of wellness programs. Participation can result in up to a 30% discount in premium costs (up to 50% with approval of the Secretary of DHHS). In addition, the ACA eliminates copays, deductibles, and other payments for some preventive care provided by private health plans, Medicare or Medicaid, and it also uses public relations strategies to increase national rates of immunization and other forms of preventive care. The ACA also requires the collection of data, including health disparity data, which will make the creation of public health approaches easier in the future.

In addition to supporting these traditional public health strategies, the ACA moves the health care system toward a greater concern for population health. The ACA, for example, encourages the formation of accountable care organizations (ACOs) as a system for delivering care. An ACO's performance is measured against its impact on outcomes relating to population health and wellness. See Susan DeVore and R. Wesley Champion, Driving Population Health through Accountable Care Organizations, 30 Health Affs. 41 (2011).

The ACA also institutes some more focused public health changes. It requires chain restaurants (those with more than 20 outlets serving essentially standardized products) to provide nutritional information on those products by posting calorie information on the menu or menu board and making additional nutritional information available to customers. It imposes the same obligations on those who sell products through vending machines, at least where customers cannot read the nutritional information already on the packaged food. The ACA also requires that employers with more than 50 employees (and others where it would not cause hardship) allow employees to express milk whenever that is necessary during the year following the birth of their children; employers must provide a clean and private space for this and allow adequate break time, although it may be unpaid time. The law also provides for public education on a host of lifestyle and preventive care issues.

As we move toward government programs that encourage wellness, is public health entering a new era in the United States—one that depends more on incentives and price regulation rather than statutory mandates? Are these new efforts—encouraging Americans to exercise, eat healthy food, stop smoking, and breast feed their children—appropriately within the realm of government?

For a discussion of the ACA and public health, see Elizabeth Weeks Leonard (ed.), Public Health Reform: Patient Protection and Affordable Care Act Implications for the Public's Health (Symposium), 39 J. L. Med. & Ethics 312, et seq (2011). For a very thoughtful summary of the overlap of law and public health, see Barry Levy, Twenty-First Century Challenges for Law and Public Health, 32 Ind. L. Rev. 1149 (1999). For a comprehensive account of the law of public health, see Lawrence Gostin and Lindsay Wiley, Public Health Law: Power, Duty Restraint (3d ed. 2016). See also Lawrence Gostin, et al., The Law and the Public's Health: A Study of Infectious Disease Law in the United States, 99 Colum. L. Rev. 59 (1999). For an interesting historical and constitutional approach to these issues, see Wendy Parmet, Populations, Public Health, and the Law (2009). For a good account of the international public health issues, see Roger Detels, et al., eds., Oxford Textbook of Public Health (4th ed. 2004).

## II. THE CONSTITUIONAL FOUNDATION OF PUBLIC HEALTH LAW

### JACOBSON V. MASSACHUSETTS

Supreme Court of the United States, 1905.
197 U.S. 11, 25 S.Ct. 358, 49 L.Ed. 643.

[The Revised Laws of that Commonwealth, c. 75, § 137, provide that "the board of health of a city or town if, in its opinion, it is necessary for the public health or safety shall require and enforce the vaccination and revaccination of all the inhabitants thereof and shall provide them with the means of free vaccination. Whoever, being over twenty-one years of age and not under guardianship, refuses or neglects to comply with such requirement shall forfeit five dollars."

\* \* \*

Proceeding under the above statutes, the Board of Health of the city of Cambridge, Massachusetts, on the twenty-seventh day of February, 1902, adopted the following regulation: "Whereas, smallpox has been prevalent to some extent in the city of Cambridge and still continues to increase; and whereas, it is necessary for the speedy extermination of the disease, that all persons not protected by vaccination should be vaccinated; and whereas, in the opinion of the board, the public health and safety require the vaccination or revaccination of all the inhabitants of Cambridge; be it ordered, that all the inhabitants of the city who have not been successfully vaccinated since March, 1, 1897, be vaccinated or revaccinated."] [Ed. Note: This description is reprinted from the syllabus of the Court.]

MR. JUSTICE HARLAN, after making the foregoing statement, delivered the opinion of the court.

We pass without extended discussion the suggestion that the particular section of the statute of Massachusetts now in question [ ] is in derogation of rights secured by the Preamble of the Constitution of the United States. Although that Preamble indicates the general purposes for which the people ordained and established the Constitution, it has never been regarded as the source of any substantive power conferred on the Government of the United States or on any of its Departments. Such powers embrace only those expressly granted in the body of the Constitution and such as may be implied from those so granted. Although, therefore, one of the declared objects of the Constitution was to secure the blessings of liberty to all under the sovereign jurisdiction and authority of the United States, no power can be exerted to that end by the United States unless, apart from the Preamble, it be found in some express delegation of power or in some power to be properly implied therefrom. [ ]

We also pass without discussion the suggestion that the above section of the statute is opposed to the spirit of the Constitution. . . . We have no need in this case to go beyond the plain, obvious meaning of the words in those provisions of the Constitution which, it is contended, must control our decision.

What, according to the judgment of the state court, is the scope and effect of the statute? What results were intended to be accomplished by it? These questions must be answered.

\* \* \*

The authority of the State to enact this statute is to be referred to what is commonly called the police power—a power which the State did not surrender when becoming a member of the Union under the Constitution. Although this court has refrained from any attempt to define the limits of that power, yet it has distinctly recognized the authority of a State to enact quarantine laws and "health laws of every description;" indeed, all laws that relate to matters completely within its territory and which do not by their necessary operation affect the people of other States. According to settled principles the police power of a State must be held to embrace, at least, such reasonable regulations established directly by legislative enactment as will protect the public health and the public safety. [ ]. It is equally true that the State may invest local bodies called into existence for purposes of local administration with authority in some appropriate way to safeguard the public health and the public safety. The mode or manner in which those results are to be accomplished is within the discretion of the State, subject, of course, so far as Federal power is concerned, only to the condition that no rule prescribed by a State, nor any regulation adopted by a local governmental agency acting under the sanction of state legislation, shall contravene the Constitution of the United States or infringe any right granted or secured by that instrument. . . .

We come, then, to inquire whether any right given, or secured by the Constitution, is invaded by the statute as interpreted by the state court. The defendant insists that his liberty is invaded when the State subjects him to fine or imprisonment for neglecting or refusing to submit to vaccination; that a compulsory vaccination law is unreasonable, arbitrary and oppressive, and, therefore, hostile to the inherent right of every freeman to care for his own body and health in such way as to him seems best; and that the execution of such a law against one who objects to vaccination, no matter for what reason, is nothing short of an assault upon his person. But the liberty secured by the Constitution of the United States to every person within its jurisdiction does not import an absolute right in each person to be, at all times and in all circumstances, wholly freed from restraint. There are manifold restraints to which every person is necessarily subject for the common good. On any other basis organized society could not exist with safety to its members. Society based on the rule that each one is a law unto himself would soon be confronted with disorder and anarchy. Real liberty for all could not exist under the operation of a principle which recognizes the right of each individual person to use his own, whether in respect of his person or his property, regardless of the injury that may be done to others. . . . The good and welfare of the Commonwealth, of which the legislature is primarily the judge, is the basis on which the police power rests in Massachusetts. [ ]

Applying these principles to the present case, it is to be observed that the legislature of Massachusetts required the inhabitants of a city or town to be vaccinated only when, in the opinion of the Board of Health, that was necessary for the public health or the public safety. The authority to determine for all what ought to be done in such an emergency must have been lodged somewhere or in some body; and surely it was appropriate for the legislature to refer that question, in the first instance, to a Board of Health, composed of persons residing in the locality affected and appointed, presumably, because of their fitness to determine such questions. To invest such a body with authority over such matters was not an unusual nor an unreasonable or arbitrary requirement. Upon the principle of self-defense, of paramount necessity, a community has the right to protect itself against an epidemic of disease which threatens the safety of its members. . . . Smallpox being prevalent and increasing at Cambridge, the court would usurp the functions of another branch of government if it adjudged, as matter of law, that the mode adopted under the sanction of the State, to protect the people at large, was arbitrary and not justified by the necessities of the case. We say necessities of the case, because it might be that an acknowledged power of a local community to protect itself against an epidemic threatening the safety of all, might be exercised in particular circumstances and in reference to particular persons in such an arbitrary, unreasonable manner, or might go so far beyond what was reasonably required for the safety of the public, as to authorize or compel the courts to interfere for the protection of such persons. . . . There is, of course, a sphere within which the individual may assert the supremacy of his own will and rightfully dispute the authority of any human government, especially of any free government existing under a written constitution, to interfere with the exercise of that will. But it is equally true that in every well-ordered society charged with the duty of conserving the safety of its members the rights of the individual in respect of his liberty may at times, under the pressure of great dangers, be subjected to such restraint, to be enforced by reasonable regulations, as the safety of the general public may demand.

* * *

Looking at the propositions embodied in the defendant's rejected offers of proof it is clear that they are more formidable by their number than by their inherent value. Those offers in the main seem to have had no purpose except to state the general theory of those of the medical profession who attach little or no value to vaccination as a means of preventing the spread of smallpox or who think that vaccination causes other diseases of the body. What everybody knows the court must know, and therefore the state court judicially knew, as this court knows, that an opposite theory accords with the common belief and is maintained by high medical authority. We must assume that when the statute in question was passed, the legislature of Massachusetts was not unaware of these opposing theories, and was compelled, of necessity, to choose between them. It was not compelled to commit a matter involving the public health and safety to the final decision of a court or jury. It is no part of the function of a court or a jury to determine which one of two modes was likely to be the most effective for the protection of the public against disease. That was for the legislative department to determine in the light of all the information it had or could obtain. . . . Upon what sound principles as to the relations existing between the different departments of government can the court review this action of the legislature? If there is any such power in the judiciary to review legislative action in respect of a matter affecting the general welfare, it can only be when that which the legislature has done comes within the rule that if a statute purporting to have been enacted to protect the public health, the public morals or the public safety, has no real or substantial relation to those objects, or is, beyond all question, a plain, palpable invasion of rights secured by the fundamental law, it is the duty of the courts to so adjudge, and thereby give effect to the Constitution." [ ]

Whatever may be thought of the expediency of this statute, it cannot be affirmed to be, beyond question, in palpable conflict with the Constitution. Nor, in view of the methods employed to stamp out the disease of smallpox, can anyone confidently assert that the means prescribed by the State to that end has no real or substantial relation to the protection of the public health and the public safety. Such an assertion would not be consistent with the experience of this and other countries whose authorities have dealt with the disease of smallpox. [The Court then summarizes the history of vaccination in Europe and America.]

\* \* \*

Since then vaccination, as a means of protecting a community against smallpox, finds strong support in the experience of this and other countries, no court, much less a jury, is justified in disregarding the action of the legislature simply because in its or their opinion that particular method was—perhaps or possibly—not the best either for children or adults.

\* \* \*

We are not prepared to hold that a minority, residing or remaining in any city or town where smallpox is prevalent, and enjoying the general protection afforded by an organized local government, may thus defy the will of its constituted authorities, acting in good faith for all, under the legislative sanction of the State [by refusing to be vaccinated]. If such be the privilege of a minority then a like privilege would belong to each individual of the community, and the spectacle would be presented of the welfare and safety of an entire population being subordinated to the notions of a single individual who chooses to remain a part of that population. . . . The safety and the health of the people of Massachusetts are, in the first instance, for that Commonwealth to guard and protect. They are matters that do not ordinarily concern the National Government. So far as they can be reached by any government, they depend, primarily, upon such action as the State in its wisdom may take; and we do not perceive that this legislation has invaded by right secured by the Federal Constitution.

Before closing this opinion we deem it appropriate, in order to prevent misapprehension as to our views, to observe . . . that the police power of a State . . . may be exerted in such circumstances or by regulations so arbitrary and oppressive in particular cases as to justify the interference of the courts to prevent wrong and oppression. Extreme cases can be readily suggested. Ordinarily such cases are not safe guides in the administration of the law. It is easy, for instance, to suppose the case of an adult who is embraced by the mere words of the act, but yet to subject whom to vaccination in a particular condition of his health or body, would be cruel and inhuman in the last degree. We are not to be understood as holding that the statute was intended to be applied to such a case, or, if it was so intended, that the judiciary would not be competent to interfere and protect the health and life of the individual concerned.

MR. JUSTICE BREWER and MR. JUSTICE PECKHAM dissent [without opinion].

### NOTES AND QUESTIONS

1. This oft-cited case established the foundation for public health regulation that came during the ensuing century. Its holding with respect to the police power plainly recognizes the authority of the state to exercise its police powers by imposing public health restrictions on willing and unwilling citizens (and others). Moreover, it clarifies that states may delegate their public health powers whether to state agencies or to local governments. *Jacobson* also recognizes that a state's power to act in the name of public health is limited by the Constitution's protection of individuals against governmental interference. The following diagram depicts the police power, its delegation, and its constitutional limitations:

2. *Jacobson* acknowledges that the due process clause in the 14th Amendment to the federal Constitution restricts the state's power to act in the name of public health. Specifically, it held that the state may not act "by regulations so arbitrary and oppressive in particular cases as to justify the interference of the courts to prevent wrong and oppression." When will the state cross this line? The Court says that "Extreme Cases can readily be suggested," but it does not actually suggest them. Can you identify these cases?

3.      Substantive due process jurisprudence has developed considerably since *Jacobson*, and, as a result, several courts have imposed standards that are more rigorous than the "non-arbitrary" test articulated in *Jacobson*. For example, three courts reviewing state orders confining individuals with tuberculosis held that state officials must prove "substantial risk" or meet a strict scrutiny standard. See City of Newark v. J.S., 279 N.J.Super. 178, 652 A.2d 265 (1993) (state must prove by clear and convincing evidence that the individual poses a substantial risk of dangerous conduct); Greene v. Edwards, 164 W.Va. 326, 263 S.E.2d 661 (1980) (same); Best v. St. Vincents Hosp., 2003 WL 21518829 (S.D.N.Y.) (confinement must be necessary to serve a substantial governmental interest). Most recently, however, two federal courts reviewing quarantine orders from the 2014 Eboa scare employed a "reasonableness" test, citing to *Jacobson*. See Hickox v. Christie, 205 F.Supp.3d 579 (D.N.J. 2016) and Liberian Community Assoc. v. Malloy, 2017 WL 4897048 (D. Conn) (appeal pending in the Second Circuit). Would *Jacobson* have been decided differently under a modern strict scrutiny standard?

4.      *Jacobson* was not the first vaccination case to be litigated in the federal courts. In Wong Wai v. Williamson, 103 F. 1 (N.D.Cal.1900), the Circuit Court faced an action by Wong Wai, "a subject of the emperor of China, residing in the city and county of San Francisco," seeking to enjoin the city from enforcing a resolution of the board of health that prohibited Chinese residents from traveling outside of the city without proof that they had been inoculated with the "Haffkine Prophylactic," which was thought to provide immunization against bubonic plague. The resolution applied only to those of Chinese extraction, although there was no evidence that they were any more likely than others to be subject to the plague. The Circuit Court recognized the public health authority of the city, but also recognized that there were limits to the exercise of this police power.

> The conditions of a great city frequently present unexpected emergencies affecting the public health, comfort, and convenience. Under such circumstances, officers charged with the duties pertaining to this department of the municipal government should be clothed with sufficient authority to deal with the conditions in a prompt and effective manner. Measures of this character, having a uniform operation, and reasonably adapted to the purpose of protecting the health and preserving the welfare of the inhabitants of a city, are constantly upheld by the courts as valid acts of legislation, however inconvenient they may prove to be, and a wide discretion has also been sanctioned in their execution. But when the municipal authority has neglected to provide suitable rules and regulations upon the subject, and the officers are left to adopt such methods as they may deem proper for the occasion, their acts are open to judicial review, and may be examined in every detail to determine whether individual rights have been respected in accordance with constitutional requirements.

\* \* \*

In the light of these well-established principles [that provide that public health measures must have an appropriate relationship with the ends they seek to serve], the action of the defendants as described in the bill of complaint cannot be justified. They are not based upon any established distinction in the conditions that are supposed to attend this plague, or the persons exposed to its contagion, but they are boldly directed against the Asiatic or Mongolian race as a class, without regard to the previous condition, habits, exposure to disease, or residence of the individual; and the only justification offered for this discrimination was a suggestion made by counsel for the defendants in the course of the argument, that this particular race is more liable to the plague than any other. No evidence has, however, been offered to support this claim, and it is not known to be a fact. This explanation must therefore be dismissed as unsatisfactory.

103 F. at 12–15. The Court went on to find that the actions of the board of health violated not only "the express provisions of the constitution of the United States, in several particulars, but also of the express provisions of our several treaties with China and of the statutes of the United States." 13 F. at 23.

5.     The Court in *Jacobson* suggests that it may be improper to apply the Massachusetts statute and the Cambridge order to an adult whose health would be placed at risk by vaccination, even though the only exception in the statute is for children whose health would be at risk. Could an adult with some legitimate health concerns about vaccination forgo it? Would this be a matter to be determined by the Board of Health, or by the courts?

6.     In a long historical footnote, the Court traces the history of vaccination from the "first compulsory act" in England in 1853. In fact, as early as 1827 the city of Boston required vaccination for school attendance, and in 1855 Massachusetts became the first state with required childhood vaccination laws associated with school attendance. The laws were fairly common by the end of the nineteenth century, but, for political and other reasons, they were not regularly enforced. Some were limited to application when there was a public health threat in the community, and some courts recognized religious defenses to the obligation to be vaccinated. See Rhea v. Board of Education, 171 N.W. 103 (N.D. 1919). Today all states provide for exemptions when the vaccination would threaten the health of the child; almost all allow for religious exemption (although the nature of those exemptions varies from state to state); and many states allow for an exemption on "moral" or other grounds. Are states Constitutionally required to have religious exemptions? If a state has a religious exemption, should that legislation also permit a "moral" exemption? Is it Constitutionally required to do so under the establishment clause of the First Amendment or the equal protection clause of the Fourteenth Amendment? These questions may soon be addressed by the new Conscience and Religious Freedom Division in the Office of Civil Rights at the U.S. Department of Health and Human Services, which, according to a Departmental press release, was created in January 2018 to "more vigorously

and effectively enforce existing laws protecting rights of conscience and religious freedom."

7.    The immunizations children must have to be enrolled in school is a matter of state law, but, as a general matter, states adopt the CDC list of recommended immunization by the Advisory Committee on Immunization Practices. In order to keep some kinds of federal funding, the states now must make an effort to enforce their own immunization laws. This issue is not entirely a scientific one, though, and vaccine manufacturers do lobby state legislatures to have their own products included on the mandatory list.

8.    While the health value of continued required immunization is now well established, those who fear government conspiracies have often had special concerns about vaccinations. It is unclear just why this has become a political issue as well as a public health issue, but it is not hard to find those who oppose vaccination with missionary zeal. The CDC, the World Health Organization (WHO), and other organizations have joined together to refute several myths about vaccination that sometimes scare parents into seeking exemptions. For a full list of the most common arguments against vaccination and the refutation of each, see the WHO's publication, 6 Common Misconceptions about Vaccinations and How to Respond to Them (2010). For an excellent account of this issue, and the basis for much of these notes, see James Hodge Jr., School Vaccination Requirements: Legal and Social Perspectives, 27 NCSL State Legislative Report, No. 14 (August 2002). See also S. Omer et al., Nonmedical Exemptions to School Immunization Requirements, 296 JAMA 1757 (2006) and S. Omer, Correspondence: Vaccination Polices and Rates of Exemption from Immunization, 2005–2011, 367 N.Eng.J.Med. 1170 (2012). For a an excellent overview of the issue and a clever proposal to finesse the opposition to immunization while respecting individuals' liberties, see Ross Silverman, No More Kidding Around: Restructuring Childhood Immunization Exceptions in Insure Public Health Protection, 12 Ann. Health L. 277 (2003).

9.    Of course, there are side effects to vaccination, and some are very serious, although a recent comprehensive study review found "no evidence of major safety concerns" associated with childhood vaccination, including current scheduling which requires delivery of multiple vaccines at one time. Institute of Medicine, Childhood Immunization Schedule and Safety: Stakeholder Concerns, Scientific Evidence, and Future Studies (2013).

10. Compensation for injuries that arise out of immunization is specifically addressed in the National Vaccine Injury Compensation Program, 42 U.S.C. § 300aa–10, et seq. This statute provides scheduled (and thus limited) compensation for those who can prove that their injury has been caused by a covered vaccine. It does not require proof of negligence or products liability for compensation. The payment is made by a government agency and the compensation payments and administration of the program are financed by an excise tax on the vaccines. Thus, the manufacturers pay the cost of the program, but they can pass that cost on and spread it out among those who are vaccinated—virtually everyone. This statute may be unique in providing that

attorneys must inform potential plaintiffs in vaccine injury cases of the existence of the law and the remedy it provides:

> It shall be the ethical obligation of any attorney who is consulted by an individual with respect to a vaccine-related injury or death to advise such individual that compensation may be available under the program for such injury or death.

42 U.S.C. § 300aa–10(b). For an excellent history of the liability litigation-induced vaccine shortages that gave rise to this no-fault compensation scheme and its predecessors, see Elizabeth Scott, The National Childhood Vaccine Injury Act Turns Fifteen, 56 Food & Drug L.J. 351 (2001). See also L. Rutkow et al., Balancing Consumer and Industry Interests in Public Health: The National Vaccine Injury Compensation Program and Its Influence During the Last Two Decades, 111 Penn St. L. Rev. 681 (2007).

## PROBLEM: EXEMPTIONS FROM IMMUNIZATION REQUIREMENTS

You are the legal counsel to the school district in Gadsden, Alabama. The Code of Alabama, § 16–30–1, et seq., requires certain immunizations as a condition of school attendance. Exemptions to this provision are found in § 16–30–3:

The provisions of this chapter shall not apply if:

> (1)  In the absence of an epidemic or immediate threat thereof, the parent or guardian of the child shall object thereto in writing on grounds that such immunization or testing conflicts with his religious tenets and practices; or

> (2)  Certification by a competent medical authority providing individual exemption from the required immunization or testing is presented the admissions officer of the school.

First grader Miranda Black's parents, who resent the heavy burden of government, have decided that they will not submit to any immunization requirement. They reason that Miranda should not have to shoulder the public health value of immunization by risking the side effects of the immunizations. Her doctor will not provide the "certification" that the school authorities want because there is no medical reason for her to avoid immunization, and thus her parents have submitted to the school authorities a statement that "compulsory immunization violates our Christian view that the government cannot make us do anything." School health officials are concerned because there were four cases of whooping cough in Gadsden during the last year—up from two the year before, and one the year before that. They attribute the increase to the increasing number of people who have obtained exemptions. The school officials have asked you how they should react to the request that Miranda be exempt. How will you advise them to proceed and why?

# III. SCIENTIFIC EVIDENCE AND PUBLIC HEALTH LAW

Public health interventions are based in epidemiological and population health data. Consequently, legislatures, courts and administrative agencies must account for such data when assessing the evaluating public health actions.

## SCHOOL BOARD OF NASSAU COUNTY V. ARLINE

Supreme Court of the United States, 1987.
480 U.S. 273, 107 S.Ct. 1123, 94 L.Ed.2d 307.

JUSTICE BRENNAN delivered the opinion of the Court.

Section 504 of the Rehabilitation Act of 1973, 87 Stat. 394, as amended, 29 U.S.C. § 794 (Act), prohibits a federally funded state program from discriminating against a handicapped individual solely by reason of his or her handicap. This case presents the questions whether a person afflicted with tuberculosis, a contagious disease, may be considered a "handicapped individual" within the meaning of § 504 of the Act, and, if so, whether such an individual is "otherwise qualified" to teach elementary school.

I

From 1966 until 1979, respondent Gene Arline taught elementary school in Nassau County, Florida. She was discharged in 1979 after suffering a third relapse of tuberculosis within two years. After she was denied relief in state administrative proceedings, she brought suit in federal court . . . .

A trial was held in the District Court, at which the principal medical evidence was provided by Marianne McEuen, M.D., an assistant director of the Community Tuberculosis Control Service of the Florida Department of Health and Rehabilitative Services. According to the medical records reviewed by Dr. McEuen, Arline was hospitalized for tuberculosis in 1957. [ ] For the next 20 years, Arline's disease was in remission. [ ] Then, in 1977, a culture revealed that tuberculosis was again active in her system; cultures taken in March 1978 and in November 1978 were also positive. [ ]

The superintendent of schools for Nassau County, Craig Marsh, then testified as to the school board's response to Arline's medical reports. After both her second relapse, in the spring of 1978, and her third relapse in November 1978, the school board suspended Arline with pay for the remainder of the school year. [ ] At the end of the 1978–1979 school year, the school board held a hearing, after which it discharged Arline, "not because she had done anything wrong," but because of the "continued reoccurence [sic] of tuberculosis." [ ]

In her trial memorandum, Arline argued that it was "not disputed that the [school board dismissed her] solely on the basis of her illness. Since the illness in this case qualifies the Plaintiff as a 'handicapped person' it is clear that she was dismissed solely as a result of her handicap in violation of Section 504." [ ] The District Court held, however, that although there was "[n]o question that she suffers a handicap," Arline was nevertheless not "a handicapped person under the terms of that statute." . . . The court then went on to state that, "even assuming" that a person with a contagious disease could be deemed a handicapped person, Arline was not "qualified" to teach elementary school. [ ]

The Court of Appeals reversed, holding that "persons with contagious diseases are within the coverage of section 504," and that Arline's condition "falls . . . neatly within the statutory and regulatory framework" of the Act. [ ] The court remanded the case "for further findings as to whether the risks of infection precluded Mrs. Arline from being 'otherwise qualified' for her job and, if so, whether it was possible to make some reasonable accommodation for her in that teaching position" or in some other position. [ ] We granted certiorari [ ] and now affirm.

## II

. . . Section 504 of the Rehabilitation Act reads in pertinent part:

"No otherwise qualified handicapped individual in the United States, as defined in section 706(7) of this title, shall, solely by reason of his handicap, be excluded from participation in, be denied the benefits of, or be subjected to discrimination under any program or activity receiving Federal financial assistance. . . ." 29 U.S.C. § 794.

[The Court held that a person suffering from a contagious disease such as tuberculosis can be a "handicapped individual" under the Act.]

\* \* \*

## IV

The remaining question is whether Arline is otherwise qualified for the job of elementary schoolteacher. To answer this question in most cases, the district court will need to conduct an individualized inquiry and make appropriate findings of fact. Such an inquiry is essential if § 504 is to achieve its goal of protecting handicapped individuals from deprivations based on prejudice, stereotypes, or unfounded fear, while giving appropriate weight to such legitimate concerns of grantees as avoiding exposing others to significant health and safety risks.[ ] The basic factors to be considered in conducting this inquiry are well established.[ ] In the context of the employment of a person handicapped with a contagious disease, we agree with *amicus* American Medical Association that this inquiry should include "[findings of] facts, based on reasonable medical judgments given the state of medical knowledge, about (a) the nature of the risk (how the disease is transmitted), (b) the duration of the risk (how long is the carrier infectious), (c) the severity of the risk (what is the potential harm to third parties) and (d) the probabilities the disease will be transmitted and will cause varying degrees of harm." [ ]

In making these findings, courts normally should defer to the reasonable medical judgments of public health officials.[] The next step in the "otherwise-qualified" inquiry is for the court to evaluate, in light of these medical findings, whether the employer could reasonably accommodate the employee under the established standards for that inquiry. [ ]

Because of the paucity of factual findings by the District Court, we, like the Court of Appeals, are unable at this stage of the proceedings to resolve whether Arline is "otherwise qualified" for her job. The District Court made no findings as to the duration and severity of Arline's condition, nor as to the probability that she would transmit the disease. Nor did the court determine whether Arline was contagious at the time she was discharged, or whether the School Board could have reasonably accommodated her.[] Accordingly, the resolution of whether Arline was otherwise qualified requires further findings of fact.

[The Court affirmed the Court of Appeals and remanded the case.]

## NOTES AND QUESTIONS

1.    While *Arline* applied the anti-discrimination provision of the Rehabilitation Act, its requirement that courts defer to the best available scientific evidence about a contagious disease has been applied in other contexts. In City of Newark v. J.C., 279 N.J.Super. 178, 652 A.2d 265 (1993), a trial court held that the City's involuntary hospitalization of a homeless man with tuberculosis did not violate the due process clause of the 14th Amendment to the federal Constitution because the man posed a significant risk of infecting others. In so holding, the Court employed a test that incorporated *Arline*'s key language.

The United States Supreme Court has recognized that "civil commitment for any purpose constitutes a significant deprivation of liberty that requires due process protection." [ ] . . . Illness alone cannot be the basis for confinement. [ ] To justify confinement it must be shown that the person is likely to pose a danger to self or to others. [ ] The proofs must show that there is a "substantial risk of dangerous conduct within the foreseeable future." [ ] These proofs must be shown by clear and convincing evidence. [ ] The terms of confinement must minimize the infringements on liberty and enhance autonomy. [ ] . . . Lesser forms of restraint must be used when they would suffice to fulfill the government interests. . . .

\* \* \*

While opinions of public health authorities must be respected, their decisions must be based upon the latest knowledge of epidemiology, virology, bacteriology, and public health. No court can substitute its medical judgment for those authorities brought to its attention or by the evidence before it. Public health decisions must be accorded due deference, *Arline, supra* . . . Nonetheless, such deference is not appropriate if those powers are exercised in an "arbitrary, unreasonable" manner. *Jacobson, supra,* [ ] Courts must guard against the risk that governmental action may be grounded in popular myths, irrational fears, or noxious fallacies rather than well-founded science.

The best way to guard against such risks is to demand an individualized, fact-specific determination as to the person under consideration. . . .

\* \* \*

Thus, it becomes possible to reconcile public health concerns, constitutional requirements, civil liberties, and the ADA all simultaneously. Good public health practice considers human rights so there is no conflict. Since coercion is a difficult and expensive means to enforce behaviors, voluntary compliance is the public health goal. Compliance is more likely when authorities demonstrate sensitivity to human rights.

\* \* \*

[Applying these standards, the Court upheld the City's involuntary isolation of J.S. in a hospital because it found that J.S. had active TB and, as a homeless person, was living on the street and in shelters where he posed a significant risk of infecting others.]

The hearing I conducted was designed to comport to all the requirements of due process and with all the requirements of a commitment hearing under *N.J.S.A.* 30:4–27.1 to –27.23. I believe my conclusions also satisfy the ADA and *Arline,* that judicial decisions in this area be based upon, "(a) the nature of the risk how the disease is transmitted), (b) the duration of the risk (how long is the carrier infectious), (c) the severity of the risk (what is the potential harm to third parties), and (d) the probabilities the disease will be transmitted and will cause varying degrees of harm." [ ]

I find that J.S. presents a significant risk to others unless isolated. Hospital confinement is the least restrictive mode of isolation proposed to me.

2.    Scott Burris has argued that the *Arline* sets a substantive due process standard for states that infringe on a person's liberty on the theory that the person poses a significant risk of spreading a contagious disease to others. See Scott Burris, Rationality Review and the Politics of Public Health, 34 Vill. L.

Rev. 933 (1989). This standard appears consistent with the ruling in *J.S.* It was also used to argue that New Jersey's quarantine of Kaci Hickox—a nurse returning from caring for Ebola patients in west Africa—was unconstitutional as was the CDC guidance on which it was based. See Robert Gatter, Ebola, Quarantine, and Flawed CDC Policy, 23 U. Miami Bus. L. Rev. 375 (2015).

3.     Just as public health actions should be based on the best available epidemiological evidence, so too should legal interventions designed to protect public health. "The work of conceptualizing, implementing, and evaluating laws to change behaviors and environments entails using the same scientific skills and methods used in the deployment of other modes of intervention in public health. We call this legal epidemiology, defined as the scientific study and deployment of law as a factor in the cause, distribution, and prevention of disease and injury in a population." Scott Burris et al., A Transdisciplinary Approach to Public Health Law: The Emerging Practice of Legal Epidemiology, 37 Ann. Rev. Public Health 135, 139 (2016). See also Wendy Parmet, Population-Based Legal Analysis: Bridging the Interdisciplinary Chasm through Public Health in Law, 66 J. Lega. Ed. 100 (2016).

4.     The Guide to Community Preventive Services (www.the communityguide.org) is "a collection of evidence-based findings" of a task force of researchers. It is a resource for identifying policy interventions that are proven effective at improving population health. Other resources for effective legal and policy interventions designed to promote public health are available at Change Lab Solutions (www.changelabsolutions.org) and at the Network for Public Health Law (www.networkforphl.org).

5.     Reconsider *Problem: Exemptions from Immunization Requirements*, above, in light of vaccination interventions that are the subject of reports from the Community Guide. Given this new information, what, if anything, would you add to or otherwise change about your advice to the school officials?

### *PROBLEM: EBOLA AND RETURNING AID WORKER*

Chris is a nurse who volunteers with the organization "Nurses Without Borders" (NWB) to provide international medical aid. He spent the last 4 weeks treating Ebola patients in Liberia. While there, Chris wore head-to-toe protective gear (including gloves and enclosed headgear) whenever he was treating patients. He never experienced a needle prick, and neither his skin nor any other part of his body ever came into direct contact with the bodily fluids of or any object that had come into contact with any patient. The CDC's Ebola factsheet states:

> Ebola . . . is a rare and deadly disease caused by infection with one of the Ebola virus species. . . .

> Ebola is spread through direct contact (through broken skin or unprotected mucous membranes in, for example, the eyes, nose, or mouth) with:

- blood or body fluids (including but not limited to feces, saliva, sweat, urine, vomit, breast milk, and semen) of a person who is sick with Ebola,

- objects (like needles and syringes) that have been contaminated with the virus, . . .

- and . . . possibly from contact with semen from a man who has recovered from Ebola (for example, by having oral, vaginal, or anal sex).

Ebola is not spread through the air or by water, or in general, by food. . . . There is no evidence that mosquitos or other insects can transmit Ebola virus. . . .

A person infected with Ebola virus is not contagious until symptoms appear. Signs and symptoms of Ebola include: fever, severe headache, fatigue, muscle pain, weakness, diarrhea, vomiting, stomach pain, unexplained bleeding or bruising. Symptoms may appear anywhere from 2 to 21 days after exposure to the virus, but the average is 8 to 10 days.

There is a 24–48 hour time period after a person infected with Ebola first experiences a fever, headache or fatigue before he exhibits the "wet symptoms" (diarrhea, vomiting, bleeding) that pose a significant risk of transmission to others. Thus, of the roughly 30,000 Ebola cases recorded over 42 years, all have resulted from an uninfected person coming into contact with the wet symptoms of an infected person. There are no recorded cases of an infected person transmitting Ebola to another while experiencing only fever, headache or fatigue.

Throughout his deployment in Liberia, Chris felt fine. A day after his last shift, he took a series of flights until he re-entered the U.S. at Newark International Airport in New Jersey. Again, Chris felt fine throughout his return trip, and he did not display any symptoms.

When Chris de-planed in New Jersey, a U.S. Department of Homeland Security (DHS) officer asked him whether he had traveled to any west African countries, and Chris replied, "Yes, I was stationed with NWB in Liberia." The DHS officer asked if Chris had had any contact with any person sick with Ebola, and Chris said he had been treating Ebola patients as part of his deployment. The officer asked Chris additional questions about his exposure to Ebola patients and his health. Chris explained that he had worn protective gear whenever he treated a patient, that he had never come into direct contact with any patient, and that he had no other exposure to Ebola other than while treating his patients. Chris also reported that his health was fine. The officer noted that Chris did not report or appear to be suffering from any symptoms of any illness. Additionally, the officer took Chris's temperature three times, and it always was normal.

The DHS officer asked Chris to wait while he informed New Jersey public health officials about Chris's status and the fact that DHS was about to permit him to enter into New Jersey. An hour later, a New Jersey public health official visited Chris and told him that, "in an abundance of caution," the state would quarantine him at a nearby hospital until the incubation period for Ebola lapsed in about 19 days.

Is the proposed quarantine of Chris constitutional? If so, why? If not, what, if any, public health action may the state of New Jersey take without violating the federal Constitution?

# IV. NON-COMMUNICABLE DISEASE AND PUBLIC HEALTH

Public health has focused primarily on infectious disease. Yet, several non-communicable diseases pose greater threats. The CDC has identified heart disease, cancer, chronic lower respiratory disease, stroke, and diabetes as among the ten leading causes of death in the U.S. Actions by public health agencies designed to reduce the incidence of these diseases—restrictions on tobacco use, warnings on cigarette boxes, disclosure of fast-food nutritional information—often face legal challenge because those actions seek to change individual lifestyles and because those actions are opposed by entrenched business interests.

### BOREALI V. AXELROD

Court of Appeals of New York, 1987.
523 N.Y.S.2d 464, 71 N.Y.2d 1, 517 N.E.2d 1350.

TITONE, J.

We hold that the Public Health Council overstepped the boundaries of its lawfully delegated authority when it promulgated a comprehensive code to govern tobacco smoking in areas that are open to the public. While the Legislature has given the Council broad authority to promulgate regulations on matters concerning the public health, the scope of the Council's authority under its enabling statute must be deemed limited by its role as an administrative, rather than a legislative, body. In this instance, the Council usurped the latter role and thereby exceeded its legislative mandate, when, following the Legislature's inability to reach an acceptable balance, the Council weighed the concerns of nonsmokers, smokers, affected businesses and the general public and, without any legislative guidance, reached its own conclusions about the proper accommodation among those competing interests. In view of the political, social and economic, rather than technical, focus of the resulting regulatory scheme, we conclude that the Council's actions were ultra vires and that the order and judgment of the courts below, which declared the Council's regulations invalid, should be affirmed.

## I.   LEGISLATIVE BACKGROUND
## AND REGULATORY SCHEME

More than two decades ago, the Surgeon General of the United States began warning the American public that tobacco smoking poses a serious health hazard. Within the past five years, there has been mounting evidence that even nonsmokers face a risk of lung cancer as a result of their exposure to tobacco smoke in the environment. As a consequence, smoking in the workplace and other indoor settings has become a cause for serious concern among health professionals [ ].

This growing concern about the deleterious effects of tobacco smoking led our State Legislature to enact a bill in 1975 restricting smoking in certain designated areas, specifically, libraries, museums, theaters and public transportation facilities [ ]. Efforts during the same year to adopt more expansive restrictions on smoking in public places were, however, unsuccessful. . . .

In late 1986 the Public Health Council (PHC) took action of its own. Purportedly acting pursuant to the broad grant of authority contained in its enabling statute [ ], the PHC published proposed rules, held public hearings and, in February of 1987, promulgated the final set of regulations prohibiting smoking in a wide variety of indoor areas that are open to the public, including schools, hospitals, auditoriums, food markets, stores, banks, taxicabs and limousines. Under these rules, restaurants with seating capacities of more than 50 people are required to provide contiguous nonsmoking areas sufficient to meet customer demand. Further, employers are required to provide smoke-free work areas for nonsmoking employees and to keep common areas free of smoke, with certain limited exceptions for cafeterias and lounges. Affected businesses are permitted to prohibit all smoking on the premises if they so choose. Expressly excluded from the regulations' coverage are restaurants with seating capacities of less than 50, conventions, trade shows, bars, private homes, private automobiles, private social functions, hotel and motel rooms and retail tobacco stores. . . .

## II.   PROCEDURAL HISTORY

[Several parties affected by the PHC's antismoking regulations sued, and a trial court set aside the regulations, holding that they exceeded PHC's statutory authority. An intermediate appellate court affirmed, and this appeal followed.]

## III.  ANALYSIS

Preliminarily, we stress that this case presents no question concerning the wisdom of the challenged regulations, the propriety of the procedures by which they were adopted or the right of government in general to promulgate restrictions on the use of tobacco in public places. The degree of scientific support for the regulations and their unquestionable value in protecting those who choose not to smoke are, likewise, not pertinent except as background information. Finally, there has been no argument made concerning the personal freedoms of smokers or their "right" to pursue in public a habit that may inflict serious harm on others who must breathe the same air. The only dispute is whether the challenged restrictions were properly adopted by an administrative agency acting under a general grant of authority and in the face of the Legislature's apparent inability to establish its own broad policy on the controversial problem of passive smoking. Accordingly, we address no other issue in this appeal.

## A.    The Delegation/Separation of Powers Issue

Section 225 (5) (a) of the Public Health Law authorizes the PHC to "deal with any matters affecting the . . . public health". At the heart of the present case is the question whether this broad grant of authority contravened the oft-recited principle that the legislative branch of government cannot cede its fundamental policymaking responsibility to an administrative agency. As a related matter, we must also inquire whether, assuming the propriety of the Legislature's grant of authority, the agency exceeded the permissible scope of its mandate by using it as a basis for engaging in inherently legislative activities. . . .

However facially broad, a legislative grant of authority must be construed, whenever possible, so that it is no broader than that which the separation of powers doctrine permits [ ]. Even under the broadest and most openended of statutory mandates, an administrative agency may not use its authority as a license to correct whatever societal evils it perceives [ ]. Here, we cannot say that the broad enabling statute in issue is itself an unconstitutional delegation of legislative authority. However, we do conclude that the agency stretched that statute beyond its constitutionally valid reach when it used the statute as a basis for drafting a code embodying its own assessment of what public policy ought to be. Our reasons follow.

Derived from the separation of powers doctrine, the principle that the legislative branch may not delegate all of its law-making powers to the executive branch has been applied with the utmost reluctance—even in the early case law. . . .

The modern view is reflected in this court's statement in *Matter of Levine v Whalen* [ ]: "Because of the constitutional provision that '[t]he legislative power of this State shall be vested in the Senate and the Assembly' (NY Const, art III, § 1), the Legislature cannot pass on its law-making functions to other bodies . . . but there is no constitutional prohibition against the delegation of power, with reasonable safeguards and standards, to an agency or commission to administer the law as enacted by the Legislature". . . .

* * *

A number of coalescing circumstances that are present in this case persuade us that the difficult-to-define line between administrative rule-making and legislative policymaking has been transgressed. While none of these circumstances, standing alone, is sufficient to warrant the conclusion that the PHC has usurped the Legislature's prerogative, all of these circumstances, when viewed in combination, paint a portrait of an agency that has improperly assumed for itself "[t]he open-ended discretion to choose ends" [ ], which characterizes the elected Legislature's role in our system of government.

First, while generally acting to further the laudable goal of protecting nonsmokers from the harmful effects of "passive smoking," the PHC has, in reality, constructed a regulatory scheme laden with exceptions based solely upon economic and social concerns. The exemptions the PHC has carved out for bars, convention centers, small restaurants, and the like, as well as the provision it has made for "waivers" based on financial hardship, have no foundation in considerations of public health. Rather, they demonstrate the agency's own effort to weigh the goal of promoting health against its social cost and to reach a suitable compromise. . . .

Striking the proper balance among health concerns, cost and privacy interests, however, is a uniquely legislative function. While it is true that many regulatory decisions involve weighing economic and social concerns against the specific values that the regulatory agency is mandated to promote, the agency in this case has not been authorized to structure its decision making in a "cost-benefit" model [ ] and, in fact, has not been given any legislative guidelines at all for determining how the competing concerns of public health and economic cost are to be weighed. Thus, to the extent that the agency has built a regulatory scheme on its own conclusions about the appropriate balance of trade-offs between health and cost to particular industries in the private sector, it was "acting solely on [its] own ideas of sound public policy" and was therefore operating outside of its proper sphere of authority [ ]. This conclusion is particularly compelling here, where the focus is on administratively created exemptions rather than on rules that promote the legislatively expressed goals, since exemptions ordinarily run counter to such goals and, consequently, cannot be justified as simple implementations of legislative values [ ]. . . .

The second, and related, consideration is that in adopting the antismoking regulations challenged here the PHC did not merely fill in the details of broad legislation describing the over-all policies to be implemented. Instead, the PHC wrote on a clean slate, creating its own comprehensive set of rules without benefit of legislative guidance. Viewed in that light, the agency's actions were a far cry from the "interstitial" rule making that typifies administrative regulatory activity [ ].

A third indicator that the PHC exceeded the scope of the authority properly delegated to it by the Legislature is the fact that the agency acted in an area in which the Legislature had repeatedly tried—and failed—to reach agreement in the face of substantial public debate and vigorous lobbying by a variety of interested factions. While we have often been reluctant to ascribe persuasive significance to legislative inaction [ ], our usual hesitancy in this area has no place here. Unlike the cases in which we have been asked to consider the Legislature's failure to act as some indirect proof of its actual intentions [ ], in this case it is appropriate for us to consider the significance of legislative inaction as evidence that the Legislature has so far been unable to reach agreement on the goals and methods that should govern in resolving a society-wide health problem. Here, the repeated failures by the Legislature to arrive at such an agreement do not automatically entitle an administrative agency to take it upon itself to fill the vacuum and impose a solution of its own. Manifestly, it is the province of the people's elected representatives, rather than appointed administrators, to resolve difficult social problems by making choices among competing ends.

Finally, although indoor smoking is unquestionably a health issue, no special expertise or technical competence in the field of health was involved in the development of the antismoking regulations challenged here. Faced with mounting evidence about the hazards to bystanders of indoor smoking, the PHC drafted a simple code describing the locales in which smoking would be prohibited and providing exemptions for various special interest groups. . . .

In summary, we conclude that while Public Health Law § 225 (5) (a) is a valid delegation of regulatory authority, it cannot be construed to encompass the policy-making activity at issue here without running afoul of the constitutional separation of powers doctrine. . . .

\* \* \*

Accordingly, the order of the Appellate Division should be affirmed.

### NOTES AND QUESTIONS

1.   *Boreali* is representative of constitutional and administrative law challenges to public health actions aimed at non-communicable diseases. Because public health measures are commonly taken by local, state and federal agencies, doctrines such as separation-of-powers, non-delegation, and *ultra vires* can curtail public health powers. For example, the same court that decided *Boreali* later set aside a "soda ban" that prohibited many businesses from selling sugary drinks in sizes larger than 16 ounces—a measure designed to help fight obesity. See New York Statewide Coalition of Hispanic Chambers

of Commerce v. New York City Dept. of Health and Mental Hygiene, 16 N.E.3d 538, 992 N.Y.S.2d 480, 23 N.Y.3d 681 (2014); c.f. NYC C.L.A.S.H., Inc. v. New York State Office of Parks, Recreation and Historic Preservation, 27 N.Y.3d 174, 51 N.E.3d 512, 32 N.Y.S.3d 1 (2016) (using the *Boreali* factors to uphold agency's outdoor smoking ban in parts of New York City's parks, historic places, and recreational facilities).

Similarly, the Supreme Court of the United States applied the *Chevron* doctrine to hold that the Food and Drug Administration (FDA) did not have authority under its enabling statute to regulate cigarettes. See Food and Drug Administration v. Brown & Williamson Tobacco Corp., 529 U.S. 120, 120 S.Ct. 1291, 146 L.Ed.2d 121 (2000). The statute authorized FDA to regulate drugs and devices, which FDA interpreted to include nicotine (a drug) delivered through cigarettes (a device). The Court held that federal cigarette legislation passed after the FDA's enabling statute—especially when combined with FDA's prior insistence that it did not have the authority to regulate cigarettes—signaled that FDA no longer had the authority to regulate cigarettes even if it once did.

2.    The First Amendment, through the commercial speech doctrine, has also been interpreted so as to limit public health authority and expand the rights of tobacco, food, and drug manufacturers. For example, in Sorrell v. IMS Health, 564 U.S. 552, 131 S.Ct. 2653 (2011), the Supreme Court struck down a Vermont statute restricting the collection and disclosure of pharmacy records for individual physicians. The Court held that the restriction suppressed protected speech under the First Amendment. It then applied heightened scrutiny, requiring the State to show that the statute "directly advanced" a "substantial governmental interest" and that it is "drawn to achieve" that interest, meaning that there must be "a fit between the legislature's ends and the means chosen to accomplish those ends." Under this standard, the Court held that Vermont's interests in protecting physician privacy, preventing harassing sales behavior by manufacturers, and preserving the doctor-patient relationship were not sufficient justifications for the restriction. Additionally, it ruled that the State failed to establish a fit between the restrictions and the State's goals of promoting public health and lowering medical costs.

By giving little weight to the State's interest in protecting public health, *Sorrel* undermines the stability of laws restricting language used to market food, tobacco and prescription drugs as well as laws mandating certain disclosures. For example, the Second Circuit ruled that off-label promotion of a pharmaceutical was protected commercial speech subject to at least heightened scrutiny. See U.S. v. Caronia, 703 F.3d 149 (2d Cir. 2012). Meanwhile, the D.C. Circuit flip-flopped on whether regulators may justify disclosure mandates based on interests other than correcting prior deception. In R.J. Reynolds Tobacco Co. v. FDA, 696 F.3d 1205 (D.C. Cir. 2012), that Court set aside FDA regulations requiring cigarette manufacturers to place graphic warnings on packaging, holding that the First Amendment requires the government to first establish that existing cigarette packaging is misleading to consumers, which it did not show. Two years later, in American Meat

Institute v. U.S. Dept. of Agriculture, 760 F.3d 18 (D.C. Cir. 2014), the same Court overruled its decision in *R.J. Reynolds*. By broadening commercial speech protection and narrowing the discretion of public health, First Amendment doctrine poses a significant challenge to improving population health. See Joshua Sharfstein, Public Health and the First Amendment, 93 Milbank Qtly 459 (2015).

## *PROBLEM: OBESITY AS A PUBLIC HEALTH PROBLEM*

As a legislator in your state, you have become very concerned about obesity in the population, and you are worried about the long range consequences of this condition on the vitality of the public. In particular, you have become concerned about the proliferation of fast-food sites that offer primarily economical but very high fat foods. You are concerned about "food deserts" in your state—areas where there are no supermarkets and limited public transportation. You are also disturbed by the relatively unhealthy foods available at the public schools throughout the state, many of which have contracts with beverage companies to run their vending machines and snack bars, and by the disappearance of mandatory physical education requirements at the high school level. There is also an indication that a comparatively sedentary lifestyle that includes watching television and playing video games contributes to what some have called the "epidemic" of obesity. Furthermore, studies have repeatedly shown that obesity alone is not a predictor for shortened lifespans or significantly greater health risks. Rather, a lack of exercise or fitness is more closely associated with health risks than is obesity. A person can be obese and healthy.

Is the problem of obesity a "public health" problem, or simply a problem for some individuals? What qualifies as "obese" for public health purposes? Is it a matter of personal responsibility that should be unrelated to the obligations of the law? Would it make any difference if you classified obesity as a "public health" problem? What legal responses might be available to the state legislature to address this problem? Are there ways to use school law, tax law, criminal law, tort law, food and drug law, insurance rate-setting, public program eligibility standards or general public health regulatory law to address this problem? What evidence is there that pulling any of these legal levers would be effective at lowering the incidence of obesity? What are the legal, political and social consequences of doing so? Are there civil liberty interests of persons who are obese (or others) that are at stake in using the law in this way?

Do you feel the same way about tobacco, gun violence, bullying, or "extreme sports" as public health problems?

# INDEX

References are to Pages